EUROPEAN UNION LAW
SELECTED DOCUMENTS

2002 Edition

By

George A. Bermann
*Beekman Professor of Law,
Jean Monnet Professor of European Union Law, and
Director, European Legal Studies Center,
Columbia University School of Law*

Roger J. Goebel
*Professor of Law and Director,
Fordham Center on European Union Law,
Fordham University School of Law*

William J. Davey
*Edwin M. Adams Professor of Law,
University of Illinois College of Law*

Eleanor M. Fox
*Walter J. Derenberg Professor of Trade Regulation,
New York University School of Law*

AMERICAN CASEBOOK SERIES®

WEST GROUP

A THOMSON COMPANY

Mat #16370207

West Group has created this publication to provide you with accurate and authoritative information concerning the subject matter covered. However, this publication was not necessarily prepared by persons licensed to practice law in a particular jurisdiction. West Group is not engaged in rendering legal or other professional advice, and this publication is not a substitute for the advice of an attorney. If you require legal or other expert advice, you should seek the services of a competent attorney or other professional.

American Casebook Series, and the West Group symbol
are registered trademarks used herein under license.

COPYRIGHT © 1993 WEST PUBLISHING CO.
COPYRIGHT © 1997 WEST GROUP
COPYRIGHT © 2002 By WEST GROUP
                610 Opperman Drive
                P.O. Box 64526
                St. Paul, MN 55164-0526
                1-800-328-9352

All rights reserved
Printed in the United States of America

ISBN 0-314-23812-3

Preface to the 2002 Edition

This Selected Documents is designed to accompany European Union Law: Cases and Materials (West Group, 2d ed. 2002). Use of the Supplement is essential for a full understanding of the materials in the casebook.

Because European Community law and European Union law are principally founded upon the application and interpretation of the Treaties establishing the European Community (EC) and European Union (EU), respectively, the EC Treaty and the Treaty on European Union (TEU), as amended through the Treaty of Amsterdam (effective 1999), are the first two documents in the volume (followed by a conversion table of article numbers necessitated by the Amsterdam Treaty's wholesale renumbering of the EC Treaty and the TEU articles). There follows the Treaty of Nice of December 2000 which, when ratified and in force, will significantly further amend the EC Treaty and the TEU in ways that the language of the Nice Treaty makes clear.

With the exception of various instruments concerning the Court of Justice and various human rights and transparency instruments, the remainder of the Selected Documents includes the more important Community legislative measures, chiefly in the form of regulations, directives and decisions that are discussed in the casebook. These documents are either fully reproduced or lightly excerpted to facilitate understanding.

The Selected Documents is organized in seven parts, corresponding to the topic coverage of the casebook. Each has an introduction briefly describing the documents which follow.

Reference should be made to the Note on Legal Sources and Citation Forms contained in the casebook for indications of the source of these and other Community documents, modes of research and citation style.

Helpful recommendations for the inclusion of certain documents were made by many of the persons thanked in the casebook Acknowledgments. We invite the suggestions of professors and other users of the Selected Documents to assist us in deciding what additional documents might be included in future editions.

Finally, we thank the staff of the information service and library of the European Union Delegations in Washington, D.C. and New York City for their assistance in obtaining recent documentation.

*

Table of Contents

	Page
PREFACE	iii

PART I. THE EUROPEAN COMMUNITY AND EUROPEAN UNION: LEGAL AND INSTITUTIONAL FRAMEWORK

1. Treaty Establishing the European Community ("The EC Treaty") 4
2. Treaty on European Union ("The TEU") 141
3. Table of Equivalences of Treaty Articles 165
4. Treaty of Nice (and Selected Protocols) 169
5. Protocol on the Statute of the Court of Justice of the European Community 214
6. Rules of Procedure of the Court of Justice of the European Community 226
7. Rules of Procedure of the Court of First Instance of the European Communities 249
8. Interinstitutional Declaration on Democracy, Transparency and Subsidiarity 251
9. Interinstitutional Agreement on Procedures for Implementing the Principle of Subsidiarity 253
10. Convention for the Protection of Human Rights and Fundamental Freedoms 255
11. Joint Declaration by the European Parliament, the Council and the Commission 265
12. Charter of Fundamental Rights of the European Union 266
13. Communication from the Commission on the Legal Nature of the Charter of Fundamental Rights of the European Union 276
14. Parliament and Council Regulation 1049/2001 of May 30, 2001, regarding public access to European Parliament, Council and Commission documents 282

PART II. THE RECEPTION AND ENFORCEMENT OF EUROPEAN LAW IN THE MEMBER STATES

PART III. THE COMMON MARKET, THE INTERNAL MARKET AND THE FOUR FREEDOMS

1. Commission Directive 70/50 on the abolition of measures which have an effect equivalent to quantitative restrictions on imports. 299
2. Council Regulation 2679/98 on the functioning of the internal market in relation to the free movement of goods. 303

TABLE OF CONTENTS

		Page
3.	Commission Communication concerning the consequences of the judgment in Case 120/78 ("Cassis de Dijon").	306
4.	Council Directive 92/32 on the approximation of the laws relating to the classification, packaging and labelling of dangerous substances.	309
5.	Council Directive 83/189 laying down a procedure for the provision of information in the field of technical standards and regulations.	325
6.	Council Directive 85/577 to protect the consumer in respect of contracts negotiated away from business premises.	331
7.	Council Regulation 1612/68 on freedom of movement for workers within the Community.	335
8.	Council Directive 68/360 on the abolition of restrictions on movement and residence within the Community for workers of Member States and their families.	341
9.	Council Directive 64/221 on the co-ordination of special measures concerning the movement and residence of foreign nationals which are justified on grounds of public policy, public security or public health.	345
10.	Council Directive 90/365 on the right of residence for employees and self-employed persons who have ceased their occupational activity.	349
11.	Council Directive 90/364 on the right of residence.	352
12.	Council Directive 93/96 on the right of residence for students.	355
13.	General Programme for the abolition of restrictions on freedom of establishment.	358
14.	Commission interpretative communication concerning the free movement of services across frontiers.	362
15.	Council Directive 86/653 on the coordination of the laws of the Member States relating to self-employed commercial agents.	368
16.	Council Directive 89/552 on the coordination of certain provisions laid down by law, regulation or administrative action in Member States concerning the pursuit of television broadcasting activities.	377
17.	First Council Directive 68/151 on coordination of safeguards which are required by Member States of companies with a view to making such safeguards equivalent throughout the Community.	388
18.	Second Council Directive 77/91 on coordination of safeguards which are required by Member States in respect of the formation of public limited liability companies and the maintenance and alteration of their capital.	393
19.	Third Council Directive 78/855 concerning mergers of public limited liability companies.	403

		Page
20.	Fourth Council Directive 78/660 on the annual accounts of certain types of companies.	414
21.	Council Regulation 2137/85 on the European Economic Interest Grouping.	423
22.	Council Directive 89/48 on a general system for the recognition of higher-education diplomas awarded on completion of profession education and training.	433
23.	Council Recommendation 89/49 concerning nationals of Member States who hold a diploma conferred in a third State.	442
24.	Council Directive 77/249 to facilitate the effective exercise by lawyers of freedom to provide services.	443
25.	Directive 98/5 of the European Parliament and of the Council to facilitate practice of the profession of lawyer on a permanent basis in a Member State other than that in which the qualification was obtained.	446
26.	Council Directive 89/104 to approximate the laws of the Member States relating to trade marks.	459

PART IV. COMPETITION POLICY

1.	Council Regulation 17/62 implementing Articles 81 and 82 (ex 85 and 86)	474
2.	Commission Notice on Agreements on Minor Importance which do not appreciably restrict competition under Article 81(1)	486
3.	Commission Notice on the Definition of the Relevant Market	491
4.	Commission Regulation 2790/1999 on the application of Article 81(3) to Vertical Agreements—block exemption	504
5.	Commission Regulation 2658/2000 on the application of Article 81(3) to Specialisation Agreements—block exemption	514
6.	Commission Regulation 2659/2000 on the application of Article 81(3) to Research and Development Agreements—block exemption	521
7.	Council Regulation 4064/1989 on the control of concentrations—Merger Regulation	531

PART V. EXTERNAL RELATIONS AND COMMERCIAL POLICY

1.	Council Regulation (EEC) No. 2913/92 of 12 October 1992 establishing the Community Customs Code.	555
2.	Council Regulation (EC) No. 384/96 of 22 December 1995 on protection against dumped imports from countries not members of the European Community.	565
3.	Council Regulation (EC) No 2026/97 of 6 October 1997 on protection against subsidized imports from countries not members of the European Community.	597

4. Council Regulation (EC) No. 3286/94 of 22 December 1994 laying down Community procedures in the field of the common commercial policy in order to ensure the exercise of the Community's rights under international trade rules, in particular those established under the auspices of the World Trade Organization. 608

PART VI. FREE MOVEMENT OF CAPITAL AND ECONOMIC AND MONETARY UNION

1. Council Directive 88/361 for the implementation of Article 67 [free movement of capital]. 620
2. Council Directive 79/279 coordinating the conditions for the admission of securities to official stock exchange listing. 624
3. Council Directive 82/121 on information to be published by companies the shares of which have been admitted to official stock-exchange listing. 637
4. Council Directive 89/592 coordinating regulations on insider dealing. 641
5. First Council Directive 77/780 on the coordination of laws, regulations and administrative provisions relating to the taking up and pursuit of the business of credit institutions. 646
6. Second Council Directive 89/646 on the coordination of laws relating to the business of credit institutions. 652
7. Council Regulation 974/98 on the introduction of the Euro, O.J. L 139/1 (May 11, 1998). 671
8. Council Regulation 1103/97 on certain provisions related to the introduction of the Euro, O.J. L 162/1 (June 19, 1997). 678

PART VII. SPECIFIC COMMUNITY POLICIES

1. Council Directive 85/337/EEC on the assessment of the effects of certain public and private projects on the environment. 686
2. Council Directive 84/450/EEC relating to the approximation of the laws, regulations and administrative provisions of the Member States concerning misleading advertising. 702
3. Council Directive 93/13/EEC on unfair terms in consumer contracts. 708
4. Council Directive 85/374/EEC on the approximation of the laws, regulations and administrative provisions of the Member States concerning liability for defective products. 716
5. Council Directive 98/59 on the approximation of the laws relating to collective redundancies. 723
6. Council Directive 2001/23 on the approximation of the laws relating to the safeguarding of employees' rights in the event of transfers of undertakings, businesses or parts of businesses. 728

		Page
7.	Council Directive 80/987 on the approximation of the laws relating to the protection of employees in the event of the insolvency of their employer.	735
8.	Community Charter of the Fundamental Social Rights of Workers.	739
9.	Council Directive 92/85 on measures to encourage improvements in the safety and health at work of pregnant workers and workers who have recently given birth or are breastfeeding.	746
10.	Council Directive 93/104 concerning certain aspects of the organization of working time.	754
11.	Council Directive 91/533 on an employer's obligation to inform employees of the conditions applicable to the contract or employment relationship.	764
12.	Council Directive 75/117 on the approximation of the laws relating to the principle of equal pay for men and women	770
13.	Council Directive 76/207 on the implementation of the principle of equal treatment for men and women as regards access to employment, vocational training and promotion, and working conditions	773
14.	Council Directive 79/7 on the progressive implementation of the principle of equal treatment for men and women in matters of social security	777
15.	Council Directive 97/80 on burden of proof in sex discrimination cases.	780
16.	Council Directive 2000/43 on equal treatment irrespective of racial or ethnic origin.	785
17.	Council Directive 2000/78 establishing general framework for equal treatment in employment and occupation.	795
18.	1968 Brussels Convention on Jurisdiction and the Enforcement of Judgments in Civil and Commercial Matters	808
19.	Protocol on the Interpretation by the Court of Justice of the Convention on Jurisdiction and the Enforcement of Judgments in Civil and Commercial Matters.	824
20.	Council Regulation 44/2001 of 22 December 2000 on Jurisdiction and the Recognition and Enforcement of Judgments in Civil and Commercial Matters.	826

EUROPEAN UNION LAW
SELECTED DOCUMENTS
2002 Edition

*

Part I

THE EUROPEAN COMMUNITY AND EUROPEAN UNION: LEGAL AND INSTITUTIONAL FRAMEWORK

INTRODUCTION

The fundamental European Community charter is the Treaty Establishing the European Community (the "EC Treaty," previously known as the "European Economic Community" or "EEC Treaty"), signed at Rome on March 25, 1957, 298 UNTS 11. The EC Treaty, as amended as of 1999 by the Treaty of Amsterdam, appears as the first document in this supplement. The other two constitutive treaties (the Treaty Establishing the European Coal and Steel Community (ECSC), April 18, 1951, 261 UNTS 140, and the Treaty Establishing the European Atomic Energy Community (Euratom), March 25, 1957, 298 UNTS 167) are not reproduced. (The ECSC Treaty passes out of existence by its own terms in 2002.)

As a text, the EC Treaty was significantly affected by a number of other agreements of a structural nature. These include (1) the Convention on Certain Institutions Common to the European Communities, March 25, 1957, (2) the Treaty Establishing a Single Council and a Single Commission of the European Communities, April 8, 1965 ("the Merger Treaty"), (3) Treaties of Accession of New Member States of 1972, 1979, 1985 and 1994, each with an annexed Act of Accession, and (4) Budgetary Treaties of 1970 and 1975. Fortunately, the modifications that these agreements introduced are now reflected in the main body of the EC Treaty itself. To the extent that the Single European Act (SEA) (effective July 1987), the Treaty of Maastricht (effective February 1992) and the Treaty of Amsterdam (effective May 1999) amended the EC Treaty, they too are reflected in the text of the EC Treaty in Document 1.

The Maastricht Treaty had, of course, the peculiarity of not only amending the existing Community treaties (including the EC Treaty) but of also being itself a new "constitutive" treaty. Indeed the Maastricht Treaty's proper name is the Treaty on European Union ("TEU"), so called because it put in place a new overarching legal entity, the European Union. Besides creating the European Union and laying down other "common provisions," the TEU introduced provisions on what have come to be known as "pillars two" and "three" because, while part (indeed "pillars") of the EU, they do not form part of the corpus of European Community law. The TEU captioned pillars two and three, respectively, "common foreign and security policy," and "cooperation in the fields of justice and home affairs." They form the legal basis for extensive intergovernmental activity conducted by the Member States under the EU banner.

Like the EC Treaty, the TEU was importantly amended by the Treaty of Amsterdam, not only in its common provisions but also in pillars two and three. The TEU, as amended at Amsterdam, constitutes Document 2 in this volume.

The Single European Act and the Maastricht and Amsterdam Treaties brought numerous Protocols and Declarations to the constitutive treaties. Protocols, by their terms, are deemed officially annexed either to the EC Treaty or to the TEU, or both. They are listed following the EC Treaty in Document 1, and a few are reproduced in full.

Document 3 is a simple conversion table, showing the roughly equivalent articles of the EC Treaty and TEU in their pre- and post-Amsterdam numberings.

Because the EC and EU are works in progress, amendments to these constitutive treaties continue apace. In December 2000 the Member States agreed on a new wave of amendments in the form of the Treaty of Nice. For want of ratification (and indeed following the Irish electorate's rejection in a referendum), the Nice Treaty remains unratified, and the constitutive treaties not as yet amended by it. Due to the likelihood of its entry into force, however, the Nice Treaty is set out as Document 4. It shows clearly which treaty articles of the EC Treaty and TEU will be amended, and precisely how, once ratification occurs. It should be consulted for possible changes whenever any particular treaty article is being considered in class or by way of reading.

Given the centrality of the Court of Justice in the evolution of EC law, the Protocol on the Statute of the Court, basically organizing it, is included (as amended) as Document 5, followed by the Rules of Procedure of the Court, as Document 6. (For the Court of First Instance, only the Table of Contents of the Court's Rules is set out, as Document 7). There follow the Interinstitutional Declaration on Democracy, Transparency and Subsidiarity of 1993 (Document 8) and the Interinstitutional Agreement on Procedures for Implementing the Principle of Subsidiarity, also of 1993 (Document 9).

Although the Community and Union remain technically without a formal written and legally enforceable Bill of Rights, the Court of Justice has made it clear that the principles of the European Human Rights Convention, together with the constitutional provisions and traditions among the Member States, are sources of fundamental rights principles that the institutions must respect and that the Court of Justice and Court of First Instance will enforce. (See Chapter 6 of the casebook). Selected provisions of the Convention and several of its protocols are set out as a separate document (Document 10). Indeed, the 1977 Joint Declaration of the Parliament, Council and Commission (Document 11) committed the institutions to respect the Convention's principles. Finally, in December 2000, the European Parliament, Council and Commission "solemnly" proclaimed a new Charter of Fundamental Rights of the European Union, albeit one that is not integrated into the Treaties or otherwise directly judicially enforceable. The Charter is set out as Document 12, followed by a Commission Communication on its "legal nature" (Document 13).

The final document in this part is Regulation 1049/2001 of the Parliament and Council regarding public access to European Parliament, Council and Commission documents. The regulation supplants Codes of Conduct voluntarily adopted by the institutions. To the extent that "freedom of information" is an aspect of EC and EU governance, this text forms part of the subject matter of Part I of the book and is accordingly dealt with in Chapter 6.

Table of Contents

PART I. THE EUROPEAN COMMUNITY AND EUROPEAN UNION: LEGAL AND INSTITUTIONAL FRAMEWORK

Doc. Page

Introduction 1
1. Treaty Establishing the European Community ("The EC Treaty") 4
2. Treaty on European Union ("The TEU") 141
3. Table of Equivalences of Treaty Articles 165
4. Treaty of Nice (and Selected Protocols) 169
5. Protocol on the Statute of the Court of Justice of the European Community 214
6. Rules of Procedure of the Court of Justice of the European Community 226
7. Rules of Procedure of the Court of First Instance of the European Communities 249
8. Interinstitutional Declaration on Democracy, Transparency and Subsidiarity 251
9. Interinstitutional Agreement on Procedures for Implementing the Principle of Subsidiarity 253
10. Convention for the Protection of Human Rights and Fundamental Freedoms 255
11. Joint Declaration by the European Parliament, the Council and the Commission 265
12. Charter of Fundamental Rights of the European Union 266
13. Communication from the Commission on the Legal Nature of the Charter of Fundamental Rights of the European Union 276
14. Parliament and Council Regulation 1049/2001 of May 30, 2001, regarding public access to European Parliament, Council and Commission documents 282

1. TREATY ESTABLISHING THE EUROPEAN COMMUNITY ("THE EC TREATY")

(As amended by the Single European Act ("SEA"), the Treaty on European Union ("TEU" or the Treaty of Maastricht) and the Treaty of Amsterdam)

consolidated version, O.J. C 340/173 (Nov. 10, 1997)

[*Eds. Note*: On a highly selected basis, the changes made to the EC Treaty by the Single European Act, the TEU and the Treaty of Amsterdam are indicated by footnote.

Note that the Treaty of Nice of December 2000, still unratified, will further amend the EC Treaty in important ways. To identify the prospective changes, see the Treaty of Nice, Document 4 in this Part. All changes to be made to the EC Treaty are indicated there.

To aid in appreciating the structure of the EC Treaty, this document begins with the Treaty's Table of Contents.

Finally, selected Protocols annexed to the EC Treaty (or both the EC Treaty and the TEU) are included at the end.]

TABLE OF CONTENTS

Preamble
- **Part One** (arts. 1–16) **—Principles**
- **Part Two** (arts. 17–22) **—Citizenship of the Union**
- **Part Three** (arts. 23–181) **—Community policies**
  - TITLE I (arts. 23–31)—Free movement of goods
    - Chapter 1 (arts. 23–27)—The Customs Union
    - Chapter 2 (arts. 28–31)—Prohibition of quantitative restrictions between Member States
  - TITLE II (arts. 32–38)—Agriculture
  - TITLE III (arts. 39–60)—Free movement of persons, services and capital
    - Chapter 1 (arts. 39–42)—Workers
    - Chapter 2 (arts. 43–48)—Right of establishment
    - Chapter 3 (arts. 49–55)—Services
    - Chapter 4 (arts. 56–60)—Capital and payments
  - TITLE IV(arts. 61–69)—Visas, asylum, immigration and other policies related to free movement of persons
  - TITLE V(arts. 70–80)—Transport
  - TITLE VI (arts. 81–97)—Common rules on competition, taxation and approximation of laws
    - Chapter 1 (arts. 81–89)—Rules on competition
      - Section 1 (arts. 81–86)—Rules applying to undertakings
      - Section 2 (arts. 87–89)—Aids granted by States
    - Chapter 2 (arts. 90–93)—Tax provisions
    - Chapter 3 (arts. 94–97)—Approximation of laws
  - TITLE VII (arts. 98–124)—Economic and monetary policy
    - Chapter 1 (arts. 98–104)—Economic policy

Chapter 2 (arts. 105–111)—Monetary policy
Chapter 3 (arts. 112–115)—Institutional provisions
Chapter 4 (arts. 116–124)—Transitional provisions
TITLE VIII (arts. 125–130)—Employment
TITLE IX (arts. 131–134)—Common commercial policy
TITLE X (art. 135)—Customs cooperation
TITLE XI (arts. 136–150)—Social policy, education, vocational training and youth
Chapter 1 (arts. 136–145)—Social provisions
Chapter 2 (arts. 146–148)—The European Social Fund
Chapter 3 (arts. 149–150)—Education, vocational training and youth
TITLE XII (arts. 151)—Culture
TITLE XIII (art. 152)—Public health
TITLE XIV (art. 153)—Consumer protection
TITLE XV (arts. 154–156)—Trans-European networks
TITLE XVI (art. 157)—Industry
TITLE XVII (arts. 158–162)—Economic and social cohesion
TITLE XVIII (arts. 163–173)—Research and technological development
TITLE XIX (arts. 174–176)—Environment
TITLE XX (arts. 177–181)—Development cooperation

Part Four (arts. 182–188)—**Association of the overseas countries and territories**

Part Five (arts. 189–280)—**Institutions of the Community**
TITLE I (arts. 189–267)—Provisions governing the institutions
Chapter 1 (arts. 189–248)—The institutions
Section 1 (arts. 189–201)—The European Parliament
Section 2 (arts. 202–210)—The Council
Section 3 (arts. 211–219)—The Commission
Section 4 (arts. 220–245)—The Court of Justice
Section 5 (arts. 246–248)—The Court of Auditors
Chapter 2 (arts. 249–256)—Provisions common to several institutions
Chapter 3 (arts. 257–262)—The Economic and Social Committee
Chapter 4 (arts. 263–265)—The Committee of the Regions
Chapter 5 (arts. 266–267)—The European Investment Bank
TITLE II (arts. 268–280)—Financial provisions

Part Six—General and final provisions
General provisions (arts. 281–312)
Final provisions (arts. 313–314)

* * *

HIS MAJESTY THE KING OF THE BELGIANS, THE PRESIDENT OF THE FEDERAL REPUBLIC OF GERMANY, THE PRESIDENT OF THE FRENCH REPUBLIC, THE PRESIDENT OF THE ITALIAN REPUBLIC, HER ROYAL HIGHNESS THE GRAND DUCHESS OF LUXEMBOURG, HER MAJESTY THE QUEEN OF THE NETHERLANDS,[1]

---

1. Denmark, Greece, Spain, Ireland, Austria, Portugal, Finland, Sweden and the United Kingdom have since become members of the European Community.

DETERMINED to lay the foundations of an ever closer union among the peoples of Europe,

RESOLVED to ensure the economic and social progress of their countries by common action to eliminate the barriers which divide Europe,

AFFIRMING as the essential objective of their efforts the constant improvements of the living and working conditions of their peoples,

RECOGNISING that the removal of existing obstacles calls for concerted action in order to guarantee steady expansion, balanced trade and fair competition,

ANXIOUS to strengthen the unity of their economies and to ensure their harmonious development by reducing the differences existing between the various regions and the backwardness of the less-favoured regions,

DESIRING to contribute, by means of a common commercial policy, to the progressive abolition of restrictions on international trade,

INTENDING to confirm the solidarity which binds Europe and the overseas countries and desiring to ensure the development of their prosperity, in accordance with the principles of the Charter of the United Nations,

RESOLVED by thus pooling their resources to preserve and strengthen peace and liberty, and calling upon the other peoples of Europe who share their ideal to join in their efforts,

DETERMINED to promote the development of the highest possible level of knowledge for their peoples through a wide access to education and through its continuous updating,

HAVE DECIDED to create a EUROPEAN COMMUNITY ...

PART ONE

PRINCIPLES

Article 1 (ex Article 1)

By this Treaty, the HIGH CONTRACTING PARTIES establish among themselves a EUROPEAN COMMUNITY.[2]

Article 2 (ex Article 2)

The Community shall have as its task, by establishing a common market and an economic and monetary union and by implementing common policies or activities referred to in Articles 3 and 4, to promote throughout the Community a harmonious, balanced and sustainable development of economic activities, a high level of employment and of social protection, equality between men and women, sustainable and non-inflationary growth, a high degree of competitiveness and convergence of economic performance, a high level of protection and improvement of the quality of the environment, the raising of the standard of living and quality

---

2. The TEU changed the name from "European Economic Community" to "European Community."

of life, and economic and social cohesion and solidarity among Member States.[3]

Article 3 (ex Article 3)[4]

1. For the purposes set out in Article 2, the activities of the Community shall include, as provided in this Treaty and in accordance with the timetable set out therein:

(a) the prohibition, as between Member States, of customs duties and quantitative restrictions on the import and export of goods, and of all other measures having equivalent effect;

(b) a common commercial policy;

(c) an internal market characterised by the abolition, as between Member States, of obstacles to the free movement of goods, persons, services and capital;

(d) measures concerning the entry and movement of persons as provided for in Title IV;

(e) a common policy in the sphere of agriculture and fisheries;

(f) a common policy in the sphere of transport;

(g) a system ensuring that competition in the internal market is not distorted;

(h) the approximation of the laws of Member States to the extent required for the functioning of the common market;

(i) the promotion of coordination between employment policies of the Member States with a view to enhancing their effectiveness by developing a coordinated strategy for employment;

(j) a policy in the social sphere comprising a European Social Fund;

(k) the strengthening of economic and social cohesion;

(l) a policy in the sphere of the environment;

(m) the strengthening of the competitiveness of Community industry;

(n) the promotion of research and technological development;

(o) encouragement for the establishment and development of trans-European networks;

(p) a contribution to the attainment of a high level of health protection;

(q) a contribution to education and training of quality and to the flowering of the cultures of the Member States;

(r) a policy in the sphere of development cooperation;

---

3. The TEU amended this article to add the "economic and monetary union" as a principal objective and to insert a number of additional economic and social goals.

4. In this list of Community activities, the TEU introduced items (d), (j) through (r), and (t) to (u), and amended significantly items (b), (c) and (e).

(s) the association of the overseas countries and territories in order to increase trade and promote jointly economic and social development;

(t) a contribution to the strengthening of consumer protection;

(u) measures in the spheres of energy, civil protection and tourism.

2. In all the activities referred to in this Article, the Community shall aim to eliminate inequalities, and to promote equality, between men and women.

Article 4 (ex Article 3a)[5]

1. For the purposes set out in Article 2, the activities of the Member States and the Community shall include, as provided in this Treaty and in accordance with the timetable set out therein, the adoption of an economic policy which is based on the close coordination of Member States' economic policies, on the internal market and on the definition of common objectives, and conducted in accordance with the principle of an open market economy with free competition.

2. Concurrently with the foregoing, and as provided in this Treaty and in accordance with the timetable and the procedures set out therein, these activities shall include the irrevocable fixing of exchange rates leading to the introduction of a single currency, the ECU, and the definition and conduct of a single monetary policy and exchange-rate policy the primary objective of both of which shall be to maintain price stability and, without prejudice to this objective, to support the general economic policies in the Community, in accordance with the principle of an open market economy with free competition.

3. These activities of the Member States and the Community shall entail compliance with the following guiding principles: stable prices, sound public finances and monetary conditions and a sustainable balance of payments.

Article 5 (ex Article 3b)[6]

The Community shall act within the limits of the powers conferred upon it by this Treaty and of the objectives assigned to it therein.

In areas which do not fall within its exclusive competence, the Community shall take action, in accordance with the principle of subsidiarity, only if and insofar as the objectives of the proposed action cannot be sufficiently achieved by the Member States and can therefore, by reason of the scale or effects of the proposed action, be better achieved by the Community.

Any action by the Community shall not go beyond what is necessary to achieve the objectives of this Treaty.

---

5. Added by the TEU.
6. Added by the TEU.

Article 6 (ex Article 3c)

Environmental protection requirements must be integrated into the definition and implementation of the Community policies and activities referred to in Article 3, in particular with a view to promoting sustainable development.

Article 7 (ex Article 4)

1. The tasks entrusted to the Community shall be carried out by the following institutions:

— a EUROPEAN PARLIAMENT,

— a COUNCIL,

— a COMMISSION,

— a COURT OF JUSTICE,

— a COURT OF AUDITORS.[7]

Each institution shall act within the limits of the powers conferred upon it by this Treaty.

2. The Council and the Commission shall be assisted by an Economic and Social Committee and a Committee of the Regions[8] acting in an advisory capacity.

Article 8 (ex Article 4a)[9]

A European System of Central Banks (hereinafter referred to as "ESCB") and a European Central Bank (hereinafter referred to as "ECB") shall be established in accordance with the procedures laid down in this Treaty; they shall act within the limits of the powers conferred upon them by this Treaty and by the Statute of the ESCB and of the ECB (hereinafter referred to as "Statute of the ESCB") annexed thereto.

Article 9 (ex Article 4b)[10]

A European Investment Bank is hereby established, which shall act within the limits of the powers conferred upon it by this Treaty and the Statute annexed thereto.

Article 10 (ex Article 5)

Member States shall take all appropriate measures, whether general or particular, to ensure fulfilment of the obligations arising out of this Treaty or resulting from action taken by the institutions of the Community. They shall facilitate the achievement of the Community's tasks.

They shall abstain from any measure which could jeopardise the attainment of the objectives of this Treaty.

---

7. Added by the TEU.
8. Added by the TEU.
9. Added by the TEU.
10. Added by the TEU.

Article 11 (ex Article 5a)[11]

1. Member States which intend to establish closer cooperation between themselves may be authorised, subject to Articles 43 and 44 of the Treaty on European Union, to make use of the institutions, procedures and mechanisms laid down by this Treaty, provided that the cooperation proposed:

(a) does not concern areas which fall within the exclusive competence of the Community;

(b) does not affect Community policies, actions or programmes;

(c) does not concern the citizenship of the Union or discriminate between nationals of Member States;

(d) remains within the limits of the powers conferred upon the Community by this Treaty; and

(e) does not constitute a discrimination or a restriction of trade between Member States and does not distort the conditions of competition between the latter.

2. The authorisation referred to in paragraph 1 shall be granted by the Council, acting by a qualified majority on a proposal from the Commission and after consulting the European Parliament.

If a member of the Council declares that, for important and stated reasons of national policy, it intends to oppose the granting of an authorisation by qualified majority, a vote shall not be taken. The Council may, acting by a qualified majority, request that the matter be referred to the Council, meeting in the composition of the Heads of State or Government, for decision by unanimity.

Member States which intend to establish closer cooperation as referred to in paragraph 1 may address a request to the Commission, which may submit a proposal to the Council to that effect. In the event of the Commission not submitting a proposal, it shall inform the Member States concerned of the reasons for not doing so.

3. Any Member State which wishes to become a party to cooperation set up in accordance with this Article shall notify its intention to the Council and to the Commission, which shall give an opinion to the Council within three months of receipt of that notification. Within four months of the date of that notification, the Commission shall decide on it and on such specific arrangements as it may deem necessary.

4. The acts and decisions necessary for the implementation of cooperation activities shall be subject to all the relevant provisions of this Treaty, save as otherwise provided for in this Article and in Articles 43 and 44 of the Treaty on European Union.

5. This Article is without prejudice to the provisions of the Protocol integrating the Schengen acquis into the framework of the European Union.

---

11. Added by the Treaty of Amsterdam.

Article 12 (ex Article 6)[12]

Within the scope of application of this Treaty, and without prejudice to any special provisions contained therein, any discrimination on grounds of nationality shall be prohibited.

The Council, acting in accordance with the procedure referred to in Article 251, may adopt rules designed to prohibit such discrimination.

Article 13 (ex Article 6a)[13]

Without prejudice to the other provisions of this Treaty and within the limits of the powers conferred by it upon the Community, the Council, acting unanimously on a proposal from the Commission and after consulting the European Parliament, may take appropriate action to combat discrimination based on sex, racial or ethnic origin, religion or belief, disability, age or sexual orientation.

Article 14 (ex Article 7a)[14]

1. The Community shall adopt measures with the aim of progressively establishing the internal market over a period expiring on 31 December 1992, in accordance with the provisions of this Article and of Articles 15, 26, 47(2), 49, 80, 93 and 95 and without prejudice to the other provisions of this Treaty.

2. The internal market shall comprise an area without internal frontiers in which the free movement of goods, persons, services and capital is ensured in accordance with the provisions of this Treaty.

3. The Council, acting by a qualified majority on a proposal from the Commission, shall determine the guidelines and conditions necessary to ensure balanced progress in all the sectors concerned.

Article 15 (ex Article 7c)[15]

When drawing up its proposals with a view to achieving the objectives set out in Article 14, the Commission shall take into account the extent of the effort that certain economies showing differences in development will have to sustain during the period of establishment of the internal market and it may propose appropriate provisions.

If these provisions take the form of derogations, they must be of a temporary nature and must cause the least possible disturbance to the functioning of the common market.

---

12. The TEU renumbered this former Article 7 as Article 6. The TEU also made the co-decision procedure applicable to action under this article. (Until the SEA in 1987 introduced parliamentary cooperation for such action, the Council acted under this article by qualified majority vote and with parliamentary consultation.) The former Article 6, regarding economic coordination, is now covered by Article 99 (ex 103).

13. The Treaty of Amsterdam eliminated the former Article 7 which detailed the establishment of the common market.

14. The first two sections were introduced as Article 8a by the SEA and were renumbered as 7a by the TEU. The third section was introduced as Article 8b by the SEA and was renumbered as 7b by the TEU.

15. Introduced as Article 8c by the SEA, this article was renumbered 7c by the TEU.

Article 16 (ex Article 7d)

Without prejudice to Articles 73, 86 and 87, and given the place occupied by services of general economic interest in the shared values of the Union as well as their role in promoting social and territorial cohesion, the Community and the Member States, each within their respective powers and within the scope of application of this Treaty, shall take care that such services operate on the basis of principles and conditions which enable them to fulfil their missions.

PART TWO[16]

CITIZENSHIP OF THE UNION

Article 17 (ex Article 8)

1. Citizenship of the Union is hereby established. Every person holding the nationality of a Member State shall be a citizen of the Union. Citizenship of the Union shall complement and not replace national citizenship.

2. Citizens of the Union shall enjoy the rights conferred by this Treaty and shall be subject to the duties imposed thereby.

Article 18 (ex Article 8a)[17]

1. Every citizen of the Union shall have the right to move and reside freely within the territory of the Member States, subject to the limitations and conditions laid down in this Treaty and by the measures adopted to give it effect.

2. The Council may adopt provisions with a view to facilitating the exercise of the rights referred to in paragraph 1; save as otherwise provided in this Treaty, the Council shall act in accordance with the procedure referred to in Article 251. The Council shall act unanimously throughout this procedure.

Article 19 (ex Article 8b)

1. Every citizen of the Union residing in a Member State of which he is not a national shall have the right to vote and to stand as a candidate at municipal elections in the Member State in which he resides, under the same conditions as nationals of that State. This right shall be exercised subject to detailed arrangements adopted by the Council, acting unanimously on a proposal from the Commission and after consulting the European Parliament; these arrangements may provide for derogations where warranted by problems specific to a Member State.

2. Without prejudice to Article 190(4) and to the provisions adopted for its implementation, every citizen of the Union residing in a Member

---

16. This Part was introduced by the TEU. It originally comprised Articles 8 to 8e, now Articles 17 to 22.

17. Prior to the Treaty of Amsterdam, this Article required the Council to act unanimously on a proposal from the Commission and after obtaining the assent of the European Parliament, rather than (as at present) to use the codecision procedure of Article 251 (ex 189b).

State of which he is not a national shall have the right to vote and to stand as a candidate in elections to the European Parliament in the Member State in which he resides, under the same conditions as nationals of that State. This right shall be exercised subject to detailed arrangements adopted by the Council, acting unanimously on a proposal from the Commission and after consulting the European Parliament; these arrangements may provide for derogations where warranted by problems specific to a Member State.

Article 20 (ex Article 8c)

Every citizen of the Union shall, in the territory of a third country in which the Member State of which he is a national is not represented, be entitled to protection by the diplomatic or consular authorities of any Member State, on the same conditions as the nationals of that State. Member States shall establish the necessary rules among themselves and start the international negotiations required to secure this protection.

Article 21 (ex Article 8d)

Every citizen of the Union shall have the right to petition the European Parliament in accordance with Article 194.

Every citizen of the Union may apply to the Ombudsman established in accordance with Article 195.

Every citizen of the Union may write to any of the institutions or bodies referred to in this Article or in Article 7 in one of the languages mentioned in Article 314 and have an answer in the same language.

Article 22 (ex Article 8e)

The Commission shall report to the European Parliament, to the Council and to the Economic and Social Committee every three years on the application of the provisions of this Part. This report shall take account of the development of the Union.

On this basis, and without prejudice to the other provisions of this Treaty, the Council, acting unanimously on a proposal from the Commission and after consulting the European Parliament, may adopt provisions to strengthen or to add to the rights laid down in this Part, which it shall recommend to the Member States for adoption in accordance with their respective constitutional requirements.

PART THREE[18]

COMMUNITY POLICIES

TITLE I: FREE MOVEMENT OF GOODS

Article 23 (ex Article 9)

1. The Community shall be based upon a customs union which shall cover all trade in goods and which shall involve the prohibition between

---

18. The TEU renumbered the former Part Two as Part Three, and changed the title to "Community Policies" from "Foundations of the Community."

Member States of customs duties on imports and exports and of all charges having equivalent effect, and the adoption of a common customs tariff in their relations with third countries.

2. The provisions of Article 25 and of Chapter 2 of this Title shall apply to products originating in Member States and to products coming from third countries which are in free circulation in Member States.

Article 24 (ex Article 10)

Products coming from a third country shall be considered to be in free circulation in a Member State if the import formalities have been complied with and any customs duties or charges having equivalent effect which are payable have been levied in that Member State, and if they have not benefited from a total or partial drawback of such duties or charges.

Chapter 1: The customs union

Article 25 (ex Article 12)[19]

Customs duties on imports and exports and charges having equivalent effect shall be prohibited between Member States. This prohibition shall also apply to customs duties of a fiscal nature.

Article 26 (ex Article 28)[20]

Common Customs Tariff duties shall be fixed by the Council acting by a qualified majority on a proposal from the Commission.

Article 27 (ex Article 29)

In carrying out the tasks entrusted to it under this Chapter the Commission shall be guided by:

(a) the need to promote trade between Member States and third countries;

(b) developments in conditions of competition within the Community insofar as they lead to an improvement in the competitive capacity of undertakings;

(c) the requirements of the Community as regards the supply of raw materials and semi-finished goods; in this connection the Commission shall take care to avoid distorting conditions of competition between Member States in respect of finished goods;

(d) the need to avoid serious disturbances in the economies of Member States and to ensure rational development of production and an expansion of consumption within the Community.

---

19. The Treaty of Amsterdam revised this article to prohibit all customs duties and charges having equivalent effect, rather than simply prohibiting the introduction of any new customs duties or charges having equivalent effect and prohibiting any increases in already applied customs duties and charges having equivalent effect. Prior to the Treaty of Amsterdam, then Articles 12 to 17 governed customs duties and charges of equivalent effect.

20. Prior to the Treaty of Amsterdam, the then Articles 18 to 29 governed the setting up of the common customs tariff.

Chapter 2: Prohibition of quantitative restrictions between Member States

Article 28 (ex Article 30)

Quantitative restrictions on imports and all measures having equivalent effect shall be prohibited between Member States.

Article 29 (ex Article 34)

Quantitative restrictions on exports, and all measures having equivalent effect, shall be prohibited between Member States.

Article 30 (ex Article 36)

The provisions of Articles 28 and 29 shall not preclude prohibitions or restrictions on imports, exports or goods in transit justified on grounds of public morality, public policy or public security; the protection of health and life of humans, animals or plants; the protection of national treasures possessing artistic, historic or archaeological value; or the protection of industrial and commercial property. Such prohibitions or restrictions shall not, however, constitute a means of arbitrary discrimination or a disguised restriction on trade between Member States.

Article 31 (ex Article 37)

1. Member States shall adjust any State monopolies of a commercial character so as to ensure that no discrimination regarding the conditions under which goods are procured and marketed exists between nationals of Member States.

The provisions of this Article shall apply to any body through which a Member State, in law or in fact, either directly or indirectly supervises, determines or appreciably influences imports or exports between Member States. These provisions shall likewise apply to monopolies delegated by the State to others.

2. Member States shall refrain from introducing any new measure which is contrary to the principles laid down in paragraph 1 or which restricts the scope of the Articles dealing with the prohibition of customs duties and quantitative restrictions between Member States.

3. If a State monopoly of a commercial character has rules which are designed to make it easier to dispose of agricultural products or obtain for them the best return, steps should be taken in applying the rules contained in this Article to ensure equivalent safeguards for the employment and standard of living of the producers concerned.

TITLE II

AGRICULTURE

Article 32 (ex Article 38)

1. The common market shall extend to agriculture and trade in agricultural products. "Agricultural products" means the products of the

soil, of stockfarming and of fisheries and products of first-stage processing directly related to these products.

2. Save as otherwise provided in Articles 33 to 38, the rules laid down for the establishment of the common market shall apply to agricultural products.

3. The products subject to the provisions of Articles 33 to 38 are listed in Annex I to this Treaty.

4. The operation and development of the common market for agricultural products must be accompanied by the establishment of a common agricultural policy.

Article 33 (ex Article 39)

1. The objectives of the common agricultural policy shall be:

(a) to increase agricultural productivity by promoting technical progress and by ensuring the rational development of agricultural production and the optimum utilisation of the factors of production, in particular labour;

(b) thus to ensure a fair standard of living for the agricultural community, in particular by increasing the individual earnings of persons engaged in agriculture;

(c) to stabilise markets;

(d) to assure the availability of supplies;

(e) to ensure that supplies reach consumers at reasonable prices.

2. In working out the common agricultural policy and the special methods for its application, account shall be taken of:

(a) the particular nature of agricultural activity, which results from the social structure of agriculture and from structural and natural disparities between the various agricultural regions;

(b) the need to effect the appropriate adjustments by degrees;

(c) the fact that in the Member States agriculture constitutes a sector closely linked with the economy as a whole.

Article 34 (ex Article 40)

1. In order to attain the objectives set out in Article 33, a common organisation of agricultural markets shall be established.

This organisation shall take one of the following forms, depending on the product concerned:

(a) common rules on competition;

(b) compulsory coordination of the various national market organisations;

(c) a European market organisation.

2. The common organisation established in accordance with paragraph 1 may include all measures required to attain the objectives set out

in Article 33, in particular regulation of prices, aids for the production and marketing of the various products, storage and carryover arrangements and common machinery for stabilising imports or exports.

The common organisation shall be limited to pursuit of the objectives set out in Article 33 and shall exclude any discrimination between producers or consumers within the Community.

Any common price policy shall be based on common criteria and uniform methods of calculation.

3. In order to enable the common organisation referred to in paragraph 1 to attain its objectives, one or more agricultural guidance and guarantee funds may be set up.

Article 35 (ex Article 41)

To enable the objectives set out in Article 33 to be attained, provision may be made within the framework of the common agricultural policy for measures such as:

> (a) an effective coordination of efforts in the spheres of vocational training, of research and of the dissemination of agricultural knowledge; this may include joint financing of projects or institutions;

> (b) joint measures to promote consumption of certain products.

Article 36 (ex Article 42)

The provisions of the Chapter relating to rules on competition shall apply to production of and trade in agricultural products only to the extent determined by the Council within the framework of Article 37(2) and (3) and in accordance with the procedure laid down therein, account being taken of the objectives set out in Article 33.

The Council may, in particular, authorise the granting of aid:

> (a) for the protection of enterprises handicapped by structural or natural conditions;

> (b) within the framework of economic development programmes.

Article 37 (ex Article 43)

1. In order to evolve the broad lines of a common agricultural policy, the Commission shall, immediately this Treaty enters into force, convene a conference of the Member States with a view to making a comparison of their agricultural policies, in particular by producing a statement of their resources and needs.

2. Having taken into account the work of the Conference provided for in paragraph 1, after consulting the Economic and Social Committee and within two years of the entry into force of this Treaty, the Commission shall submit proposals for working out and implementing the common agricultural policy, including the replacement of the national organisations by one of the forms of common organisation provided for in Article 34(1), and for implementing the measures specified in this Title.

These proposals shall take account of the interdependence of the agricultural matters mentioned in this Title.

The Council shall, on a proposal from the Commission and after consulting the European Parliament, acting by a qualified majority, make regulations, issue directives, or take decisions, without prejudice to any recommendations it may also make.

3. The Council may, acting by a qualified majority and in accordance with paragraph 2, replace the national market organisations by the common organisation provided for in Article 34(1) if:

(a) the common organisation offers Member States which are opposed to this measure and which have an organisation of their own for the production in question equivalent safeguards for the employment and standard of living of the producers concerned, account being taken of the adjustments that will be possible and the specialisation that will be needed with the passage of time;

(b) such an organisation ensures conditions for trade within the Community similar to those existing in a national market.

4. If a common organisation for certain raw materials is established before a common organisation exists for the corresponding processed products, such raw materials as are used for processed products intended for export to third countries may be imported from outside the Community.

Article 38 (ex Article 46)

Where in a Member State a product is subject to a national market organisation or to internal rules having equivalent effect which affect the competitive position of similar production in another Member State, a countervailing charge shall be applied by Member States to imports of this product coming from the Member State where such organisation or rules exist, unless that State applies a countervailing charge on export.

The Commission shall fix the amount of these charges at the level required to redress the balance; it may also authorise other measures, the conditions and details of which it shall determine.

TITLE III

FREE MOVEMENT OF PERSONS, SERVICES AND CAPITAL

Chapter 1: Workers

Article 39 (ex Article 48)

1. Freedom of movement for workers shall be secured within the Community.

2. Such freedom of movement shall entail the abolition of any discrimination based on nationality between workers of the Member States as regards employment, remuneration and other conditions of work and employment.

3. It shall entail the right, subject to limitations justified on grounds of public policy, public security or public health:

(a) to accept offers of employment actually made;

(b) to move freely within the territory of Member States for this purpose;

(c) to stay in a Member State for the purpose of employment in accordance with the provisions governing the employment of nationals of that State laid down by law, regulation or administrative action;

(d) to remain in the territory of a Member State after having been employed in that State, subject to conditions which shall be embodied in implementing regulations to be drawn up by the Commission.

4. The provisions of this Article shall not apply to employment in the public service.

Article 40 (ex Article 49)[21]

The Council shall, acting in accordance with the procedure referred to in Article 251 and after consulting the Economic and Social Committee, issue directives or make regulations setting out the measures required to bring about freedom of movement for workers, as defined in Article 39, in particular:

(a) by ensuring close cooperation between national employment services;

(b) by abolishing those administrative procedures and practices and those qualifying periods in respect of eligibility for available employment, whether resulting from national legislation or from agreements previously concluded between Member States, the maintenance of which would form an obstacle to liberalisation of the movement of workers;

(c) by abolishing all such qualifying periods and other restrictions provided for either under national legislation or under agreements previously concluded between Member States as imposed on workers of other Member States conditions regarding the free choice of employment other than those imposed on workers of the State concerned;

(d) by setting up appropriate machinery to bring offers of employment into touch with applications for employment and to facilitate the achievement of a balance between supply and demand in the employment market in such a way as to avoid serious threats to the standard of living and level of employment in the various regions and industries.

21. The TEU amended the first paragraph to require that legislation be adopted by the codecision procedure, then Article 189b (now Article 251). In 1987, the SEA had amended the article to require the cooperation procedure, described in then Article 189c (now Article 252). The initial Treaty had authorized legislation by simple majority vote of the Council, with no reference to the European Parliament.

Article 41 (ex Article 50)

Member States shall, within the framework of a joint programme, encourage the exchange of young workers.

Article 42 (ex Article 51)

The Council shall, acting in accordance with the procedure referred to in Article 251, adopt such measures in the field of social security as are necessary to provide freedom of movement for workers; to this end, it shall make arrangements to secure for migrant workers and their dependents:

(a) aggregation, for the purpose of acquiring and retaining the right to benefit and of calculating the amount of benefit, of all periods taken into account under the laws of the several countries;

(b) payment of benefits to persons resident in the territories of Member States.

The Council shall act unanimously throughout the procedure referred to in Article 251.

Chapter 2: Right of establishment

Article 43 (ex Article 52)

Within the framework of the provisions set out below, restrictions on the freedom of establishment of nationals of a Member State in the territory of another Member State shall be prohibited. Such prohibition shall also apply to restrictions on the setting-up of agencies, branches or subsidiaries by nationals of any Member State established in the territory of any Member State.

Freedom of establishment shall include the right to take up and pursue activities as self-employed persons and to set up and manage undertakings, in particular companies or firms within the meaning of the second paragraph of Article 48, under the conditions laid down for its own nationals by the law of the country where such establishment is effected, subject to the provisions of the Chapter relating to capital.

Article 44 (ex Article 54)[22]

1. In order to attain freedom of establishment as regards a particular activity, the Council, acting in accordance with the procedure referred to in Article 251 and after consulting the Economic and Social Committee, shall act by means of directives.

2. The Council and the Commission shall carry out the duties devolving upon them under the preceding provisions, in particular:

---

22. The TEU amended section 1 to require that directives be adopted by the codecision procedure (now Article 251). In 1987, the SEA had previously amended the article to require the cooperation procedure (now Article 252). The original Treaty provision had required the Council during the first stage to act unanimously in adopting directives after consultation of the European Parliament, and thereafter by qualified majority.

(a) by according, as a general rule, priority treatment to activities where freedom of establishment makes a particularly valuable contribution to the development of production and trade;

(b) by ensuring close cooperation between the competent authorities in the Member States in order to ascertain the particular situation within the Community of the various activities concerned;

(c) by abolishing those administrative procedures and practices, whether resulting from national legislation or from agreements previously concluded between Member States, the maintenance of which would form an obstacle to freedom of establishment;

(d) by ensuring that workers of one Member State employed in the territory of another Member State may remain in that territory for the purpose of taking up activities therein as self-employed persons, where they satisfy the conditions which they would be required to satisfy if they were entering that State at the time when they intended to take up such activities;

(e) by enabling a national of one Member State to acquire and use land and buildings situated in the territory of another Member State, insofar as this does not conflict with the principles laid down in Article 33(2);

(f) by effecting the progressive abolition of restrictions on freedom of establishment in every branch of activity under consideration, both as regards the conditions for setting up agencies, branches or subsidiaries in the territory of a Member State and as regards the subsidiaries in the territory of a Member State and as regards the conditions governing the entry of personnel belonging to the main establishment into managerial or supervisory posts in such agencies, branches or subsidiaries;

(g) by coordinating to the necessary extent the safeguards which, for the protection of the interests of members and other, are required by Member States of companies or firms within the meaning of the second paragraph of Article [48] with a view to making such safeguards equivalent throughout the Community;

(h) by satisfying themselves that the conditions of establishment are not distorted by aids granted by Member States.

Article 45 (ex Article 55)

The provisions of this Chapter shall not apply, so far as any given Member State is concerned, to activities which in that State are connected, even occasionally, with the exercise of official authority.

The Council may, acting by a qualified majority on a proposal from the Commission, rule that the provisions of this Chapter shall not apply to certain activities.

Article 46 (ex Article 56)

1. The provisions of this Chapter and measures taken in pursuance thereof shall not prejudice the applicability of provisions laid down by law, regulation or administrative action providing for special treatment for foreign nationals on grounds of public policy, public security or public health.

2. The Council shall, acting in accordance with the procedure referred to in Article 251, issue directives for the coordination of the abovementioned provisions.[23]

Article 47 (ex Article 57)[24]

1. In order to make it easier for persons to take up and pursue activities as self-employed persons, the Council shall, acting in accordance with the procedure referred to in Article 251, issue directives for the mutual recognition of diplomas, certificates and other evidence of formal qualifications.

2. For the same purpose, the Council shall, acting in accordance with the procedure referred to in Article 251, issue directives for the coordination of the provisions laid down by law, regulation or administrative action in Member States concerning the taking-up and pursuit of activities as self-employed persons. The Council, acting unanimously throughout the procedure referred to in Article 251, shall decide on directives the implementation of which involves in at least one Member State amendment of the existing principles laid down by law governing the professions with respect to training and conditions of access for natural persons. In other cases the Council shall act by qualified majority.

3. In the case of the medical and allied and pharmaceutical professions, the progressive abolition of restrictions shall be dependent upon coordination of the conditions for their exercise in the various Member States.

Article 48 (ex Article 58)

Companies or firms formed in accordance with the law of a Member State and having their registered office, central administration or principal place of business within the Community shall, for the purposes of this

---

23. The TEU amended section 2 to require that after the end of the second stage, directives should be adopted by the codecision procedure (now Article 251). In 1987, the SEA had previously amended the article to require use of the cooperation procedure (now Article 252). The original Treaty provision had permitted the Council to act by qualified majority, but without reference to the European Parliament.

24. The Treaty of Amsterdam amended the first and second sentences of section 2 to require that directives be adopted by the codecision procedure, now described in Article 251, while amending the last sentence of section 2 to require the Council to act by qualified majority. The TEU had previously amended section 1 and the last sentence of section 2 to require that directives be adopted by the codecision procedure (now Article 251). In 1987, the SEA had already amended both sections to require that the cooperation procedure (now Article 252). Originally, the Treaty in section 1 had required the Council to act by qualified majority (after consultation of the European Parliament) after the end of the first stage, while permitting the Council in the last sentence of section 2 to act by qualified majority vote, without reference to the European Parliament.

Chapter, be treated in the same way as natural persons who are nationals of Member States.

"Companies or firms" means companies or firms constituted under civil or commercial law, including cooperative societies, and other legal persons governed by public or private law, save for those which are non-profit-making.

Chapter 3: Services

Article 49 (ex Article 59)

Within the framework of the provisions set out below, restrictions on freedom to provide services within the Community shall be prohibited in respect of nationals of Member States who are established in a State of the Community other than that of the person for whom the services are intended.

The Council may, acting by a qualified majority on a proposal from the Commission, extend the provisions of the Chapter to nationals of a third country who provide services and who are established within the Community.[25]

Article 50 (ex Article 60)

Services shall be considered to be "services" within the meaning of this Treaty where they are normally provided for remuneration, insofar as they are not governed by the provisions relating to freedom of movement for goods, capital and persons.

"Services" shall in particular include:

(a) activities of an industrial character;

(b) activities of a commercial character;

(c) activities of craftsmen;

(d) activities of the professions.

Without prejudice to the provisions of the Chapter relating to the right of establishment, the person providing a service may, in order to do so, temporarily pursue his activity in the State where the service is provided, under the same conditions as are imposed by that State on its own nationals.

Article 51 (ex Article 61)

1. Freedom to provide services in the field of transport shall be governed by the provisions of the Title relating to transport.

2. The liberalisation of banking and insurance services connected with movements of capital shall be effected in step with the liberalisation of movement of capital.

---

25. In 1987, the SEA amended the second paragraph of Article 49 (ex 59) to permit Council action by qualified majority, instead of unanimity.

Article 52 (ex Article 63)

1. In order to achieve the liberalisation of a specific service, the Council shall, on a proposal from the Commission and after consulting the Economic and Social Committee and the European Parliament, issue directives acting by a qualified majority.

2. As regards the directives referred to in paragraph 1, priority shall as a general rule be given to those services which directly affect production costs or the liberalisation of which helps to promote trade in goods.

Article 53 (ex Article 64)

The Member States declare their readiness to undertake the liberalisation of services beyond the extent required by the directives issued pursuant to Article 52(1), if their general economic situation and the situation of the economic sector concerned so permit.

To this end, the Commission shall make recommendations to the Member States concerned.

Article 54 (ex Article 65)

As long as restrictions on freedom to provide services have not been abolished, each Member State shall apply such restrictions without distinction on grounds of nationality or residence to all persons providing services within the meaning of the first paragraph of Article 49.

Article 55 (ex Article 66)

The provisions of Articles 45 to 48 shall apply to the matters covered by this Chapter.

Chapter 4: Capital and payments[26]

Article 56 (ex Article 73b)

1. Within the framework of the provisions set out in this Chapter, all restrictions on the movement of capital between Member States and between Member States and third countries shall be prohibited.

2. Within the framework of the provisions set out in this Chapter, all restrictions on payments between Member States and between Member States and third countries shall be prohibited.

Article 57 (ex Article 73c)

1. The provisions of Article 56 shall be without prejudice to the application to third countries of any restrictions which exist on 31 December 1993 under national or Community law adopted in respect of the movement of capital to or from third countries involving direct investment—including in real estate—establishment, the provision of financial services or the admission of securities to capital markets.

---

26. The TEU introduced Article 73b through 73h (the latter provision having since been repealed) in place of the previous Articles 67–73.

2. Whilst endeavouring to achieve the objective of free movement of capital between Member States and third countries to the greatest extent possible and without prejudice to the other Chapters of this Treaty, the Council may, acting by a qualified majority on a proposal from the Commission, adopt measures on the movement of capital to or from third countries involving direct investment—including investment in real estate—establishment, the provision of financial services or the admission of securities to capital markets. Unanimity shall be required for measures under this paragraph which constitute a step back in Community law as regards the liberalisation of the movement of capital to or from third countries.

Article 58 (ex Article 73d)

1. The provisions of Article 56 shall be without prejudice to the right of Member States:

(a) to apply the relevant provisions of their tax law which distinguish between taxpayers who are not in the same situation with regard to their place of residence or with regard to the place where their capital is invested;

(b) to take all requisite measures to prevent infringements of national law and regulations, in particular in the field of taxation and the prudential supervision of financial institutions, or to lay down procedures for the declaration of capital movements for purposes of administrative or statistical information, or to take measures which are justified on grounds of public policy or public security.

2. The provisions of this Chapter shall be without prejudice to the applicability of restrictions on the right of establishment which are compatible with this Treaty.

3. The measures and procedures referred to in paragraphs 1 and 2 shall not constitute a means of arbitrary discrimination or a disguised restriction on the free movement of capital and payments as defined in Article 56.

Article 59 (ex Article 73f)

Where, in exceptional circumstances, movements of capital to or from third countries cause, or threaten to cause, serious difficulties for the operation of economic and monetary union, the Council, acting by a qualified majority on a proposal from the Commission and after consulting the ECB, may take safeguard measures with regard to third countries for a period not exceeding six months if such measures are strictly necessary.

Article 60 (ex Article 73g)

1. If, in the cases envisaged in Article 301, action by the Community is deemed necessary, the Council may, in accordance with the procedure provided for in Article 301, take the necessary urgent measures on the movement of capital and on payments as regards the third countries concerned.

2. Without prejudice to Article 297 and as long as the Council has not taken measures pursuant to paragraph 1, a Member State may, for serious political reasons and on grounds of urgency, take unilateral measures against a third country with regard to capital movements and payments. The Commission and the other Member States shall be informed of such measures by the date of their entry into force at the latest.

The Council may, acting by a qualified majority on a proposal from the Commission, decide that the Member State concerned shall amend or abolish such measures. The President of the Council shall inform the European Parliament of any such decision taken by the Council.

TITLE IV (ex Title IIIa)[27]
VISAS, ASYLUM, IMMIGRATION AND OTHER POLICIES RELATED TO FREE MOVEMENT OF PERSONS

Article 61 (ex Article 73i)

In order to establish progressively an area of freedom, security and justice, the Council shall adopt:

(a) within a period of five years after the entry into force of the Treaty of Amsterdam, measures aimed at ensuring the free movement of persons in accordance with Article 14, in conjunction with directly related flanking measures with respect to external border controls, asylum and immigration, in accordance with the provisions of Article 62(2) and (3) and Article 63(1)(a) and (2)(a), and measures to prevent and combat crime in accordance with the provisions of Article 31(e) of the Treaty on European Union;

(b) other measures in the fields of asylum, immigration and safeguarding the rights of nationals of third countries, in accordance with the provisions of Article 63;

(c) measures in the field of judicial cooperation in civil matters as provided for in Article 65;

(d) appropriate measures to encourage and strengthen administrative cooperation, as provided for in Article 66;

(e) measures in the field of police and judicial cooperation in criminal matters aimed at a high level of security by preventing and combating crime within the Union in accordance with the provisions of the Treaty on European Union.

Article 62 (ex Article 73j)

The Council, acting in accordance with the procedure referred to in Article 67, shall, within a period of five years after the entry into force of the Treaty of Amsterdam, adopt:

---

27. The Treaty of Amsterdam introduced this new Title IV on visas, asylum, immigration and other policies related to the free movement of persons. Prior to the Treaty of Amsterdam, these matters were governed under the "third pillar" on justice and home affairs. The Treaty of Amsterdam transferred these matters (including the essential provisions of the 1990 Schengen Convention) to pillar one.

(1) measures with a view to ensuring, in compliance with Article 14, the absence of any controls on persons, be they citizens of the Union or nationals of third countries, when crossing internal borders;

(2) measures on the crossing of the external borders of the Member States which shall establish:

(a) standards and procedures to be followed by Member States in carrying out checks on persons at such borders;

(b) rules on visas for intended stays of no more than three months, including:

(i) the list of third countries whose nationals must be in possession of visas when crossing the external borders and those whose nationals are exempt from that requirement;

(ii) the procedures and conditions for issuing visas by Member States;

(iii) a uniform format for visas;

(iv) rules on a uniform visa;

(3) measures setting out the conditions under which nationals of third countries shall have the freedom to travel within the territory of the Member States during a period of no more than three months.

Article 63 (ex Article 73k)

The Council, acting in accordance with the procedure referred to in Article 67, shall, within a period of five years after the entry into force of the Treaty of Amsterdam, adopt:

(1) measures on asylum, in accordance with the Geneva Convention of 28 July 1951 and the Protocol of 31 January 1967 relating to the status of refugees and other relevant treaties, within the following areas:

(a) criteria and mechanisms for determining which Member State is responsible for considering an application for asylum submitted by a national of a third country in one of the Member States,

(b) minimum standards on the reception of asylum seekers in Member States,

(c) minimum standards with respect to the qualification of nationals of third countries as refugees,

(d) minimum standards on procedures in Member States for granting or withdrawing refugee status;

(2) measures on refugees and displaced persons within the following areas:

(a) minimum standards for giving temporary protection to displaced persons from third countries who cannot return to their country of origin and for persons who otherwise need international protection,

(b) promoting a balance of effort between Member States in receiving and bearing the consequences of receiving refugees and displaced persons;

(3) measures on immigration policy within the following areas:

(a) conditions of entry and residence, and standards on procedures for the issue by Member States of long term visas and residence permits, including those for the purpose of family reunion,

(b) illegal immigration and illegal residence, including repatriation of illegal residents;

(4) measures defining the rights and conditions under which nationals of third countries who are legally resident in a Member State may reside in other Member States.

Measures adopted by the Council pursuant to points 3 and 4 shall not prevent any Member State from maintaining or introducing in the areas concerned national provisions which are compatible with this Treaty and with international agreements.

Measures to be adopted pursuant to points 2(b), 3(a) and 4 shall not be subject to the five year period referred to above.

Article 64 (ex Article 73l)

1. This Title shall not affect the exercise of the responsibilities incumbent upon Member States with regard to the maintenance of law and order and the safeguarding of internal security.

2. In the event of one or more Member States being confronted with an emergency situation characterised by a sudden inflow of nationals of third countries and without prejudice to paragraph 1, the Council may, acting by qualified majority on a proposal from the Commission, adopt provisional measures of a duration not exceeding six months for the benefit of the Member States concerned.

Article 65 (ex Article 73m)

Measures in the field of judicial cooperation in civil matters having cross-border implications, to be taken in accordance with Article 67 and insofar as necessary for the proper functioning of the internal market, shall include:

(a) improving and simplifying:

— the system for cross-border service of judicial and extrajudicial documents;

— cooperation in the taking of evidence;

— the recognition and enforcement of decisions in civil and commercial cases, including decisions in extrajudicial cases;

(b) promoting the compatibility of the rules applicable in the Member States concerning the conflict of laws and of jurisdiction;

(c) eliminating obstacles to the good functioning of civil proceedings, if necessary by promoting the compatibility of the rules on civil procedure applicable in the Member States.

Article 66 (ex Article 73n)

The Council, acting in accordance with the procedure referred to in Article 67, shall take measures to ensure cooperation between the relevant departments of the administrations of the Member States in the areas covered by this Title, as well as between those departments and the Commission.

Article 67 (ex Article 73o)

1. During a transitional period of five years following the entry into force of the Treaty of Amsterdam, the Council shall act unanimously on a proposal from the Commission or on the initiative of a Member State and after consulting the European Parliament.

2. After this period of five years:

— the Council shall act on proposals from the Commission the Commission shall examine any request made by a Member State that it submit a proposal to the Council;

— the Council, acting unanimously after consulting the European Parliament, shall take a decision with a view to providing for all or parts of the areas covered by this Title to be governed by the procedure referred to in Article 251 and adapting the provisions relating to the powers of the Court of Justice.

3. By derogation from paragraphs 1 and 2, measures referred to in Article 62(2)(b) (i) and (iii) shall, from the entry into force of the Treaty of Amsterdam, be adopted by the Council acting by a qualified majority on a proposal from the Commission and after consulting the European Parliament.

4. By derogation from paragraph 2, measures referred to in Article 62(2)(b) (ii) and (iv) shall, after a period of five years following the entry into force of the Treaty of Amsterdam, be adopted by the Council acting in accordance with the procedure referred to in Article 251.

Article 68 (ex Article 73p)

1. Article 234 shall apply to this Title under the following circumstances and conditions: where a question on the interpretation of this Title or on the validity or interpretation of acts of the institutions of the Community based on this Title is raised in a case pending before a court or a tribunal of a Member State against whose decisions there is no judicial remedy under national law, that court or tribunal shall, if it considers that a decision on the question is necessary to enable it to give judgment, request the Court of Justice to give a ruling thereon.

2. In any event, the Court of Justice shall not have jurisdiction to rule on any measure or decision taken pursuant to Article 62(1) relating to the maintenance of law and order and the safeguarding of internal security.

3. The Council, the Commission or a Member State may request the Court of Justice to give a ruling on a question of interpretation of this Title or of acts of the institutions of the Community based on this Title. The ruling given by the Court of Justice in response to such a request shall not apply to judgments of courts or tribunals of the Member States which have become res judicata.

Article 69 (ex Article 73q)

The application of this Title shall be subject to the provisions of the Protocol on the position of the United Kingdom and Ireland and to the Protocol on the position of Denmark and without prejudice to the Protocol on the application of certain aspects of Article 14 of the Treaty establishing the European Community to the United Kingdom and to Ireland.

TITLE V (ex Title IV)
TRANSPORT
Article 70 (ex Article 74)

The objectives of this Treaty shall, in matters governed by this Title, be pursued by Member States within the framework of a common transport policy.

Article 71 (ex Article 75)[28]

1. For the purpose of implementing Article 70, and taking into account the distinctive features of transport, the Council shall, acting in accordance with the procedure referred to in Article 251 and after consulting the Economic and Social Committee and the Committee of the Regions, lay down:

(a) common rules applicable to international transport to or from the territory of a Member State or passing across the territory of one or more Member States;

(b) the conditions under which non-resident carriers may operate transport services within a Member State;

(c) measures to improve transport safety;

(d) any other appropriate provisions.

2. By way of derogation from the procedure provided for in paragraph 1, where the application of provisions concerning the principles of the regulatory system for transport would be liable to have a serious effect on the standard of living and on employment in certain areas and on the

---

28. The TEU had amended this article (i) to add section 1(c), (ii) to require the cooperation procedure of then Article 189c (now 252) for the adoption of rules under section 1, and (iii) to require a proposal from the Commission and consultation of the Parliament and the Economic and Social Committee.

operation of transport facilities, they shall be laid down by the Council acting unanimously on a proposal from the Commission, after consulting the European Parliament and the Economic and Social Committee. In so doing, the Council shall take into account the need for adaptation to the economic development which will result from establishing the common market.

Article 72 (ex Article 76)

Until the provisions referred to in Article 71(1) have been laid down, no Member State may, without the unanimous approval of the Council, make the various provisions governing the subject on 1 January 1958 or, for acceding States, the date of their accession less favourable in their direct or indirect effect on carriers of other Member States as compared with carriers who are nationals of that State.

Article 73 (ex Article 77)

Aids shall be compatible with this Treaty if they meet the needs of coordination of transport or if they represent reimbursement for the discharge of certain obligations inherent in the concept of a public service.

Article 74 (ex Article 78)

Any measures taken within the framework of this Treaty in respect of transport rates and conditions shall take account of the economic circumstances of carriers.

Article 75 (ex Article 79)

1. In the case of transport within the Community, discrimination which takes the form of carriers charging different rates and imposing different conditions for the carriage of the same goods over the same transport links on grounds of the country of origin or of destination of the goods in question shall be abolished.

2. Paragraph 1 shall not prevent the Council from adopting other measures in pursuance of Article 71(1).

3. The Council shall, acting by a qualified majority on a proposal from the Commission and after consulting the Economic and Social Committee, lay down rules for implementing the provisions of paragraph 1.

The Council may in particular lay down the provisions needed to enable the institutions of the Community to secure compliance with the rule laid down in paragraph 1 and to ensure that users benefit from it to the full.

4. The Commission shall, acting on its own initiative or on application by a Member State, investigate any cases of discrimination falling within paragraph 1 and, after consulting any Member State concerned, shall take the necessary decisions within the framework of the rules laid down in accordance with the provisions of paragraph 3.

Article 76 (ex Article 80)

1. The imposition by a Member State, in respect of transport operations carried out within the Community, of rates and conditions involving any element of support or protection in the interest of one or more particular undertakings or industries shall be prohibited, unless authorised by the Commission.

2. The Commission shall, acting on its own initiative or on application by a Member State, examine the rates and conditions referred to in paragraph 1, taking account in particular of the requirements of an appropriate regional economic policy, the needs of underdeveloped areas and the problems of areas seriously affected by political circumstances on the one hand, and of the effects of such rates and conditions on competition between the different modes of transport on the other.

After consulting each Member State concerned, the Commission shall take the necessary decisions.

3. The prohibition provided for in paragraph 1 shall not apply to tariffs fixed to meet competition.

Article 77 (ex Article 81)

Charges or dues in respect of the crossing of frontiers which are charged by a carrier in addition to the transport rates shall not exceed a reasonable level after taking the costs actually incurred thereby into account.

Member States shall endeavour to reduce these costs progressively.

The Commission may make recommendations to Member States for the application of this Article.

Article 78 (ex Article 82)

The provisions of this Title shall not form an obstacle to the application of measures taken in the Federal Republic of Germany to the extent that such measures are required in order to compensate for the economic disadvantages caused by the division of Germany to the economy of certain areas of the Federal Republic affected by that division.

Article 79 (ex Article 83)

An Advisory Committee consisting of experts designated by the governments of Member States shall be attached to the Commission. The Commission, whenever it considers it desirable, shall consult the Committee on transport matters without prejudice to the powers of the Economic and Social Committee.

Article 80 (ex Article 84)[29]

1. The provisions of this Title shall apply to transport by rail, road and inland waterway.

---

29. The SEA amended this article to permit Council action by qualified majority (rather than unanimity) and to add the final sentence.

2. The Council may, acting by a qualified majority, decide whether, to what extent and by what procedure appropriate provisions may be laid down for sea and air transport.

The procedural provisions of Article 71 shall apply.

TITLE VI (ex Title V)[30]

COMMON RULES ON COMPETITION, TAXATION AND APPROXIMATION OF LAWS

Chapter 1: Rules on competition

Section 1: Rules applying to undertakings

Article 81 (ex Article 85)

1. The following shall be prohibited as incompatible with the common market: all agreements between undertakings, decisions by associations of undertakings and concerted practices which may affect trade between Member States and which have as their object or effect the prevention, restriction or distortion of competition within the common market, and in particular those which:

(a) directly or indirectly fix purchase or selling prices or any other trading conditions;

(b) limit or control production, markets, technical development, or investment;

(c) share markets or sources of supply;

(d) apply dissimilar conditions to equivalent transactions with other trading parties, thereby placing them at a competitive disadvantage;

(e) make the conclusion of contracts subject to acceptance by the other parties of supplementary obligations which, by their nature or according to commercial usage, have no connection with the subject of such contracts.

2. Any agreements or decisions prohibited pursuant to this Article shall be automatically void.

3. The provisions of paragraph 1 may, however, be declared inapplicable in the case of:

— any agreement or category of agreements between undertakings;

— any decision or category of decisions by associations of undertakings;

— any concerted practice or category of concerted practices;

---

30. The TEU introduced this Title designation to replace the former "Part Three: Policy of the Community, Title 1 Common Rules."

which contributes to improving the production or distribution of goods or to promoting technical or economic progress, while allowing consumers a fair share of the resulting benefit, and which does not:

(a) impose on the undertakings concerned restrictions which are not indispensable to the attainment of these objectives;

(b) afford such undertakings the possibility of eliminating competition in respect of a substantial part of the products in question.

Article 82 (ex Article 86)

Any abuse by one or more undertakings of a dominant position within the common market or in a substantial part of it shall be prohibited as incompatible with the common market insofar as it may affect trade between Member States.

Such abuse may, in particular, consist in:

(a) directly or indirectly imposing unfair purchase or selling prices or other unfair trading conditions;

(b) limiting production, markets or technical development to the prejudice of consumers;

(c) applying dissimilar conditions to equivalent transactions with other trading parties, thereby placing them at a competitive disadvantage;

(d) making the conclusion of contracts subject to acceptance by the other parties of supplementary obligations which, by their nature or according to commercial usage, have no connection with the subject of such contracts.

Article 83 (ex Article 87)

1. The appropriate regulations or directives to give effect to the principles set out in Articles 81 and 82 shall be laid down by the Council, acting by a qualified majority on a proposal from the Commission and after consulting the European Parliament.[31]

2. The regulations or directives referred to in paragraph 1 shall be designed in particular:

(a) to ensure compliance with the prohibitions laid down in Article 81(1) and in Article 82 by making provision for fines and periodic penalty payments;

(b) to lay down detailed rules for the application of Article 81(3), taking into account the need to ensure effective supervision on the one hand, and to simplify administration to the greatest possible extent on the other;

---

31. The Treaty of Amsterdam amended paragraph 1 to require the Council to act by qualified majority rather than unanimously.

(c) to define, if need be, in the various branches of the economy, the scope of the provisions of Articles 81 and 82;

(d) to define the respective functions of the Commission and of the Court of Justice in applying the provisions laid down in this paragraph;

(e) to determine the relationship between national laws and the provisions contained in this Section or adopted pursuant to this Article.

Article 84 (ex Article 88)

Until the entry into force of the provisions adopted in pursuance of Article 83, the authorities in Member States shall rule on the admissibility of agreements, decisions and concerted practices and on abuse of a dominant position in the common market in accordance with the law of their country and with the provisions of Article 81, in particular paragraph 3, and of Article 82.

Article 85 (ex Article 89)

1. Without prejudice to Article 84, the Commission shall ensure the application of the principles laid down in Articles 81 and 82. On application by a Member State or on its own initiative, and in cooperation with the competent authorities in the Member States, who shall give it their assistance, the Commission shall investigate cases of suspected infringement of these principles. If it finds that there has been an infringement, it shall propose appropriate measures to bring it to an end.

2. If the infringement is not brought to an end, the Commission shall record such infringement of the principles in a reasoned decision. The Commission may publish its decision and authorise Member States to take the measures, the conditions and details of which it shall determine, needed to remedy the situation.

Article 86 (ex Article 90)

1. In the case of public undertakings and undertakings to which Member States grant special or exclusive rights, Member States shall neither enact nor maintain in force any measure contrary to the rules contained in this Treaty, in particular to those rules provided for in Article 12 and Articles 81 to 89.

2. Undertakings entrusted with the operation of services of general economic interest or having the character of a revenue-producing monopoly shall be subject to the rules contained in this Treaty, in particular to the rules on competition, insofar as the application of such rules does not obstruct the performance, in law or in fact, of the particular tasks assigned to them. The development of trade must not be affected to such an extent as would be contrary to the interests of the Community.

3. The Commission shall ensure the application of the provisions of this Article and shall, where necessary, address appropriate directives or decisions to Member States.

Section 2: Aids granted by States

Article 87 (ex Article 92)

1. Save as otherwise provided in this Treaty, any aid granted by a Member State or through State resources in any form whatsoever which distorts or threatens to distort competition by favouring certain undertakings or the production of certain goods shall, insofar as it affects trade between Member States, be incompatible with the common market.

2. The following shall be compatible with the common market:

(a) aid having a social character, granted to individual consumers, provided that such aid is granted without discrimination related to the origin of the products concerned;

(b) aid to make good the damage caused by natural disasters or exceptional occurrences;

(c) aid granted to the economy of certain areas of the Federal Republic of Germany affected by the division of Germany, insofar as such aid is required in order to compensate for the economic disadvantages caused by that division;

3. The following may be considered to be compatible with the common market:

(a) aid to promote the economic development of areas where the standard of living is abnormally low or where there is serious underemployment;

(b) aid to promote the execution of an important project of common European interest or to remedy a serious disturbance in the economy of a Member State;

(c) aid to facilitate the development of certain economic activities or of certain economic areas, where such aid does not adversely affect trading conditions to an extent contrary to the common interest;

(d) aid to promote culture and heritage conservation where such aid does not affect trading conditions and competition in the Community to an extent that is contrary to the common interest;[32]

(e) such other categories of aid as may be specified by decision of the Council acting by a qualified majority on a proposal from the Commission.

Article 88 (ex Article 93)

1. The Commission shall, in cooperation with Member States, keep under constant review all systems of aid existing in those States. It shall propose to the latter any appropriate measures required by the progressive development or by the functioning of the common market.

2. If, after giving notice to the parties concerned to submit their comments, the Commission finds that aid granted by a State or through

---

32. The TEU inserted paragraph 3(d), renumbering the former paragraph (d) as (e).

State resources is not compatible with the common market having regard to Article 87, or that such aid is being misused, it shall decide that the State concerned shall abolish or alter such aid within a period of time to be determined by the Commission.

If the State concerned does not comply with this decision within the prescribed time, the Commission or any other interested State may, in derogation from the provisions of Articles 226 and 227, refer the matter to the Court of Justice direct.

On application by a Member State, the Council may, acting unanimously, decide that aid which that State is granting or intends to grant shall be considered to be compatible with the common market, in derogation from the provisions of Article 87 or from the regulations provided for in Article 89, if such a decision is justified by exceptional circumstances. If, as regards the aid in question, the Commission has already initiated the procedure provided for in the first subparagraph of this paragraph, the fact that the State concerned has made its application to the Council shall have the effect of suspending that procedure until the Council has made its attitude known.

If, however, the Council has not made its attitude known within three months of the said application being made, the Commission shall give its decision on the case.

3. The Commission shall be informed, in sufficient time to enable it to submit its comments, of any plans to grant or alter aid. If it considers that any such plan is not compatible with the common market having regard to Article 87, it shall without delay initiate the procedure provided for in paragraph 2. The Member State concerned shall not put its proposed measures into effect until this procedure has resulted in a final decision.

Article 89 (ex Article 94)[33]

The Council, acting by a qualified majority on a proposal from the Commission and after consulting the European Parliament, may make any appropriate regulations for the application of Articles 87 and 88 and may in particular determine the conditions in which Article 88(3) shall apply and the categories of aid exempted from this procedure.

Chapter 2: Tax provisions

Article 90 (ex Article 95)

No Member State shall impose, directly or indirectly, on the products of other Member States any internal taxation of any kind in excess of that imposed directly or indirectly on similar domestic products.

Furthermore, no Member State shall impose on the products of other Member States any internal taxation of such a nature as to afford indirect protection to other products.

---

33. The TEU added the requirement of parliamentary consultation.

Article 91 (ex Article 96)

Where products are exported to the territory of any Member State, any repayment of internal taxation shall not exceed the internal taxation imposed on them whether directly or indirectly.

Article 92 (ex Article 98)

In the case of charges other than turnover taxes, excise duties and other forms of indirect taxation, remissions and repayments in respect of exports to other Member States may not be granted and countervailing charges in respect of imports from Member States may not be imposed unless the measures contemplated have been previously approved for a limited period by the Council acting by a qualified majority on a proposal from the Commission.

Article 93 (ex Article 99)[34]

The Council shall, acting unanimously on a proposal from the Commission and after consulting the European Parliament and the Economic and Social Committee, adopt provisions for the harmonisation of legislation concerning turnover taxes, excise duties and other forms of indirect taxation to the extent that such harmonisation is necessary to ensure the establishment and the functioning of the internal market within the time-limit laid down in Article 14.

Chapter 3: Approximation of laws

Article 94 (ex Article 100)[35]

The Council shall, acting unanimously on a proposal from the Commission and after consulting the European Parliament and the Economic and Social Committee, issue directives for the approximation of such laws, regulations or administrative provisions of the Member States as directly affect the establishment or functioning of the common market.

Article 95 (ex Article 100a)[36]

1. By way of derogation from Article 94 and save where otherwise provided in this Treaty, the following provisions shall apply for the achievement of the objectives set out in Article 14. The Council shall, acting in accordance with the procedure referred to in Article 251 and after consulting the Economic and Social Committee, adopt the measures for the approximation of the provisions laid down by law, regulation or administra-

---

34. The TEU added the requirement that the Council consult ECOSOC. Previously, the SEA in 1987 required parliamentary consultation and inserted the cross-reference to the internal market provision, now Article 14.

35. The TEU added the requirement that the Council consult Parliament and ECOSOC before adopting directives under this Article.

36. In 1987, the SEA introduced Article 100a (now 95). The TEU the required use of the codecision procedure of the then 189b (now 251), in place of the cooperation procedure of then Article 189c (now 252).

tive action in Member States which have as their object the establishment and functioning of the internal market.

2. Paragraph 1 shall not apply to fiscal provisions, to those relating to the free movement of persons nor to those relating to the rights and interests of employed persons.

3. The Commission, in its proposals envisaged in paragraph 1 concerning health, safety, environmental protection and consumer protection, will take as a base a high level of protection, taking account in particular of any new development based on scientific facts. Within their respective powers, the European Parliament and the Council will also seek to achieve this objective.[37]

4. If, after the adoption by the Council or by the Commission of a harmonisation measure, a Member State deems it necessary to maintain national provisions on grounds of major needs referred to in Article 30, or relating to the protection of the environment or the working environment, it shall notify the Commission of these provisions as well as the grounds for maintaining them.[38]

5. Moreover, without prejudice to paragraph 4, if, after the adoption by the Council or by the Commission of a harmonisation measure, a Member State deems it necessary to introduce national provisions based on new scientific evidence relating to the protection of the environment or the working environment on grounds of a problem specific to that Member State arising after the adoption of the harmonisation measure, it shall notify the Commission of the envisaged provisions as well as the grounds for introducing them.

6. The Commission shall, within six months of the notifications as referred to in paragraphs 4 and 5, approve or reject the national provisions involved after having verified whether or not they are a means of arbitrary discrimination or a disguised restriction on trade between Member States and whether or not they shall constitute an obstacle to the functioning of the internal market.

In the absence of a decision by the Commission within this period the national provisions referred to in paragraphs 4 and 5 shall be deemed to have been approved.

When justified by the complexity of the matter and in the absence of danger for human health, the Commission may notify the Member State concerned that the period referred to in this paragraph may be extended for a further period of up to six months.

7. When, pursuant to paragraph 6, a Member State is authorised to maintain or introduce national provisions derogating from a harmonisation

---

37. The Treaty of Amsterdam amended paragraph 3 to specify that the institutions should take account of any new development based on scientific facts.

38. The Treaty of Amsterdam amended paragraph 4 to include reference to harmonization measures by the Commission and to require a Member State to provide the Commission with notice and the grounds for maintaining a national provision.

measure, the Commission shall immediately examine whether to propose an adaptation to that measure.

8. When a Member State raises a specific problem on public health in a field which has been the subject of prior harmonisation measures, it shall bring it to the attention of the Commission which shall immediately examine whether to propose appropriate measures to the Council.

9. By way of derogation from the procedure laid down in Articles 226 and 227, the Commission and any Member State may bring the matter directly before the Court of Justice if it considers that another Member State is making improper use of the powers provided for in this Article.

10. The harmonisation measures referred to above shall, in appropriate cases, include a safeguard clause authorising the Member States to take, for one or more of the non-economic reasons referred to in Article [30], provisional measures subject to a Community control procedure.

Article 96 (ex Article 101)

Where the Commission finds that a difference between the provisions laid down by law, regulation or administrative action in Member States is distorting the conditions of competition in the common market and that the resultant distortion needs to be eliminated, it shall consult the Member States concerned.

If such consultation does not result in an agreement eliminating the distortion in question, the Council shall, on a proposal from the Commission, acting by a qualified majority, issue the necessary directives. The Commission and the Council may take any other appropriate measures provided for in this Treaty.

Article 97 (ex Article 102)

1. Where there is a reason to fear that the adoption or amendment of a provision laid down by law, regulation or administrative action may cause distortion within the meaning of Article 96, a Member State desiring to proceed therewith shall consult the Commission. After consulting the Member States, the Commission shall recommend to the States concerned such measures as may be appropriate to avoid the distortion in question.

2. If a State desiring to introduce or amend its own provisions does not comply with the recommendation addressed to it by the Commission, other Member States shall not be required, in pursuance of Article 96, to amend their own provisions in order to eliminate such distortion. If the Member State which has ignored the recommendation of the Commission causes distortion detrimental only to itself, the provisions of Article 96 shall not apply.

TITLE VII (ex Title VI)[39]
ECONOMIC AND MONETARY POLICY

Chapter 1: Economic policy

Article 98 (ex Article 102a)

Member States shall conduct their economic policies with a view to contributing to the achievement of the objectives of the Community, as defined in Article 2, and in the context of the broad guidelines referred to in Article 99(2). The Member States and the Community shall act in accordance with the principle of an open market economy with free competition, favouring an efficient allocation of resources, and in compliance with the principles set out in Article 4.

Article 99 (ex Article 103)

1. Member States shall regard their economic policies as a matter of common concern and shall coordinate them within the Council, in accordance with the provisions of Article 98.

2. The Council shall, acting by a qualified majority on a recommendation from the Commission, formulate a draft for the broad guidelines of the economic policies of the Member States and of the Community, and shall report its findings to the European Council.

The European Council shall, acting on the basis of the report from the Council, discuss a conclusion on the broad guidelines of the economic policies of the Member States and of the Community.

On the basis of this conclusion, the Council shall, acting by a qualified majority, adopt a recommendation setting out these broad guidelines. The Council shall inform the European Parliament of its recommendation.

3. In order to ensure closer coordination of economic policies and sustained convergence of the economic performances of the Member States, the Council shall, on the basis of reports submitted by the Commission, monitor economic developments in each of the Member States and in the Community as well as the consistency of economic policies with the broad guidelines referred to in paragraph 2, and regularly carry out an overall assessment.

For the purpose of this multilateral surveillance, Member States shall forward information to the Commission about important measures taken by them in the field of their economic policy and such other information as they deem necessary.

4. Where it is established, under the procedure referred to in paragraph 3, that the economic policies of a Member State are not consistent with the broad guidelines referred to in paragraph 2 or that they risk jeopardising the proper functioning of economic and monetary union, the Council may, acting by a qualified majority on a recommendation from the

---

39. The TEU introduced this title as Title VI, which, prior to the Treaty of Amsterdam, was comprised of four chapters and Articles 102a to 109m, in replacement of a prior Title II, Economic Policy, comprising Articles 102a to 109.

Commission, make the necessary recommendations to the Member State concerned. The Council may, acting by a qualified majority on a proposal from the Commission, decide to make its recommendations public.

The President of the Council and the Commission shall report to the European Parliament on the results of multilateral surveillance. The President of the Council may be invited to appear before the competent committee of the European Parliament if the Council has made its recommendations public.

5. The Council, acting in accordance with the procedure referred to in Article 252, may adopt detailed rules for the multilateral surveillance procedure referred to in paragraphs 3 and 4 of this Article.

Article 100 (ex Article 103a)

1. Without prejudice to any other procedures provided for in this Treaty, the Council may, acting unanimously on a proposal from the Commission, decide upon the measures appropriate to the economic situation, in particular if severe difficulties arise in the supply of certain products.

2. Where a Member State is in difficulties or is seriously threatened with severe difficulties caused by exceptional occurrences beyond its control, the Council may, acting unanimously on a proposal from the Commission, grant, under certain conditions, Community financial assistance to the Member State concerned. Where the severe difficulties are caused by natural disasters, the Council shall act by qualified majority. The President of the Council shall inform the European Parliament of the decision taken.

Article 101 (ex Article 104)

1. Overdraft facilities or any other type of credit facility with the ECB or with the central banks of the Member States (hereinafter referred to as "national central banks") in favour of Community institutions or bodies, central governments, regional, local or other public authorities, other bodies governed by public law, or public undertakings of Member States shall be prohibited, as shall the purchase directly from them by the ECB or national central banks of debt instruments.

2. Paragraph 1 shall not apply to publicly owned credit institutions which, in the context of the supply of reserves by central banks, shall be given the same treatment by national central banks and the ECB as private credit institutions.

Article 102 (ex Article 104a)

1. Any measure, not based on prudential considerations, establishing privileged access by Community institutions or bodies, central governments, regional, local or other public authorities, other bodies governed by public law, or public undertakings of Member States to financial institutions, shall be prohibited.

2. The Council, acting in accordance with the procedure referred to in Article 252, shall, before 1 January 1994, specify definitions for the application of the prohibition referred to in paragraph 1.

Article 103 (ex Article 104b)

1. The Community shall not be liable for or assume the commitments of central governments, regional, local or other public authorities, other bodies governed by public law, or public undertakings of any Member State, without prejudice to mutual financial guarantees for the joint execution of a specific project. A Member State shall not be liable for or assume the commitments of central governments, regional, local or other public authorities, other bodies governed by public law, or public undertakings of another Member State, without prejudice to mutual financial guarantees for the joint execution of a specific project.

2. If necessary, the Council, acting in accordance with the procedure referred to in Article 252, may specify definitions for the application of the prohibition referred to in Article 101 and in this Article.

Article 104 (ex Article 104c)

1. Member States shall avoid excessive government deficits.

2. The Commission shall monitor the development of the budgetary situation and of the stock of government debt in the Member States with a view to identifying gross errors. In particular it shall examine compliance with budgetary discipline on the basis of the following two criteria:

(a) whether the ratio of the planned or actual government deficit to gross domestic product exceeds a reference value, unless:

— either the ratio has declined substantially and continuously and reached a level that comes close to the reference value;

— or, alternatively, the excess over the reference value is only exceptional and temporary and the ratio remains close to the reference value;

(b) whether the ratio of government debt to gross domestic product exceeds a reference value, unless the ratio is sufficiently diminishing and approaching the reference value at a satisfactory pace.

The reference values are specified in the Protocol on the excessive deficit procedure annexed to this Treaty.

3. If a Member State does not fulfil the requirements under one or both of these criteria, the Commission shall prepare a report. The report of the Commission shall also take into account whether the government deficit exceeds government investment expenditure and take into account all other relevant factors, including the medium-term economic and budgetary position of the Member State.

The Commission may also prepare a report if, notwithstanding the fulfilment of the requirements under the criteria, it is of the opinion that there is a risk of an excessive deficit in a Member State.

4. The Committee provided for in Article 114 shall formulate an opinion on the report of the Commission.

5. If the Commission considers that an excessive deficit in a Member State exists or may occur, the Commission shall address an opinion to the Council.

6. The Council shall, acting by a qualified majority on a recommendation from the Commission, and having considered any observations which the Member State concerned may wish to make, decide after an overall assessment whether an excessive deficit exists.

7. Where the existence of an excessive deficit is decided according to paragraph 6, the Council shall make recommendations to the Member State concerned with a view to bringing that situation to an end within a given period. Subject to the provisions of paragraph 8, these recommendations shall not be made public.

8. Where it establishes that there has been no effective action in response to its recommendations within the period laid down, the Council may make its recommendations public.

9. If a Member State persists in failing to put into practice the recommendations of the Council, the Council may decide to give notice to the Member State to take, within a specified time-limit, measures for the deficit reduction which is judged necessary by the Council in order to remedy the situation.

In such a case, the Council may request the Member State concerned to submit reports in accordance with a specific timetable in order to examine the adjustment efforts of that Member State.

10. The rights to bring actions provided for in Articles 226 and 227 may not be exercised within the framework of paragraphs 1 to 9 of this Article.

11. As long as a Member State fails to comply with a decision taken in accordance with paragraph 9, the Council may decide to apply or, as the case may be, intensify one or more of the following measures:

— to require the Member State concerned to publish additional information, to be specified by the Council, before issuing bonds and securities;

— to invite the European Investment Bank to reconsider its lending policy towards the Member State concerned;

— to require the Member State concerned to make a non-interest-bearing deposit of an appropriate size with the Community until the excessive deficit has, in the view of the Council, been corrected;

— to impose fines of an appropriate size.

The President of the Council shall inform the European Parliament of the decisions taken.

12. The Council shall abrogate some or all of its decisions referred to in paragraphs 6 to 9 and 11 to the extent that the excessive deficit in the Member State concerned has, in the view of the Council, been corrected. If

the Council has previously made public recommendations, it shall, as soon as the decision under paragraph 8 has been abrogated, make a public statement that an excessive deficit in the Member State concerned no longer exists.

13. When taking the decisions referred to in paragraphs 7 to 9, 11 and 12, the Council shall act on a recommendation from the Commission by a majority of two-thirds of the votes of its members weighted in accordance with Article 205(2), excluding the votes of the representative of the Member State concerned.

14. Further provisions relating to the implementation of the procedure described in this Article are set out in the Protocol on the excessive deficit procedure annexed to this Treaty.

The Council shall, acting unanimously on a proposal from the Commission and after consulting the European Parliament and the ECB, adopt the appropriate provisions which shall then replace the said Protocol.

Subject to the other provisions of this paragraph, the Council shall, before 1 January 1994, acting by a qualified majority on a proposal from the Commission and after consulting the European Parliament, lay down detailed rules and definitions for the application of the provisions of the said Protocol.

Chapter 2: Monetary policy

Article 105 (ex Article 105)

1. The primary objective of the ESCB shall be to maintain price stability. Without prejudice to the objective of price stability, the ESCB shall support the general economic policies in the Community with a view to contributing to the achievement of the objectives of the Community as laid down in Article 2. The ESCB shall act in accordance with the principle of an open market economy with free competition, favouring an efficient allocation of resources, and in compliance with the principles set out in Article 4.

2. The basic tasks to be carried out through the ESCB shall be:

— to define and implement the monetary policy of the Community;

— to conduct foreign exchange operations consistent with the provisions of Article 111;

— to hold and manage the official foreign reserves of the Member States;

— to promote the smooth operation of payment systems.

3. The third indent of paragraph 2 shall be without prejudice to the holding and management by the governments of Member States of foreign-exchange working balances.

4. The ECB shall be consulted:

— on any proposed Community act in its fields of competence;

— by national authorities regarding any draft legislative provision in its fields of competence, but within the limits and under the conditions set out by the Council in accordance with the procedure laid down in Article 107(6).

The ECB may submit opinions to the appropriate Community institutions or bodies or to national authorities on matters in its fields of competence.

5. The ESCB shall contribute to the smooth conduct of policies pursued by the competent authorities relating to the prudential supervision of credit institutions and the stability of the financial system.

6. The Council may, acting unanimously on a proposal from the Commission and after consulting the ECB and after receiving the assent of the European Parliament, confer upon the ECB specific tasks concerning policies relating to the prudential supervision of credit institutions and other financial institutions with the exception of insurance undertakings.

Article 106 (ex Article 105a)

1. The ECB shall have the exclusive right to authorise the issue of banknotes within the Community. The ECB and the national central banks may issue such notes. The banknotes issued by the ECB and the national central banks shall be the only such notes to have the status of legal tender within the Community.

2. Member States may issue coins subject to approval by the ECB of the volume of the issue. The Council may, acting in accordance with the procedure referred to in Article 252 and after consulting the ECB, adopt measures to harmonise the denominations and technical specifications of all coins intended for circulation to the extent necessary to permit their smooth circulation within the Community.

Article 107 (ex Article 106)

1. The ESCB shall be composed of the ECB and of the national central banks.

2. The ECB shall have legal personality.

3. The ESCB shall be governed by the decision-making bodies of the ECB which shall be the Governing Council and the Executive Board.

4. The Statute of the ESCB is laid down in a Protocol annexed to this Treaty.

5. Articles 5.1, 5.2, 5.3, 17, 18, 19.1, 22, 23, 24, 26, 32.2, 32.3, 32.4, 32.6, 33.1(a) and 36 of the Statute of the ESCB may be amended by the Council, acting either by a qualified majority on a recommendation from the ECB and after consulting the Commission or unanimously on a proposal from the Commission and after consulting the ECB. In either case, the assent of the European Parliament shall be required.

6. The Council, acting by a qualified majority either on a proposal from the Commission and after consulting the European Parliament and

the ECB or on a recommendation from the ECB and after consulting the European Parliament and the Commission, shall adopt the provisions referred to in Articles 4, 5.4, 19.2, 20, 28.1, 29.2, 30.4 and 34.3 of the Statute of the ESCB.

Article 108 (ex Article 107)

When exercising the powers and carrying out the tasks and duties conferred upon them by this Treaty and the Statute of the ESCB, neither the ECB, nor a national central bank, nor any member of their decision-making bodies shall seek or take instructions from Community institutions or bodies, from any government of a Member State or from any other body. The Community institutions and bodies and the governments of the Member States undertake to respect this principle and not to seek to influence the members of the decision-making bodies of the ECB or of the national central banks in the performance of their tasks.

Article 109 (ex Article 108)

Each Member State shall ensure, at the latest at the date of the establishment of the ESCB, that its national legislation including the statutes of its national central bank is compatible with this Treaty and the Statute of the ESCB.

Article 110 (ex Article 108a)

1. In order to carry out the tasks entrusted to the ESCB, the ECB shall, in accordance with the provisions of this Treaty and under the conditions laid down in the Statute of the ESCB:

— make regulations to the extent necessary to implement the tasks defined in Article 3.1, first indent, Articles 19.1, 22 and 25.2 of the Statute of the ESCB and in cases which shall be laid down in the acts of the Council referred to in Article 107(6);

— take decisions necessary for carrying out the tasks entrusted to the ESCB under this Treaty and the Statute of the ESCB;

— make recommendations and deliver opinions.

2. A regulation shall have general application. It shall be binding in its entirety and directly applicable in all Member States.

Recommendations and opinions shall have no binding force.

A decision shall be binding in its entirety upon those to whom it is addressed.

Articles 253 to 256 shall apply to regulations and decisions adopted by the ECB.

The ECB may decide to publish its decisions, recommendations and opinions.

3. Within the limits and under the conditions adopted by the Council under the procedure laid down in Article 107(6), the ECB shall be entitled

to impose fines or periodic penalty payments on undertakings for failure to comply with obligations under its regulations and decisions.

Article 111 (Article 109)

1. By way of derogation from Article 300, the Council may, acting unanimously on a recommendation from the ECB or from the Commission, and after consulting the ECB in an endeavour to reach a consensus consistent with the objective of price stability, after consulting the European Parliament, in accordance with the procedure in paragraph 3 for determining the arrangements, conclude formal agreements on an exchange-rate system for the ECU in relation to non-Community currencies. The Council may, acting by a qualified majority on a recommendation from the ECB or from the Commission, and after consulting the ECB in an endeavour to reach a consensus consistent with the objective of price stability, adopt, adjust or abandon the central rates of the ECU within the exchange-rate system. The President of the Council shall inform the European Parliament of the adoption, adjustment or abandonment of the ECU central rates.

2. In the absence of an exchange-rate system in relation to one or more non-Community currencies as referred to in paragraph 1, the Council, acting by a qualified majority either on a recommendation from the Commission and after consulting the ECB or on a recommendation from the ECB, may formulate general orientations for exchange-rate policy in relation to these currencies. These general orientations shall be without prejudice to the primary objective of the ESCB to maintain price stability.

3. By way of derogation from Article 300, where agreements concerning monetary or foreign exchange regime matters need to be negotiated by the Community with one or more States or international organisations, the Council, acting by a qualified majority on a recommendation from the Commission and after consulting the ECB, shall decide the arrangements for the negotiation and for the conclusion of such agreements. These arrangements shall ensure that the Community expresses a single position. The Commission shall be fully associated with the negotiations.

Agreements concluded in accordance with this paragraph shall be binding on the institutions of the Community, on the ECB and on Member States.

4. Subject to paragraph 1, the Council shall, on a proposal from the Commission and after consulting the ECB, acting by a qualified majority decide on the position of the Community at international level as regards issues of particular relevance to economic and monetary union and, acting unanimously, decide its representation in compliance with the allocation of powers laid down in Articles 99 and 105.

5. Without prejudice to Community competence and Community agreements as regards economic and monetary union, Member States may negotiate in international bodies and conclude international agreements.

Chapter 3: Institutional provisions

Article 112 (ex Article 109a)

1. The Governing Council of the ECB shall comprise the members of the Executive Board of the ECB and the Governors of the national central banks.

2 (a) The Executive Board shall comprise the President, the Vice-President and four other members.

(b) The President, the Vice-President and the other members of the Executive Board shall be appointed from among persons of recognised standing and professional experience in monetary or banking matters by common accord of the governments of the Member States at the level of Heads of State or Government, on a recommendation from the Council, after it has consulted the European Parliament and the Governing Council of the ECB.

Their term of office shall be eight years and shall not be renewable.

Only nationals of Member States may be members of the Executive Board.

Article 113 (ex Article 109b)

1. The President of the Council and a member of the Commission may participate, without having the right to vote, in meetings of the Governing Council of the ECB.

The President of the Council may submit a motion for deliberation to the Governing Council of the ECB.

2. The President of the ECB shall be invited to participate in Council meetings when the Council is discussing matters relating to the objectives and tasks of the ESCB.

3. The ECB shall address an annual report on the activities of the ESCB and on the monetary policy of both the previous and current year to the European Parliament, the Council and the Commission, and also to the European Council. The President of the ECB shall present this report to the Council and to the European Parliament, which may hold a general debate on that basis.

The President of the ECB and the other members of the Executive Board may, at the request of the European Parliament or on their own initiative, be heard by the competent committees of the European Parliament.

Article 114 (ex Article 109c)

1. In order to promote coordination of the policies of Member States to the full extent needed for the functioning of the internal market, a Monetary Committee with advisory status is hereby set up.

It shall have the following tasks:

— to keep under review the monetary and financial situation of the Member States and of the Community and the general payments system of the Member States and to report regularly thereon to the Council and to the Commission;

— to deliver opinions at the request of the Council or of the Commission, or on its own initiative for submission to those institutions;

— without prejudice to Article 207, to contribute to the preparation of the work of the Council referred to in Articles 59, 60, 99(2), (3), (4) and (5), 100, 102, 103, 104, 116(2), 117(6), 119, 120, 121(2) and 122(1);

—to examine, at least once a year, the situation regarding the movement of capital and the freedom of payments, as they result from the application of this Treaty and of measures adopted by the Council; the examination shall cover all measures relating to capital movements and payments; the Committee shall report to the Commission and to the Council on the outcome of this examination.

The Member States and the Commission shall each appoint two members of the Monetary Committee.

2. At the start of the third stage, an Economic and Financial Committee shall be set up. The Monetary Committee provided for in paragraph 1 shall be dissolved.

The Economic and Financial Committee shall have the following tasks:

— to deliver opinions at the request of the Council or of the Commission, or on its own initiative for submission to those institutions;

— to keep under review the economic and financial situation of the Member States and of the Community and to report regularly thereon to the Council and to the Commission, in particular on financial relations with third countries and international institutions;

— without prejudice to Article 207, to contribute to the preparation of the work of the Council referred to in Articles 59, 60, 99(2), (3), (4) and (5), 100, 102, 103, 104, 105(6), 106(2), 107(5) and (6), 111, 119, 120(2) and (3), 122(2), 123(4) and (5), and to carry out other advisory and preparatory tasks assigned to it by the Council;

— to examine, at least once a year, the situation regarding the movement of capital and the freedom of payments, as they result from the application of this Treaty and of measures adopted by the Council; the examination shall cover all measures relating to capital movements and payments; the Committee shall report to the Commission and to the Council on the outcome of this examination.

The Member States, the Commission and the ECB shall each appoint no more than two members of the Committee.

3. The Council shall, acting by a qualified majority on a proposal from the Commission and after consulting the ECB and the Committee referred to in this Article, lay down detailed provisions concerning the composition of the Economic and Financial Committee. The President of the Council shall inform the European Parliament of such a decision.

4. In addition to the tasks set out in paragraph 2, if and as long as there are Member States with a derogation as referred to in Articles 122 and 123, the Committee shall keep under review the monetary and financial situation and the general payments system of those Member States and report regularly thereon to the Council and to the Commission.

Article 115 (ex Article 109d)

For matters within the scope of Articles 99(4), 104 with the exception of paragraph 14, 111, 121, 122 and 123(4) and (5), the Council or a Member State may request the Commission to make a recommendation or a proposal, as appropriate. The Commission shall examine this request and submit its conclusions to the Council without delay.

Chapter 4: Transitional provisions

Article 116 (ex Article 109e)

1. The second stage for achieving economic and monetary union shall begin on 1 January 1994.

2. Before that date:

(a) each Member State shall:

— adopt, where necessary, appropriate measures to comply with the prohibitions laid down in Article 56 and in Articles 101 and 102(1);

— adopt, if necessary, with a view to permitting the assessment provided for in subparagraph (b), multiannual programmes intended to ensure the lasting convergence necessary for the achievement of economic and monetary union, in particular with regard to price stability and sound public finances;

(b) the Council shall, on the basis of a report from the Commission, assess the progress made with regard to economic and monetary convergence, in particular with regard to price stability and sound public finances, and the progress made with the implementation of Community law concerning the internal market.

3. The provisions of Articles 101, 102(1), 103(1) and 104 with the exception of paragraphs 1, 9, 11 and 14 shall apply from the beginning of the second stage.

The provisions of Articles 100(2), 104(1), (9) and (11), 105, 106, 108, 111, 112, 113 and 114(2) and (4) shall apply from the beginning of the third stage.

4. In the second stage, Member States shall endeavour to avoid excessive government deficits.

5. During the second stage, each Member State shall, as appropriate, start the process leading to the independence of its central bank, in accordance with Article 109.

Article 117 (ex Article 109f)

1. At the start of the second stage, a European Monetary Institute (hereinafter referred to as "EMI") shall be established and take up its duties; it shall have legal personality and be directed and managed by a Council, consisting of a President and the Governors of the national central banks, one of whom shall be Vice-President.

The President shall be appointed by common accord of the governments of the Member States at the level of Heads of State or Government, on a recommendation from the Council of the EMI, and after consulting the European Parliament and the Council. The President shall be selected from among persons of recognised standing and professional experience in monetary or banking matters. Only nationals of Member States may be President of the EMI. The Council of the EMI shall appoint the Vice-President.

The Statute of the EMI is laid down in a Protocol annexed to this Treaty.

2. The EMI shall:

— strengthen cooperation between the national central banks;

— strengthen the coordination of the monetary policies of the Member States, with the aim of ensuring price stability;

— monitor the functioning of the European Monetary System;

— hold consultations concerning issues falling within the competence of the national central banks and affecting the stability of financial institutions and markets;

— take over the tasks of the European Monetary Cooperation Fund, which shall be dissolved; the modalities of dissolution are laid down in the Statute of the EMI;

— facilitate the use of the ECU and oversee its development, including the smooth functioning of the ECU clearing system.

3. For the preparation of the third stage, the EMI shall:

— prepare the instruments and the procedures necessary for carrying out a single monetary policy in the third stage;

— promote the harmonisation, where necessary, of the rules and practices governing the collection, compilation and distribution of statistics in the areas within its field of competence;

— prepare the rules for operations to be undertaken by the national central banks within the framework of the ESCB;

— promote the efficiency of cross-border payments;

— supervise the technical preparation of ECU banknotes.

At the latest by 31 December 1996, the EMI shall specify the regulatory, organisational and logistical framework necessary for the ESCB to perform its tasks in the third stage. This framework shall be submitted for decision to the ECB at the date of its establishment.

4. The EMI, acting by a majority of two thirds of the members of its Council, may:

— formulate opinions or recommendations on the overall orientation of monetary policy and exchange-rate policy as well as on related measures introduced in each Member State;

— submit opinions or recommendations to governments and to the Council on policies which might affect the internal or external monetary situation in the Community and, in particular, the functioning of the European Monetary System;

— make recommendations to the monetary authorities of the Member States concerning the conduct of their monetary policy.

5. The EMI, acting unanimously, may decide to publish its opinions and its recommendations.

6. The EMI shall be consulted by the Council regarding any proposed Community act within its field of competence.

Within the limits and under the conditions set out by the Council, acting by a qualified majority on a proposal from the Commission and after consulting the European Parliament and the EMI, the EMI shall be consulted by the authorities of the Member States on any draft legislative provision within its field of competence.

7. The Council may, acting unanimously on a proposal from the Commission and after consulting the European Parliament and the EMI, confer upon the EMI other tasks for the preparation of the third stage.

8. Where this Treaty provides for a consultative role for the ECB, references to the ECB shall be read as referring to the EMI before the establishment of the ECB.

9. During the second stage, the term "ECB" used in Articles 230, 232, 233, 234, 237 and 288 shall be read as referring to the EMI.

Article 118 (ex Article 109g)

The currency composition of the ECU basket shall not be changed.

From the start of the third stage, the value of the ECU shall be irrevocably fixed in accordance with Article 123(4).

Article 119 (ex Article 109h)

1. Where a Member State is in difficulties or is seriously threatened with difficulties as regards its balance of payments either as a result of an overall disequilibrium in its balance of payments, or as a result of the type of currency at its disposal, and where such difficulties are liable in particular to jeopardise the functioning of the common market or the progressive implementation of the common commercial policy, the Commission shall immediately investigate the position of the State in question and the action which, making use of all the means at its disposal, that State has taken or may take in accordance with the provisions of this Treaty. The Commission shall state what measures it recommends the State concerned to take.

If the action taken by a Member State and the measures suggested by the Commission do not prove sufficient to overcome the difficulties which have arisen or which threaten, the Commission shall, after consulting the Committee referred to in Article 114, recommend to the Council the granting of mutual assistance and appropriate methods therefor.

The Commission shall keep the Council regularly informed of the situation and of how it is developing.

2. The Council, acting by a qualified majority, shall grant such mutual assistance; it shall adopt directives or decisions laying down the conditions and details of such assistance, which may take such forms as:

(a) a concerted approach to or within any other international organisations to which Member States may have recourse;

(b) measures needed to avoid deflection of trade where the State which is in difficulties maintains or reintroduces quantitative restrictions against third countries;

(c) the granting of limited credits by other Member States, subject to their agreement.

3. If the mutual assistance recommended by the Commission is not granted by the Council or if the mutual assistance granted and the measures taken are insufficient, the Commission shall authorise the State which is in difficulties to take protective measures, the conditions and details of which the Commission shall determine.

Such authorisation may be revoked and such conditions and details may be changed by the Council acting by a qualified majority.

4. Subject to Article 122(6), this Article shall cease to apply from the beginning of the third stage.

Article 120 (ex Article 109i)

1. Where a sudden crisis in the balance of payments occurs and a decision within the meaning of Article 119(2) is not immediately taken, the Member State concerned may, as a precaution, take the necessary protective measures. Such measures must cause the least possible disturbance in the functioning of the common market and must not be wider in scope than is strictly necessary to remedy the sudden difficulties which have arisen.

2. The Commission and the other Member States shall be informed of such protective measures not later than when they enter into force. The Commission may recommend to the Council the granting of mutual assistance under Article 119.

3. After the Commission has delivered an opinion and the Committee referred to in Article 114 has been consulted, the Council may, acting by a qualified majority, decide that the State concerned shall amend, suspend or abolish the protective measures referred to above.

4. Subject to Article 122(6), this Article shall cease to apply from the beginning of the third stage.

Article 121 (ex Article 109j)

1. The Commission and the EMI shall report to the Council on the progress made in the fulfilment by the Member States of their obligations regarding the achievement of economic and monetary union. These reports shall include an examination of the compatibility between each Member State's national legislation, including the statutes of its national central bank, and Articles 108 and 109 of this Treaty and the Statute of the ESCB. The reports shall also examine the achievement of a high degree of sustainable convergence by reference to the fulfilment by each Member State of the following criteria:

— the achievement of a high degree of price stability; this will be apparent from a rate of inflation which is close to that of, at most, the three best performing Member States in terms of price stability;

— the sustainability of the government financial position; this will be apparent from having achieved a government budgetary position without a deficit that is excessive as determined in accordance with Article 104(6);

— the observance of the normal fluctuation margins provided for by the exchange-rate mechanism of the European Monetary System, for at least two years, without devaluing against the currency of any other Member State;

— the durability of convergence achieved by the Member State and of its participation in the exchange-rate mechanism of the European Monetary System being reflected in the long-term interest-rate levels.

The four criteria mentioned in this paragraph and the relevant periods over which they are to be respected are developed further in a Protocol annexed to this Treaty. The reports of the Commission and the EMI shall also take account of the development of the ECU, the results of the integration of markets, the situation and development of the balances of payments on current account and an examination of the development of unit labour costs and other price indices.

2. On the basis of these reports, the Council, acting by a qualified majority on a recommendation from the Commission, shall assess:

— for each Member State, whether it fulfils the necessary conditions for the adoption of a single currency;

— whether a majority of the Member States fulfil the necessary conditions for the adoption of a single currency,

and recommend its findings to the Council, meeting in the composition of the Heads of State or Government. The European Parliament shall be consulted and forward its opinion to the Council, meeting in the composition of the Heads of State or Government.

3. Taking due account of the reports referred to in paragraph 1 and the opinion of the European Parliament referred to in paragraph 2, the Council, meeting in the composition of the Heads of State or Government, shall, acting by a qualified majority, not later than 31 December 1996:

— decide, on the basis of the recommendations of the Council referred to in paragraph 2, whether a majority of the Member States fulfil the necessary conditions for the adoption of a single currency;

— decide whether it is appropriate for the Community to enter the third stage,

and if so:

— set the date for the beginning of the third stage.

4. If by the end of 1997 the date for the beginning of the third stage has not been set, the third stage shall start on 1 January 1999. Before 1 July 1998, the Council, meeting in the composition of the Heads of State or Government, after a repetition of the procedure provided for in paragraphs 1 and 2, with the exception of the second indent of paragraph 2, taking into account the reports referred to in paragraph 1 and the opinion of the European Parliament, shall, acting by a qualified majority and on the basis of the recommendations of the Council referred to in paragraph 2, confirm which Member States fulfil the necessary conditions for the adoption of a single currency.

Article 122 (ex Article 109k)

1. If the decision has been taken to set the date in accordance with Article 121(3), the Council shall, on the basis of its recommendations referred to in Article 121(2), acting by a qualified majority on a recommendation from the Commission, decide whether any, and if so which, Member States shall have a derogation as defined in paragraph 3 of this Article. Such Member States shall in this Treaty be referred to as "Member States with a derogation".

If the Council has confirmed which Member States fulfil the necessary conditions for the adoption of a single currency, in accordance with Article 121(4), those Member States which do not fulfil the conditions shall have a derogation as defined in paragraph 3 of this Article. Such Member States shall in this Treaty be referred to as "Member States with a derogation".

2. At least once every two years, or at the request of a Member State with a derogation, the Commission and the ECB shall report to the Council in accordance with the procedure laid down in Article 121(1). After consulting the European Parliament and after discussion in the Council, meeting in the composition of the Heads of State or Government, the Council shall, acting by a qualified majority on a proposal from the Commission, decide which Member States with a derogation fulfil the necessary conditions on the basis of the criteria set out in Article 121(1), and abrogate the derogations of the Member States concerned.

3. A derogation referred to in paragraph 1 shall entail that the following Articles do not apply to the Member State concerned: Articles 104(9) and (11), 105(1), (2), (3) and (5), 106, 110, 111, and 112(2)(b). The exclusion of such a Member State and its national central bank from rights and obligations within the ESCB is laid down in Chapter IX of the Statute of the ESCB.

4. In Articles 105(1), (2) and (3), 106, 110, 111 and 112(2)(b), "Member States" shall be read as "Member States without a derogation".

5. The voting rights of Member States with a derogation shall be suspended for the Council decisions referred to in the Articles of this Treaty mentioned in paragraph 3. In that case, by way of derogation from Articles 205 and 250(1), a qualified majority shall be defined as two-thirds of the votes of the representatives of the Member States without a derogation weighted in accordance with Article 205(2), and unanimity of those Member States shall be required for an act requiring unanimity.

6. Articles 119 and 120 shall continue to apply to a Member State with a derogation.

Article 123 (ex Article 109l)

1. Immediately after the decision on the date for the beginning of the third stage has been taken in accordance with Article 121(3), or, as the case may be, immediately after 1 July 1998:

— the Council shall adopt the provisions referred to in Article 107(6);

— the governments of the Member States without a derogation shall appoint, in accordance with the procedure set out in Article 50 of the Statute of the ESCB, the President, the Vice–President and the other members of the Executive Board of the ECB. If there are Member States with a derogation, the number of members of the Executive Board may be smaller than provided for in Article 11.1 of the Statute of the ESCB, but in no circumstances shall it be less than four.

As soon as the Executive Board is appointed, the ESCB and the ECB shall be established and shall prepare for their full operation as described in this Treaty and the Statute of the ESCB. The full exercise of their powers shall start from the first day of the third stage.

2. As soon as the ECB is established, it shall, if necessary, take over tasks of the EMI. The EMI shall go into liquidation upon the establishment of the ECB; the modalities of liquidation are laid down in the Statute of the EMI.

3. If and as long as there are Member States with a derogation, and without prejudice to Article 107(3) of this Treaty, the General Council of the ECB referred to in Article 45 of the Statute of the ESCB shall be constituted as a third decision-making body of the ECB.

4. At the starting date of the third stage, the Council shall, acting with the unanimity of the Member States without a derogation, on a proposal from the Commission and after consulting the ECB, adopt the conversion rates at which their currencies shall be irrevocably fixed and at which irrevocably fixed rate the ECU shall be substituted for these currencies, and the ECU will become a currency in its own right. This measure shall by itself not modify the external value of the ECU. The Council shall, acting according to the same procedure, also take the other measures necessary for the rapid introduction of the ECU as the single currency of those Member States.

5. If it is decided, according to the procedure set out in Article 122(2), to abrogate a derogation, the Council shall, acting with the unanimity of the Member States without a derogation and the Member State concerned, on a proposal from the Commission and after consulting the ECB, adopt the rate at which the ECU shall be substituted for the currency of the Member State concerned, and take the other measures necessary for the introduction of the ECU as the single currency in the Member State concerned.

Article 124 (ex Article 109m)

1. Until the beginning of the third stage, each Member State shall treat its exchange-rate policy as a matter of common interest. In so doing, Member States shall take account of the experience acquired in cooperation within the framework of the European Monetary System (EMS) and in developing the ECU, and shall respect existing powers in this field.

2. From the beginning of the third stage and for as long as a Member State has a derogation, paragraph 1 shall apply by analogy to the exchange-rate policy of that Member State.

TITLE VIII (ex Title VIa)[40]

EMPLOYMENT

Article 125 (ex Article 109n)

Member States and the Community shall, in accordance with this Title, work towards developing a coordinated strategy for employment and particularly for promoting a skilled, trained and adaptable workforce and labour markets responsive to economic change with a view to achieving the objectives defined in Article 2 of the Treaty on European Union and in Article 2 of this Treaty.

Article 126 (ex Article 109o)

1. Member States, through their employment policies, shall contribute to the achievement of the objectives referred to in Article 125 in a way consistent with the broad guidelines of the economic policies of the Member States and of the Community adopted pursuant to Article 99(2).

2. Member States, having regard to national practices related to the responsibilities of management and labour, shall regard promoting employment as a matter of common concern and shall coordinate their action in this respect within the Council, in accordance with the provisions of Article 128.

Article 127 (ex Article 109p)

1. The Community shall contribute to a high level of employment by encouraging cooperation between Member States and by supporting and, if necessary, complementing their action. In doing so, the competences of the Member States shall be respected.

---

40. The Treaty of Amsterdam introduced the new Title VIII on employment.

2. The objective of a high level of employment shall be taken into consideration in the formulation and implementation of Community policies and activities.

Article 128 (ex Article 109q)

1. The European Council shall each year consider the employment situation in the Community and adopt conclusions thereon, on the basis of a joint annual report by the Council and the Commission.

2. On the basis of the conclusions of the European Council, the Council, acting by a qualified majority on a proposal from the Commission and after consulting the European Parliament, the Economic and Social Committee, the Committee of the Regions and the Employment Committee referred to in Article 130, shall each year draw up guidelines which the Member States shall take into account in their employment policies. These guidelines shall be consistent with the broad guidelines adopted pursuant to Article 99(2).

3. Each Member State shall provide the Council and the Commission with an annual report on the principal measures taken to implement its employment policy in the light of the guidelines for employment as referred to in paragraph 2.

4. The Council, on the basis of the reports referred to in paragraph 3 and having received the views of the Employment Committee, shall each year carry out an examination of the implementation of the employment policies of the Member States in the light of the guidelines for employment. The Council, acting by a qualified majority on a recommendation from the Commission, may, if it considers it appropriate in the light of that examination, make recommendations to Member States.

5. On the basis of the results of that examination, the Council and the Commission shall make a joint annual report to the European Council on the employment situation in the Community and on the implementation of the guidelines for employment.

Article 129 (ex Article 109r)

The Council, acting in accordance with the procedure referred to in Article 251 and after consulting the Economic and Social Committee and the Committee of the Regions, may adopt incentive measures designed to encourage cooperation between Member States and to support their action in the field of employment through initiatives aimed at developing exchanges of information and best practices, providing comparative analysis and advice as well as promoting innovative approaches and evaluating experiences, in particular by recourse to pilot projects.

Those measures shall not include harmonisation of the laws and regulations of the Member States.

Article 130 (ex Article 109s)

The Council, after consulting the European Parliament, shall establish an Employment Committee with advisory status to promote coordination between Member States on employment and labour market policies. The tasks of the Committee shall be:

— to monitor the employment situation and employment policies in the Member States and the Community;

— without prejudice to Article 207, to formulate opinions at the request of either the Council or the Commission or on its own initiative, and to contribute to the preparation of the Council proceedings referred to in Article 128.

In fulfilling its mandate, the Committee shall consult management and labour.

Each Member State and the Commission shall appoint two members of the Committee.

TITLE IX (ex Title VII)[41]

COMMERCIAL POLICY POLICY

Article 131 (ex Article 110)[42]

By establishing a customs union between themselves Member States aim to contribute, in the common interest, to the harmonious development of world trade, the progressive abolition of restrictions on international trade and the lowering of customs barriers.

The common commercial policy shall take into account the favourable effect which the abolition of customs duties between Member States may have on the increase in the competitive strength of undertakings in those States.

Article 132 (ex Article 112)

1. Without prejudice to obligations undertaken by them within the framework of other international organisations, Member States shall progressively harmonise the systems whereby they grant aid for exports to third countries, to the extent necessary to ensure that competition between undertakings of the Community is not distorted.

On a proposal from the Commission, the Council shall, acting by a qualified majority, issue any directives needed for this purpose.

2. The preceding provisions shall not apply to such a drawback of customs duties or charges having equivalent effect nor to such a repayment of indirect taxation including turnover taxes, excise duties and other indirect taxes as is allowed when goods are exported from a Member State to a third country, insofar as such a drawback or repayment does not exceed the amount imposed, directly or indirectly, on the products exported.

---

41. The TEU designated this new Title VII in replacement of the previous Chapter 4 on commercial policy.

42. The TEU deleted the former Article 111 which had dealt with coordination of trade policy and legislative procedures applicable during the transitional period.

Article 133 (ex Article 113)[43]

1. The common commercial policy shall be based on uniform principles, particularly in regard to changes in tariff rates, the conclusion of tariff and trade agreements, the achievement of uniformity in measures of liberalisation, export policy and measures to protect trade such as those to be taken in the event of dumping or subsidies.

2. The Commission shall submit proposals to the Council for implementing the common commercial policy.

3. Where agreements with one or more States or international organisations need to be negotiated, the Commission shall make recommendations to the Council, which shall authorise the Commission to open the necessary negotiations.

The Commission shall conduct these negotiations in consultation with a special committee appointed by the Council to assist the Commission in this task and within the framework of such directives as the Council may issue to it.

The relevant provisions of Article 300 shall apply.

4. In exercising the powers conferred upon it by this Article, the Council shall act by a qualified majority.

5. The Council, acting unanimously on a proposal from the Commission and after consulting the European Parliament, may extend the application of paragraphs 1 to 4 to international negotiations and agreements on services and intellectual property insofar as they are not covered by these paragraphs.

Article 134 (ex Article 115)[44]

In order to ensure that the execution of measures of commercial policy taken in accordance with this Treaty by any Member State is not obstructed by deflection of trade, or where differences between such measures lead to economic difficulties in one or more Member States, the Commission shall recommend the methods for the requisite cooperation between Member States. Failing this, the Commission may authorise Member States to take the necessary protective measures, the conditions and details of which it shall determine.

In case of urgency, Member States shall request authorisation to take the necessary measures themselves from the Commission, which shall take a decision as soon as possible; the Member States concerned shall then notify the measures to the other Member States. The Commission may

---

43. The TEU amended this article to insert "one or more States or international organisations" in place of "third countries" in paragraph 3, and to address the manner of Council action, now covered in Article 300.

44. The TEU amended the second sentence of paragraph one to replace "shall" with "may." The TEU also amended the second paragraph to require Member States to obtain Commission authorization for any necessary measures. The TEU deleted Article 116, which had required the Member States to take common action in international organizations insofar as the common market was concerned.

decide at any time that the Member States concerned shall amend or abolish the measures in question.

In the selection of such measures, priority shall be given to those which cause the least disturbance of the functioning of the common market.

TITLE X (ex Title VIIa)

CUSTOMS COOPERATION

Article 135 (ex Article 116)

Within the scope of application of this Treaty, the Council, acting in accordance with the procedure referred to in Article 251, shall take measures in order to strengthen customs cooperation between Member States and between the latter and the Commission. These measures shall not concern the application of national criminal law or the national administration of justice.

TITLE XI (ex Title VIII)[45]

SOCIAL POLICY, EDUCATION, VOCATIONAL TRAINING AND YOUTH

Chapter 1: Social Provisions

Article 136 (ex Article 117)[46]

The Community and the Member States, having in mind fundamental social rights such as those set out in the European Social Charter signed at Turin on 18 October 1961 and in the 1989 Community Charter of the Fundamental Social Rights of Workers, shall have as their objectives the promotion of employment, improved living and working conditions, so as to make possible their harmonisation while the improvement is being maintained, proper social protection, dialogue between management and labour, the development of human resources with a view to lasting high employment and the combating of exclusion.

To this end the Community and the Member States shall implement measures which take account of the diverse forms of national practices, in particular in the field of contractual relations, and the need to maintain the competitiveness of the Community economy.

They believe that such a development will ensue not only from the functioning of the common market, which will favour the harmonisation of social systems, but also from the procedures provided for in this Treaty and from the approximation of provisions laid down by law, regulation or administrative action.

---

45. The TEU gave this title a new name and renumbered it as Title VIII, in place of the former Title III, Social Policy.

46. The Treaty of Amsterdam amended the first paragraph to more fully develop the signatories' commitment to the rights of workers. It also inserted a new second paragraph to take account of the diversity of national practices and the need to maintain economic competition.

Article 137 (ex Article 118)[47]

1. With a view to achieving the objectives of Article 136, the Community shall support and complement the activities of the Member States in the following fields:

— improvement in particular of the working environment to protect workers' health and safety;

— working conditions;

— the information and consultation of workers;

— the integration of persons excluded from the labour market, without prejudice to Article 150;

— equality between men and women with regard to labour market opportunities and treatment at work.

2. To this end, the Council may adopt, by means of directives, minimum requirements for gradual implementation, having regard to the conditions and technical rules obtaining in each of the Member States. Such directives shall avoid imposing administrative, financial and legal constraints in a way which would hold back the creation and development of small and medium-sized undertakings.

The Council shall act in accordance with the procedure referred to in Article 251 after consulting the Economic and Social Committee and the Committee of the Regions.

The Council, acting in accordance with the same procedure, may adopt measures designed to encourage cooperation between Member States through initiatives aimed at improving knowledge, developing exchanges of information and best practices, promoting innovative approaches and evaluating experiences in order to combat social exclusion.

3. However, the Council shall act unanimously on a proposal from the Commission, after consulting the European Parliament, the Economic and Social Committee and the Committee of the Regions in the following areas:

— social security and social protection of workers;

— protection of workers where their employment contract is terminated;

— representation and collective defence of the interests of workers and employers, including co-determination, subject to paragraph 6;

— conditions of employment for third-country nationals legally residing in Community territory;

— financial contributions for promotion of employment and job-creation, without prejudice to the provisions relating to the Social Fund.

---

47. The Treaty of Amsterdam altered and added to the list of concerns in section 1, changed the body responsible for achieving the stated goals from the Commission to the Council, empowered the Council to issue directives rather than deliver opinions, required the Council to consult the Committee of the Regions, and permitted the Council to adopt measures that would encourage cooperation between Member States. The Amsterdam Treaty also added new paragraphs 3 to 6.

4. A Member State may entrust management and labour, at their joint request, with the implementation of directives adopted pursuant to paragraphs 2 and 3.

In this case, it shall ensure that, no later than the date on which a directive must be transposed in accordance with Article 249, management and labour have introduced the necessary measures by agreement, the Member State concerned being required to take any necessary measure enabling it at any time to be in a position to guarantee the results imposed by that directive.

5. The provisions adopted pursuant to this Article shall not prevent any Member State from maintaining or introducing more stringent protective measures compatible with this Treaty.

6. The provisions of this Article shall not apply to pay, the right of association, the right to strike or the right to impose lock-outs.

Article 138 (ex Article 118a)[48]

1. The Commission shall have the task of promoting the consultation of management and labour at Community level and shall take any relevant measure to facilitate their dialogue by ensuring balanced support for the parties.

2. To this end, before submitting proposals in the social policy field, the Commission shall consult management and labour on the possible direction of Community action.

3. If, after such consultation, the Commission considers Community action advisable, it shall consult management and labour on the content of the envisaged proposal. Management and labour shall forward to the Commission an opinion or, where appropriate, a recommendation.

4. On the occasion of such consultation, management and labour may inform the Commission of their wish to initiate the process provided for in Article 139. The duration of the procedure shall not exceed nine months, unless the management and labour concerned and the Commission decide jointly to extend it.

The Treaty of Amsterdam changed the objective of this article from the improvement the health and safety of workers in the working environment and the harmonization of conditions in that area to promoting the consultation of management and labour and facilitating their dialogue. It changed the body responsible for this objective from the Council to the Commission. In 1987, the SEA introduced this article. The TEU made the cross-reference to the cooperation procedure of Article 189c, replacing the previous description of the cooperation procedure.

---

48. The Treaty of Amsterdam changed the objective of this article from improvement of the health and safety of workers in the working environment (including by harmonizing working conditions) to promoting consultation and dialogue between management and labor. It changed the body responsible for attaining this objective from the Council to the Commission. The article was originally introduced by the SEA in 1987, while the TEU made the cross-reference to the cooperation procedure.

Article 139 (ex Article 118b)[49]

1. Should management and labour so desire, the dialogue between them at Community level may lead to contractual relations, including agreements.

2. Agreements concluded at Community level shall be implemented either in accordance with the procedures and practices specific to management and labour and the Member States or, in matters covered by Article 137, at the joint request of the signatory parties, by a Council decision on a proposal from the Commission.

The Council shall act by qualified majority, except where the agreement in question contains one or more provisions relating to one of the areas referred to in Article 137(3), in which case it shall act unanimously.

Article 140 (ex Article 118c)

With a view to achieving the objectives of Article 136 and without prejudice to the other provisions of this Treaty, the Commission shall encourage cooperation between the Member States and facilitate the coordination of their action in all social policy fields under this chapter, particularly in matters relating to:

— employment

— labour law and working conditions

— basic and advanced vocational training

— social security

— prevention of occupational accidents and diseases

— occupational hygiene

— the right of association and collective bargaining between employers and workers.

To this end, the Commission shall act in close contact with Member States by making studies, delivering opinions and arranging consultations both on problems arising at national level and on those of concern to international organisations.

Before delivering the opinions provided for in this Article, the Commission shall consult the Economic and Social Committee.

Article 141 (ex Article 119)[50]

1. Each Member State shall ensure that the principle of equal pay for male and female workers for equal work or work of equal value is applied.

2. For the purpose of this Article, "pay" means the ordinary basic or minimum wage or salary and any other consideration, whether in cash or

49. The original Article 118b, added by the SEA in 1987, simply called upon the Commission to endeavor to develop dialogue between management and labor. The Treaty of Amsterdam added the second and final paragraphs.

50. The Treaty of Amsterdam added paragraphs 3 and 4.

in kind, which the worker receives directly or indirectly, in respect of his employment, from his employer.

Equal pay without discrimination based on sex means:

(a) that pay for the same work at piece rates shall be calculated on the basis of the same unit of measurement;

(b) that pay for work at time rates shall be the same for the same job.

3. The Council, acting in accordance with the procedure referred to in Article 251, and after consulting the Economic and Social Committee, shall adopt measures to ensure the application of the principle of equal opportunities and equal treatment of men and women in matters of employment and occupation, including the principle of equal pay for equal work or work of equal value.

4. With a view to ensuring full equality in practice between men and women in working life, the principle of equal treatment shall not prevent any Member State from maintaining or adopting measures providing for specific advantages in order to make it easier for the under-represented sex to pursue a vocational activity or to prevent or compensate for disadvantages in professional careers.

Article 142 (ex Article 119a)

Member States shall endeavour to maintain the existing equivalence between paid holiday schemes.

Article 143 (ex Article 120)

The Commission shall draw up a report each year on progress in achieving the objectives of Article 136, including the demographic situation in the Community. It shall forward the report to the European Parliament, the Council and the Economic and Social Committee.

The European Parliament may invite the Commission to draw up reports on particular problems concerning the social situation.

Article 144 (ex Article 121)

The Council may, acting unanimously and after consulting the Economic and Social Committee, assign to the Commission tasks in connection with the implementation of common measures, particularly as regards social security for the migrant workers referred to in Articles 39 to 42.

Article 145 (ex Article 122)

The Commission shall include a separate chapter on social developments within the Community in its annual report to the European Parliament.

The European Parliament may invite the Commission to draw up reports on any particular problems concerning social conditions.

Chapter 2: The European Social Fund

Article 146 (ex Article 123)[51]

In order to improve employment opportunities for workers in the internal market and to contribute thereby to raising the standard of living, a European Social Fund is hereby established in accordance with the provisions set out below; it shall aim to render the employment of workers easier and to increase their geographical and occupational mobility within the Community, and to facilitate their adaptation to industrial changes and to changes in production systems, in particular through vocational training and retraining.

Article 147 (ex Article 124)

The Fund shall be administered by the Commission.

The Commission shall be assisted in this task by a Committee presided over by a Member of the Commission and composed of representatives of governments, trade unions and employers' organisations.

Article 148 (ex Article 125)[52]

The Council, acting in accordance with the procedure referred to in Article 251 and after consulting the Economic and Social Committee and the Committee of the Regions, shall adopt implementing decisions relating to the European Social Fund.

Chapter 3: Education, vocational training and youth

Article 149 (ex Article 126)[53]

1. The Community shall contribute to the development of quality education by encouraging cooperation between Member States and, if necessary, by supporting and supplementing their action, while fully respecting the responsibility of the Member States for the content of teaching and the organisation of education systems and their cultural and linguistic diversity.

2. Community action shall be aimed at:

— developing the European dimension in education, particularly through the teaching and dissemination of the languages of the Member States;

— encouraging mobility of students and teachers, inter alia by encouraging the academic recognition of diplomas and periods of study;

— promoting cooperation between educational establishments;

---

51. The TEU amended this article to refer to the internal market, rather than the common market, and to add the final two clauses.

52. The TEU introduced this article, repealing a longer text contained in the then Articles 125 to 127 which had set specific goals for and limits on the Fund's operations. The TEU also enabled the Council to act by a qualified majority vote after consulting Parliament.

53. Added by the TEU.

— developing exchanges of information and experience on issues common to the education systems of the Member States;

— encouraging the development of youth exchanges and of exchanges of socio-educational instructors;

— encouraging the development of distance education.

3. The Community and the Member States shall foster cooperation with third countries and the competent international organisations in the field of education, in particular the Council of Europe.

4. In order to contribute to the achievement of the objectives referred to in this Article, the Council:

— acting in accordance with the procedure referred to in Article 251, after consulting the Economic and Social Committee and the Committee of the Regions, shall adopt incentive measures, excluding any harmonisation of the laws and regulations of the Member States;

— acting by a qualified majority on a proposal from the Commission, shall adopt recommendations.

Article 150 (ex Article 127)[54]

1. The Community shall implement a vocational training policy which shall support and supplement the action of the Member States, while fully respecting the responsibility of the Member States for the content and organisation of vocational training.

2. Community action shall aim to:

— facilitate adaptation to industrial changes, in particular through vocational training and retraining;

— improve initial and continuing vocational training in order to facilitate vocational integration and reintegration into the labour market;

— facilitate access to vocational training and encourage mobility of instructors and trainees and particularly young people;

— stimulate cooperation on training between educational or training establishments and firms;

— develop exchanges of information and experience on issues common to the training systems of the Member States.

3. The Community and the Member States shall foster cooperation with third countries and the competent international organisations in the sphere of vocational training.

4. The Council, acting in accordance with the procedure referred to in Article 251 and after consulting the Economic and Social Committee and the Committee of the Regions, shall adopt measures to contribute to the

---

54. The TEU introduced this article in place of the former Article 128 which required the Council to "lay down general principles for implementing a common vocational training policy," taking action by simple majority vote without reference to the Parliament.

achievement of the objectives referred to in this Article, excluding any harmonisation of the laws and regulations of the Member States.

TITLE XII (ex Title IX)
CULTURE
Article 151 (ex Article 128)

1. The Community shall contribute to the flowering of the cultures of the Member States, while respecting their national and regional diversity and at the same time bringing the common cultural heritage to the fore.

2. Action by the Community shall be aimed at encouraging cooperation between Member States and, if necessary, supporting and supplementing their action in the following areas:

— improvement of the knowledge and dissemination of the culture and history of the European peoples;

— conservation and safeguarding of cultural heritage of European significance;

— non-commercial cultural exchanges;

— artistic and literary creation, including in the audiovisual sector.

3. The Community and the Member States shall foster cooperation with third countries and the competent international organisations in the sphere of culture, in particular the Council of Europe.

4. The Community shall take cultural aspects into account in its action under other provisions of this Treaty, in particular in order to respect and to promote the diversity of its cultures.

5. In order to contribute to the achievement of the objectives referred to in this Article, the Council:

— acting in accordance with the procedure referred to in Article 251 and after consulting the Committee of the Regions, shall adopt incentive measures, excluding any harmonisation of the laws and regulations of the Member States. The Council shall act unanimously throughout the procedure referred to in Article 251;

— acting unanimously on a proposal from the Commission, shall adopt recommendations.

TITLE XIII (ex Title X)[55]
PUBLIC HEALTH
Article 152 (ex Article 129)

1. A high level of human health protection shall be ensured in the definition and implementation of all Community policies and activities.

---

55. The TEU introduced Title X (now Title XIII) on Public Health, including former Article 129. The prior Articles 129 and 130, dealing with the European Investment Bank, were replaced by the present Articles 266 and 267. The Treaty of Amsterdam amended this article to add paragraph 4(a), 4(b) and 5.

Community action, which shall complement national policies, shall be directed towards improving public health, preventing human illness and diseases, and obviating sources of danger to human health. Such action shall cover the fight against the major health scourges, by promoting research into their causes, their transmission and their prevention, as well as health information and education.

The Community shall complement the Member States' action in reducing drugs-related health damage, including information and prevention.

2. The Community shall encourage cooperation between the Member States in the areas referred to in this Article and, if necessary, lend support to their action.

Member States shall, in liaison with the Commission, coordinate among themselves their policies and programmes in the areas referred to in paragraph 1. The Commission may, in close contact with the Member States, take any useful initiative to promote such coordination.

3. The Community and the Member States shall foster cooperation with third countries and the competent international organisations in the sphere of public health.

4. The Council, acting in accordance with the procedure referred to in Article 251 and after consulting the Economic and Social Committee and the Committee of the Regions, shall contribute to the achievement of the objectives referred to in this Article through adopting:

(a) measures setting high standards of quality and safety of organs and substances of human origin, blood and blood derivatives these measures shall not prevent any Member State from maintaining or introducing more stringent protective measures;

(b) by way of derogation from Article 37, measures in the veterinary and phytosanitary fields which have as their direct objective the protection of public health;

(c) incentive measures designed to protect and improve human health, excluding any harmonisation of the laws and regulations of the Member States.

The Council, acting by a qualified majority on a proposal from the Commission, may also adopt recommendations for the purposes set out in this Article.

5. Community action in the field of public health shall fully respect the responsibilities of the Member States for the organisation and delivery of health services and medical care. In particular, measures referred to in paragraph 4(a) shall not affect national provisions on the donation or medical use of organs and blood.

TITLE XIV (ex Title XI)[56]
CONSUMER PROTECTION
Article 153 (ex Article 129a)

1. In order to promote the interests of consumers and to ensure a high level of consumer protection, the Community shall contribute[to protecting the health, safety and economic interests of consumers, as well as to promoting their right to information, education and to organise themselves in order to safeguard their interests.

2. Consumer protection requirements shall be taken into account in defining and implementing other Community policies and activities.

3. The Community shall contribute to the attainment of the objectives referred to in paragraph 1 through:

(a) measures adopted pursuant to Article 95 in the context of the completion of the internal market;

(b) measures which support, supplement and monitor the policy pursued by the Member States.

4. The Council, acting in accordance with the procedure referred to in Article 251 and after consulting the Economic and Social Committee, shall adopt the measures referred to in paragraph 3(b).

5. Measures adopted pursuant to paragraph 4 shall not prevent any Member State from maintaining or introducing more stringent protective measures. Such measures must be compatible with this Treaty. The Commission shall be notified of them.

TITLE XV (ex Title XII)[57]
TRANS–EUROPEAN NETWORKS
Article 154 (ex Article 129b)

1. To help achieve the objectives referred to in Articles 14 and 158 and to enable citizens of the Union, economic operators and regional and local communities to derive full benefit from the setting-up of an area without internal frontiers, the Community shall contribute to the establishment and development of trans-European networks in the areas of transport, telecommunications and energy infrastructures.

2. Within the framework of a system of open and competitive markets, action by the Community shall aim at promoting the interconnection and interoperability of national networks as well as access to such networks. It shall take account in particular of the need to link island, landlocked and peripheral regions with the central regions of the Community.

---

56. The TEU introduced this title on consumer protection and the former article 129a. The article was revised by the Treaty of Amsterdam to add paragraphs 1 and 2, extending the article's objectives from attaining a high level of consumer protection to promoting the interests of consumers.

57. The TEU introduced this title, as well as its Articles 129b to 129d (now 154 to 156).

Article 155 (ex Article 129c)

1. In order to achieve the objectives referred to in Article 154, the Community:

— shall establish a series of guidelines covering the objectives, priorities and broad lines of measures envisaged in the sphere of trans-European networks these guidelines shall identify projects of common interest;

— shall implement any measures that may prove necessary to ensure the interoperability of the networks, in particular in the field of technical standardisation;

— may support projects of common interest supported by Member States, which are identified in the framework of the guidelines referred to in the first indent, particularly through feasibility studies, loan guarantees or interest-rate subsidies; the Community may also contribute, through the Cohesion Fund set up pursuant to Article 161, to the financing of specific projects in Member States in the area of transport infrastructure.

The Community's activities shall take into account the potential economic viability of the projects.

2. Member States shall, in liaison with the Commission, coordinate among themselves the policies pursued at national level which may have a significant impact on the achievement of the objectives referred to in Article 154. The Commission may, in close cooperation with the Member State, take any useful initiative to promote such coordination.

3. The Community may decide to cooperate with third countries to promote projects of mutual interest and to ensure the interoperability of networks.

Article 156 (ex Article 129d)

The guidelines and other measures referred to in Article 155(1) shall be adopted by the Council, acting in accordance with the procedure referred to in Article 251 and after consulting the Economic and Social Committee and the Committee of the Regions.

Guidelines and projects of common interest which relate to the territory of a Member State shall require the approval of the Member State concerned.

TITLE XVI (ex Title XIII)[58]
INDUSTRY
Article 157 (ex Article 130)

1. The Community and the Member States shall ensure that the conditions necessary for the competitiveness of the Community's industry exist.

---

58. The TEU introduced this title on industry and its Article 130 (now 157).

For that purpose, in accordance with a system of open and competitive markets, their action shall be aimed at:

— speeding up the adjustment of industry to structural changes;

— encouraging an environment favourable to initiative and to the development of undertakings throughout the Community, particularly small and medium-sized undertakings;

— encouraging an environment favourable to cooperation between undertakings;

— fostering better exploitation of the industrial potential of policies of innovation, research and technological development.

2. The Member States shall consult each other in liaison with the Commission and, where necessary, shall coordinate their action. The Commission may take any useful initiative to promote such coordination.

3. The Community shall contribute to the achievement of the objectives set out in paragraph 1 through the policies and activities it pursues under other provisions of this Treaty. The Council, acting unanimously on a proposal from the Commission, after consulting the European Parliament and the Economic and Social Committee, may decide on specific measures in support of action taken in the Member States to achieve the objectives set out in paragraph 1.

This Title shall not provide a basis for the introduction by the Community of any measure which could lead to a distortion of competition.

TITLE XVII (ex Title XIV)[59]

ECONOMIC AND SOCIAL COHESION

Article 158 (ex Article 130a)

In order to promote its overall harmonious development, the Community shall develop and pursue its actions leading to the strengthening of its economic and social cohesion.

In particular, the Community shall aim at reducing disparities between the levels of development of the various regions and the backwardness of the least favoured regions or islands, including rural areas.

Article 159 (ex Article 130b)[60]

Member States shall conduct their economic policies and shall coordinate them in such a way as, in addition, to attain the objectives set out in Article 158. The formulation and implementation of the Community's policies and actions and the implementation of the internal market shall

---

59. The TEU renumbered Title V as Title XIV and amended the last sentence of then Article 130a to insert "the levels of development of" and "including rural areas." Title V and Article 130a were initially added by the SEA in 1987.

60. The SEA introduced the first paragraph and the TEU added the other two paragraphs.

take into account the objectives set out in Article 158 and shall contribute to their achievement. The Community shall also support the achievement of these objectives by the action it takes through the Structural Funds (European Agricultural Guidance and Guarantee Fund, Guidance Section; European Social Fund; European Regional Development Fund), the European Investment Bank and the other existing financial instruments.

The Commission shall submit a report to the European Parliament, the Council, the Economic and Social Committee and the Committee of the Regions every three years on the progress made towards achieving economic and social cohesion and on the manner in which the various means provided for in this Article have contributed to it. This report shall, if necessary, be accompanied by appropriate proposals.

If specific actions prove necessary outside the Funds and without prejudice to the measures decided upon within the framework of the other Community policies, such actions may be adopted by the Council acting unanimously on a proposal from the Commission and after consulting the European Parliament, the Economic and Social Committee and the Committee of the Regions.

Article 160 (ex Article 130c)[61]

The European Regional Development Fund is intended to help to redress the main regional imbalances in the Community through participation in the development and structural adjustment of regions whose development is lagging behind and in the conversion of declining industrial regions.

Article 161 (ex Article 130d)[62]

Without prejudice to Article 162, the Council, acting unanimously on a proposal from the Commission and after obtaining the assent of the European Parliament and consulting the Economic and Social Committee and the Committee of the Regions, shall define the tasks, priority objectives and the organisation of the Structural Funds, which may involve grouping the Funds. The Council, acting by the same procedure, shall also define the general rules applicable to them and the provisions necessary to ensure their effectiveness and the coordination of the Funds with one another and with the other existing financial instruments.

A Cohesion Fund set up by the Council in accordance with the same procedure shall provide a financial contribution to projects in the fields of environment and trans-European networks in the area of transport infrastructure.

---

61. Added by the SEA.

62. The SEA introduced this article, which the TEU then amended, principally to give the Council ongoing authority to set the objectives and structure of the Funds and to see to the creation of the Cohesion Fund. The TEU also required the assent (rather than merely the consultation) of the Parliament and the advice of the Committee of the Regions.

Article 162 (ex Article 130e)[63]

Implementing decisions relating to the European Regional Development Fund shall be taken by the Council, acting in accordance with the procedure referred to in Article 251 and after consulting the Economic and Social Committee and the Committee of the Regions.

With regard to the European Agricultural Guidance and Guarantee Fund, Guidance Section, and the European Social Fund, Articles 37 and 148 respectively shall continue to apply.

TITLE XVIII (ex Title XV)[64]
RESEARCH AND TECHNOLOGICAL DEVELOPMENT

Article 163 (ex Article 130f)

1. The Community shall have the objective of strengthening the scientific and technological bases of Community industry and encouraging it to become more competitive at international level, while promoting all the research activities deemed necessary by virtue of other Chapters of this Treaty.

2. For this purpose the Community shall, throughout the Community, encourage undertakings, including small and medium-sized undertakings, research centres and universities in their research and technological development activities of high quality; it shall support their efforts to cooperate with one another, aiming, notably, at enabling undertakings to exploit the internal market potential to the full, in particular through the opening-up of national public contracts, the definition of common standards and the removal of legal and fiscal obstacles to that cooperation.

3. All Community activities under this Treaty in the area of research and technological development, including demonstration projects, shall be decided on and implemented in accordance with the provisions of this Title.

Article 164 (ex Article 130g)

In pursuing these objectives, the Community shall carry out the following activities, complementing the activities carried out in the Member States:

(a) implementation of research, technological development and demonstration programmes, by promoting cooperation with and between undertakings, research centres and universities;

(b) promotion of cooperation in the field of Community research, technological development and demonstration with third countries and international organisations;

(c) dissemination and optimisation of the results of activities in Community research, technological development and demonstration;

---

63. The SEA introduced this article, which the TEU slightly reworded, requiring the Committee of the Regions to be consulted.

64. In 1987, the SEA introduced this title, then numbered VI. The TEU slightly revised the articles, which after Amsterdam were renumbered Articles 163 to 173.

(d) stimulation of the training and mobility of researchers in the Community.

Article 165 (ex Article 130h)

1. The Community and the Member States shall coordinate their research and technological development activities so as to ensure that national policies and Community policy are mutually consistent.

2. In close cooperation with the Member State, the Commission may take any useful initiative to promote the coordination referred to in paragraph 1.

Article 166 (ex Article 130i)[65]

1. A multiannual framework programme, setting out all the activities of the Community, shall be adopted by the Council, acting in accordance with the procedure referred to in Article 251 after consulting the Economic and Social Committee.

The framework programme shall:

— establish the scientific and technological objectives to be achieved by the activities provided for in Article [164] and fix the relevant priorities;

— indicate the broad lines of such activities;

— fix the maximum overall amount and the detailed rules for Community financial participation in the framework programme and the respective shares in each of the activities provided for.

2. The framework programme shall be adapted or supplemented as the situation changes.

3. The framework programme shall be implemented through specific programmes developed within each activity. Each specific programme shall define the detailed rules for implementing it, fix its duration and provide for the means deemed necessary. The sum of the amounts deemed necessary, fixed in the specific programmes, may not exceed the overall maximum amount fixed for the framework programme and each activity.

4. The Council, acting by a qualified majority on a proposal from the Commission and after consulting the European Parliament and the Economic and Social Committee, shall adopt the specific programmes.

Article 167 (ex Article 130j)[66]

For the implementation of the multiannual framework programme the Council shall:

— determine the rules for the participation of undertakings, research centres and universities;

---

65. The SEA introduced Articles 130i and 130k. The TEU combined the two and elaborated the text, Inn particular, the TEU called for application of the codecision procedure of the then Article 189b (but with unanimity in the Council) to set the framework program, instead of merely requiring parliamentary consultation. The TEU then deleted Article 130q which had previously laid out the legislative procedure.

66. Added by the TEU.

— lay down the rules governing the dissemination of research results.

Article 168 (ex Article 130k)[67]

In implementing the multiannual framework programme, supplementary programmes may be decided on involving the participation of certain Member States only, which shall finance them subject to possible Community participation.

The Council shall adopt the rules applicable to supplementary programmes, particularly as regards the dissemination of knowledge and access by other Member States.

Article 169 (ex Article 130l)

In implementing the multiannual framework programme the Community may make provision, in agreement with the Member States concerned, for participation in research and development programmes undertaken by several Member States, including participation in the structures created for the execution of those programmes.

Article 170 (ex Article 130m)

In implementing the multiannual framework programme the Community may make provision for cooperation in Community research, technological development and demonstration with third countries or international organisations.

The detailed arrangements for such cooperation may be the subject of agreements between the Community and the third parties concerned, which shall be negotiated and concluded in accordance with Article 300.

Article 171 (ex Article 130n)

The Community may set up joint undertakings or any other structure necessary for the efficient execution of Community research, technological development and demonstration programmes.

Article 172 (ex Article 130o)[68]

The Council, acting by qualified majority on a proposal from the Commission and after consulting the European Parliament and the Economic and Social Committee, shall adopt the provisions referred to in Article 171.

The Council, acting in accordance with the procedure referred to in Article 251 and after consulting the Economic and Social Committee, shall adopt the provisions referred to in Articles 167, 168 and 169. Adoption of the supplementary programmes shall require the agreement of the Member States concerned.

---

67. The SEA introduced this article, formerly numbered Articles 130l to 130o. Because the TEU merged the previous Articles 130k and 130i, the former Articles 130l to 130o became Articles 130k to 130n.

68. Added by the TEU.

Article 173 (ex Article 130p)[69]

At the beginning of each year the Commission shall send a report to the European Parliament and the Council. The report shall include information on research and technological development activities and the dissemination of results during the previous year, and the work programme for the current year.

TITLE XIX (ex Title XVI)[70]
ENVIRONMENT

Article 174 (ex Article 130r)[71]

1. Community policy on the environment shall contribute to pursuit of the following objectives:

— preserving, protecting and improving the quality of the environment;

— protecting human health;

— prudent and rational utilisation of natural resources;

— promoting measures at international level to deal with regional or worldwide environmental problems.

2. Community policy on the environment shall aim at a high level of protection taking into account the diversity of situations in the various regions of the Community. It shall be based on the precautionary principle and on the principles that preventive action should be taken, that environmental damage should as a priority be rectified at source and that the polluter should pay.

In this context, harmonisation measures answering environmental protection requirements shall include, where appropriate, a safeguard clause allowing Member States to take provisional measures, for non-economic environmental reasons, subject to a Community inspection procedure.

3. In preparing its policy on the environment, the Community shall take account of:

— available scientific and technical data;

— environmental conditions in the various regions of the Community;

— the potential benefits and costs of action or lack of action;

— the economic and social development of the Community as a whole and the balanced development of its regions.

69. The TEU introduced this article. The former Article 130p had covered the issue of financing,, now dealt with in Article 166 (ex 130i).

70. In 1987, the SEA introduced this title, then numbered VII, and its Articles 130r to 130t (now 174 to 176).

71. The text, which was introduced by the SEA in 1987, was amended by the TEU to add the promotion of international measures as a policy objective in section 1, the mandate for "a high level of protection" in section 2, and the possibility of safeguard clauses for particular States in section 2. The SEA text also included a statement of the subsidiarity principle in a section 4, which was deleted by the TEU due to the insertion of a general subsidiarity principle in Article 3b (now 5).

4. Within their respective spheres of competence, the Community and the Member States shall cooperate with third countries and with the competent international organisations. The arrangements for Community cooperation may be the subject of agreements between the Community and the third parties concerned, which shall be negotiated and concluded in accordance with Article 300.

The previous subparagraph shall be without prejudice to Member States' competence to negotiate in international bodies and to conclude international agreements.

Article 175 (ex Article 130s)[72]

1. The Council, acting in accordance with the procedure referred to in Article 251 and after consulting the Economic and Social Committee and the Committee of the Regions, shall decide what action is to be taken by the Community in order to achieve the objectives referred to in Article 174.

2. By way of derogation from the decision-making procedure provided for in paragraph 1 and without prejudice to Article 95, the Council, acting unanimously on a proposal from the Commission and after consulting the European Parliament, the Economic and Social Committee and the Committee of the Regions, shall adopt:

— provisions primarily of a fiscal nature;

— measures concerning town and country planning, land use with the exception of waste management and measures of a general nature, and management of water resources;

— measures significantly affecting a Member State's choice between different energy sources and the general structure of its energy supply.

The Council may, under the conditions laid down in the preceding subparagraph, define those matters referred to in this paragraph on which decisions are to be taken by a qualified majority.

3. In other areas, general action programmes setting out priority objectives to be attained shall be adopted by the Council, acting in accordance with the procedure referred to in Article 251 and after consulting the Economic and Social Committee and the Committee of the Regions.

The Council, acting under the terms of paragraph 1 or paragraph 2 according to the case, shall adopt the measures necessary for the implementation of these programmes.

4. Without prejudice to certain measures of a Community nature, the Member States shall finance and implement the environment policy.

5. Without prejudice to the principle that the polluter should pay, if a measure based on the provisions of paragraph 1 involves costs deemed

---

72. This article, added by the SEA, was significantly amended by the TEU, chiefly to use the cooperation procedure of Article 189c (now 252) as the usual legislative process for adopting environmental rules, in place of the parliamentary cooperation procedure and Council unanimity. However, the TEU retained the latter procedures for the measures specified in section 2.

disproportionate for the public authorities of a Member State, the Council shall, in the act adopting that measure, lay down appropriate provisions in the form of:

— temporary derogations, and/or

— financial support from the Cohesion Fund set up pursuant to Article 161.

Article 176 (ex Article 130t)[73]

The protective measures adopted pursuant to Article 175 shall not prevent any Member State from maintaining or introducing more stringent protective measures. Such measures must be compatible with this Treaty. They shall be notified to the Commission.

TITLE XX (ex Title XVII)[74]
DEVELOPMENT COOPERATION

Article 177 (ex Article 130u)

1. Community policy in the sphere of development cooperation, which shall be complementary to the policies pursued by the Member States, shall foster:

— the sustainable economic and social development of the developing countries, and more particularly the most disadvantaged among them;

— the smooth and gradual integration of the developing countries into the world economy;

— the campaign against poverty in the developing countries.

2. Community policy in this area shall contribute to the general objective of developing and consolidating democracy and the rule of law, and to that of respecting human rights and fundamental freedoms.

3. The Community and the Member States shall comply with the commitments and take account of the objectives they have approved in the context of the United Nations and other competent international organisations.

Article 178 (ex Article 130v)

The Community shall take account of the objectives referred to in Article 177 in the policies that it implements which are likely to affect developing countries.

Article 179 (ex Article 130w)

1. Without prejudice to the other provisions of this Treaty, the Council, acting in accordance with the procedure referred to in Article 251, shall adopt the measures necessary to further the objectives referred to in Article 177. Such measures may take the form of multiannual programmes.

---

73. Added by the SEA. The TEU added the final two sentences.

74. The TEU introduced this Title and its Articles 130u to 130y (now 177 to 181).

2. The European Investment Bank shall contribute, under the terms laid down in its Statute, to the implementation of the measures referred to in paragraph 1.

3. The provisions of this Article shall not affect cooperation with the African, Caribbean and Pacific countries in the framework of the ACP–EC Convention.

Article 180 (ex Article 130x)

1. The Community and the Member States shall coordinate their policies on development cooperation and shall consult each other on their aid programmes, including in international organisations and during international conferences. They may undertake joint action. Member States shall contribute if necessary to the implementation of Community aid programmes.

2. The Commission may take any useful initiative to promote the coordination referred to in paragraph 1.

Article 181 (ex Article 130y)

Within their respective spheres of competence, the Community and the Member States shall cooperate with third countries and with the competent international organisations. The arrangements for Community cooperation may be the subject of agreements between the Community and the third parties concerned, which shall be negotiated and concluded in accordance with Article 300.

The previous paragraph shall be without prejudice to Member States' competence to negotiate in international bodies and to conclude international agreements.

PART FOUR

ASSOCIATION OF THE OVERSEAS COUNTRIES AND TERRITORIES

Article 182 (ex Article 131)

The Member States agree to associate with the Community the non-European countries and territories which have special relations with Denmark, France, the Netherlands and the United Kingdom. These countries and territories (hereinafter called the "countries and territories") are listed in Annex II to this Treaty.

The purpose of association shall be to promote the economic and social development of the countries and territories and to establish close economic relations between them and the Community as a whole.

In accordance with the principles set out in the Preamble to this Treaty, association shall serve primarily to further the interests and prosperity of the inhabitants of these countries and territories in order to lead them to the economic, social and cultural development to which they aspire.

Article 183 (ex Article 132)

Association shall have the following objectives.

(1) Member States shall apply to their trade with the countries and territories the same treatment as they accord each other pursuant to this Treaty.

(2) Each country or territory shall apply to its trade with Member States and with the other countries and territories the same treatment as that which it applies to the European State with which is has special relations.

(3) The Member States shall contribute to the investments required for the progressive development of these countries and territories.

(4) For investments financed by the Community, participation in tenders and supplies shall be open on equal terms to all natural and legal persons who are nationals of a Member State or of one of the countries and territories.

(5) In relations between Member States and the countries and territories the right of establishment of nationals and companies or firms shall be regulated in accordance with the provisions and procedures laid down in the Chapter relating to the right of establishment and on a non-discriminatory basis, subject to any special provisions laid down pursuant to Article 187.

Article 184 (ex Article 133)

1. Customs duties on imports into the Member States of goods originating in the countries and territories shall be prohibited in conformity with the [prohibition] of customs duties between Member States in accordance with the provisions of this Treaty.

2. Customs duties on imports into each country or territory from Member States or from the other countries or territories shall be prohibited in accordance with the provisions of Article 25.

3. The countries and territories may, however, levy customs duties which meet the needs of their development and industrialisation or produce revenue for their budgets.

The duties referred to in the preceding subparagraph may not exceed the level of those imposed on imports of products from the Member State with which each country or territory has special relations.

4. Paragraph 2 shall not apply to countries and territories which, by reason of the particular international obligations by which they are bound, already apply a non-discriminatory customs tariff.

5. The introduction of or any change in customs duties imposed on goods imported into the countries and territories shall not, either in law or in fact, give rise to any direct or indirect discrimination between imports from the various Member States.

Article 185 (ex Article 134)

If the level of the duties applicable to goods from a third country on entry into a country or territory is liable, when the provisions of Article 184(1) have been applied, to cause deflections of trade to the detriment of any Member State, the latter may request the Commission to propose to the other Member States the measures needed to remedy the situation.

Article 186 (ex Article 135)

Subject to the provisions relating to public health, public security or public policy, freedom of movement within Member States for workers from the countries and territories, and within the countries and territories for workers from Member States, shall be governed by agreements to be concluded subsequently with the unanimous approval of Member States.

Article 187 (ex Article 136)

The Council, acting unanimously, shall, on the basis of the experience acquired under the association of the countries and territories with the Community and of the principles set out in this Treaty, lay down provisions as regards the detailed rules and the procedure for the association of the countries and territories with the Community.

Article 188 (ex Article 136a)

The provisions of Articles 182 to 187 shall apply to Greenland, subject to the specific provisions for Greenland set out in the Protocol on special arrangements for Greenland, annexed to this Treaty.

PART FIVE

INSTITUTIONS OF THE COMMUNITY

TITLE I

PROVISIONS GOVERNING THE INSTITUTIONS

Chapter 1. The institutions

Section 1: The European Parliament[75]

Article 189 (ex Article 137)[76]

The European Parliament, which shall consist of representatives of the peoples of the States brought together in the Community, shall exercise the powers conferred upon it by this Treaty.

The number of Members of the European Parliament shall not exceed seven hundred.

---

75. The Treaty of Rome gave this body the title "Assembly." The SEA changed this designation to "European Parliament."

76. The TEU deleted the words "advisory and supervisory," which formerly described the European Parliament's powers.

Article 190 (ex Article 138)

1. The representatives in the European Parliament of the peoples of the States brought together in the Community shall be elected by direct universal suffrage.

2. The number of representatives elected in each Member State shall be as follows:

Belgium	25	France	87	Austria	21
Denmark	16	Ireland	15	Portugal	25
Germany	99	Italy	87	Finland	16
Greece	25	Luxembourg	6	Sweden	22
Spain	64	Netherlands	31	United Kingdom	87

In the event of amendments to this paragraph, the number of representatives elected in each Member State must ensure appropriate representation of the peoples of the States brought together in the Community.

3. Representatives shall be elected for a term of five years.

4. The European Parliament shall draw up a proposal for elections by direct universal suffrage in accordance with a uniform procedure in all Member States or in accordance with principles common to all Member States.

The Council shall, acting unanimously after obtaining the assent of the European Parliament, which shall act by a majority of its component members, lay down the appropriate provisions, which it shall recommend to Member States for adoption in accordance with their respective constitutional requirements.

5. The European Parliament shall, after seeking an opinion from the Commission and with the approval of the Council acting unanimously, lay down the regulations and general conditions governing the performance of the duties of its Members.

Article 191 (ex Article 138a)[77]

Political parties at European level are important as a factor for integration within the Union. They contribute to forming a European awareness and to expressing the political will of the citizens of the Union.

Article 192 (ex Article 138b)[78]

Insofar as provided in this Treaty, the European Parliament shall participate in the process leading up to the adoption of Community acts by exercising its powers under the procedures laid down in Articles 251 and 252 and by giving its assent or delivering advisory opinions.

The European Parliament may, acting by a majority of its Members, request the Commission to submit any appropriate proposal on matters on

---

77. Added by the TEU.
78. Added by the TEU.

which it considers that a Community act is required for the purpose of implementing this Treaty.

Article 193 (ex Article 138c)[79]

In the course of its duties, the European Parliament may, at the request of a quarter of its Members, set up a temporary Committee of Inquiry to investigate, without prejudice to the powers conferred by this Treaty on other institutions or bodies, alleged contraventions or maladministration in the implementation of Community law, except where the alleged facts are being examined before a court and while the case is still subject to legal proceedings.

The temporary Committee of Inquiry shall cease to exist on the submission of its report.

The detailed provisions governing the exercise of the right of inquiry shall be determined by common accord of the European Parliament, the Council and the Commission.

Article 194 (ex Article 138d)[80]

Any citizen of the Union, and any natural or legal person residing or having its registered office in a Member State, shall have the right to address, individually or in association with other citizens or persons, a petition to the European Parliament on a matter which comes within the Community's fields of activity and which affects him, her or it directly.

Article 195 (ex Article 138e)[81]

1. The European Parliament shall appoint an Ombudsman empowered to receive complaints from any citizen of the Union or any natural or legal person residing or having its registered office in a Member State concerning instances of maladministration in the activities of the Community institutions or bodies, with the exception of the Court of Justice and the Court of First Instance acting in their judicial role.

In accordance with his duties, the Ombudsman shall conduct inquiries for which he finds grounds, either on his own initiative or on the basis of complaints submitted to him direct or through a Member of the European Parliament, except where the alleged facts are or have been the subject of legal proceedings. Where the Ombudsman establishes an instance of maladministration, he shall refer the matter to the institution concerned, which shall have a period of three months in which to inform him of its views. The Ombudsman shall then forward a report to the European Parliament and the institution concerned. The person lodging the complaint shall be informed of the outcome of such inquiries.

The Ombudsman shall submit an annual report to the European Parliament on the outcome of his inquiries.

79. Added by the TEU.
80. Added by the TEU.
81. Added by the TEU.

2. The Ombudsman shall be appointed after each election of the European Parliament for the duration of its term of office. The Ombudsman shall be eligible for reappointment.

The Ombudsman may be dismissed by the Court of Justice at the request of the European Parliament if he no longer fulfils the conditions required for the performance of his duties or if he is guilty of serious misconduct.

3. The Ombudsman shall be completely independent in the performance of his duties. In the performance of those duties he shall neither seek nor take instructions from any body. The Ombudsman may not, during his term of office, engage in any other occupation, whether gainful or not.

4. The European Parliament shall, after seeking an opinion from the Commission and with the approval of the Council acting by a qualified majority, lay down the regulations and general conditions governing the performance of the Ombudsman's duties.

Article 196 (ex Article 139)

The European Parliament shall hold an annual session. It shall meet, without requiring to be convened, on the second Tuesday in March.

The European Parliament may meet in extraordinary session at the request of a majority of its Members or at the request of the Council or of the Commission.

Article 197 (ex Article 140)

The European Parliament shall elect its President and its officers from among its Members.

Members of the Commission may attend all meetings and shall, at their request, be heard on behalf of the Commission.

The Commission shall reply orally or in writing to questions put to it by the European Parliament or by its Members.

The Council shall be heard by the European Parliament in accordance with the conditions laid down by the Council in its Rules of Procedure.

Article 198 (ex Article 141)

Save as otherwise provided in this Treaty, the European Parliament shall act by an absolute majority of the votes cast.

The Rules of Procedure shall determine the quorum.

Article 199 (ex Article 142)

The European Parliament shall adopt its Rules of Procedure, acting by a majority of its Members.

The proceedings of the European Parliament shall be published in the manner laid down in its Rules of Procedure.

Article 200 (ex Article 143)

The European Parliament shall discuss in open session the annual general report submitted to it by the Commission.

Article 201 (ex Article 144)[82]

If a motion of censure on the activities of the Commission is tabled before it, the European Parliament shall not vote thereon until at least three days after the motion has been tabled and only by open vote.

If the motion of censure is carried by a two-thirds majority of the votes cast, representing a majority of the Members of the European Parliament, the Members of the Commission shall resign as a body. They shall continue to deal with current business until they are replaced in accordance with Article 214. In this case, the term of office of the Members of the Commission appointed to replace them shall expire on the date on which the term of office of the Members of the Commission obliged to resign as a body would have expired.

Section 2. The Council

Article 202 (ex Article 145)

To ensure that the objectives set out in this Treaty are attained the Council shall, in accordance with the provisions of this Treaty:

— ensure coordination of the general economic policies of the Member States;

— have power to take decisions;

— confer on the Commission, in the acts which the Council adopts, powers for the implementation of the rules which the Council lays down. The Council may impose certain requirements in respect of the exercise of these powers. The Council may also reserve the right, in specific cases, to exercise directly implementing powers itself. The procedures referred to above must be consonant with principles and rules to be laid down in advance by the Council, acting unanimously on a proposal from the Commission and after obtaining the Opinion of the European Parliament.[83]

Article 203 (ex Article 146)[84]

The Council shall consist of a representative of each Member State at ministerial level, authorised to commit the government of that Member State.

The office of President shall be held in turn by each Member State in the Council for a term of six months in the order decided by the Council acting unanimously.

---

82. The TEU amended this article to add the final sentence.

83. In 1987, the SEA inserted the last indent concerning the delegation of powers to the Commission.

84. The TEU amended the first paragraph to insert the words "at ministerial level, authorized to commit the government."

Article 204 (ex Article 147)

The Council shall meet when convened by its President on his own initiative or at the request of one of its members or of the Commission.

Article 205 (ex Article 148)[85]

1. Save as otherwise provided in this Treaty, the Council shall act by a majority of its members.

2. Where the Council is required to act by a qualified majority, the votes of its members shall be weighted as follows:

Belgium	5	France	10	Austria	4
Denmark	3	Ireland	3	Portugal	5
Germany	10	Italy	10	Finland	3
Greece	5	Luxembourg	2	Sweden	4
Spain	8	Netherlands	5	United Kingdom	10

For their adoption, acts of the Council shall require at least:

— 62 votes in favour where this Treaty requires them to be adopted on a proposal from the Commission,

— 62 votes in favour, cast by at least 10 members, in other cases.

3. Abstentions by members present in person or represented shall not prevent the adoption by the Council of acts which require unanimity.

Article 206 (ex Article 150)

Where a vote is taken, any member of the Council may also act on behalf of not more than one other member.

Article 207 (ex Article 151)[86]

1. A committee consisting of the Permanent Representatives of the Member States shall be responsible for preparing the work of the Council and for carrying out the tasks assigned to it by the Council. The Committee may adopt procedural decisions in cases provided for in the Council's Rules of Procedure.

2. The Council shall be assisted by a General Secretariat, under the responsibility of a Secretary–General, High Representative for the common foreign and security policy, who shall be assisted by a Deputy Secretary-General responsible for the running of the General Secretariat. The Secretary-General [and the Deputy Secretary–General] shall be appointed by the Council acting unanimously.

The Council shall decide on the organisation of the General Secretariat.

---

85. This article's specification of the weighted votes and the minimum required for a qualified majority have been changed each time new States have acceded to the Community. The TEU repealed former Article 149 which had been earlier amended by the SEA to introduce the cooperation procedure.

86. The TEU amended this article to introduce section 2, giving Treaty status to the General Secretariat.

3. The Council shall adopt its Rules of Procedure.

For the purpose of applying Article 255(3), the Council shall elaborate in these Rules the conditions under which the public shall have access to Council documents. For the purpose of this paragraph, the Council shall define the cases in which it is to be regarded as acting in its legislative capacity, with a view to allowing greater access to documents in those cases, while at the same time preserving the effectiveness of its decision-making process. In any event, when the Council acts in its legislative capacity, the results of votes and explanations of vote as well as statements in the minutes shall be made public.

Article 208 (ex Article 152)

The Council may request the Commission to undertake any studies the Council considers desirable for the attainment of the common objectives, and to submit to it any appropriate proposals.

Article 209 (ex Article 153)

The Council shall, after receiving an opinion from the Commission, determine the rules governing the committees provided for in this Treaty.

Article 210 (ex Article 154)

The Council shall, acting by a qualified majority, determine the salaries, allowances and pensions of the President and Members of the Commission, and of the President, Judges, Advocates-General and Registrar of the Court of Justice. It shall also, again by a qualified majority, determine any payment to be made instead of remuneration.

Section 3. The Commission

Article 211 (ex Article 155)

In order to ensure the proper functioning and development of the common market, the Commission shall:

— ensure that the provisions of this Treaty and the measures taken by the institutions pursuant thereto are applied;

— formulate recommendations or deliver opinions on matters dealt with in this Treaty, if it expressly so provides or if the Commission considers it necessary;

— have its own power of decision and participate in the shaping of measures taken by the Council and by the European Parliament in the manner provided for in this Treaty;

— exercise the powers conferred on it by the Council for the implementation of the rules laid down by the latter.

Article 212 (ex Article 156)

The Commission shall publish annually, not later than one month before the opening of the session of the European Parliament, a general report on the activities of the Community.

Article 213 (ex Article 157)[87]

1. The Commission shall consist of 20 Members, who shall be chosen on the grounds of their general competence and whose independence is beyond doubt.

The number of Members of the Commission may be altered by the Council, acting unanimously.

Only nationals of Member States may be Members of the Commission.

The Commission must include at least one national of each of the Member States, but may not include more than two Members having the nationality of the same State.

2. The Members of the Commission shall, in the general interest of the Community, be completely independent in the performance of their duties.

In the performance of these duties, they shall neither seek nor take instructions from any government or from any other body. They shall refrain from any action incompatible with their duties. Each Member State undertakes to respect this principle and not to seek to influence the Members of the Commission in the performance of their tasks.

The Members of the Commission may not, during their term of office, engage in any other occupation, whether gainful or not. When entering upon their duties they shall give a solemn undertaking that, both during and after their term of office, they will respect the obligations arising therefrom and in particular their duty to behave with integrity and discretion as regards the acceptance, after they have ceased to hold office, of certain appointments or benefits. In the event of any breach of these obligations, the Court of Justice may, on application by the Council or the Commission, rule that the Member concerned be, according to the circumstances, either compulsorily retired in accordance with Article 216 or deprived of his right to a pension or other benefits in its stead.

Article 214 (ex Article 158)[88]

1. The Members of the Commission shall be appointed, in accordance with the procedure referred to in paragraph 2, for a period of five years, subject, if need be, to Article 201.

Their term of office shall be renewable.

2. The governments of the Member States shall nominate by common accord the person they intend to appoint as President of the Commission the nomination shall be approved by the European Parliament.

---

87. The number of members of the Commission has been increased each time new States join the Community, most recently in 1995.

88. The TEU substantially modified this article. Initially, members of the Commission served four years and were named by common accord of the Member States without reference to the European Parliament. The original treaty text made no reference to the office of the President of the Commission.

The governments of the Member States shall, by common accord with the nominee for President, nominate the other persons whom they intend to appoint as Members of the Commission.

The President and the other Members of the Commission thus nominated shall be subject as a body to a vote of approval by the European Parliament. After approval by the European Parliament, the President and the other Members of the Commission shall be appointed by common accord of the governments of the Member States.

Article 215 (ex Article 159)

Apart from normal replacement, or death, the duties of a Member of the Commission shall end when he resigns or is compulsorily retired.

The vacancy thus caused shall be filled for the remainder of the Member's term of office by a new Member appointed by common accord of the governments of the Member States. The Council may, acting unanimously, decide that such a vacancy need not be filled.

In the event of resignation, compulsory retirement or death, the President shall be replaced for the remainder of his term of office. The procedure laid down in Article 214(2) shall be applicable for the replacement of the President.[89]

Save in the case of compulsory retirement under Article 216, Members of the Commission shall remain in office until they have been replaced.

Article 216 (ex Article 160)

If any Member of the Commission no longer fulfils the conditions required for the performance of his duties or if he has been guilty of serious misconduct, the Court of Justice may, on application by the Council or the Commission, compulsorily retire him.

Article 217 (ex Article 161)[90]

The Commission may appoint a Vice-President or two Vice-Presidents from among its Members.

Article 218 (ex Article 162)

1. The Council and the Commission shall consult each other and shall settle by common accord their methods of cooperation.

2. The Commission shall adopt its Rules of Procedure so as to ensure that both it and its departments operate in accordance with the provisions of this Treaty. It shall ensure that these rules are published.

Article 219 (ex Article 163)

The Commission shall work under the political guidance of its President.

---

89. The TEU added the third paragraph.
90. The TEU substantially amended this article, which formerly provided that the President and six Vice-Presidents should be appointed by common accord of the Member States for two year renewable terms.

The Commission shall act by a majority of the number of Members provided for in Article 213.

A meeting of the Commission shall be valid only if the number of Members laid down in its Rules of Procedure is present.

Section 4. The Court of Justice

Article 220 (ex Article 164)

The Court of Justice shall ensure that in the interpretation and application of this Treaty the law is observed.

Article 221 (ex Article 165)[91]

The Court of Justice shall consist of 15 Judges.

The Court of Justice shall sit in plenary session. It may, however, form chambers, each consisting of three, five or seven Judges, either to undertake certain preparatory inquiries or to adjudicate on particular categories of cases in accordance with rules laid down for these purposes.

The Court of Justice shall sit in plenary session when a Member State or a Community institution that is a party to the proceedings so requests.

Should the Court of Justice so request, the Council may, acting unanimously, increase the number of Judges and make the necessary adjustments to the second and third paragraphs of this Article and to the second paragraph of Article 223.

Article 222 (ex Article 166)

The Court of Justice shall be assisted by eight Advocates–General. However, a ninth Advocate–General shall be appointed as from 1 January 1995 until 6 October 2000.[92]

It shall be the duty of the Advocate–General, acting with complete impartiality and independence, to make, in open court, reasoned submissions on cases brought before the Court of Justice, in order to assist the Court in the performance of the task assigned to it in Article 220.

Should the Court of Justice so request, the Council may, acting unanimously, increase the number of Advocates–General and make the necessary adjustments to the third paragraph of Article 223.

Article 223 (ex Article 167)

The Judges and Advocates–General shall be chosen from persons whose independence is beyond doubt and who possess the qualifications required for appointment to the highest judicial offices in their respective

---

[91]. The number of judges set in the first paragraph has been increased to parallel the number of Member States each time new States have joined the Community, most recently in 1995. The TEU amended this article's second paragraph to create seven-Judge chambers. The TEU also amended the third paragraph to eliminate the requirement that the Court sit in plenary session in Article 234 (ex 177) proceedings.

[92]. The Act of Accession in 1995 increased the permanent number of Advocates–General from six to eight, and a ninth was added to serve until 2000.

countries or who are jurisconsults of recognised competence; they shall be appointed by common accord of the governments of the Member States for a term of six years.

Every three years there shall be a partial replacement of the Judges. Eight and seven Judges shall be replaced alternately.

Every three years there shall be a partial replacement of the Advocates–General. Four Advocates–General shall be replaced on each occasion.

Retiring Judges and Advocates–General shall be eligible for reappointment.

The Judges shall elect the President of the Court of Justice from among their number for a term of three years. He may be re-elected.

Article 224 (ex Article 168)

The Court of Justice shall appoint its Registrar and lay down the rules governing his service.

Article 225 (ex Article 168a)[93]

1. A Court of First Instance shall be attached to the Court of Justice with jurisdiction to hear and determine at first instance, subject to a right of appeal to the Court of Justice on points of law only and in accordance with the conditions laid down by the Statute, certain classes of action or proceeding defined in accordance with the conditions laid down in paragraph 2. The Court of First Instance shall not be competent to hear and determine questions referred for a preliminary ruling under Article 234.

2. At the request of the Court of Justice and after consulting the European Parliament and the Commission, the Council, acting unanimously, shall determine the classes of action or proceeding referred to in paragraph 1 and the composition of the Court of First Instance and shall adopt the necessary adjustments and additional provisions to the Statute of the Court of Justice. Unless the Council decides otherwise, the provisions of this Treaty relating to the Court of Justice, in particular the provisions of the Protocol on the Statute of the Court of Justice, shall apply to the Court of First Instance.

3. The members of the Court of First Instance shall be chosen from persons whose independence is beyond doubt and who possess the ability required for appointment to judicial office; they shall be appointed by common accord of the governments of the Member States for a term of six years. The membership shall be partially renewed every three years. Retiring members shall be eligible for reappointment.

---

93. Added by the SEA in 1987. The TEU amended this article to name this Court officially the Court of First Instance. The TEU also amended sections 1 and 2 to enable the Council to set freely the classes of action or proceeding to be heard by the Court of First Instance. The initial text had limited the Court of First Instance's potential jurisdiction to actions or proceedings "brought by natural or legal persons."

4. The Court of First Instance shall establish its Rules of Procedure in agreement with the Court of Justice. Those rules shall require the unanimous approval of the Council.

Article 226 (ex Article 169)

If the Commission considers that a Member State has failed to fulfil an obligation under this Treaty, it shall deliver a reasoned opinion on the matter after giving the State concerned the opportunity to submit its observations.

If the State concerned does not comply with the opinion within the period laid down by the Commission, the latter may bring the matter before the Court of Justice.

Article 227 (ex Article 170)

A Member State which considers that another Member State has failed to fulfil an obligation under this Treaty may bring the matter before the Court of Justice.

Before a Member State brings an action against another Member State for an alleged infringement of an obligation under this Treaty, it shall bring the matter before the Commission.

The Commission shall deliver a reasoned opinion after each of the States concerned has been given the opportunity to submit its own case and its observations on the other party's case both orally and in writing.

If the Commission has not delivered an opinion within three months of the date on which the matter was brought before it, the absence of such opinion shall not prevent the matter from being brought before the Court of Justice.

Article 228 (ex Article 171)[94]

1. If the Court of Justice finds that a Member State has failed to fulfil an obligation under this Treaty, the State shall be required to take the necessary measures to comply with the judgment of the Court of Justice.

2. If the Commission considers that the Member State concerned has not taken such measures it shall, after giving that State the opportunity to submit its observations, issue a reasoned opinion specifying the points on which the Member State concerned has not complied with the judgment of the Court of Justice.

If the Member State concerned fails to take the necessary measures to comply with the Court's judgment within the time-limit laid down by the Commission, the latter may bring the case before the Court of Justice. In so doing it shall specify the amount of the lump sum or penalty payment to be paid by the Member State concerned which it considers appropriate in the circumstances.

---

94. The TEU amended this article to insert section 2.

If the Court of Justice finds that the Member State concerned has not complied with its judgment it may impose a lump sum or penalty payment on it.

This procedure shall be without prejudice to Article 227.

Article 229 (ex Article 172)[95]

Regulations adopted jointly by the European Parliament and the Council, and by the Council, pursuant to the provisions of this Treaty, may give the Court of Justice unlimited jurisdiction with regard to the penalties provided for in such regulations.

Article 230 (ex Article 173)[96]

The Court of Justice shall review the legality of acts adopted jointly by the European Parliament and the Council, of acts of the Council, of the Commission and of the ECB, other than recommendations and opinions, and of acts of the European Parliament intended to produce legal effects vis-à-vis third parties.

It shall for this purpose have jurisdiction in actions brought by a Member State, the Council or the Commission on grounds of lack of competence, infringement of an essential procedural requirement, infringement of this Treaty or of any rule of law relating to its application, or misuse of powers.

The Court of Justice shall have jurisdiction under the same conditions in actions brought by the European Parliament, by the Court of Auditors and by the ECB for the purpose of protecting their prerogatives.

Any natural or legal person may, under the same conditions, institute proceedings against a decision addressed to that person or against a decision which, although in the form of a regulation or a decision addressed to another person, is of direct and individual concern to the former.

The proceedings provided for in this Article shall be instituted within two months of the publication of the measure, or of its notification to the plaintiff, or, in the absence thereof, of the day on which it came to the knowledge of the latter, as the case may be.

Article 231 (ex Article 174)

If the action is well founded, the Court of Justice shall declare the act concerned to be void.

In the case of a regulation, however, the Court of Justice shall, if it considers this necessary, state which of the effects of the regulation which it has declared void shall be considered as definitive.

---

95. The TEU amended this article to refer to regulations "adopted jointly by the European Parliament and the Council," in addition to those adopted by the Council alone.

96. The TEU amended the first paragraph of this article to give the Court of Justice the power to review "acts adopted jointly by the European Parliament and the Council," acts of the ECB, and acts of the Parliament. The TEU also inserted the third paragraph.

Article 232 (ex Article 175)[97]

Should the European Parliament, the Council or the Commission, in infringement of this Treaty, fail to act, the Member States and the other institutions of the Community may bring an action before the Court of Justice to have the infringement established.

The action shall be admissible only if the institution concerned has first been called upon to act. If, within two months of being so called upon, the institution concerned has not defined its position, the action may be brought within a further period of two months.

Any natural or legal person may, under the conditions laid down in the preceding paragraphs, complain to the Court of Justice that an institution of the Community has failed to address to that person any act other than a recommendation or an opinion.

The Court of Justice shall have jurisdiction, under the same conditions, in actions or proceedings brought by the ECB in the areas falling within the latter's field of competence and in actions or proceedings brought against the latter.

Article 233 (ex Article 176)[98]

The institution or institutions whose act has been declared void or whose failure to act has been declared contrary to this Treaty shall be required to take the necessary measures to comply with the judgment of the Court of Justice.

This obligation shall not affect any obligation which may result from the application of the second paragraph of Article 288.

This Article shall also apply to the ECB.

Article 234 (ex Article 177)

The Court of Justice shall have jurisdiction to give preliminary rulings concerning:

(a) the interpretation of this Treaty;

(b) the validity and interpretation of acts of the institutions of the Community and of the ECB;[99]

(c) the interpretation of the statutes of bodies established by an act of the Council, where those statutes so provide.

Where such a question is raised before any court or tribunal of a Member State, that court or tribunal may, if it considers that a decision on the question is necessary to enable it to give judgment, request the Court of Justice to give a ruling thereon.

---

97. The TEU amended the first paragraph of this article to enable actions against the European Parliament to be brought before the Court of Justice. The TEU also inserted the fourth paragraph.

98. The TEU added "or institutions" in the first paragraph, and added the third paragraph.

99. The TEU added the ECB in paragraph (b).

Where any such question is raised in a case pending before a court or tribunal of a Member State against whose decisions there is no judicial remedy under national law, that court or tribunal shall bring the matter before the Court of Justice.

Article 235 (ex Article 178)

The Court of Justice shall have jurisdiction in disputes relating to compensation for damage provided for in the second paragraph of Article 288.

Article 236 (ex Article 179)

The Court of Justice shall have jurisdiction in any dispute between the Community and its servants within the limits and under the conditions laid down in the Staff Regulations or the Conditions of Employment.

Article 237 (ex Article 180)

The Court of Justice shall, within the limits hereinafter laid down, have jurisdiction in disputes concerning:

(a) the fulfilment by Member States of obligations under the Statute of the European Investment Bank. In this connection, the Board of Directors of the Bank shall enjoy the powers conferred upon the Commission by Article 226;

(b) measures adopted by the Board of Governors of the European Investment Bank. In this connection, any Member State, the Commission or the Board of Directors of the Bank may institute proceedings under the conditions laid down in Article 230;

(c) measures adopted by the Board of Directors of the European Investment Bank. Proceedings against such measures may be instituted only by Member States or by the Commission, under the conditions laid down in Article 230, and solely on the grounds of non-compliance with the procedure provided for in Article 21(2), (5), (6) and (7) of the Statute of the Bank;

(d) the fulfilment by national central banks of obligations under this Treaty and the Statute of the ESCB. In this connection the powers of the Council of the ECB in respect of national central banks shall be the same as those conferred upon the Commission in respect of Member States by Article 226. If the Court of Justice finds that a national central bank has failed to fulfil an obligation under this Treaty, that bank shall be required to take the necessary measures to comply with the judgment of the Court of Justice.[100]

Article 238 (ex Article 181)

The Court of Justice shall have jurisdiction to give judgment pursuant to any arbitration clause contained in a contract concluded by or on behalf

---

100. The TEU amended this article to insert paragraph (d).

of the Community, whether that contract be governed by public or private law.

Article 239 (ex Article 182)

The Court of Justice shall have jurisdiction in any dispute between Member States which relates to the subject matter of this Treaty if the dispute is submitted to it under a special agreement between the parties.

Article 240 (ex Article 183)

Save where jurisdiction is conferred on the Court of Justice by this Treaty, disputes to which the Community is a party shall not on that ground be excluded from the jurisdiction of the courts or tribunals of the Member States.

Article 241 (ex Article 184)[101]

Notwithstanding the expiry of the period laid down in the fifth paragraph of Article 230, any party may, in proceedings in which a regulation adopted jointly by the European Parliament and the Council, or a regulation of the Council, of the Commission, or of the ECB is at issue, plead the grounds specified in the second paragraph of Article 230 in order to invoke before the Court of Justice the inapplicability of that regulation.

Article 242 (ex Article 185)

Actions brought before the Court of Justice shall not have suspensory effect. The Court of Justice may, however, if it considers that circumstances so require, order that application of the contested act be suspended.

Article 243 (ex Article 186)

The Court of Justice may in any cases before it prescribe any necessary interim measures.

Article 244 (ex Article 187)

The judgments of the Court of Justice shall be enforceable under the conditions laid down in Article 256.

Article 245 (ex Article 188)

The Statute of the Court of Justice is laid down in a separate Protocol.

The Council may, acting unanimously at the request of the Court of Justice and after consulting the Commission and the European Parliament, amend the provisions of Title III of the Statute.[102]

The Court of Justice shall adopt its Rules of Procedure. These shall require the unanimous approval of the Council.

---

101. The TEU amended this article to include regulations "jointly adopted by the European Parliament and the Council," and regulations of the ECB.

102. The SEA amended this article to insert the second paragraph.

Section 5. The Court of Auditors[103]

Article 246 (ex Article 188a)

The Court of Auditors shall carry out the audit.

Article 247 (ex Article 188b)

1. The Court of Auditors shall consist of 15 Members.

2. The Members of the Court of Auditors shall be chosen from among persons who belong or have belonged in their respective countries to external audit bodies or who are especially qualified for this office. Their independence must be beyond doubt.

3. The Members of the Court of Auditors shall be appointed for a term of six years by the Council, acting unanimously after consulting the European Parliament.

The Members of the Court of Auditors shall be eligible for reappointment.

They shall elect the President of the Court of Auditors from among their number for a term of three years. The President may be re-elected.

4. The Members of the Court of Auditors shall, in the general interest of the Community, be completely independent in the performance of their duties.

In the performance of these duties, they shall neither seek nor take instructions from any government or from any other body. They shall refrain from any action incompatible with their duties.

5. The Members of the Court of Auditors may not, during their term of office, engage in any other occupation, whether gainful or not. When entering upon their duties they shall give a solemn undertaking that, both during and after their term of office, they will respect the obligations arising therefrom and in particular their duty to behave with integrity and discretion as regards the acceptance, after they have ceased to hold office, of certain appointments or benefits.

6. Apart from normal replacement, or death, the duties of a Member of the Court of Auditors shall end when he resigns, or is compulsorily retired by a ruling of the Court of Justice pursuant to paragraph 7.

The vacancy thus caused shall be filled for the remainder of the Member's term of office.

Save in the case of compulsory retirement, Members of the Court of Auditors shall remain in office until they have been replaced.

7. A Member of the Court of Auditors may be deprived of his office or of his right to a pension or other benefits in its stead only if the Court of Justice, at the request of the Court of Auditors, finds that he no longer

---

103. The TEU introduced this section and Articles 246 to 248 (ex 188a to 188c), replacing the former Articles 206 and 206a.

fulfils the requisite conditions or meets the obligations arising from his office.

8. The Council, acting by a qualified majority, shall determine the conditions of employment of the President and the Members of the Court of Auditors and in particular their salaries, allowances and pensions. It shall also, by the same majority, determine any payment to be made instead of remuneration.

9. The provisions of the Protocol on the privileges and immunities of the European Communities applicable to the Judges of the Court of Justice shall also apply to the Members of the Court of Auditors.

Article 248 (ex Article 188c)

1. The Court of Auditors shall examine the accounts of all revenue and expenditure of the Community. It shall also examine the accounts of all revenue and expenditure of all bodies set up by the Community insofar as the relevant constituent instrument does not preclude such examination.

The Court of Auditors shall provide the European Parliament and the Council with a statement of assurance as to the reliability of the accounts and the legality and regularity of the underlying transactions which shall be published in the Official Journal of the European Communities.

2. The Court of Auditors shall examine whether all revenue has been received and all expenditure incurred in a lawful and regular manner and whether the financial management has been sound. In doing so, it shall report in particular on any cases of irregularity.

The audit of revenue shall be carried out on the basis both of the amounts established as due and the amounts actually paid to the Community.

The audit of expenditure shall be carried out on the basis both of commitments undertaken and payments made.

These audits may be carried out before the closure of accounts for the financial year in question.

3. The audit shall be based on records and, if necessary, performed on the spot in the other institutions of the Community, on the premises of any body which manages revenue or expenditure on behalf of the Community and in the Member States, including on the premises of any natural or legal person in receipt of payments from the budget. In the Member States the audit shall be carried out in liaison with national audit bodies or, if these do not have the necessary powers, with the competent national departments. The Court of Auditors and the national audit bodies of the Member States shall cooperate in a spirit of trust while maintaining their independence. These bodies or departments shall inform the Court of Auditors whether they intend to take part in the audit.

The other institutions of the Community, any bodies managing revenue or expenditure on behalf of the Community, any natural or legal person in receipt of payments from the budget, and the national audit bodies or, if these do not have the necessary powers, the competent national departments, shall forward to the Court of Auditors, at its request, any document or information necessary to carry out its task.

In respect of the European Investment Bank's activity in managing Community expenditure and revenue, the Court's rights of access to information held by the Bank shall be governed by an agreement between the Court, the Bank and the Commission. In the absence of an agreement, the Court shall nevertheless have access to information necessary for the audit of Community expenditure and revenue managed by the Bank.

4. The Court of Auditors shall draw up an annual report after the close of each financial year. It shall be forwarded to the other institutions of the Community and shall be published, together with the replies of these institutions to the observations of the Court of Auditors, in the Official Journal of the European Communities.

The Court of Auditors may also, at any time, submit observations, particularly in the form of special reports, on specific questions and deliver opinions at the request of one of the other institutions of the Community.

It shall adopt its annual reports, special reports or opinions by a majority of its Members.

It shall assist the European Parliament and the Council in exercising their powers of control over the implementation of the budget.

Chapter 2. Provisions common to several institutions

Article 249 (ex Article 189)

In order to carry out their task and in accordance with the provisions of this Treaty, the European Parliament acting jointly with the Council, the Council and the Commission shall make regulations and issue directives, take decisions, make recommendations or deliver opinions.[104]

A regulation shall have general application. It shall be binding in its entirety and directly applicable in all Member States.

A directive shall be binding, as to the result to be achieved, upon each Member State to which it is addressed, but shall leave to the national authorities the choice of form and methods.

A decision shall be binding in its entirety upon those to whom it is addressed.

Recommendations and opinions shall have no binding force.

Article 250 (ex Article 189a)

1. Where, in pursuance of this Treaty, the Council acts on a proposal from the Commission, unanimity shall be required for an act constituting an amendment to that proposal, subject to Article 251(4) and (5).

---

104. The TEU amended the first paragraph to insert "the European Parliament acting jointly with the Council."

2. As long as the Council has not acted, the Commission may alter its proposal at any time during the procedures leading to the adoption of a Community act.

Article 251 (ex Article 189b)[105]

1. Where reference is made in this Treaty to this Article for the adoption of an act, the following procedure shall apply.

2. The Commission shall submit a proposal to the European Parliament and the Council.

The Council, acting by a qualified majority after obtaining the opinion of the European Parliament,

— if it approves all the amendments contained in the European Parliament's opinion, may adopt the proposed act thus amended;

— if the European Parliament does not propose any amendments, may adopt the proposed act;

— shall otherwise adopt a common position and communicate it to the European Parliament. The Council shall inform the European Parliament fully of the reasons which led it to adopt its common position. The Commission shall inform the European Parliament fully of its position.

If, within three months of such communication, the European Parliament:

(a) approves the common position or has not taken a decision, the act in question shall be deemed to have been adopted in accordance with that common position;

(b) rejects, by an absolute majority of its component members, the common position, the proposed act shall be deemed not to have been adopted;

(c) proposes amendments to the common position by an absolute majority of its component members, the amended text shall be forwarded to the Council and to the Commission, which shall deliver an opinion on those amendments.

3. If, within three months of the matter being referred to it, the Council, acting by a qualified majority, approves all the amendments of the European Parliament, the act in question shall be deemed to have been adopted in the form of the common position thus amended; however, the Council shall act unanimously on the amendments on which the Commission has delivered a negative opinion. If the Council does not approve all the amendments, the President of the Council, in agreement with the President of the European Parliament, shall within six weeks convene a meeting of the Conciliation Committee.

4. The Conciliation Committee, which shall be composed of the members of the Council or their representatives and an equal number of

---

105. Added by the TEU. The text sets forth what is commonly called the codecision procedure. The Treaty of Amsterdam amended sections 2 and 6 to further increase Parliament's power.

representatives of the European Parliament, shall have the task of reaching agreement on a joint text, by a qualified majority of the members of the Council or their representatives and by a majority of the representatives of the European Parliament. The Commission shall take part in the Conciliation Committee's proceedings and shall take all the necessary initiatives with a view to reconciling the positions of the European Parliament and the Council. In fulfilling this task, the Conciliation Committee shall address the common position on the basis of the amendments proposed by the European Parliament.

5. If, within six weeks of its being convened, the Conciliation Committee approves a joint text, the European Parliament, acting by an absolute majority of the votes cast, and the Council, acting by a qualified majority, shall each have a period of six weeks from that approval in which to adopt the act in question in accordance with the joint text. If either of the two institutions fails to approve the proposed act within that period, it shall be deemed not to have been adopted.

6. Where the Conciliation Committee does not approve a joint text, the proposed act shall be deemed not to have been adopted.

7. The periods of three months and six weeks referred to in this Article shall be extended by a maximum of one month and two weeks respectively at the initiative of the European Parliament or the Council.

Article 252 (ex Article 189c)[106]

Where reference is made in this Treaty to this Article for the adoption of an act, the following procedure shall apply:

(a) The Council, acting by a qualified majority on a proposal from the Commission and after obtaining the opinion of the European Parliament, shall adopt a common position.

(b) The Council's common position shall be communicated to the European Parliament. The Council and the Commission shall inform the European Parliament fully of the reasons which led the Council to adopt its common position and also of the Commission's position.

If, within three months of such communication, the European Parliament approves this common position or has not taken a decision within that period, the Council shall definitively adopt the act in question in accordance with the common position.

(c) The European Parliament may, within the period of three months referred to in point (b), by an absolute majority of its component Members, propose amendments to the Council's common position. The European Parliament may also, by the same majority, reject the Council's common position. The result of the proceedings shall be transmitted to the Council and the Commission.

106. This legislative mode, commonly called the cooperation procedure, was introduced as Article 149(2) by the SEA in 1987. The TEU moved the description of the procedure to Article 189c (now 252).

If the European Parliament has rejected the Council's common position, unanimity shall be required for the Council to act on a second reading.

(d) The Commission shall, within a period of one month, re-examine the proposal on the basis of which the Council adopted its common position, by taking into account the amendments proposed by the European Parliament.

The Commission shall forward to the Council, at the same time as its re-examined proposal, the amendments of the European Parliament which it has not accepted, and shall express its opinion on them. The Council may adopt these amendments unanimously.

(e) The Council, acting by a qualified majority, shall adopt the proposal as re-examined by the Commission.

Unanimity shall be required for the Council to amend the proposal as re-examined by the Commission.

(f) In the cases referred to in points (c), (d) and (e), the Council shall be required to act within a period of three months. If no decision is taken within this period, the Commission proposal shall be deemed not to have been adopted.

(g) The periods referred to in points (b) and (f) may be extended by a maximum of one month by common accord between the Council and the European Parliament.

Article 253 (ex Article 190)[107]

Regulations, directives and decisions adopted jointly by the European Parliament and the Council, and such acts adopted by the Council or the Commission, shall state the reasons on which they are based and shall refer to any proposals or opinions which were required to be obtained pursuant to this Treaty.

Article 254 (ex Article 191)[108]

1. Regulations, directives and decisions adopted in accordance with the procedure referred to in Article 251 shall be signed by the President of the European Parliament and by the President of the Council and published in the Official Journal of the European Communities. They shall enter into force on the date specified in them or, in the absence thereof, on the twentieth day following that of their publication.

2. Regulations of the Council and of the Commission, as well as directives of those institutions which are addressed to all Member States, shall be published in the Official Journal of the European Communities. They shall enter into force on the date specified in them or, in the absence thereof, on the twentieth day following that of their publication.

---

107. The TEU amended this article to include regulations, directives and decisions "adopted jointly by the European Parliament and the Council."

108. The TEU inserted section 1 and required that Commission regulations, as well as Council and Commission directives "addressed to all the Member States" must be published in the Official Journal.

3. Other directives, and decisions, shall be notified to those to whom they are addressed and shall take effect upon such notification.

Article 255 (ex Article 191a)

1. Any citizen of the Union, and any natural or legal person residing or having its registered office in a Member State, shall have a right of access to European Parliament, Council and Commission documents, subject to the principles and the conditions to be defined in accordance with paragraphs 2 and 3.

2. General principles and limits on grounds of public or private interest governing this right of access to documents shall be determined by the Council, acting in accordance with the procedure referred to in Article 251 within two years of the entry into force of the Treaty of Amsterdam.

3. Each institution referred to above shall elaborate in its own Rules of Procedure specific provisions regarding access to its documents.

Article 256 (ex Article 192)

Decisions of the Council or of the Commission which impose a pecuniary obligation on persons other than States, shall be enforceable.

Enforcement shall be governed by the rules of civil procedure in force in the State in the territory of which it is carried out. The order for its enforcement shall be appended to the decision, without other formality than verification of the authenticity of the decision, by the national authority which the government of each Member State shall designate for this purpose and shall make known to the Commission and to the Court of Justice.

When these formalities have been completed on application by the party concerned, the latter may proceed to enforcement in accordance with the national law, by bringing the matter directly before the competent authority.

Enforcement may be suspended only by a decision of the Court of Justice. However, the courts of the country concerned shall have jurisdiction over complaints that enforcement is being carried out in an irregular manner.

Chapter 3. The Economic and Social Committee

Article 257 (ex Article 193)

An Economic and Social Committee is hereby established. It shall have advisory status.

The Committee shall consist of representatives of the various categories of economic and social activity, in particular, representatives of producers, farmers, carriers, workers, dealers, craftsmen, professional occupations and representatives of the general public.

Article 258 (ex Article 194)[109]

The number of members of the Economic and Social Committee shall be as follows:

Belgium	12	France	24	Austria	12
Denmark	9	Ireland	9	Portugal	12
Germany	24	Italy	24	Finland	9
Greece	12	Luxembourg	6	Sweden	12
Spain	21	Netherlands	12	United Kingdom	24

The members of the Committee shall be appointed by the Council, acting unanimously, for four years. Their appointments shall be renewable.

The members of the Committee may not be bound by any mandatory instructions. They shall be completely independent in the performance of their duties, in the general interest of the Community.

The Council, acting by a qualified majority, shall determine the allowances of members of the Committee.

Article 259 (ex Article 195)[110]

1. For the appointment of the members of the Committee, each Member State shall provide the Council with a list containing twice as many candidates as there are seats allotted to its nationals.

The composition of the Committee shall take account of the need to ensure adequate representation of the various categories of economic and social activity.

2. The Council shall consult the Commission. It may obtain the opinion of European bodies which are representative of the various economic and social sectors to which the activities of the Community are of concern.

Article 260 (ex Article 196)

The Committee shall elect its chairman and officers from among its members for a term of two years.

It shall adopt its Rules of Procedure.

The Committee shall be convened by its chairman at the request of the Council or of the Commission. It may also meet on its own initiative.

Article 261 (ex Article 197)

The Committee shall include specialised sections for the principal fields covered by this Treaty.

---

[109]. The number of members from each Member State has been modified each time new States join the Community, most recently in 1995. The TEU amended the third paragraph to add the obligation of complete independence, and also inserted the fourth paragraph.

[110]. The TEU amended the second paragraph, eliminating the requirement that the Council, acting unanimously, approve the rules of procedure. The TEU also added the last sentence.

These specialised sections shall operate within the general terms of reference of the Committee. They may not be consulted independently of the Committee.

Subcommittees may also be established within the Committee to prepare on specific questions or in specific fields, draft opinions to be submitted to the Committee for its consideration.

The Rules of Procedure shall lay down the methods of composition and the terms of reference of the specialised sections and of the subcommittees.

Article 262 (ex Article 198)

The Committee must be consulted by the Council or by the Commission where this Treaty so provides. The Committee may be consulted by these institutions in all cases in which they consider it appropriate. It may issue an opinion on its own initiative in cases in which it considers such action appropriate.[111]

The Council or the Commission shall, if it considers it necessary, set the Committee, for the submission of its opinion, a time-limit which may not be less than one month from the date on which the chairman receives notification to this effect. Upon expiry of the time-limit, the absence of an opinion shall not prevent further action.

The opinion of the Committee and that of the specialised section, together with a record of the proceedings, shall be forwarded to the Council and to the Commission.

The Committee may be consulted by the European Parliament.

Chapter 4. The Committee of the Regions[112]

Article 263 (ex Article 198a)

A Committee consisting of representatives of regional and local bodies, hereinafter referred to as the Committee of the Regions, is hereby established with advisory status.

The number of members of the Committee of the Regions shall be as follows:

Belgium	12	France	24	Austria	12
Denmark	9	Ireland	9	Portugal	12
Germany	24	Italy	24	Finland	9
Greece	12	Luxembourg	6	Sweden	12
Spain	21	Netherlands	12	United Kingdom	24

The members of the Committee and an equal number of alternate members shall be appointed for four years by the Council acting unanimously on proposals from the respective Member States. Their term of office shall be renewable. No member of the Committee shall at the same time be a Member of the European Parliament.

---

111. The TEU added the final sentence in the first paragraph.

112. The TEU introduced this chapter and Articles 263 to 265 (ex Article 198a to c).

The members of the Committee may not be bound by any mandatory instructions. They shall be completely independent in the performance of their duties, in the general interest of Community.

Article 264 (ex Article 198b)[113]

The Committee of the Regions shall elect its chairman and officers from among its members for a term of two years.

It shall adopt its Rules of Procedure.

The Committee shall be convened by its chairman at the request of the Council or of the Commission. It may also meet on its own initiative.

Article 265 (ex Article 198c)

The Committee of the Regions shall be consulted by the Council or by the Commission where this Treaty so provides and in all other cases, in particular those which concern cross-border cooperation, in which one of these two institutions considers it appropriate.

The Council or the Commission shall, if it considers it necessary, set the Committee, for the submission of its opinion, a time-limit which may not be less than one month from the date on which the chairman receives notification to this effect. Upon expiry of the time-limit, the absence of an opinion shall not prevent further action.

Where the Economic and Social Committee is consulted pursuant to Article 262, the Committee of the Regions shall be informed by the Council or the Commission of the request for an opinion. Where it considers that specific regional interests are involved, the Committee of the Regions may issue an opinion on the matter.

The Committee of the Regions may be consulted by the European Parliament.

It may issue an opinion on its own initiative in cases in which it considers such action appropriate.

The opinion of the Committee, together with a record of the proceedings, shall be forwarded to the Council and to the Commission.

Chapter 5. The European Investment Bank[114]

Article 266 (ex Article 198d)

The European Investment Bank shall have legal personality.

The members of the European Investment Bank shall be the Member States.

The Statute of the European Investment Bank is laid down in a Protocol annexed to this Treaty.

---

113. The Treaty of Amsterdam amended this article so as to dispense with the requirement that the Committee of Regions submit its Rules of Procedure to the unanimous approval of the Council.

114. The TEU introduced this chapter and Articles 198d and e (now 266 and 267), which essentially replaced the former Articles 129 and 130.

Article 267 (ex Article 198e)

The task of the European Investment Bank shall be to contribute, by having recourse to the capital market and utilising its own resources, to the balanced and steady development of the common market in the interest of the Community. For this purpose the Bank shall, operating on a non-profit-making basis, grant loans and give guarantees which facilitate the financing of the following projects in all sectors of the economy:

(a) projects for developing less-developed regions;

(b) projects for modernising or converting undertakings or for developing fresh activities called for by the progressive establishment of the common market, where these projects are of such a size or nature that they cannot be entirely financed by the various means available in the individual Member States;

(c) projects of common interest to several Member States which are of such a size or nature that they cannot be entirely financed by the various means available in the individual Member States.

In carrying out its task, the Bank shall facilitate the financing of investment programmes in conjunction with assistance from the Structural Funds and other Community financial instruments.

TITLE II

FINANCIAL PROVISIONS

Article 268 (ex Article 199)[115]

All items of revenue and expenditure of the Community, including those relating to the European Social Fund, shall be included in estimates to be drawn up for each financial year and shall be shown in the budget.

Administrative expenditure occasioned for the institutions by the provisions of the Treaty on European Union relating to common foreign and security policy and to cooperation in the fields of justice and home affairs shall be charged to the budget. The operational expenditure occasioned by the implementation of the said provisions may, under the conditions referred to therein, be charged to the budget.

The revenue and expenditure shown in the budget shall be in balance.

Article 269 (ex Article 201)[116]

Without prejudice to other revenue, the budget shall be financed wholly from own resources.

The Council, acting unanimously on a proposal from the Commission and after consulting the European Parliament, shall lay down provisions relating to the system of own resources of the Community, which it shall

---

115. The TEU added the second and third paragraphs, while deleting Article 200, which had set out the initial six Member States' percentage contributions to budget revenue.

116. The TEU introduced this article, repealing the initial text which had foreseen the creation of a system of the Community's own resources.

Article 270 (ex Article 201a)[117]

With a view to maintaining budgetary discipline, the Commission shall not make any proposal for a Community act, or alter its proposals, or adopt any implementing measure which is likely to have appreciable implications for the budget without providing the assurance that that proposal or that measure is capable of being financed within the limit of the Community's own resources arising under provisions laid down by the Council pursuant to Article 269.

Article 271 (ex Article 202)

The expenditure shown in the budget shall be authorised for one financial year, unless the regulations made pursuant to Article 279 provide otherwise.

In accordance with conditions to be laid down pursuant to Article 279, any appropriations, other than those relating to staff expenditure, that are unexpended at the end of the financial year may be carried forward to the next financial year only.

Appropriations shall be classified under different chapters grouping items of expenditure according to their nature or purpose and subdivided, as far as may be necessary, in accordance with the regulations made pursuant to Article 279.

The expenditure of the European Parliament, the Council, the Commission and the Court of Justice shall be set out in separate parts of the budget, without prejudice to special arrangements for certain common items of expenditure.

Article 272 (ex Article 203)

1. The financial year shall run from 1 January to 31 December.

2. Each institution of the Community shall, before 1 July, draw up estimates of its expenditure. The Commission shall consolidate these estimates in a preliminary draft budget. It shall attach thereto an opinion which may contain different estimates.

The preliminary draft budget shall contain an estimate of revenue and an estimate of expenditure.

3. The Commission shall place the preliminary draft budget before the Council not later than 1 September of the year preceding that in which the budget is to be implemented.

The Council shall consult the Commission and, where appropriate, the other institutions concerned whenever it intends to depart from the preliminary draft budget.

---

117. Added by the TEU.

The Council, acting by a qualified majority, shall establish the draft budget and forward it to the European Parliament.

4. The draft budget shall be placed before the European Parliament not later than 5 October of the year preceding that in which the budget is to be implemented.

The European Parliament shall have the right to amend the draft budget, acting by a majority of its Members, and to propose to the Council, acting by an absolute majority of the votes cast, modifications to the draft budget relating to expenditure necessarily resulting from this Treaty or from acts adopted in accordance therewith.

If, within 45 days of the draft budget being placed before it, the European Parliament has given its approval, the budget shall stand as finally adopted. If within this period the European Parliament has not amended the draft budget nor proposed any modifications thereto, the budget shall be deemed to be finally adopted.

If within this period the European Parliament has adopted amendments or proposed modifications, the draft budget together with the amendments or proposed modifications shall be forwarded to the Council.

5. After discussing the draft budget with the Commission and, where appropriate, with the other institutions concerned, the Council shall act under the following conditions:

(a) the Council may, acting by a qualified majority, modify any of the amendments adopted by the European Parliament;

(b) with regard to the proposed modifications:

— where a modification proposed by the European Parliament does not have the effect of increasing the total amount of the expenditure of an institution, owing in particular to the fact that the increase in expenditure which it would involve would be expressly compensated by one or more proposed modifications correspondingly reducing expenditure, the Council may, acting by a qualified majority, reject the proposed modification. In the absence of a decision to reject it, the proposed modification shall stand as accepted;

— where a modification proposed by the European Parliament has the effect of increasing the total amount of the expenditure of an institution, the Council may, acting by a qualified majority, accept this proposed modification. In the absence of a decision to accept it, the proposed modification shall stand as rejected;

— where, in pursuance of one of the two preceding subparagraphs, the Council has rejected a proposed modification, it may, acting by a qualified majority, either retain the amount shown in the draft budget or fix another amount.

The draft budget shall be modified on the basis of the proposed modifications accepted by the Council.

If, within 15 days of the draft being placed before it, the Council has not modified any of the amendments adopted by the European Parliament and if the modifications proposed by the latter have been accepted, the budget shall be deemed to be finally adopted. The Council shall inform the European Parliament that it has not modified any of the amendments and that the proposed modifications have been accepted.

If within this period the Council has modified one or more of the amendments adopted by the European Parliament or if the modifications proposed by the latter have been rejected or modified, the modified draft budget shall again be forwarded to the European Parliament. The Council shall inform the European Parliament of the results of its deliberations.

6. Within 15 days of the draft budget being placed before it, the European Parliament, which shall have been notified of the action taken on its proposed modifications, may, acting by a majority of its Members and three-fifths of the votes cast, amend or reject the modifications to its amendments made by the Council and shall adopt the budget accordingly. If within this period the European Parliament has not acted, the budget shall be deemed to be finally adopted.

7. When the procedure provided for in this Article has been completed, the President of the European Parliament shall declare that the budget has been finally adopted.

8. However, the European Parliament, acting by a majority of its Members and two-thirds of the votes cast, may, if there are important reasons, reject the draft budget and ask for a new draft to be submitted to it.

9. A maximum rate of increase in relation to the expenditure of the same type to be incurred during the current year shall be fixed annually for the total expenditure other than that necessarily resulting from this Treaty or from acts adopted in accordance therewith.

The Commission shall, after consulting the Economic Policy Committee, declare what this maximum rate is as it results from:

— the trend, in terms of volume, of the gross national product within the Community;

— the average variation in the budgets of the Member States; and

— the trend of the cost of living during the preceding financial year.

The maximum rate shall be communicated, before 1 May, to all the institutions of the Community. The latter shall be required to conform to this during the budgetary procedure, subject to the provisions of the fourth and fifth subparagraphs of this paragraph.

If, in respect of expenditure other than that necessarily resulting from this Treaty or from acts adopted in accordance therewith, the actual rate of increase in the draft budget established by the Council is over half the maximum rate, the European Parliament may, exercising its right of amendment, further increase the total amount of that expenditure to a limit not exceeding half the maximum rate.

Where the European Parliament, the Council or the Commission consider that the activities of the Communities require that the rate determined according to the procedure laid down in this paragraph should be exceeded, another rate may be fixed by agreement between the Council, acting by a qualified majority, and the European Parliament, acting by a majority of its Members and three-fifths of the votes cast.

10. Each institution shall exercise the powers conferred upon it by this Article, with due regard for the provisions of the Treaty and for acts adopted in accordance therewith, in particular those relating to the Communities' own resources and to the balance between revenue and expenditure.

Article 273 (ex Article 204)

If, at the beginning of a financial year, the budget has not yet been voted, a sum equivalent to not more than one-twelfth of the budget appropriations for the preceding financial year may be spent each month in respect of any chapter or other subdivision of the budget in accordance with the provisions of the Regulations made pursuant to Article 279; this arrangement shall not, however, have the effect of placing at the disposal of the Commission appropriations in excess of one-twelfth of those provided for in the draft budget in course of preparation.

The Council may, acting by a qualified majority, provided that the other conditions laid down in the first subparagraph are observed, authorise expenditure in excess of one-twelfth.

If the decision relates to expenditure which does not necessarily result from this Treaty or from acts adopted in accordance therewith, the Council shall forward it immediately to the European Parliament; within 30 days the European Parliament, acting by a majority of its Members and three-fifths of the votes cast, may adopt a different decision on the expenditure in excess of the one-twelfth referred to in the first subparagraph. This part of the decision of the Council shall be suspended until the European Parliament has taken its decision. If within the said period the European Parliament has not taken a decision which differs from the decision of the Council, the latter shall be deemed to be finally adopted.

The decisions referred to in the second and third subparagraphs shall lay down the necessary measures relating to resources to ensure application of this Article.

Article 274 (ex Article 205)[118]

The Commission shall implement the budget, in accordance with the provisions of the regulations made pursuant to Article 279, on its own responsibility and within the limits of the appropriations, having regard to the principles of sound financial management. Member States shall cooperate with the Commission to ensure that the appropriations are used in accordance with the principles of sound financial management.

---

118. The TEU amended this article to add to the first sentence the language, "having regard to the principles of sound financial management."

The regulations shall lay down detailed rules for each institution concerning its part in effecting its own expenditure.

Within the budget, the Commission may, subject to the limits and conditions laid down in the regulations made pursuant to Article 279, transfer appropriations from one chapter to another or from one subdivision to another.

Article 275 (ex Article 205a)

The Commission shall submit annually to the Council and to the European Parliament the accounts of the preceding financial year relating to the implementation of the budget. The Commission shall also forward to them a financial statement of the assets and liabilities of the Community.

Article 276 (ex Article 206)[119]

1. The European Parliament, acting on a recommendation from the Council which shall act by a qualified majority, shall give a discharge to the Commission in respect of the implementation of the budget. To this end, the Council and the European Parliament in turn shall examine the accounts and the financial statement referred to in Article 275, the annual report by the Court of Auditors together with the replies of the institutions under audit to the observations of the Court of Auditors, the statement of assurance referred to in Article 248(1), second subparagraph and any relevant special reports by the Court of Auditors.

2. Before giving a discharge to the Commission, or for any other purpose in connection with the exercise of its powers over the implementation of the budget, the European Parliament may ask to hear the Commission give evidence with regard to the execution of expenditure or the operation of financial control systems. The Commission shall submit any necessary information to the European Parliament at the latter's request.

3. The Commission shall take all appropriate steps to act on the observations in the decisions giving discharge and on other observations by the European Parliament relating to the execution of expenditure, as well as on comments accompanying the recommendations on discharge adopted by the Council.

At the request of the European Parliament or the Council, the Commission shall report on the measures taken in the light of these observations and comments and in particular on the instructions given to the departments which are responsible for the implementation of the budget. These reports shall also be forwarded to the Court of Auditors.

Article 277 (ex Article 207)

The budget shall be drawn up in the unit of account determined in accordance with the provisions of the regulations made pursuant to Article 279.

---

119. The TEU moved the former Article 206b, with a slight addition, to Article 206(1), and added sections 2 and 3, which after the Treaty of Amsterdam is now covered by Article 276. The pre-TEU Articles 206 and 206a, dealing with the Court of Auditors, were moved, as modified, to the present Articles 246 to 248.

Article 278 (ex Article 208)

The Commission may, provided it notifies the competent authorities of the Member States concerned, transfer into the currency of one of the Member States its holdings in the currency of another Member State, to the extent necessary to enable them to be used for purposes which come within the scope of this Treaty. The Commission shall as far as possible avoid making such transfers if it possesses cash or liquid assets in the currencies which it needs.

The Commission shall deal with each Member State through the authority designated by the State concerned. In carrying out financial operations the Commission shall employ the services of the bank of issue of the Member State concerned or of any other financial institution approved by that State.

Article 279 (ex Article 209)[120]

The Council, acting unanimously on a proposal from the Commission and after consulting the European Parliament and obtaining the opinion of the Court of Auditors, shall:

(a) make Financial Regulations specifying in particular the procedure to be adopted for establishing and implementing the budget and for presenting and auditing accounts;

(b) determine the methods and procedure whereby the budget revenue provided under the arrangements relating to the Community's own resources shall be made available to the Commission, and determine the measures to be applied, if need be, to meet cash requirements;

(c) lay down rules concerning the responsibility of financial controllers, authorising officers and accounting officers, and concerning appropriate arrangements for inspection.

Article 280 (ex Article 209a)[121]

1. The Community and the Member States shall counter fraud and any other illegal activities affecting the financial interests of the Community through measures to be taken in accordance with this Article, which shall act as a deterrent and be such as to afford effective protection in the Member States.

2. Member States shall take the same measures to counter fraud affecting the financial interests of the Community as they take to counter fraud affecting their own financial interests.

3. Without prejudice to other provisions of this Treaty, the Member States shall coordinate their action aimed at protecting the financial interests of the Community against fraud. To this end they shall organise,

---

120. The TEU amended this article to add the words "financial controllers" to paragraph (c).

121. The TEU added this article, which originally only comprised paragraphs (2) and (3). The Treaty of Amsterdam added paragraphs (1), (4) and (5).

together with the Commission, close and regular cooperation between the competent authorities.

4. The Council, acting in accordance with the procedure referred to in Article 251, after consulting the Court of Auditors, shall adopt the necessary measures in the fields of the prevention of and fight against fraud affecting the financial interests of the Community with a view to affording effective and equivalent protection in the Member States. These measures shall not concern the application of national criminal law or the national administration of justice.

5. The Commission, in cooperation with Member States, shall each year submit to the European Parliament and to the Council a report on the measures taken for the implementation of this Article.

PART SIX

GENERAL AND FiNAL PROVISIONS

Article 281 (ex Article 210)

The Community shall have legal personality.

Article 282 (ex Article 211)

In each of the Member States, the Community shall enjoy the most extensive legal capacity accorded to legal persons under their laws; it may, in particular, acquire or dispose of movable and immovable property and may be a party to legal proceedings. To this end, the Community shall be represented by the Commission.

Article 283 (ex Article 212)

The Council shall, acting by a qualified majority on a proposal from the Commission and after consulting the other institutions concerned, lay down the Staff Regulations of officials of the European Communities and the Conditions of Employment of other servants of those Communities.

Article 284 (ex Article 213)

The Commission may, within the limits and under conditions laid down by the Council in accordance with the provisions of this Treaty, collect any information and carry out any checks required for the performance of the tasks entrusted to it.

Article 285 (ex Article 213a)

1. Without prejudice to Article 5 of the Protocol on the Statute of the European System of Central Banks and of the European Central Bank, the Council, acting in accordance with the procedure referred to in Article 251, shall adopt measures for the production of statistics where necessary for the performance of the activities of the Community.

2. The production of Community statistics shall conform to impartiality, reliability, objectivity, scientific independence, cost-effectiveness and

statistical confidentiality it shall not entail excessive burdens on economic operators.

Article 286 (ex Article 213b)

1. From 1 January 1999, Community acts on the protection of individuals with regard to the processing of personal data and the free movement of such data shall apply to the institutions and bodies set up by, or on the basis of, this Treaty.

2. Before the date referred to in paragraph 1, the Council, acting in accordance with the procedure referred to in Article 251, shall establish an independent supervisory body responsible for monitoring the application of such Community acts to Community institutions and bodies and shall adopt any other relevant provisions as appropriate.

Article 287 (ex Article 214)

The members of the institutions of the Community, the members of committees, and the officials and other servants of the Community shall be required, even after their duties have ceased, not to disclose information of the kind covered by the obligation of professional secrecy, in particular information about undertakings, their business relations or their cost components.

Article 288 (ex Article 215)

The contractual liability of the Community shall be governed by the law applicable to the contract in question.

In the case of non-contractual liability, the Community shall, in accordance with the general principles common to the laws of the Member States, make good any damage caused by its institutions or by its servants in the performance of their duties.

The preceding paragraph shall apply under the same conditions to damage caused by the ECB or by its servants in the performance of their duties.[122]

The personal liability of its servants towards the Community shall be governed by the provisions laid down in their Staff Regulations or in the Conditions of Employment applicable to them.

Article 289 (ex Article 216)

The seat of the institutions of the Community shall be determined by common accord of the Governments of the Member States.

Article 290 (ex Article 217)

The rules governing the languages of the institutions of the Community shall, without prejudice to the provisions contained in the Rules of Procedure of the Court of Justice, be determined by the Council, acting unanimously.

---

122. The TEU added the third paragraph.

Article 291 (ex Article 218)

The Community shall enjoy in the territories of the Member States such privileges and immunities as are necessary for the performance of its tasks, under the conditions laid down in the Protocol of 8 April 1965 on the privileges and immunities of the European Communities. The same shall apply to the European Central Bank, the European Monetary Institute, and the European Investment Bank.

Article 292 (ex Article 219)

Member States undertake not to submit a dispute concerning the interpretation or application of this Treaty to any method of settlement other than those provided for therein.

Article 293 (ex Article 220)

Member States shall, so far as is necessary, enter into negotiations with each other with a view to securing for the benefit of their nationals:

— the protection of persons and the enjoyment and protection of rights under the same conditions as those accorded by each State to its own nationals;

— the abolition of double taxation within the Community;

— the mutual recognition of companies or firms within the meaning of the second paragraph of Article 48, the retention of legal personality in the event of transfer of their seat from one country to another, and the possibility of mergers between companies or firms governed by the laws of different countries;

— the simplification of formalities governing the reciprocal recognition and enforcement of judgments of courts or tribunals and of arbitration awards.

Article 294 (ex Article 221)

Member States shall accord nationals of the other Member States the same treatment as their own nationals as regards participation in the capital of companies or firms within the meaning of Article 48, without prejudice to the application of the other provisions of this Treaty.

Article 295 (ex Article 222)

This Treaty shall in no way prejudice the rules in Member States governing the system of property ownership.

Article 296 (ex Article 223)

1. The provisions of this Treaty shall not preclude the application of the following rules:

    (a) no Member State shall be obliged to supply information the disclosure of which it considers contrary to the essential interests of its security;

(b) any Member State may take such measures as it considers necessary for the protection of the essential interests of its security which are connected with the production of or trade in arms, munitions and war material; such measures shall not adversely affect the conditions of competition in the common market regarding products which are not intended for specifically military purposes.

2. The Council may, acting unanimously on a proposal from the Commission, make changes to the list, which it drew up on 15 April 1958, of the products to which the provisions of paragraph 1(b) apply.

Article 297 (ex Article 224)

Member States shall consult each other with a view to taking together the steps needed to prevent the functioning of the common market being affected by measures which a Member State may be called upon to take in the event of serious internal disturbances affecting the maintenance of law and order, in the event of war, serious international tension constituting a threat of war, or in order to carry out obligations it has accepted for the purpose of maintaining peace and international security.

Article 298 (ex Article 225)

If measures taken in the circumstances referred to in Articles 296 and 297 have the effect of distorting the conditions of competition in the common market, the Commission shall, together with the State concerned, examine how these measures can be adjusted to the rules laid down in the Treaty.

By way of derogation from the procedure laid down in Articles 226 and 227, the Commission or any Member State may bring the matter directly before the Court of Justice if it considers that another Member State is making improper use of the powers provided for in Articles 296 and 297. The Court of Justice shall give its ruling in camera.

Article 299 (ex Article 227)[123]

1. This Treaty shall apply to the Kingdom of Belgium, the Kingdom of Denmark, the Federal Republic of Germany, the Hellenic Republic, the Kingdom of Spain, the French Republic, Ireland, the Italian Republic, the Grand Duchy of Luxembourg, the Kingdom of the Netherlands, the Republic of Austria, the Portuguese Republic, the Republic of Finland, the Kingdom of Sweden and the United Kingdom of Great Britain and Northern Ireland.

2. The provisions of this Treaty shall apply to the French overseas departments, the Azores, Madeira and the Canary Islands.

---

123. The Treaty of Amsterdam amended section 2 concerning the Treaty's force on the French overseas departments, the Azores, Madeira and the Canary Islands, and moved subsection 5(d), initially added in 1995, to its own section 5. The first paragraph of this article has been amended each time new States join the Community, most recently in 1995. (The TEU deleted a reference to Algeria as a French overseas department.)

However, taking account of the structural social and economic situation of the French overseas departments, the Azores, Madeira and the Canary Islands, which is compounded by their remoteness, insularity, small size, difficult topography and climate, economic dependence on a few products, the permanence and combination of which severely restrain their development, the Council, acting by a qualified majority on a proposal from the Commission and after consulting the European Parliament, shall adopt specific measures aimed, in particular, at laying down the conditions of application of the present Treaty to those regions, including common policies.

The Council shall, when adopting the relevant measures referred to in the second subparagraph, take into account areas such as customs and trade policies, fiscal policy, free zones, agriculture and fisheries policies, conditions for supply of raw materials and essential consumer goods, State aids and conditions of access to structural funds and to horizontal Community programmes.

The Council shall adopt the measures referred to in the second subparagraph taking into account the special characteristics and constraints of the outermost regions without undermining the integrity and the coherence of the Community legal order, including the internal market and common policies.

3. The special arrangements for association set out in Part Four of this Treaty shall apply to the overseas countries and territories listed in Annex II to this Treaty.

This Treaty shall not apply to those overseas countries and territories having special relations with the United Kingdom of Great Britain and Northern Ireland which are not included in the aforementioned list.

4. The provisions of this Treaty shall apply to the European territories for whose external relations a Member State is responsible.

5. The provisions of this Treaty shall apply to the Aland Islands in accordance with the provisions set out in Protocol No 2 to the Act concerning the conditions of accession of the Republic of Austria, the Republic of Finland and the Kingdom of Sweden.

6. Notwithstanding the preceding paragraphs:

(a) this Treaty shall not apply to the Faeroe Islands;

(b) this Treaty shall not apply to the Sovereign Base Areas of the United Kingdom of Great Britain and Northern Ireland in Cyprus;

(c) this Treaty shall apply to the Channel Islands and the Isle of Man only to the extent necessary to ensure the implementation of the arrangements for those islands set out in the Treaty concerning the accession of new Member States to the European Economic Community and to the European Atomic Energy Community signed on 22 January 1972.

Article 300 (ex Article 228)[124]

1. Where this Treaty provides for the conclusion of agreements between the Community and one or more States or international organisations, the Commission shall make recommendations to the Council, which shall authorise the Commission to open the necessary negotiations. The Commission shall conduct these negotiations in consultation with special committees appointed by the Council to assist it in this task and within the framework of such directives as the Council may issue to it.

In exercising the powers conferred upon it by this paragraph, the Council shall act by a qualified majority, except in the cases where the first subparagraph of paragraph 2 provides that the Council shall act unanimously.

2. Subject to the powers vested in the Commission in this field, the signing, which may be accompanied by a decision on provisional application before entry into force, and the conclusion of the agreements shall be decided on by the Council, acting by a qualified majority on a proposal from the Commission. The Council shall act unanimously when the agreement covers a field for which unanimity is required for the adoption of internal rules and for the agreements referred to in Article 310.

By way of derogation from the rules laid down in paragraph 3, the same procedures shall apply for a decision to suspend the application of an agreement, and for the purpose of establishing the positions to be adopted on behalf of the Community in a body set up by an agreement based on Article 310, when that body is called upon to adopt decisions having legal effects, with the exception of decisions supplementing or amending the institutional framework of the agreement.

The European Parliament shall be immediately and fully informed on any decision under this paragraph concerning the provisional application or the suspension of agreements, or the establishment of the Community position in a body set up by an agreement based on Article 310.

3. The Council shall conclude agreements after consulting the European Parliament, except for the agreements referred to in Article 133(3), including cases where the agreement covers a field for which the procedure referred to in Article 251 or that referred to in Article 252 is required for the adoption of internal rules. The European Parliament shall deliver its opinion within a time-limit which the Council may lay down according to the urgency of the matter. In the absence of an opinion within that time-limit, the Council may act.

By way of derogation from the previous subparagraph, agreements referred to in Article 310, other agreements establishing a specific institutional framework by organising cooperation procedures, agreements having important budgetary implications for the Community and agreements

---

124. The TEU substantially modified this article, introducing most of the text. Section 6 was formerly Article 228(1) second paragraph, and section 7 was formerly Article 228(2).

entailing amendment of an act adopted under the procedure referred to in Article 251 shall be concluded after the assent of the European Parliament has been obtained.

The Council and the European Parliament may, in an urgent situation, agree upon a time-limit for the assent.

4. When concluding an agreement, the Council may, by way of derogation from paragraph 2, authorise the Commission to approve modifications on behalf of the Community where the agreement provides for them to be adopted by a simplified procedure or by a body set up by the agreement; it may attach specific conditions to such authorisation.

5. When the Council envisages concluding an agreement which calls for amendments to this Treaty, the amendments must first be adopted in accordance with the procedure laid down in Article 48 of the Treaty on European Union.

6. The Council, the Commission or a Member State may obtain the opinion of the Court of Justice as to whether an agreement envisaged is compatible with the provisions of this Treaty. Where the opinion of the Court of Justice is adverse, the agreement may enter into force only in accordance with Article 48 of the Treaty on European Union.

7. Agreements concluded under the conditions set out in this Article shall be binding on the institutions of the Community and on Member States.

Article 301 (ex Article 228a)[125]

Where it is provided, in a common position or in a joint action adopted according to the provisions of the Treaty on European Union relating to the common foreign and security policy, for an action by the Community to interrupt or to reduce, in part or completely, economic relations with one or more third countries, the Council shall take the necessary urgent measures. The Council shall act by a qualified majority on a proposal from the Commission.

Article 302 (ex Article 229)

It shall be for the Commission to ensure the maintenance of all appropriate relations with the organs of the United Nations and of its specialised agencies.

The Commission shall also maintain such relations as are appropriate with all international organisations.

---

125. Added by the TEU.

Article 303 (ex Article 230)

The Community shall establish all appropriate forms of cooperation with the Council of Europe.

Article 304 (ex Article 231)[126]

The Community shall establish close cooperation with the Organisation for Economic Cooperation and Development, the details of which shall be determined by common accord.

Article 305 (ex Article 232)

1. The provisions of this Treaty shall not affect the provisions of the Treaty establishing the European Coal and Steel Community, in particular as regards the rights and obligations of Member States, the powers of the institutions of that Community and the rules laid down by that Treaty for the functioning of the common market in coal and steel.

2. The provisions of this Treaty shall not derogate from those of the Treaty establishing the European Atomic Energy Community.

Article 306 (ex Article 233)

The provisions of this Treaty shall not preclude the existence or completion of regional unions between Belgium and Luxembourg, or between Belgium, Luxembourg and the Netherlands, to the extent that the objectives of these regional unions are not attained by application of this Treaty.

Article 307 (ex Article 234)

The rights and obligations arising from agreements concluded before 1 January 1958 or, for acceding States, before the date of their accession, between one or more Member States on the one hand, and one or more third countries on the other, shall not be affected by the provisions of this Treaty.

To the extent that such agreements are not compatible with this Treaty, the Member State or States concerned shall take all appropriate steps to eliminate the incompatibilities established. Member States shall, where necessary, assist each other to this end and shall, where appropriate, adopt a common attitude.

In applying the agreements referred to in the first paragraph, Member States shall take into account the fact that the advantages accorded under this Treaty by each Member State form an integral part of the establishment of the Community and are thereby inseparably linked with the creation of common institutions, the conferring of powers upon them and the granting of the same advantages by all the other Member States.

Article 308 (ex Article 235)[127]

If action by the Community should prove necessary to attain, in the course of the operation of the common market, one of the objectives of the

---

126. The TEU substituted the current name of the OECD for its original name, the Organization for European Economic Cooperation.

127. The TEU deleted the former Article 236's account of the amendment procedure, now transferred to Article 48 of the TEU, as well as the former Article 237's account of

Community and this Treaty has not provided the necessary powers, the Council shall, acting unanimously on a proposal from the Commission and after consulting the European Parliament, take the appropriate measures.

Article 309 (ex Article 236)

1. Where a decision has been taken to suspend the voting rights of the representative of the government of a Member State in accordance with Article 7(2) of the Treaty on European Union, these voting rights shall also be suspended with regard to this Treaty.

2. Moreover, where the existence of a serious and persistent breach by a Member State of principles mentioned in Article 6(1) of the Treaty on European Union has been determined in accordance with Article 7(1) of that Treaty, the Council, acting by a qualified majority, may decide to suspend certain of the rights deriving from the application of this Treaty to the Member State in question. In doing so, the Council shall take into account the possible consequences of such a suspension on the rights and obligations of natural and legal persons.

The obligations of the Member State in question under this Treaty shall in any case continue to be binding on that State.

3. The Council, acting by a qualified majority, may decide subsequently to vary or revoke measures taken in accordance with paragraph 2 in response to changes in the situation which led to their being imposed.

4. When taking decisions referred to in paragraphs 2 and 3, the Council shall act without taking into account the votes of the representative of the government of the Member State in question. By way of derogation from Article 205(2) a qualified majority shall be defined as the same proportion of the weighted votes of the members of the Council concerned as laid down in Article 205(2).

This paragraph shall also apply in the event of voting rights being suspended in accordance with paragraph 1. In such cases, a decision requiring unanimity shall be taken without the vote of the representative of the government of the Member State in question.

Article 310 (ex Article 238)[128]

The Community may conclude with one or more States or international organisations agreements establishing an association involving reciprocal rights and obligations, common action and special procedure.

Article 311 (ex Article 239)

The protocols annexed to this Treaty by common accord of the Member States shall form an integral part thereof.

---

the process for admission of new States, now transferred to Article 49 of the TEU.

128. The TEU amended this article, deleting the second and third paragraphs, which are now covered in Article 300 (ex 228).

Article 312 (ex Article 240)

This Treaty is concluded for an unlimited period.

FINAL PROVISIONS

Article 313 (ex Article 247)

This Treaty shall be ratified by the High Contracting Parties in accordance with their respective constitutional requirements. The instruments of ratification shall be deposited with the Government of the Italian Republic.

This Treaty shall enter into force on the first day of the month following the deposit of the instrument of ratification by the last signatory State to take this step. If, however, such deposit is made less than 15 days before the beginning of the following month, this Treaty shall not enter into force until the first day of the second month after the date of such deposit.

Article 314 (ex Article 248)

This Treaty, drawn up in a single original in the Dutch, French, German, and Italian languages, all four texts being equally authentic, shall be deposited in the archives of the Government of the Italian Republic, which shall transmit a certified copy to each of the Governments of the other signatory States.

Pursuant to the Accession Treaties, the Danish, English, Finnish, Greek, Irish, Portuguese, Spanish and Swedish versions of this Treaty shall also be authentic.

[Annexes omitted. Annex I is the list of products referred to in Article 32 of the Treaty. Annex II is a list of the overseas countries and territories.]

PROTOCOLS ANNEXED TO THE EC TREATY BY THE TREATY OF MAASTRICHT

1. Protocol on the acquisition of property in Denmark
2. Protocol concerning Article 119 of the Treaty establishing the European Community
3. Protocol on the Statute of the European System of Central Banks and of the European Central Bank
4. Protocol on the Statute of the European Monetary Institute
5. Protocol on the excessive deficit procedure referred to in Article 109j [now 121] of the Treaty establishing the European Community **[reprinted below]**
6. Protocol on the convergence criteria referred to in Article 109j [now 121] of the Treaty establishing the European Community **[reprinted below]**

7. Protocol amending the Protocol on the privileges and immunities of the European Communities
8. Protocol on Denmark
9. Protocol on Portugal
10. Protocol on the transition to the third stage of economic and monetary union [**reprinted below**]
11. Protocol on certain provisions relating to the United Kingdom of Great Britain and Northern Ireland
12. Protocol on certain provisions relating to Denmark
13. Protocol on France
14. Protocol on social policy, to which is annexed an agreement concluded between the Member States of the European Community with the exception of the United Kingdom of Great Britain and Northern Ireland, to which two declarations are attached
15. Protocol on economic and social cohesion
16. Protocol on the Economic and Social Committee and the Committee of the Regions
17. Protocol annexed to the Treaty on European Union and to the Treaties establishing the European Communities [**reprinted below**]

PROTOCOLS ANNEXED TO THE EC TREATY AND/OR THE TEU BY THE TREATY OF AMSTERDAM

1. Protocol on Article 17 of the Treaty on European Union
2. Protocol integrating the Schengen *acquis* into the framework of the European Union [**reprinted below**]
3. Protocol on the application of certain aspects of Article 14 [ex 7a] of the Treaty establishing the European Community to the United Kingdom and Ireland [**reprinted below**]
4. Protocol on the position of the United Kingdom and Ireland [**reprinted below**]
5. Protocol on the position of Denmark [**reprinted below**]
6. Protocol on the institutions with the prospect of enlargement of the European Union
7. Protocol on the location of the seats of the institutions and of certain bodies and departments of the European Communities and of Europol
8. Protocol on the role of national parliaments in the European Union [**reprinted below**]
9. Protocol on the Statute of the European Investment Bank
10. Protocol on asylum for nationals of Member States of the European Union [**reprinted below**]
11. Protocol on the application of the principles of subsidiarity and proportionality [**reprinted below**]

12. Protocol on external relations of the Member States with regard to the crossing of external borders
13. Protocol on the system of public broadcasting in the Member States
14. Protocol on protection and welfare of animals

Protocol on the excessive deficit procedure referred to in Article 109j [now 121] of the Treaty establishing the European Community

Article 1

The reference values referred to in Article 104c(2) [now 104(2)] of this Treaty are:

— 3% for the ratio of the planned or actual government deficit to gross domestic product at market prices
— 60% for the ratio of government debt to gross domestic product at market prices.

Article 2

In Article 104c [now 104] of this Treaty and in this Protocol:

— government means general government, that is central government, regional or local government and social security funds, to the exclusion of commercial operations, as defined in the European System of Integrated Economic Accounts
— deficit means net borrowing as defined in the European System of Integrated Economic Accounts
— investment means gross fixed capital formation as defined in the European System of Integrated Economic Accounts
— debt means total gross debt at nominal value outstanding at the end of the year and consolidated between and within the sectors of general government as defined in the first indent.

Article 3

In order to ensure the effectiveness of the excessive deficit procedure, the governments of the Member States shall be responsible under this procedure for the deficits of general government as defined in the first indent of Article 2. The Member States shall ensure that national procedures in the budgetary area enable them to meet their obligations in this area deriving from this Treaty. The Member States shall report their planned and actual deficits and the levels of their debt promptly and regularly to the Commission.

Article 4

The statistical data to be used for the application of this Protocol shall be provided by the Commission.

Protocol on the convergence criteria referred to in Article 109j [now 121] of the Treaty establishing the European Community

Article 1

The criterion on price stability referred to in the first indent of Article 109j(1) [now 121 (1)] of this Treaty shall mean that a Member State has a price performance that is sustainable and an average rate of inflation, observed over a period of one year before the examination, that does not exceed by more than 1 percentage points that of, at most, the three best performing Member States in terms of price stability. Inflation shall be measured by means of the consumer price index on a comparable basis, taking into account differences in national definitions.

Article 2

The criterion on the government budgetary position referred to in the second indent of Article 109j(1) [now 121(1)] of this Treaty shall mean that at the time of the examination the Member State is not the subject of a Council decision under Article 104c(6) of this Treaty that an excessive deficit exists.

Article 3

The criterion on participation in the Exchange Rate Mechanism of the European Monetary System referred to in the third indent of Article 109j(1) [now 121] of this Treaty shall mean that a Member State has respected the normal fluctuation margins provided for by the Exchange Rate Mechanism of the European Monetary System without severe tensions for at least the last two years before the examination. In particular, the Member State shall not have devalued its currency's bilateral central rate against any other Member State's currency on its own initiative for the same period.

Article 4

The criterion on the convergence of interest rates referred to in the fourth indent of Article 109j(1) [121(1)] of this Treaty shall mean that, observed over a period of one year before the examination, a Member State has had an average nominal long-term interest rate that does not exceed by more than 2 percentage points that of, at most, the three best performing Member States in terms of price stability. Interest rates shall be measured on the basis of long term government bonds or comparable securities, taking into account differences in national definitions.

Article 5

The statistical data to be used for the application of this Protocol shall be provided by the Commission.

Article 6

The Council shall, acting unanimously on a proposal from the Commission and after consulting the European Parliament, the EMI or the ECB as the case may be, and the Committee referred to in Article 109c [now 114], adopt appropriate provisions to lay down the details of the convergence criteria referred to in Article 109j [121] of this Treaty, which shall then replace this Protocol.

Protocol on the transition to the third stage of economic and monetary union

THE HIGH CONTRACTING PARTIES,

Declare the irreversible character of the Community's movement to the third stage of Economic and Monetary Union by signing the new Treaty provisions on Economic and Monetary Union.

Therefore all Member States shall, whether they fulfil the necessary conditions for the adoption of a single currency or not, respect the will for the Community to enter swiftly into the third stage, and therefore no Member State shall prevent the entering into the third stage.

If by the end of 1997 the date of the beginning of the third stage has not been set, the Member States concerned, the Community institutions and other bodies involved shall expedite all preparatory work during 1998, in order to enable the Community to enter the third stage irrevocably on 1 January 1999 and to enable the ECB and the ESCB to start their full functioning from this date.

Protocol annexed to the Treaty on European Union and to the Treaties establishing the European Communities

Nothing in the Treaty on European Union, or in the Treaties establishing the European Communities, or in the Treaties or Acts modifying or supplementing those Treaties, shall affect the application in Ireland of Article 40.3.3. of the Constitution of Ireland.

Protocol integrating the Schengen *acquis* into the framework of the European Union

Article 1

The Kingdom of Belgium, the Kingdom of Denmark, the Federal Republic of Germany, the Hellenic Republic, the Kingdom of Spain, the French Republic, the Italian Republic, the Grand Duchy of Luxembourg, the Kingdom of the Netherlands, the Republic of Austria, the Portuguese Republic, the Republic of Finland and the Kingdom of Sweden, signatories to the Schengen agreements, are authorised to establish closer cooperation among themselves within the scope of those agreements and related provisions, as they are listed in the Annex to this Protocol, hereinafter referred to as the Schengen acquis. This cooperation shall be conducted within the institutional and legal framework of the European Union and with respect for the relevant provisions of the Treaty on European Union and of the Treaty establishing the European Community.

Article 2

1. From the date of entry into force of the Treaty of Amsterdam, the Schengen acquis, including the decisions of the Executive Committee established by the Schengen agreements which have been adopted before this date, shall immediately apply to the thirteen Member States referred to in Article 1, without prejudice to the provisions of paragraph 2 of this Article. From the same date, the Council will substitute itself for the said Executive Committee.

The Council, acting by the unanimity of its Members referred to in Article 1, shall take any measure necessary for the implementation of this paragraph. The Council, acting unanimously, shall determine, in conformity with the relevant provisions of the Treaties, the legal basis for each of the provisions or decisions which constitute the Schengen acquis.

With regard to such provisions and decisions and in accordance with that determination, the Court of Justice of the European Communities shall exercise the powers conferred upon it by the relevant applicable provisions of the Treaties. In any event, the Court of Justice shall have no jurisdiction on measures or decisions relating to the maintenance of law and order and the safeguarding of internal security.

As long as the measures referred to above have not been taken and without prejudice to Article 5(2), the provisions or decisions which constitute the Schengen acquis shall be regarded as acts based on Title VI of the Treaty on European Union.

2. The provisions of paragraph 1 shall apply to the Member States which have signed accession protocols to the Schengen agreements, from the dates decided by the Council, acting with the unanimity of its Members mentioned in Article 1, unless the conditions for the accession of any of those States to the Schengen acquis are met before the date of the entry into force of the Treaty of Amsterdam.

Article 3

Following the determination referred to in Article 2(1), second subparagraph, Denmark shall maintain the same rights and obligations in relation to the other signatories to the Schengen agreements, as before the said determination with regard to those parts of the Schengen acquis that are determined to have a legal basis in Title IIIa of the Treaty establishing the European Community.

With regard to those parts of the Schengen acquis that are determined to have legal base in Title VI of the Treaty on European Union, Denmark shall continue to have the same rights and obligations as the other signatories to the Schengen agreements.

Article 4

Ireland and the United Kingdom of Great Britain and Northern Ireland, which are not bound by the Schengen acquis, may at any time request to take part in some or all of the provisions of this acquis.

The Council shall decide on the request with the unanimity of its members referred to in Article 1 and of the representative of the Government of the State concerned.

Article 5

1. Proposals and initiatives to build upon the Schengen acquis shall be subject to the relevant provisions of the Treaties.

In this context, where either Ireland or the United Kingdom or both have not notified the President of the Council in writing within a reasonable period that they wish to take part, the authorisation referred to in Article 5a of the Treaty establishing the European Community or Article K.12 of the Treaty on European Union shall be deemed to have been granted to the Members States referred to in Article 1 and to Ireland or the United Kingdom where either of them wishes to take part in the areas of cooperation in question.

2. The relevant provisions of the Treaties referred to in the first subparagraph of paragraph 1 shall apply even if the Council has not adopted the measures referred to in Article 2(1), second subparagraph.

Article 6

The Republic of Iceland and the Kingdom of Norway shall be associated with the implementation of the Schengen acquis and its further development on the basis of the Agreement signed in Luxembourg on 19 December 1996. Appropriate procedures shall be agreed to that effect in an Agreement to be concluded with those States by the Council, acting by the unanimity of its Members mentioned in Article 1. Such Agreement shall include provisions on the contribution of Iceland and Norway to any financial consequences resulting from the implementation of this Protocol.

A separate Agreement shall be concluded with Iceland and Norway by the Council, acting unanimously, for the establishment of rights and obligations between Ireland and the United Kingdom of Great Britain and Northern Ireland on the one hand, and Iceland and Norway on the other, in domains of the Schengen acquis which apply to these States.

Article 7

The Council shall, acting by a qualified majority, adopt the detailed arrangements for the integration of the Schengen Secretariat into the General Secretariat of the Council.

Article 8

For the purposes of the negotiations for the admission of new Member States into the European Union, the Schengen acquis and further measures taken by the institutions within its scope shall be regarded as an acquis which must be accepted in full by all States candidates for admission.

Annex: Schengen acquis:

1. The Agreement, signed in Schengen on 14 June 1985, between the Governments of the States of the Benelux Economic Union, the Federal Republic of Germany and the French Republic on the gradual abolition of checks at their common borders.

2. The Convention, signed in Schengen on 19 June 1990, between the Kingdom of Belgium, the Federal Republic of Germany, the French Republic, the Grand Duchy of Luxembourg and the Kingdom of the Netherlands, implementing the Agreement on the gradual abolition of checks at their common borders, signed in Schengen on 14 June 1985, with related Final Act and common declarations.

3. The Accession Protocols and Agreements to the 1985 Agreement and the 1990 Implementation Convention with Italy (signed in Paris on 27 November 1990), Spain and Portugal (signed in Bonn on 25 June 1991), Greece (signed in Madrid on 6 November 1992), Austria (signed in Brussels

on 28 April 1995) and Denmark, Finland and Sweden (signed in Luxembourg on 19 December 1996), with related Final Acts and declarations.

4. Decisions and declarations adopted by the Executive Committee established by the 1990 Implementation Convention, as well as acts adopted for the implementation of the Convention by the organs upon which the Executive Committee has conferred decision making powers.

Protocol on the application of certain aspects of Article 14 [ex 7a] of the Treaty establishing the European Community to the United Kingdom and to Ireland

Article 1

The United Kingdom shall be entitled, notwithstanding Article 7a [now 14] of the Treaty establishing the European Community, any other provision of that Treaty or of the Treaty on European Union, any measure adopted under those Treaties, or any international agreement concluded by the Community or by the Community and its Member States with one or more third States, to exercise at its frontiers with other Member States such controls on persons seeking to enter the United Kingdom as it may consider necessary for the purpose:

(a) of verifying the right to enter the United Kingdom of citizens of States which are Contracting Parties to the Agreement on the European Economic Area and of their dependents exercising rights conferred by Community law, as well as citizens of other States on whom such rights have been conferred by an agreement by which the United Kingdom is bound and

(b) of determining whether or not to grant other persons permission to enter the United Kingdom.

Nothing in Article 7a [now 14] of the Treaty establishing the European Community or in any other provision of that Treaty or of the Treaty on European Union or in any measure adopted under them shall prejudice the right of the United Kingdom to adopt or exercise any such controls. References to the United Kingdom in this Article shall include territories for whose external relations the United Kingdom is responsible.

Article 2

The United Kingdom and Ireland may continue to make arrangements between themselves relating to the movement of persons between their territories (the Common Travel Area), while fully respecting the rights of persons referred to in Article 1, first paragraph, point (a) of this Protocol. Accordingly, as long as they maintain such arrangements, the provisions of Article 1 of this Protocol shall apply to Ireland under the same terms and conditions as for the United Kingdom. Nothing in Article 7a of the Treaty establishing the European Community, in any other provision of that Treaty or of the Treaty on European Union or in any measure adopted under them, shall affect any such arrangements.

Article 3

The other Member States shall be entitled to exercise at their frontiers or at any point of entry into their territory such controls on persons seeking to enter their territory from the United Kingdom or any territories whose external relations are under its responsibility for the same purposes stated in Article 1 of this Protocol, or from Ireland as long as the provisions of Article 1 of this Protocol apply to Ireland.

Nothing in Article 7a [now 14] of the Treaty establishing the European Community or in any other provision of that Treaty or of the Treaty on European Union or in any measure adopted under them shall prejudice the right of the other Member States to adopt or exercise any such controls.

Protocol on the position of the United Kingdom and Ireland

Article 1

Subject to Article 3, the United Kingdom and Ireland shall not take part in the adoption by the Council of proposed measures pursuant to Title IIIa [now IV] of the Treaty establishing the European Community. By way of derogation from Article 148(2) [now 205(2)] of the Treaty establishing the European Community, a qualified majority shall be defined as the same proportion of the weighted votes of the members of the Council concerned as laid down in the said Article 148(2) [now 205(2)]. The unanimity of the members of the Council, with the exception of the representatives of the governments of the United Kingdom and Ireland, shall be necessary for decisions of the Council which must be adopted unanimously.

Article 2

In consequence of Article 1 and subject to Articles 3, 4 and 6, none of the provisions of Title IIIa [now IV] of the Treaty establishing the European Community, no measure adopted pursuant to that Title, no provision of any international agreement concluded by the Community pursuant to that Title, and no decision of the Court of Justice interpreting any such provision or measure shall be binding upon or applicable in the United Kingdom or Ireland and no such provision, measure or decision shall in any way affect the competences, rights and obligations of those States and no such provision, measure or decision shall in any way affect the *acquis communautaire* nor form part of Community law as they apply to the United Kingdom or Ireland.

Article 3

1. The United Kingdom or Ireland may notify the President of the Council in writing, within three months after a proposal or initiative has been presented to the Council pursuant to Title IIIa [now IV] of the Treaty establishing the European Community, that it wishes to take part in the adoption and application of any such proposed measure, whereupon that State shall be entitled to do so. By way of derogation from Article 148(2) [now 205(2)] of the Treaty establishing the European Community, a qualified majority shall be defined as the same proportion of the weighted votes of the members of the Council concerned as laid down in the said Article 148(2) [now 205(2)].

The unanimity of the members of the Council, with the exception of a member which has not made such a notification, shall be necessary for decisions of the Council which must be adopted unanimously. A measure adopted under this paragraph shall be binding upon all Member States which took part in its adoption.

2. If after a reasonable period of time a measure referred to in paragraph 1 cannot be adopted with the United Kingdom or Ireland taking part, the Council may adopt such measure in accordance with Article 1 without the participation of the United Kingdom or Ireland. In that case Article 2 applies.

Article 4

The United Kingdom or Ireland may at any time after the adoption of a measure by the Council pursuant to Title IIIa [now IV] of the Treaty establishing the European Community notify its intention to the Council and to the Commission that it wishes to accept that measure. In that case, the procedure provided for in Article 5a(3) [now 11(3)] of the Treaty establishing the European Community shall apply mutatis mutandis.

Article 5

A Member State which is not bound by a measure adopted pursuant to Title IIIa [now IV] of the Treaty establishing the European Community shall bear no financial consequences of that measure other than administrative costs entailed for the institutions.

Article 6

Where, in cases referred to in this Protocol, the United Kingdom or Ireland is bound by a measure adopted by the Council pursuant to Title IIIa [now IV] of the Treaty establishing the European Community, the relevant provisions of that Treaty, including Article 73p [now 68], shall apply to that State in relation to that measure.

Article 7

Articles 3 and 4 shall be without prejudice to the Protocol integrating the Schengen *acquis* into the framework of the European Union.

Article 8

Ireland may notify the President of the Council in writing that it no longer wishes to be covered by the terms of this Protocol. In that case, the normal treaty provisions will apply to Ireland.

Protocol on the position of Denmark

Part I

Article 1

Denmark shall not take part in the adoption by the Council of proposed measures pursuant to Title IIIa [now IV] of the Treaty establishing the European Community. By way of derogation from Article 148(2) [now 205(2)] of the Treaty establishing the European Community, a qualified majority shall be defined as the same proportion of the weighted votes of the members of the Council concerned as laid down in the said

Article 148(2) [now 205(2)]. The unanimity of the members of the Council, with the exception of the representative of the government of Denmark, shall be necessary for the decisions of the Council which must be adopted unanimously.

Article 2

None of the provisions of Title IIIa [now IV] of the Treaty establishing the European Community, no measure adopted pursuant to that Title, no provision of any international agreement concluded by the Community pursuant to that Title, and no decision of the Court of Justice interpreting any such provision or measure shall be binding upon or applicable in Denmark and no such provision, measure or decision shall in any way affect the competences, rights and obligations of Denmark and no such provision, measure or decision shall in any way affect the *acquis communautaire* nor form part of Community law as they apply to Denmark.

Article 3

Denmark shall bear no financial consequences of measures referred to in Article 1, other than administrative costs entailed for the institutions.

Article 4

Articles 1, 2 and 3 shall not apply to measures determining the third countries whose nationals must be in possession of a visa when crossing the external borders of the Member States, or measures relating to a uniform format for visas.

Article 5

1. Denmark shall decide within a period of 6 months after the Council has decided on a proposal or initiative to build upon the Schengen *acquis* under the provisions of Title IIIa [now IV] of the Treaty establishing the European Community, whether it will implement this decision in its national law. If it decides to do so, this decision will create an obligation under international law between Denmark and the other Member States referred to in Article 1 of the Protocol integrating the Schengen *acquis* into the framework of the European Union as well as Ireland or the United Kingdom if those Member States take part in the areas of cooperation in question.

2. If Denmark decides not to implement a decision of the Council as referred to in paragraph 1, the Member States referred to in Article 1 of the Protocol integrating the Schengen *acquis* into the framework of the European Union will consider appropriate measures to be taken.

Part II

Article 6

With regard to measures adopted by the Council in the field of Articles J.3(1) [now 13(1)] and J.7 [now 17] of the Treaty on European Union, Denmark does not participate in the elaboration and the implementation of decisions and actions of the Union which have defence implications, but will not prevent the development of closer cooperation between Member States in this area. Therefore Denmark shall not participate in their adoption. Denmark shall not be obliged to contribute to the financing of operational expenditure arising from such measures.

Part III

Article 7

At any time Denmark may, in accordance with its constitutional requirements, inform the other Member States that it no longer wishes to avail itself of all or part of this Protocol. In that event, Denmark will apply in full all relevant measures then in force taken within the framework of the European Union.

Protocol on the role of national parliaments in the European Union

I. Information for National Parliaments of Member States

1. All Commission consultation documents (green and white papers and communications) shall be promptly forwarded to national parliaments of the Member States.

2. Commission proposals for legislation as defined by the Council in accordance with Article 151 (3) [now 207(3)] of the Treaty establishing the European Community, shall be made available in good time so that the government of each Member State may ensure that its own national parliament receives them as appropriate.

3. A six-week period shall elapse between a legislative proposal or a proposal for a measure to be adopted under Title VI of the Treaty on European Union being made available in all languages to the European Parliament and the Council by the Commission and the date when it is placed on a Council agenda for decision either for the adoption of an act or for adoption of a common position pursuant to Article 189b or 189c [now 251 or 252] of the Treaty establishing the European Community, subject to exceptions on grounds of urgency, the reasons for which shall be stated in the act or common position.

II. The Conference of European Affairs Committees

4. The Conference of European Affairs Committees, hereinafter referred to as COSAC, established in Paris on 16–17 November 1989, may make any contribution it deems appropriate for the attention of the institutions of the European Union, in particular on the basis of draft legal texts which representatives of governments of the Member States may decide by common accord to forward to it, in view of the nature of their subject matter.

5. COSAC may examine any legislative proposal or initiative in relation to the establishment of an area of freedom, security and justice which might have a direct bearing on the rights and freedoms of individuals. The European Parliament, the Council and the Commission shall be informed of any contribution made by COSAC under this point.

6. COSAC may address to the European Parliament, the Council and the Commission any contribution which it deems appropriate on the legislative activities of the Union, notably in relation to the application of

the principle of subsidiarity, the area of freedom, security and justice as well as questions regarding fundamental rights.

7. Contributions made by COSAC shall in no way bind national parliaments or prejudge their position.

Protocol on asylum for nationals of Member States of the European Union

Sole Article

Given the level of protection of fundamental rights and freedoms by the Member States of the European Union, Member States shall be regarded as constituting safe countries of origin in respect of each other for all legal and practical purposes in relation to asylum matters. Accordingly, any application for asylum made by a national of a Member State may be taken into consideration or declared admissible for processing by another Member State only in the following cases:

(a) if the Member State of which the applicant is a national proceeds after the entry into force of the Treaty of Amsterdam, availing itself of the provisions of Article 15 of the Convention for the Protection of Human Rights and Fundamental Freedoms, to take measures derogating in its territory from its obligations under that Convention

(b) if the procedure referred to in Article F.1(1) [now 7(1)] of the Treaty on European Union has been initiated and until the Council takes a decision in respect thereof

(c) if the Council, acting on the basis of Article F.1(1) [now 7(1)] of the Treaty on European Union, has determined, in respect of the Member State which the applicant is a national, the existence of a serious and persistent breach by that Member State of principles mentioned in Article F(1) [now 6(1)];

(d) if a Member State should so decide unilaterally in respect of the application of a national of another Member State in that case the Council shall be immediately informed the application shall be dealt with on the basis of the presumption that it is manifestly unfounded without affecting in any way, whatever the cases may be, the decision-making power of the Member State.

Protocol on the application of the principles of subsidiarity and proportionality

(1) In exercising the powers conferred on it, each institution shall ensure that the principle of subsidiarity is complied with. It shall also ensure compliance with the principle of proportionality, according to which any action by the Community shall not go beyond what is necessary to achieve the objectives of the Treaty.

(2) The application of the principles of subsidiarity and proportionality shall respect the general provisions and the objectives of the Treaty, particularly as regards the maintaining in full of the acquis communautaire and the institutional balance it shall not affect the principles developed by

the Court of Justice regarding the relationship between national and Community law, and it should take into account Article F(4) [now 7(4)] of the Treaty on European Union, according to which 'the Union shall provide itself with the means necessary to attain its objectives and carry through its policies.

(3) The principle of subsidiarity does not call into question the powers conferred on the European Community by the Treaty, as interpreted by the Court of Justice. The criteria referred to in the second paragraph of Article 3b of the Treaty shall relate to areas for which the Community does not have exclusive competence. The principle of subsidiarity provides a guide as to how those powers are to be exercised at the Community level. Subsidiarity is a dynamic concept and should be applied in the light of the objectives set out in the Treaty. It allows Community action within the limits of its powers to be expanded where circumstances so require, and conversely, to be restricted or discontinued where it is no longer justified.

(4) For any proposed Community legislation, the reasons on which it is based shall be stated with a view to justifying its compliance with the principles of subsidiarity and proportionality the reasons for concluding that a Community objective can be better achieved by the Community must be substantiated by qualitative or, wherever possible, quantitative indicators.

(5) For Community action to be justified, both aspects of the subsidiarity principle shall be met: the objectives of the proposed action cannot be sufficiently achieved by Member States' action in the framework of their national constitutional system and can therefore be better achieved by action on the part of the Community.

The following guidelines should be used in examining whether the abovementioned condition is fulfilled:

— the issue under consideration has transnational aspects which cannot be satisfactorily regulated by action by Member States
— actions by Member States alone or lack of Community action would conflict with the requirements of the Treaty (such as the need to correct distortion of competition or avoid disguised restrictions on trade or strengthen economic and social cohesion) or would otherwise significantly damage Member States' interests
— action at Community level would produce clear benefits by reason of its scale or effects compared with action at the level of the Member States.

(6) The form of Community action shall be as simple as possible, consistent with satisfactory achievement of the objective of the measure and the need for effective enforcement. The Community shall legislate only to the extent necessary. Other things being equal, directives should be preferred to regulations and framework directives to detailed measures. Directives as provided for in Article 189 [now 249] of the Treaty, while binding upon each Member State to which they are addressed as to the result to be achieved, shall leave to the national authorities the choice of form and methods.

(7) Regarding the nature and the extent of Community action, Community measures should leave as much scope for national decision as possible, consistent with securing the aim of the measure and observing the requirements of the Treaty. While respecting Community law, care should be taken to respect well established national arrangements and the organisation and working of Member States' legal systems. Where appropriate and subject to the need for proper enforcement, Community measures should provide Member States with alternative ways to achieve the objectives of the measures.

(8) Where the application of the principle of subsidiarity leads to no action being taken by the Community, Member States are required in their action to comply with the general rules laid down in Article 5 [now 10] of the Treaty, by taking all appropriate measures to ensure fulfilment of their obligations under the Treaty and by abstaining from any measure which could jeopardise the attainment of the objectives of the Treaty.

(9) Without prejudice to its right of initiative, the Commission should:

— except in cases of particular urgency or confidentiality, consult widely before proposing legislation and, wherever appropriate, publish consultation documents

— justify the relevance of its proposals with regard to the principle of subsidiarity whenever necessary, the explanatory memorandum accompanying a proposal will give details in this respect. The financing of Community action in whole or in part from the Community budget shall require an explanation

— take duly into account the need for any burden, whether financial or administrative, falling upon the Community, national governments, local authorities, economic operators and citizens, to be minimised and proportionate to the objective to be achieved

— submit an annual report to the European Council, the European Parliament and the Council on the application of Article 3b [now 5] of the Treaty. This annual report shall also be sent to the Committee of the Regions and to the Economic and Social Committee.

(10) The European Council shall take account of the Commission report referred to in the fourth indent of point 9 within the report on the progress achieved by the Union which it is required to submit to the European Parliament in accordance with Article D [now 4] of the Treaty on European Union.

(11) While fully observing the procedures applicable, the European Parliament and the Council shall, as an integral part of the overall examination of Commission proposals, consider their consistency with Article 3b [now 5] of the Treaty. This concerns the original Commission proposal as well as amendments which the European Parliament and the Council envisage making to the proposal.

(12) In the course of the procedures referred to in Articles 189b [now 251] and 189c [now 252] of the Treaty, the European Parliament shall be informed of the Council's position on the application of Article 3b [now 5]

of the Treaty, by way of a statement of the reasons which led the Council to adopt its common position. The Council shall inform the European Parliament of the reasons on the basis of which all or part of a Commission proposal is deemed to be inconsistent with Article 3b [now 5] of the Treaty.

(13) Compliance with the principle of subsidiarity shall be reviewed in accordance with the rules laid down by the Treaty.

2. TREATY ON EUROPEAN UNION ("THE TEU")

(As amended by the Treaty of Amsterdam)

consolidated version, O.J. C 340/173 (Nov. 10, 1997)

[*Eds. Note*: The TEU was signed at Maastricht, the Netherlands, on February 7, 1992. Commonly known as the Treaty of Maastricht, it entered into force on November 1, 1993. The TEU was subsequently amended by the Treaty of Amsterdam. On a highly selected basis, the changes made to the TEU by the Amsterdam Treaty are indicated by footnote.

Note that the Treaty of Nice of December 2000, still unratified, will further amend the TEU in important ways. To identify the prospective changes, see the Treaty of Nice, Document 4 in this Part. All changes to be made to the TEU are indicated there.

To aid in appreciating the structure of the TEU, this document begins with the Treaty's Table of Contents. Note that Titles II, III and IV of the TEU, which contain amendments to the EC Treaty, the Coal and Steel Community Treaty and the Euratom Treaty, respectively, are omitted from the text.

For a list of Protocols annexed to both the EC Treaty and the TEU, see Document 1 in this volume. A selected number of Protocols are reproduced.]

Table of Contents

Preamble
TITLE I (arts. 1–7)—Common Provisions
TITLE II (art. 8)—Provisions amending the Treaty establishing the European Economic Community with a view to establishing the European Community
TITLE III (art. 9)—Provisions amending the Treaty establishing the European Coal and Steel Community
TITLE IV (art. 10)—Provisions amending the Treaty establishing the European Atomic Energy Community
TITLE V (arts. 11–28)—Provision son a Common Foreign and Security Policy
TITLE VI (arts. 29–42)—Provisions on Police and Judicial Cooperation in Criminal Matters
TITLE VII (arts. 43–45)—Provisions on Closer Cooperation
TITLE VIII—Final Provisions (arts. 46–53)

HIS MAJESTY THE KING OF THE BELGIANS, HER MAJESTY THE QUEEN OF DENMARK, THE PRESIDENT OF THE FEDERAL REPUBLIC OF GERMANY, THE PRESIDENT OF THE HELLENIC REPUBLIC, HIS MAJESTY THE KING OF SPAIN, THE PRESIDENT OF THE FRENCH REPUBLIC, THE PRESIDENT OF IRELAND, THE PRESIDENT OF THE ITALIAN REPUBLIC, HIS ROYAL HIGHNESS THE GRAND DUKE OF LUXEMBOURG, HER MAJESTY THE QUEEN OF THE NETHERLANDS, THE PRESIDENT OF THE PORTUGUESE REPUBLIC, HER MAJESTY THE QUEEN OF THE UNITED KINGDOM

OF GREAT BRITAIN AND NORTHERN IRELAND,[1]

RESOLVED to mark a new stage in the process of European integration undertaken with the establishment of the European Communities,

RECALLING the historic importance of the ending of the division of the European continent and the need to create firm bases for the construction of the future Europe,

CONFIRMING their attachment to the principles of liberty, democracy and respect for human rights and fundamental freedoms and of the rule of law,

CONFIRMING their attachment to fundamental social rights as defined in the European Social Charter signed at Turin on 18 October 1961 and in the 1989 Community Charter of the Fundamental Social Rights of Workers,[2]

DESIRING to deepen the solidarity between their peoples while respecting their history, their culture and their traditions,

DESIRING to enhance further the democratic and efficient functioning of the institutions so as to enable them better to carry out, within a single institutional framework, the tasks entrusted to them,

RESOLVED to achieve the strengthening and the convergence of their economies and to establish an economic and monetary union including, in accordance with the provisions of this Treaty, a single and stable currency,

DETERMINED to promote economic and social progress for their peoples, taking into account the principle of sustainable development and within the context of the accomplishment of the internal market and of reinforced cohesion and environmental protection, and to implement policies ensuring that advances in economic integration are accompanied by parallel progress in other fields,

RESOLVED to establish a citizenship common to nationals of their countries,

RESOLVED to implement a common foreign and security policy including the progressive framing of a common defence policy, which might lead to a common defence in accordance with the provisions of Article 17, thereby reinforcing the European identity and its independence in order to promote peace, security and progress in Europe and in the world,

RESOLVED to facilitate the free movement of persons, while ensuring the safety and security of their peoples, by establishing an area of freedom, security and justice, in accordance with the provisions of this Treaty,

RESOLVED to continue the process of creating an ever closer union among the peoples of Europe, in which decisions are taken as closely as possible to the citizen in accordance with the principle of subsidiarity,

---

1. Denmark, Greece, Spain, Ireland, Austria, Portugal, Finland, Sweden and the United Kingdom have since become members of the European Union.

2. Added by the Treaty of Amsterdam.

IN VIEW of further steps to be taken in order to advance European integration,

HAVE DECIDED to establish a European Union ...

TITLE I
COMMON PROVISIONS
Article 1 (ex Article A)

By this Treaty, the HIGH CONTRACTING PARTIES establish among themselves a EUROPEAN UNION, hereinafter called "the Union".

This Treaty marks a new stage in the process of creating an ever closer union among the peoples of Europe, in which decisions are taken as openly as possible and as closely as possible to the citizen.[3]

The Union shall be founded on the European Communities, supplemented by the policies and forms of cooperation established by this Treaty. Its task shall be to organise, in a manner demonstrating consistency and solidarity, relations between the Member States and between their peoples.

Article 2 (ex Article B)

The Union shall set itself the following objectives:

— to promote economic and social progress and a high level of employment and to achieve balanced and sustainable development, in particular through the creation of an area without internal frontiers, through the strengthening of economic and social cohesion and through the establishment of economic and monetary union, ultimately including a single currency in accordance with the provisions of this Treaty[4]

— to assert its identity on the international scene, in particular through the implementation of a common foreign and security policy including the progressive framing of a common defence policy, which might lead to a common defence, in accordance with the provisions of Article 17

— to strengthen the protection of the rights and interests of the nationals of its Member States through the introduction of a citizenship of the Union

— to maintain and develop the Union as an area of freedom, security and justice, in which the free movement of persons is assured in conjunction with appropriate measures with respect to external border controls, asylum, immigration and the prevention and combating of crime[5]

— to maintain in full the *acquis communautaire* and build on it with a view to considering to what extent the policies and forms of cooperation introduced by this Treaty may need to be revised with the aim of ensuring the effectiveness of the mechanisms and the institutions of the Community.

---

3. The Treaty of Amsterdam added the language "as openly as possible."

4. The Treaty of Amsterdam added the language "and a high level of employment."

5. The Treaty of Amsterdam added this indent.

The objectives of the Union shall be achieved as provided in this Treaty and in accordance with the conditions and the timetable set out therein while respecting the principle of subsidiarity as defined in Article 5 of the Treaty establishing the European Community.

Article 3 (ex Article C)

The Union shall be served by a single institutional framework which shall ensure the consistency and the continuity of the activities carried out in order to attain its objectives while respecting and building upon the acquis communautaire.

The Union shall in particular ensure the consistency of its external activities as a whole in the context of its external relations, security, economic and development policies. The Council and the Commission shall be responsible for ensuring such consistency and shall cooperate to this end. They shall ensure the implementation of these policies, each in accordance with its respective powers.

Article 4 (ex Article D)

The European Council shall provide the Union with the necessary impetus for its development and shall define the general political guidelines thereof.

The European Council shall bring together the Heads of State or Government of the Member States and the President of the Commission. They shall be assisted by the Ministers for Foreign Affairs of the Member States and by a Member of the Commission. The European Council shall meet at least twice a year, under the chairmanship of the Head of State or Government of the Member State which holds the Presidency of the Council.

The European Council shall submit to the European Parliament a report after each of its meetings and a yearly written report on the progress achieved by the Union.

Article 5 (ex Article E)

The European Parliament, the Council, the Commission, the Court of Justice and the Court of Auditors[6] shall exercise their powers under the conditions and for the purposes provided for, on the one hand, by the provisions of the Treaties establishing the European Communities and of the subsequent Treaties and Acts modifying and supplementing them and, on the other hand, by the other provisions of this Treaty.

Article 6 (ex Article F)[7]

1. The Union is founded on the principles of liberty, democracy, respect for human rights and fundamental freedoms, and the rule of law, principles which are common to the Member States.

---

6. The Treaty of Amsterdam added the Court of Auditors as an institution.

7. The Treaty of Amsterdam added paragraphs 1 and 3.

2. The Union shall respect fundamental rights, as guaranteed by the European Convention for the Protection of Human Rights and Fundamental Freedoms signed in Rome on 4 November 1950 and as they result from the constitutional traditions common to the Member States, as general principles of Community law.

3. The Union shall respect the national identities of its Member States.

4. The Union shall provide itself with the means necessary to attain its objectives and carry through its policies.

Article 7 (ex Article F.1)[8]

1. The Council, meeting in the composition of the Heads of State or Government and acting by unanimity on a proposal by one third of the Member States or by the Commission and after obtaining the assent of the European Parliament, may determine the existence of a serious and persistent breach by a Member State of principles mentioned in Article 6(1), after inviting the government of the Member State in question to submit its observations.

2. Where such a determination has been made, the Council, acting by a qualified majority, may decide to suspend certain of the rights deriving from the application of this Treaty to the Member State in question, including the voting rights of the representative of the government of that Member State in the Council. In doing so, the Council shall take into account the possible consequences of such a suspension on the rights and obligations of natural and legal persons.

The obligations of the Member State in question under this Treaty shall in any case continue to be binding on that State.

3. The Council, acting by a qualified majority, may decide subsequently to vary or revoke measures taken under paragraph 2 in response to changes in the situation which led to their being imposed.

4. For the purposes of this Article, the Council shall act without taking into account the vote of the representative of the government of the Member State in question. Abstentions by members present in person or represented shall not prevent the adoption of decisions referred to in paragraph 1. A qualified majority shall be defined as the same proportion of the weighted votes of the members of the Council concerned as laid down in Article 205(2) of the Treaty establishing the European Community.

This paragraph shall also apply in the event of voting rights being suspended pursuant to paragraph 2.

5. For the purposes of this Article, the European Parliament shall act by a two-thirds majority of the votes cast, representing a majority of its members.

8. Added by the Treaty of Amsterdam.

[TITLES II, III and IV omitted]

TITLE V

PROVISIONS ON A COMMON FOREIGN AND SECURITY POLICY

Article 11 (ex Article J.1)

1. The Union shall define and implement a common foreign and security policy covering all areas of foreign and security policy, the objectives of which shall be:

— to safeguard the common values, fundamental interests, independence and integrity of the Union in conformity with the principles of the United Nations Charter[9]

— to strengthen the security of the Union in all ways

— to preserve peace and strengthen international security, in accordance with the principles of the United Nations Charter, as well as the principles of the Helsinki Final Act and the objectives of the Paris Charter, including those on external borders [10]

— to promote international cooperation

— to develop and consolidate democracy and the rule of law, and respect for human rights and fundamental freedoms.

2. The Member States shall support the Union's external and security policy actively and unreservedly in a spirit of loyalty and mutual solidarity.

The Member States shall work together to enhance and develop their mutual political solidarity. They shall refrain from any action which is contrary to the interests of the Union or likely to impair its effectiveness as a cohesive force in international relations.

The Council shall ensure that these principles are complied with.

Article 12 (ex Article J.2)

The Union shall pursue the objectives set out in Article 11 by:

— defining the principles of and general guidelines for the common foreign and security policy

— deciding on common strategies

— adopting joint actions

— adopting common positions

— strengthening systematic cooperation between Member States in the conduct of policy.

Article 13 (ex Article J.3)

1. The European Council shall define the principles of and general guidelines for the common foreign and security policy, including for mat-

---

[9]. The requirement to conform with the United Nations Charter was added by the Amsterdam Treaty.

[10]. The Amsterdam Treaty added the reference to external borders.

ters with defence implications.[11]

2. The European Council shall decide on common strategies to be implemented by the Union in areas where the Member States have important interests in common.

Common strategies shall set out their objectives, duration and the means to be made available by the Union and the Member States.[12]

3. The Council shall take the decisions necessary for defining and implementing the common foreign and security policy on the basis of the general guidelines defined by the European Council.[13]

The Council shall recommend common strategies to the European Council and shall implement them, in particular by adopting joint actions and common positions.

The Council shall ensure the unity, consistency and effectiveness of action by the Union.[14]

Article 14 (ex Article J.4)[15]

1. The Council shall adopt joint actions. Joint actions shall address specific situations where operational action by the Union is deemed to be required. They shall lay down their objectives, scope, the means to be made available to the Union, if necessary their duration, and the conditions for their implementation.[16]

2. If there is a change in circumstances having a substantial effect on a question subject to joint action, the Council shall review the principles and objectives of that action and take the necessary decisions. As long as the Council has not acted, the joint action shall stand.

3. Joint actions shall commit the Member States in the positions they adopt and in the conduct of their activity.

4. The Council may request the Commission to submit to it any appropriate proposals relating to the common foreign and security policy to ensure the implementation of a joint action.[17]

5. Whenever there is any plan to adopt a national position or take national action pursuant to a joint action, information shall be provided in time to allow, if necessary, for prior consultations within the Council. The obligation to provide prior information shall not apply to measures which are merely a national transposition of Council decisions.

---

11. The substance of this paragraph was found in ex Article J.8(1). The Amsterdam Treaty added the "defence implications" clause.

12. Paragraph 2 was added by the Amsterdam Treaty.

13. The substance of the first sentence of this paragraph 3 was found in ex Article J.8(2).

14. The last two sentences of this article were added by the Amsterdam Treaty.

15. The substance of this article was found in ex Article J.3.

16. The Treaty of Amsterdam deleted a provision for qualified majority voting when the Council adopts joint actions under this paragraph.

17. Paragraph 4 was added by the Amsterdam Treaty.

6. In cases of imperative need arising from changes in the situation and failing a Council decision, Member States may take the necessary measures as a matter of urgency having regard to the general objectives of the joint action. The Member State concerned shall inform the Council immediately of any such measures.

7. Should there be any major difficulties in implementing a joint action, a Member State shall refer them to the Council which shall discuss them and seek appropriate solutions. Such solutions shall not run counter to the objectives of the joint action or impair its effectiveness.

Article 15 (ex Article J.5)

The Council shall adopt common positions. Common positions shall define the approach of the Union to a particular matter of a geographical or thematic nature. Member States shall ensure that their national policies conform to the common positions.[18]

Article 16 (ex Article J.6)

Member States shall inform and consult one another within the Council on any matter of foreign and security policy of general interest in order to ensure that the Union's influence is exerted as effectively as possible by means of concerted and convergent action.[19]

Article 17 (ex Article J.7)

1. The common foreign and security policy shall include all questions relating to the security of the Union, including the progressive framing of a common defence policy, in accordance with the second subparagraph, which might lead to a common defence, should the European Council so decide. It shall in that case recommend to the Member States the adoption of such a decision in accordance with their respective constitutional requirements.[20]

The Western European Union (WEU) is an integral part of the development of the Union providing the Union with access to an operational capability notably in the context of paragraph 2. It supports the Union in framing the defence aspects of the common foreign and security policy as set out in this Article. The Union shall accordingly foster closer institutional relations with the WEU with a view to the possibility of the integration of the WEU into the Union, should the European Council so decide. It shall in that case recommend to the Member States the adoption of such a decision in accordance with their respective constitutional requirements.

The policy of the Union in accordance with this Article shall not prejudice the specific character of the security and defence policy of certain Member States and shall respect the obligations of certain Member States, which see their common defence realised in the North Atlantic Treaty

---

[18]. The Treaty of Amsterdam added the definition of common positions.

[19]. The previous version of this article, found at former Article J.2(3), only required Member States to "coordinate" their action in international organizations and at international conferences.

[20]. Participation by the European Council was added by the Amsterdam Treaty.

Organisation (NATO), under the North Atlantic Treaty and be compatible with the common security and defence policy established within that framework.

The progressive framing of a common defence policy will be supported, as Member States consider appropriate, by cooperation between them in the field of armaments.[21]

2. Questions referred to in this Article shall include humanitarian and rescue tasks, peacekeeping tasks and tasks of combat forces in crisis management, including peacemaking.[22]

3. The Union will avail itself of the WEU to elaborate and implement decisions and actions of the Union which have defence implications.[23]

The competence of the European Council to establish guidelines in accordance with Article 13 shall also obtain in respect of the WEU for those matters for which the Union avails itself of the WEU.[24]

When the Union avails itself of the WEU to elaborate and implement decisions of the Union on the tasks referred to in paragraph 2 all Member States of the Union shall be entitled to participate fully in the tasks in question. The Council, in agreement with the institutions of the WEU, shall adopt the necessary practical arrangements to allow all Member States contributing to the tasks in question to participate fully and on an equal footing in planning and decision-taking in the WEU.[25]

Decisions having defence implications dealt with under this paragraph shall be taken without prejudice to the policies and obligations referred to in paragraph 1, third subparagraph.

4. The provisions of this Article shall not prevent the development of closer cooperation between two or more Member States on a bilateral level, in the framework of the WEU and the Atlantic Alliance, provided such cooperation does not run counter to or impede that provided for in this Title.

5. With a view to furthering the objectives of this Article, the provisions of this Article will be reviewed in accordance with Article 48.[26]

Article 18 (ex Article J.8)[27]

1. The Presidency shall represent the Union in matters coming within the common foreign and security policy.

2. The Presidency shall be responsible for the implementation of decisions taken under this Title in that capacity it shall in principle express

---

21. This sentence was added by the Amsterdam Treaty. The Amsterdam Treaty also deleted Article J.4(3), which removed issues having defense implications under this article from the procedural requirements of the current Article 14 (ex J.3).

22. Paragraph 2 was added by the Treaty of Amsterdam.

23. This sentence derives from former Article J.4(2).

24. This paragraph was added by the Amsterdam Treaty.

25. This paragraph was added by the Amsterdam Treaty.

26. The substance of this paragraph is found in former Article J.4(6).

27. The substance of paragraphs 1, 2 and 4 is found in former Article J.5.

the position of the Union in international organisations and international conferences.[28]

3. The Presidency shall be assisted by the Secretary–General of the Council who shall exercise the function of High Representative for the common foreign and security policy.[29]

4. The Commission shall be fully associated in the tasks referred to in paragraphs 1 and 2. The Presidency shall be assisted in those tasks if need be by the next Member State to hold the Presidency.[30]

5. The Council may, whenever it deems it necessary, appoint a special representative with a mandate in relation to particular policy issues.[31]

Article 19 (ex Article J.9)

1. Member States shall coordinate their action in international organisations and at international conferences. They shall uphold the common positions in such fora.

In international organisations and at international conferences where not all the Member States participate, those which do take part shall uphold the common positions.[32]

2. Without prejudice to paragraph 1 and Article 14(3), Member States represented in international organisations or international conferences where not all the Member States participate shall keep the latter informed of any matter of common interest.

Member States which are also members of the United Nations Security Council will concert and keep the other Member States fully informed. Member States which are permanent members of the Security Council will, in the execution of their functions, ensure the defence of the positions and the interests of the Union, without prejudice to their responsibilities under the provisions of the United Nations Charter.[33]

Article 20 (ex Article J.10)[34]

The diplomatic and consular missions of the Member States and the Commission Delegations in third countries and international conferences, and their representations to international organisations, shall cooperate in ensuring that the common positions and joint actions adopted by the Council are complied with and implemented.

They shall step up cooperation by exchanging information, carrying out joint assessments and contributing to the implementation of the provisions

---

28. The Treaty of Amsterdam changed the Presidency's responsibility for "implementation of common measures" to responsibility for "decisions."

29. This paragraph was added by the Amsterdam Treaty.

30. Previously, the TEU provided for the Presidency to be assisted by both the next and the previous Member States to hold the Presidency.

31. This paragraph was added by the Amsterdam Treaty.

32. The substance of this article is found in former Article J.2(3).

33. The substance of this article is found in former Article J.5(4).

34. The substance of this article is found in former Article J.6.

referred to in Article 20 of the Treaty establishing the European Community.

Article 21 (ex Article J.11)[35]

The Presidency shall consult the European Parliament on the main aspects and the basic choices of the common foreign and security policy and shall ensure that the views of the European Parliament are duly taken into consideration. The European Parliament shall be kept regularly informed by the Presidency and the Commission of the development of the Union's foreign and security policy.

The European Parliament may ask questions of the Council or make recommendations to it. It shall hold an annual debate on progress in implementing the common foreign and security policy.

Article 22 (ex Article J.12)[36]

1. Any Member State or the Commission may refer to the Council any question relating to the common foreign and security policy and may submit proposals to the Council.

2. In cases requiring a rapid decision, the Presidency, of its own motion, or at the request of the Commission or a Member State, shall convene an extraordinary Council meeting within forty-eight hours or, in an emergency, within a shorter period.

Article 23 (ex Article J.13)[37]

1. Decisions under this Title shall be taken by the Council acting unanimously. Abstentions by members present in person or represented shall not prevent the adoption of such decisions.

When abstaining in a vote, any member of the Council may qualify its abstention by making a formal declaration under the present subparagraph. In that case, it shall not be obliged to apply the decision, but shall accept that the decision commits the Union. In a spirit of mutual solidarity, the Member State concerned shall refrain from any action likely to conflict with or impede Union action based on that decision and the other Member States shall respect its position. If the members of the Council qualifying their abstention in this way represent more than one third of the votes weighted in accordance with Article 205(2) of the Treaty establishing the European Community, the decision shall not be adopted.

2. By derogation from the provisions of paragraph 1, the Council shall act by qualified majority:

— when adopting joint actions, common positions or taking any other decision on the basis of a common strategy

---

35. The substance of this article is found in former Article J.7.

36. The substance of this article is found in former Articles J.8(3) and (4).

37. This article was largely amended by the Amsterdam Treaty, except for the requirement of Council unanimity for decisions under this Title.

— when adopting any decision implementing a joint action or a common position.

If a member of the Council declares that, for important and stated reasons of national policy, it intends to oppose the adoption of a decision to be taken by qualified majority, a vote shall not be taken. The Council may, acting by a qualified majority, request that the matter be referred to the European Council for decision by unanimity.

The votes of the members of the Council shall be weighted in accordance with Article 205(2) of the Treaty establishing the European Community. For their adoption, decisions shall require at least 62 votes in favour, cast by at least 10 members.

This paragraph shall not apply to decisions having military or defence implications.

3. For procedural questions, the Council shall act by a majority of its members.

Article 24 (ex Article J.14)

When it is necessary to conclude an agreement with one or more States or international organisations in implementation of this Title, the Council, acting unanimously, may authorise the Presidency, assisted by the Commission as appropriate, to open negotiations to that effect. Such agreements shall be concluded by the Council acting unanimously on a recommendation from the Presidency. No agreement shall be binding on a Member State whose representative in the Council states that it has to comply with the requirements of its own constitutional procedure the other members of the Council may agree that the agreement shall apply provisionally to them.

The provisions of this Article shall also apply to matters falling under Title VI.

Article 25 (ex Article J.15)[38]

Without prejudice to Article 207 of the Treaty establishing the European Community, a Political Committee shall monitor the international situation in the areas covered by the common foreign and security policy and contribute to the definition of policies by delivering opinions to the Council at the request of the Council or on its own initiative. It shall also monitor the implementation of agreed policies, without prejudice to the responsibility of the Presidency and the Commission.

Article 26 (ex Article J.16)[39]

The Secretary–General of the Council, High Representative for the common foreign and security policy, shall assist the Council in matters coming within the scope of the common foreign and security policy, in particular through contributing to the formulation, preparation and imple-

---

38. The substance of this article is found in former Article J.8(5).

39. Added by the Treaty of Amsterdam.

mentation of policy decisions, and, when appropriate and acting on behalf of the Council at the request of the Presidency, through conducting political dialogue with third parties.

Article 27 (ex Article J.17)[40]

The Commission shall be fully associated with the work carried out in the common foreign and security policy field.

Article 28 (ex Article J.18)

1. Articles 189, 190, 196 to 199, 203, 204, 206 to 209, 213 to 219, 255 and 290 of the Treaty establishing the European Community shall apply to the provisions relating to the areas referred to in this Title.

2. Administrative expenditure which the provisions relating to the areas referred to in this Title entail for the institutions shall be charged to the budget of the European Communities.

3. Operational expenditure to which the implementation of those provisions gives rise shall also be charged to the budget of the European Communities, except for such expenditure arising from operations having military or defence implications and cases where the Council acting unanimously decides otherwise.[41]

In cases where expenditure is not charged to the budget of the European Communities it shall be charged to the Member States in accordance with the gross national product scale, unless the Council acting unanimously decides otherwise. As for expenditure arising from operations having military or defence implications, Member States whose representatives in the Council have made a formal declaration under Article 23(1), second subparagraph, shall not be obliged to contribute to the financing thereof.[42]

4. The budgetary procedure laid down in the Treaty establishing the European Community shall apply to the expenditure charged to the budget of the European Communities.[43]

TITLE VI

PROVISIONS ON POLICE AND JUDICIAL COOPERATION IN CRIMINAL MATTERS

Article 29 (ex Article K.1)[44]

Without prejudice to the powers of the European Community, the Union's objective shall be to provide citizens with a high level of safety within an area of freedom, security and justice by developing common

---

40. The substance of this article is found in former Article J.9.

41. The previous version of this section required a unanimous decision by the Council for operational expenditures to be charged to the EC.

42. This section's inclusion of military and defence expenditures was added by the Amsterdam Treaty.

43. The substance of this article is found in former Article J.11.

44. The substance of this article is found in former Article K.1(4)–(9).

action among the Member States in the fields of police and judicial cooperation in criminal matters and by preventing and combating racism and xenophobia.

That objective shall be achieved by preventing and combating crime, organised or otherwise, in particular terrorism, trafficking in persons and offences against children, illicit drug trafficking and illicit arms trafficking, corruption and fraud, through:

— closer cooperation between police forces, customs authorities and other competent authorities in the Member States, both directly and through the European Police Office (Europol), in accordance with the provisions of Articles 30 and 32

— closer cooperation between judicial and other competent authorities of the Member States in accordance with the provisions of Articles 31(a) to (d) and 32

— approximation, where necessary, of rules on criminal matters in the Member States, in accordance with the provisions of Article 31(e).[45]

Article 30 (ex Article K.2)[46]

1. Common action in the field of police cooperation shall include:

(a) operational cooperation between the competent authorities, including the police, customs and other specialised law enforcement services of the Member States in relation to the prevention, detection and investigation of criminal offences

(b) the collection, storage, processing, analysis and exchange of relevant information, including information held by law enforcement services on reports on suspicious financial transactions, in particular through Europol, subject to appropriate provisions on the protection of personal data

(c) cooperation and joint initiatives in training, the exchange of liaison officers, secondments, the use of equipment, and forensic research

(d) the common evaluation of particular investigative techniques in relation to the detection of serious forms of organised crime.

2. The Council shall promote cooperation through Europol and shall in particular, within a period of five years after the date of entry into force of the Treaty of Amsterdam:

(a) enable Europol to facilitate and support the preparation, and to encourage the coordination and carrying out, of specific investigative actions by the competent authorities of the Member States, including operational actions of joint teams comprising representatives of Europol in a support capacity

(b) adopt measures allowing Europol to ask the competent authorities of the Member States to conduct and coordinate their investiga-

---

45. The last indent was added by the Amsterdam Treaty.

46. Added by the Treaty of Amsterdam.

tions in specific cases and to develop specific expertise which may be put at the disposal of Member States to assist them in investigating cases of organised crime

(c) promote liaison arrangements between prosecuting/investigating officials specialising in the fight against organised crime in close cooperation with Europol

(d) establish a research, documentation and statistical network on cross-border crime.

Article 31 (ex Article K.3)[47]

Common action on judicial cooperation in criminal matters shall include:

(a) facilitating and accelerating cooperation between competent ministries and judicial or equivalent authorities of the Member States in relation to proceedings and the enforcement of decisions

(b) facilitating extradition between Member States

(c) ensuring compatibility in rules applicable in the Member States, as may be necessary to improve such cooperation

(d) preventing conflicts of jurisdiction between Member States

(e) progressively adopting measures establishing minimum rules relating to the constituent elements of criminal acts and to penalties in the fields of organised crime, terrorism and illicit drug trafficking.

Article 32 (ex Article K.4)[48]

The Council shall lay down the conditions and limitations under which the competent authorities referred to in Articles 30 and 31 may operate in the territory of another Member State in liaison and in agreement with the authorities of that State.

Article 33 (ex Article K.5)[49]

This Title shall not affect the exercise of the responsibilities incumbent upon Member States with regard to the maintenance of law and order and the safeguarding of internal security.

Article 34 (ex Article K.6)[50]

1. In the areas referred to in this Title, Member States shall inform and consult one another within the Council with a view to coordinating their action. To that end, they shall establish collaboration between the relevant departments of their administrations.

2. The Council shall take measures and promote cooperation, using the appropriate form and procedures as set out in this Title, contributing to

---

47. Added by the Treaty of Amsterdam.
48. Added by the Treaty of Amsterdam.
49. The substance of this article is found in former Article K.2(2).
50. The substance of this article is found in former Article K.3.

the pursuit of the objectives of the Union. To that end, acting unanimously[51] on the initiative of any Member State or of the Commission, the Council may:

(a) adopt common positions defining the approach of the Union to a particular matter;[52]

(b) adopt framework decisions for the purpose of approximation of the laws and regulations of the Member States. Framework decisions shall be binding upon the Member States as to the result to be achieved but shall leave to the national authorities the choice of form and methods. They shall not entail direct effect;[53]

(c) adopt decisions for any other purpose consistent with the objectives of this Title, excluding any approximation of the laws and regulations of the Member States. These decisions shall be binding and shall not entail direct effect the Council, acting by a qualified majority, shall adopt measures necessary to implement those decisions at the level of the Union;[54]

(d) establish conventions which it shall recommend to the Member States for adoption in accordance with their respective constitutional requirements. Member States shall begin the procedures applicable within a time limit to be set by the Council.

Unless they provide otherwise, conventions shall, once adopted by at least half of the Member States, enter into force for those Member States. Measures implementing conventions shall be adopted within the Council by a majority of two-thirds of the Contracting Parties.[55]

3. Where the Council is required to act by a qualified majority, the votes of its members shall be weighted as laid down in Article 205(2) of the Treaty establishing the European Community, and for their adoption acts of the Council shall require at least 62 votes in favour, cast by at least 10 members.[56]

4. For procedural questions, the Council shall act by a majority of its members.[57]

Article 35 (ex Article K.7)[58]

1. The Court of Justice of the European Communities shall have jurisdiction, subject to the conditions laid down in this Article, to give

---

51. The Treaty of Amsterdam added the requirement of Council unanimity.

52. Prior to the Treaty of Amsterdam, this article only sought to promote cooperation in contributing to the pursuit of the objectives of the Union.

53. This paragraph was added by the Amsterdam Treaty.

54. This paragraph was added by the Amsterdam Treaty.

55. Prior to the Amsterdam Treaty, the Commission was not permitted to take initiative on judicial cooperation on criminal matters, customs cooperation, or police cooperation. The first sentence of this paragraph was added by the Amsterdam Treaty.

56. The substance of this paragraph is found in former Article K.4(3).

57. This paragraph was added by the Amsterdam Treaty.

58. This article, based on former Article K.3(2), was significantly expanded by Amsterdam. Previously the article merely al-

preliminary rulings on the validity and interpretation of framework decisions and decisions, on the interpretation of conventions established under this Title and on the validity and interpretation of the measures implementing them.

2. By a declaration made at the time of signature of the Treaty of Amsterdam or at any time thereafter, any Member State shall be able to accept the jurisdiction of the Court of Justice to give preliminary rulings as specified in paragraph 1.

3. A Member State making a declaration pursuant to paragraph 2 shall specify that either:

(a) any court or tribunal of that State against whose decisions there is no judicial remedy under national law may request the Court of Justice to give a preliminary ruling on a question raised in a case pending before it and concerning the validity or interpretation of an act referred to in paragraph 1 if that court or tribunal considers that a decision on the question is necessary to enable it to give judgment, or

(b) any court or tribunal of that State may request the Court of Justice to give a preliminary ruling on a question raised in a case pending before it and concerning the validity or interpretation of an act referred to in paragraph 1 if that court or tribunal considers that a decision on the question is necessary to enable it to give judgment.

4. Any Member State, whether or not it has made a declaration pursuant to paragraph 2, shall be entitled to submit statements of case or written observations to the Court in cases which arise under paragraph 1.

5. The Court of Justice shall have no jurisdiction to review the validity or proportionality of operations carried out by the police or other law enforcement services of a Member State or the exercise of the responsibilities incumbent upon Member States with regard to the maintenance of law and order and the safeguarding of internal security.

6. The Court of Justice shall have jurisdiction to review the legality of framework decisions and decisions in actions brought by a Member State or the Commission on grounds of lack of competence, infringement of an essential procedural requirement, infringement of this Treaty or of any rule of law relating to its application, or misuse of powers. The proceedings provided for in this paragraph shall be instituted within two months of the publication of the measure.

7. The Court of Justice shall have jurisdiction to rule on any dispute between Member States regarding the interpretation or the application of acts adopted under Article 34(2) whenever such dispute cannot be settled by the Council within six months of its being referred to the Council by one of its members. The Court shall also have jurisdiction to rule on any dispute between Member States and the Commission regarding the interpretation or the application of conventions established under Article 34(2)(d).

lowed conventions to confer jurisdiction on the Court of Justice.

Article 36 (ex Article K.8)[59]

1. A Coordinating Committee shall be set up consisting of senior officials. In addition to its coordinating role, it shall be the task of the Committee to:

— give opinions for the attention of the Council, either at the Council's request or on its own initiative

— contribute, without prejudice to Article 207 of the Treaty establishing the European Community, to the preparation of the Council's discussions in the areas referred to in Article 29.

2. The Commission shall be fully associated with the work in the areas referred to in this Title.

Article 37 (ex Article K.9)[60]

Within international organisations and at international conferences in which they take part, Member States shall defend the common positions adopted under the provisions of this Title.

Articles 18 and 19 shall apply as appropriate to matters falling under this Title.[61]

Article 38 (ex Article K.10)[62]

Agreements referred to in Article 24 may cover matters falling under this Title.

Article 39 (ex Article K.11)[63]

1. The Council shall consult the European Parliament before adopting any measure referred to in Article 34(2)(b), (c) and (d). The European Parliament shall deliver its opinion within a time-limit which the Council may lay down, which shall not be less than three months. In the absence of an opinion within that time-limit, the Council may act.[64]

2. The Presidency and the Commission shall regularly inform the European Parliament of discussions in the areas covered by this Title.

3. The European Parliament may ask questions of the Council or make recommendations to it. Each year, it shall hold a debate on the progress made in the areas referred to in this Title.

Article 40 (ex Article K.12)[65]

1. Member States which intend to establish closer cooperation between themselves may be authorised, subject to Articles 43 and 44, to make

---

59. The substance of this article is found in former Article K.4.

60. The substance of this article is found in former Article K.5.

61. This sentence was added by the Amsterdam Treaty.

62. Added by the Treaty of Amsterdam.

63. The substance of this article is found in former Article K.6.

64. The previous version only required the Parliament's views be taken into consideration.

65. The Treaty of Amsterdam significantly expanded this article, which was previously Article K.7.

use of the institutions, procedures and mechanisms laid down by the Treaties provided that the cooperation proposed:

(a) respects the powers of the European Community, and the objectives laid down by this Title

(b) has the aim of enabling the Union to develop more rapidly into an area of freedom, security and justice.

2. The authorisation referred to in paragraph 1 shall be granted by the Council, acting by a qualified majority at the request of the Member States concerned and after inviting the Commission to present its opinion the request shall also be forwarded to the European Parliament.

If a member of the Council declares that, for important and stated reasons of national policy, it intends to oppose the granting of an authorisation by qualified majority, a vote shall not be taken. The Council may, acting by a qualified majority, request that the matter be referred to the European Council for decision by unanimity.

The votes of the members of the Council shall be weighted in accordance with Article 205(2) of the Treaty establishing the European Community. For their adoption, decisions shall require at least 62 votes in favour, cast by at least 10 members.

3. Any Member State which wishes to become a party to cooperation set up in accordance with this Article shall notify its intention to the Council and to the Commission, which shall give an opinion to the Council within three months of receipt of that notification, possibly accompanied by a recommendation for such specific arrangements as it may deem necessary for that Member State to become a party to the cooperation in question. Within four months of the date of that notification, the Council shall decide on the request and on such specific arrangements as it may deem necessary. The decision shall be deemed to be taken unless the Council, acting by a qualified majority, decides to hold it in abeyance in this case, the Council shall state the reasons for its decision and set a deadline for reexamining it. For the purposes of this paragraph, the Council shall act under the conditions set out in Article 44.

4. The provisions of Articles 29 to 41 shall apply to the closer cooperation provided for by this Article, save as otherwise provided for in this Article and in Articles 43 and 44.

The provisions of the Treaty establishing the European Community concerning the powers of the Court of Justice of the European Communities and the exercise of those powers shall apply to paragraphs 1, 2 and 3.

5. This Article is without prejudice to the provisions of the Protocol integrating the Schengen acquis into the framework of the European Union.

Article 41 (ex Article K.13)[66]

1. Articles 189, 190, 195, 196 to 199, 203, 204, 205(3), 206 to 209, 213 to 219, 255 and 290 of the Treaty establishing the European Community shall apply to the provisions relating to the areas referred to in this Title.

2. Administrative expenditure which the provisions relating to the areas referred to in this Title entail for the institutions shall be charged to the budget of the European Communities.

3. Operational expenditure to which the implementation of those provisions gives rise shall also be charged to the budget of the European Communities, except where the Council acting unanimously decides otherwise. In cases where expenditure is not charged to the budget of the European Communities it shall be charged to the Member States in accordance with the gross national product scale, unless the Council acting unanimously decides otherwise.

4. The budgetary procedure laid down in the Treaty establishing the European Community shall apply to the expenditure charged to the budget of the European Communities.[67]

Article 42 (ex Article K.14)

The Council, acting unanimously on the initiative of the Commission or a Member State, and after consulting the European Parliament,[68] may decide that action in areas referred to in Article 29 shall fall under Title IV of the Treaty establishing the European Community, and at the same time determine the relevant voting conditions relating to it. It shall recommend the Member States to adopt that decision in accordance with their respective constitutional requirements.

TITLE VII (ex Title VIa)[69]

PROVISIONS ON CLOSER COOPERATION

Article 43 (ex Article K.15)

1. Member States which intend to establish closer cooperation between themselves may make use of the institutions, procedures and mechanisms laid down by this Treaty and the Treaty establishing the European Community provided that the cooperation:

   (a) is aimed at furthering the objectives of the Union and at protecting and serving its interests

   (b) respects the principles of the said Treaties and the single institutional framework of the Union

---

66. The substance of paragraphs 1 through 3 is found in former Article K.8.

67. This paragraph was added by the Amsterdam Treaty.

68. The requirement of parliamentary consultation was added by the Amsterdam Treaty.

69. This title was added by the Amsterdam Treaty.

(c) is only used as a last resort, where the objectives of the said Treaties could not be attained by applying the relevant procedures laid down therein

(d) concerns at least a majority of Member States

(e) does not affect the *'acquis communautaire'* and the measures adopted under the other provisions of the said Treaties

(f) does not affect the competences, rights, obligations and interests of those Member States which do not participate therein

(g) is open to all Member States and allows them to become parties to the cooperation at any time, provided that they comply with the basic decision and with the decisions taken within that framework

(h) complies with the specific additional criteria laid down in Article 11 of the Treaty establishing the European Community and Article 40 of this Treaty, depending on the area concerned, and is authorised by the Council in accordance with the procedures laid down therein.

2. Member States shall apply, as far as they are concerned, the acts and decisions adopted for the implementation of the cooperation in which they participate. Member States not participating in such cooperation shall not impede the implementation thereof by the participating Member States.

Article 44 (ex Article K.16)

1. For the purposes of the adoption of the acts and decisions necessary for the implementation of the cooperation referred to in Article 43, the relevant institutional provisions of this Treaty and of the Treaty establishing the European Community shall apply. However, while all members of the Council shall be able to take part in the deliberations, only those representing participating Member States shall take part in the adoption of decisions. The qualified majority shall be defined as the same proportion of the weighted votes of the members of the Council concerned as laid down in Article 205(2) of the Treaty establishing the European Community. Unanimity shall be constituted by only those Council members concerned.

2. Expenditure resulting from implementation of the cooperation, other than administrative costs entailed for the institutions, shall be borne by the participating Member States, unless the Council, acting unanimously, decides otherwise.

Article 45 (ex Article K.17)

The Council and the Commission shall regularly inform the European Parliament of the development of closer cooperation established on the basis of this Title.

TITLE VIII (ex Title VII)
FINAL PROVISIONS

Article 46 (ex Article L)[70]

The provisions of the Treaty establishing the European Community, the Treaty establishing the European Coal and Steel Community and the Treaty establishing the European Atomic Energy Community concerning the powers of the Court of Justice of the European Communities and the exercise of those powers shall apply only to the following provisions of this Treaty:

(a) provisions amending the Treaty establishing the European Economic Community with a view to establishing the European Community, the Treaty establishing the European Coal and Steel Community and the Treaty establishing the European Atomic Energy Community

(b) provisions of Title VI, under the conditions provided for by Article 35

(c) provisions of Title VII, under the conditions provided for by Article 11 of the Treaty establishing the European Community and Article 40 of this Treaty

(d) Article 6(2) with regard to action of the institutions, insofar as the Court has jurisdiction under the Treaties establishing the European Communities and under this Treaty

(e) Articles 46 to 53.

Article 47 (ex Article M)

Subject to the provisions amending the Treaty establishing the European Economic Community with a view to establishing the European Community, the Treaty establishing the European Coal and Steel Community and the Treaty establishing the European Atomic Energy Community, and to these final provisions, nothing in this Treaty shall affect the Treaties establishing the European Communities or the subsequent Treaties and Acts modifying or supplementing them.

Article 48 (ex Article N)

The government of any Member State or the Commission may submit to the Council proposals for the amendment of the Treaties on which the Union is founded.

If the Council, after consulting the European Parliament and, where appropriate, the Commission, delivers an opinion in favour of calling a conference of representatives of the governments of the Member States, the conference shall be convened by the President of the Council for the purpose of determining by common accord the amendments to be made to those Treaties. The European Central Bank shall also be consulted in the case of institutional changes in the monetary area.

---

70. Paragraphs (b), (d), and (e) were added by the Amsterdam Treaty.

The amendments shall enter into force after being ratified by all the Member States in accordance with their respective constitutional requirements.

Article 49 (ex Article O)

Any European State which respects the principles set out in Article 6(1)[71] may apply to become a member of the Union. It shall address its application to the Council, which shall act unanimously after consulting the Commission and after receiving the assent of the European Parliament, which shall act by an absolute majority of its component members.

The conditions of admission and the adjustments to the Treaties on which the Union is founded which such admission entails shall be the subject of an agreement between the Member States and the applicant State. This agreement shall be submitted for ratification by all the contracting States in accordance with their respective constitutional requirements.

Article 50 (ex Article P)

1. Articles 2 to 7 and 10 to 19 of the Treaty establishing a Single Council and a Single Commission of the European Communities, signed in Brussels on 8 April 1965, are hereby repealed.

2. Article 2, Article 3(2) and Title III of the Single European Act signed in Luxembourg on 17 February 1986 and in The Hague on 28 February 1986 are hereby repealed.

Article 51 (ex Article Q)

This Treaty is concluded for an unlimited period.

Article 52 (ex Article R)

1. This Treaty shall be ratified by the High Contracting Parties in accordance with their respective constitutional requirements. The instruments of ratification shall be deposited with the Government of the Italian Republic.

2. This Treaty shall enter into force on 1 January 1993, provided that all the instruments of ratification have been deposited, or, failing that, on the first day of the month following the deposit of the instrument of ratification by the last signatory State to take this step.

Article 53 (ex Article S)

This Treaty, drawn up in a single original in the Danish, Dutch, English, French, German, Greek, Irish, Italian, Portuguese and Spanish languages, the texts in each of these languages being equally authentic, shall be deposited in the archives of the government of the Italian Republic,

---

[71]. The requirement that the applicant state respect Article 6(1)'s principles was added by the Treaty of Amsterdam.

which will transmit a certified copy to each of the governments of the other signatory States.

Pursuant to the Accession Treaty of 1994, the Finnish and Swedish versions of this Treaty shall also be authentic.[72]

---

72. This sentence was added by the Amsterdam Treaty.

3. TABLE OF EQUIVALENCES OF TREATY ARTICLES

[*Eds. Note*: The Treaty of Amsterdam, effective May 1999, renumbered the treaty articles of the Treaty Establishing the European Community and the Treaty on European Union. The conversion table (or "table of equivalences") referred to in Article 12 of the Treaty of Amsterdam is reproduced below.]

Numbering of the Treaty on European Union and the EC Treaty *before* and *after* the entry into force of the Treaty of Amsterdam

A. Treaty on European Union (TEU)

Before	After	Before	After	Before	After
Title I	*Title I*	Art J.7	Art 17	Art K.9	Art 37
Art A	Art 1	Art J.8	Art 18	Art K.10	Art 38
Art B	Art 2	Art J.9	Art 19	Art K.11	Art 39
Art C	Art 3	Art J.10	Art 20	Art K.12	Art 40
Art D	Art 4	Art J.11	Art 21	Art K.13	Art 41
Art E	Art 5	Art J.12	Art 22	Art K.14	Art 42
Art F	Art 6	Art J.13	Art 23	*Title VIa*	*Title VII*
Art F.1	Art 7	Art J.14	Art 24	Art K.15	Art 43
Title II	*Title II*	Art J.15	Art 25	Art K.16	Art 44
Art G	Art 8	Art J.16	Art 26	Art K.17	Art 45
Title III	*Title III*	Art J.17	Art 27	*Title VII*	*Title VIII*
Art H	Art 9	Art J.18	Art 28	Art L	Art 46
Title IV	*Title IV*	*Title VI*	*Title VI*	Art M	Art 47
Art I	Art 10	Art K.1	Art 29	Art N	Art 48
Title V	*Title V*	Art K.2	Art 30	Art O	Art 49
Art J.1	Art 11	Art K.3	Art 31	Art P	Art 50
Art J.2	Art 12	Art K.4	Art 32	Art Q	Art 51
Art J.3	Art 13	Art K.5	Art 33	Art R	Art 52
Art J.4	Art 14	Art K.6	Art 34	Art S	Art 53
Art J.5	Art 15	Art K.7	Art 35		
Art J.6	Art 16	Art K.8	Art 36		

B. Treaty establishing the European Community (EC)

Before	After	Before	After	Before	After
Part One	*Part One*	Art 7	– (repealed)	Art 9	Art 23
Art 1	Art 1	Art 7a	Art 14	Art 10	Art 24
Art 2	Art 2	Art 7b	– (repealed)	Art 11	– (repealed)
Art 3	Art 3	Art 7c	Art 15	Chapter 1	Chapter 1
Art 3a	Art 4	Art 7d	Art 16	Section 1	(deleted)
Art 3b	Art 5	*Part Two*	*Part Two*	Art 12	Art 25
Art 3c	Art 6	Art 8	Art 17	Art 13	– (repealed)
Art 4	Art 7	Art 8a	Art 18	Art 14	– (repealed)
Art 4a	Art 8	Art 8b	Art 19	Art 15	– (repealed)
Art 4b	Art 9	Art 8c	Art 20	Art 16	– (repealed)
Art 5	Art 10	Art 8d	Art 21	Art 17	– (repealed)

Art 5a	Art 11	Art 8e	Art 22	Art 18	– (repealed)
Art 6	Art 12	*Part Three*	*Part Three*	Art 19	– (repealed)
Art 6a	Art 13	*Title I*	*Title I*	Art 20	– (repealed)
Art 21	– (repealed)	Art 62	– (repealed)	Art 86	Art 82
Art 22	– (repealed)	Art 63	Art 52	Art 87	Art 83
Art 23	– (repealed)	Art 64	Art 53	Art 88	Art 84
Art 24	– (repealed)	Art 65	Art 54	Art 89	Art 85
Art 25	– (repealed)	Art 66	Art 55	Art 90	Art 86
Art 26	– (repealed)	*Chapter 4*	*Chapter 4*	*Section 2*	*(deleted)*
Art 27	– (repealed)	Art 67	– (repealed)	Art 91	– (repealed)
Art 28	Art 26	Art 68	– (repealed)	*Section 3*	*Section 2*
Art 29	Art 27	Art 69	– (repealed)	Art 92	Art 87
Chapter 2	*Chapter 2*	Art 70	– (repealed)	Art 93	Art 88
Art 30	Art 28	Art 71	– (repealed)	Art 94	Art 89
Art 31	– (repealed)	Art 72	– (repealed)	*Chapter 2*	*Chapter 2*
Art 32	– (repealed)	Art 73	– (repealed)	Art 95	Art 90
Art 33	– (repealed)	Art 73a	– (repealed)	Art 96	Art 91
Art 34	Art 29	Art 73b	Art 56	Art 97	– (repealed)
Art 35	– (repealed)	Art 73c	Art 57	Art 98	Art 92
Art 36	Art 30	Art 73d	Art 58	Art 99	Art 93
Art 37	Art 31	Art 73e	– (repealed)	*Chapter 3*	*Chapter 3*
Title II	*Title II*	Art 73f	Art 59	Art 100	Art 94
Art 38	Art 32	Art 73g	Art 60	Art 100a	Art 95
Art 39	Art 33	Art 73h	– (repealed)	Art 100b	– (repealed)
Art 40	Art 34	*Title IIIa*	*Title IV*	Art 100c	– (repealed)
Art 41	Art 35	Art 73i	Art 61	Art 100d	– (repealed)
Art 42	Art 36	Art 73j	Art 62	Art 101	Art 96
Art 43	Art 37	Art 73k	Art 63	Art 102	Art 97
Art 44	– (repealed)	Art 73l	Art 64	*Title VI*	*Title VII*
Art 45	– (repealed)	Art 73m	Art 65	*Chapter 1*	*Chapter 1*
Art 46	Art 38	Art 73n	Art 66	Art 102a	Art 98
Art 47	– (repealed)	Art 73o	Art 67	Art 103	Art 99
Title III	*Title III*	Art 73p	Art 68	Art 103a	Art 100
Chapter 1	*Chapter 1*	Art 73q	Art 69	Art 104	Art 101
Art 48	Art 39	*Title IV*	*Title V*	Art 104a	Art 102
Art 49	Art 40	Art 74	Art 70	Art 104b	Art 103
Art 50	Art 41	Art 75	Art 71	Art 104c	Art 104
Art 51	Art 42	Art 76	Art 72	*Chapter 2*	*Chapter 2*
Chapter 2	*Chapter 2*	Art 77	Art 73	Art 105	Art 105
Art 52	Art 43	Art 78	Art 74	Art 105a	Art 106
Art 53	– (repealed)	Art 79	Art 75	Art 106	Art 107
Art 54	Art 44	Art 80	Art 76	Art 107	Art 108
Art 55	Art 45	Art 81	Art 77	Art 108	Art 109
Art 56	Art 46	Art 82	Art 78	Art 108a	Art 110
Art 57	Art 47	Art 83	Art 79	Art 109	Art 111
Art 58	Art 48	Art 84	Art 80	*Chapter 3*	*Chapter 3*
Chapter 3	*Chapter 3*	*Title V*	*Title VI*	Art 109a	Art 112
Art 59	Art 49	*Chapter 1*	*Chapter 1*	Art 109b	Art 113

Art 60	Art 50	Section 1	Section 1		
Art 61	Art 51	Art 85	Art 81		
Art 109c	Art 114	Chapter 3	Chapter 3	Part Four	Part Four
Art 109d	Art 115	Art 126	Art 149	Art 131	Art 182
Chapter 4	Chapter 4	Art 127	Art 150	Art 132	Art 183
Art 109e	Art 116	Title IX	Title XII	Art 133	Art 184
Art 109f	Art 117	Art 128	Art 151	Art 134	Art 185
Art 109g	Art 118	Title X	Title XIII	Art 135	Art 186
Art 109h	Art 119	Art 129	Art 152	Art 136	Art 187
Art 109i	Art 120	Title XI	Title XIV	Art 136a	Art 188
Art 109j	Art 121	Art 129a	Art 153	Part Five	Part Five
Art 109k	Art 122	Title XII	Title XV	Title I	Title I
Art 109l	Art 123	Art 129b	Art 154	Chapter I	Chapter I
Art 109m	Art 124	Art 129c	Art 155	Section 1	Section 1
Title VIa	Title VIII	Art 129d	Art 156	Art 137	Art 189
Art 109n	Art 125	Title XIII	Title XVI	Art 138	Art 190
Art 109o	Art 126	Art 130	Art 157	Art 138a	Art 191
Art 109p	Art 127	Title XIV	Title XVII	Art 138b	Art 192
Art 109q	Art 128	Art 130a	Art 158	Art 138c	Art 193
Art 109r	Art 129	Art 130b	Art 159	Art 138d	Art 194
Art 109s	Art 130	Art 130c	Art 160	Art 138e	Art 195
Title VII	Title IX	Art 130d	Art 161	Art 139	Art 196
Art 110	Art 131	Art 130e	Art 162	Art 140	Art 197
Art 111	– (repealed)	Title XV	Title XVIII	Art 141	Art 198
Art 112	Art 132	Art 130f	Art 163	Art 142	Art 199
Art 113s	Art 133	Art 130g	Art 164	Art 143	Art 200
Art 114	– (repealed)	Art 130h	Art 165	Art 144	Art 201
Art 115	Art 134	Art 130i	Art 166	Section 2	Section 2
Art 116	– (repealed)	Art 130j	Art 167	Art 145	Art 202
Title VIIa	Title X	Art 130k	Art 168	Art 146	Art 203
Art 116 (new)	Art 135	Art 130l	Art 169	Art 147	Art 204
Title VIII	Title XI	Art 130m	Art 170	Art 148	Art 205
Chapter 1	Chapter 1	Art 130n	Art 171	Art 149	– (repealed)
Art 117	Art 136	Art 130o	Art 172	Art 150	Art 206
Art 118	Art 137	Art 130p	Art 173	Art 151	Art 207
Art 118a	Art 138	Art 130q	– (repealed)	Art 152	Art 208
Art 118b	Art 139	Title XVI	Title XIX	Art 153	Art 209
Art 118c	Art 140	Art 130r	Art 174	Art 154	Art 210
Art 119	Art 141	Art 130s	Art 175	Section 3	Section 3
Art 119a	Art 142	Art 130t	Art 176	Art 155	Art 211
Art 120	Art 143	Title XVII	Title XX	Art 156	Art 212
Art 121	Art 144	Art 130u	Art 177	Art 157	Art 213
Art 122	Art 145	Art 130v	Art 178	Art 158	Art 214
Chapter 2	Chapter 2	Art 130w	Art 179	Art 159	Art 215
Art 123	Art 146	Art 130x	Art 180	Art 160	Art 216
Art 124	Art 147	Art 130y	Art 181	Art 161	Art 217
Art 125	Art 148			Art 162	Art 218
Art 163	Art 219	Art 191	Art 254	Art 213a	Art 285

Section 4	*Section 4*	Art 191a	Art 255	Art 213b	Art 286
Art 164	Art 220	*Chapter 3*	*Chapter 3*	Art 214	Art 287
Art 165	Art 221	Art 192	Art 256	Art 215	Art 288
Art 166	Art 222	Art 193	Art 257	Art 216	Art 289
Art 167	Art 223	Art 194	Art 258	Art 217	Art 290
Art 168	Art 224	Art 195	Art 259	Art 218	Art 291
Art 168a	Art 225	Art 196	Art 260	Art 219	Art 292
Art 169	Art 226	Art 197	Art 261	Art 220	Art 293
Art 170	Art 227	Art 198	Art 262	Art 221	Art 294
Art 171	Art 228	*Chapter 4*	*Chapter 4*	Art 222	Art 295
Art 172	Art 229	Art 198a	Art 263	Art 223	Art 296
Art 173	Art 230	Art 198b	Art 264	Art 224	Art 297
Art 174	Art 231	Art 198c	Art 265	Art 225	Art 298
Art 175	Art 232	*Chapter 5*	*Chapter 5*	Art 226	– (repealed)
Art 176	Art 233	Art 198d	Art 266	Art 227	Art 299
Art 177	Art 234	Art 198e	Art 267	Art 228	Art 300
Art 178	Art 235	*Title II*	*Title II*	Art 228a	Art 301
Art 179	Art 236	Art 199	Art 268	Art 229	Art 302
Art 180	Art 237	Art 200	– (repealed)	Art 230	Art 303
Art 181	Art 238	Art 201	Art 269	Art 231	Art 304
Art 182	Art 239	Art 201a	Art 270	Art 232	Art 305
Art 183	Art 240	Art 202	Art 271	Art 233	Art 306
Art 184	Art 241	Art 203	Art 272	Art 234	Art 307
Art 185	Art 242	Art 204	Art 273	Art 235	Art 308
Art 186	Art 243	Art 205	Art 274	Art 236	Art 309
Art 187	Art 244	Art 205a	Art 275	Art 237	– (repealed)
Art 188	Art 245	Art 206	Art 276	Art 238	Art 310
Section 5	*Section 5*	Art 206a	– (repealed)	Art 239	Art 311
Art 188a	Art 246	Art 207	Art 277	Art 240	Art 312
Art 188b	Art 247	Art 208	Art 278	Art 241	– (repealed)
Art 188c	Art 248	Art 209	Art 279	Art 242	– (repealed)
Chapter 2	*Chapter 2*	Art 209a	Art 280	Art 243	– (repealed)
Art 189	Art 249	*Part Six*	*Part Six*	Art 244	– (repealed)
Art 189a	Art 250	Art 210	Art 281	Art 245	– (repealed)
Art 189b	Art 251	Art 211	Art 282	Art 246	– (repealed)
Art 189c	Art 252	Art 212	Art 283	Art 247	Art 313
Art 190	Art 253	Art 213	Art 284	Art 248	Art 314

4. TREATY OF NICE (AND SELECTED PROTOCOLS)

signed at Nice, Feb. 26, 2001, O.J. C80/1 (March 10, 2001)

[*Eds. Note*: The Treaty of Nice amends the Treaty Establishing the European Community (EC Treaty) and the Treaty on European Union (TEU) (as well as the treaties establishing the Coal and Steel Community and Euratom). At the time of this writing, the Nice Treaty remains unratified. It is reproduced below, insofar as the amendments to the EC Treaty and the TEU are concerned. The EC Treaty and TEU articles being amended or replaced may be found in Documents 1 and 2 of this Selected Documents, respectively.

The Nice Treaty contains numerous Protocols and Declarations. They are all listed following the text of the Nice Treaty below. Two Protocols in particular are reproduced: the Protocol on the Enlargement of the European Union and the Protocol on the Statute of the Court of Justice.]

PART ONE: SUBSTANTIVE AMENDMENTS
Article 1

The Treaty on European Union shall be amended in accordance with the provisions of this Article.

1. Article 7 shall be replaced by the following:

"Article 7

1. On a reasoned proposal by one third of the Member States, by the European Parliament or by the Commission, the Council, acting by a majority of four-fifths of its members after obtaining the assent of the European Parliament, may determine that there is a clear risk of a serious breach by a Member State of principles mentioned in Article 6(1), and address appropriate recommendations to that State. Before making such a determination, the Council shall hear the Member State in question and, acting in accordance with the same procedure, may call on independent persons to submit within a reasonable time limit a report on the situation in the Member State in question.

The Council shall regularly verify that the grounds on which such a determination was made continue to apply.

2. The Council, meeting in the composition of the Heads of State or Government and acting by unanimity on a proposal by one third of the Member States or by the Commission and after obtaining the assent of the European Parliament, may determine the existence of a serious and persistent breach by a Member State of principles mentioned in Article 6(1), after inviting the government of the Member State in question to submit its observations.

3. Where a determination under paragraph 2 has been made, the Council, acting by a qualified majority, may decide to suspend certain of the rights deriving from the application of this Treaty to the Member State in question, including the voting rights of the representative of the government of that Member State in the Council. In doing so, the Council shall

take into account the possible consequences of such a suspension on the rights and obligations of natural and legal persons.

The obligations of the Member State in question under this Treaty shall in any case continue to be binding on that State.

4. The Council, acting by a qualified majority, may decide subsequently to vary or revoke measures taken under paragraph 3 in response to changes in the situation which led to their being imposed.

5. For the purposes of this Article, the Council shall act without taking into account the vote of the representative of the government of the Member State in question. Abstentions by members present in person or represented shall not prevent the adoption of decisions referred to in paragraph 2. A qualified majority shall be defined as the same proportion of the weighted votes of the members of the Council concerned as laid down in Article 205(2) of the Treaty establishing the European Community.

This paragraph shall also apply in the event of voting rights being suspended pursuant to paragraph 3.

6. For the purposes of paragraphs 1 and 2, the European Parliament shall act by a two-thirds majority of the votes cast, representing a majority of its Members."

2. *Article 17 shall be replaced by the following:*

"Article 17

1. The common foreign and security policy shall include all questions relating to the security of the Union, including the progressive framing of a common defence policy, which might lead to a common defence, should the European Council so decide. It shall in that case recommend to the Member States the adoption of such a decision in accordance with their respective constitutional requirements.

The policy of the Union in accordance with this Article shall not prejudice the specific character of the security and defence policy of certain Member States and shall respect the obligations of certain Member States, which see their common defence realised in the North Atlantic Treaty Organisation (NATO), under the North Atlantic Treaty and be compatible with the common security and defence policy established within that framework.

The progressive framing of a common defence policy will be supported, as Member States consider appropriate, by cooperation between them in the field of armaments.

2. Questions referred to in this Article shall include humanitarian and rescue tasks, peacekeeping tasks and tasks of combat forces in crisis management, including peacemaking.

3. Decisions having defence implications dealt with under this Article shall be taken without prejudice to the policies and obligations referred to in paragraph 1, second subparagraph.

4. The provisions of this Article shall not prevent the development of closer cooperation between two or more Member States on a bilateral level, in the framework of the Western European Union (WEU) and NATO, provided such cooperation does not run counter to or impede that provided for in this Title.

5. With a view to furthering the objectives of this Article, the provisions of this Article will be reviewed in accordance with Article 48."

3. In Article 23(2), first subparagraph, the following third indent shall be added:

"—when appointing a special representative in accordance with Article 18(5)."

4. Article 24 shall be replaced by the following:

"Article 24

1. When it is necessary to conclude an agreement with one or more States or international organisations in implementation of this Title, the Council may authorise the Presidency, assisted by the Commission as appropriate, to open negotiations to that effect. Such agreements shall be concluded by the Council on a recommendation from the Presidency.

2. The Council shall act unanimously when the agreement covers an issue for which unanimity is required for the adoption of internal decisions.

3. When the agreement is envisaged in order to implement a joint action or common position, the Council shall act by a qualified majority in accordance with Article 23(2).

4. The provisions of this Article shall also apply to matters falling under Title VI. When the agreement covers an issue for which a qualified majority is required for the adoption of internal decisions or measures, the Council shall act by a qualified majority in accordance with Article 34(3).

5. No agreement shall be binding on a Member State whose representative in the Council states that it has to comply with the requirements of its own constitutional procedure; the other members of the Council may agree that the agreement shall nevertheless apply provisionally.

6. Agreements concluded under the conditions set out by this Article shall be binding on the institutions of the Union."

5. Article 25 shall be replaced by the following:

"Article 25

Without prejudice to Article 207 of the Treaty establishing the European Community, a Political and Security Committee shall monitor the international situation in the areas covered by the common foreign and security policy and contribute to the definition of policies by delivering opinions to the Council at the request of the Council or on its own initiative. It shall also monitor the implementation of agreed policies, without prejudice to the responsibility of the Presidency and the Commission.

Within the scope of this Title, this Committee shall exercise, under the responsibility of the Council, political control and strategic direction of crisis management operations.

The Council may authorise the Committee, for the purpose and for the duration of a crisis management operation, as determined by the Council, to take the relevant decisions concerning the political control and strategic direction of the operation, without prejudice to Article 47."

6. *The following Articles shall be inserted:*

"Article 27a

1. Enhanced cooperation in any of the areas referred to in this Title shall be aimed at safeguarding the values and serving the interests of the Union as a whole by asserting its identity as a coherent force on the international scene. It shall respect:

— the principles, objectives, general guidelines and consistency of the common foreign and security policy and the decisions taken within the framework of that policy;

— the powers of the European Community, and

— consistency between all the Union's policies and its external activities.

2. Articles 11 to 27 and Articles 27b to 28 shall apply to the enhanced cooperation provided for in this Article, save as otherwise provided in Article 27c and Articles 43 to 45.

Article 27b

Enhanced cooperation pursuant to this Title shall relate to implementation of a joint action or a common position. It shall not relate to matters having military or defence implications.

Article 27c

Member States which intend to establish enhanced cooperation between themselves under Article 27b shall address a request to the Council to that effect.

The request shall be forwarded to the Commission and to the European Parliament for information. The Commission shall give its opinion particularly on whether the enhanced cooperation proposed is consistent with Union policies. Authorisation shall be granted by the Council, acting in accordance with the second and third subparagraphs of Article 23(2) and in compliance with Articles 43 to 45.

Article 27d

Without prejudice to the powers of the Presidency or of the Commission, the Secretary–General of the Council, High Representative for the common foreign and security policy, shall in particular ensure that the European Parliament and all members of the Council are kept fully informed of the implementation of enhanced cooperation in the field of the common foreign and security policy.

Article 27e

Any Member State which wishes to participate in enhanced cooperation established in accordance with Article 27c shall notify its intention to the Council and inform the Commission. The Commission shall give an opinion to the Council within three months of the date of receipt of that notification. Within four months of the date of receipt of that notification, the Council shall take a decision on the request and on such specific arrangements as it may deem necessary. The decision shall be deemed to be taken unless the Council, acting by a qualified majority within the same period, decides to hold it in abeyance; in that case, the Council shall state the reasons for its decision and set a deadline for re-examining it.

For the purposes of this Article, the Council shall act by a qualified majority. The qualified majority shall be defined as the same proportion of the weighted votes and the same proportion of the number of the members of the Council concerned as those laid down in the third subparagraph of Article 23(2)."

7. In Article 29, second paragraph, the second indent shall be replaced by the following:

"—closer cooperation between judicial and other competent authorities of the Member States, including cooperation through the European Judicial Cooperation Unit ("Eurojust"), in accordance with the provisions of Articles 31 and 32;"

8. Article 31 shall be replaced by the following:

"Article 31

1. Common action on judicial cooperation in criminal matters shall include:

(a) facilitating and accelerating cooperation between competent ministries and judicial or equivalent authorities of the Member States, including, where appropriate, cooperation through Eurojust, in relation to proceedings and the enforcement of decisions;

(b) facilitating extradition between Member States;

(c) ensuring compatibility in rules applicable in the Member States, as may be necessary to improve such cooperation;

(d) preventing conflicts of jurisdiction between Member States;

(e) progressively adopting measures establishing minimum rules relating to the constituent elements of criminal acts and to penalties in the fields of organised crime, terrorism and illicit drug trafficking.

2. The Council shall encourage cooperation through Eurojust by:

(a) enabling Eurojust to facilitate proper coordination between Member States' national prosecuting authorities;

(b) promoting support by Eurojust for criminal investigations in cases of serious cross-border crime, particularly in the case of organised crime, taking account, in particular, of analyses carried out by Europol;

(c) facilitating close cooperation between Eurojust and the European Judicial Network, particularly, in order to facilitate the execution of letters rogatory and the implementation of extradition requests."

9. *Article 40 shall be replaced by the following Articles 40, 40a and 40b:*

"Article 40

1. Enhanced cooperation in any of the areas referred to in this Title shall have the aim of enabling the Union to develop more rapidly into an area of freedom, security and justice, while respecting the powers of the European Community and the objectives laid down in this Title.

2. Articles 29 to 39 and Articles 40a to 41 shall apply to the enhanced cooperation provided for by this Article, save as otherwise provided in Article 40a and in Articles 43 to 45.

3. The provisions of the Treaty establishing the European Community concerning the powers of the Court of Justice and the exercise of those powers shall apply to this Article and to Articles 40a and 40b.

Article 40a

1. Member States which intend to establish enhanced cooperation between themselves under Article 40 shall address a request to the Commission, which may submit a proposal to the Council to that effect. In the event of the Commission not submitting a proposal, it shall inform the Member States concerned of the reasons for not doing so. Those Member States may then submit an initiative to the Council designed to obtain authorisation for the enhanced cooperation concerned.

2. The authorisation referred to in paragraph 1 shall be granted, in compliance with Articles 43 to 45, by the Council, acting by a qualified majority, on a proposal from the Commission or on the initiative of at least eight Member States, and after consulting the European Parliament. The votes of the members of the Council shall be weighted in accordance with Article 205(2) of the Treaty establishing the European Community.

A member of the Council may request that the matter be referred to the European Council. After that matter has been raised before the European Council, the Council may act in accordance with the first subparagraph of this paragraph.

Article 40b

Any Member State which wishes to participate in enhanced cooperation established in accordance with Article 40a shall notify its intention to the Council and to the Commission, which shall give an opinion to the Council within three months of the date of receipt of that notification, possibly accompanied by a recommendation for such specific arrangements as it may deem necessary for that Member State to become a party to the cooperation in question. The Council shall take a decision on the request within four months of the date of receipt of that notification. The decision shall be deemed to be taken unless the Council, acting by a qualified majority within the same period, decides to hold it in abeyance; in that case, the Council shall state the reasons for its decision and set a deadline for re-examining it.

For the purposes of this Article, the Council shall act under the conditions set out in Article 44(1)."

10. The heading of Title VII shall be replaced by the following: "Provisions on enhanced cooperation".

11. Article 43 shall be replaced by the following:

"Article 43

Member States which intend to establish enhanced cooperation between themselves may make use of the institutions, procedures and mechanisms laid down by this Treaty and by the Treaty establishing the European Community provided that the proposed cooperation:

(a) is aimed at furthering the objectives of the Union and of the Community, at protecting and serving their interests and at reinforcing their process of integration;

(b) respects the said Treaties and the single institutional framework of the Union;

(c) respects the acquis communautaire and the measures adopted under the other provisions of the said Treaties;

(d) remains within the limits of the powers of the Union or of the Community and does not concern the areas which fall within the exclusive competence of the Community;

(e) does not undermine the internal market as defined in Article 14(2) of the Treaty establishing the European Community, or the economic and social cohesion established in accordance with Title XVII of that Treaty;

(f) does not constitute a barrier to or discrimination in trade between the Member States and does not distort competition between them;

(g) involves a minimum of eight Member States;

(h) respects the competences, rights and obligations of those Member States which do not participate therein;

(i) does not affect the provisions of the Protocol integrating the Schengen acquis into the framework of the European Union;

(j) is open to all the Member States, in accordance with Article 43b."

12. The following Articles shall be inserted:

"Article 43a

Enhanced cooperation may be undertaken only as a last resort, when it has been established within the Council that the objectives of such cooperation cannot be attained within a reasonable period by applying the relevant provisions of the Treaties.

Article 43b

When enhanced cooperation is being established, it shall be open to all Member States. It shall also be open to them at any time, in accordance with Articles 27e and 40b of this Treaty and with Article 11a of the Treaty establishing the European Community, subject to compliance with the basic decision and with the decisions taken within that framework. The Commission and the Member States participating in enhanced cooperation shall ensure that as many Member States as possible are encouraged to take part."

13. Article 44 shall be replaced by the following Articles 44 and 44a:

"Article 44

1. For the purposes of the adoption of the acts and decisions necessary for the implementation of enhanced cooperation referred to in Article 43, the relevant institutional provisions of this Treaty and of the Treaty establishing the European Community shall apply. However, while all members of the Council shall be able to take part in the deliberations, only those representing Member States participating in enhanced cooperation shall take part in the adoption of decisions. The qualified majority shall be defined as the same proportion of the weighted votes and the same proportion of the number of the Council members concerned as laid down in Article 205(2) of the Treaty establishing the European Community, and in the second and third subparagraphs of Article 23(2) of this Treaty as regards enhanced cooperation established on the basis of Article 27c. Unanimity shall be constituted by only those Council members concerned.

Such acts and decisions shall not form part of the Union acquis.

2. Member States shall apply, as far as they are concerned, the acts and decisions adopted for the implementation of the enhanced cooperation in which they participate. Such acts and decisions shall be binding only on those Member States which participate in such cooperation and, as appropriate, shall be directly applicable only in those States. Member States which do not participate in such cooperation shall not impede the implementation thereof by the participating Member States.

Article 44a

Expenditure resulting from implementation of enhanced cooperation, other than administrative costs entailed for the institutions, shall be borne by the participating Member States, unless all members of the Council, acting unanimously after consulting the European Parliament, decide otherwise."

14. Article 45 shall be replaced by the following:

"Article 45

The Council and the Commission shall ensure the consistency of activities undertaken on the basis of this Title and the consistency of such activities with the policies of the Union and the Community, and shall cooperate to that end."

15. Article 46 shall be replaced by the following:

"Article 46

The provisions of the Treaty establishing the European Community, the Treaty establishing the European Coal and Steel Community and the Treaty establishing the European Atomic Energy Community concerning the powers of the Court of Justice of the European Communities and the exercise of those powers shall apply only to the following provisions of this Treaty:

(a) provisions amending the Treaty establishing the European Economic Community with a view to establishing the European Community, the Treaty establishing the European Coal and Steel Community and the Treaty establishing the European Atomic Energy Community;

(b) provisions of Title VI, under the conditions provided for by Article 35;

(c) provisions of Title VII, under the conditions provided for by Articles 11 and 11a of the Treaty establishing the European Community and Article 40 of this Treaty;

(d) Article 6(2) with regard to action of the institutions, insofar as the Court has jurisdiction under the Treaties establishing the European Communities and under this Treaty;

(e) the purely procedural stipulations in Article 7, with the Court acting at the request of the Member State concerned within one month from the date of the determination by the Council provided for in that Article;

(f) Articles 46 to 53."

Article 2

The Treaty establishing the European Community shall be amended in accordance with the provisions of this Article.

1. Article 11 shall be replaced by the following Articles 11 and 11a:

"Article 11

1. Member States which intend to establish enhanced cooperation between themselves in one of the areas referred to in this Treaty shall address a request to the Commission, which may submit a proposal to the Council to that effect. In the event of the Commission not submitting a proposal, it shall inform the Member States concerned of the reasons for not doing so.

2. Authorisation to establish enhanced cooperation as referred to in paragraph 1 shall be granted, in compliance with Articles 43 to 45 of the Treaty on European Union, by the Council, acting by a qualified majority on a proposal from the Commission and after consulting the European Parliament. When enhanced cooperation relates to an area covered by the procedure referred to in Article 251 of this Treaty, the assent of the European Parliament shall be required.

A member of the Council may request that the matter be referred to the European Council. After that matter has been raised before the European Council, the Council may act in accordance with the first subparagraph of this paragraph.

3. The acts and decisions necessary for the implementation of enhanced cooperation activities shall be subject to all the relevant provisions of this Treaty, save as otherwise provided in this Article and in Articles 43 to 45 of the Treaty on European Union.

Article 11a

Any Member State which wishes to participate in enhanced cooperation established in accordance with Article 11 shall notify its intention to the Council and to the Commission, which shall give an opinion to the Council within three months of the date of receipt of that notification. Within four months of the date of receipt of that notification, the Commission shall take a decision on it, and on such specific arrangements as it may deem necessary."

2. In Article 13, the current text shall become paragraph 1 and the following paragraph 2 shall be added:

"2. By way of derogation from paragraph 1, when the Council adopts Community incentive measures, excluding any harmonisation of the laws and regulations of the Member States, to support action taken by the Member States in order to contribute to the achievement of the objectives referred to in paragraph 1, it shall act in accordance with the procedure referred to in Article 251."

3. Article 18 shall be replaced by the following:

"Article 18

1. Every citizen of the Union shall have the right to move and reside freely within the territory of the Member States, subject to the limitations and conditions laid down in this Treaty and by the measures adopted to give it effect.

2. If action by the Community should prove necessary to attain this objective and this Treaty has not provided the necessary powers, the Council may adopt provisions with a view to facilitating the exercise of the rights referred to in paragraph 1. The Council shall act in accordance with the procedure referred to in Article 251.

3. Paragraph 2 shall not apply to provisions on passports, identity cards, residence permits or any other such document or to provisions on social security or social protection."

4. In Article 67, the following paragraph shall be added:

"5. By derogation from paragraph 1, the Council shall adopt, in accordance with the procedure referred to in Article 251:

— the measures provided for in Article 63(1) and (2)(a) provided that the Council has previously adopted, in accordance with paragraph 1 of this

Article, Community legislation defining the common rules and basic principles governing these issues;

— the measures provided for in Article 65 with the exception of aspects relating to family law."

5. *Article 100 shall be replaced by the following:*

"Article 100

1. Without prejudice to any other procedures provided for in this Treaty, the Council, acting by a qualified majority on a proposal from the Commission, may decide upon the measures appropriate to the economic situation, in particular if severe difficulties arise in the supply of certain products.

2. Where a Member State is in difficulties or is seriously threatened with severe difficulties caused by natural disasters or exceptional occurrences beyond its control, the Council, acting by a qualified majority on a proposal from the Commission, may grant, under certain conditions, Community financial assistance to the Member State concerned. The President of the Council shall inform the European Parliament of the decision taken."

6. *Article 111(4) shall be replaced by the following:*

"4. Subject to paragraph 1, the Council, acting by a qualified majority on a proposal from the Commission and after consulting the ECB, shall decide on the position of the Community at international level as regards issues of particular relevance to economic and monetary union and on its representation, in compliance with the allocation of powers laid down in Articles 99 and 105."

7. *Article 123(4) shall be replaced by the following:*

"4. At the starting date of the third stage, the Council shall, acting with the unanimity of the Member States without a derogation, on a proposal from the Commission and after consulting the ECB, adopt the conversion rates at which their currencies shall be irrevocably fixed and at which irrevocably fixed rate the ECU shall be substituted for these currencies, and the ECU will become a currency in its own right. This measure shall by itself not modify the external value of the ECU. The Council, acting by a qualified majority of the said Member States, on a proposal from the Commission and after consulting the ECB, shall take the other measures necessary for the rapid introduction of the ECU as the single currency of those Member States. The second sentence of Article 122(5) shall apply."

8. *Article 133 shall be replaced by the following:*

"Article 133

1. The common commercial policy shall be based on uniform principles, particularly in regard to changes in tariff rates, the conclusion of tariff and trade agreements, the achievement of uniformity in measures of liberalisation, export policy and measures to protect trade such as those to be taken in the event of dumping or subsidies.

2. The Commission shall submit proposals to the Council for implementing the common commercial policy.

3. Where agreements with one or more States or international organisations need to be negotiated, the Commission shall make recommendations to the Council, which shall authorise the Commission to open the necessary negotiations. The Council and the Commission shall be responsible for ensuring that the agreements negotiated are compatible with internal Community policies and rules.

The Commission shall conduct these negotiations in consultation with a special committee appointed by the Council to assist the Commission in this task and within the framework of such directives as the Council may issue to it. The Commission shall report regularly to the special committee on the progress of negotiations.

The relevant provisions of Article 300 shall apply.

4. In exercising the powers conferred upon it by this Article, the Council shall act by a qualified majority.

5. Paragraphs 1 to 4 shall also apply to the negotiation and conclusion of agreements in the fields of trade in services and the commercial aspects of intellectual property, insofar as those agreements are not covered by the said paragraphs and without prejudice to paragraph 6.

By way of derogation from paragraph 4, the Council shall act unanimously when negotiating and concluding an agreement in one of the fields referred to in the first subparagraph, where that agreement includes provisions for which unanimity is required for the adoption of internal rules or where it relates to a field in which the Community has not yet exercised the powers conferred upon it by this Treaty by adopting internal rules.

The Council shall act unanimously with respect to the negotiation and conclusion of a horizontal agreement insofar as it also concerns the preceding subparagraph or the second subparagraph of paragraph 6.

This paragraph shall not affect the right of the Member States to maintain and conclude agreements with third countries or international organisations insofar as such agreements comply with Community law and other relevant international agreements.

6. An agreement may not be concluded by the Council if it includes provisions which would go beyond the Community's internal powers, in particular by leading to harmonisation of the laws or regulations of the Member States in an area for which this Treaty rules out such harmonisation.

In this regard, by way of derogation from the first subparagraph of paragraph 5, agreements relating to trade in cultural and audiovisual services, educational services, and social and human health services, shall fall within the shared competence of the Community and its Member States. Consequently, in addition to a Community decision taken in accordance with the relevant provisions of Article 300, the negotiation of such agreements shall require the common accord of the Member States. Agreements thus negotiated shall be concluded jointly by the Community and the Member States.

The negotiation and conclusion of international agreements in the field of transport shall continue to be governed by the provisions of Title V and Article 300.

7. Without prejudice to the first subparagraph of paragraph 6, the Council, acting unanimously on a proposal from the Commission and after consulting the European Parliament, may extend the application of paragraphs 1 to 4 to international negotiations and agreements on intellectual property insofar as they are not covered by paragraph 5."

9. *Article 137 shall be replaced by the following:*

"Article 137

1. With a view to achieving the objectives of Article 136, the Community shall support and complement the activities of the Member States in the following fields:

(a) improvement in particular of the working environment to protect workers' health and safety;

(b) working conditions;

(c) social security and social protection of workers;

(d) protection of workers where their employment contract is terminated;

(e) the information and consultation of workers;

(f) representation and collective defence of the interests of workers and employers, including co-determination, subject to paragraph 5;

(g) conditions of employment for third-country nationals legally residing in Community territory;

(h) the integration of persons excluded from the labour market, without prejudice to Article 150;

(i) equality between men and women with regard to labour market opportunities and treatment at work;

(j) the combating of social exclusion;

(k) the modernisation of social protection systems without prejudice to point (c).

2. To this end, the Council:

(a) may adopt measures designed to encourage cooperation between Member States through initiatives aimed at improving knowledge, developing exchanges of information and best practices, promoting innovative approaches and evaluating experiences, excluding any harmonisation of the laws and regulations of the Member States;

(b) may adopt, in the fields referred to in paragraph 1(a) to (i), by means of directives, minimum requirements for gradual implementation, having regard to the conditions and technical rules obtaining in each of the Member States. Such directives shall avoid imposing administrative, financial and legal constraints in a way which would hold back the creation and development of small and medium-sized undertakings.

The Council shall act in accordance with the procedure referred to in Article 251 after consulting the Economic and Social Committee and the Committee of the Regions, except in the fields referred to in paragraph 1(c), (d), (f) and (g) of this Article, where the Council shall act unanimously on a proposal from the Commission, after consulting the European Parliament and the said Committees. The Council, acting unanimously on a proposal from the Commission, after consulting the European Parliament, may decide to render the procedure referred to in Article 251 applicable to paragraph 1(d), (f) and (g) of this Article.

3. A Member State may entrust management and labour, at their joint request, with the implementation of directives adopted pursuant to paragraph 2.

In this case, it shall ensure that, no later than the date on which a directive must be transposed in accordance with Article 249, management and labour have introduced the necessary measures by agreement, the Member State concerned being required to take any necessary measure enabling it at any time to be in a position to guarantee the results imposed by that directive.

4. The provisions adopted pursuant to this Article:

— shall not affect the right of Member States to define the fundamental principles of their social security systems and must not significantly affect the financial equilibrium thereof;

— shall not prevent any Member State from maintaining or introducing more stringent protective measures compatible with this Treaty.

5. The provisions of this Article shall not apply to pay, the right of association, the right to strike or the right to impose lock-outs."

10. *In Article 139(2), the second subparagraph shall be replaced by the following:*

"The Council shall act by a qualified majority, except where the agreement in question contains one or more provisions relating to one of the areas for which unanimity is required pursuant to Article 137(2). In that case, it shall act unanimously."

11. *Article 144 shall be replaced by the following:*

"Article 144

The Council, after consulting the European Parliament, shall establish a Social Protection Committee with advisory status to promote cooperation on social protection policies between Member States and with the Commission. The tasks of the Committee shall be:

— to monitor the social situation and the development of social protection policies in the Member States and the Community;

— to promote exchanges of information, experience and good practice between Member States and with the Commission;

— without prejudice to Article 207, to prepare reports, formulate opinions or undertake other work within its fields of competence, at the request of either the Council or the Commission or on its own initiative.

In fulfilling its mandate, the Committee shall establish appropriate contacts with management and labour.

Each Member State and the Commission shall appoint two members of the Committee."

12. Article 157(3) shall be replaced by the following:

"3. The Community shall contribute to the achievement of the objectives set out in paragraph 1 through the policies and activities it pursues under other provisions of this Treaty. The Council, acting in accordance with the procedure referred to in Article 251 and after consulting the Economic and Social Committee, may decide on specific measures in support of action taken in the Member States to achieve the objectives set out in paragraph 1.

This Title shall not provide a basis for the introduction by the Community of any measure which could lead to a distortion of competition or contains tax provisions or provisions relating to the rights and interests of employed persons."

13. In Article 159, the third paragraph shall be replaced by the following:

"If specific actions prove necessary outside the Funds and without prejudice to the measures decided upon within the framework of the other Community policies, such actions may be adopted by the Council acting in accordance with the procedure referred to in Article 251 and after consulting the Economic and Social Committee and the Committee of the Regions."

14. In Article 161, the following third paragraph shall be added:

"From 1 January 2007, the Council shall act by a qualified majority on a proposal from the Commission after obtaining the assent of the European Parliament and after consulting the Economic and Social Committee and the Committee of the Regions if, by that date, the multiannual financial perspective applicable from 1 January 2007 and the Interinstitutional Agreement relating thereto have been adopted. If such is not the case, the procedure laid down by this paragraph shall apply from the date of their adoption."

15. Article 175(2) shall be replaced by the following:

'2. By way of derogation from the decision-making procedure provided for in paragraph 1 and without prejudice to Article 95, the Council, acting unanimously on a proposal from the Commission and after consulting the

European Parliament, the Economic and Social Committee and the Committee of the Regions, shall adopt:

(a) provisions primarily of a fiscal nature;

(b) measures affecting:

— town and country planning;

— quantitative management of water resources or affecting, directly or indirectly, the availability of those resources;

— land use, with the exception of waste management;

(c) measures significantly affecting a Member State's choice between different energy sources and the general structure of its energy supply.

The Council may, under the conditions laid down in the first subparagraph, define those matters referred to in this paragraph on which decisions are to be taken by a qualified majority.'

16. *In Part Three, the following Title shall be added:*

"Title XXI

ECONOMIC, FINANCIAL AND TECHNICAL COOPERATION WITH THIRD COUNTRIES

Article 181a

1. Without prejudice to the other provisions of this Treaty, and in particular those of Title XX, the Community shall carry out, within its spheres of competence, economic, financial and technical cooperation measures with third countries. Such measures shall be complementary to those carried out by the Member States and consistent with the development policy of the Community.

Community policy in this area shall contribute to the general objective of developing and consolidating democracy and the rule of law, and to the objective of respecting human rights and fundamental freedoms.

2. The Council, acting by a qualified majority on a proposal from the Commission and after consulting the European Parliament, shall adopt the measures necessary for the implementation of paragraph 1. The Council shall act unanimously for the association agreements referred to in Article 310 and for the agreements to be concluded with the States which are candidates for accession to the Union.

3. Within their respective spheres of competence, the Community and the Member States shall cooperate with third countries and the competent international organisations. The arrangements for Community cooperation may be the subject of agreements between the Community and the third parties concerned, which shall be negotiated and concluded in accordance with Article 300.

The first subparagraph shall be without prejudice to the Member States' competence to negotiate in international bodies and to conclude international agreements."

17. In Article 189, the second paragraph shall be replaced by the following:

"The number of Members of the European Parliament shall not exceed 732."

18. Article 190(5) shall be replaced by the following:

"5. The European Parliament, after seeking an opinion from the Commission and with the approval of the Council acting by a qualified majority, shall lay down the regulations and general conditions governing the performance of the duties of its Members. All rules or conditions relating to the taxation of Members or former Members shall require unanimity within the Council."

19. In Article 191, the following second paragraph shall be added:

"The Council, acting in accordance with the procedure referred to in Article 251, shall lay down the regulations governing political parties at European level and in particular the rules regarding their funding."

20. Article 207(2) shall be replaced by the following:

"2. The Council shall be assisted by a General Secretariat, under the responsibility of a Secretary–General, High Representative for the common foreign and security policy, who shall be assisted by a Deputy Secretary–General responsible for the running of the General Secretariat. The Secretary–General and the Deputy Secretary–General shall be appointed by the Council, acting by a qualified majority.

The Council shall decide on the organisation of the General Secretariat."

21. Article 210 shall be replaced by the following:

"Article 210

The Council shall, acting by a qualified majority, determine the salaries, allowances and pensions of the President and Members of the Commission, and of the President, Judges, Advocates–General and Registrar of the Court of Justice and of the Members and Registrar of the Court of First Instance. It shall also, again by a qualified majority, determine any payment to be made instead of remuneration."

22. Article 214(2) shall be replaced by the following:

"2. The Council, meeting in the composition of Heads of State or Government and acting by a qualified majority, shall nominate the person it intends to appoint as President of the Commission; the nomination shall be approved by the European Parliament.

The Council, acting by a qualified majority and by common accord with the nominee for President, shall adopt the list of the other persons whom it intends to appoint as Members of the Commission, drawn up in accordance with the proposals made by each Member State.

The President and the other Members of the Commission thus nominated shall be subject as a body to a vote of approval by the European Parliament. After approval by the European Parliament, the President and the other Members of the Commission shall be appointed by the Council, acting by a qualified majority."

23. *Article 215 shall be replaced by the following:*

"Article 215

Apart from normal replacement, or death, the duties of a Member of the Commission shall end when he resigns or is compulsorily retired.

A vacancy caused by resignation, compulsory retirement or death shall be filled for the remainder of the Member's term of office by a new Member appointed by the Council, acting by a qualified majority. The Council may, acting unanimously, decide that such a vacancy need not be filled.

In the event of resignation, compulsory retirement or death, the President shall be replaced for the remainder of his term of office. The procedure laid down in Article 214(2) shall be applicable for the replacement of the President.

Save in the case of compulsory retirement under Article 216, Members of the Commission shall remain in office until they have been replaced or until the Council has decided that the vacancy need not be filled, as provided for in the second paragraph of this Article."

24. *Article 217 shall be replaced by the following:*

"Article 217

1. The Commission shall work under the political guidance of its President, who shall decide on its internal organisation in order to ensure that it acts consistently, efficiently and on the basis of collegiality.

2. The responsibilities incumbent upon the Commission shall be structured and allocated among its Members by its President. The President may reshuffle the allocation of those responsibilities during the Commission's term of office. The Members of the Commission shall carry out the duties devolved upon them by the President under his authority.

3. After obtaining the approval of the College, the President shall appoint Vice-Presidents from among its Members.

4. A Member of the Commission shall resign if the President so requests, after obtaining the approval of the College."

25. *In Article 219, the first paragraph shall be deleted.*

26. *Article 220 shall be replaced by the following:*

"Article 220

The Court of Justice and the Court of First Instance, each within its jurisdiction, shall ensure that in the interpretation and application of this Treaty the law is observed.

In addition, judicial panels may be attached to the Court of First Instance under the conditions laid down in Article 225a in order to exercise, in certain specific areas, the judicial competence laid down in this Treaty."

27. Article 221 shall be replaced by the following:

"Article 221

The Court of Justice shall consist of one judge per Member State.

The Court of Justice shall sit in chambers or in a Grand Chamber, in accordance with the rules laid down for that purpose in the Statute of the Court of Justice.

When provided for in the Statute, the Court of Justice may also sit as a full Court."

28. Article 222 shall be replaced by the following:

"Article 222

The Court of Justice shall be assisted by eight Advocates–General. Should the Court of Justice so request, the Council, acting unanimously, may increase the number of Advocates–General.

It shall be the duty of the Advocate–General, acting with complete impartiality and independence, to make, in open court, reasoned submissions on cases which, in accordance with the Statute of the Court of Justice, require his involvement."

29. Article 223 shall be replaced by the following:

"Article 223

The Judges and Advocates–General of the Court of Justice shall be chosen from persons whose independence is beyond doubt and who possess the qualifications required for appointment to the highest judicial offices in their respective countries or who are jurisconsults of recognised competence; they shall be appointed by common accord of the governments of the Member States for a term of six years.

Every three years there shall be a partial replacement of the Judges and Advocates–General, in accordance with the conditions laid down in the Statute of the Court of Justice.

The Judges shall elect the President of the Court of Justice from among their number for a term of three years. He may be re-elected.

Retiring Judges and Advocates–General may be reappointed.

The Court of Justice shall appoint its Registrar and lay down the rules governing his service.

The Court of Justice shall establish its Rules of Procedure. Those Rules shall require the approval of the Council, acting by a qualified majority."

30. Article 224 shall be replaced by the following:

"Article 224

The Court of First Instance shall comprise at least one judge per Member State. The number of Judges shall be determined by the Statute of the Court of Justice. The Statute may provide for the Court of First Instance to be assisted by Advocates–General.

The members of the Court of First Instance shall be chosen from persons whose independence is beyond doubt and who possess the ability required for appointment to high judicial office. They shall be appointed by common accord of the governments of the Member States for a term of six years. The membership shall be partially renewed every three years. Retiring members shall be eligible for reappointment.

The Judges shall elect the President of the Court of First Instance from among their number for a term of three years. He may be re-elected.

The Court of First Instance shall appoint its Registrar and lay down the rules governing his service.

The Court of First Instance shall establish its Rules of Procedure in agreement with the Court of Justice. Those Rules shall require the approval of the Council, acting by a qualified majority.

Unless the Statute of the Court of Justice provides otherwise, the provisions of this Treaty relating to the Court of Justice shall apply to the Court of First Instance."

31. *Article 225 shall be replaced by the following:*

"Article 225

1. The Court of First Instance shall have jurisdiction to hear and determine at first instance actions or proceedings referred to in Articles 230, 232, 235, 236 and 238, with the exception of those assigned to a judicial panel and those reserved in the Statute for the Court of Justice. The Statute may provide for the Court of First Instance to have jurisdiction for other classes of action or proceeding.

Decisions given by the Court of First Instance under this paragraph may be subject to a right of appeal to the Court of Justice on points of law only, under the conditions and within the limits laid down by the Statute.

2. The Court of First Instance shall have jurisdiction to hear and determine actions or proceedings brought against decisions of the judicial panels set up under Article 225a.

Decisions given by the Court of First Instance under this paragraph may exceptionally be subject to review by the Court of Justice, under the conditions and within the limits laid down by the Statute, where there is a serious risk of the unity or consistency of Community law being affected.

3. The Court of First Instance shall have jurisdiction to hear and determine questions referred for a preliminary ruling under Article 234, in specific areas laid down by the Statute.

Where the Court of First Instance considers that the case requires a decision of principle likely to affect the unity or consistency of Community law, it may refer the case to the Court of Justice for a ruling.

Decisions given by the Court of First Instance on questions referred for a preliminary ruling may exceptionally be subject to review by the Court of Justice, under the conditions and within the limits laid down by the Statute, where there is a serious risk of the unity or consistency of Community law being affected."

32. The following Article shall be inserted:

"Article 225a

The Council, acting unanimously on a proposal from the Commission and after consulting the European Parliament and the Court of Justice or at the request of the Court of Justice and after consulting the European Parliament and the Commission, may create judicial panels to hear and determine at first instance certain classes of action or proceeding brought in specific areas.

The decision establishing a judicial panel shall lay down the rules on the organisation of the panel and the extent of the jurisdiction conferred upon it.

Decisions given by judicial panels may be subject to a right of appeal on points of law only or, when provided for in the decision establishing the panel, a right of appeal also on matters of fact, before the Court of First Instance.

The members of the judicial panels shall be chosen from persons whose independence is beyond doubt and who possess the ability required for appointment to judicial office. They shall be appointed by the Council, acting unanimously.

The judicial panels shall establish their Rules of Procedure in agreement with the Court of Justice. Those Rules shall require the approval of the Council, acting by a qualified majority.

Unless the decision establishing the judicial panel provides otherwise, the provisions of this Treaty relating to the Court of Justice and the provisions of the Statute of the Court of Justice shall apply to the judicial panels."

33. The following Article shall be inserted:

"Article 229a

Without prejudice to the other provisions of this Treaty, the Council, acting unanimously on a proposal from the Commission and after consulting the European Parliament, may adopt provisions to confer jurisdiction, to the extent that it shall determine, on the Court of Justice in disputes relating to the application of acts adopted on the basis of this Treaty which create Community industrial property rights. The Council shall recommend those provisions to the Member States for adoption in accordance with their respective constitutional requirements."

34. In Article 230, the second and third paragraphs shall be replaced by the following:

"It shall for this purpose have jurisdiction in actions brought by a Member State, the European Parliament, the Council or the Commission on grounds of lack of competence, infringement of an essential procedural requirement, infringement of this Treaty or of any rule of law relating to its application, or misuse of powers.

The Court of Justice shall have jurisdiction under the same conditions in actions brought by the Court of Auditors and by the ECB for the purpose of protecting their prerogatives."

35. *Article 245 shall be replaced by the following:*

"Article 245

The Statute of the Court of Justice shall be laid down in a separate Protocol.

The Council, acting unanimously at the request of the Court of Justice and after consulting the European Parliament and the Commission, or at the request of the Commission and after consulting the European Parliament and the Court of Justice, may amend the provisions of the Statute, with the exception of Title I."

36. *Article 247 shall be amended as follows:*

   (a) Paragraph 1 shall be replaced by the following:

"1. The Court of Auditors shall consist of one national from each Member State.";

   (b) Paragraph 3 shall be replaced by the following:

"3. The Members of the Court of Auditors shall be appointed for a term of six years. The Council, acting by a qualified majority after consulting the European Parliament, shall adopt the list of Members drawn up in accordance with the proposals made by each Member State. The term of office of the Members of the Court of Auditors shall be renewable.

They shall elect the President of the Court of Auditors from among their number for a term of three years. The President may be re-elected."

37. *Article 248 shall be amended as follows:*

   (a) paragraph 1 shall be replaced by the following:

"1. The Court of Auditors shall examine the accounts of all revenue and expenditure of the Community. It shall also examine the accounts of all revenue and expenditure of all bodies set up by the Community insofar as the relevant constituent instrument does not preclude such examination.

The Court of Auditors shall provide the European Parliament and the Council with a statement of assurance as to the reliability of the accounts and the legality and regularity of the underlying transactions which shall be published in the Official Journal of the European Union. This statement may be supplemented by specific assessments for each major area of Community activity.";

   (b) paragraph 4 shall be replaced by the following:

"4. The Court of Auditors shall draw up an annual report after the close of each financial year. It shall be forwarded to the other institutions of the Community and shall be published, together with the replies of these institutions to the observations of the Court of Auditors, in the Official Journal of the European Union.

The Court of Auditors may also, at any time, submit observations, particularly in the form of special reports, on specific questions and deliver opinions at the request of one of the other institutions of the Community.

It shall adopt its annual reports, special reports or opinions by a majority of its Members. However, it may establish internal chambers in order to adopt certain categories of reports or opinions under the conditions laid down by its Rules of Procedure.

It shall assist the European Parliament and the Council in exercising their powers of control over the implementation of the budget.

The Court of Auditors shall draw up its Rules of Procedure. Those rules shall require the approval of the Council, acting by a qualified majority."

38. In Article 254(1) and (2), the words Official Journal of the European Communities shall be replaced by Official Journal of the European Union.

39. Article 257 shall be replaced by the following:

"Article 257

An Economic and Social Committee is hereby established. It shall have advisory status.

The Committee shall consist of representatives of the various economic and social components of organised civil society, and in particular representatives of producers, farmers, carriers, workers, dealers, craftsmen, professional occupations, consumers and the general interest."

40. Article 258 shall be replaced by the following:

"Article 258

The number of members of the Economic and Social Committee shall not exceed 350.

The number of members of the Committee shall be as follows:

Belgium	12	France	24	Austria	12
Denmark	9	Ireland	9	Portugal	12
Germany	24	Italy	24	Finland	9
Greece	12	Luxembourg	6	Sweden	12
Spain	21	Netherlands	12	United Kingdom	24

The members of the Committee may not be bound by any mandatory instructions. They shall be completely independent in the performance of their duties, in the general interest of the Community.

The Council, acting by a qualified majority, shall determine the allowances of members of the Committee."

41. In Article 259, paragraph 1 shall be replaced by the following:

"1. The members of the Committee shall be appointed for four years, on proposals from the Member States. The Council, acting by a qualified majority, shall adopt the list of members drawn up in accordance with the proposals made by each Member State. The term of office of the members of the Committee shall be renewable."

42. *Article 263 shall be replaced by the following:*

"Article 263

A Committee, hereinafter referred to as "the Committee of the Regions", consisting of representatives of regional and local bodies who either hold a regional or local authority electoral mandate or are politically accountable to an elected assembly, is hereby established with advisory status.

The number of members of the Committee of the Regions shall not exceed 350.

The number of members of the Committee shall be as follows:

Belgium	12	France	24	Austria	12
Denmark	9	Ireland	9	Portugal	12
Germany	24	Italy	24	Finland	9
Greece	12	Luxembourg	6	Sweden	12
Spain	21	Netherlands	12	United Kingdom	24

The members of the Committee and an equal number of alternate members shall be appointed for four years, on proposals from the respective Member States. Their term of office shall be renewable. The Council, acting by a qualified majority, shall adopt the list of members and alternate members drawn up in accordance with the proposals made by each Member State. When the mandate referred to in the first paragraph on the basis of which they were proposed comes to an end, the term of office of members of the Committee shall terminate automatically and they shall then be replaced for the remainder of the said term of office in accordance with the same procedure. No member of the Committee shall at the same time be a Member of the European Parliament.

The members of the Committee may not be bound by any mandatory instructions. They shall be completely independent in the performance of their duties, in the general interest of the Community."

43. *Article 266 shall be replaced by the following:*

"Article 266

The European Investment Bank shall have legal personality.

The members of the European Investment Bank shall be the Member States.

The Statute of the European Investment Bank is laid down in a Protocol annexed to this Treaty. The Council, acting unanimously, at the request of the European Investment Bank and after consulting the European Parliament and the Commission, or at the request of the Commission and after consulting the European Parliament and the European Investment Bank, may amend Articles 4, 11 and 12 and Article 18(5) of the Statute of the Bank."

44. *Article 279 shall be replaced by the following:*

"Article 279

1. The Council, acting unanimously on a proposal from the Commission and after consulting the European Parliament and obtaining the opinion of the Court of Auditors, shall:

(a) make Financial Regulations specifying in particular the procedure to be adopted for establishing and implementing the budget and for presenting and auditing accounts;

(b) lay down rules concerning the responsibility of financial controllers, authorising officers and accounting officers, and concerning appropriate arrangements for inspection.

From 1 January 2007, the Council shall act by a qualified majority on a proposal from the Commission and after consulting the European Parliament and obtaining the opinion of the Court of Auditors.

2. The Council, acting unanimously on a proposal from the Commission and after consulting the European Parliament and obtaining the opinion of the Court of Auditors, shall determine the methods and procedure whereby the budget revenue provided under the arrangements relating to the Community's own resources shall be made available to the Commission, and determine the measures to be applied, if need be, to meet cash requirements."

45. Article 290 shall be replaced by the following:

"Article 290

The rules governing the languages of the institutions of the Community shall, without prejudice to the provisions contained in the Statute of the Court of Justice, be determined by the Council, acting unanimously."

46. Article 300 shall be amended as follows:

(a) in paragraph 2, the second and third subparagraphs shall be replaced by the following:

"By way of derogation from the rules laid down in paragraph 3, the same procedures shall apply for a decision to suspend the application of an agreement, and for the purpose of establishing the positions to be adopted on behalf of the Community in a body set up by an agreement, when that body is called upon to adopt decisions having legal effects, with the exception of decisions supplementing or amending the institutional framework of the agreement.

The European Parliament shall be immediately and fully informed of any decision under this paragraph concerning the provisional application or the suspension of agreements, or the establishment of the Community position in a body set up by an agreement";

(b) paragraph 6 shall be replaced by the following:

"6. The European Parliament, the Council, the Commission or a Member State may obtain the opinion of the Court of Justice as to whether an agreement envisaged is compatible with the provisions of this Treaty. Where the opinion of the Court of Justice is adverse, the agreement may enter into force only in accordance with Article 48 of the Treaty on European Union."

47. Article 309 shall be amended as follows:

(a) in paragraph 1, the terms 'Article 7(2)' shall be replaced by 'Article 7(3)';

(b) in paragraph 2, the terms 'Article 7(1)' shall be replaced by 'Article 7(2)'.

[Articles 3 and 4 contain amendments, respectively, to the Treaty Establishing the European Atomic Energy Community Treaty and the Treaty Establishing the European Coal and Steel Community. Article 5 amends the Protocol on the Statute of the European System of Central Banks and of the European Central Bank. Article 6 amends the Protocol on the privileges and immunities of the European Communities.]

PART TWO: TRANSITIONAL AND FINAL PROVISIONS

Article 7

The Protocols on the Statute of the Court of Justice annexed to the Treaty establishing the European Community and to the Treaty establishing the European Atomic Energy Community are hereby repealed and replaced by the Protocol on the Statute of the Court of Justice annexed by this Treaty to the Treaty on European Union, to the Treaty establishing the European Community and to the Treaty establishing the European Atomic Energy Community.

* * *

Article 11

This Treaty is concluded for an unlimited period.

Article 12

. . .

2. This Treaty shall enter into force on the first day of the second month following that in which the instrument of ratification is deposited by the last signatory State to fulfil that formality.

PROTOCOLS

PROTOCOL ANNEXED TO THE TREATY ON EUROPEAN UNION AND TO THE TREATIES ESTABLISHING THE EUROPEAN COMMUNITIES ON THE ENLARGEMENT OF THE EUROPEAN UNION

Article 1. Repeal of the Protocol on the institutions

The Protocol on the institutions with the prospect of enlargement of the European Union, annexed to the Treaty on European Union and to the Treaties establishing the European Communities, is hereby repealed.

Article 2. Provisions concerning the European Parliament

1. On 1 January 2004 and with effect from the start of the 2004–2009 term, in Article 190(2) of the Treaty establishing the European Community

and in Article 108(2) of the Treaty establishing the European Atomic Energy Community, the first subparagraph shall be replaced by the following:

"The number of representatives elected in each Member State shall be as follows:

Belgium	22	France	72	Austria	17
Denmark	13	Ireland	12	Portugal	22
Germany	99	Italy	72	Finland	13
Greece	22	Luxembourg	6	Sweden	18
Spain	50	Netherlands	25	United Kingdom	72"

2. Subject to paragraph 3, the total number of representatives in the European Parliament for the 2004–2009 term shall be equal to the number of representatives specified in Article 190(2) of the Treaty establishing the European Community and in Article 108(2) of the Treaty establishing the European Atomic Energy Community plus the number of representatives of the new Member States resulting from the accession treaties signed by 1 January 2004 at the latest.

3. If the total number of members referred to in paragraph 2 is less than 732, a pro rata correction shall be applied to the number of representatives to be elected in each Member State, so that the total number is as close as possible to 732, without such a correction leading to the number of representatives to be elected in each Member State being higher than that provided for in Article 190(2) of the Treaty establishing the European Community and in Article 108(2) of the Treaty establishing the European Atomic Energy Community for the 1999–2004 term.

The Council shall adopt a decision to that effect.

4. By way of derogation from the second paragraph of Article 189 of the Treaty establishing the European Community and from the second paragraph of Article 107 of the Treaty establishing the European Atomic Energy Community, in the event of the entry into force of accession treaties after the adoption of the Council decision provided for in the second subparagraph of paragraph 3 of this Article, the number of members of the European Parliament may temporarily exceed 732 for the period for which that decision applies. The same correction as that referred to in the first subparagraph of paragraph 3 of this Article shall be applied to the number of representatives to be elected in the Member States in question.

Article 3: Provisions concerning the weighting of votes in the Council

1. On 1 January 2005:

(a) in Article 205 of the Treaty establishing the European Community and in Article 118 of the Treaty establishing the European Atomic Energy Community:

(i) paragraph 2 shall be replaced by the following:

"2. Where the Council is required to act by a qualified majority, the votes of its members shall be weighted as follows:

Belgium	12	France	29	Austria	10
Denmark	7	Ireland	7	Portugal	12
Germany	29	Italy	29	Finland	7
Greece	12	Luxembourg	4	Sweden	10
Spain	27	Netherlands	13	United Kingdom	29

Acts of the Council shall require for their adoption at least 169 votes in favour cast by a majority of the members where this Treaty requires them to be adopted on a proposal from the Commission.

In other cases, for their adoption acts of the Council shall require at least 169 votes in favour, cast by at least two-thirds of the members."

(ii) the following paragraph 4 shall be added:

"4. When a decision is to be adopted by the Council by a qualified majority, a member of the Council may request verification that the Member States constituting the qualified majority represent at least 62% of the total population of the Union. If that condition is shown not to have been met, the decision in question shall not be adopted."

(b) In Article 23(2) of the Treaty on European Union, the third subparagraph shall be replaced by the following text:

"The votes of the members of the Council shall be weighted in accordance with Article 205(2) of the Treaty establishing the European Community. For their adoption, decisions shall require at least 169 votes in favour cast by at least two-thirds of the members. When a decision is to be adopted by the Council by a qualified majority, a member of the Council may request verification that the Member States constituting the qualified majority represent at least 62% of the total population of the Union. If that condition is shown not to have been met, the decision in question shall not be adopted."

(c) In Article 34 of the Treaty on European Union, paragraph 3 shall be replaced by the following:

"3. Where the Council is required to act by a qualified majority, the votes of its members shall be weighted as laid down in Article 205(2) of the Treaty establishing the European Community, and for their adoption acts of the Council shall require at least 169 votes in favour, cast by at least two-thirds of the members. When a decision is to be adopted by the Council by a qualified majority, a member of the Council may request verification that the Member States constituting the qualified majority represent at least 62% of the total population of the Union. If that condition is shown not to have been met, the decision in question shall not be adopted."

2. At the time of each accession, the threshold referred to in the second subparagraph of Article 205(2) of the Treaty establishing the European Community and in the second subparagraph of Article 118(2) of the Treaty establishing the European Atomic Energy Community shall be

calculated in such a way that the qualified majority threshold expressed in votes does not exceed the threshold resulting from the table in the Declaration on the enlargement of the European Union, included in the Final Act of the Conference which adopted the Treaty of Nice.

Article 4: Provisions concerning the Commission

1. On 1 January 2005 and with effect from when the first Commission following that date takes up its duties, Article 213(1) of the Treaty establishing the European Community and Article 126(1) of the Treaty establishing the European Atomic Energy Community shall be replaced by the following:

"1. The Members of the Commission shall be chosen on the grounds of their general competence and their independence shall be beyond doubt.

The Commission shall include one national of each of the Member States.

The number of Members of the Commission may be altered by the Council, acting unanimously."

2. When the Union consists of 27 Member States, Article 213(1) of the Treaty establishing the European Community and Article 126(1) of the Treaty establishing the European Atomic Energy Community shall be replaced by the following:

"1. The Members of the Commission shall be chosen on the grounds of their general competence and their independence shall be beyond doubt.

The number of Members of the Commission shall be less than the number of Member States. The Members of the Commission shall be chosen according to a rotation system based on the principle of equality, the implementing arrangements for which shall be adopted by the Council, acting unanimously.

The number of Members of the Commission shall be set by the Council, acting unanimously."

This amendment shall apply as from the date on which the first Commission following the date of accession of the twenty-seventh Member State of the Union takes up its duties.

3. The Council, acting unanimously after signing the treaty of accession of the twenty-seventh Member State of the Union, shall adopt:

— the number of Members of the Commission;

— the implementing arrangements for a rotation system based on the principle of equality containing all the criteria and rules necessary for determining the composition of successive colleges automatically on the basis of the following principles:

(a) Member States shall be treated on a strictly equal footing as regards determination of the sequence of, and the time spent by, their nationals as Members of the Commission; consequently, the difference between the total number of terms of office held by nationals of any given pair of Member States may never be more than one;

(b) subject to point (a), each successive college shall be so composed as to reflect satisfactorily the demographic and geographical range of all the Member States of the Union.

4. Any State which accedes to the Union shall be entitled, at the time of its accession, to have one of its nationals as a Member of the Commission until paragraph 2 applies.

PROTOCOL ANNEXED TO THE TREATY ON EUROPEAN UNION, TO THE TREATY ESTABLISHING THE EUROPEAN COMMUNITY AND TO THE TREATY ESTABLISHING THE EUROPEAN ATOMIC ENERGY COMMUNITY ON THE STATUTE OF THE COURT OF JUSTICE

[This Protocol would, upon ratification of the Treaty of Nice, replace the existing Statute of the Court of Justice, document 5 in this Supplement.]

Article 1

The Court of Justice shall be constituted and shall function in accordance with the provisions of the Treaty on European Union (EU Treaty), of the Treaty establishing the European Community (EC Treaty), of the Treaty establishing the European Atomic Energy Community (EAEC Treaty) and of this Statute.

TITLE I: JUDGES AND ADVOCATES–GENERAL

Article 2

Before taking up his duties each Judge shall, in open court, take an oath to perform his duties impartially and conscientiously and to preserve the secrecy of the deliberations of the Court.

Article 3

The Judges shall be immune from legal proceedings. After they have ceased to hold office, they shall continue to enjoy immunity in respect of acts performed by them in their official capacity, including words spoken or written.

The Court, sitting as a full Court, may waive the immunity.

Where immunity has been waived and criminal proceedings are instituted against a Judge, he shall be tried, in any of the Member States, only by the court competent to judge the members of the highest national judiciary.

Articles 12 to 15 and Article 18 of the Protocol on the privileges and immunities of the European Communities shall apply to the Judges, Advocates–General, Registrar and Assistant Rapporteurs of the Court, without prejudice to the provisions relating to immunity from legal proceedings of Judges which are set out in the preceding paragraphs.

Article 4

The Judges may not hold any political or administrative office.

They may not engage in any occupation, whether gainful or not, unless exemption is exceptionally granted by the Council.

When taking up their duties, they shall give a solemn undertaking that, both during and after their term of office, they will respect the obligations arising therefrom, in particular the duty to behave with integrity and discretion as regards the acceptance, after they have ceased to hold office, of certain appointments or benefits.

Any doubt on this point shall be settled by decision of the Court.

Article 5

Apart from normal replacement, or death, the duties of a Judge shall end when he resigns.

Where a Judge resigns, his letter of resignation shall be addressed to the President of the Court for transmission to the President of the Council. Upon this notification a vacancy shall arise on the bench.

Save where Article 6 applies, a Judge shall continue to hold office until his successor takes up his duties.

Article 6

A Judge may be deprived of his office or of his right to a pension or other benefits in its stead only if, in the unanimous opinion of the Judges and Advocates–General of the Court, he no longer fulfils the requisite conditions or meets the obligations arising from his office. The Judge concerned shall not take part in any such deliberations.

The Registrar of the Court shall communicate the decision of the Court to the President of the European Parliament and to the President of the Commission and shall notify it to the President of the Council.

In the case of a decision depriving a Judge of his office, a vacancy shall arise on the bench upon this latter notification.

Article 7

A Judge who is to replace a member of the Court whose term of office has not expired shall be appointed for the remainder of his predecessor's term.

Article 8

The provisions of Articles 2 to 7 shall apply to the Advocates–General.

TITLE II: ORGANISATION

Article 9

When, every three years, the Judges are partially replaced, eight and seven Judges shall be replaced alternately.

When, every three years, the Advocates–General are partially replaced, four Advocates–General shall be replaced on each occasion.

Article 10

The Registrar shall take an oath before the Court to perform his duties impartially and conscientiously and to preserve the secrecy of the deliberations of the Court.

Article 11

The Court shall arrange for replacement of the Registrar on occasions when he is prevented from attending the Court.

Article 12

Officials and other servants shall be attached to the Court to enable it to function. They shall be responsible to the Registrar under the authority of the President.

Article 13

On a proposal from the Court, the Council may, acting unanimously, provide for the appointment of Assistant Rapporteurs and lay down the rules governing their service. The Assistant Rapporteurs may be required, under conditions laid down in the Rules of Procedure, to participate in preparatory inquiries in cases pending before the Court and to cooperate with the Judge who acts as Rapporteur.

The Assistant Rapporteurs shall be chosen from persons whose independence is beyond doubt and who possess the necessary legal qualifications; they shall be appointed by the Council. They shall take an oath before the Court to perform their duties impartially and conscientiously and to preserve the secrecy of the deliberations of the Court.

Article 14

The Judges, the Advocates–General and the Registrar shall be required to reside at the place where the Court has its seat.

Article 15

The Court shall remain permanently in session. The duration of the judicial vacations shall be determined by the Court with due regard to the needs of its business.

Article 16

The Court shall form chambers consisting of three and five Judges. The Judges shall elect the Presidents of the chambers from among their number. The Presidents of the chambers of five Judges shall be elected for three years. They may be re-elected once.

The Grand Chamber shall consist of eleven Judges. It shall be presided over by the President of the Court. The Presidents of the chambers of five

Judges and other Judges appointed in accordance with the conditions laid down in the Rules of Procedure shall also form part of the Grand Chamber.

The Court shall sit in a Grand Chamber when a Member State or an institution of the Communities that is party to the proceedings so requests.

The Court shall sit as a full Court where cases are brought before it pursuant to Article 195(2), Article 213(2), Article 216 or Article 247(7) of the EC Treaty or Article 107d(2), Article 126(2), Article 129 or Article 160b(7) of the EAEC Treaty.

Moreover, where it considers that a case before it is of exceptional importance, the Court may decide, after hearing the Advocate–General, to refer the case to the full Court.

Article 17

Decisions of the Court shall be valid only when an uneven number of its members is sitting in the deliberations.

Decisions of the chambers consisting of either three or five Judges shall be valid only if they are taken by three Judges.

Decisions of the Grand Chamber shall be valid only if nine Judges are sitting.

Decisions of the full Court shall be valid only if eleven Judges are sitting.

In the event of one of the Judges of a chamber being prevented from attending, a Judge of another chamber may be called upon to sit in accordance with conditions laid down in the Rules of Procedure.

Article 18

No Judge or Advocate–General may take part in the disposal of any case in which he has previously taken part as agent or adviser or has acted for one of the parties, or in which he has been called upon to pronounce as a member of a court or tribunal, of a commission of inquiry or in any other capacity.

If, for some special reason, any Judge or Advocate–General considers that he should not take part in the judgment or examination of a particular case, he shall so inform the President. If, for some special reason, the President considers that any Judge or Advocate–General should not sit or make submissions in a particular case, he shall notify him accordingly.

Any difficulty arising as to the application of this Article shall be settled by decision of the Court.

A party may not apply for a change in the composition of the Court or of one of its chambers on the grounds of either the nationality of a Judge or the absence from the Court or from the chamber of a Judge of the nationality of that party.

TITLE III: PROCEDURE

Article 19

The Member States and the institutions of the Communities shall be represented before the Court by an agent appointed for each case; the agent may be assisted by an adviser or by a lawyer.

The States, other than the Member States, which are parties to the Agreement on the European Economic Area and also the EFTA Surveillance Authority referred to in that Agreement shall be represented in same manner.

Other parties must be represented by a lawyer.

Only a lawyer authorised to practise before a court of a Member State or of another State which is a party to the Agreement on the European Economic Area may represent or assist a party before the Court.

Such agents, advisers and lawyers shall, when they appear before the Court, enjoy the rights and immunities necessary to the independent exercise of their duties, under conditions laid down in the Rules of Procedure.

As regards such advisers and lawyers who appear before it, the Court shall have the powers normally accorded to courts of law, under conditions laid down in the Rules of Procedure.

University teachers being nationals of a Member State whose law accords them a right of audience shall have the same rights before the Court as are accorded by this Article to lawyers.

Article 20

The procedure before the Court shall consist of two parts: written and oral.

The written procedure shall consist of the communication to the parties and to the institutions of the Communities whose decisions are in dispute, of applications, statements of case, defences and observations, and of replies, if any, as well as of all papers and documents in support or of certified copies of them.

Communications shall be made by the Registrar in the order and within the time laid down in the Rules of Procedure.

The oral procedure shall consist of the reading of the report presented by a Judge acting as Rapporteur, the hearing by the Court of agents, advisers and lawyers and of the submissions of the Advocate–General, as well as the hearing, if any, of witnesses and experts.

Where it considers that the case raises no new point of law, the Court may decide, after hearing the Advocate–General, that the case shall be determined without a submission from the Advocate–General.

Article 21

A case shall be brought before the Court by a written application addressed to the Registrar. The application shall contain the applicant's name and permanent address and the description of the signatory, the name of the party or names of the parties against whom the application is made, the subject-matter of the dispute, the form of order sought and a brief statement of the pleas in law on which the application is based.

The application shall be accompanied, where appropriate, by the measure the annulment of which is sought or, in the circumstances referred to in Article 232 of the EC Treaty and Article 148 of the EAEC Treaty, by documentary evidence of the date on which an institution was, in accordance with those Articles, requested to act. If the documents are not submitted with the application, the Registrar shall ask the party concerned to produce them within a reasonable period, but in that event the rights of the party shall not lapse even if such documents are produced after the time-limit for bringing proceedings.

Article 22

A case governed by Article 18 of the EAEC Treaty shall be brought before the Court by an appeal addressed to the Registrar. The appeal shall contain the name and permanent address of the applicant and the description of the signatory, a reference to the decision against which the appeal is brought, the names of the respondents, the subject-matter of the dispute, the submissions and a brief statement of the grounds on which the appeal is based.

The appeal shall be accompanied by a certified copy of the decision of the Arbitration Committee which is contested.

If the Court rejects the appeal, the decision of the Arbitration Committee shall become final.

If the Court annuls the decision of the Arbitration Committee, the matter may be re-opened, where appropriate, on the initiative of one of the parties in the case, before the Arbitration Committee. The latter shall conform to any decisions on points of law given by the Court.

Article 23

In the cases governed by Article 35(1) of the EU Treaty, by Article 234 of the EC Treaty and by Article 150 of the EAEC Treaty, the decision of the court or tribunal of a Member State which suspends its proceedings and refers a case to the Court shall be notified to the Court by the court or tribunal concerned. The decision shall then be notified by the Registrar of the Court to the parties, to the Member States and to the Commission, and also to the Council or to the European Central Bank if the act the validity or interpretation of which is in dispute originates from one of them, and to the European Parliament and the Council if the act the validity or interpretation of which is in dispute was adopted jointly by those two institutions.

Within two months of this notification, the parties, the Member States, the Commission and, where appropriate, the European Parliament, the Council and the European Central Bank, shall be entitled to submit statements of case or written observations to the Court.

In the cases governed by Article 234 of the EC Treaty, the decision of the national court or tribunal shall, moreover, be notified by the Registrar of the Court to the States, other than the Member States, which are parties to the Agreement on the European Economic Area and also to the EFTA Surveillance Authority referred to in that Agreement which may, within two months of notification, where one of the fields of application of that Agreement is concerned, submit statements of case or written observations to the Court.

Article 24

The Court may require the parties to produce all documents and to supply all information which the Court considers desirable. Formal note shall be taken of any refusal.

The Court may also require the Member States and institutions not being parties to the case to supply all information which the Court considers necessary for the proceedings.

Article 25

The Court may at any time entrust any individual, body, authority, committee or other organisation it chooses with the task of giving an expert opinion.

Article 26

Witnesses may be heard under conditions laid down in the Rules of Procedure.

Article 27

With respect to defaulting witnesses the Court shall have the powers generally granted to courts and tribunals and may impose pecuniary penalties under conditions laid down in the Rules of Procedure.

Article 28

Witnesses and experts may be heard on oath taken in the form laid down in the Rules of Procedure or in the manner laid down by the law of the country of the witness or expert.

Article 29

The Court may order that a witness or expert be heard by the judicial authority of his place of permanent residence.

The order shall be sent for implementation to the competent judicial authority under conditions laid down in the Rules of Procedure. The documents drawn up in compliance with the letters rogatory shall be returned to the Court under the same conditions.

The Court shall defray the expenses, without prejudice to the right to charge them, where appropriate, to the parties.

Article 30

A Member State shall treat any violation of an oath by a witness or expert in the same manner as if the offence had been committed before one of its courts with jurisdiction in civil proceedings. At the instance of the Court, the Member State concerned shall prosecute the offender before its competent court.

Article 31

The hearing in court shall be public, unless the Court, of its own motion or on application by the parties, decides otherwise for serious reasons.

Article 32

During the hearings the Court may examine the experts, the witnesses and the parties themselves. The latter, however, may address the Court only through their representatives.

Article 33

Minutes shall be made of each hearing and signed by the President and the Registrar.

Article 34

The case list shall be established by the President.

Article 35

The deliberations of the Court shall be and shall remain secret.

Article 36

Judgments shall state the reasons on which they are based. They shall contain the names of the Judges who took part in the deliberations.

Article 37

Judgments shall be signed by the President and the Registrar. They shall be read in open court.

Article 38

The Court shall adjudicate upon costs.

Article 39

The President of the Court may, by way of summary procedure, which may, in so far as necessary, differ from some of the rules contained in this Statute and which shall be laid down in the Rules of Procedure, adjudicate upon applications to suspend execution, as provided for in Article 242 of the EC Treaty and Article 157 of the EAEC Treaty, or to prescribe interim measures in pursuance of Article 243 of the EC Treaty or Article 158 of the EAEC Treaty, or to suspend enforcement in accordance with the fourth paragraph of Article 256 of the EC Treaty or the third paragraph of Article 164 of the EAEC Treaty.

Should the President be prevented from attending, his place shall be taken by another Judge under conditions laid down in the Rules of Procedure.

The ruling of the President or of the Judge replacing him shall be provisional and shall in no way prejudice the decision of the Court on the substance of the case.

Article 40

Member States and institutions of the Communities may intervene in cases before the Court.

The same right shall be open to any other person establishing an interest in the result of any case submitted to the Court, save in cases between Member States, between institutions of the Communities or between Member States and institutions of the Communities.

Without prejudice to the second paragraph, the States, other than the Member States, which are parties to the Agreement on the European Economic Area, and also the EFTA Surveillance Authority referred to in that Agreement, may intervene in cases before the Court where one of the fields of application that Agreement is concerned.

An application to intervene shall be limited to supporting the form of order sought by one of the parties.

Article 41

Where the defending party, after having been duly summoned, fails to file written submissions in defence, judgment shall be given against that party by default. An objection may be lodged against the judgment within one month of it being notified. The objection shall not have the effect of staying enforcement of the judgment by default unless the Court decides otherwise.

Article 42

Member States, institutions of the Communities and any other natural or legal persons may, in cases and under conditions to be determined by the Rules of Procedure, institute third-party proceedings to contest a judgment rendered without their being heard, where the judgment is prejudicial to their rights.

Article 43

If the meaning or scope of a judgment is in doubt, the Court shall construe it on application by any party or any institution of the Communities establishing an interest therein.

Article 44

An application for revision of a judgment may be made to the Court only on discovery of a fact which is of such a nature as to be a decisive factor, and which, when the judgment was given, was unknown to the Court and to the party claiming the revision.

The revision shall be opened by a judgment of the Court expressly recording the existence of a new fact, recognising that it is of such a character as to lay the case open to revision and declaring the application admissible on this ground.

No application for revision may be made after the lapse of 10 years from the date of the judgment.

Article 45

Periods of grace based on considerations of distance shall be determined by the Rules of Procedure.

No right shall be prejudiced in consequence of the expiry of a time-limit if the party concerned proves the existence of unforeseeable circumstances or of force majeure.

Article 46

Proceedings against the Communities in matters arising from non-contractual liability shall be barred after a period of five years from the occurrence of the event giving rise thereto. The period of limitation shall be interrupted if proceedings are instituted before the Court or if prior to such proceedings an application is made by the aggrieved party to the relevant institution of the Communities. In the latter event the proceedings must be instituted within the period of two months provided for in Article 230 of the EC Treaty and Article 146 of the EAEC Treaty; the provisions of the second paragraph of Article 232 of the EC Treaty and the second paragraph of Article 148 of the EAEC Treaty, respectively, shall apply where appropriate.

TITLE IV: THE COURT OF FIRST INSTANCE OF THE EUROPEAN COMMUNITIES

Article 47

Articles 2 to 8, Articles 14 and 15, the first, second, fourth and fifth paragraphs of Article 17 and Article 18 shall apply to the Court of First Instance and its members. The oath referred to in Article 2 shall be taken before the Court of Justice and the decisions referred to in Articles 3, 4 and 6 shall be adopted by that Court after hearing the Court of First Instance.

The fourth paragraph of Article 3 and Articles 10, 11 and 14 shall apply to the Registrar of the Court of First Instance mutatis mutandis.

Article 48

The Court of First Instance shall consist of 15 Judges.

Article 49

The members of the Court of First Instance may be called upon to perform the task of an Advocate–General.

It shall be the duty of the Advocate–General, acting with complete impartiality and independence, to make, in open court, reasoned submissions on certain cases brought before the Court of First Instance in order to assist the Court of First Instance in the performance of its task.

The criteria for selecting such cases, as well as the procedures for designating the Advocates–General, shall be laid down in the Rules of Procedure of the Court of First Instance.

A member called upon to perform the task of Advocate–General in a case may not take part in the judgment of the case.

Article 50

The Court of First Instance shall sit in chambers of three or five Judges. The Judges shall elect the Presidents of the chambers from among their number. The Presidents of the chambers of five Judges shall be elected for three years. They may be re-elected once.

The composition of the chambers and the assignment of cases to them shall be governed by the Rules of Procedure. In certain cases governed by the Rules of Procedure, the Court of First Instance may sit as a full court or be constituted by a single Judge.

The Rules of Procedure may also provide that the Court of First Instance may sit in a Grand Chamber in cases and under the conditions specified therein.

Article 51

By way of exception to the rule laid down in Article 225(1) of the EC Treaty and Article 140a(1) of the EAEC Treaty, the Court of Justice shall have jurisdiction in actions brought by the Member States, by the institutions of the Communities and by the European Central Bank.

Article 52

The President of the Court of Justice and the President of the Court of First Instance shall determine, by common accord, the conditions under which officials and other servants attached to the Court of Justice shall render their services to the Court of First Instance to enable it to function. Certain officials or other servants shall be responsible to the Registrar of the Court of First Instance under the authority of the President of the Court of First Instance.

Article 53

The procedure before the Court of First Instance shall be governed by Title III.

Such further and more detailed provisions as may be necessary shall be laid down in its Rules of Procedure. The Rules of Procedure may derogate from the fourth paragraph of Article 40 and from Article 41 in order to take account of the specific features of litigation in the field of intellectual property.

Notwithstanding the fourth paragraph of Article 20, the Advocate-General may make his reasoned submissions in writing.

Article 54

Where an application or other procedural document addressed to the Court of First Instance is lodged by mistake with the Registrar of the Court of Justice, it shall be transmitted immediately by that Registrar to the Registrar of the Court of First Instance; likewise, where an application or other procedural document addressed to the Court of Justice is lodged by mistake with the Registrar of the Court of First Instance, it shall be transmitted immediately by that Registrar to the Registrar of the Court of Justice.

Where the Court of First Instance finds that it does not have jurisdiction to hear and determine an action in respect of which the Court of Justice has jurisdiction, it shall refer that action to the Court of Justice; likewise, where the Court of Justice finds that an action falls within the jurisdiction of the Court of First Instance, it shall refer that action to the Court of First Instance, whereupon that Court may not decline jurisdiction.

Where the Court of Justice and the Court of First Instance are seised of cases in which the same relief is sought, the same issue of interpretation is raised or the validity of the same act is called in question, the Court of First Instance may, after hearing the parties, stay the proceedings before it until such time as the Court of Justice shall have delivered judgment. Where applications are made for the same act to be declared void, the Court of First Instance may also decline jurisdiction in order that the Court of Justice may rule on such applications. In the cases referred to in this paragraph, the Court of Justice may also decide to stay the proceedings before it; in that event, the proceedings before the Court of First Instance shall continue.

Article 55

Final decisions of the Court of First Instance, decisions disposing of the substantive issues in part only or disposing of a procedural issue concerning a plea of lack of competence or inadmissibility, shall be notified by the Registrar of the Court of First Instance to all parties as well as all Member States and the institutions of the Communities even if they did not intervene in the case before the Court of First Instance.

Article 56

An appeal may be brought before the Court of Justice, within two months of the notification of the decision appealed against, against final decisions of the Court of First Instance and decisions of that Court disposing of the substantive issues in part only or disposing of a procedural issue concerning a plea of lack of competence or inadmissibility.

Such an appeal may be brought by any party which has been unsuccessful, in whole or in part, in its submissions. However, interveners other than the Member States and the institutions of the Communities may bring such an appeal only where the decision of the Court of First Instance directly affects them.

With the exception of cases relating to disputes between the Communities and their servants, an appeal may also be brought by Member States and institutions of the Communities which did not intervene in the proceedings before the Court of First Instance. Such Member States and institutions shall be in the same position as Member States or institutions which intervened at first instance.

Article 57

Any person whose application to intervene has been dismissed by the Court of First Instance may appeal to the Court of Justice within two weeks from the notification of the decision dismissing the application.

The parties to the proceedings may appeal to the Court of Justice against any decision of the Court of First Instance made pursuant to Article 242 or Article 243 or the fourth paragraph of Article 256 of the EC Treaty or Article 157 or Article 158 or the third paragraph of Article 164 of the EAEC Treaty within two months from their notification.

The appeal referred to in the first two paragraphs of this Article shall be heard and determined under the procedure referred to in Article 39.

Article 58

An appeal to the Court of Justice shall be limited to points of law. It shall lie on the grounds of lack of competence of the Court of First Instance, a breach of procedure before it which adversely affects the interests of the appellant as well as the infringement of Community law by the Court of First Instance.

No appeal shall lie regarding only the amount of the costs or the party ordered to pay them.

Article 59

Where an appeal is brought against a decision of the Court of First Instance, the procedure before the Court of Justice shall consist of a written part and an oral part. In accordance with conditions laid down in the Rules of Procedure, the Court of Justice, having heard the Advocate-General and the parties, may dispense with the oral procedure.

Article 60

Without prejudice to Articles 242 and 243 of the EC Treaty or Articles 157 and 158 of the EAEC Treaty, an appeal shall not have suspensory effect.

By way of derogation from Article 244 of the EC Treaty and Article 159 of the EAEC Treaty, decisions of the Court of First Instance declaring a regulation to be void shall take effect only as from the date of expiry of the period referred to in the first paragraph of Article 56 of this Statute or, if an appeal shall have been brought within that period, as from the date of dismissal of the appeal, without prejudice, however, to the right of a party to apply to the Court of Justice, pursuant to Articles 242 and 243 of the EC Treaty or Articles 157 and 158 of the EAEC Treaty, for the suspension of the effects of the regulation which has been declared void or for the prescription of any other interim measure.

Article 61

If the appeal is well founded, the Court of Justice shall quash the decision of the Court of First Instance. It may itself give final judgment in the matter, where the state of the proceedings so permits, or refer the case back to the Court of First Instance for judgment.

Where a case is referred back to the Court of First Instance, that Court shall be bound by the decision of the Court of Justice on points of law.

When an appeal brought by a Member State or an institution of the Communities, which did not intervene in the proceedings before the Court of First Instance, is well founded, the Court of Justice may, if it considers this necessary, state which of the effects of the decision of the Court of First Instance which has been quashed shall be considered as definitive in respect of the parties to the litigation.

Article 62

In the cases provided for in Article 225(2) and (3) of the EC Treaty and Article 140a(2) and (3) of the EAEC Treaty, where the First Advocate-General considers that there is a serious risk of the unity or consistency of Community law being affected, he may propose that the Court of Justice review the decision of the Court of First Instance.

The proposal must be made within one month of delivery of the decision by the Court of First Instance. Within one month of receiving the proposal made by the First Advocate-General, the Court of Justice shall decide whether or not the decision should be reviewed.

TITLE V: FINAL PROVISIONS

Article 63

The Rules of Procedure of the Court of Justice and of the Court of First Instance shall contain any provisions necessary for applying and, where required, supplementing this Statute.

Article 64

Until the rules governing the language arrangements applicable at the Court of Justice and the Court of First Instance have been adopted in this Statute, the provisions of the Rules of Procedure of the Court of Justice and of the Rules of Procedure of the Court of First Instance governing language arrangements shall continue to apply. Those provisions may only be amended or repealed in accordance with the procedure laid down for amending this Statute.

PROTOCOLS ANNEXED TO THE TREATY ESTABLISHING THE EUROPEAN COMMUNITY

[The Nice Treaty contains 2 Protocols to be annexed to the EC Treaty: a Protocol on the financial consequences of the expiry of the ECSC Treaty and a Protocol on Article 67 of the EC Treaty, according to which: "From 1 May 2004, the Council shall act by a qualified majority, on a proposal from the Commission and after consulting the European Parliament, in order to adopt the measures referred to in Article 66 of the [EC] Treaty ..."]

DECLARATIONS ADOPTED BY THE INTERGOVERNMENTAL CONFERENCE AND ANNEXED TO THE FINAL ACT

[Adopted by the IGC and annexed to the Nice Treaty are the following:

1. Declaration on the European security and defence policy
2. Declaration on Article 31(2) of the Treaty on European Union
3. Declaration on Article 10 of the Treaty establishing the European Community
4. Declaration on the third paragraph of Article 21 of the Treaty establishing the European Community
5. Declaration on Article 67 of the Treaty establishing the European Community
6. Declaration on Article 100 of the Treaty establishing the European Community
7. Declaration on Article 111 of the Treaty establishing the European Community
8. Declaration on Article 137 of the Treaty establishing the European Community
9. Declaration on Article 175 of the Treaty establishing the European Community
10. Declaration on Article 181a of the Treaty establishing the European Community
11. Declaration on Article 191 of the Treaty establishing the European Community
12. Declaration on Article 225 of the Treaty establishing the European Community
13. Declaration on Article 225(2) and (3) of the Treaty establishing the European Community
14. Declaration on Article 225(2) and (3) of the Treaty establishing the European Community
15. Declaration on Article 225(3) of the Treaty establishing the European Community
16. Declaration on Article 225a of the Treaty establishing the European Community

17. Declaration on Article 229a of the Treaty establishing the European Community

18. Declaration on the Court of Auditors

19. Declaration on Article 10.6 of the Statute of the European System of Central Banks and of the European Central Bank

20. Declaration on the enlargement of the European Union

21. Declaration on the qualified majority threshold and the number of votes for a blocking minority in an enlarged Union

22. Declaration on the venue for European Councils

23. Declaration on the future of the Union

24. Declaration on Article 2 of the Protocol on the financial consequences of the expiry of the ECSC Treaty and on the Research Fund for Coal and Steel

The Conference also noted a number of Declarations by Member States:

1. Declaration by Luxembourg

2. Declaration by Greece, Spain and Portugal on Article 161 of the Treaty establishing the European Community

3. Declaration by Denmark, Germany, the Netherlands and Austria on Article 161 of the Treaty establishing the European Community.]

5. PROTOCOL ON THE STATUTE OF THE COURT OF JUSTICE OF THE EUROPEAN COMMUNITY

(Signed at Brussels, April 17, 1957, 298 UNTS 147 (1958), as amended by Council Decision 88/591, O.J. C 215/1 (Aug. 21, 1989), Council Decision 94/993/EC, OJ 1994 L379/1 (Dec. 31, 1994), Council Decision 95/208/EC, OJ 1995 L131/33 (June 15, 1995), and the Treaty of Amsterdam, O.J. 1997 C340/68)

[*Eds. Note*: The Treaty of Nice has attached to it a new Protocol on the Statute of the Court of Justice which, upon ratification of the Nice Treaty, will replace this Protocol. The text of the new Protocol appears immediately following the Treaty of Nice in Document 4 of this Part.]

Article 1

The Court established by Article 7 [ex 4] of this Treaty shall be constituted and shall function in accordance with the provisions of this Treaty and of this Statute.

Title I

Judges and Advocates General

Article 2

Before taking up his duties each Judge shall, in open court, take an oath to perform his duties impartially and conscientiously and to preserve the secrecy of the deliberations of the Court.

Article 3

The Judges shall be immune from legal proceedings. After they have ceased to hold office, they shall continue to enjoy immunity in respect of acts performed by them in their official capacity, including words spoken or written.

The Court, sitting in plenary session, may waive the immunity.

Where immunity has been waived and criminal proceedings are instituted against a Judge, he shall be tried, in any of the Member States, only by the Court competent to judge the members of the highest national judiciary.

Articles 12 to 15 and 18 of the Protocol on the privileges and immunities of the European Communities shall apply to the Judges, Advocates General, Registrar and Assistant Rapporteurs of the Court of Justice, without prejudice to the provisions relating to immunity from legal proceedings of Judges which are set out in the preceding paragraphs.

Article 4

The Judges may not hold any political or administrative office.

They may not engage in any occupation, whether gainful or not, unless exemption is exceptionally granted by the Council.

When taking up their duties, they shall give a solemn undertaking that, both during and after their term of office, they will respect the obligations arising therefrom, in particular the duty to behave with integrity and discretion as regards the acceptance, after they have ceased to hold office, of certain appointments or benefits.

Any doubt on this point shall be settled by decision of the Court.

Article 5

Apart from normal replacement, or death, the duties of a Judge shall end when he resigns.

Where a Judge resigns, his letter of resignation shall be addressed to the President of the Court for transmission to the President of the Council. Upon this notification a vacancy shall arise on the bench.

Save where Article 6 applies, a Judge shall continue to hold office until his successor takes up his duties.

Article 6

A Judge may be deprived of his office or of his right to a pension or other benefits in its stead only if, in the unanimous opinion of the Judges and Advocates General of the Court, he no longer fulfils the requisite conditions or meets the obligations arising from his office. The Judge concerned shall not take part in any such deliberations.

The Registrar of the Court shall communicate the decision of the Court to the President of the European Parliament and to the President of the Commission and shall notify it to the President of the Council.

In the case of a decision depriving a Judge of his office, a vacancy shall arise on the bench upon this latter notification.

Article 7

A Judge who is to replace a member of the Court whose term of office has not expired shall be appointed for the remainder of his predecessor's term.

Article 8

The provisions of Articles 2 to 7 shall apply to the Advocates General.

Title II

Organisation

Article 9

The Registrar shall take an oath before the Court to perform his duties impartially and conscientiously and to preserve the secrecy of the deliberations of the Court.

Article 10

The Court shall arrange for replacement of the Registrar on occasions when he is prevented from attending the Court.

Article 11

Officials and other servants shall be attached to the Court to enable it to function. They shall be responsible to the Registrar under the authority of the President.

Article 12

On a proposal from the Court, the Council may, acting unanimously, provide for the appointment of Assistant Rapporteurs and lay down the rules governing their service. The Assistant Rapporteurs may be required, under conditions laid down in the Rules of Procedure, to participate in preparatory inquiries in cases pending before the Court and to cooperate with the Judge who acts as Rapporteur.

The Assistant Rapporteurs shall be chosen from persons whose independence is beyond doubt and who possess the necessary legal qualifications; they shall be appointed by the Council. They shall take an oath before the Court to perform their duties impartially and conscientiously and to preserve the secrecy of the deliberations of the Court.

Article 13

The Judges, the Advocates General and the Registrar shall be required to reside at the place where the Court has its seat.

Article 14

The Court shall remain permanently in session. The duration of the judicial vacations shall be determined by the Court with due regard to the needs of its business.

Article 15

Decisions of the Court shall be valid only when an uneven number of its members is sitting in the deliberations. Decisions of the full Court shall be valid if nine members are sitting. Decisions of the Chambers consisting of three or five Judges shall be valid only if three Judges are sitting. Decisions of the Chambers consisting of seven Judges shall be valid only if five Judges are sitting. In the event of one of the Judges of a Chamber being prevented from attending, a Judge of another Chamber may be called upon to sit in accordance with conditions laid down in the Rules of Procedure.

Article 16

No Judge or Advocate General may take part in the disposal of any case in which he has previously taken part as agent or adviser or has acted for one of the parties, or in which he has been called upon to pronounce as a Member of a court or tribunal, of a commission of inquiry or in any other capacity.

If, for some special reason, any Judge or Advocate General considers that he should not take part in the judgment or examination of a particular case, he shall so inform the President. If, for some special reason, the President considers that any Judge or Advocate General should not sit or make submissions in a particular case, he shall notify him accordingly.

Any difficulty arising as to the application of this Article shall be settled by decision of the Court.

A party may not apply for a change in the composition of the Court or of one of its Chambers on the grounds of either the nationality of a Judge or the absence from the Court or from the Chamber of a Judge of the nationality of that party.

Title III

Procedure

Article 17

The States and the institutions of the Community shall be represented before the Court by an agent appointed for each case; the agent may be assisted by an adviser or by a lawyer.

The States, other than the Member States, which are parties to the Agreement on the European Economic Area, and also the EFTA Surveillance Authority referred to in that Agreement, shall be represented in the same manner.

Other parties must be represented by a lawyer.

Only a lawyer authorised to practise before a court of a Member State or of another State which is a party to the Agreement on the European Economic Area may represent or assist a party before the Court.

Such agents, advisers and lawyers shall, when they appear before the Court, enjoy the rights and immunities necessary to the independent exercise of their duties, under conditions laid down in the Rules of Procedure.

As regards such advisers and lawyers who appear before it, the Court shall have the powers normally accorded to courts of law, under conditions laid down in the Rules of Procedure.

University teachers being nationals of a Member State whose law accords them a right of audience shall have the same rights before the Court as are accorded by this Article to lawyers.

Article 18

The procedure before the Court shall consist of two parts: written and oral.

The written procedure shall consist of the communication to the parties and to the institutions of the Community whose decisions are in dispute, of applications, statements of case, defences and observations, and of replies, if any, as well as of all papers and documents in support or of certified copies of them.

Communications shall be made by the Registrar in the order and within the time laid down in the rules of procedure.

The oral procedure shall consist of the reading of the report presented by a Judge acting as Rapporteur, the hearing by the Court of agents, advisers and lawyers and of the submissions of the Advocate General, as well as the hearing, if any, of witnesses and experts.

Article 19

A case shall be brought before the Court by a written application addressed to the Registrar. The application shall contain the applicant's name and permanent address and the description of the signatory, the name of the party or names of the parties against whom the application is made, the subject-matter of the dispute, the form of order sought and a brief statement of the pleas in law on which the application is based.

The application shall be accompanied, where appropriate, by the measure the annulment of which is sought or, in the circumstances referred to in Article 232 [ex 175] of this Treaty, by documentary evidence of the date on which an institution was, in accordance with that Article, requested to act. If the documents are not submitted with the application, the Registrar shall ask the party concerned to produce them within a reasonable period, but in that event the rights of the party shall not lapse even if such documents are produced after the time-limit for bringing proceedings.

Article 20

In the cases governed by Article 234 [ex 177] of this Treaty the decision of the court or tribunal of a Member State which suspends its proceedings and refers a case to the Court shall be notified to the Court by the court or tribunal concerned. The decision shall then be notified by the Registrar of the Court to the parties, to the Member States and to the Commission, and also to the Council or to the European Central Bank if the act the validity or interpretation of which is in dispute originates from one of them, and to the European Parliament and the Council if the act the validity or interpretation of which is in dispute was adopted jointly by those two institutions.

Within two months of this notification, the parties, the Member States, the Commission and, where appropriate, the European Parliament, the Council and the European Central Bank, shall be entitled to submit statements of case or written observations to the Court.

The decision of the aforesaid court or tribunal shall, moreover, be notified by the Registrar of the Court to the States, other than the Member States, which are parties to the Agreement on the European Economic Area and also to the EFTA Surveillance Authority referred to in that Agreement which may, within two months of notification, submit statements of case or written observations to the Court.

Article 21

The Court may require the parties to produce all documents and to supply all information which the Court considers desirable. Formal note shall be taken of any refusal.

The Court may also require the Member States and institutions not being parties to the case to supply all information which the Court considers necessary for the proceedings.

Article 22

The Court may at any time entrust any individual, body, authority, committee or other organisation it chooses with the task of giving an expert opinion.

Article 23

Witnesses may be heard under conditions laid down in the Rules of Procedure.

Article 24

With respect to defaulting witnesses the Court shall have the powers generally granted to courts and tribunals and may impose pecuniary penalties under conditions laid down in the Rules of Procedure.

Article 25

Witnesses and experts may be heard on oath taken in the form laid down in the Rules of Procedure or in the manner laid down by the law of the country of the witness or expert.

Article 26

The Court may order that a witness or expert be heard by the judicial authority of his place of permanent residence.

The order shall be sent for implementation to the competent judicial authority under conditions laid down in the Rules of Procedure. The documents drawn up in compliance with the letters rogatory shall be returned to the Court under the same conditions.

The Court shall defray the expenses, without prejudice to the right to charge them, where appropriate, to the parties.

Article 27

A Member State shall treat any violation of an oath by a witness or expert in the same manner as if the offence had been committed before one of its courts with jurisdiction in civil proceedings. At the instance of the Court, the Member State concerned shall prosecute the offender before its competent court.

Article 28

The hearing in court shall be public, unless the Court, of its own motion or on application by the parties, decides otherwise for serious reasons.

Article 29

During the hearings the Court may examine the experts, the witnesses and the parties themselves. The latter, however, may address the Court only through their representatives.

Article 30

Minutes shall be made of each hearing and signed by the President and the Registrar.

Article 31

The case list shall be established by the President.

Article 32

The deliberations of the Court shall be and shall remain secret.

Article 33

Judgments shall state the reasons on which they are based. They shall contain the names of the Judges who took part in the deliberations.

Article 34

Judgments shall be signed by the President and the Registrar. They shall be read in open court.

Article 35

The Court shall adjudicate upon costs.

Article 36

The President of the Court may, by way of summary procedure, which may, in so far as necessary, differ from some of the rules contained in this Statute and which shall be laid down in the Rules of Procedure, adjudicate upon applications to suspend execution, as provided for in Article 242 [ex 185] of this Treaty, or to prescribe interim measures in pursuance of Article 243 [ex 186] or to suspend enforcement in accordance with the last paragraph of Article 256 [ex 192].

Should the President be prevented from attending, his place shall be taken by another Judge under conditions laid down in the Rules of Procedure.

The ruling of the President or of the Judge replacing him shall be provisional and shall in no way prejudice the decision of the Court on the substance of the case.

Article 37

Member States and institutions of the Community may intervene in cases before the Court.

The same right shall be open to any other person establishing an interest in the result of any case submitted to the Court, save in cases between Member States, between institutions of the Community or between Member States and institutions of the Community.

Without prejudice to the preceding paragraph, the States, other than the Member States, which are parties to the Agreement on the European Economic Area, and also the EFTA Surveillance Authority referred to in that Agreement, may intervene in cases before the Court where one of the fields of application of that Agreement is concerned.

An application to intervene shall be limited to supporting the form of order sought by one of the parties.

Article 38

Where the defending party, after having been duly summoned, fails to file written submissions in defence, judgment shall be given against that party by default. An objection may be lodged against the judgment within one month of it being notified. The objection shall not have the effect of staying enforcement of the judgment by default unless the Court decides otherwise.

Article 39

Member States, institutions of the Community and any other natural or legal persons may, in cases and under conditions to be determined by the Rules of Procedure, institute third-party proceedings to contest a judgment rendered without their being heard, where the judgment is prejudicial to their rights.

Article 40

If the meaning or scope of a judgment is in doubt, the Court shall construe it on application by any party or any institution of the Community establishing an interest therein.

Article 41

An application for revision of a judgment may be made to the Court only on discovery of a fact which is of such a nature as to be a decisive factor, and which, when the judgment was given, was unknown to the Court and to the party claiming the revision.

The revision shall be opened by a judgment of the Court expressly, recording the existence of a new fact, recognising that it is of such a character as to lay the case open to revision and declaring the application admissible on this ground.

No application for revision may be made after the lapse of 10 years from the date of the judgment.

Article 42

Periods of grace based on considerations of distance shall be determined by the Rules of Procedure.

No right shall be prejudiced in consequence of the expiry of a time-limit if the party concerned proves the existence of unforeseeable circumstances or of force majeure.

Article 43

Proceedings against the Community in matters arising from non-contractual liability shall be barred after a period of five years from the occurrence of the event giving rise thereto. The period of limitation shall be interrupted if proceedings are instituted before the Court or if prior to such proceedings an application is made by the aggrieved party to the relevant institution of the Community. In the latter event the proceedings must be instituted within the period of two months provided for in Article 230 [ex 173]; the provisions of the second paragraph of Article 232 [ex 175] shall apply where appropriate.

Title IV

The Court of First Instance of the European Communities

Article 44

Articles 2 to 8 and 13 to 16 of this Statute shall apply to the Court of First Instance and its members. The oath referred to in Article 2 shall be taken before the Court of Justice and the decisions referred to in Articles 3, 4 and 6 shall be adopted by that Court after hearing the Court of First Instance.

Article 45

The Court of First Instance shall appoint its Registrar and lay down the rules governing his service. Articles 9, 10 and 13 of this Statute shall apply to the Registrar of the Court of First Instance mutatis mutandis.

The President of the Court of Justice and the President of the Court of First Instance shall determine, by common accord, the conditions under which officials and other servants attached to the Court of Justice shall render their services to the Court of First Instance to enable it to function. Certain officials or other servants shall be responsible to the Registrar of the Court of First Instance under the authority of the President of the Court of First Instance.

Article 46

The procedure before the Court of First Instance shall be governed by Title III of this Statute, with the exception of Article 20.

Such further and more detailed provisions as may be necessary shall be laid down in the Rules of Procedure established in accordance with Article 225 [ex 168a(4)] of the Treaty. The Rules of Procedure may derogate from the fourth paragraph of Article 37 and from Article 38 of this Statute in order to take account of the specific features of litigation in the field of intellectual property.

Notwithstanding the fourth paragraph of Article 18 of this Statute, the Advocate General may make his reasoned submissions in writing.

Article 47

Where an application or other procedural document addressed to the Court of First Instance is lodged by mistake with the Registrar of the Court of Justice it shall be transmitted immediately by that Registrar to the Registrar of the Court of First Instance; likewise, where an application or other procedural document addressed to the Court of Justice is lodged by mistake with the Registrar of the Court of First Instance, it shall be transmitted immediately by that Registrar to the Registrar of the Court of Justice.

Where the Court of First Instance finds that it does not have jurisdiction to hear and determine an action in respect of which the Court of Justice has jurisdiction, it shall refer that action to the Court of Justice; likewise, where the Court of Justice finds that an action falls within the jurisdiction of the Court of First Instance, it shall refer that action to the Court of First Instance, whereupon that Court may not decline jurisdiction.

Where the Court of Justice and the Court of First Instance are seised of cases in which the same relief is sought, the same issue of interpretation is raised or the validity of the same act is called in question, the Court of First Instance may, after hearing the parties, stay the proceedings before it until such time as the Court of Justice shall have delivered judgment. Where applications are made for the same act to be declared void, the Court of First Instance may also decline jurisdiction in order that the Court of Justice may rule on such applications. In the cases referred to in this subparagraph, the Court of Justice may also decide to stay the proceedings before it; in that event, the proceedings before the Court of First Instance shall continue.

Article 48

Final decisions of the Court of First Instance, decisions disposing of the substantive issues in part only or disposing of a procedural issue concerning a plea of lack of competence or inadmissibility, shall be notified by the Registrar of the Court of First Instance to all parties as well as all Member States and the Community institutions even if they did not intervene in the case before the Court of First Instance.

Article 49

An appeal may be brought before the Court of Justice, within two months of the notification of the decision appealed against, against final decisions of the Court of First Instance and decisions of that Court disposing of the substantive issues in part only or disposing of a procedural issue concerning a plea of lack of competence or inadmissibility.

Such an appeal may be brought by any party which has been unsuccessful, in whole or in part, in its submissions. However, interveners other than the Member States and the Community institutions may bring such an appeal only where the decision of the Court of First Instance directly affects them.

With the exception of cases relating to disputes between the Community and its servants, an appeal may also be brought by Member States and Community institutions which did not intervene in the proceedings before the Court of First Instance. Such Member States and institutions shall be in the same position as Member States or institutions which intervened at first instance.

Article 50

Any person whose application to intervene has been dismissed by the Court of First Instance may appeal to the Court of Justice within two weeks of the notification of the decision dismissing the application.

The parties to the proceedings may appeal to the Court of Justice against any decision of the Court of First Instance made pursuant to Article 242 [ex 185] or 243 [ex 186] or the fourth paragraph of Article 256, para. 4 [ex 192] of this Treaty within two months from their notification.

The appeal referred to in the first two paragraphs of this Article shall be heard and determined under the procedure referred to in Article 36 of this Statute.

Article 51

An appeal to the Court of Justice shall be limited to points of law. It shall lie on the grounds of lack of competence of the Court of First Instance, a breach of procedure before it which adversely affects the interests of the appellant as well as the infringement of Community law by the Court of First Instance.

No appeal shall lie regarding only the amount of the costs or the party ordered to pay them.

Article 52

Where an appeal is brought against a decision of the Court of First Instance, the procedure before the Court of Justice shall consist of a written part and an oral part. In accordance with conditions laid down in the Rules of Procedure the Court of Justice, having heard the Advocate General and the parties, may dispense with the oral procedure.

Article 53

Without prejudice to Articles 242 and 243 [ex 185 and 186] of this Treaty, an appeal shall not have suspensory effect.

By way of derogation from Article 244 [ex 187] of this Treaty, decisions of the Court of First Instance declaring a regulation to be void shall take effect only as from the date of expiry of the period referred to in the first paragraph of Article 49 of this Statute or, if an appeal shall have been brought within that period, as from the date of dismissal of the appeal, without prejudice, however, to the right of a party to apply to the Court of Justice, pursuant to Articles 242 and 243 [ex 185 and 186] of this Treaty, for the suspension of the effects of the regulation which has been declared void or for the prescription of any other interim measure.

Article 54

If the appeal is well founded, the Court of Justice shall quash the decision of the Court of First Instance. It may itself give final judgment in the matter, where the state of the proceedings so permits, or refer the case back to the Court of First Instance for judgment.

Where a case is referred back to the Court of First Instance, that Court shall be bound by the decision of the Court of Justice on points of law.

When an appeal brought by a Member State or a Community institution, which did not intervene in the proceedings before the Court of First Instance, is well founded the Court of Justice may, if it considers this necessary, state which of the effects of the decision of the Court of First Instance which has been quashed shall be considered as definitive in respect of the parties to the litigation.

Article 55

The Rules of Procedure of the Court provided for in Article 245 [ex 188] of this Treaty shall contain, apart from the provisions contemplated by this Statute, any other provisions necessary for applying and, where required, supplementing it.

Article 56

The Council may, acting unanimously, make such further adjustments to the provisions of this Statute as may be required by reason of measures taken by the Council in accordance with the last paragraph of Article 221, para. 4 [ex 165] of this Treaty.

6. RULES OF PROCEDURE OF THE COURT OF JUSTICE OF THE EUROPEAN COMMUNITY

(consolidated version published in O.J. C 34/1 (Feb. 1, 2001), reflecting the republication of June 19, 1991, O.J. L 176/7 (July 4, 1991), as amended on Feb. 21, 1995, O.J. L 44/61 (Feb. 28, 1995), on March 11, 1997, O.J. L 103/1 (Apr. 19, 1997), on May 16, 2000, O.J. L 122/43 (May 24, 2000), on Nov. 28, 2000, O. L 322/1 (Dec. 19, 2000), and on April 3, 2001, O.J. L 119/1 (April 27, 2001))

[Eds. Note: Due to scarcity of space, this Document contains, in addition to the full Table of Contents of the Rules of Procedure, only selected provisions of the Rules]

Table of Contents

Interpretation (art. 1)
TITLE I: ORGANISATION OF THE COURT
  Ch. 1 (arts. 2–6) Judges and Advocates General (Articles 2 to 6)
  Ch. 2 (arts. 7–11) Presidency of the Court and constitution of the Chambers (Articles 7 to 11)
  Ch. 3 (arts. 12–23) Registry
    sec. 1 (arts. 12–19) The Registrar and Assistant Registrars
    sec. 2 (arts. 20–23) Other departments
  Ch. 4 (art. 24) Assistant Rapporteurs
  Ch. 5 (arts. 25–28) The working of the Court
  Ch. 6 (arts. 29–31) Languages
  Ch. 7 (arts. 32–36) Rights and obligations of agents, advisers and lawyers
TITLE II: PROCEDURE
  Ch. 1 (arts. 37–44a) Written procedure
  Ch. 2 (arts. 45–54a) Preparatory inquiries and other preparatory measures
    sec. 1 (arts. 45–46) Measures of inquiry
    sec. 2 (arts. 47–53) The summoning and examination of witnesses and experts (Articles 47 to 53)
    sec. 3 (art. 54) Closure of the preparatory inquiry (Article 54)
    sec. 4 (art. 54a) Preparatory measures (Article 54a)
  Ch. 3 (arts. 55–62) Oral procedure
  Ch. 3a (art. 62a) Expedited procedures
  Ch. 4 (arts. 63–68) Judgments
  Ch. 5 (arts. 69–75) Costs
  Ch. 6 (art. 76) Legal aid
  Ch. 7 (arts. 77–78) Discontinuance
  Ch. 8 (art. 79) Service
  Ch. 9 (arts. 80–82) Time-limits
  Ch. 10 (art. 82a) Stay of proceedings
TITLE III: SPECIAL FORMS OF PROCEDURE
  Ch. 1 (arts. 83–90) Suspension of operation or enforcement and other interim measures
  Ch. 2 (arts. 91–92) Preliminary issues

Ch. 3 (art. 93) Intervention
Ch. 4 (art. 94) Judgments by default and applications to set them aside
Ch. 5 (arts. 95–96) Cases assigned to Chambers
Ch. 6 (arts. 97–100) Exceptional review procedures
  sec. 1 (art. 97) Third-party proceedings
  sec. 2 (arts. 98–100) Revision
Ch. 7 (art. 101) Appeals against decisions of the Arbitration Committee
Ch. 8 (art. 102) Interpretation of judgments
Ch. 9 (arts. 103–104a) Preliminary rulings and other references for interpretation
Ch. 10 (arts. 105–06) Special procedures under Articles 103 to 105 of the EAEC Treaty
Ch. 11 (arts. 107–09) Opinions
Ch. 12 (art. 109a) Requests for interpretation under Article 68 of the EC Treaty
Ch. 13 (art. 109b) Settlement of the disputes referred to in Article 35 of the Union Treaty
TITLE IV: APPEALS AGAINST DECISIONS OF THE COURT OF FIRST INSTANCE
  (arts. 110–23)
TITLE V: PROCEDURES PROVIDED FOR BY THE EEA AGREEMENT
  (arts. 123a–123b)
Miscellaneous provisions (arts. 124–27)
Annex: Decision on official holidays

SELECTED RULES OF PROCEDURE

TITLE I

ORGANISATION OF THE COURT

* * *

Chapter 2: Presidency of the Court and Constitution of the Chambers

Article 7

1. The Judges shall, immediately after the partial replacement provided for in Article 223 of the EC Treaty ... elect one of their number as President of the Court for a term of three years.

2. If the office of the President of the Court falls vacant before the normal date of expiry thereof, the Court shall elect a successor for the remainder of the term.

3. The elections provided for in this Article shall be by secret ballot. If a Judge obtains an absolute majority he shall be elected. If no Judge obtains an absolute majority, a second ballot shall be held and the Judge obtaining the most votes shall be elected. Where two or more Judges obtain an equal number of votes the oldest of them shall be deemed elected.

Article 8

The President shall direct the judicial business and the administration of the Court; he shall preside at hearings and deliberations.

Article 9

1. The Court shall set up Chambers in accordance with the provisions of the second paragraph of Article 221 of the EC Treaty ... and shall decide which Judges shall be attached to them. ...

2. As soon as an application initiating proceedings has been lodged, the President shall assign the case to one of the Chambers for any preparatory inquiries and shall designate a Judge from that Chamber to act as Rapporteur.

3. The Court shall lay down criteria by which, as a rule, cases are to be assigned to Chambers.

4. These Rules shall apply to proceedings before the Chambers.

In cases assigned to a Chamber the powers of the President of the Court shall be exercised by the President of the Chamber.

Article 10

1. The Court shall appoint for a period of one year the Presidents of the Chambers and the First Advocate General.

The provisions of Article 7(2) and (3) shall apply.

* * *

2. The First Advocate General shall assign each case to an Advocate General as soon as the Judge–Rapporteur has been designated by the President. He shall take the necessary steps if an Advocate General is absent or prevented from acting.

* * *

Chapter 5: The Working of the Court

Article 25

1. The dates and times of the sittings of the Court shall be fixed by the President.

2. The dates and times of the sittings of the Chambers shall be fixed by their respective Presidents.

3. The Court and the Chambers may choose to hold one or more sittings in a place other than that in which the Court has its seat.

Article 26

1. Where, by reason of a Judge being absent or prevented from attending, there is an even number of Judges, the most junior Judge within the meaning of Article 6 of these Rules shall abstain from taking part in the deliberations unless he is the Judge–Rapporteur. In that case the Judge

immediately senior to him shall abstain from taking part in the deliberations.

2. If after the Court has been convened it is found that the quorum referred to in Article 15 of the EC Statute, Article 18 of the ECSC Statute and Article 15 of the EAEC Statute has not been attained, the President shall adjourn the sitting until there is a quorum.

3. If in any Chamber the quorum referred to in Article 15 of the EC Statute, Article 18 of the ECSC Statute and Article 15 of the EAEC Statute has not been attained, the President of that Chamber shall so inform the President of the Court who shall designate another Judge to complete the Chamber.

Article 27

1. The Court and Chambers shall deliberate in closed session.

2. Only those Judges who were present at the oral proceedings and the Assistant Rapporteur, if any, entrusted with the consideration of the case may take part in the deliberations.

3. Every Judge taking part in the deliberations shall state his opinion and the reasons for it.

4. Any Judge may require that any questions be formulated in the language of his choice and communicated in writing to the Court or Chamber before being put to the vote.

5. The conclusions reached by the majority of the Judges after final discussion shall determine the decision of the Court. Votes shall be cast in reverse order to the order of precedence laid down in Article 6 of these Rules.

6. Differences of view on the substance, wording or order of questions, or on the interpretation of the voting shall be settled by decision of the Court or Chamber.

7. Where the deliberations of the Court concern questions of its own administration, the Advocates General shall take part and have a vote. The Registrar shall be present, unless the Court decides to the contrary.

8. Where the Court sits without the Registrar being present it shall, if necessary, instruct the most junior Judge within the meaning of Article 6 of these Rules to draw up minutes. The minutes shall be signed by that Judge and by the President.

* * *

Chapter 6: Languages

Article 29

1. The language of a case shall be Danish, Dutch, English, Finnish, French, German, Greek, Irish, Italian, Portuguese, Spanish or Swedish.

2. The language of a case shall be chosen by the applicant, except that:

(a) where the defendant is a Member State or a natural or legal person having the nationality of a Member State, the language of the case shall be the official language of that State; where that State has more than one official language, the applicant may choose between them;

(b) at the joint request of the parties, the use of another of the languages mentioned in paragraph 1 for all or part of the proceedings may be authorised;

(c) at the request of one of the parties, and after the opposite party and the Advocate General have been heard, the use of another of the languages mentioned in paragraph 1 as the language of the case for all or part of the proceedings may be authorised by way of derogation from subparagraphs (a) and (b); such a request may not be submitted by an institution of the European Communities.

In cases to which Article 103 of these Rules applies, the language of the case shall be the language of the national court or tribunal which refers the matter to the Court. At the duly substantiated request of one of the parties to the main proceedings, and after the opposite party and the Advocate General have been heard, the use of another of the languages mentioned in paragraph 1 may be authorised for the oral procedure.

Requests as above may be decided on by the President; the latter may and, where he wishes to accede to a request without the agreement of all the parties, must refer the request to the Court.

3. The language of the case shall in particular be used in the written and oral pleadings of the parties and in supporting documents, and also in the minutes and decisions of the Court.

Any supporting documents expressed in another language must be accompanied by a translation into the language of the case.

In the case of lengthy documents, translations may be confined to extracts. However, the Court or Chamber may, of its own motion or at the request of a party, at any time call for a complete or fuller translation.

Notwithstanding the foregoing provisions, a Member State shall be entitled to use its official language when intervening in a case before the Court or when taking part in any reference of a kind mentioned in Article 103. This provision shall apply both to written statements and to oral addresses. The Registrar shall cause any such statement or address to be translated into the language of the case.

The States, other than the Member States, which are parties to the EEA Agreement, and also the EFTA Surveillance Authority, may be authorised to use one of the languages mentioned in paragraph 1, other than the language of the case, when they intervene in a case before the Court or participate in preliminary ruling proceedings envisaged by Article 20 of the EC Statute. This provision shall apply both to written statements and oral addresses. The Registrar shall cause any such statement or address to be translated into the language of the case.

4. Where a witness or expert states that he is unable adequately to express himself in one of the languages referred to in paragraph (1) of this Article, the Court or Chamber may authorise him to give his evidence in another language. The Registrar shall arrange for translation into the language of the case.

5. The President of the Court and the Presidents of Chambers in conducting oral proceedings, the Judge–Rapporteur both in his preliminary report and in his report for the hearing, Judges and Advocates General in putting questions and Advocates General in delivering their opinions may use one of the languages referred to in paragraph 1 of this Article other than the language of the case. The Registrar shall arrange for translation into the language of the case.

Article 30

1. The Registrar shall, at the request of any Judge, of the Advocate General or of a party, arrange for anything said or written in the course of the proceedings before the Court or a Chamber to be translated into the languages he chooses from those referred to in Article 29(1).

2. Publications of the Court shall be issued in the languages referred to in Article 1 of Council Regulation No 1.

Article 31

The texts of documents drawn up in the language of the case or in any other language authorised by the Court pursuant to Article 29 of these Rules shall be authentic.

Chapter 7: Rights and Obligations of Agents, Advisers and Lawyers

Article 32

1. Agents, advisers and lawyers appearing before the Court or before any judicial authority to which the Court has addressed letters rogatory, shall enjoy immunity in respect of words spoken or written by them concerning the case or the parties.

2. Agents, advisers and lawyers shall enjoy the following further privileges and facilities:

(a) papers and documents relating to the proceedings shall be exempt from both search and seizure; in the event of a dispute the customs officials or police may seal those papers and documents; they shall then be immediately forwarded to the Court for inspection in the presence of the Registrar and of the person concerned;

* * *

Article 34

The privileges, immunities and facilities specified in Article 32 of these Rules are granted exclusively in the interests of the proper conduct of proceedings.

The Court may waive the immunity where it considers that the proper conduct of proceedings will not be hindered thereby.

Article 35

1. Any adviser or lawyer whose conduct towards the Court, a Chamber, a Judge, an Advocate General or the Registrar is incompatible with the dignity of the Court, or who uses his rights for purposes other than those for which they were granted, may at any time be excluded from the proceedings by an order of the Court or Chamber, after the Advocate General has been heard; the person concerned shall be given an opportunity to defend himself.

The order shall have immediate effect.

* * *

TITLE II
PROCEDURE
Chapter 1: Written Procedure

Article 37

1. The original of every pleading must be signed by the party's agent or lawyer.

The original, accompanied by all annexes referred to therein, shall be lodged together with five copies for the Court and a copy for every other party to the proceedings. Copies shall be certified by the party lodging them.

2. Institutions shall in addition produce, within time-limits laid down by the Court, translations of all pleadings into the other languages provided for by Article 1 of Council Regulation No 1. The second subparagraph of paragraph 1 of this Article shall apply.

3. All pleadings shall bear a date. In the reckoning of time-limits for taking steps in proceedings, only the date of lodgment at the Registry shall be taken into account.

4. To every pleading there shall be annexed a file containing the documents relied on in support of it, together with a schedule listing them.

5. Where in view of the length of a document only extracts from it are annexed to the pleading, the whole document or a full copy of it shall be lodged at the Registry.

* * *

Article 38

1. An application of the kind referred to in Article 19 of the EC Statute ... shall state:

(a) the name and address of the applicant;

(b) the designation of the party against whom the application is made;

(c) the subject-matter of the proceedings and a summary of the pleas in law on which the application is based;

(d) the form of order sought by the applicant;

(e) where appropriate, the nature of any evidence offered in support.

* * *

3. The lawyer acting for a party must lodge at the Registry a certificate that he is authorised to practise before a court of a Member State or of another State which is a party to the EEA Agreement.

4. The application shall be accompanied, where appropriate, by the documents specified in the second paragraph of Article 19 of the EC Statute [of the Court of Justice]....

* * *

Article 39

The application shall be served on the defendant....

Article 40

1. Within one month after service on him of the application, the defendant shall lodge a defence, stating:

(a) the name and address of the defendant;

(b) the arguments of fact and law relied on;

(c) the form of order sought by the defendant;

(d) the nature of any evidence offered by him.

The provisions of Article 38(2) to (5) of these Rules shall apply to the defence.

2. The time-limit laid down in paragraph 1 of this Article may be extended by the President on a reasoned application by the defendant.

Article 41

1. The application initiating the proceedings and the defence may be supplemented by a reply from the applicant and by a rejoinder from the defendant.

2. The President shall fix the time-limits within which these pleadings are to be lodged.

Article 42

1. In reply or rejoinder a party may offer further evidence. The party must, however, give reasons for the delay in offering it.

2. No new plea in law may be introduced in the course of proceedings unless it is based on matters of law or of fact which come to light in the course of the procedure.

If in the course of the procedure one of the parties puts forward a new plea in law which is so based, the President may, even after the expiry of the normal procedural time-limits, acting on a report of the Judge–Rapporteur and after hearing the Advocate General, allow the other party time to answer on that plea.

The decision on the admissibility of the plea shall be reserved for the final judgment.

Article 43

The Court may, at any time, after hearing the parties and the Advocate General, if the assignment referred to in Article 10(2) has taken place, order that two or more cases concerning the same subject-matter shall, on account of the connection between them, be joined for the purposes of the written or oral procedure or of the final judgment. The cases may subsequently be disjoined. The President may refer these matters to the Court.

Article 44

1. The President shall fix a date on which the Judge–Rapporteur is to present his preliminary report to the Court, either

(a) after the rejoinder has been lodged, or

(b) where no reply or no rejoinder has been lodged within the time-limit fixed in accordance with Article 41(2), or

(c) where the party concerned has waived his right to lodge a reply or rejoinder, or

(d) where the expedited procedure referred to in Article 62a is to be applied, when the President fixes a date for the hearing.

2. The preliminary report shall contain recommendations as to whether a preparatory inquiry or any other preparatory step should be undertaken and whether the case should be referred to a Chamber. It shall also contain the Judge–Rapporteur's recommendation, if any, as to the possible omission of the oral part of the procedure as provided for in Article 44a.

The Court shall decide, after hearing the Advocate General, what action to take upon the recommendations of the Judge–Rapporteur.

3. Where the Court orders a preparatory inquiry and does not undertake it itself, it shall assign the inquiry to the Chamber.

Where the Court decides to open the oral procedure without an inquiry, the President shall fix the opening date.

Article 44a

Without prejudice to any special provisions laid down in these Rules, the procedure before the Court shall also include an oral part. However, after the pleadings referred to in Article 40(1) and, as the case may be, in Article 41(1) have been lodged, the Court, acting on a report from the Judge–Rapporteur and after hearing the Advocate General, and if none of the parties has submitted an application setting out the reasons for which he wishes to be heard, may decide otherwise. The application shall be submitted within a period of one month from notification to the party of the close of the written procedure. That period may be extended by the President.

Chapter 2: Preparatory Inquiries and Other Preparatory Measures

Section 1: Measures of inquiry

Article 45

1. The Court, after hearing the Advocate General, shall prescribe the measures of inquiry that it considers appropriate by means of an order setting out the facts to be proved. Before the Court decides on the measures of inquiry referred to in paragraph 2(c), (d) and (e) the parties shall be heard.

The order shall be served on the parties.

2. Without prejudice to Articles 21 and 22 of the EC Statute, ... the following measures of inquiry may be adopted:

   (a) the personal appearance of the parties;

   (b) a request for information and production of documents;

   (c) oral testimony;

   (d) the commissioning of an expert's report;

   (e) an inspection of the place or thing in question.

3. The measures of inquiry which the Court has ordered may be conducted by the Court itself, or be assigned to the Judge–Rapporteur.

The Advocate General shall take part in the measures of inquiry.

4. Evidence may be submitted in rebuttal and previous evidence may be amplified.

Article 46

1. A Chamber to which a preparatory inquiry has been assigned may exercise the powers vested in the Court by Articles 45 and 47 to 53 of these Rules; the powers vested in the President of the Court may be exercised by the President of the Chamber.

2. Articles 56 and 57 of these Rules shall apply to proceedings before the Chamber.

3. The parties shall be entitled to attend the measures of inquiry.

Section 2: The summoning and examination of witnesses and experts

Article 47

1. The Court may, either of its own motion or on application by a party, and after hearing the Advocate General, order that certain facts be proved by witnesses. The order of the Court shall set out the facts to be established.

The Court may summon a witness of its own motion or on application by a party or at the instance of the Advocate General.

An application by a party for the examination of a witness shall state precisely about what facts and for what reasons the witness should be examined.

2. The witness shall be summoned by an order of the Court containing the following information:

(a) the surname, forenames, description and address of the witness;

(b) an indication of the facts about which the witness is to be examined;

(c) where appropriate, particulars of the arrangements made by the Court for reimbursement of expenses incurred by the witness, and of the penalties which may be imposed on defaulting witnesses.

The order shall be served on the parties and the witnesses.

* * *

4. After the identity of the witness has been established, the President shall inform him that he will be required to vouch the truth of his evidence in the manner laid down in these Rules.

The witness shall give his evidence to the Court, the parties having been given notice to attend. After the witness has given his main evidence the President may, at the request of a party or of his own motion, put questions to him.

The other Judges and the Advocate General may do likewise.

Subject to the control of the President, questions may be put to witnesses by the representatives of the parties.

* * *

6. The Registrar shall draw up minutes in which the evidence of each witness is reproduced.

The minutes shall be signed by the President or by the Judge-Rapporteur responsible for conducting the examination of the witness, and by the Registrar. Before the minutes are thus signed, witnesses must be given an opportunity to check the content of the minutes and to sign them.

The minutes shall constitute an official record.

Article 48

1. Witnesses who have been duly summoned shall obey the summons and attend for examination.

2. If a witness who has been duly summoned fails to appear before the Court, the Court may impose upon him a pecuniary penalty not exceeding EUR 5000(2) and may order that a further summons be served on the witness at his own expense.

The same penalty may be imposed upon a witness who, without good reason, refuses to give evidence or to take the oath or where appropriate to make a solemn affirmation equivalent thereto.

3. If the witness proffers a valid excuse to the Court, the pecuniary penalty imposed on him may be cancelled. The pecuniary penalty imposed may be reduced at the request of the witness where he establishes that it is disproportionate to his income.

* * *

Article 49

1. The Court may order that an expert's report be obtained. The order appointing the expert shall define his task and set a time-limit within which he is to make his report.

2. The expert shall receive a copy of the order, together with all the documents necessary for carrying out his task. He shall be under the supervision of the Judge–Rapporteur, who may be present during his investigation and who shall be kept informed of his progress in carrying out his task.

The Court may request the parties or one of them to lodge security for the costs of the expert's report.

3. At the request of the expert, the Court may order the examination of witnesses. Their examination shall be carried out in accordance with Article 47 of these Rules.

4. The expert may give his opinion only on points which have been expressly referred to him.

5. After the expert has made his report, the Court may order that he be examined, the parties having been given notice to attend. Subject to the control of the President, questions may be put to the expert by the representatives of the parties.

* * *

Article 52

The Court may, on application by a party or of its own motion, issue letters rogatory for the examination of witnesses or experts, as provided for in the supplementary rules mentioned in Article 125 of these Rules.

Article 53

1. The Registrar shall draw up minutes of every hearing. The minutes shall be signed by the President and by the Registrar and shall constitute an official record.

* * *

Section 3: Closure of the preparatory inquiry

Article 54

Unless the Court prescribes a period within which the parties may lodge written observations, the President shall fix the date for the opening of the oral procedure after the preparatory inquiry has been completed.

Where a period had been prescribed for the lodging of written observations, the President shall fix the date for the opening of the oral procedure after that period has expired.

Section 4: Preparatory Measures

Article 54a

The Judge–Rapporteur and the Advocate General may request the parties to submit within a specified period all such information relating to the facts, and all such documents or other particulars, as they may consider relevant. The information and/or documents provided shall be communicated to the other parties.

Chapter 3: Oral Procedure

* * *

Article 56

1. The proceedings shall be opened and directed by the President, who shall be responsible for the proper conduct of the hearing.

2. The oral proceedings in cases heard in camera shall not be published.

Article 57

The President may in the course of the hearing put questions to the agents, advisers or lawyers of the parties.

The other Judges and the Advocate General may do likewise.

Article 58

A party may address the Court only through his agent, adviser or lawyer.

Article 59

1. The Advocate General shall deliver his opinion orally at the end of the oral procedure.

2. After the Advocate General has delivered his opinion, the President shall declare the oral procedure closed.

Article 60

The Court may at any time, in accordance with Article 45(1), after hearing the Advocate General, order any measure of inquiry to be taken or that a previous inquiry be repeated or expanded. The Court may direct the Chamber or the Judge–Rapporteur to carry out the measures so ordered.

Article 61

The Court may after hearing the Advocate General order the reopening of the oral procedure.

Article 62

1. The Registrar shall draw up minutes of every hearing. The minutes shall be signed by the President and by the Registrar and shall constitute an official record.

2. The parties may inspect the minutes at the Registry and obtain copies at their own expense.

Chapter 3a: Expedited Procedures

Article 62a

1. On application by the applicant or the defendant, the President may exceptionally decide, on the basis of a recommendation by the Judge–Rapporteur and after hearing the other party and the Advocate General, that a case is to be determined pursuant to an expedited procedure derogating from the provisions of these Rules, where the particular urgency of the case requires the Court to give its ruling with the minimum of delay.

An application for a case to be decided under an expedited procedure shall be made by a separate document lodged at the same time as the application initiating the proceedings or the defence, as the case may be.

2. Under the expedited procedure, the originating application and the defence may be supplemented by a reply and a rejoinder only if the President considers this to be necessary.

An intervener may lodge a statement in intervention only if the President considers this to be necessary.

3. Once the defence has been lodged or, if the decision to adjudicate under an expedited procedure is not made until after that pleading has been lodged, once that decision has been taken, the President shall fix a date for the hearing, which shall be communicated forthwith to the parties. He may postpone the date of the hearing where the organisation of measures of inquiry or of other preparatory measures so requires.

Without prejudice to Article 42, the parties may supplement their arguments and offer further evidence in the course of the oral procedure. They must, however, give reasons for the delay in offering such further evidence.

4. The Court shall give its ruling after hearing the Advocate General.

Chapter 4: Judgments

Article 63

The judgment shall contain:

— a statement that it is the judgment of the Court,
— the date of its delivery,
— the names of the President and of the Judges taking part in it,
— the name of the Advocate General,
— the name of the Registrar,
— the description of the parties,
— the names of the agents, advisers and lawyers of the parties,
— a statement of the forms of order sought by the parties,
— a statement that the Advocate General has been heard,
— a summary of the facts,
— the grounds for the decision,
— the operative part of the judgment, including the decision as to costs.

Article 64

1. The judgment shall be delivered in open court; the parties shall be given notice to attend to hear it.

* * *

Article 65

The judgment shall be binding from the date of its delivery.

* * *

Chapter 5: Costs

Article 69

1. A decision as to costs shall be given in the final judgment or in the order which closes the proceedings.

2. The unsuccessful party shall be ordered to pay the costs if they have been applied for in the successful party's pleadings.

Where there are several unsuccessful parties the Court shall decide how the costs are to be shared.

3. Where each party succeeds on some and fails on other heads, or where the circumstances are exceptional, the Court may order that the costs be shared or that the parties bear their own costs.

The Court may order a party, even if successful, to pay costs which the Court considers that party to have unreasonably or vexatiously caused the opposite party to incur.

4. The Member States and institutions which intervene in the proceedings shall bear their own costs.

The States, other than the Member States, which are parties to the EEA Agreement, and also the EFTA Surveillance Authority, shall bear their own costs if they intervene in the proceedings. The Court may order an intervener other than those mentioned in the preceding subparagraphs to bear his own costs.

* * *

6. Where a case does not proceed to judgment the costs shall be in the discretion of the Court.

Article 70

Without prejudice to the second subparagraph of Article 69(3) of these Rules, in proceedings between the Communities and their servants the institutions shall bear their own costs.

* * *

Article 72

Proceedings before the Court shall be free of charge, except that:

(a) where a party has caused the Court to incur avoidable costs the Court may, after hearing the Advocate General, order that party to refund them;

(b) where copying or translation work is carried out at the request of a party, the cost shall, in so far as the Registrar considers it excessive, be paid for by that party on the scale of charges referred to in Article 16(5) of these Rules.

Article 73

Without prejudice to the preceding Article, the following shall be regarded as recoverable costs:

(a) sums payable to witnesses and experts under Article 51 of these Rules;

(b) expenses necessarily incurred by the parties for the purpose of the proceedings, in particular the travel and subsistence expenses and the remuneration of agents, advisers or lawyers.

Chapter : Legal Aid

Article 76

1. A party who is wholly or in part unable to meet the costs of the proceedings may at any time apply for legal aid.

The application shall be accompanied by evidence of the applicant's need of assistance, and in particular by a document from the competent authority certifying his lack of means.

2. If the application is made prior to proceedings which the applicant wishes to commence, it shall briefly state the subject of such proceedings.

The application need not be made through a lawyer.

3. The President shall designate a Judge to act as Rapporteur. The Chamber to which the latter belongs shall, after considering the written observations of the opposite party and after hearing the Advocate General, decide whether legal aid should be granted in full or in part, or whether it should be refused. The Chamber shall consider whether there is manifestly no cause of action.

* * *

TITLE III

SPECIAL FORMS

Chapter 1: Suspension of Operation or Enforcement and Other Interim Measures

Article 83

1. An application to suspend the operation of any measure adopted by an institution, made pursuant to Article 242 of the EC Treaty ... shall be admissible only if the applicant is challenging that measure in proceedings before the Court.

An application for the adoption of any other interim measure referred to in Article 243 of the EC Treaty ... shall be admissible only if it is made by a party to a case before the Court and relates to that case.

2. An application of a kind referred to in paragraph 1 of this Article shall state the subject-matter of the proceedings, the circumstances giving rise to urgency and the pleas of fact and law establishing a prima facie case for the interim measures applied for.

* * *

Article 84

1. The application shall be served on the opposite party, and the President shall prescribe a short period within which that party may submit written or oral observations.

2. The President may order a preparatory inquiry. The President may grant the application even before the observations of the opposite party have been submitted. This decision may be varied or cancelled even without any application being made by any party.

Article 85

The President shall either decide on the application himself or refer it to the Court.

* * *

Article 86

1. The decision on the application shall take the form of a reasoned order, from which no appeal shall lie. The order shall be served on the parties forthwith.

2. The enforcement of the order may be made conditional on the lodging by the applicant of security, of an amount and nature to be fixed in the light of the circumstances.

* * *

4. The order shall have only an interim effect, and shall be without prejudice to the decision of the Court on the substance of the case.

Article 87

On application by a party, the order may at any time be varied or cancelled on account of a change in circumstances.

Article 88

Rejection of an application for an interim measure shall not bar the party who made it from making a further application on the basis of new facts.

Article 89

The provisions of this Chapter shall apply to applications to suspend the enforcement of a decision of the Court or of any measure adopted by another institution, submitted pursuant to Articles 244 and 256 of the EC Treaty....

The order granting the application shall fix, where appropriate, a date on which the interim measure is to lapse.

* * *

Chapter 2: Preliminary Issues

Article 91

1. A party applying to the Court for a decision on a preliminary objection or other preliminary plea not going to the substance of the case shall make the application by a separate document.

The application must state the pleas of fact and law relied on and the form of order sought by the applicant; any supporting documents must be annexed to it.

2. As soon as the application has been lodged, the President shall prescribe a period within which the opposite party may lodge a document containing a statement of the form of order sought by that party and its pleas in law.

3. Unless the Court decides otherwise, the remainder of the proceedings shall be oral.

4. The Court shall, after hearing the Advocate General, decide on the application or reserve its decision for the final judgment.

* * *

Article 92

1. Where it is clear that the Court has no jurisdiction to take cognisance of an action or where the action is manifestly inadmissible, the Court may, by reasoned order, after hearing the Advocate General and without taking further steps in the proceedings, give a decision on the action.

2. The Court may at any time of its own motion consider whether there exists any absolute bar to proceeding with a case or declare, after hearing the parties, that the action has become devoid of purpose and that there is no need to adjudicate on it; it shall give its decision in accordance with Article 91(3) and (4) of these Rules.

* * *

Chapter 5: Cases Assigned to Chambers

Article 95

1. The Court may assign any case brought before it to a Chamber in so far as the difficulty or importance of the case or particular circumstances are not such as to require that the Court decide it in plenary session.

2. The decision so to assign a case shall be taken by the Court at the end of the written procedure upon consideration of the preliminary report presented by the Judge–Rapporteur and after the Advocate General has been heard.

However, a case may not be so assigned if a Member State or an institution of the Communities, being a party to the proceedings, has requested that the case be decided in plenary session. In this subparagraph the expression 'party to the proceedings' means any Member State or any institution which is a party to or an intervener in the proceedings or which has submitted written observations in any reference of a kind mentioned in Article 103 of these Rules.

The request referred to in the preceding subparagraph may not be made in proceedings between the Communities and their servants.

3. A Chamber may at any stage refer a case back to the Court.

* * *

Chapter 9: Preliminary Rulings and Other References for Interpretation

Article 103

1. In cases governed by Article 20 of the EC Statute ..., the procedure shall be governed by the provisions of these Rules, subject to adaptations necessitated by the nature of the reference for a preliminary ruling.

* * *

3. In cases provided for in Article 35(1) of the Union Treaty ..., the text of the decision to refer the matter shall be served on the parties in the case, the Member States, the Commission and the Council.

These parties, States and institutions may, within two months from the date of such service, lodge written statements of case or written observations.

* * *

Article 104

1. The decisions of national courts or tribunals referred to in Article 103 shall be communicated to the Member States in the original version, accompanied by a translation into the official language of the State to which they are addressed.

* * *

2. As regards the representation and attendance of the parties to the main proceedings in the preliminary ruling procedure the Court shall take account of the rules of procedure of the national court or tribunal which made the reference.

3. Where a question referred to the Court for a preliminary ruling is identical to a question on which the Court has already ruled, where the answer to such a question may be clearly deduced from existing case-law or where the answer to the question admits of no reasonable doubt, the Court may, after informing the court or tribunal which referred the question to it, hearing any observations submitted by the persons referred to in Article 20 of the EC Statute ... and Article 103(3) of these Rules and hearing the Advocate General, give its decision by reasoned order in which, if appropriate, reference is made to its previous judgment or to the relevant case-law.

4. Without prejudice to paragraph (3) of this Article, the procedure before the Court in the case of a reference for a preliminary ruling shall also include an oral part. However, after the statements of case or written observations referred to in Article 20 of the EC Statute, ... have been submitted, the Court, acting on a report from the Judge–Rapporteur, after informing the persons who under the aforementioned provisions are entitled to submit such statements or observations, may, after hearing the Advocate General, decide otherwise, provided that none of those persons has submitted an application setting out the reasons for which he wishes to be heard. The application shall be submitted within a period of one month from service on the party or person of the written statements of case or written observations which have been lodged. That period may be extended by the President.

5. The Court may, after hearing the Advocate General, request clarification from the national court.

6. It shall be for the national court or tribunal to decide as to the costs of the reference.

* * *

Article 104a

At the request of the national court, the President may exceptionally decide, on a proposal from the Judge-Rapporteur and after hearing the Advocate General, to apply an accelerated procedure derogating from the provisions of these Rules to a reference for a preliminary ruling, where the circumstances referred to establish that a ruling on the question put to the Court is a matter of exceptional urgency.

In that event, the President may immediately fix the date for the hearing, which shall be notified to the parties in the main proceedings and to the other persons referred to in Article 20 of the EC Statute ... and Article 103(3) of these Rules when the decision making the reference is served.

The parties and other interested persons referred to in the preceding paragraph may lodge statements of case or written observations within a period prescribed by the President, which shall not be less than 15 days. The President may request the parties and other interested persons to restrict the matters addressed in their statement of case or written observations to the essential points of law raised by the question referred.

The statements of case or written observations, if any, shall be notified to the parties and to the other persons referred to above prior to the hearing.

The Court shall rule after hearing the Advocate General.

* * *

TITLE IV

APPEALS AGAINST DECISIONS OF THE COURT OF FIRST INSTANCE

Article 110

Without prejudice to the arrangements laid down in Article 29(2)(b) and (c) and the fourth subparagraph of Article 29(3) of these Rules, in appeals against decisions of the Court of First Instance ... the language of the case shall be the language of the decision of the Court of First Instance against which the appeal is brought.

Article 111

1. An appeal shall be brought by lodging an application at the Registry of the Court of Justice or of the Court of First Instance.

* * *

Article 112

1. An appeal shall contain:

    (a) the name and address of the appellant;

    (b) the names of the other parties to the proceedings before the Court of First Instance;

(c) the pleas in law and legal arguments relied on;

(d) the form or order sought by the appellant.

* * *

Article 113

1. An appeal may seek:

— to set aside, in whole or in part, the decision of the Court of First Instance;

— the same form of order, in whole or in part, as that sought at first instance and shall not seek a different form of order.

2. The subject-matter of the proceedings before the Court of First Instance may not be changed in the appeal.

* * *

Article 115

1. Any party to the proceedings before the Court of First Instance may lodge a response within two months after service on him of notice of the appeal. The time-limit for lodging a response shall not be extended.

2. A response shall contain:

   (a) the name and address of the party lodging it;

   (b) the date on which notice of the appeal was served on him;

   (c) the pleas in law and legal arguments relied on;

   (d) the form of order sought by the respondent.

* * *

Article 116

1. A response may seek:

— to dismiss, in whole or in part, the appeal or to set aside, in whole or in part, the decision of the Court of First Instance;

— the same form of order, in whole or in part, as that sought at first instance and shall not seek a different form of order.

2. The subject-matter of the proceedings before the Court of First Instance may not be changed in the response.

Article 117

1. The appeal and the response may be supplemented by a reply and a rejoinder where the President, on application made by the appellant within seven days of service of the response, considers such further pleading necessary and expressly allows the submission of a reply in order to enable the appellant to put forward his point of view or in order to provide a basis for the decision on the appeal. The President shall prescribe

the date by which the reply is to be submitted and, upon service of that pleading, the date by which the rejoinder is to be submitted.

2. Where the response seeks to set aside, in whole or in part, the decision of the Court of First Instance on a plea in law which was not raised in the appeal, the appellant or any other party may submit a reply on that plea alone within two months of the service of the response in question. Paragraph 1 shall apply to any further pleading following such a reply.

* * *

Article 119

Where the appeal is, in whole or in part, clearly inadmissible or clearly unfounded, the Court may at any time, acting on a report from the Judge-Rapporteur and after hearing the Advocate General, by reasoned order dismiss the appeal in whole or in part.

Article 120

After the submission of pleadings as provided for in Article 115(1) and, if any, Article 117(1) and(2) of these Rules, the Court, acting on a report from the Judge-Rapporteur and after hearing the Advocate General and the parties, may decide to dispense with the oral part of the procedure unless one of the parties submits an application setting out the reasons for which he wishes to be heard. The application shall be submitted within a period of one month from notification to the party of the close of the written procedure. That period may be extended by the President.

* * *

Article 122

Where the appeal is unfounded or where the appeal is well founded and the Court itself gives final judgment in the case, the Court shall make a decision as to costs....

* * *

7. RULES OF PROCEDURE OF THE COURT OF FIRST INSTANCE OF THE EUROPEAN COMMUNITIES

May 2, 1991, OJ 2001 C34/39 (Feb. 1, 2001)

[Eds. Note: For reasons of space, only the Table of Contents of the Rules are reprinted below.]

Table of Contents

Interpretation (art. 1)
TITLE 1 ORGANISATION OF THE COURT OF FIRST INSTANCE
    Ch. 1 (arts. 2–9) President and Members of the Court of First Instance
    Ch. 2 (arts. 10–19) Constitution of the Chambers and Designation of Judge–Rapporteurs and Advocates General
    Ch. 3 (arts. 20–30) Registry
    Ch. 4 (arts. 31–34) The Working of the Court of First Instance
    Ch. 5 (arts. 35–37) Languages
    Ch. 6 (arts. 38–42) Rights and Obligations of agents, Advisers and Lawyers
TITLE 2 PROCEDURE
    Ch. 1 (arts. 43–54) Written procedure
    Ch. 2 (arts. 55–63) Oral Procedure
    Ch. 3 (arts. 64–76) Measures of Organisation of Procedure and Measures of Inquiry
        sec. 1 (art. 64) Measures of Organisation of Procedure
        sec. 2 (arts. 65–67) Measures of Inquiry
        sec. 3 (arts. 68–76) The summoning and examination of witnesses and experts
    Ch. 3a (art. 76a) Expedited Procedures
    Ch. 4 (arts. 77–80) Stay of Proceedings and Declining of Jurisdiction by the Court of First Instance
    Ch. 5 (arts. 81–86) Judgments
    Ch. 6 (arts. 87–93) Costs
    Ch. 7 (arts. 94–97) Legal Aid
    Ch. 8 (arts. 98–99) Discontinuance
    Ch. 9 (art. 100) Service
    Ch. 10 (arts. 101–03) Time–Limits
TITLE 3 SPECIAL FORMS OF PROCEDURE
    Ch. 1 (arts. 104–10) Suspension of Operation or Enforcement and Other Interim Measures
    Ch. 2 (arts. 111–14) Preliminary Issues
    Ch. 3 (arts. 115–16) Intervention
    Ch. 4 (arts.117–21) Judgments of the Court of First Instance Delivered after its Decision Has Been Set Aside and the Case Referred Back to it
    Ch. 5 (art. 122) Judgments by Default and Applications to Set Them Aside
    Ch. 6 (arts. 123–29)

sec. 1 (arts. 123–24) Third–Party Proceedings
sec. 2 (arts. 125–29) Revision

TITLE IV PROCEEDINGS RELATING TO INTELLECTUAL PROPERTY RIGHTS
(arts. 130–36)

FINAL PROVISIONS (arts. 136–37)

8. INTERINSTITUTIONAL DECLARATION ON DEMOCRACY, TRANSPARENCY AND SUBSIDIARITY

(Bull. EC 10/93, page 118)

1. The European Parliament, the Council and the Commission, as institutions of the European Union, will, within the framework of the legislative procedure, respect in full the democratic principles on which the systems of government of the Member States are based; they reaffirm their attachment to the implementation of transparency by the institutions.

2. As soon as Parliament has adopted its resolution on the annual legislative programme proposed by the Commission, the Council will state its position on the programme in a declaration and undertake to implement as soon as possible the provisions to which it attaches priority, on the basis of formal Commission proposals and in compliance with the procedures laid down by the Treaties.

3. In order to increase the transparency of the Community, the institutions recall the measures which they have already taken in this direction:

The European Parliament, in amending its Rules of Procedure on 15 September 1993, has confirmed the public nature of meetings of its committees and of its plenary sittings.

The Council has agreed to take steps:

☐ to open some of its debates to the public;

☐ to publish records and explanations of its voting;

☐ to publish the common positions which it adopts under the procedures laid down in Articles 189b and 189c, and the statement of reasons accompanying them;

☐ to improve information for the press and the public on its work and decisions;

☐ to improve general information on its role and activities;

☐ to simplify and consolidate Community legislation in cooperation with the other institutions;

☐ to provide access to its archives.

The Commission has already taken or is in the process of taking the following measures:

☐ wider consultations before presenting proposals, in particular publication of Green or White Papers on the topics listed in the 1993 legislative programme;

☐ flagging in the legislative programme of upcoming proposals which would appear to be suitable for wide-ranging preliminary consultations;

☐ introduction of a notification procedure, consisting of the publication in the Official Journal of a brief summary of any measure planned by the Commission, with the setting of a deadline by which interested parties may submit their comments;

☐ publication of work programmes and legislative programmes in the Official Journal to publicize action planned by the Commission;

☐ finalization of the work programme by October with a view to enhancing openness;

☐ publication in the legislative programme of plans for the consolidation of Community legislation;

☐ provision of easier public access to documents held by the Commission with effect from 1 January 1994;

☐ improving knowledge of existing databases and their accessibility, including improving the existing relay network;

☐ publication each week in the Official Journal of lists of documents on general topics; wider public access to documents on specific topics;

☐ preparation of an interinstitutional yearbook giving details of each institution's organization chart;

☐ faster publication of Commission documents in all Community languages;

☐ adoption of a new information and communication policy occupying a larger place in Commission activities; enhanced coordination of information activities both inside and outside the Commission;

☐ adoption of additional measures to facilitate the general public's understanding of Commission business, in particular by making available the necessary resources and equipment to provide a suitable response to requests from the media;

☐ improvement in the treatment of telephone, mail and personal contacts between citizens and the Commission;

☐ promotion of the establishment of self-regulation by special interest groups by asking them to draft a code of conduct and a directory;

☐ creation by the Commission of a database on special interest groups as an instrument for use by the general public and by Community officials.

4. Interinstitutional Agreement on procedures for implementing the principle of subsidiarity.

5. Draft Decision of the European Parliament laying down the regulations and general conditions governing the performance of the ombudsman's duties.

6. Arrangements for the proceedings of the Conciliation Committee under Article 189b.

7. The three institutions will adopt all these texts in accordance with their internal procedures.

The agreements established at the Interinstitutional Conference on 25 October 1993 are aimed at implementing the Treaty on European Union and at strengthening the democratic, transparent nature of the European Union. They may be added to or amended by common agreement at the initiative of any of the three institutions.

9. INTERINSTITUTIONAL AGREEMENT ON PROCEDURES FOR IMPLEMENTING THE PRINCIPLE OF SUBSIDIARITY

(Bull. EC 10/93, p. 119)

The European Parliament, the Council and the Commission,

Having regard to the Treaty on European Union signed in Maastricht on 7 February 1992, and in particular Article B thereof,

Having regard to the Treaty establishing the European Community, and in particular Article 3b thereof, as resulting from the Treaty on European Union,

Having regard to the conclusions of the European Council, meeting in Edinburgh, concerning subsidiarity, transparency and democracy,

Have agreed on the following measures:

General provisions

☐ The purpose of the procedures for implementing the principle of subsidiarity shall be to govern the manner in which the powers assigned to the Community institutions by the Treaties, in order to enable them to achieve the objectives laid down by the Treaties, are exercised.

☐ Such procedures shall not call into question the *acquis communautaire,* the provisions of the Treaties concerning the powers conferred on the institutions or the institutional balance.

Procedures

☐ In exercising its right of initiative, the Commission shall take into account the principle of subsidiarity and show that it has been observed. The European Parliament and the Council shall do likewise, in exercising the powers conferred on them by Articles 138b and 152 respectively of the Treaty establishing the European Community.

☐ The explanatory memorandum for any Commission proposal shall include a justification of the proposal under the principle of subsidiarity.

☐ Any amendment which may be made to the Commission's text, whether by the European Parliament or the Council, must, if it entails more extensive or intensive intervention by the Community, be accompanied by a justification under the principle of subsidiarity and Article 3b.

☐ The three institutions shall, under their internal procedures, regularly check that action envisaged complies with the provisions concerning subsidiarity as regards both the choice of legal instruments and the content of a proposal. Such checks must form an integral part of the substantive examination.

Review of compliance with the principle of subsidiarity

☐ Compliance with the principle of subsidiarity shall be reviewed under the normal Community process, in accordance with the rules laid down by the Treaties.

☐ The Commission shall draw up an annual report for the European Parliament and the Council on compliance with the principle of subsidiarity. The European Parliament shall hold a public debate on that report, with the participation of the Council and the Commission.

Final provisions

☐ In the event of general difficulties concerning the application of this Agreement, the President of the European Parliament, the President of the Council or the President of the Commission may request that an interinstitutional conference be convened in order to overcome such difficulties or to supplement or amend this Agreement.

☐ This Interinstitutional Agreement shall apply as from the entry into force of the Treaty on European Union.

10. CONVENTION FOR THE PROTECTION OF HUMAN RIGHTS AND FUNDAMENTAL FREEDOMS

(Signed at Rome, Nov. 4, 1950, effective Sept. 3, 1953)
1955 UNTS 220 (no. 2889)

(as amended by Protocol No. 11, ETS No. 155, eff. Nov. 1, 1998)

The governments signatory hereto, being members of the Council of Europe,

Considering the Universal Declaration of Human Rights proclaimed by the General Assembly of the United Nations on 10th December 1948;

Considering that this Declaration aims at securing the universal and effective recognition and observance of the Rights therein declared;

Considering that the aim of the Council of Europe is the achievement of greater unity between its members and that one of the methods by which that aim is to be pursued is the maintenance and further realisation of human rights and fundamental freedoms;

Reaffirming their profound belief in those fundamental freedoms which are the foundation of justice and peace in the world and are best maintained on the one hand by an effective political democracy and on the other by a common understanding and observance of the human rights upon which they depend;

Being resolved, as the governments of European countries which are like-minded and have a common heritage of political traditions, ideals, freedom and the rule of law, to take the first steps for the collective enforcement of certain of the rights stated in the Universal Declaration,

Have agreed as follows:

Article 1—Obligation to respect human rights

The High Contracting Parties shall secure to everyone within their jurisdiction the rights and freedoms defined in Section I of this Convention.

Section I—Rights and freedoms

Article 2—Right to life

1. Everyone's right to life shall be protected by law. No one shall be deprived of his life intentionally save in the execution of a sentence of a court following his conviction of a crime for which this penalty is provided by law.

2. Deprivation of life shall not be regarded as inflicted in contravention of this article when it results from the use of force which is no more than absolutely necessary:

    a. in defence of any person from unlawful violence;

    b. in order to effect a lawful arrest or to prevent the escape of a person lawfully detained;

c. in action lawfully taken for the purpose of quelling a riot or insurrection.

Article 3—Prohibition of torture

No one shall be subjected to torture or to inhuman or degrading treatment or punishment.

Article 4—Prohibition of slavery and forced labour

1. No one shall be held in slavery or servitude.

2. No one shall be required to perform forced or compulsory labour.

3. For the purpose of this article the term "forced or compulsory labour" shall not include:

    a. any work required to be done in the ordinary course of detention imposed according to the provisions of Article 5 of this Convention or during conditional release from such detention;

    b. any service of a military character or, in case of conscientious objectors in countries where they are recognised, service exacted instead of compulsory military service;

    c. any service exacted in case of an emergency or calamity threatening the life or well-being of the community;

    d. any work or service which forms part of normal civic obligations.

Article 5—Right to liberty and security

1. Everyone has the right to liberty and security of person. No one shall be deprived of his liberty save in the following cases and in accordance with a procedure prescribed by law:

    a. the lawful detention of a person after conviction by a competent court;

    b. the lawful arrest or detention of a person for non-compliance with the lawful order of a court or in order to secure the fulfilment of any obligation prescribed by law;

    c. the lawful arrest or detention of a person effected for the purpose of bringing him before the competent legal authority on reasonable suspicion of having committed an offence or when it is reasonably considered necessary to prevent his committing an offence or fleeing after having done so;

    d. the detention of a minor by lawful order for the purpose of educational supervision or his lawful detention for the purpose of bringing him before the competent legal authority;

    e. the lawful detention of persons for the prevention of the spreading of infectious diseases, of persons of unsound mind, alcoholics or drug addicts or vagrants;

    f. the lawful arrest or detention of a person to prevent his effecting an unauthorised entry into the country or of a person against whom action is being taken with a view to deportation or extradition.

2. Everyone who is arrested shall be informed promptly, in a language which he understands, of the reasons for his arrest and of any charge against him.

3. Everyone arrested or detained in accordance with the provisions of paragraph 1.c of this article shall be brought promptly before a judge or other officer authorised by law to exercise judicial power and shall be entitled to trial within a reasonable time or to release pending trial. Release may be conditioned by guarantees to appear for trial.

4. Everyone who is deprived of his liberty by arrest or detention shall be entitled to take proceedings by which the lawfulness of his detention shall be decided speedily by a court and his release ordered if the detention is not lawful.

5. Everyone who has been the victim of arrest or detention in contravention of the provisions of this article shall have an enforceable right to compensation.

Article 6—Right to a fair trial

1. In the determination of his civil rights and obligations or of any criminal charge against him, everyone is entitled to a fair and public hearing within a reasonable time by an independent and impartial tribunal established by law. Judgment shall be pronounced publicly but the press and public may be excluded from all or part of the trial in the interests of morals, public order or national security in a democratic society, where the interests of juveniles or the protection of the private life of the parties so require, or to the extent strictly necessary in the opinion of the court in special circumstances where publicity would prejudice the interests of justice.

2. Everyone charged with a criminal offence shall be presumed innocent until proved guilty according to law.

3. Everyone charged with a criminal offence has the following minimum rights:

    a. to be informed promptly, in a language which he understands and in detail, of the nature and cause of the accusation against him;

    b. to have adequate time and facilities for the preparation of his defence;

    c. to defend himself in person or through legal assistance of his own choosing or, if he has not sufficient means to pay for legal assistance, to be given it free when the interests of justice so require;

    d. to examine or have examined witnesses against him and to obtain the attendance and examination of witnesses on his behalf under the same conditions as witnesses against him;

    e. to have the free assistance of an interpreter if he cannot understand or speak the language used in court.

Article 7—No punishment without law

1. No one shall be held guilty of any criminal offence on account of any act or omission which did not constitute a criminal offence under national or international law at the time when it was committed. Nor shall a heavier penalty be imposed than the one that was applicable at the time the criminal offence was committed.

2. This article shall not prejudice the trial and punishment of any person for any act or omission which, at the time when it was committed, was criminal according to the general principles of law recognised by civilised nations.

Article 8—Right to respect for private and family life

1. Everyone has the right to respect for his private and family life, his home and his correspondence.

2. There shall be no interference by a public authority with the exercise of this right except such as is in accordance with the law and is necessary in a democratic society in the interests of national security, public safety or the economic well-being of the country, for the prevention of disorder or crime, for the protection of health or morals, or for the protection of the rights and freedoms of others.

Article 9—Freedom of thought, conscience and religion

1. Everyone has the right to freedom of thought, conscience and religion; this right includes freedom to change his religion or belief and freedom, either alone or in community with others and in public or private, to manifest his religion or belief, in worship, teaching, practice and observance.

2. Freedom to manifest one's religion or beliefs shall be subject only to such limitations as are prescribed by law and are necessary in a democratic society in the interests of public safety, for the protection of public order, health or morals, or for the protection of the rights and freedoms of others.

Article 10—Freedom of expression

1. Everyone has the right to freedom of expression. This right shall include freedom to hold opinions and to receive and impart information and ideas without interference by public authority and regardless of frontiers. This article shall not prevent States from requiring the licensing of broadcasting, television or cinema enterprises.

2. The exercise of these freedoms, since it carries with it duties and responsibilities, may be subject to such formalities, conditions, restrictions or penalties as are prescribed by law and are necessary in a democratic society, in the interests of national security, territorial integrity or public safety, for the prevention of disorder or crime, for the protection of health or morals, for the protection of the reputation or rights of others, for preventing the disclosure of information received in confidence, or for maintaining the authority and impartiality of the judiciary.

Article 11—Freedom of assembly and association

1. Everyone has the right to freedom of peaceful assembly and to freedom of association with others, including the right to form and to join trade unions for the protection of his interests.

2. No restrictions shall be placed on the exercise of these rights other than such as are prescribed by law and are necessary in a democratic society in the interests of national security or public safety, for the prevention of disorder or crime, for the protection of health or morals or for the protection of the rights and freedoms of others. This article shall not prevent the imposition of lawful restrictions on the exercise of these rights by members of the armed forces, of the police or of the administration of the State.

Article 12—Right to marry

Men and women of marriageable age have the right to marry and to found a family, according to the national laws governing the exercise of this right.

Article 13—Right to an effective remedy

Everyone whose rights and freedoms as set forth in this Convention are violated shall have an effective remedy before a national authority notwithstanding that the violation has been committed by persons acting in an official capacity.

Article 14—Prohibition of discrimination

The enjoyment of the rights and freedoms set forth in this Convention shall be secured without discrimination on any ground such as sex, race, colour, language, religion, political or other opinion, national or social origin, association with a national minority, property, birth or other status.

Article 15—Derogation in time of emergency

1. In time of war or other public emergency threatening the life of the nation any High Contracting Party may take measures derogating from its obligations under this Convention to the extent strictly required by the exigencies of the situation, provided that such measures are not inconsistent with its other obligations under international law.

2. No derogation from Article 2, except in respect of deaths resulting from lawful acts of war, or from Articles 3, 4 (paragraph 1) and 7 shall be made under this provision.

3. Any High Contracting Party availing itself of this right of derogation shall keep the Secretary General of the Council of Europe fully informed of the measures which it has taken and the reasons therefor. It shall also inform the Secretary General of the Council of Europe when such measures have ceased to operate and the provisions of the Convention are again being fully executed.

Article 16—Restrictions on political activity of aliens

Nothing in Articles 10, 11 and 14 shall be regarded as preventing the High Contracting Parties from imposing restrictions on the political activity of aliens.

Article 17—Prohibition of abuse of rights

Nothing in this Convention may be interpreted as implying for any State, group or person any right to engage in any activity or perform any act aimed at the destruction of any of the rights and freedoms set forth herein or at their limitation to a greater extent than is provided for in the Convention.

Article 18—Limitation on use of restrictions on rights

The restrictions permitted under this Convention to the said rights and freedoms shall not be applied for any purpose other than those for which they have been prescribed.

[Section II deals with the European Court of Human Rights, including its jurisdiction and procedure.]

[Section III contains miscellaneous provisions, including Article 53:]

Article 53—Safeguard for existing human rights

Nothing in this Convention shall be construed as limiting or derogating from any of the human rights and fundamental freedoms which may be ensured under the laws of any High Contracting Party or under any other agreement to which it is a Party.

PROTOCOL TO THE CONVENTION FOR THE PROTECTION OF HUMAN RIGHTS AND FUNDAMENTAL FREEDOMS

(Signed at Paris, March 20, 1952)
(as amended by Protocol No. 11, ETS No. 155, eff. Nov. 1, 1998)

Article 1—Protection of property

Every natural or legal person is entitled to the peaceful enjoyment of his possessions. No one shall be deprived of his possessions except in the public interest and subject to the conditions provided for by law and by the general principles of international law.

The preceding provisions shall not, however, in any way impair the right of a State to enforce such laws as it deems necessary to control the use of property in accordance with the general interest or to secure the payment of taxes or other contributions or penalties.

Article 2—Right to education

No person shall be denied the right to education. In the exercise of any functions which it assumes in relation to education and to teaching, the State shall respect the right of parents to ensure such education and teaching in conformity with their own religious and philosophical convictions.

Article 3—Right to free elections

The High Contracting Parties undertake to hold free elections at reasonable intervals by secret ballot, under conditions which will ensure the free expression of the opinion of the people in the choice of the legislature.

* * *

PROTOCOL NO. 4 TO THE CONVENTION FOR THE PROTECTION OF HUMAN RIGHTS AND FUNDAMENTAL FREEDOMS

(Signed at Strasbourg, Sept. 16, 1963)

(as amended by Protocol No. 11, ETS No. 155, eff. Nov. 1, 1998)

Article 1—Prohibition of imprisonment for debt

No one shall be deprived of his liberty merely on the ground of inability to fulfil a contractual obligation.

Article 2—Freedom of movement

1. Everyone lawfully within the territory of a State shall, within that territory, have the right to liberty of movement and freedom to choose his residence.

2. Everyone shall be free to leave any country, including his own.

3. No restrictions shall be placed on the exercise of these rights other than such as are in accordance with law and are necessary in a democratic society in the interests of national security or public safety, for the maintenance of *ordre public*, for the prevention of crime, for the protection of health or morals, or for the protection of the rights and freedoms of others.

4. The rights set forth in paragraph 1 may also be subject, in particular areas, to restrictions imposed in accordance with law and justified by the public interest in a democratic society.

Article 3—Prohibition of expulsion of nationals

1. No one shall be expelled, by means either of an individual or of a collective measure, from the territory of the State of which he is a national.

2. No one shall be deprived of the right to enter the territory of the state of which he is a national.

Article 4—Prohibition of collective expulsion of aliens

Collective expulsion of aliens is prohibited.

* * *

Article 5—Relationship to the Convention

As between the High Contracting Parties the provisions of Articles 1, 2, 3 and 4 of this Protocol shall be regarded as additional articles to the Convention and all the provisions of the Convention shall apply accordingly.

Article 6—Signature and ratification

This Protocol shall be open for signature by the members of the Council of Europe, who are the signatories of the Convention; it shall be ratified at the same time as or after the ratification of the Convention. It shall enter into force after the deposit of ten instruments of ratification. As regards any signatory ratifying subsequently, the Protocol shall enter into force at the date of the deposit of its instrument of ratification.

The instruments of ratification shall be deposited with the Secretary General of the Council of Europe, who will notify all members of the names of those who have ratified.

Done at Paris on the 20th day of March 1952, in English and French, both texts being equally authentic, in a single copy which shall remain deposited in the archives of the Council of Europe. The Secretary General shall transmit certified copies to each of the signatory governments.

PROTOCOL NO. 6 TO THE CONVENTION FOR THE PROTECTION OF HUMAN RIGHTS AND FUNDAMENTAL FREEDOMS

(Signed at Strasbourg, April 28, 1983)

(as amended by Protocol No. 11, ETS No. 155, eff. Nov. 1, 1998)

Article 1—Abolition of the death penalty

The death penalty shall be abolished. No one shall be condemned to such penalty or executed.

Article 2—Death penalty in time of war

A State may make provision in its law for the death penalty in respect of acts committed in time of war or of imminent threat of war; such penalty shall be applied only in the instances laid down in the law and in accordance with its provisions. The State shall communicate to the Secretary General of the Council of Europe the relevant provisions of that law.

Article 3—Prohibition of derogations

No derogation from the provisions of this Protocol shall be made under Article 15 of the Convention.

Article 4—Prohibition of reservations

No reservation may be made under Article 57 of the Convention in respect of the provisions of this Protocol.

* * *

PROTOCOL NO. 7 TO THE CONVENTION FOR THE PROTECTION OF HUMAN RIGHTS AND FUNDAMENTAL FREEDOMS

(Signed at Strasbourg, Nov. 22, 1984)

(as amended by Protocol No. 11, ETS No. 155, eff. Nov. 1, 1998)

Article 1—Procedural safeguards relating to expulsion of aliens

1. An alien lawfully resident in the territory of a State shall not be expelled therefrom except in pursuance of a decision reached in accordance with law and shall be allowed:

a. to submit reasons against his expulsion,

b. to have his case reviewed, and

c. to be represented for these purposes before the competent authority or a person or persons designated by that authority.

2. An alien may be expelled before the exercise of his rights under paragraph 1.a, b and c of this Article, when such expulsion is necessary in the interests of public order or is grounded on reasons of national security.

Article 2—Right of appeal in criminal matters

1. Everyone convicted of a criminal offence by a tribunal shall have the right to have his conviction or sentence reviewed by a higher tribunal. The exercise of this right, including the grounds on which it may be exercised, shall be governed by law.

2. This right may be subject to exceptions in regard to offences of a minor character, as prescribed by law, or in cases in which the person concerned was tried in the first instance by the highest tribunal or was convicted following an appeal against acquittal.

Article 3—Compensation for wrongful conviction

When a person has by a final decision been convicted of a criminal offence and when subsequently his conviction has been reversed, or he has been pardoned, on the ground that a new or newly discovered fact shows conclusively that there has been a miscarriage of justice, the person who has suffered punishment as a result of such conviction shall be compensated according to the law or the practice of the State concerned, unless it is proved that the non-disclosure of the unknown fact in time is wholly or partly attributable to him.

Article 4—Right not to be tried or punished twice

1. No one shall be liable to be tried or punished again in criminal proceedings under the jurisdiction of the same State for an offence for which he has already been finally acquitted or convicted in accordance with the law and penal procedure of that State.

2. The provisions of the preceding paragraph shall not prevent the reopening of the case in accordance with the law and penal procedure of the State concerned, if there is evidence of new or newly discovered facts, or if there has been a fundamental defect in the previous proceedings, which could affect the outcome of the case.

3. No derogation from this Article shall be made under Article 15 of the Convention.

Article 5—Equality between spouses

Spouses shall enjoy equality of rights and responsibilities of a private law character between them, and in their relations with their children, as to marriage, during marriage and in the event of its dissolution. This Article shall not prevent States from taking such measures as are necessary in the interests of the children.

* * *

PROTOCOL NO. 12 TO THE CONVENTION FOR THE PROTECTION OF HUMAN RIGHTS AND FUNDAMENTAL FREEDOMS

(Signed at Rome, Nov. 4, 2000)

Article 1—General prohibition of discrimination

1. The enjoyment of any right set forth by law shall be secured without discrimination on any ground such as sex, race, colour, language, religion, political or other opinion, national or social origin, association with a national minority, property, birth or other status.

2. No one shall be discriminated against by any public authority on any ground such as those mentioned in paragraph 1.

* * *

11. JOINT DECLARATION BY THE EUROPEAN PARLIAMENT, THE COUNCIL AND THE COMMISSION

(Signed at Luxembourg, April 5, 1977)
O.J. C 103/1 (April 27, 1977)

THE EUROPEAN PARLIAMENT, THE COUNCIL AND THE COMMISSION,

Whereas the Treaties establishing the European Communities are based on the principle of respect for the law;

Whereas, as the Court of Justice has recognized, that law comprises, over and above the rules embodied in the treaties and secondary Community legislation, the general principles of law and in particular the fundamental rights, principles and rights on which the constitutional law of the Member States is based;

Whereas, in particular, all the Member States are Contracting Parties to the European Convention for the Protection of Human Rights and Fundamental Freedoms signed in Rome on 4 November 1950,

HAVE ADOPTED THE FOLLOWING DECLARATION:

1. The European Parliament, the Council and the Commission stress the prime importance they attach to the protection of fundamental rights, as derived in particular from the constitutions of the Member States and the European Convention for the Protection of Human Rights and Fundamental Freedoms.

2. In the exercise of their powers and in pursuance of the aims of the European Communities they respect and will continue to respect these rights.

12. CHARTER OF FUNDAMENTAL RIGHTS OF THE EUROPEAN UNION

O.J. C 364/1 (Dec. 18, 2000)

SOLEMN PROCLAMATION (done at Nice, Dec. 7, 2000)

The European Parliament, the Council and the Commission solemnly proclaim the text below as the Charter of fundamental rights of the European Union.

PREAMBLE

The peoples of Europe, in creating an ever closer union among them, are resolved to share a peaceful future based on common values.

Conscious of its spiritual and moral heritage, the Union is founded on the indivisible, universal values of human dignity, freedom, equality and solidarity; it is based on the principles of democracy and the rule of law. It places the individual at the heart of its activities, by establishing the citizenship of the Union and by creating an area of freedom, security and justice.

The Union contributes to the preservation and to the development of these common values while respecting the diversity of the cultures and traditions of the peoples of Europe as well as the national identities of the Member States and the organisation of their public authorities at national, regional and local levels; it seeks to promote balanced and sustainable development and ensures free movement of persons, goods, services and capital, and the freedom of establishment.

To this end, it is necessary to strengthen the protection of fundamental rights in the light of changes in society, social progress and scientific and technological developments by making those rights more visible in a Charter.

This Charter reaffirms, with due regard for the powers and tasks of the Community and the Union and the principle of subsidiarity, the rights as they result, in particular, from the constitutional traditions and international obligations common to the Member States, the Treaty on European Union, the Community Treaties, the European Convention for the Protection of Human Rights and Fundamental Freedoms, the Social Charters adopted by the Community and by the Council of Europe and the case-law of the Court of Justice of the European Communities and of the European Court of Human Rights.

Enjoyment of these rights entails responsibilities and duties with regard to other persons, to the human community and to future generations.

The Union therefore recognises the rights, freedoms and principles set out hereafter.

CHAPTER I
DIGNITY

Article 1. Human dignity

Human dignity is inviolable. It must be respected and protected.

Article 2. Right to life

1. Everyone has the right to life.
2. No one shall be condemned to the death penalty, or executed.

Article 3. Right to the integrity of the person

1. Everyone has the right to respect for his or her physical and mental integrity.
2. In the fields of medicine and biology, the following must be respected in particular:

— the free and informed consent of the person concerned, according to the procedures laid down by law,

— the prohibition of eugenic practices, in particular those aiming at the selection of persons,

— the prohibition on making the human body and its parts as such a source of financial gain,

— the prohibition of the reproductive cloning of human beings.

Article 4. Prohibition of torture and inhuman or degrading treatment or punishment

No one shall be subjected to torture or to inhuman or degrading treatment or punishment.

Article 5. Prohibition of slavery and forced labour

1. No one shall be held in slavery or servitude.
2. No one shall be required to perform forced or compulsory labour.
3. Trafficking in human beings is prohibited.

CHAPTER II

FREEDOMS

Article 6. Right to liberty and security

Everyone has the right to liberty and security of person.

Article 7. Respect for private and family life

Everyone has the right to respect for his or her private and family life, home and communications.

Article 8. Protection of personal data

1. Everyone has the right to the protection of personal data concerning him or her.
2. Such data must be processed fairly for specified purposes and on the basis of the consent of the person concerned or some other legitimate basis laid down by law. Everyone has the right of access to data which has been collected concerning him or her, and the right to have it rectified.

3. Compliance with these rules shall be subject to control by an independent authority.

Article 9. Right to marry and right to found a family

The right to marry and the right to found a family shall be guaranteed in accordance with the national laws governing the exercise of these rights.

Article 10. Freedom of thought, conscience and religion

1. Everyone has the right to freedom of thought, conscience and religion. This right includes freedom to change religion or belief and freedom, either alone or in community with others and in public or in private, to manifest religion or belief, in worship, teaching, practice and observance.

2. The right to conscientious objection is recognised, in accordance with the national laws governing the exercise of this right.

Article 11. Freedom of expression and information

1. Everyone has the right to freedom of expression. This right shall include freedom to hold opinions and to receive and impart information and ideas without interference by public authority and regardless of frontiers.

2. The freedom and pluralism of the media shall be respected.

Article 12. Freedom of assembly and of association

1. Everyone has the right to freedom of peaceful assembly and to freedom of association at all levels, in particular in political, trade union and civic matters, which implies the right of everyone to form and to join trade unions for the protection of his or her interests.

2. Political parties at Union level contribute to expressing the political will of the citizens of the Union.

Article 13. Freedom of the arts and sciences

The arts and scientific research shall be free of constraint. Academic freedom shall be respected.

Article 14. Right to education

1. Everyone has the right to education and to have access to vocational and continuing training.

2. This right includes the possibility to receive free compulsory education.

3. The freedom to found educational establishments with due respect for democratic principles and the right of parents to ensure the education and teaching of their children in conformity with their religious, philosophical and pedagogical convictions shall be respected, in accordance with the national laws governing the exercise of such freedom and right.

Article 15. Freedom to choose an occupation and right to engage in work

1. Everyone has the right to engage in work and to pursue a freely chosen or accepted occupation.

2. Every citizen of the Union has the freedom to seek employment, to work, to exercise the right of establishment and to provide services in any Member State.

3. Nationals of third countries who are authorised to work in the territories of the Member States are entitled to working conditions equivalent to those of citizens of the Union.

Article 16. Freedom to conduct a business

The freedom to conduct a business in accordance with Community law and national laws and practices is recognised.

Article 17. Right to property

1. Everyone has the right to own, use, dispose of and bequeath his or her lawfully acquired possessions. No one may be deprived of his or her possessions, except in the public interest and in the cases and under the conditions provided for by law, subject to fair compensation being paid in good time for their loss. The use of property may be regulated by law in so far as is necessary for the general interest.

2. Intellectual property shall be protected.

Article 18. Right to asylum

The right to asylum shall be guaranteed with due respect for the rules of the Geneva Convention of 28 July 1951 and the Protocol of 31 January 1967 relating to the status of refugees and in accordance with the Treaty establishing the European Community.

Article 19. Protection in the event of removal, expulsion or extradition

1. Collective expulsions are prohibited.

2. No one may be removed, expelled or extradited to a State where there is a serious risk that he or she would be subjected to the death penalty, torture or other inhuman or degrading treatment or punishment.

CHAPTER III
EQUALITY

Article 20. Equality before the law

Everyone is equal before the law.

Article 21. Non-discrimination

1. Any discrimination based on any ground such as sex, race, colour, ethnic or social origin, genetic features, language, religion or belief, political or any other opinion, membership of a national minority, property, birth, disability, age or sexual orientation shall be prohibited.

2. Within the scope of application of the Treaty establishing the European Community and of the Treaty on European Union, and without prejudice to the special provisions of those Treaties, any discrimination on grounds of nationality shall be prohibited.

Article 22. Cultural, religious and linguistic diversity

The Union shall respect cultural, religious and linguistic diversity.

Article 23. Equality between men and women

Equality between men and women must be ensured in all areas, including employment, work and pay.

The principle of equality shall not prevent the maintenance or adoption of measures providing for specific advantages in favour of the under-represented sex.

Article 24. The Rights of the Child

1. Children shall have the right to such protection and care as is necessary for their well-being. They may express their views freely. Such views shall be taken into consideration on matters which concern them in accordance with their age and maturity.

2. In all actions relating to children, whether taken by public authorities or private institutions, the child's best interests must be a primary consideration.

3. Every child shall have the right to maintain on a regular basis a personal relationship and direct contact with both his or her parents, unless that is contrary to his or her interests.

Article 25. The rights of the elderly

The Union recognises and respects the rights of the elderly to lead a life of dignity and independence and to participate in social and cultural life.

Article 26. Integration of persons with disabilities

The Union recognises and respects the right of persons with disabilities to benefit from measures designed to ensure their independence, social and occupational integration and participation in the life of the community.

CHAPTER IV

SOLIDARITY

Article 27. Workers' right to information and consultation within the undertaking

Workers or their representatives must, at the appropriate levels, be guaranteed information and consultation in good time in the cases and under the conditions provided for by Community law and national laws and practices.

Article 28. Right of collective bargaining and action

Workers and employers, or their respective organisations, have, in accordance with Community law and national laws and practices, the right to negotiate and conclude collective agreements at the appropriate levels and, in cases of conflicts of interest, to take collective action to defend their interests, including strike action.

Article 29. Right of access to placement services

Everyone has the right of access to a free placement service.

Article 30. Protection in the event of unjustified dismissal

Every worker has the right to protection against unjustified dismissal, in accordance with Community law and national laws and practices.

Article 31. Fair and just working conditions

1. Every worker has the right to working conditions which respect his or her health, safety and dignity.

2. Every worker has the right to limitation of maximum working hours, to daily and weekly rest periods and to an annual period of paid leave.

Article 32. Prohibition of child labour and protection of young people at work

The employment of children is prohibited. The minimum age of admission to employment may not be lower than the minimum school-leaving age, without prejudice to such rules as may be more favourable to young people and except for limited derogations.

Young people admitted to work must have working conditions appropriate to their age and be protected against economic exploitation and any work likely to harm their safety, health or physical, mental, moral or social development or to interfere with their education.

Article 33. Family and professional life

1. The family shall enjoy legal, economic and social protection.

2. To reconcile family and professional life, everyone shall have the right to protection from dismissal for a reason connected with maternity and the right to paid maternity leave and to parental leave following the birth or adoption of a child.

Article 34. Social security and social assistance

1. The Union recognises and respects the entitlement to social security benefits and social services providing protection in cases such as maternity, illness, industrial accidents, dependency or old age, and in the case of loss of employment, in accordance with the rules laid down by Community law and national laws and practices.

2. Everyone residing and moving legally within the European Union is entitled to social security benefits and social advantages in accordance with Community law and national laws and practices.

3. In order to combat social exclusion and poverty, the Union recognises and respects the right to social and housing assistance so as to ensure a decent existence for all those who lack sufficient resources, in accordance with the rules laid down by Community law and national laws and practices.

Article 35. Health care

Everyone has the right of access to preventive health care and the right to benefit from medical treatment under the conditions established by national laws and practices. A high level of human health protection shall be ensured in the definition and implementation of all Union policies and activities.

Article 36. Access to services of general economic interest

The Union recognises and respects access to services of general economic interest as provided for in national laws and practices, in accordance with the Treaty establishing the European Community, in order to promote the social and territorial cohesion of the Union.

Article 37. Environmental protection

A high level of environmental protection and the improvement of the quality of the environment must be integrated into the policies of the Union and ensured in accordance with the principle of sustainable development.

Article 38. Consumer protection

Union policies shall ensure a high level of consumer protection.

CHAPTER V

CITIZENS' RIGHTS

Article 39. Right to vote and to stand as a candidate at elections to the European Parliament

1. Every citizen of the Union has the right to vote and to stand as a candidate at elections to the European Parliament in the Member State in which he or she resides, under the same conditions as nationals of that State.

2. Members of the European Parliament shall be elected by direct universal suffrage in a free and secret ballot.

Article 40. Right to vote and to stand as a candidate at municipal elections

Every citizen of the Union has the right to vote and to stand as a candidate at municipal elections in the Member State in which he or she resides under the same conditions as nationals of that State.

Article 41. Right to good administration

1. Every person has the right to have his or her affairs handled impartially, fairly and within a reasonable time by the institutions and bodies of the Union.

2. This right includes:

— the right of every person to be heard, before any individual measure which would affect him or her adversely is taken;

— the right of every person to have access to his or her file, while respecting the legitimate interests of confidentiality and of professional and business secrecy;

— the obligation of the administration to give reasons for its decisions.

3. Every person has the right to have the Community make good any damage caused by its institutions or by its servants in the performance of their duties, in accordance with the general principles common to the laws of the Member States.

4. Every person may write to the institutions of the Union in one of the languages of the Treaties and must have an answer in the same language.

Article 42. Right of access to documents

Any citizen of the Union, and any natural or legal person residing or having its registered office in a Member State, has a right of access to European Parliament, Council and Commission documents.

Article 43. Ombudsman

Any citizen of the Union and any natural or legal person residing or having its registered office in a Member State has the right to refer to the Ombudsman of the Union cases of maladministration in the activities of the Community institutions or bodies, with the exception of the Court of Justice and the Court of First Instance acting in their judicial role.

Article 44. Right to petition

Any citizen of the Union and any natural or legal person residing or having its registered office in a Member State has the right to petition the European Parliament.

Article 45. Freedom of movement and of residence

1. Every citizen of the Union has the right to move and reside freely within the territory of the Member States.

2. Freedom of movement and residence may be granted, in accordance with the Treaty establishing the European Community, to nationals of third countries legally resident in the territory of a Member State.

Article 46. Diplomatic and consular protection

Every citizen of the Union shall, in the territory of a third country in which the Member State of which he or she is a national is not represented, be entitled to protection by the diplomatic or consular authorities of any Member State, on the same conditions as the nationals of that Member State.

CHAPTER VI

JUSTICE

Article 47. Right to an effective remedy and to a fair trial

Everyone whose rights and freedoms guaranteed by the law of the Union are violated has the right to an effective remedy before a tribunal in compliance with the conditions laid down in this Article.

Everyone is entitled to a fair and public hearing within a reasonable time by an independent and impartial tribunal previously established by law. Everyone shall have the possibility of being advised, defended and represented.

Legal aid shall be made available to those who lack sufficient resources in so far as such aid is necessary to ensure effective access to justice.

Article 48. Presumption of innocence and right of defence

1. Everyone who has been charged shall be presumed innocent until proved guilty according to law.

2. Respect for the rights of the defence of anyone who has been charged shall be guaranteed.

Article 49. Principles of legality and proportionality of criminal offences and penalties

1. No one shall be held guilty of any criminal offence on account of any act or omission which did not constitute a criminal offence under national law or international law at the time when it was committed. Nor shall a heavier penalty be imposed than that which was applicable at the time the criminal offence was committed. If, subsequent to the commission of a criminal offence, the law provides for a lighter penalty, that penalty shall be applicable.

2. This Article shall not prejudice the trial and punishment of any person for any act or omission which, at the time when it was committed, was criminal according to the general principles recognised by the community of nations.

3. The severity of penalties must not be disproportionate to the criminal offence.

Article 50. Right not to be tried or punished twice in criminal proceedings for the same criminal offence

No one shall be liable to be tried or punished again in criminal proceedings for an offence for which he or she has already been finally acquitted or convicted within the Union in accordance with the law.

CHAPTER VII

GENERAL PROVISIONS

Article 51. Scope

1. The provisions of this Charter are addressed to the institutions and bodies of the Union with due regard for the principle of subsidiarity and to the Member States only when they are implementing Union law. They shall therefore respect the rights, observe the principles and promote the application thereof in accordance with their respective powers.

2. This Charter does not establish any new power or task for the Community or the Union, or modify powers and tasks defined by the Treaties.

Article 52. Scope of guaranteed rights

1. Any limitation on the exercise of the rights and freedoms recognised by this Charter must be provided for by law and respect the essence of those rights and freedoms. Subject to the principle of proportionality, limitations may be made only if they are necessary and genuinely meet objectives of general interest recognised by the Union or the need to protect the rights and freedoms of others.

2. Rights recognised by this Charter which are based on the Community Treaties or the Treaty on European Union shall be exercised under the conditions and within the limits defined by those Treaties.

3. In so far as this Charter contains rights which correspond to rights guaranteed by the Convention for the Protection of Human Rights and Fundamental Freedoms, the meaning and scope of those rights shall be the same as those laid down by the said Convention. This provision shall not prevent Union law providing more extensive protection.

Article 53. Level of protection

Nothing in this Charter shall be interpreted as restricting or adversely affecting human rights and fundamental freedoms as recognised, in their respective fields of application, by Union law and international law and by international agreements to which the Union, the Community or all the Member States are party, including the European Convention for the Protection of Human Rights and Fundamental Freedoms, and by the Member States' constitutions.

Article 54. Prohibition of abuse of rights

Nothing in this Charter shall be interpreted as implying any right to engage in any activity or to perform any act aimed at the destruction of any of the rights and freedoms recognised in this Charter or at their limitation to a greater extent than is provided for herein.

13. COMMUNICATION FROM THE COMMISSION ON THE LEGAL NATURE OF THE CHARTER OF FUNDAMENTAL RIGHTS OF THE EUROPEAN UNION

COM (2000) 644, O.J. C 364/1 (Oct., 10, 2000)

(footnotes deleted)

THE CHARACTERISTICS OF THE DRAFT CHARTER

1. The challenge of preparing the draft Charter has been taken up: at the formal session of the Convention on 2 October 2000, the President of the Convention responsible for preparing it recorded that there was broad consensus on the draft and sent it to the President of the European Council.

The draft Charter offers great potential value added. By bringing together in a single instrument the rights hitherto scattered over a range of national and international instruments, it enshrines the very essence of the European acquis regarding fundamental rights.

2. This is a balanced text that makes ambitious innovations:

— all personal rights—civil, political, economic and social rights and the rights of citizens of the European Union—are brought together in a single instrument. It thus throws into the sharpest relief the principle of the indivisibility of rights. The draft Charter breaks with the distinction hitherto made in both European and international documents between civil and political rights on the one side and economic and social rights on the other, enumerating all rights around a few major principles: human dignity, fundamental freedoms, equality, solidarity, citizenship and justice:

— in respect for the principle of universalism, the rights set forth in the draft are generally given to all persons, irrespective of their nationality or residence. The position is different for the rights that are most directly bound up with citizenship of the Union, which are given only to citizens (such as participation in elections to the European Parliament or in local elections), and for certain rights that are related to a particular status (rights of children, certain social rights of workers, for example);

— the draft is decidedly contemporary in that it sets forth rights which, without being strictly new, such as data protection and rights linked to bioethics, are designed to meet the challenges of current and future development of information technologies and genetic engineering;

— the draft also meets the strong and legitimate contemporary demand for transparency and impartiality in the operation of the Community administration, incorporating the rights of access to administrative documents of the Community institutions and the right to sound administration that sum up the tenor of the decisions of the Court of Justice;

— the gender-neutral language used in the text also deserves highlighting. The draft is addressed to everybody, with no predominance of one gender over the other;

— in formal terms, it is drafted clearly and concisely and it will be easy for all those to whom it is addressed to understand. This was the first condition that had to be met in order to satisfy the demand from the Cologne European Council for 'a Charter of fundamental rights ... to make their overriding importance and relevance more visible to the Union's citizens'. It is also a condition for the enjoyment of all the benefits of certainty as to the law that the Charter must offer in areas where Union law applies.

3. In the light of the characteristics of the draft—which satisfies the requests made by the Commission in its Communication of 13 September—the Commission representative was able to indicate his full approval of the draft Charter.

The Commission is convinced that the value added by the draft is real and that this value added is the basis for the future success of the Charter, irrespective of its ultimate legal nature.

THE NATURE AND EFFECTS OF THE CHARTER

4. The question of the nature of the Charter has been at the centre of the debate ever since the Cologne European Council decided to prepare a draft Charter. The Heads of State or Government decided to answer this question in two stages:

— first, the Charter should be solemnly proclaimed by the European Parliament, the Commission and the Council,

— then, "It will then have to be considered whether and, if so, how the Charter should be integrated into the treaties."

5. There have been a number of expressions of opinion on the question.

The European Parliament, in two resolutions passed on 16 March and 2 October 2000, resolutely supported a mandatory Charter incorporated in the Treaties. So did the Economic and Social Committee and the Committee of the Regions in opinions given at their September 2000 sessions.

The same call was made virtually unanimously by the representatives of civil society at the hearings organised by the Convention. It is unlikely that the expectations aroused in public opinion by the decision to prepare the Charter could be satisfied by mere proclamation by the Community institutions without incorporation of the Charter in the Treaties.

Many members of the Convention, belonging to different component groups and political trends, supported a Charter incorporated in the Treaties.

Lastly, the Commission, in its Communication of 13 September, undertook to present a Communication on the nature of the Charter.

6. The Commission had an opportunity to express an opinion on the nature of the Charter when answering an oral question in the European Parliament last December. It stated that the Convention, both during its proceedings and in its final outcome, should leave open the two options as to the Charter's final status, as envisaged by the Heads of State or Government—a legally mandatory instrument incorporated in the Treaties or a solemn political declaration.

The Commission also stated that the draft Charter should meet two fundamental objectives: visibility for the citizen and the certainty as to the law that the Charter must offer in areas where Union law applies.

7. It is in this spirit, notably at the instigation of the President of the Convention, Mr Herzog, that from the very outset the Convention's proceedings were directed towards producing a text 'as if' it were to be incorporated in the Treaties, thus leaving the final choice to the European Council.

8. This "as if" doctrine clearly inspired the Convention. If a Charter had been prepared solely for presentation as a political declaration, the general provisions of the draft, which are the most important and the most difficult ones (Chapter VII), would have been superfluous.

The importance of these clauses must be emphasised: they are the guarantee of the Charter's future success.

They are the place where it is specified just what the Charter is—an instrument to verify respect for fundamental rights by the institutions and the Member States when they act under Union law. This is made clear by Article 51, which provides that the Charter is addressed to the Union institutions and bodies and to the Member States, when they give effect to Union law.

9. But these provisions also seek to offer an appropriate response to the highly important questions that will arise in the event of incorporation of the Charter in the Treaties.

The Commission considers that the draft Charter offers an acceptable response:

— respect for the autonomy of Union law: it is also important that the Charter be incorporated harmoniously into the Union legal system and that its underlying legal principles be respected. This applies in particular to the autonomy of the Community legal order in relation to international law and the national law of the Member States; the Charter is drafted in such a way as to respect that autonomy. In particular, the explicit recognition by the last sentence of Article 52(3) is perfectly satisfactory: there is nothing to preclude Union law from giving more extensive protection than the European Convention;

— the relationship between the Charter and the European Convention for the Protection of Human Rights and Fundamental Freedoms: the risk of disparity between the rights and freedoms secured by the European Convention and those set forth in the Charter, and the risk of the case-law of the Luxembourg and Strasbourg courts diverging, was carefully analysed while the draft Charter was being prepared. The solutions adopted by Article 52(3) of the draft are entirely satisfactory; there was the same broad consensus on them as on the other provisions of the draft, and the Council of Europe observers in the Convention also supported them: the rights set forth in the Charter correspond in their meaning and scope to rights already secured by the European Convention, without prejudice to the principle of the autonomy of Union law. The risk of the case-law of the European Court of Human Rights diverging from that of the Court of Justice of the European Communities should thereby be removed. If the draft Charter is silent on the question of Union accession to the European Convention, of course, it must be acknowledged that the question remains open. The existence of the Charter will not render the question of accession any less interesting, the effect being to introduce external monitoring of fundamental rights at Union level; by the same token accession to the Convention would not make the preparation of the Union Charter any less valuable;

— the relationship between the Charter and the Union's powers, and respect for the principle of subsidiarity: in no case will the Charter be a means of extending the Community's powers and the Union's tasks. And the subsidiarity principle must be respected. Article 51 of the draft is perfectly clear; this is borne out by paragraph 5 of the Preamble, stating, 'just in case', how attentive the authors of the draft were to these points;

— the relationship between the Charter and the national Constitutions: it might have been feared that the Charter would make it necessary for Member States to amend their constitutions. This will manifestly not be the case, not just because of one of the general provisions of the draft but also because of the definition of the rights it sets forth. In any event, proper account has been taken of observations on the need to attain this objective, made throughout the Convention's proceedings, in particular by government representatives. At the end of the day it is clear that the Charter will not replace national Constitutions in the area within its scope—respect for fundamental rights at national level. And it is clear that the relationship between Union primary law, which would include the Charter if it is incorporated in the Treaties, and national law will remain unchanged;

— a major advance in certainty as to the law: at this time it seems clear to the Commission that the Charter will not endanger certainty as to the law relating to fundamental rights. Quite the contrary: it will increase it in no small measure. The Charter will offer a clear guide for the interpretation of fundamental rights by the Court of Justice which in the current situation has to use disparate, sometimes uncertain, sources of inspiration. It must also be stressed that the Charter makes no change to the redress procedures and court architecture provided for by the Treaties, since it opens up no new procedures for seeking redress in the Community courts.

10. Consequently, given the foregoing considerations, it is reasonable to assume that the Charter will produce all its effects, legal and others, whatever its nature. As the Commission said in the European Parliament on 3 October 2000, it is clear that it would be difficult for the Council and the Commission, who are to proclaim it solemnly, to ignore in the future, in their legislative function, an instrument prepared at the request of the European Council by the full range of sources of national and European legitimacy acting in concert.

Likewise, it is highly likely that the Court of Justice will seek inspiration in it, as it already does in other fundamental rights instruments. It can reasonably be expected that the Charter will become mandatory through the Court's interpretation of it as belonging to the general principles of Community law.

11. The Commission considers that the Charter, by reason of its content, its tight drafting and its high political and symbolic value, ought properly to be incorporated in the Treaties sooner or later. For the Commission, this incorporation is not a question to be addressed in theoretical or doctrinal terms. It must be addressed in terms of legal effectiveness and common sense. It is therefore preferable, for the sake of visibility and certainty as to the law, for the Charter to be made mandatory in its own right and not just through its judicial interpretation.

In practice, the real question is when and how it should be incorporated in the Treaties.

WHAT SHOULD BE DECIDED TODAY

12. The Commission is aware of the importance attached to the Charter being able to have full effect in the future. It does not wish to overload an already heavy political agenda. It will be for the Heads of State or Government to take up that challenge. But the Commission's political assessment is that any decision on the matter must be based on clear criteria that have already been put forward:

* evaluation of the content of the Charter,
* greater certainty as to the law,
* visibility of rights for citizens,
* a firm foundation for the European venture in the values protected by fundamental rights.

Irrespective of all this, the Commission emphasises that the Heads of State or Government have a number of options regarding both the technicalities of incorporation in the Treaties and the timing.

Regarding timing, the European Council might consider entering the question on the agenda for the current Intergovernmental Conference. It could take a decision to that effect at the Biarritz meeting. But this question cannot be considered without regard for the scope of the proceedings as already defined by the European Council for the present Intergovernmental Conference or for the prospect of reorganising the Treaties as proposed by the Commission at that conference in its communication of 12 July 2000, "A Basic Treaty for the European Union".

As the Commission sees it, there is a very close link between reorganisation of the Treaties and incorporation of the Charter in them. Consequently the Heads of State or Government should at the very least decide at Nice to launch some kind of process in this direction, clearly setting objectives and procedural and other details.

This is the only way forward that provided a basis for an effort to educate the citizen and give practical form to the technical details that will bring a sound result within reach.

Regarding the technical details, the European Council might in due course envisage, for example, straightforward incorporation of the articles of the Charter in the Treaty on European Union in a Title headed 'Fundamental Rights', or incorporation of the Charter in a Protocol annexed to the Treaties.

In any event, the question arises whether Article 6(2) of the Treaty on European Union can be kept in its present form. At the very least it must be generally obvious that, while leaving open the possibility of future developments, there can be no question of pretending to ignore the Charter as a solemn political declaration, in the light of Article 6(2). The Commission considers that this question should be discussed by the Intergovernmental Conference after the Biarritz European Council. The point would be to consider the possibility of amending this provision of the Treaty on European Union, bearing in mind the sequence determined by the conclusions of the Cologne European Council: proclamation of the Charter by the European Council at Nice, then incorporation in the Treaties.

14. PARLIAMENT AND COUNCIL REGULATION 1049/2001 OF MAY 30, 2001

regarding public access to European Parliament, Council and Commission documents

O.J. L 145/43 (May 31, 2001)

THE EUROPEAN PARLIAMENT AND THE COUNCIL OF THE EUROPEAN UNION,

Having regard to the Treaty establishing the European Community, and in particular Article 255(2) thereof,

Having regard to the proposal from the Commission (1),

Acting in accordance with the procedure referred to in Article 251 of the Treaty (2),

Whereas:

(1) The second subparagraph of Article 1 of the Treaty on European Union enshrines the concept of openness, stating that the Treaty marks a new stage in the process of creating an ever closer union among the peoples of Europe, in which decisions are taken as openly as possible and as closely as possible to the citizen.

(2) Openness enables citizens to participate more closely in the decision-making process and guarantees that the administration enjoys greater legitimacy and is more effective and more accountable to the citizen in a democratic system. Openness contributes to strengthening the principles of democracy and respect for fundamental rights as laid down in Article 6 of the EU Treaty and in the Charter of Fundamental Rights of the European Union.

(3) The conclusions of the European Council meetings held at Birmingham, Edinburgh and Copenhagen stressed the need to introduce greater transparency into the work of the Union institutions. This Regulation consolidates the initiatives that the institutions have already taken with a view to improving the transparency of the decision-making process.

(4) The purpose of this Regulation is to give the fullest possible effect to the right of public access to documents and to lay down the general principles and limits on such access in accordance with Article 255(2) of the EC Treaty.

(5) Since the question of access to documents is not covered by provisions of the Treaty establishing the European Coal and Steel Community and the Treaty establishing the European Atomic Energy Community, the European Parliament, the Council and the Commission should, in accordance with Declaration No 41 attached to the Final Act of the Treaty of Amsterdam, draw guidance from this Regulation as regards documents concerning the activities covered by those two Treaties.

(6) Wider access should be granted to documents in cases where the institutions are acting in their legislative capacity, including under delegated powers, while at the same time preserving the effectiveness of the

institutions' decision-making process. Such documents should be made directly accessible to the greatest possible extent.

(7) In accordance with Articles 28(1) and 41(1) of the EU Treaty, the right of access also applies to documents relating to the common foreign and security policy and to police and judicial cooperation in criminal matters. Each institution should respect its security rules.

(8) In order to ensure the full application of this Regulation to all activities of the Union, all agencies established by the institutions should apply the principles laid down in this Regulation.

(9) On account of their highly sensitive content, certain documents should be given special treatment. Arrangements for informing the European Parliament of the content of such documents should be made through interinstitutional agreement.

(10) In order to bring about greater openness in the work of the institutions, access to documents should be granted by the European Parliament, the Council and the Commission not only to documents drawn up by the institutions, but also to documents received by them. In this context, it is recalled that Declaration No 35 attached to the Final Act of the Treaty of Amsterdam provides that a Member State may request the Commission or the Council not to communicate to third parties a document originating from that State without its prior agreement.

(11) In principle, all documents of the institutions should be accessible to the public. However, certain public and private interests should be protected by way of exceptions. The institutions should be entitled to protect their internal consultations and deliberations where necessary to safeguard their ability to carry out their tasks. In assessing the exceptions, the institutions should take account of the principles in Community legislation concerning the protection of personal data, in all areas of Union activities.

(12) All rules concerning access to documents of the institutions should be in conformity with this Regulation.

(13) In order to ensure that the right of access is fully respected, a two-stage administrative procedure should apply, with the additional possibility of court proceedings or complaints to the Ombudsman.

(14) Each institution should take the measures necessary to inform the public of the new provisions in force and to train its staff to assist citizens exercising their rights under this Regulation. In order to make it easier for citizens to exercise their rights, each institution should provide access to a register of documents.

(15) Even though it is neither the object nor the effect of this Regulation to amend national legislation on access to documents, it is nevertheless clear that, by virtue of the principle of loyal cooperation which governs relations between the institutions and the Member States, Member States should take care not to hamper the proper application of this Regulation and should respect the security rules of the institutions.

(16) This Regulation is without prejudice to existing rights of access to documents for Member States, judicial authorities or investigative bodies.

(17) In accordance with Article 255(3) of the EC Treaty, each institution lays down specific provisions regarding access to its documents in its rules of procedure. Council Decision 93/731/EC of 20 December 1993 on public access to Council documents (3), Commission Decision 94/90/ECSC, EC, Euratom of 8 February 1994 on public access to Commission documents (4), European Parliament Decision 97/632/EC, ECSC, Euratom of 10 July 1997 on public access to European Parliament documents (5), and the rules on confidentiality of Schengen documents should therefore, if necessary, be modified or be repealed,

HAVE ADOPTED THIS REGULATION:

Article 1

Purpose

The purpose of this Regulation is:

(a) to define the principles, conditions and limits on grounds of public or private interest governing the right of access to European Parliament, Council and Commission (hereinafter referred to as 'the institutions') documents provided for in Article 255 of the EC Treaty in such a way as to ensure the widest possible access to documents,

(b) to establish rules ensuring the easiest possible exercise of this right, and

(c) to promote good administrative practice on access to documents.

Article 2

Beneficiaries and scope

1. Any citizen of the Union, and any natural or legal person residing or having its registered office in a Member State, has a right of access to documents of the institutions, subject to the principles, conditions and limits defined in this Regulation.

2. The institutions may, subject to the same principles, conditions and limits, grant access to documents to any natural or legal person not residing or not having its registered office in a Member State.

3. This Regulation shall apply to all documents held by an institution, that is to say, documents drawn up or received by it and in its possession, in all areas of activity of the European Union.

4. Without prejudice to Articles 4 and 9, documents shall be made accessible to the public either following a written application or directly in electronic form or through a register. In particular, documents drawn up or received in the course of a legislative procedure shall be made directly accessible in accordance with Article 12.

5. Sensitive documents as defined in Article 9(1) shall be subject to special treatment in accordance with that Article.

6. This Regulation shall be without prejudice to rights of public access to documents held by the institutions which might follow from instruments of international law or acts of the institutions implementing them.

Article 3

Definitions

For the purpose of this Regulation:

(a) "document" shall mean any content whatever its medium (written on paper or stored in electronic form or as a sound, visual or audiovisual recording) concerning a matter relating to the policies, activities and decisions falling within the institution's sphere of responsibility;

(b) "third party" shall mean any natural or legal person, or any entity outside the institution concerned, including the Member States, other Community or non-Community institutions and bodies and third countries.

Article 4

Exceptions

1. The institutions shall refuse access to a document where disclosure would undermine the protection of:

(a) the public interest as regards:

— public security,

— defence and military matters,

— international relations,

— the financial, monetary or economic policy of the Community or a Member State;

(b) privacy and the integrity of the individual, in particular in accordance with Community legislation regarding the protection of personal data.

2. The institutions shall refuse access to a document where disclosure would undermine the protection of:

— commercial interests of a natural or legal person, including intellectual property,

— court proceedings and legal advice,

— the purpose of inspections, investigations and audits,

unless there is an overriding public interest in disclosure.

3. Access to a document, drawn up by an institution for internal use or received by an institution, which relates to a matter where the decision

has not been taken by the institution, shall be refused if disclosure of the document would seriously undermine the institution's decision-making process, unless there is an overriding public interest in disclosure.

Access to a document containing opinions for internal use as part of deliberations and preliminary consultations within the institution concerned shall be refused even after the decision has been taken if disclosure of the document would seriously undermine the institution's decision-making process, unless there is an overriding public interest in disclosure.

4. As regards third-party documents, the institution shall consult the third party with a view to assessing whether an exception in paragraph 1 or 2 is applicable, unless it is clear that the document shall or shall not be disclosed.

5. A Member State may request the institution not to disclose a document originating from that Member State without its prior agreement.

6. If only parts of the requested document are covered by any of the exceptions, the remaining parts of the document shall be released.

7. The exceptions as laid down in paragraphs 1 to 3 shall only apply for the period during which protection is justified on the basis of the content of the document. The exceptions may apply for a maximum period of 30 years. In the case of documents covered by the exceptions relating to privacy or commercial interests and in the case of sensitive documents, the exceptions may, if necessary, continue to apply after this period.

Article 5

Documents in the Member States

Where a Member State receives a request for a document in its possession, originating from an institution, unless it is clear that the document shall or shall not be disclosed, the Member State shall consult with the institution concerned in order to take a decision that does not jeopardise the attainment of the objectives of this Regulation.

The Member State may instead refer the request to the institution.

Article 6

Applications

1. Applications for access to a document shall be made in any written form, including electronic form, in one of the languages referred to in Article 314 of the EC Treaty and in a sufficiently precise manner to enable the institution to identify the document. The applicant is not obliged to state reasons for the application.

2. If an application is not sufficiently precise, the institution shall ask the applicant to clarify the application and shall assist the applicant in doing so, for example, by providing information on the use of the public registers of documents.

3. In the event of an application relating to a very long document or to a very large number of documents, the institution concerned may confer with the applicant informally, with a view to finding a fair solution.

4. The institutions shall provide information and assistance to citizens on how and where applications for access to documents can be made.

Article 7

Processing of initial applications

1. An application for access to a document shall be handled promptly. An acknowledgement of receipt shall be sent to the applicant. Within 15 working days from registration of the application, the institution shall either grant access to the document requested and provide access in accordance with Article 10 within that period or, in a written reply, state the reasons for the total or partial refusal and inform the applicant of his or her right to make a confirmatory application in accordance with paragraph 2 of this Article.

2. In the event of a total or partial refusal, the applicant may, within 15 working days of receiving the institution's reply, make a confirmatory application asking the institution to reconsider its position.

3. In exceptional cases, for example in the event of an application relating to a very long document or to a very large number of documents, the time-limit provided for in paragraph 1 may be extended by 15 working days, provided that the applicant is notified in advance and that detailed reasons are given.

4. Failure by the institution to reply within the prescribed time-limit shall entitle the applicant to make a confirmatory application.

Article 8

Processing of confirmatory applications

1. A confirmatory application shall be handled promptly. Within 15 working days from registration of such an application, the institution shall either grant access to the document requested and provide access in accordance with Article 10 within that period or, in a written reply, state the reasons for the total or partial refusal. In the event of a total or partial refusal, the institution shall inform the applicant of the remedies open to him or her, namely instituting court proceedings against the institution and/or making a complaint to the Ombudsman, under the conditions laid down in Articles 230 and 195 of the EC Treaty, respectively.

2. In exceptional cases, for example in the event of an application relating to a very long document or to a very large number of documents, the time limit provided for in paragraph 1 may be extended by 15 working days, provided that the applicant is notified in advance and that detailed reasons are given.

3. Failure by the institution to reply within the prescribed time limit shall be considered as a negative reply and entitle the applicant to institute

court proceedings against the institution and/or make a complaint to the Ombudsman, under the relevant provisions of the EC Treaty.

Article 9

Treatment of sensitive documents

1. Sensitive documents are documents originating from the institutions or the agencies established by them, from Member States, third countries or International Organisations, classified as 'TRES SECRET/TOP SECRET', 'SECRET' or 'CONFIDENTIEL' in accordance with the rules of the institution concerned, which protect essential interests of the European Union or of one or more of its Member States in the areas covered by Article 4(1)(a), notably public security, defence and military matters.

2. Applications for access to sensitive documents under the procedures laid down in Articles 7 and 8 shall be handled only by those persons who have a right to acquaint themselves with those documents. These persons shall also, without prejudice to Article 11(2), assess which references to sensitive documents could be made in the public register.

3. Sensitive documents shall be recorded in the register or released only with the consent of the originator.

4. An institution which decides to refuse access to a sensitive document shall give the reasons for its decision in a manner which does not harm the interests protected in Article 4.

5. Member States shall take appropriate measures to ensure that when handling applications for sensitive documents the principles in this Article and Article 4 are respected.

6. The rules of the institutions concerning sensitive documents shall be made public.

7. The Commission and the Council shall inform the European Parliament regarding sensitive documents in accordance with arrangements agreed between the institutions.

Article 10

Access following an application

1. The applicant shall have access to documents either by consulting them on the spot or by receiving a copy, including, where available, an electronic copy, according to the applicant's preference. The cost of producing and sending copies may be charged to the applicant. This charge shall not exceed the real cost of producing and sending the copies. Consultation on the spot, copies of less than 20 A4 pages and direct access in electronic form or through the register shall be free of charge.

2. If a document has already been released by the institution concerned and is easily accessible to the applicant, the institution may fulfil its obligation of granting access to documents by informing the applicant how to obtain the requested document.

3. Documents shall be supplied in an existing version and format (including electronically or in an alternative format such as Braille, large print or tape) with full regard to the applicant's preference.

Article 11

Registers

1. To make citizens' rights under this Regulation effective, each institution shall provide public access to a register of documents. Access to the register should be provided in electronic form. References to documents shall be recorded in the register without delay.

2. For each document the register shall contain a reference number (including, where applicable, the interinstitutional reference), the subject matter and/or a short description of the content of the document and the date on which it was received or drawn up and recorded in the register. References shall be made in a manner which does not undermine protection of the interests in Article 4.

3. The institutions shall immediately take the measures necessary to establish a register which shall be operational by 3 June 2002.

Article 12

Direct access in electronic form or through a register

1. The institutions shall as far as possible make documents directly accessible to the public in electronic form or through a register in accordance with the rules of the institution concerned.

2. In particular, legislative documents, that is to say, documents drawn up or received in the course of procedures for the adoption of acts which are legally binding in or for the Member States, should, subject to Articles 4 and 9, be made directly accessible.

3. Where possible, other documents, notably documents relating to the development of policy or strategy, should be made directly accessible.

4. Where direct access is not given through the register, the register shall as far as possible indicate where the document is located.

Article 13

Publication in the Official Journal

1. In addition to the acts referred to in Article 254(1) and (2) of the EC Treaty and the first paragraph of Article 163 of the Euratom Treaty, the following documents shall, subject to Articles 4 and 9 of this Regulation, be published in the Official Journal:

(a) Commission proposals;

(b) common positions adopted by the Council in accordance with the procedures referred to in Articles 251 and 252 of the EC Treaty and the reasons underlying those common positions, as well as the European Parliament's positions in these procedures;

(c) framework decisions and decisions referred to in Article 34(2) of the EU Treaty;

(d) conventions established by the Council in accordance with Article 34(2) of the EU Treaty;

(e) conventions signed between Member States on the basis of Article 293 of the EC Treaty;

(f) international agreements concluded by the Community or in accordance with Article 24 of the EU Treaty.

2. As far as possible, the following documents shall be published in the Official Journal:

(a) initiatives presented to the Council by a Member State pursuant to Article 67(1) of the EC Treaty or pursuant to Article 34(2) of the EU Treaty;

(b) common positions referred to in Article 34(2) of the EU Treaty;

(c) directives other than those referred to in Article 254(1) and (2) of the EC Treaty, decisions other than those referred to in Article 254(1) of the EC Treaty, recommendations and opinions.

3. Each institution may in its rules of procedure establish which further documents shall be published in the Official Journal.

Article 14

Information

1. Each institution shall take the requisite measures to inform the public of the rights they enjoy under this Regulation.

2. The Member States shall cooperate with the institutions in providing information to the citizens.

Article 15

Administrative practice in the institutions

1. The institutions shall develop good administrative practices in order to facilitate the exercise of the right of access guaranteed by this Regulation.

2. The institutions shall establish an interinstitutional committee to examine best practice, address possible conflicts and discuss future developments on public access to documents.

Article 16

Reproduction of documents

This Regulation shall be without prejudice to any existing rules on copyright which may limit a third party's right to reproduce or exploit released documents.

Article 17

Reports

1. Each institution shall publish annually a report for the preceding year including the number of cases in which the institution refused to grant access to documents, the reasons for such refusals and the number of sensitive documents not recorded in the register.

2. At the latest by 31 January 2004, the Commission shall publish a report on the implementation of the principles of this Regulation and shall make recommendations, including, if appropriate, proposals for the revision of this Regulation and an action programme of measures to be taken by the institutions.

Article 18

Application measures

1. Each institution shall adapt its rules of procedure to the provisions of this Regulation. The adaptations shall take effect from 3 December 2001.

2. Within six months of the entry into force of this Regulation, the Commission shall examine the conformity of Council Regulation (EEC, Euratom) No. 354/83 of 1 February 1983 concerning the opening to the public of the historical archives of the European Economic Community and the European Atomic Energy Community (6) with this Regulation in order to ensure the preservation and archiving of documents to the fullest extent possible.

3. Within six months of the entry into force of this Regulation, the Commission shall examine the conformity of the existing rules on access to documents with this Regulation.

Article 19

Entry into force

This Regulation shall enter into force on the third day following that of its publication in the Official Journal of the European Communities.

It shall be applicable from 3 December 2001.

This Regulation shall be binding in its entirety and directly applicable in all Member States.

*

Part II

THE RECEPTION AND ENFORCEMENT OF EUROPEAN LAW IN THE MEMBER STATES

There are no documents corresponding to this Part.

*

Part III

THE COMMON MARKET, THE INTERNAL MARKET AND THE FOUR FREEDOMS

INTRODUCTION

The process of harmonization to achieve the free movement of goods, persons, services and capital and thereby to attain an integrated internal market has produced a tremendous volume of legislation, chiefly in the form of directives. As described in Chapter 14 of the casebook, a substantial number of such directives were adopted in the 1960s and 1970s.

The program of legislation outlined in the Commission White Paper on Completing the Internal Market, COM (85) 310 (June 1985), discussed in Chapter 14, has engendered another substantial body of legislation. Rather than reproducing the White Paper, which is now largely of historical interest, a number of the more important achievements of the White Paper program are printed hereafter.

The legislation reproduced hereafter represents the most important items discussed in the casebook, presented in the sequence of the casebook chapters. To achieve the widest possible sampling of legislation, some items have been lightly excerpted. Whereas clauses which essentially duplicate specific articles in the legislation, and text which is too detailed or technical to be of pedagogical interest, have been deleted. Footnote references in recent legislation to the initial Commission proposal and reports of Parliament and the Economic and Social Council have been retained to facilitate further research.

The significance of each of the printed documents is indicated in its coverage in the casebook. We indicate here only the reason for the selection of the reproduced documents and make cross-references to casebook coverage or citation of related documents, sector by sector.

Free movement of goods. Directive 70/50 provides a valuable illustrative list of Member State measures which restrict the free movement of goods. The Commission Communication on *Cassis de Dijon* constitutes a policy view on the implications of that judgment.

Technical and safety legislation. The dangerous substances directive 92/32 is a model illustrating the early wave of harmonization legislation covering dangerous solvents, pharmaceuticals, paints and varnishes, cosmetics, etc., reviewed in Chapter 14A. Directive 83/189 is an important part of the program for a new approach to technical harmonization, covered in Chapter 14D, because it serves to reduce the risk that newly adopted national regulations or standards will hinder the free movement of goods.

Free movement of workers. Regulation 1612/68 is the fundamental expression of the rules enabling workers and their families to achieve complete integration into the host State employment and social environment. It is supplemented by Directive 68/360 on rights of residence and Directive 64/221, which narrowly limits the Member States' power to restrict free movement on grounds of public policy, public security or public health. Accessory regulations, as the right to continued residence after ceasing work and the right of education for dependent children, are mentioned in Chapter 15A.

The People's Europe program. The three directives 93/96, 90/365 and 90/364, covering respectively a right of residence for students, for retired persons, and for virtually all persons not engaged in an occupational activity, represent the principal achievement of the People's Europe program. Chapter 16A reviews other important legislation in this program, such as the directives harmonizing conditions for drivers' licenses and for the control of the sale and ownership of weapons, as well as those enabling voting in local elections and elections for the European Parliament. Chapter 16C describes the Erasmus and related programs to encourage student mobility and cooperation among higher education institutions.

Right of establishment and freedom to provide services. The General Programme for the abolition of restrictions on the freedom of establishment remains important because of its descriptive list of discriminatory Member State rules, practices and conditions. The corresponding program with regard to services is mentioned in Chapter 17A. The 1993 Communication on free movement of services constitutes a significant statement of policy in this field, largely based upon Court of Justice judgments. Directive 86/653 on commercial agents is an excellent illustration of harmonization directives intended to facilitate establishment by creating common rules in a particular sector. Directive 89/552 on television broadcasting is not only a rare example of harmonizing rules in a trans-border services sector; it also illustrates the Community's efforts to promote cultural interests, as discussed in Chapter 16C.

Company law. Harmonization in this field is important because it promotes commercial enterprise by reducing disparities in the structure and operations of companies, particularly those created in the larger stock corporation form. The First and Second Directives, 68/151 and 77/91, provide rules on the capital and shareholding structure of companies, as well as on mandatory disclosures to shareholders and third parties. The Third Directive 78/855 is likewise a key one since it creates a modern system for executing corporate mergers. Chapter 17D mentions other company law directives, as well as the well-known draft Fifth directive on internal shareholding and management structure and the proposal for a Community stock corporation, both unfortunately too long for reproduction. Chapter 17D also discusses the Fourth Directive 78/660 on annual accounts and the accessory Seventh and Eighth directives. Finally, the European Economic Interest Grouping Regulation is printed, because it constitutes a useful initiative in facilitating joint ventures.

Professional rights. Directive 89/48 on the recognition of higher education diplomas is a major internal market program achievement, facilitating the right of establishment for a wide variety of professions, including lawyers. It follows a new approach of mutual trust, making no attempt to harmonize educational standards, the approach used for earlier directives for the medical and accessory professions. The earlier directives are discussed in Chapter 18A. Directive 77/249 on lawyers' trans-border services is not only important in facilitating rights of practice by Community lawyers; it is also a rare example of a directive limited to services. Directive 98/5 on lawyers' right of establishment substantially liberlizes community legal practice rights.

Intellectual property rights. The trademark harmonization Directive 89/104 is the first measure adopted in the effort to produce an integrated system of intellectual property rights, thus reducing the tendency of national rights to partition the market for goods and services. Other recent important legislation, such as the Community Trademark Regulation and a series of new initiatives in copyright law, are reviewed in Chapter 19E.

Table of Contents

Doc.		Page
1.	Commission Directive 70/50 on the abolition of measures which have an effect equivalent to quantitative restrictions on imports.	299
2.	Council Regulation 2679/98 on the functioning of the internal market in relation to the free movement of goods.	303
3.	Commission Communication concerning the consequences of the judgment in Case 120/78 ("Cassis de Dijon").	306
4.	Council Directive 92/32 on the approximation of the laws relating to the classification, packaging and labelling of dangerous substances.	309
5.	Council Directive 83/189 laying down a procedure for the provision of information in the field of technical standards and regulations.	325
6.	Council Directive 85/577 to protect the consumer in respect of contracts negotiated away from business premises.	331
7.	Council Regulation 1612/68 on freedom of movement for workers within the Community.	335
8.	Council Directive 68/360 on the abolition of restrictions on movement and residence within the Community for workers of Member States and their families.	341
9.	Council Directive 64/221 on the co-ordination of special measures concerning the movement and residence of foreign nationals which are justified on grounds of public policy, public security or public health.	345
10.	Council Directive 90/365 on the right of residence for employees and self-employed persons who have ceased their occupational activity.	349
11.	Council Directive 90/364 on the right of residence.	352
12.	Council Directive 93/96 on the right of residence for students.	355
13.	General Programme for the abolition of restrictions on freedom of establishment.	358

Doc.		
14.	Commission interpretative communication concerning the free movement of services across frontiers.	362
15.	Council Directive 86/653 on the coordination of the laws of the Member States relating to self-employed commercial agents.	368
16.	Council Directive 89/552 on the coordination of certain provisions laid down by law, regulation or administrative action in Member States concerning the pursuit of television broadcasting activities.	377
17.	First Council Directive 68/151 on coordination of safeguards which are required by Member States of companies with a view to making such safeguards equivalent throughout the Community.	388
18.	Second Council Directive 77/91 on coordination of safeguards which are required by Member States in respect of the formation of public limited liability companies and the maintenance and alteration of their capital.	393
19.	Third Council Directive 78/855 concerning mergers of public limited liability companies.	403
20.	Fourth Council Directive 78/660 on the annual accounts of certain types of companies.	414
21.	Council Regulation 2137/85 on the European Economic Interest Grouping.	423
22.	Council Directive 89/48 on a general system for the recognition of higher-education diplomas awarded on completion of profession education and training.	433
23.	Council Recommendation 89/49 concerning nationals of Member States who hold a diploma conferred in a third State.	442
24.	Council Directive 77/249 to facilitate the effective exercise by lawyers of freedom to provide services.	443
25.	Directive 98/5 of the European Parliament and of the Council to facilitate practice of the profession of lawyer on a permanent basis in a Member State other than that in which the qualification was obtained.	446
26.	Council Directive 89/104 to approximate the laws of the Member States relating to trade marks.	459

1. COMMISSION DIRECTIVE 70/50/EEC

of 22 December 1969

based on the provisions of Article 33(7), on the abolition of measures which have an effect equivalent to quantitative restrictions on imports and are not covered by other provisions adopted in pursuance of the EEC Treaty

J.O. L 13/29 (Jan. 19, 1970), English Spec. Ed. 1970-I, 17

THE COMMISSION OF THE EUROPEAN COMMUNITIES,

Having regard to the provisions of the Treaty establishing the European Economic Community, and in particular Article 33(7) thereof;

Whereas for the purpose of Article 30 *et seq.* 'measures' means laws, regulations, administrative provisions, administrative practices, and all instruments issuing from a public authority, including recommendations;

Whereas for the purposes of this Directive 'administrative practices' means any standard and regularly followed procedure of a public authority; whereas 'recommendations' means any instruments issuing from a public authority which, while not legally binding on the addressees thereof, cause them to pursue a certain conduct;

Whereas the formalities to which imports are subject do not as a general rule have an effect equivalent to that of quantitative restrictions and, consequently, are not covered by this Directive;

Whereas certain measures adopted by Member States, other than those applicable equally to domestic and imported products, which were operative at the date of entry into force of the Treaty and are not covered by other provisions adopted in pursuance of the Treaty, either preclude importation or make it more difficult or costly than the disposal of domestic production;

* * *

Whereas such measures hinder imports which could otherwise take place, and thus have an effect equivalent to quantitative restrictions on imports;

Whereas effects on the free movement of goods of measures which relate to the marketing of products and which apply equally to domestic and imported products are not as a general rule equivalent to those of quantitative restrictions, since such effects are normally inherent in the disparities between rules applied by Member States in this respect;

Whereas, however, such measures may have a restrictive effect on the free movement of goods over and above that which is intrinsic to such rules;

Whereas such is the case where imports are either precluded or made more difficult or costly than the disposal of domestic production and where such effect is not necessary for the attainment of an objective within the scope of the powers for the regulation of trade left to Member States by the

Treaty; whereas such is in particular the case where the said objective can be attained just as effectively by other means which are less of a hindrance to trade; whereas such is also the case where the restrictive effect of these provisions on the free movement of goods is out of proportion to their purpose;

Whereas these measures accordingly have an effect equivalent to that of quantitative restrictions on imports;

* * *

Whereas the provisions concerning the abolition of quantitative restrictions and measures having equivalent effect between Member States apply both to products originating in and exported by Member States and to products originating in third countries and put into free circulation in the other Member States;

* * *

HAS ADOPTED THIS DIRECTIVE:

Article 1

The purpose of this Directive is to abolish the measures referred to in Articles 2 and 3, which were operative at the date of entry into force of the EEC Treaty.

Article 2

1. This Directive covers measures, other than those applicable equally to domestic or imported products, which hinder imports which could otherwise take place, including measures which make importation more difficult or costly than the disposal of domestic production.

2. In particular, it covers measures which make imports or the disposal, at any marketing stage, of imported products subject to a condition—other than a formality—which is required in respect of imported products only, or a condition differing from that required for domestic products and more difficult to satisfy. Equally, it covers, in particular, measures which favour domestic products or grant them a preference, other than an aid, to which conditions may or may not be attached.

3. The measures referred to must be taken to include those measures which:

   (a) lay down, for imported products only, minimum or maximum prices below or above which imports are prohibited, reduced or made subject to conditions liable to hinder importation;

   (b) lay down less favourable prices for imported products than for domestic products;

   (c) fix profit margins or any other price components for imported products only or fix these differently for domestic products and for imported products, to the detriment of the latter;

(d) preclude any increase in the price of the imported product corresponding to the supplementary costs and charges inherent in importation;

(e) fix the prices of products solely on the basis of the cost price or the quality of domestic products at such a level as to create a hindrance to importation;

(f) lower the value of an imported product, in particular by causing a reduction in its intrinsic value, or increase its costs;

(g) make access of imported products to the domestic market conditional upon having an agent or representative in the territory of the importing Member State;

(h) lay down conditions of payment in respect of imported products only, or subject imported products to conditions which are different from those laid down for domestic products and more difficult to satisfy;

(i) require for imports only, the giving of guarantees or making of payments on account;

(j) subject imported products only to conditions, in respect in particular of shape, size, weight, composition, presentation, identification or putting up, or subject imported products to conditions which are different from those for domestic products and more difficult to satisfy;

(k) hinder the purchase by private individuals of imported products only, or encourage, require or give preference to the purchase of domestic products only;

(*l*) totally or partially preclude the use of national facilities or equipment in respect of imported products only, or totally or partially confine the use of such facilities or equipment to domestic products only;

(m) prohibit or limit publicity in respect of imported products only, or totally or partially confine publicity to domestic products only;

(n) prohibit, limit or require stocking in respect of imported products only; totally or partially confine the use of stocking facilities to domestic products only, or make the stocking of imported products subject to conditions which are different from those required for domestic products and more difficult to satisfy;

(o) make importation subject to the granting of reciprocity by one or more Member States;

(p) prescribe that imported products are to conform, totally or partially, to rules other than those of the importing country;

(q) specify time limits for imported products which are insufficient or excessive in relation to the normal course of the various transactions to which these time limits apply;

(r) subject imported products to controls or, other than those inherent in the customs clearance procedure, to which domestic products are not subject or which are stricter in respect of imported products than they are in respect of domestic products, without this being necessary in order to ensure equivalent protection;

(s) confine names which are not indicative of origin or source to domestic products only.

Article 3

This Directive also covers measures governing the marketing of products which deal, in particular, with shape, size, weight, composition, presentation, identification or putting up and which are equally applicable to domestic and imported products, where the restrictive effect of such measures on the free movement of goods exceeds the effects intrinsic to trade rules.

This is the case, in particular, where:

— the restrictive effects on the free movement of goods are out of proportion to their purpose;

— the same objective can be attained by other means which are less of a hindrance to trade.

Article 4

1. Member States shall take all necessary steps in respect of products which must be allowed to enjoy free movement pursuant to Articles 9 and 10 of the Treaty to abolish measures having an effect equivalent to quantitative restrictions on imports and covered by this Directive.

2. Member States shall inform the Commission of measures taken pursuant to this Directive.

Article 5

1. This Directive does not apply to measures:

(a) which fall under Article 37(1) of the EEC Treaty;

(b) which are referred to in Article 44 of the EEC Treaty or form an integral part of a national organization of an agricultural market not yet replaced by a common organization.

2. This Directive shall apply without prejudice to the application, in particular, of Articles 36 and 223 of the EEC Treaty.

Article 6

This Directive is addressed to the Member States.

2. COUNCIL REGULATION (EC) 2679/98

of 7 December 1998

on the functioning of the internal market in relation to the free movement of goods among the Member States

O.J. L 337/8 (Dec. 12, 1998)

THE COUNCIL OF THE EUROPEAN UNION,

Having regard to the Treaty establishing the European Community, and in particular Article 235 thereof,

Having regard to the proposal from the Commission,

Having regard to the opinion of the European Parliament,

Having regard to the opinion of the Economic and Social Committee,

(1) Whereas, as provided for in Article 7a of the Treaty, the internal market comprises an area without internal frontiers in which, in particular, the free movement of goods is ensured in accordance with Articles 30 to 36 of the Treaty;

(2) Whereas breaches of this principle, such as occur when in a given Member State the free movement of goods is obstructed by actions of private individuals, may cause grave disruption to the proper functioning of the internal market and inflict serious losses on the individuals affected;

(3) Whereas, in order to ensure fulfilment of the obligations arising from the Treaty, and, in particular, to ensure the proper functioning of the internal market, Member States should, on the one hand, abstain from adopting measures or engaging in conduct liable to constitute an obstacle to trade and, on the other hand, take all necessary and proportionate measures with a view to facilitating the free movement of goods in their territory;

(4) Whereas such measures must not affect the exercise of fundamental rights, including the right or freedom to strike;

(5) Whereas this Regulation does not prevent any actions which may be necessary in certain cases at Community level to respond to problems in the functioning of the internal market, taking into account, where appropriate, the application of this Regulation;

(6) Whereas Member States have exclusive competence as regards the maintenance of public order and the safeguarding of internal security as well as in determining whether, when and which measures are necessary and proportionate in order to facilitate the free movement of goods in their territory in a given situation;

(7) Whereas there should be adequate and rapid exchange of information between the Member States and the Commission on obstacles to the free movement of goods;

(8) Whereas a Member State on the territory of which obstacles to the free movement of goods occur should take all necessary and proportionate measures to restore as soon as possible the free movement of goods in their territory in order to avoid the risk that the disruption or loss in question will continue, increase or intensify and that there may be a breakdown in trade and in the contractual relations which underlie it; whereas such Member State should inform the Commission and, if requested, other Member States of the measures it has taken or intends to take in order fo fulfil this objective;

(9) Whereas the Commission, in fulfilment of its duty under the Treaty, should notify the Member State concerned of its view that a breach has occurred and the Member State should respond to that notification;

(10) Whereas the Treaty provides for no powers, other than those in Article 235 thereof, for the adoption of this Regulation,

HAS ADOPTED THIS REGULATION:

Article 1

For the purpose of this Regulation:

1. the term 'obstacle' shall mean an obstacle to the free movement of goods among Member States which is attributable to a Member State, whether it involves action or inaction on its part, which may constitute a breach of Articles 30 to 36 of the Treaty and which:

(a) leads to serious disruption of the free movement of goods by physically or otherwise preventing, delaying or diverting their import into, export from or transport across a Member State,

(b) causes serious loss to the individuals affected, and

(c) requires immediate action in order to prevent any continuation, increase or intensification of the disruption or loss in question;

2. the term 'inaction' shall cover the case when the competent authorities of a Member State, in the presence of an obstacle caused by actions taken by private individuals, fail to take all necessary and proportionate measures within their powers with a view to removing the obstacle and ensuring the free movement of goods in their territory.

Article 2

This Regulation may not be interpreted as affecting in any way the exercise of fundamental rights as recognised in Member States, including the right or freedom to strike. These rights may also include the right or freedom to take other actions covered by the specific industrial relations systems in Member States.

Article 3

1. When an obstacle occurs or when there is a threat thereof

(a) any Member State (whether or not it is the Member State concerned) which has relevant information shall immediately transmit it to the Commission, and

(b) the Commission shall immediately transmit to the Member States that information and any information from any other source which it may consider relevant.

2. The Member State concerned shall respond as soon as possible to requests for information from the Commission and from other Member States concerning the nature of the obstacle or threat and the action which it has taken or proposes to take. Information exchange between Member States shall also be transmitted to the Commission.

Article 4

1. When an obstacle occurs, and subject to Article 2, the Member State concerned shall

(a) take all necessary and proportionate measures so that the free movement of goods is assured in the territory of the Member State in accordance with the Treaty, and

(b) inform the Commission of the actions which its authorities have taken or intend to take.

2. The Commission shall immediately transmit the information received under paragraph 1(b) to the other Member States.

Article 5

1. Where the Commission considers that an obstacle is occurring in a Member State, it shall notify the Member State concerned of the reasons that have led the Commission to such a conclusion and shall request the Member State to take all necessary and proportionate measures to remove the said obstacle within a period which it shall determine with reference to the urgency of the case.

2. In reaching its conclusion, the Commission shall have regard to Article 2.

3. The Commission may publish in the Official Journal of the European Communities the text of the notification which it has sent to the Member State concerned and shall immediately transmit the text to any party which requests it.

4. The Member State shall, within five working days of receipt of the text, either:

— inform the Commission of the steps which it has taken or intends to take to implement paragraph 1, or

— communicate a reasoned submission as to why there is no obstacle constituting a breach of Articles 30 to 36 of the Treaty.

5. In exceptional cases, the Commission may allow an extension of the deadline mentioned in paragraph 4 if the Member State submits a duly substantiated request and the grounds cited are deemed acceptable.

This Regulation shall be binding in its entirety and directly applicable in all Member States.

3. COMMUNICATION FROM THE COMMISSION CONCERNING THE CONSEQUENCES OF THE JUDGMENT GIVEN BY THE COURT OF JUSTICE ON 20 FEBRUARY 1979 IN CASE 120/78 ('CASSIS DE DIJON')

O.J. C 256/2 (Mar. 10, 1980)

The following is the text of a letter which has been sent to the Member States; the European Parliament and the Council have also been notified of it.

In the Commission's Communication of 6 November 1978 on 'Safeguarding free trade within the Community', it was emphasized that the free movement of goods is being affected by a growing number of restrictive measures.

The judgment delivered by the Court of Justice on 20 February 1979 in Case 120/78 (the 'Cassis de Dijon' case), * * * has given the Commission some interpretative guidance enabling it to monitor more strictly the application of the Treaty rules on the free movement of goods, particularly Articles 30 to 36 of the EEC Treaty.

The Court gives a very general definition of the barriers to free trade which are prohibited by the provisions of Article 30 *et seq.* of the EEC Treaty. These are taken to include 'any national measure capable of hindering, directly or indirectly, actually or potentially, intra-Community trade'.

In its judgment of 20 February 1979 the Court indicates the scope of this definition as it applies to technical and commercial rules.

Any product lawfully produced and marketed in one Member State must, in principle, be admitted to the market of any other Member State.

Technical and commercial rules, even those equally applicable to national and imported products, may create barriers to trade only where those rules are necessary to satisfy mandatory requirements and to serve a purpose which is in the general interest and for which they are an essential guarantee. This purpose must be such as to take precedence over the requirements of the free movement of goods, which constitutes one of the fundamental rules of the Community.

The conclusions in terms of policy which the Commission draws from this new guidance are set out below.

— Whereas Member States may, with respect to domestic products and in the absence of relevant Community provisions, regulate the terms on which such products are marketed, the case is different for products imported from other Member States.

Any product imported from another Member State must in principle be admitted to the territory of the importing Member State if it has been lawfully produced, that is, conforms to rules and processes of manufacture that are customarily and traditionally accepted in the exporting country, and is marketed in the territory of the latter.

This principle implies that Member States, when drawing up commercial or technical rules liable to affect the free movement of goods, may not take an exclusively national viewpoint and take account only of requirements confined to domestic products. The proper functioning of the common market demands that each Member State also give consideration to the legitimate requirements of the other Member States.

— Only under very strict conditions does the Court accept exceptions to this principle; barriers to trade resulting from differences between commercial and technical rules are only admissible:

- if the rules are necessary, that is appropriate and not excessive, in order to satisfy mandatory requirements (public health, protection of consumers or the environment, the fairness of commercial transactions, etc.);
- if the rules serve a purpose in the general interest which is compelling enough to justify an exception to a fundamental rule of the Treaty such as the free movement of goods;
- if the rules are essential for such a purpose to be attained, i.e. are the means which are the most appropriate and at the same time least hinder trade.

The Court's interpretation has induced the Commission to set out a number of guidelines.

— The principles deduced by the Court imply that a Member State may not in principle prohibit the sale in its territory of a product lawfully produced and marketed in another Member State even if the product is produced according to technical or quality requirements which differ from those imposed on its domestic products. Where a product 'suitably and satisfactorily' fulfils the legitimate objective of a Member State's own rules (public safety, protection of the consumer or the environment, etc.), the importing country cannot justify prohibiting its sale in its territory by claiming that the way it fulfils the objective is different from that imposed on domestic products.

In such a case, an absolute prohibition of sale could not be considered 'necessary' to satisfy a 'mandatory requirement' because it would not be an 'essential guarantee' in the sense defined in the Court's judgment.

The Commission will therefore have to tackle a whole body of commercial rules which lay down that products manufactured and marketed in one Member State must fulfil technical or qualitative conditions in order to be admitted to the market of another and specifically in all cases where the trade barriers occasioned by such rules are inadmissible according to the very strict criteria set out by the Court.

The Commission is referring in particular to rules covering the composition, designation, presentation and packaging of products as well as rules requiring compliance with certain technical standards.

— The Commission's work of harmonization will henceforth have to be directed mainly at national laws having an impact on the functioning of the common market where barriers to trade to be removed arise from national provisions which are admissible under the criteria set by the Court.

The Commission will be concentrating on sectors deserving priority because of their economic relevance to the creation of a single internal market.

To forestall later difficulties, the Commission will be informing Member States of potential objections, under the terms of Community law, to provisions they may be considering introducing which come to the attention of the Commission.

It will be producing suggestions soon on the procedures to be followed in such cases.

The Commission is confident that this approach will secure greater freedom of trade for the Community's manufacturers, so strengthening the industrial base of the Community, while meeting the expectations of consumers.

4. COUNCIL DIRECTIVE 92/32/EEC

of 30 April 1992

amending for the seventh time Directive 67/548/EEC on the approximation of the laws, regulations and administrative provisions relating to the classification, packaging and labelling of dangerous substances

O.J. L 154/1 (June 5, 1992)

THE COUNCIL OF THE EUROPEAN COMMUNITIES,

Having regard to the Treaty establishing the European Economic Community, and in particular Article 100a thereof,

Having regard to the proposal from the Commission,

In cooperation with the European Parliament,

Having regard to the opinion of the Economic and Social Committee,

Whereas disparity between the laws, regulations and administrative provisions relating to the classification, packaging and labelling of dangerous substances and to the notification of new substances in the Member States may lead to barriers to trade between Member States and create unequal conditions of competition; whereas the disparity between these measures in the Member States has a direct impact on the functioning of the internal market and does not guarantee the same level of protection of public health and the environment;

Whereas measures for the approximation of the provisions of the Member States which have as their object the establishment and functioning of the internal market shall, inasmuch as they concern health, safety and the protection of man and the environment, take as their basis a high level of protection;

Whereas, in order to protect man and the environment from potential risks which could arise from the placing on the market of new substances, it is necessary to lay down appropriate measures and in particular to amend and reinforce the provisions of Council Directive 67/548/EEC, as last amended by Directive 90/517/EEC;

Whereas any new substance placed on the market should be notified to the competent authorities by means of a notification containing certain information; * * *

Whereas it is necessary to lay down measures to make it possible to introduce a notification procedure under which a notification made in one Member State is then valid for the Community; whereas it may be worthwhile, in the case of substances manufactured outside the Community, for the manufacturer to appoint an exclusive representative in the Community for the purpose of notification;

Whereas, in order to forecast the effects on man and the environment, it is advisable that any new substance that is notified be the subject of an assessment of the risks, and whereas uniform principles for risk assessment should be laid down;

Whereas it is, moreover, important to follow closely the evolution and use of new substances placed on the market and whereas it is therefore necessary to institute a system which allows all new substances to be listed;

Whereas the Commission, pursuant to Article 13(1) of Directive 67/548/EEC, drew up * * * an inventory of substances on the Community market as at 18 September 1981 (EINECS); whereas that inventory was published in the *Official Journal of the European Communities*;

Whereas it is appropriate to reduce to a minimum the number of animals used for experimental purposes, in accordance with Council Directive 86/609/EEC of 24 November 1986 on the approximation of the laws, regulations and administrative provisions of the Member States regarding the protection of animals used for experimental and other scientific purposes; whereas all appropriate measures should be taken to avoid the duplication of tests on animals;

Whereas Council Directive 87/18/EEC of 18 December 1986 on the harmonization of laws, regulations and administrative provisions relating to the application of the principles of good laboratory practice and the verification of their application for tests on chemical substances specifies the Community principles of good laboratory practice which must be followed for tests on chemicals;

Whereas, in order to promote environmental protection and safety and health at work, it is desirable for safety data on dangerous substances to be available to professional users;

Whereas provisions should be adopted at Community level on the classification and labelling of substances in order to promote the protection of the population and, in particular, of the workers who use them;

Whereas, in order to ensure an adequate level of protection for man and the environment, it is necessary to introduce measures for the packaging and provisional labelling of dangerous substances not appearing in Annex I to Directive 67/548/EEC; whereas, for the same reason, it is necessary to make the indication of safety advice mandatory;

Whereas Article 2 of Directive 67/548/EEC classifies substances and preparations as toxic, harmful, corrosive or irritant by the use of general definitions; whereas experience has shown that it is necessary for this classification to be improved upon; whereas it seems appropriate to provide precise criteria for classification; whereas, in addition, Article 3 of the Directive provides for an assessment of the environmental hazard, making it necessary to enumerate certain characteristics and parameters of assessment and to establish a phased test programme;

Whereas it is desirable to add a new common danger symbol, 'dangerous for the environment', to appear on packaging;

Whereas the confidential nature of certain information covered by individual or commercial secrecy should be guaranteed;

Whereas Member States should be allowed to take safeguard measures, under certain conditions;

Whereas the Commission should be given the powers necessary to adapt all the Annexes to Directive 67/548/EEC to technical progress,

HAS ADOPTED THIS DIRECTIVE:

Article 1

Directive 67/548/EEC is hereby amended as follows:

1. Article 1 to 23 shall be replaced by the following Articles:

Article 1

Objectives and Scope

1. The purpose of this Directive is to approximate the laws, regulations and administrative provisions of the Member States on:

(a) the notification of substances;

(b) the exchange of information on notified substances;

(c) the assessment of the potential risk to man and the environment of notified substances;

(d) the classification, packaging and labelling of substances dangerous to man or the environment,

where such substances are placed on the market in the Member States.

2. This Directive shall not apply to the following preparations in the finished state, intended for the final user:

(a) medicinal products for human or veterinary use, as defined in Directive 65/65/EEC, as last amended by Directive 87/21/EEC;

(b) cosmetic products defined by Directive 76/768/EEC, as last amended by Directive 86/199/EEC;

(c) mixtures of substances which, in the form of waste, are covered by Directives 75/442/EEC and 78/319/EEC;

(d) foodstuffs;

(e) animal feedingstuffs;

(f) pesticides;

(g) radioactive substances as defined by Directive 80/836/EEC;

(h) other substances or preparations for which Community notification or approval procedures exist and for which requirements are equivalent to those laid down in this Directive.

Not later than 12 months after notification of this Directive, the Commission, in accordance with the procedure laid down in Article 29 (4)(a), shall establish a list of substances and preparations referred to above. This list will be re-examined periodically and as necessary revised in accordance with the said procedure.

* * *

Article 2

Definitions

1. For the purpose of this Directive:

(a) "substances" means chemical elements and their compounds in the natural state or obtained by any production process, including any additive necessary to preserve the stability of the products and any impurity deriving from the process used, but excluding any solvent which may be separated without affecting the stability of the substance or changing its composition;

(b) "preparations" means mixtures or solutions composed of two or more substances;

* * *

(d) "notification" means the documents, with the requisite information, presented to the competent authority of a Member State:

— for substances manufactured within the Community, by the manufacturer who places a substance either on its own or in a preparation on the market,

— for substances manufactured outside the Community, by any person established in the Community who is responsible for placing the substance either on its own or in a preparation on the Community market, or alternatively by the person established within the Community who is, for the purposes of submitting a notification for a given substance placed on the Community market, either on its own or in a preparation, designated by the manfacturer as his sole representative.

The person submitting the notification, as described above, shall be referred to as "the notifier".

(e) "placing on the market" means the making available to third parties. Importation into the Community customs territory shall be deemed to be placing on the market for the purposes of this Directive;

(f) "scientific research and development" means scientific experimentation, analysis or chemical research carried out under controlled conditions; it includes the determination of intrinsic properties, performance and efficacy as well as scientific investigation related to product development;

(g) "process-orientated research and development" means the further development of a substance in the course of which pilot plant or production trials are used to test the fields of application of the substance;

(h) "EINECS" means the European Inventory of Existing Commercial Substances. This inventory contains the definitive list of all substances deemed to be on the Community market on 18 September 1981.

2. The following are "dangerous" within the meaning of this Directive:

(a) explosive substances and preparations: solid, liquid, pasty or gelatinous substances and preparations which may also react exothermically without atmospheric oxygen thereby quickly evolving gases, and which, under defined test conditions, detonate, quickly deflagrate or upon heating explode when partially confined;

(b) oxidizing substances and preparations: substances and preparations which give rise to a highly exothermic reaction in contact with other substances, particularly flammable substances;

(c) extremely flammable substances and preparations: liquid substances and preparations having an extremely low flash-point and a low boiling-point and gaseous substances and preparations which are flammable in contact with air at ambient temperature and pressure;

(d) highly flammable substances and preparations:

— substances and preparations which may become hot and finally catch fire in contact with air at ambient temperature without any application of energy, or

— solid substances and preparations which may readily catch fire after brief contact with a source of ignition and which continue to burn or to be consumed after removal of the source of ignition, or

— liquid substances and preparations having a very low flash-point, or

— substances and preparations which, in contact with water or damp air, evolve highly flammable gases in dangerous quantities;

(e) flammable substances and preparations: liquid substances and preparations having a low flash-point;

(f) very toxic substances and preparations: substances and preparations which in very low quantities cause death or acute or chronic damage to health when inhaled, swallowed or absorbed via the skin;

(g) toxic substances and preparations: substances and preparations which in low quantities cause death or acute or chronic damage to health when inhaled, swallowed or absorbed via the skin;

(h) harmful substances and preparations: substances and preparations which may cause death or acute or chronic damage to health when inhaled, swallowed or absorbed via the skin;

(i) corrosive substances and preparations: substances and preparations which may, on contact with living tissues, destroy them;

(j) irritant substances and preparations: non-corrosive substances and preparations which, through immediate, prolonged or repeated contact with the skin or mucous membrane, may cause inflammation;

(k) sensitizing substances and preparations: substances and preparations which, if they are inhaled or if they penetrate the skin, are capable of eliciting a reaction of hypersensitization such that on further exposure to the substance or preparation, characteristic adverse effects are produced;

(*l*) carcinogenic substances and preparations: substances or preparations which, if they are inhaled or ingested or if they penetrate the skin, may induce cancer or increase its incidence;

(m) mutagenic substances and preparations: substances and preparations which, if they are inhaled or ingested or if they penetrate the skin, may induce heritable genetic defects or increase their incidence;

(n) substances and preparations which are toxic for reproduction: substances and preparations which, if they are inhaled or ingested or if they penetrate the skin, may produce, or increase the incidence of, non-heritable adverse effects in the progeny and/or an impairment of male or female reproductive functions or capacity;

(o) substances and preparations which are dangerous for the environment: substances and preparations which, were they to enter the environment, would present or may present an immediate or delayed danger for one or more components of the environment.

Article 3

Testing and assessment of the properties of substances

1. Tests on chemicals carried out within the framework of this Directive shall as a general principle be conducted according to the methods laid down in Annex V. * * *

Laboratory tests shall be carried out in compliance with the principles of good laboratory practice provided for in Directive 87/18/EEC and with the provisions of Directive 86/609/EEC.

2. The real or potential risk to man and the environment shall be assessed on the basis of the principles adopted, by 30 April 1993, in accordance with the procedure laid down in Article 29(4)(b). These principles shall be regularly reviewed and, where appropriate, revised in accordance with the same procedure.

Article 4

Classification

1. Substances shall be classified on the basis of their intrinsic properties according to the categories laid down in Article 2(2). * * *

2. The general principles of the classification and labelling of substances and preparations shall be applied according to the criteria in Annex

VI, save where contrary requirements for dangerous preparations are specified in separate Directives.

* * *

Article 5

Duties of the Member States

1. Without prejudice to Article 13, Member States shall take all the necessary measures to ensure that substances cannot be placed on the market on their own or in preparations unless they have been:

— notified to the competent authority of one of the Member States in accordance with this Directive,

— packaged and labelled in accordance with Articles 22 to 25 and with the criteria in Annex VI, and in accordance with the results of the tests provided for in Annexes VII and VIII, save in the case of preparations where provisions exist in other Directives.

In addition, Member States shall take all the necessary measures to ensure that the provisions concerning safety data sheets as laid down in Article 27 are observed.

2. The measures referred to in the second indent of paragraph 1 shall apply until the substance is listed in Annex I or until a decision not to list it has been taken in accordance with the procedure laid down in Article 29.

Article 6

Obligation to carry out investigations

Manufacturers, distributors and importers of dangerous substances which appear in the EINECS but which have not yet been introduced into Annex I shall be obliged to carry out an investigation to make themselves aware of the relevant and accessible data which exist concerning the properties of such substances. On the basis of this information, they shall package and provisionally label these substances according to the rules laid down in Articles 22 to 25 and the criteria in Annex VI.

Article 7

Full notification

1. Without prejudice to Articles 1(2), 8(1), 13 and 16(1), any notifier of a substance shall be required to submit to the competent authority referred to in Article 16(1) of the Member State in which the substance is manufactured, or in the case of a manufacturer located outside the Community, the Member State within which the notifier is established, a notification including:

— a technical dossier supplying the information necessary for evaluating the foreseeable risks, whether immediate or delayed, which the substance may entail for man and the environment, and containing all available relevant data for this purpose. As a minimum, the dossier shall contain the information and results of the studies referred to in

Annex VII.A, together with a detailed and full description of the studies conducted and of the methods used or a bibliographical reference to them,

— a declaration concerning the unfavourable effects of the substance in terms of the various foreseeable uses,

— the proposed classification and labelling of the substance in accordance with this Directive,

— in the case of dangerous substances only, a proposal for a safety data sheet as provided for in Article 27,

— in the case of a manufacturer located outside the Community, the notifier shall, in accordance with Article 2(1)(d), second indent, include, if appropriate, a statement from the manufacturer to the effect that, for the purpose of submitting a notification for the substance in question, he is designated as the manufacturer's sole representative,

— if so desired, a statement by the notifier requesting, on reasoned grounds, that the notification be exempted from the provisions of Article 15(2) for a maximum period which shall not in any case exceed one year following the date of notification.

Besides the information referred to above, the notifier may also provide the authority with a preliminary assessment of the risks, which he has made in accordance with the principles laid down in Article 3(2).

* * *

Article 8

Reduced notification requirements for substances placed on the market in quantities of less than one tonne per annum per manufacturer

[Text omitted]

Article 10

Placing of notified substances on the market

1. Substances notified under Article 7 may, in the absence of any indication to the contrary from the competent authority, be placed on the market no sooner than 60 days after receipt by the authority of a dossier in conformity with the requirements of this Directive.

* * *

Article 11

Substances manufactured outside the Community

Where, for substances manufactured outside the Community, more than one notification exists for a substance manufactured by the same manufacturer, the cumulative yearly tonnages placed on the Community market shall be determined by the Commission and the national authorities on the basis of the information submitted under Articles 7(1), 8(1) and

14. The obligation to carry out supplementary testing in accordance with Article 7(2) will fall collectively on all notifiers.

Article 12

Polymers [text omitted]

Article 13

Exemptions [text omitted]

Article 14

Follow-up information

1. Any notifier of a substance already notified in conformity with Articles 7(1) or 8(1) shall be responsible on his own initiative for informing in writing the competent authority to which the initial notification was submitted of:

— changes in the annual or total quantities placed on the Community market by him or, in the case of a substance manufactured outside the Community for which the notifier has been designated as sole representative, by him and/or others,

— new knowledge of the effects of the substance on man and/or the environment of which he may reasonably be expected to have become aware,

— new uses for which the substance is placed on the market of which he may reasonably be expected to have become aware,

— any change in the composition of the substances as given in Annex VII. A, B or C, section 1.3,

— any change in his status (manufacturer or importer).

2. Any importer of a substance produced by a manufacturer established outside the Community who imports the substance within the framework of a notification previously submitted by a sole representative in accordance with Article 2(1)(d) shall be required to ensure that the sole representative is provided with up-to-date information concerning the quantities of the substance introduced by him on to the Community market.

Article 15

Renotification of the same substance and avoidance of duplicating testing on vertebrate animals [text omitted]

Article 16

Rights and duties of the authorities

1. Member States shall appoint the competent authority or authorities responsible for receiving the information provided for in Articles 7 to 14 and examining its conformity with the requirements of this Directive.

Moreover, if it can be shown to be necessary for the evaluation of the risk which may be caused by a substance, the competent authorities may ask for further information, verification and/or confirmatory tests concerning the substances or their transformation products, of which they have been notified or have received information under this Directive; this may also include requesting any of the information referred to in Annex VIII earlier than provided for in Article 7(2). Additionally, the competent authorities may:

— carry out such sampling as is necessary for control purposes,

— require the notifier to supply such quantities of the notified substance as it deems necessary for the carrying out of verification tests,

— take appropriate measures relating to safe use of a substance pending the introduction of Community provisions.

In the case of substances notified in accordance with Articles 7(1) and 8(1) and (2), the competent authority which received notification shall carry out an assessment of the risks in accordance with the general principles laid down in Article 3(2). The assessment shall include recommendations on the most appropriate method for testing the substance and, where appropriate, also include recommendations on measures which will enable the risk for man and the environment in connection with the marketing of the substance to be lessened. The assessment shall be updated from time to time in the light of additional information provided under this Article or Articles 7(2), 8(3) and 14(1).

2. In the case of notifications submitted in conformity with Article 7, within a period of 60 days following receipt of the notification, the authority shall inform the notifier in writing as to whether the notification has, or has not, been accepted as being in conformity with this Directive.

If the dossier is accepted, the authority shall at the same time advise the notifier of the official number which has been allocated to the notification. If the dossier is not accepted, the authority shall inform the notifier as to what further information he is required to provide in order to bring the dossier into conformity with this Directive.

* * *

6. Without prejudice to Article 19(1), Member States and the Commission shall ensure that any information concerning commercial exploitation or manufacturing is kept secret.

Article 17

Involvement of the Commission in the notification procedure

When a Member State has received the notification dossier referred to in Articles 7(1) and 8(1), or information on the supplementary testing carried out in accordance with Articles 7(2) and 8(3), or follow-up information submitted in conformity with Article 14, it shall as soon as possible send the Commission a copy of the dossier or of the further information or a summary thereof.

In the case of the further information referred to in Article 16(1), the competent authority shall notify the Commission of the tests chosen, the reasons for their choice, the results and, if appropriate, an assessment of the results. In the case of information received in conformity with Article 13(2), the competent authority shall forward to the Commission such elements as would be of common interest for the Commission and the other competent authorities.

The assessment of the risks referred to in Article 16(1) or a summary of that assessment shall be forwarded to the Commission as soon as it becomes available.

Article 18

Duties of the Commission

1. On receipt of the dossiers and information referred to in Article 17, the Commission shall forward copies to the Member States. In addition, the Commission may also forward any other relevant information it has collected pursuant to this Directive, as it sees fit.

2. The competent authority of any Member State may consult directly the competent authority which received the original notification, or the Commission, on specific details of the data contained in the dossier required under this Directive or the assessment of the risks provided for in Article 16(1); it may also suggest that further tests or information be requested or that the assessment of the risks be modified. * * *

Article 19

Confidentiality of data

1. If he considers that there is a confidentiality problem, the notifier may indicate the information provided for in Articles 7, 8 and 14 which he considers to be commercially sensitive and disclosure of which might harm him industrially or commercially, and which he therefore wishes to be kept secret from all persons other than the competent authorities and the Commission. Full justification must be given in such cases.

* * *

4. Confidential information brought to the attention either of the Commission or of a Member State shall be kept secret.

In all cases such information:

— may be brought to the attention only of the authorities whose responsibilities are specified in Article 16(1),

— may, however, be divulged to persons directly involved in administrative or legal proceedings involving sanctions which are undertaken for the purpose of controlling substances placed on the market and to persons who are to participate or be heard in legislative proceedings.

Article 20

Exchange of the summary dossier [text omitted]

Article 21

Lists of existing and new substances

1. The Commission shall keep a list of all substances notified under this Directive. This list shall be compiled in accordance with the provisions of Commission Decision 85/71/EEC.

2. The Commission shall allocate an EEC number to each substance contained on the EINECS inventory and on the list referred to in paragraph 1.

Article 22

Packaging

1. Member States shall take all necessary measures to ensure that dangerous substances cannot be placed on the market unless their packaging satisfies the following requirements:

 (a) it shall be so designed and constructed that its contents cannot escape; this requirement shall not apply where special safety devices are prescribed;

 (b) the materials constituting the packaging and fastenings must not be susceptible to adverse attack by the contents, or liable to form dangerous compounds with the contents;

 (c) packaging and fastenings must be strong and solid throughout to ensure that they will not loosen and will safely meet the normal stresses and strains of handling;

 (d) containers fitted with replaceable fastening devices shall be so designed that the packaging can be refastened repeatedly without the contents escaping;

 (e) every container of whatever capacity, containing substances sold or made available to the general public and labelled "very toxic", "toxic" or "corrosive", as defined in this Directive, must have a child-resistant fastening and a tactile warning of danger;

 (f) every container, of whatever capacity, containing substances sold or made available to the general public and labelled "harmful", "extremely flammable" or "highly flammable" as defined in this Directive must bear a tactile warning of danger.

2. Member States may also prescribe that packaging shall be closed initially with a seal in such a way that when the packaging is opened for the first time the seal is irreparably damaged.

* * *

Article 23

Labelling

1. Member States shall take all necessary measures to ensure that dangerous substances cannot be placed on the market unless the labelling on their packaging satisfies the following requirements.

2. Every package shall show clearly and indelibly the following:

(a) the name of the substance under one of the designations given in Annex I. If the substance is not yet listed in Annex I, the name must be given using an internationally recognized designation;

(b) the name and full address including the telephone number of the person established in the Community who is responsible for placing the substance on the market whether it be the manufacturer, the importer or the distributor;

(c) danger symbols, when laid down, and indication of the danger involved in the use of the substance. The design of the danger symbols and the wording of the indications of danger shall comply with those laid down in Annex II. The symbol shall be printed in black on an orange-yellow background. The danger symbols and indications of danger to be used for each substance shall be those indicated in Annex I.

* * *

Article 24

Implementation of labelling requirements

1. Where the particulars required by Article 23 appear on a label, that label shall be firmly affixed to one or more surfaces of the packaging so that these particulars can be read horizontally when the package is set down normally. The dimensions of the label shall be as follows:

Capacity of the package	*Dimensions (in millimetres)*
— not exceeding 3 litres	at least 52 × 74
— greater than 3 litres but not exceeding 50 litres	at least 74 × 105
— greater than 50 litres but not exceeding 500 litres	at least 105 × 148
— greater than 500 litres	at least 148 × 210

Each symbol shall cover at least one-tenth of the surface area of the label but not be less than 1 cm^2. The entire surface of the label shall adhere to the package immediately containing the substance.

* * *

2. A label is not required where the particulars are clearly shown on the package itself, as specified in paragraph 1.

3. The colour and presentation of the label—or, in the case of paragraph 2, of the package—shall be such that the danger symbol and its background stand out clearly.

* * *

5. Member States may make the placing on the market of dangerous substances in their territories subject to the use of the official language or languages in respect of the labelling thereof.

* * *

Article 25

Exemptions from labelling and packaging requirements [text omitted]

Article 26

Advertisement [text omitted]

Any advertisement for a substance which belongs to one or more of the categories referred to in Article 2(2) shall be prohibited if no mention is made therein of the category or categories concerned.

Article 27

Safety data sheet

1. To enable professional users in particular to take the necessary measures as regards the protection of the environment and health and safety at the workplace, at, or if appropriate, before the first delivery of a dangerous substance, any manufacturer, importer or distributor shall communicate to the recipient a safety data sheet. This sheet must contain the information necessary for protection of man and the environment.

* * *

Article 28

Adaptation to technical progress [text omitted]

The amendments necessary for adapting the Annexes to technical progress shall be adopted in accordance with the procedure laid down in Article 29.

Article 29

Procedure for adaptation to technical progress [text omitted]

Article 30

Free movement clause

Member States may not prohibit, restrict or impede the placing on the market of substances which comply with the requirements of this Directive, on grounds relating to notification, classification, packaging or labelling within the meaning of this Directive.

Article 31

Safeguard clause

1. Where, in the light of new information, a Member State has justifiable reasons to consider that a substance, which has been accepted as satisfying the requirements of the Directive, nevertheless constitutes a

danger for man or the environment, by reason of classification, packaging or labelling which is no longer appropriate, it may temporarily reclassify or, if necessary, prohibit the placing on the market of that substance or subject it to special conditions in its territory. It shall immediately inform the Commission and the other Member States of such action and give reasons for its decision.

2. The Commission shall take a decision in accordance with the procedure referred to in Article 29(4)(a).

3. If, subsequent to the decision taken in accordance with paragraph 2, the Commission considers that for cases falling under paragraph 1 above, technical adaptations to the Annexes of this Directive are necessary, it shall take a decision on the matter in accordance with the procedure provided for in Article 29.

Article 32

Reports

1. Every three years, Member States shall forward to the Commission a report on the implementation of this Directive in their respective territories. The first report shall be submitted three years after the implementation of this Directive.

2. Every three years, the Commission shall prepare a composite report based on the information referred to in paragraph 1, which shall be forwarded to the Member States.

* * *

Article 3

1. Member States shall bring into force the laws, regulations and administrative provisions necessary to comply with this Directive not later than 31 October 1993. They shall forthwith inform the Commission thereof.

* * *

3. Member States shall communicate to the Commission the texts of the provisions of national law which they adopt in the field governed by this Directive.

Article 4

This Directive is addressed to the Member States.

[Annexes omitted, except for Annex II]

ANNEXE II – ANLAGE II – BIJLAGE II – ALLEGATO II – ANNEX II

E

Explosif
Explosionsgefährlich
Ontplofbaar
Esplosivo
Explosive

O

Comburant
Brandfördernd
Oxyderend
Comburente
Oxidising

F

Facilement inflammable
Leicht entzündlich
Licht ontvlambaar
Facilmente infiammabile
Easily flammable

T

Toxique
Gift
Vergiftig
Tossico
Toxic

C

Corrosif
Ätzend
Corrosief
Corrosivo
Corrosive

Xn

Nocif
Gesundheitsschädlich
Schadelijk
Nocivo
Harmful

Xi

Irritant
Reizstoff
Irriterend
Irritante
Irritant

N.B. The current text of Annex II provides also the Finnish, Greek, Portugese, Spanish and Swedish equivalents of these words.

5. COUNCIL DIRECTIVE 83/189/EEC

of 28 March 1983

laying down a procedure for the provision of information in the field of technical standards and regulations

O.J. L 109/8 (Apr. 26, 1983)

THE COUNCIL OF THE EUROPEAN COMMUNITIES.

Having regard to the Treaty establishing the European Economic Community, and in particular Articles 100 and 213 thereof,

Having regard to the proposal from the Commission,

Having regard to the opinion of the European Parliament,

Having regard to the opinion of the Economic and Social Committee,

Whereas the prohibition of quantitative restrictions on the movement of goods and of measures having an equivalent effect is one of the basic principles of the Community;

Whereas barriers to trade resulting from technical regulations relating to products may be allowed only where they are necessary in order to meet essential requirements and have an objective in the public interest of which they constitute the main guarantee;

Whereas it is essential for the Commission to have the necessary information at its disposal before the adoption of technical provisions; whereas, consequently, the Member States which are required to facilitate the achievement of its task pursuant to Article 5 of the Treaty must notify it of their projects in the field of technical regulations;

* * *

Whereas, * * * the Member State in question must, pursuant to the general obligations laid down in Article 5 of the Treaty, defer implementation of the contemplated measure for a period sufficient to allow either a joint examination of * * * amendments [proposed by the Commission or other Member States] or the preparation of the proposal for a Council Directive or of the Commission Directive; whereas the time limits laid down in the Agreement of the representatives of the Governments of the Member States meeting within the Council of 28 May 1969 providing for standstill and notification to the Commission, as amended by the Agreement of 5 March 1973, have proved inadequate in the cases concerned and should accordingly be extended;

Whereas the procedure concerning the standstill arrangement and notification of the Commission contained in the abovementioned Agreement of 28 May 1969 remains applicable to products subject to that procedure which are not covered by this Directive;

Whereas, in practice, national technical standards may have the same effects on the free movement of goods as technical regulations;

Whereas it would therefore appear necessary to inform the Commission of draft standards under similar conditions to those which apply to technical regulations; whereas, pursuant to Article 213 of the Treaty, the Commission may, within the limits and under the conditions laid down by the Council in accordance with the provisions of the Treaty, collect any information and carry out any checks required for the performance of the tasks entrusted to it;

* * *

HAS ADOPTED THIS DIRECTIVE:

Article 1

For the purposes of this Directive, the following meanings shall apply:

1. 'technical specification', a specification contained in a document which lays down the characteristics required of a product such as levels of quality, performance, safety or dimensions, including the requirements applicable to the product as regards terminology, symbols, testing and test methods, packaging, marking or labeling;

2. 'standard', a technical specification approved by a recognized standardizing body for repeated or continuous application, with which compliance is not compulsory;

3. 'standards programme', document listing the subjects for which it is intended to draw up or alter a standard;

4. 'draft standard', document containing the text of the technical specifications concerning a given subject, which is being considered for adoption in accordance with the national standards procedure, as that document stands after the preparatory work and as circulated for public comment or scrutiny;

5. 'technical regulation', technical specifications, including the relevant administrative provisions, the observance of which is compulsory, *de jure* or *de facto*, in the case of marketing or use in a Member State or a major part thereof, except those laid down by local authorities;

6. 'draft technical regulation', the text of a technical specification including administrative provisions, formulated with the aim of enacting it or of ultimately having it enacted as a technical regulation, the text being at a stage or preparation at which substantial amendments can still be made;

7. 'product', any industrially manufactured product and any agricultural product.

> [Directive 88/182, O.J. L 81/75 (Mar. 26, 1988), amended the definition to include agricultural products, medicinal products and cosmetics.]

Article 2

1. The Commission and the standards institutions in List 1 annexed hereto shall be informed each year, not later than 31 January, of the

standards programmes drawn up by the national institutions in List 2 annexed hereto. This information shall be brought up to date every quarter. The Commission may amend or supplement these lists on the basis of communications from the Member States.

2. Standards programmes shall indicate in particular whether the standard:

— will be the transposition in full of an existing international or European standard,

— will be the transposition of an international or European standard incorporating certain national divergences or amendments,

— will be a new national standard,

— will constitute an amendment of a national standard.

* * *

3. The Commission shall keep this information at the disposal of the Member States in a form in which the different programmes can be compared.

Article 3

The Commission and the standards institutions shall be informed if one or more standards institutions:

— wish to be involved passively or actively (by sending an observer) in activities planned by other standards institutions,

— wish a European standard or any other document leading to uniform technical specifications to be drawn up.

Article 4

At least every four months the standards institutions referred to in List 1 and the Commission shall receive all new draft standards, except where such standards merely transpose the full text of an international or European standard.

When a draft is communicated it shall be indicated whether the standard will be:

— the transposition of an international or European standard incorporating certain national divergences or amendments,

— a new national standard, or

— an amendment of a national standard.

Article 5

A Standing Committee shall be set up consisting of representatives appointed by the Member States who may call on the assistance of experts or advisers; its chairman shall be a representative of the Commission.

The Committee shall draw up its own rules of procedure.

Article 6

1. The Committee shall meet at least twice a year with the representatives of the standards institutions referred to in List 1.

2. The Commission shall submit to the Committee a report on the implementation and application of the abovementioned procedures and proposals aimed at eliminating existing or foreseeable barriers to trade.

3. The Committee shall express its opinion on the communications and proposals referred to in paragraph 2 and may in this connection propose, in particular, that the Commission:

— request the European standards institutions to draw up a European standard within a given time limit,

— ensure where necessary, in order to avoid the risk of barriers to trade, that initially the Member States concerned decide amongst themselves on appropriate measures,

— take all appropriate measures.

* * *

5. The Committee may be consulted by the Commission on any preliminary draft technical regulation received by the latter.

* * *

7. The proceedings of the Committee and the information to be submitted to it shall be confidential.

However, the Committee and the national authorities may, provided that the necessary precautions are taken, consult, for an expert opinion, natural or legal persons, including persons in the private sector.

Article 7

1. Member States shall take all appropriate measures to ensure that their standards institutions do not draw up or introduce standards in the field in question while the European standard referred to in the first indent of Article 6(3) is being drawn up. This undertaking shall lapse unless a European standard has been introduced within six months following expiry of the time limit fixed in accordance with the said indent.

* * *

Article 8

1. Member States shall immediately communicate to the Commission any draft technical regulation, except where such technical regulation merely transposes the full text of an international or European standard, in which case information regarding the relevant standard shall suffice; they shall also let the Commission have a brief statement of the grounds which make the enactment of such a technical regulation necessary, where these are not already made clear in the draft.

The Commission shall immediately notify the other Member States of any draft it has received; it may also refer this draft to the Committee for its opinion.

2. The Commission and the Member States may make comments to the Member State which has forwarded a draft technical regulation, that Member State shall take such comments into account as far as possible in the subsequent preparation of the technical regulation.

3. At the express request of a Member State or the Commission, Member States shall communicate to them, without delay, the definitive text of a technical regulation.

4. The information supplied under this Article shall be confidential.

However, the Committee and the national authorities may, provided that the necessary precautions are taken, consult, for an expert opinion, natural or legal persons, including persons in the private sector.

Article 9

1. Without prejudice to paragraph 2, Member States shall postpone the adoption of a draft technical regulation for six months from the date of the notification referred to in Article 8(1) if the Commission or another Member State delivers a detailed opinion, within three months of that date, to the effect that the measure envisaged must be amended in order to eliminate or reduce any barriers which it might create to the free movement of goods.

2. The period in paragraph 1 shall be 12 months if, within three months following the notification referred to in Article 8(1), the Commission gives notice of its intention of proposing or adopting a Directive on the subject.

3. Paragraphs 1 and 2 shall not apply in those cases where, for urgent reasons relating to the protection of public health or safety, a Member State is obliged to prepare technical regulations in a very short space of time in order to enact and introduce them immediately without any consultations being possible. In such cases the Member State in question shall in the notification provided for in Article 8 state the grounds warranting the urgent adoption of the measures.

Article 10

Articles 8 and 9 shall not apply where Member States honour their obligations arising out of Community Directives or commitments arising out of an international agreement where they result in the adoption of uniform technical specifications in the Community.

Article 11

No later than four years following the date of notification of this Directive the Commission, in close cooperation with the Committee referred to in Article 5, shall review the operation of the procedures laid down in this Directive and, if need be, submit any relevant proposals for amending them.

Article 12

1. Member States shall bring into force the measures necessary in order to comply with this Directive within 12 months following its notification and shall forthwith inform the Commission thereof.

2. Member States shall ensure that the texts of the main provisions of national law which they adopt in the field governed by this Directive are communicated to the Commission.

Article 13

This Directive is addressed to the Member States.

ANNEX I

European standardization bodies

CEN Comité Européen de Normalisation

Cenelee Comité Européen de Normalisation Electrotechnique

ETSI European Telecommunications Standards Institute

[other annexes omitted.]

[The preceding text has been retained for pedagogical purposes. This directive was substantially amended by Council Directive 94/10/EEC, O.J. L 100/30 (Apr. 19, 1994). The recitals indicate that, among other things, the amendments were intended to "define more clearly the information which has to be notified and to make the procedure more flexible and less cumbersome," and to cover more precisely the status of *de facto* technical regulations.

The chief substantive amendments are as follows:

Article 1(2) was amended to distinguish between an international standard, a European standard, and a national standard;

Article 1 was amended to insert a new (9), defining *de facto* regulations as including, i.e., laws or regulations which refer to "professional codes or codes of practice which in turn refer to technical specifications";

Article 4 was amended to impose on Member States the duty to ensure that their standardization bodies comply with the directive's obligations;

Article 9 was amended to extend the Member State's duty to postpone action on a draft technical regulation from 12 to 18 months whenever the Council has adopted a relevant common position within the initial 12 month period;

Article 11 was amended to require the Commission to provide the European Parliament and the Council with bi-annual reports on the application of the directive, and to publish annually in the Official Journal lists of standardization work entrusted to European standardization bodies pursuant to the directive.

The amendments became effective July 1, 1995.]

6. COUNCIL DIRECTIVE 85/577/EEC

of 20 December 1985

to protect the consumer in respect of contracts negotiated away from business premises

O.J. L 372/31 (Dec. 31, 1985)

THE COUNCIL OF THE EUROPEAN COMMUNITIES,

Having regard to the Treaty establishing the European Economic Community, and in particular Article 100 thereof,

Having regard to the proposal from the Commission,

Having regard to the opinion of the European Parliament,

Having regard to the opinion of the Economic and Social Committee,

Whereas it is a common form of commercial practice in the Member States for the conclusion of a contract or a unilateral engagement between a trader and consumer to be made away from the business premises of the trader, and whereas such contracts and engagements are the subject of legislation which differs from one Member State to another;

Whereas any disparity between such legislation may directly affect the functioning of the common market; whereas it is therefore necessary to approximate laws in this field;

* * *

Whereas the special feature of contracts concluded away from the business premises of the trader is that as a rule it is the trader who initiates the contract negotiations, for which the consumer is unprepared or which he does not except; whereas the consumer is often unable to compare the quality and price of the offer with other offers; whereas this surprise element generally exists not only in contracts made at the doorstep but also in other forms of contract concluded by the trader away from his business premises;

Whereas the consumer should be given a right of cancellation over a period of at least seven days in order to enable him to assess the obligations arising under the contract;

Whereas appropriate measures should be taken to ensure that the consumer is informed in writing of this period for reflection;

Whereas the freedom of Member States to maintain or introduce a total or partial prohibition on the conclusion of contracts away from business premises, inasmuch as they consider this to be in the interest of consumers, must not be affected;

HAS ADOPTED THIS DIRECTIVE:

Article 1

1. This Directive shall apply to contracts under which a trader supplies goods or services to a consumer and which are concluded:

— during an excursion organized by the trader away from his business premises, or

— during a visit by a trader

    (i) to the consumer's home or to that of another consumer;

    (ii) to the consumer's place of work;

    where the visit does not take place at the express request of the consumer.

* * *

Article 2

For the purposes of this Directive:

'consumer' means a natural person who, in transactions covered by this Directive, is acting for purposes which can be regarded as outside his trade or profession;

'trader' means a natural or legal person who, for the transaction in question, acts in his commercial or professional capacity, and anyone acting in the name or on behalf of a trader.

Article 3

1. The Member States may decide that this Directive shall apply only to contracts for which the payment to be made by the consumer exceeds a specified amount. This amount may not exceed 60 [Euro].

The Council, acting on a proposal from the Commission, shall examine and, if necessary, revise this amount for the first time no later than four years after notification of the Directive and thereafter every two years, taking into account economic and monetary developments in the Community.

2. This Directive shall not apply to:

(a) contracts for the construction, sale and rental of immovable property or contracts concerning other rights relating to immovable property.

Contracts for the supply of goods and for their incorporation in immovable property or contracts for repairing immovable property shall fall within the scope of this Directive;

b) contracts for the supply of foodstuffs or beverages or other goods intended for current consumption in the household and supplied by regular roundsmen;

(c) contracts for the supply of goods or services, provided that all three of the following conditions are met:

    (i) the contract is concluded on the basis of a trader's catalogue which the consumer has a proper opportunity of reading in the absence of the trader's representative,

(ii) there is intended to be continuity of contact between the trader's representative and the consumer in relation to that or any subsequent transaction,

(iii) both the catalogue and the contract clearly inform the consumer of his right to return goods to the supplier within a period of not less than seven days of receipt or otherwise to cancel the contract within that period without obligation of any kind other than to take reasonable care of the goods;

(d) insurance contracts;

(e) contracts for securities.

* * *

Article 4

In the case of transactions within the scope of Article 1, traders shall be required to give consumers written notice of their right of cancellation within the period laid down in Article 5, together with the name and address of a person against whom that right may be exercised.

Such notice shall be dated and shall state particulars enabling the contract to be identified. It shall be given to the consumer:

(a) in the case of Article 1(1), at the time of conclusion of the contract;

* * *

Member States shall ensure that their national legislation lays down appropriate consumer protection measures in cases where the information referred to in this Article is not supplied.

Article 5

1. The consumer shall have the right to renounce the effects of his undertaking by sending notice within a period of not less than seven days from receipt by the consumer of the notice referred to in Article 4, in accordance with the procedure laid down by national law. It shall be sufficient if the notice is dispatched before the end of such period.

2. The giving of the notice shall have the effect of releasing the consumer from any obligations under the cancelled contract.

Article 6

The consumer may not waive the rights conferred on him by this Directive.

Article 7

If the consumer exercises his right of renunciation, the legal effects of such renunciation shall be governed by national laws, particularly regarding the reimbursement of payments for goods or services provided and the return of goods received.

Article 8

This Directive shall not prevent Member States from adopting or maintaining more favourable provisions to protect consumers in the field which it covers.

Article 9

1. Member States shall take the measures necessary to comply with this Directive within 24 months of its notification. They shall forthwith inform the Commission thereof.

2. Member States shall ensure that the texts of the main provisions of national law which they adopt in the field covered by this Directive are communicated to the Commission.

Article 10

This Directive is addressed to the Member States.

7. REGULATION (EEC) 1612/68 OF THE COUNCIL

of 15 October 1968

on freedom of movement for workers within the Community

O.J. English Spec. Ed. 1968–II, 475

THE COUNCIL OF THE EUROPEAN COMMUNITIES,

Having regard to the Treaty establishing the European Economic Community, and in particular Article 49 thereof;

Having regard to the proposal from the Commission;

Having regard to the Opinion of the European Parliament;[1]

Having regard to the Opinion of the Economic and Social Committee;[2]

Whereas freedom of movement for workers should be secured within the Community by the end of the transitional period at the latest; whereas the attainment of this objective entails the abolition of any discrimination based on nationality between workers of the Member States as regards employment, remuneration and other conditions of work and employment, as well as the right of such workers to move freely within the Community in order to pursue activities as employed persons subject to any limitations justified on grounds of public policy, public security or public health;

Whereas by reason in particular of the early establishment of the customs union and in order to ensure the simultaneous completion of the principal foundations of the Community, provisions should be adopted to enable the objectives laid down in Articles 48 and 49 of the Treaty in the field of freedom of movement to be achieved and to perfect measures adopted successively under Regulation No. 15[3] on the first steps for attainment of freedom of movement and under Council Regulation No. 38/54/EEC[4] of 25 March 1964 on freedom of movement for workers within the Community;

Whereas freedom of movement constitutes a fundamental right of workers and their families; whereas mobility of labour within the Community must be one of the means by which the worker is guaranteed the possibility of improving his living and working conditions and promoting his social advancement, while helping to satisfy the requirements of the economies of the Member States; whereas the right of all workers in the Member States to pursue the activity of their choice within the Community should be affirmed;

Whereas such right must be enjoyed without discrimination by permanent, seasonal and frontier workers and by those who pursue their activities for the purpose of providing services;

Whereas the right of freedom of movement, in order that it may be exercised, by objective standards, in freedom and dignity, requires that equality of treatment shall be ensured in fact and in law in respect of all

1. OJ No. 268, 6.11.1967, p. 9.
2. OJ No. 298, 7.12.1967, p. 10.
3. OJ No. 57, 26.8.1961, p. 1073/61.
4. OJ No. 62, 17.4.1964, p. 965/64.

matters relating to the actual pursuit of activities as employed persons and to eligibility for housing, and also that obstacles to the mobility of workers shall be eliminated, in particular as regards the worker's right to be joined by his family and the conditions for the integration of that family into the host country;

Whereas the principle of non-discrimination between Community workers entails that all nationals of Member States have the same priority as regards employment as is enjoyed by national workers;

* * *

HAS ADOPTED THIS REGULATION:

PART I

EMPLOYMENT AND WORKERS' FAMILIES

Title I. Eligibility for employment

Article 1

1. Any national of a Member State, shall, irrespective of his place of residence, have the right to take up an activity as an employed person, and to pursue such activity, within the territory of another Member State in accordance with the provisions laid down by law, regulation or administrative action governing the employment of nationals of that State.

2. He shall, in particular, have the right to take up available employment in the territory of another Member State with the same priority as nationals of that State.

Article 2

Any national of a Member State and any employer pursuing an activity in the territory of a Member State may exchange their applications for and offers of employment, and may conclude and perform contracts of employment in accordance with the provisions in force laid down by law, regulation or administrative action, without any discrimination resulting therefrom.

Article 3

1. Under this Regulation, provisions laid down by law, regulation or administrative action or administrative practices of a Member State shall not apply:

— where they limit application for and offers of employment, or the right of foreign nationals to take up and pursue employment or subject these to conditions not applicable in respect of their own nationals; or

— where, though applicable irrespective of nationality, their exclusive or principal aim or effect is to keep nationals of other Member States away from the employment offered.

This provision shall not apply to conditions relating to linguistic knowledge required by reason of the nature of the post to be filled.

2. There shall be included in particular among the provisions or practices of a Member State referred to in the first subparagraph of paragraph 1 those which:

(a) prescribe a special recruitment procedure for foreign nationals;

(b) limit or restrict the advertising of vacancies in the press or through any other medium or subject it to conditions other than those applicable in respect of employers pursuing their activities in the territory of that Member State;

(c) subject eligibility for employment to conditions of registration with employment offices or impede recruitment of individual workers, where persons who do not reside in the territory of that State are concerned.

Article 4

1. Provisions laid down by law, regulation or administrative action of the Member States which restrict by number or percentage the employment of foreign nationals in any undertaking, branch of activity or region, or at a national level, shall not apply to nationals of the other Member States.

2. When in a Member State the granting of any benefit to undertakings is subject to a minimum percentage of national workers being employed, nationals of the other Member States shall be counted as national workers, subject to the provisions of the Council Directive of 15 October 1963.[2]

Article 5

A national of a Member State who seeks employment in the territory of another Member State shall receive the same assistance there as that afforded by the employment offices in that State to their own nationals seeking employment.

Article 6

1. The engagement and recruitment of a national of one Member State for a post in another Member State shall not depend on medical, vocational or other criteria which are discriminatory on grounds of nationality by comparison with those applied to nationals of the other Member State who wish to pursue the same activity.

2. Nevertheless, a national who holds an offer in his name from an employer in a Member State other than that of which he is a national may have to undergo a vocational test, if the employer expressly requests this when making his offer of employment.

Title II. Employment and equality of treatment

Article 7

1. A worker who is a national of a Member State may not, in the territory of another Member State, be treated differently from national

---

2. OJ No. 159, 2.11.1963, p. 2661/63.

workers by reason of his nationality in respect of any conditions of employment and work, in particular as regards remuneration, dismissal, and should he become unemployed, reinstatement or re-employment;

2. He shall enjoy the same social and tax advantages as national workers.

3. He shall also, by virtue of the same right and under the same conditions as national workers, have access to training in vocational schools and retraining centres.

4. Any clause of a collective or individual agreement or of any other collective regulation concerning eligibility for employment, employment, remuneration and other conditions of work or dismissal shall be null and void in so far as it lays down or authorises discriminatory conditions in respect of workers who are nationals of the other Member States.

Article 8

1. A worker who is a national of a Member State and who is employed in the territory of another Member State shall enjoy equality of treatment as regards membership of trade unions and the exercise of rights attaching thereto, including the right to vote [and to be eligible for the administration or management posts of a trade union]; he may be excluded from taking part in the management of bodies governed by public law and from holding an office governed by public law. Furthermore, he shall have the right of eligibility for workers' representative bodies in the undertaking. The provisions of this Article shall not affect laws or regulations in certain Member States which grant more extensive rights to workers coming from the other Member States. [Insert added by Council Regulation 312/76, O.J. L 39/2 (Feb. 14, 1976).]

* * *

Article 9

1. A worker who is a national of a Member State and who is employed in the territory of another Member State shall enjoy all the rights and benefits accorded to national workers in matters of housing, including ownership of the housing he needs.

2. Such worker may, with the same right as nationals, put his name down on the housing lists in the region in which he is employed, where such lists exist; he shall enjoy the resultant benefits and priorities.

If his family has remained in the country whence he came, they shall be considered for this purpose as residing in the said region, where national workers benefit from a similar presumption.

Title III. Workers' families

Article 10

1. The following shall, irrespective of their nationality, have the right to install themselves with a worker who is a national of one Member State and who is employed in the territory of another Member State:

(a) his spouse and their descendants who are under the age of 21 years or are dependents;

(b) dependent relatives in the ascending line of the worker and his spouse.

2. Member States shall facilitate the admission of any member of the family not coming within the provisions of paragraph 1 if dependent on the worker referred to above or living under his roof in the country whence he comes.

3. For the purposes of paragraphs 1 and 2, the worker must have available for his family housing considered as normal for national workers in the region where he is employed; this provision, however must not give rise to discrimination between national workers and workers from the other Member States.

Article 11

Where a national of a Member State is pursuing an activity as an employed or self-employed person in the territory of another Member State, his spouse and those of the children who are under the age of 21 years or dependent on him shall have the right to take up any activity as an employed person throughout the territory of that same State, even if they are not nationals of any Member State.

Article 12

The children of a national of a Member State who is or has been employed in the territory of another Member State shall be admitted to that State's general educational, apprenticeship and vocational training courses under the same conditions as the nationals of that State, if such children are residing in its territory.

Member States shall encourage all efforts to enable such children to attend these courses under the best possible conditions.

PART II

CLEARANCE OF VACANCIES AND APPLICATIONS FOR EMPLOYMENT

Title I. Co-operation between the Member States and with the Commission

Article 13

1. The Member States or the Commission shall instigate or together undertake any study of employment or unemployment which they consider necessary for securing freedom of movement for workers within the Community.

The central employment services of the Member States shall co-operate closely with each other and with the Commission with a view to acting jointly as regards the clearing of vacancies and applications for employment within the Community and the resultant placing of workers in employment.

2. To this end the Member States shall designate specialist services which shall be entrusted with organising work in the fields referred to above and co-operating with each other and with the departments of the Commission.

> [Omitted articles 14–48 describe the composition, role and operating procedures of specialist services, the European Co-ordination Office for vacancy clearance, and Advisory and Technical committees.]

8. COUNCIL DIRECTIVE 68/360/EEC

of 15 October 1968

on the abolition of restrictions on movement and residence within the Community for workers of Member States and their families

O.J. English Spec. Ed. 1968–II, 485

THE COUNCIL OF THE EUROPEAN COMMUNITIES,

Having regard to the Treaty establishing the European Economic Community, and in particular Article 49 thereof;

Having regard to the proposal from the Commission;

Having regard to the Opinion of the European Parliament;

Having regard to the Opinion of the Economic and Social Committee;

Whereas Council Regulation (EEC) No. 1612/68 fixed the provisions governing freedom of movement for workers within the Community; whereas, consequently, measures should be adopted for the abolition of restrictions which still exist concerning movement and residence within the Community, which conform to the rights and privileges accorded by the said Regulation to nationals of any Member State who move in order to pursue activities as employed persons and to members of their families;

Whereas the rules applicable to residence should, as far as possible, bring the position of workers from other Member States and members of their families into line with that of nationals;

* * *

HAS ADOPTED THIS DIRECTIVE:

Article 1

Member States shall, acting as provided in this Directive, abolish restrictions on the movement and residence of nationals of the said States and of members of their families to whom Regulation (EEC) No. 1612/68 applies.

Article 2

1. Member States shall grant the nationals referred to in Article 1 the right to leave their territory in order to take up activities as employed persons and to pursue such activities in the territory of another Member State. Such right shall be exercised simply on production of a valid identity card or passport. Members of the family shall enjoy the same right as the national on whom they are dependent.

2. Member States shall, acting in accordance with their laws, issue to such nationals, or renew, an identity card or passport, which shall state in particular the holder's nationality.

3. The passport must be valid at least for all Member States and for countries through which the holder must pass when travelling between

Member States. Where a passport is the only document on which the holder may lawfully leave the country, its period of validity shall be not less than five years.

4. Member States may not demand from the nationals referred to in Article 1 any exit visa or any equivalent document.

Article 3

1. Member States shall allow the persons referred to in Article 1 to enter their territory simply on production of a valid identity card or passport.

2. No entry visa or equivalent document may be demanded save from members of the family who are not nationals of a Member State. Member States shall accord to such persons every facility for obtaining any necessary visas.

Article 4

1. Member States shall grant the right of residence in their territory to the persons referred to in Article 1 who are able to produce the documents listed in paragraph 3.

2. As proof of the right of residence, a document entitled 'Residence Permit for a National of a Member State of the EEC' shall be issued. This document must include a statement that it has been issued pursuant to Regulation (EEC) No. 1612/68 and to the measures taken by the Member States for the implementation of the present Directive. The text of such statement is given in the Annex to this Directive.

3. For the issue of a Residence Permit for a National of a Member State of the EEC, Member States may require only the production of the following documents;

— by the worker;
  (a) the document with which he entered their territory;
  (b) a confirmation of engagement from the employer or a certificate of employment;
— by the members of the worker's family:
  (c) the document with which they entered the territory;
  (d) a document issued by the competent authority of the State of origin or the State whence they came, proving their relationship;
  (e) in the cases referred to in Article 10(1) and (2) of Regulation (EEC) No. 1612/68, a document issued by the competent authority of the State of origin or the State whence they came, testifying that they are dependent on the worker or that they live under his roof in such country.

4. A member of the family who is not a national of a Member State shall be issued with a residence document which shall have the same validity as that issued to the worker on whom he is dependent.

Article 5

Completion of the formalities for obtaining a residence permit shall not hinder the immediate beginning of employment under a contract concluded by the applicants.

Article 6

1. The residence permit:

(a) must be valid throughout the territory of the Member State which issued it;

(b) must be valid for at least five years from the date of issue and be automatically renewable.

2. Breaks in residence not exceeding six consecutive months and absence on military service shall not affect the validity of a residence permit.

3. Where a worker is employed for a period exceeding three months but not exceeding a year in the service of an employer in the host State or in the employ of a person providing services, the host Member State shall issue him a temporary residence permit, the validity of which may be limited to the expected period of the employment.

Subject to the provisions of Article 8(1)(c), a temporary residence permit shall be issued also to a seasonal worker employed for a period of more than three months. The period of employment must be shown in the documents referred to in paragraph 4(3)(b).

Article 7

1. A valid residence permit may not be withdrawn from a worker solely on the grounds that he is no longer in employment, either because he is temporarily incapable of work as a result of illness or accident, or because he is involuntarily unemployed, this being duly confirmed by the competent employment office.

2. When the residence permit is renewed for the first time, the period of residence may be restricted, but not to less than twelve months, where the worker has been involuntarily unemployed in the Member State for more than twelve consecutive months.

Article 8

1. Member States shall, without issuing a residence permit, recognise the right of residence in their territory of:

(a) a worker pursuing an activity as an employed person, where the activity is not expected to last for more than three months. The document with which the person concerned entered the territory and a statement by the employer on the expected duration of the employment shall be sufficient to cover his stay * * *.

(b) a worker who, while having his residence in the territory of a Member State to which he returns as a rule, each day or at least once a week, is employed in the territory of another Member State. The competent authority of the State where he is employed may issue such worker with a special permit valid for five years and automatically renewable;

(c) a seasonal worker who holds a contract of employment stamped by the competent authority of the Member State on whose territory he has come to pursue his activity.

* * *

Article 9

1. The residence documents granted to nationals of a Member State of the EEC referred to in this Directive shall be issued and renewed free of charge or on payment of an amount not exceeding the dues and taxes charged for the issue of identity cards to nationals.

* * *

Article 10

Member States shall not derogate from the provisions of this Directive save on grounds of public policy, public security or public health.

* * *

Article 14

This Directive is addressed to the Member States.

ANNEX

Text of the statement referred to in Article 4(2):

'This permit is issued pursuant to Regulation (EEC) No. 1612/68 of the Council of the European Communities of 15 October 1968 and to the measures taken in implementation of the Council Directive of 15 October 1968.

In accordance with the provisions of the above-mentioned Regulation, the holder of this permit has the right to take up and pursue an activity as an employed person in ___[1] territory under the same conditions as ___ workers.'

---

[1] Belgian, German, French, Italian, Luxembourg, Netherlands, according to the country issuing the permit.

9. COUNCIL DIRECTIVE 64/221/EEC

of 25 February 1964

on the co-ordination of special measures concerning the movement and residence of foreign nationals which are justified on grounds of public policy, public security or public health

O.J. English Spec. Ed. 1963–1964, 117

THE COUNCIL OF THE EUROPEAN ECONOMIC COMMUNITY,

Having regard to the Treaty establishing the European Economic Community, and in particular Article 56(2) thereof;

Having regard to Council Regulation No. 15 of 16 August 1961[1] on initial measures to bring about free movement of workers within the Community, and in particular Article 47 thereof;

* * *

Having regard to the General Programmes for the abolition of restrictions on freedom of establishment and on freedom to provide services, and in particular Title II of each such programme;

* * *

Whereas co-ordination of provisions laid down by law, regulation or administrative action which provide for special treatment for foreign nationals on grounds of public policy, public security or public health should in the first place deal with the conditions for entry and residence of nationals of Member States moving within the Community either in order to pursue activities as employed or self-employed persons, or as recipients of services;

* * *

Whereas, in each Member State, nationals of other Member States should have adequate legal remedies available to them in respect of the decisions of the administration in such matters;

* * *

HAS ADOPTED THIS DIRECTIVE:

Article 1

1. The provisions of this Directive shall apply to any national of a Member State who resides in or travels to another Member State of the Community, either in order to pursue an activity as an employed or self-employed person, or as a recipient of services.

2. These provisions shall apply also to the spouse and to members of the family who come within the provisions of the regulations and directives adopted in this field in pursuance of the Treaty.

---

1. OJ No. 57, 26.8.1961, p. 1073/61.

Article 2

1. This Directive relates to all measures concerning entry into their territory, issue or renewal of residence permits, or expulsion from their territory, taken by Member States on grounds of public policy, public security or public health.

2. Such grounds shall not be invoked to service economic ends.

Article 3

1. Measures taken on grounds of public policy or of public security shall be based exclusively on the personal conduct of the individual concerned.

2. Previous criminal convictions shall not in themselves constitute grounds for the taking of such measures.

3. Expiry of the identity card or passport used by the person concerned to enter the host country and to obtain a residence permit shall not justify expulsion from the territory.

4. The State which issued the identity card or passport shall allow the holder of such document to re-enter its territory without any formality even if the document is no longer valid or the nationality of the holder is in dispute.

Article 4

1. The only diseases or disabilities justifying refusal of entry into a territory or refusal to issue a first residence permit shall be those listed in the Annex to this Directive.

2. Diseases or disabilities occurring after a first residence permit has been issued shall not justify refusal to renew the residence permit or expulsion from the territory.

3. Member States shall not introduce new provisions or practices which are more restrictive than those in force at the date of notification of this Directive.

Article 5

1. A decision to grant or to refuse a first residence permit shall be taken as soon as possible and in any event not later than six months from the date of application for the permit.

The person concerned shall be allowed to remain temporarily in the territory pending a decision either to grant or to refuse a residence permit.

2. The host country may, in cases where this is considered essential, request the Member State of origin of the applicant, and if need be other Member States, to provide information concerning any previous police record. Such enquiries shall not be made as a matter of routine. The Member State consulted shall give its reply within two months.

Article 6

The person concerned shall be informed of the grounds of public policy, public security, or public health upon which the decision taken in his case is based, unless this is contrary to the interests of the security of the State involved.

Article 7

The person concerned shall be officially notified of any decision to refuse the issue or renewal of a residence permit or to expel him from the territory. The period allowed for leaving the territory shall be stated in this notification. Save in cases of urgency, this period shall be not less than fifteen days if the person concerned has not yet been granted a residence permit and not less than one month in all other cases.

Article 8

The person concerned shall have the same legal remedies in respect of any decision concerning entry, or refusing the issue or renewal of a residence permit, or ordering expulsion from the territory, as are available to nationals of the State concerned in respect of acts of the administration.

Article 9

1. Where there is no right of appeal to a court of law, or where such appeal may be only in respect of the legal validity of the decision, or where the appeal cannot have suspensory effect, a decision refusing renewal of a residence permit or ordering the expulsion of the holder of a residence permit from the territory shall not be taken by the administrative authority, save in cases of urgency, until an opinion has been obtained from a competent authority of the host country before which the person concerned enjoys such rights of defence and of assistance or representation as the domestic law of that country provides for.

This authority shall not be the same as that empowered to take the decision refusing renewal of the residence permit or ordering expulsion.

2. Any decision refusing the issue of a first residence permit or ordering expulsion of the person concerned before the issue of the permit shall, where that person so requests, be referred for consideration to the authority whose prior opinion is required under paragraph I. The person concerned shall then be entitled to submit his defence in person, except where this would be contrary to the interests of national security.

* * *

Article 11

This Directive is addressed to the Member States.

ANNEX

A. Diseases which might endanger public health:

1. Diseases subject to quarantine listed in International Health Regulation No. 2 of the World Health Organisation of 25 May 1951;

2. Tuberculosis of the respiratory system in an active state or showing a tendency to develop;

3. Syphilis;

4. Other infectious diseases or contagious parasitic diseases if they are the subject of provisions for the protection of nationals of the host country.

B. Diseases and disabilities which might threaten public policy or public security:

1. Drug addiction;

2. Profound mental disturbance; manifest conditions of psychotic disturbance with agitation, delirium, hallucinations or confusion.

10. COUNCIL DIRECTIVE 90/365/EEC

of 28 June 1990

on the right of residence for employees and self-employed persons who have ceased their occupational activity

O.J. L 180/28 (July 13, 1990)

THE COUNCIL OF THE EUROPEAN COMMUNITIES,

Having regard to the Treaty establishing the European Economic Community, and in particular Article 235 thereof,

Having regard to the proposal from the Commission,[1]

Having regard to the opinion of the European Parliament,[2]

Having regard to the opinion of the Economic and Social Committee,[3]

Whereas Article 3(c) of the Treaty provides that the activities of the Community shall include, as provided in the Treaty, the abolition, as between Member States, of obstacles to freedom of movement for persons;

Whereas Article 8a of the Treaty provides that the internal market must be established by 31 December 1992; whereas the internal market comprises an area without internal frontiers in which the free movement of goods, persons, services and capital is ensured, in accordance with the provisions of the Treaty;

Whereas Articles 48 and 52 of the Treaty provide for freedom of movement for workers and self-employed persons, which entails the right of residence in the Member States in which they pursue their occupational activity; whereas it is desirable that this right of residence also be granted to persons who have ceased their occupational activity even if they have not exercised their right to freedom of movement during their working life;

Whereas beneficiaries of the right of residence must not become an unreasonable burden on the public finances of the host Member State;

Whereas under Article 10 of Regulation (EEC) No. 1408/71,[4] as amended by Regulation (EEC) No. 1390/81,[5] recipients of invalidity or old age cash benefits or pensions for accidents at work or occupational diseases are entitled to continue to receive these benefits and pensions even if they reside in the territory of a Member State other than that in which the institution responsible for payment is situated;

Whereas this right can only be genuinely exercised if it is also granted to members of the family;

* * *

Whereas the Treaty does not provide, for the action concerned, powers other than those of Article 235,

---

1. OJ No. C 191, 28.7.1989, p. 3; and OJ No. C 26, 3.2.1990, p. 19.
2. Opinion delivered on 13 June 1990 (not yet published in the Official Journal).
3. OJ No. C 329, 30.12.1989, p. 25.
4. OJ No. L 149, 5.7.1971, p. 2.
5. OJ No. L 143, 29. 5. 1981, p. 1.

HAS ADOPTED THIS DIRECTIVE:

Article 1

1. Member States shall grant the right of residence to nationals of Member States who have pursued an activity as an employee or self-employed person and to members of their families as defined in paragraph 2, provided that they are recipients of an invalidity or early retirement pension, or old age benefits, or of a pension in respect of an industrial accident or disease of an amount sufficient to avoid becoming a burden on the social security system of the host Member State during their period of residence and provided they are covered by sickness insurance in respect of all risks in the host Member State.

The resources of the applicant shall be deemed sufficient where they are higher than the level of resources below which the host Member State may grant social assistance to its nationals, taking into account the personal circumstances of persons admitted pursuant to paragraph 2.

Where the second subparagraph cannot be applied in a Member State the resources of the applicant shall be deemed sufficient if they are higher than the level of the minimum social security pension paid by the host Member State.

2. The following shall, irrespective of their nationality, have the right to install themselves in another Member State with the holder of the right of residence:

   (a) his or her spouse and their descendants who are dependents;

   (b) dependent relatives in the ascending line of the holder of the right of residence and his or her spouse.

Article 2

1. Exercise of the right of residence shall be evidenced by means of the issue of a document known as a 'Residence permit for a national of a Member State of the EEC', whose validity may be limited to five years on a renewable basis. However, the Member States may, when they deem it to be necessary, require revalidation of the permit at the end of the first two years of residence. Where a member of the family does not hold the nationality of a Member State, he or she shall be issued with a residence document of the same validity as that issued to the national on whom he or she depends.

For the purposes of issuing the residence permit or document, the Member State may require only that the applicant present a valid identity card or passport and provide proof that he or she meets the conditions laid down in Article 1.

2. Articles 2, 3, 6(1)(a) and (2) and Article 9 of Directive 68/360/EEC shall apply *mutatis mutandis* to the beneficiaries of this Directive.

The spouse and the dependent children of a national of a Member State entitled to the right of residence within the territory of a Member State shall be entitled to take up any employed or self-employed activity anywhere within the territory of that Member State, even if they are not nationals of a Member State.

Member States shall not derogate from the provisions of this Directive save on grounds of public policy, public security or public health. In that event, Directive 64/221/EEC shall apply.

3. This Directive shall not affect existing law on the acquisition of second homes.

Article 3

The right of residence shall remain for as long as beneficiaries of that right fulfil the conditions laid down in Article 1.

Article 4

The Commission shall, not more than three years after the date of implementation of this Directive, and at three-yearly intervals thereafter, draw up a report on the application of this Directive and submit it to the European Parliament and the Council.

Article 5

Member States shall bring into force the laws, regulations and administrative provisions necessary to comply with this Directive not later than 30 June 1992. They shall forthwith inform the Commission thereof.

Article 6

This Directive is addressed to the Member States.

11. COUNCIL DIRECTIVE 90/364/EEC

of 28 June 1990

on the right of residence

O.J. L 180/26 (July 13, 1990)

THE COUNCIL OF THE EUROPEAN COMMUNITIES,

Having regard to the Treaty establishing the European Economic Community, and in particular Article 235 thereof,

Having regard to the proposal from the Commission,

Having regard to the opinion of the European Parliament,

Having regard to the opinion of the Economic and Social Committee,

Whereas Article 3(c) of the Treaty provides that the activities of the Community shall include, as provided in the Treaty, the abolition, as between Member States, of obstacles to freedom of movement for persons;

Whereas Article 8a of the Treaty provides that the internal market must be established by 31 December 1992; whereas the internal market comprises an area without internal frontiers in which the free movement of goods, persons, services and capital is ensured in accordance with the provisions of the Treaty;

Whereas national provisions on the right of nationals of the Member States to reside in a Member State other than their own must be harmonized to ensure such freedom of movement;

Whereas beneficiaries of the right of residence must not become an unreasonable burden on the public finances of the host Member State;

Whereas this right can only be genuinely exercised if it is also granted to members of the family;

* * *

Whereas the Treaty does not provide, for the action concerned, powers other than those of Article 235,

HAS ADOPTED THIS DIRECTIVE:

Article 1

1. Member States shall grant the right of residence to nationals of Member States who do not enjoy this right under other provisions of Community law and to members of their families as defined in paragraph 2, provided that they themselves and the members of their families are covered by sickness insurance in respect of all risks in the host Member State and have sufficient resources to avoid becoming a burden on the social assistance system of the host Member State during their period of residence.

The resources referred to in the first subparagraph shall be deemed sufficient where they are higher than the level of resources below which the host Member State may grant social assistance to its nationals, taking into account the personal circumstances of the applicant and, where appropriate, the personal circumstances of persons admitted pursuant to paragraph 2.

Where the second subparagraph cannot be applied in a Member State, the resources of the applicant shall be deemed sufficient if they are higher than the level of the minimum social security pension paid by the host Member State.

2. The following shall, irrespective of their nationality, have the right to install themselves in another Member State with the holder of the right of residence:

(a) his or her spouse and their descendants who are dependents;

(b) dependent relatives in the ascending line of the holder of the right of residence and his or her spouse.

Article 2

1. Exercise of the right of residence shall be evidenced by means of the issue of a document known as a 'Residence permit for a national of a Member State of the EEC', the validity of which may be limited to five years on a renewable basis. However, the Member States may, when they deem it to be necessary, require revalidation of the permit at the end of the first two years of residence. Where a member of the family does not hold the nationality of a Member State, he or she shall be issued with a residence document of the same validity as that issued to the national on whom he or she depends.

For the purpose of issuing the residence permit or document, the Member State may require only that the applicant present a valid identity card or passport and provide proof that he or she meets the conditions laid down in Article 1.

2. Articles 2, 3, 6(1)(a) and (2) and Article 9 of Directive 68/360/EEC shall apply *mutatis mutandis* to the beneficiaries of this Directive.

The spouse and the dependent children of a national of a Member State entitled to the right of residence within the territory of a Member State shall be entitled to take up any employed or self-employed activity anywhere within the territory of that Member State, even if they are not nationals of a Member State.

Member States shall not derogate from the provisions of this Directive save on grounds of public policy, public security or public health. In that event, Directive 64/221/EEC shall apply.

3. This Directive shall not affect existing law on the acquisition of second homes.

Article 3

The right of residence shall remain for as long as beneficiaries of that right fulfil the conditions laid down in Article 1.

Article 4

The Commission shall, not more than three years after the date of implementation of this Directive, and at three-yearly intervals thereafter, draw up a report on the application of this Directive and submit it to the European Parliament and the Council.

Article 5

Member States shall bring into force the laws, regulations and administrative provisions necessary to comply with this Directive not later than 30 June 1992. They shall forthwith inform the Commission thereof.

Article 6

This Directive is addressed to the Member States.

12. COUNCIL DIRECTIVE 93/96/EEC

of 29 October 1993

on the right of residence for students

O.J. L 317/59 (December 18, 1993)

THE COUNCIL OF THE EUROPEAN COMMUNITIES,

Having regard to the Treaty establishing the European Economic Community, and in particular the second paragraph of Article 7 thereof,

Having regard to the proposal from the Commission,

In cooperation with the European Parliament,

Having regard to the opinion of the Economic and Social Committee,

Whereas Article 3(c) of the Treaty provides that the activities of the Community shall include, as provided in the Treaty, the abolition, as between Member States, of obstacles to freedom of movement for persons;

Whereas Article 8a of the Treaty provides that the internal market must be established by 31 December 1992; whereas the internal market comprises an area without internal frontiers in which the free movement of goods, persons, services and capital is ensured in accordance with the provisions of the Treaty;

Whereas, as the Court of Justice has ruled, Articles 128 and 7 of the Treaty prohibit any discrimination between nationals of the Member States as regards access to vocational training in the Community; whereas access by a national of one Member State to vocational training in another Member State implies, for that national, a right of residence in that other Member State;

* * *

Whereas the right of residence for students forms part of a set of related measures designed to promote vocational training;

Whereas beneficiaries of the right of residence must not become an unreasonable burden on the public finances of the host Member State;

Whereas, in the present state of Community law, as established by the case law of the Court of Justice, assistance granted to students, does not fall within the scope of the Treaty within the meaning of Article 7 thereof;

Whereas the right of residence can only be genuinely exercised if it is also granted to the spouse and their dependent children;

* * *

Whereas this Directive does not apply to students who enjoy the right of residence by virtue of the fact that they are or have been effectively engaged in economic activities or are members of the family of a migrant worker;

Whereas, by its judgment of 7 July 1992 in Case C-295/90, the Court of Justice annulled Council Directive 90/366/EEC of 28 June 1990 on the right of residence for students[1], while maintaining the effects of the annulled Directive until the entry into force of a directive adopted on the appropriate legal basis;

Whereas the effects of Directive 90/366/EEC should be maintained during the period up to 31 December 1993, the date by which Member States are to have adopted the laws, regulations and administrative provisions necessary to comply with this Directive,

HAS ADOPTED THIS DIRECTIVE:

Article 1

In order to lay down conditions to facilitate the exercise of the right of residence and with a view to guaranteeing access to vocational training in a non-discriminatory manner for a national of a Member State who has been accepted to attend a vocational training course in another Member State, the Member States shall recognize the right of residence for any student who is a national of a Member State and who does not enjoy this right under other provisions of Community law, and to the student's spouse and their dependent children, where the student assures the relevant national authority, by means of a declaration or by such alternative means as the student may choose that are at least equivalent, that he has sufficient resources to avoid becoming a burden on the social assistance system of the host Member State during their period of residence, provided that the student is enrolled in a recognized educational establishment for the principal purpose of following a vocational training course there and that he is covered by sickness insurance in respect of all risks in the host Member State.

Article 2

1. The right of residence shall be restricted to the duration of the course of studies in question.

The right of residence shall be evidenced by means of the issue of a document known as a 'residence permit for a national of a Member State of the Community', the validity of which may be limited to the duration of the course of studies or to one year where the course lasts longer; in the latter event it shall be renewable annually. Where a member of the family does not hold the nationality of a Member State, he or she shall be issued with a residence document of the same validity as that issued to the national on whom he or she depends.

For the purpose of issuing the residence permit or document, the Member State may require only that the applicant present a valid identity card or passport and provide proof that he or she meets the conditions laid down in Article 1.

2. Articles 2, 3 and 9 of Directive 68/360/EEC shall apply *mutatis mutandis* to the beneficiaries of this Directive.

---

1. OJ No. L 180, 13.7.1990. p. 30.

The spouse and the dependent children of a national of a Member State entitled to the right of residence within the territory of a Member State shall be entitled to take up any employed or self-employed activity anywhere within the territory of that Member State, even if they are not nationals of a Member State.

Member States shall not derogate from the provisions of this Directive save on grounds of public policy, public security or public health: in that event, Articles 2 to 9 of Directive 64/221/EEC shall apply.

Article 3

This Directive shall not establish any entitlement to the payment of maintenance grants by the host Member State on the part of students benefiting from the right of residence.

Article 4

The right of residence shall remain for as long as beneficiaries of that right fulfil the conditions laid down in Article 1.

Article 5

The Commission shall, not more than three years after the date of implementation of this Directive, and at three-yearly intervals thereafter, draw up a report on the application of this Directive and submit it to the European Parliament and the Council.

The Commission shall pay particular attention to any difficulties to which the implementation of Article 1 might give rise in the Member States; it shall, if appropriate, submit proposals to the Council with the aim of remedying such difficulties.

Article 6

Member States shall bring into force the law, regulations and administrative provisions necessary to comply with this Directive not later than 31 December 1993. They shall forthwith inform the Commission thereof.

For the period preceding that date, the effects of Directive 90/366/EEC shall be maintained.

When Member States adopt those measures, they shall contain a reference to this Directive or shall be accompanied by such a reference on the occasion of their official publication. The methods of making such references shall be laid down by the Member States.

Article 7

This Directive is addressed to the Member States.

13. GENERAL PROGRAMME

for the abolition of restrictions on freedom of establishment

O.J. English Spec. Ed. 1974, IX, 7

The Council of the European Economic Community,

Having regard to the provisions of the Treaty, and in particular Articles 54 and 132(5) thereof;

Having regard to the proposal from the Commission;

Having regard to the Opinion of the Economic and Social Committee;

Having regard to the Opinion of the European Parliament;

Has adopted this General Programme for the abolition of restrictions on freedom of establishment within the European Economic Community.

Title I

Beneficiaries

[T]he persons entitled to benefit from the abolition of restrictions on freedom of establishment as set out in this General Programme are:

— nationals of Member States or of the overseas countries and territories, and

— companies and firms formed under the law of a Member State or of an overseas country or territory and having either the seat prescribed by their statutes, or their centre of administration, or their main establishment situated within the Community or in an overseas country or territory,

who wish to establish themselves in order to pursue activities as self-employed persons in a Member State; and

— nationals of Member States or of the overseas countries and territories who are established in a Member State or in an overseas country or territory, and

— companies and firms as above, provided that, where only the seat prescribed by their statutes is situated within the Community or in an overseas country or territory, their activity shows a real and continuous link with the economy of a Member State or of an overseas country or territory; such link shall not be one of nationality, whether of the members of the company or firm, or of the persons holding managerial or supervisory posts therein, or of the holders of the capital,

who wish to set up agencies, branches or subsidiaries in a Member State.

Title II

Entry and Residence

The following steps are to be taken before the end of the second year of the second stage of the transitional period:

A. The provisions laid down by law, Regulation or administrative action which in any Member State govern the entry and residence of nationals of other Member States will, where such provisions are not justified on grounds of public policy, public security or public health, and are liable to hinder those nationals in taking up or pursuing activities as self-employed persons, be so amended, in particular by the abrogation of those having an economic purpose, as to eliminate this source of hindrance;

B. The abolition of provisions laid down by law, Regulation or administrative action which in a Member State prohibit nationals of other Member States working in paid employment in that State from staying on and taking up an activity there in a self-employed capacity even though such nationals satisfy the requirements which they would have to meet if they were entering the Member State in question at the time when they wished to take up the activity concerned.

Title III

Restrictions

Subject to the exceptions or special provisions laid down in the Treaty and in particular to:

— Article 55 concerning activities which are connected with the exercise of official authority in a Member State; and to

— Article 56 concerning provisions on special treatment for foreign nationals on grounds of public policy, public security or public health,

the following restrictions are to be eliminated in accordance with the timetable laid down under Title IV:

A. Any measure which, pursuant to any provision laid down by law, Regulation or administrative action in a Member State, or as the result of the application of such a provision, or of administrative practices, prohibits or hinders nationals of other Member States in their pursuit of an activity as a self-employed person by treating nationals of other Member States differently from nationals of the country concerned.

Such restrictive provisions and practices are in particular those which, in respect of foreign nationals only:

(a) prohibit the taking up or pursuit of an activity as a self-employed person;

(b) make the taking up or pursuit of an activity as a self-employed person subject to an authorization or to the issue of a document such as a foreign trader's permit;

(c) impose additional conditions in respect of the granting of any authorization required for the taking up or pursuit of an activity as a self-employed person;

(d) make the taking up or pursuit of an activity as a self-employed person subject to a period of prior residence or training in the host country;

(e) make the taking up or pursuit of an activity as a self-employed person more costly by through (sic) taxation or other financial burdens, such as a requirement that the person concerned shall lodge a deposit or provide security in the host country;

(f) limit or hinder, by making it more costly or more difficult, access to sources of supply or to distribution outlets;

(g) prohibit or hinder access to any vocational training which is necessary or useful for the pursuit of an activity as a self-employed person;

(h) prohibit foreign nationals from becoming members of companies or firms, or restrict their rights as members, in particular as regards the functions which they may perform within the company or firm;

(i) deny or restrict the right to participate in social security schemes, in particular sickness, accident, invalidity or old age insurance schemes, or the right to receive family allowances;

(j) grant less favourable treatment in the event of nationalization, expropriation or requisition.

The like shall apply to provisions and practices which, in respect of foreign nationals only, exclude, limit or impose conditions on the power to exercise rights normally attaching to an activity as a self-employed person, and in particular the power:

(a) to enter into contracts, in particular contracts for work, business or agricultural tenancies, and contracts of employment, and to enjoy all rights arising under such contracts;

(b) to submit tenders for or to act directly as a party or as a subcontractor in contracts with the State or with any other legal person governed by public law;

(c) to obtain licences or authorizations issued by the State or by any other legal person governed by public law;

(d) to acquire, use or dispose of movable or immovable property or rights therein;

(e) to acquire, use or dispose of intellectual property and all rights deriving therefrom;

(f) to borrow, and in particular to have access to the various forms of credit;

(g) to receive aids granted by the State, whether direct or indirect;

(h) to be a party to legal or administrative proceedings;

(i) to join professional or trade organizations;

where the professional or trade activities of the person concerned necessarily involve the exercise of such power.

Furthermore, included among the abovementioned provisions and practices are those which limit or impair the freedom of personnel belonging to the main establishment in one Member State to take up managerial or supervisory posts in agencies, branches or subsidiaries in another Member State.

B. Any requirements imposed, pursuant to any provision laid down by law, Regulation or administrative action or in consequence of any administrative practice, in respect of the taking up or pursuit of an activity as a self-employed person where, although applicable irrespective of nationality, their effect is exclusively or principally, to hinder the taking up or pursuit of such activity by foreign nationals.

Title IV

Timetable

[The omitted text in Titles IV–VII, together with annexes, sets forth the timetable for legislative action, sector by sector.]

14. COMMISSION INTERPRETATIVE COMMUNICATION CONCERNING THE FREE MOVEMENT OF SERVICES ACROSS FRONTIERS

O.J.C. 334/3 (Dec. 9, 1993)

I. INTRODUCTION

The service sector is a cornerstone of the internal market. In an area without internal frontiers, not only must the growth of the service sector be fostered in order to generate employment, but businesses and consumers must be afforded unhindered access to a broader range of services which are both cheaper, more efficient and more appropriate to their needs.

As the Commission stated in 1985, 'despite the provisions of Articles 59 and 62 of the Treaty, progress on the freedom to provide services across internal frontiers has been much slower than the progress achieved on free movement of goods' because 'firms and individuals have not yet succeeded in taking full advantage of this freedom'[1].

The Court of Justice recently handed down a series of important judgments concerning the interpretation of the provisions of the EEC Treaty on the free movement of services. This case-law, which the Court itself has felt ought to be summarized and consolidated[2], gives the Commission useful guidance on how the Treaty's rules should be applied with a view to ensuring the orderly functioning and development of the internal market.

The purpose of this communication is to inform the ordinary citizen about how Article 59 has been interpreted by the Court[3]. It answers the need for transparency of Community rules as required by the Edinburgh European Council in that it facilitates a decentralized and correct application of the Treaty's rules in Member States with a minimum of intervention on the part of the Community authorities. As provided by the White Paper on completing the internal market, the communication will serve as a guide for public authorities as regards their obligations, and for Community citizens as regards the rights they enjoy[4].

II. FIELD OF APPLICATION

Articles 59 and 60 of the Treaty establish the principle of the free movement[5] of services[6]. This principle became directly applicable and unconditional on the expiry of the transitional period[7].

---

1. Commission White Paper on completing the internal market, 14 June 1985, points 95 and 98.
2. Case C-288/89 *Mediawet* [1991] ECR 1-4007, paragraphs 10 to 15.
3. It is not concerned with the other provisions on services, whether they be provisions of primary law (e.g. Article 75, which deals with transport) or of secondary law (e.g. harmonization directives).
4. Point 155 of the White Paper.
5. Community competence is limited to services of a 'cross-border' nature.
6. For the purposes of Article 60 of the EEC Treaty, this term covers remunerated economic activities.
7. Case 33/74, *Van Binsbergen* [1974] ECR 1299, paragraph 24.

The Court has given a general definition of the obstacles to the free movement of services prohibited by Articles 59 *et seq.* of the EEC Treaty. These articles cover cross-border trade in services of a temporary nature, as opposed to the right of establishment[8].

Where the service is of a 'permanent' nature, the rules on the right of establishment apply (Article 52). On the question of where to draw the dividing line between 'temporary' and 'permanent', the Court has held that the rules on the free movement of services may not be relied upon with a view to circumventing the rules which would be applicable were a person to establish himself in another Member State[9].

The Court has likewise held that a Member State may not make the provision of services in its territory subject to compliance with all the conditions required for establishment and thereby deprive of all practical effectiveness the provisions of the Treaty whose object is, precisely, to guarantee the freedom to provide services[10].

On this issue of the temporary nature of a service, the Court has ruled that Articles 59 and 60 of the Treaty cannot be interpreted as meaning that the domestic legislation applicable to nationals of a State which normally covers a 'permanent' activity pursued by persons established in that State may be applied in its entirety and in the same way to activities of a 'temporary' nature pursued by persons established in other Member States[11].

III. PRINCIPLES OF APPLICATION

1. The prohibition of restrictions on the free movement of services

In the Court's view, the concept of restriction on the free movement of services involves more than just discrimination. Unjustified or disproportionate restrictions are also prohibited even if they apply without distinction to services provided by nationals of the State in question and to those provided by non-nationals.

The Court has thus held that Article 59 requires 'not only the abolition of any discrimination against a person providing services on account of his nationality but also

— the abolition of any restriction on the freedom to provide services imposed on the ground that the person providing a service is

---

8. In the transport sector, with particular reference to the laying-down of common rules applicable to international transport and the conditions under which non-resident carriers may operate transport services, application of the principle of free movement of services is governed by the common transport policy (see Articles 61(1) and 75 of the EEC Treaty and the judgment of the Court of Justice in Case 13/83 *Parliament v. Council* [1985] ECR 1513, paragraphs 62 and 63).

9. Case 205/84 *Commission v. Germany* [1986] ECR 3755, paragraph 22.

10. Case C-180/89 *Commission v. Italy* [1991] ECR I-709, paragraph 15; Case C-76/90 *Sager* [1991] ECR I-4221, paragraph 13.

11. Case C-294/89 *Commission v. France* [1991] ECR I-3591, paragraph 26.

established in a Member State other than the one in which the service is provided'[12], and

— 'the abolition of any restriction, even if it applies without distinction to national providers of services and to those of other Member States, when it is liable to prohibit or otherwise impede the activities of a provider of services established in another Member State where he lawfully provides similar services'[13].

In principle, the expression 'liable to prohibit or otherwise impede'[14] covers any measure which might hinder trade in services between Member States, e.g. those which affect the ability of the service provider to provide a service[15], those which increase the cost of the service[16] or discourage its provision[17], and those which prevent potential customers from having recourse to the services of their choice[18]. The freedom to provide services thus protects not only those who provide, but also those who receive, services[19].

2. Exceptions, exemptions and derogations and the limits thereto: necessity and proportionality

That is not to say, however, that all such measures are prohibited outright by Article 59.

It is in the light of the principles of necessity and proportionality that it has to be examined whether a provision of domestic law contains restrictions on freedom to provide services and, if so, whether those restrictions are justified by overriding reasons relating to the public interest[20].

In its decisions[21], the Court thus introduces practical criteria for applying these principles, based, *inter alia,* on the specific situation of the service provider (who operates from the country in which he is established), the type of activity concerned (its simplicity) and protection of the recipient of the service (possibility of his suffering loss or damage in the event of non-compliance with the rules of the country in which the service is provided).

Restrictions are compatible with Article 59 only if it is established that:

12. Case C-154/89 *Commission v. France* [1991] ECR I-659, paragraph 12; Case C-288/89, cited above, paragraph 10.

13. Case C-76/90, cited above, paragraph 12.

14. Case C-33/74, cited above, paragraph 10; Case C-76/90, cited above, paragraph 12.

15. Case C-113/89 *Rush Portuguesa* [1990] ECR I-1417, paragraph 12.

16. Case 205/84, cited above, paragraph 28.

17. Judgment of 28 January 1992 in Case C-204/90 *Bachmann,* not yet reported, paragraph 31; judgment of 28 January 1992 in Case C-300/90 *Commission v. Belgium,* not yet reported, paragraph 22.

18. Judgment of 26 February 1991 in Case C-180/89 *Commission v. Italy,* not yet reported, paragraph 16.

19. Joined Cases 286/82 and 26/83 *Luisi and Carbone* [1984] ECR 377, paragraphs 10 and 16.

20. Case C-288/89, cited above, paragraph 16.

21. Case C-76/90, cited above, paragraphs 14 and 18.

(a) *'with regard to the activity in question, there are overriding reasons relating to the public interest which justify restrictions on the freedom to provide services'*[22]

On the reasons that may be invoked, the Court draws a clear distinction between discriminatory and non-discriminatory measures.

'National rules which are not applicable to services without discrimination as regards their origin are compatible with Community law only if they can be brought within the scope of an express exemption, such as that contained in Article 56 of the Treaty'[23]. These exemptions relate to public policy, public security or public health.

On the other hand, national rules which are applicable without discrimination may be justified, in the words used by the Court, by a number of other mandatory requirements or overriding reasons in the public interest[24]. In view of the specific nature of certain professional activities, the imposition of specific requirements for the purpose of applying rules governing these types of activity is, therefore, not necessarily incompatible with the Treaty[25].

Such requirements are primarily those referred to in Article 56, but also those mentioned in other articles of the Treaty; they relate in particular to public morality, the protection of workers and consumers, industrial and commercial property and the protection of national treasures possessing artistic, historic or archaeological value[26].

Other mandatory requirements and legitimate objectives worthy of protection may also qualify, such as professional rules designed to protect the recipients of services[27], the protection of intellectual property[28], the protection of workers[29], the protection of consumers[30], the taking into account of 'Coherence' in the tax system[30bis], professional ethics[31], good standing and independence, the operation of the judicial system[32], the turning to account of the historical heritage and the widest possible dissemination of knowledge of a country's historical, artistic and cultural heritage[33].

On the other hand, 'economic aims cannot constitute grounds of public policy within the meaning of Article 56'[34]. The same applies to

---

22. Case C–180/89, cited above, paragraph 18.

23. Case C–288/89, cited above, paragraph 11.

24. Case 205/84, cited above, paragraph 29; Case C–76/90, cited above, paragraph 15.

25. Judgment of 20 May 1992 in Case C–106/91 *Ramrath*, not yet reported, paragraph 29.

26. Article 36 of the EEC Treaty.

27. Joined Cases 110/78 and 111/78 *Van Wesemael* [1979] ECR 35, paragraph 28.

28. Case 62/79 *Coditel* [1980] ECR 881.

29. Case 279/80 *Webb* [1981] ECR 3305, paragraph 19; Joined Cases 62 and 63/81 [1982] ECR 223, paragraph 14; Case C–113/89 cited above, paragraph 18.

30. Case 220/83 *Commission v. France* [1986] ECR 3663, paragraph 20.

30bis Judgment of 28 January 1992 in Case C–204/90 *Bachmann*.

31. Case 33/74, cited above, paragraph 12.

32. Case 33/74, cited above, paragraph 14.

33. Case C–180/89, cited above, paragraph 20; Case C–154/89, cited above, paragraph 17; Case C–198/89 *Commission v. Greece* [1991] ECR I–727, paragraph 21.

34. Case 352/85 *Bond van Adverteerders* [1989] ECR 2085, paragraph 34; Case C–288/89, cited above, paragraph 11.

considerations of an administrative nature, aimed, for example, at making it easier for the authorities of the State in which the service is provided to perform their task. Such considerations cannot justify derogation by a Member State from the rules of Community law. That principle applies with even greater force where the derogation in question amounts to preventing the exercise of one of the fundamental freedoms guaranteed by the Treaty[35];

(b) *'the public interest is not already protected by the rules of the State of establishment'*[36]

Admittedly, Member States have the right and indeed the duty to safeguard the public interest within their territory. This does not mean, however, that 'all national legislation applicable to nationals of that State and usually applied to the permanent activities of persons established therein may be similarly applied in their entirety to the temporary activities of persons who are established in other Member States'[37].

It should be emphasized that the conditions laid down by the Member State in which the service is provided 'may not duplicate equivalent statutory conditions which have already been satisfied in the State in which the undertaking is established' and that 'the supervisory authority of the State in which the service is provided must take into account supervision and verifications which have already been carried out in the Member State of establishment'[38].

Consequently, restrictions on the freedom to provide services 'come within the scope of Article 59 if the application of the national legislation to foreign persons providing services is not justified by overriding reasons relating to the public interest or if the requirements embodied in that legislation are already satisfied by the rules imposed on those persons in the Member State in which they are established'[39];

and

(c) *'the same result cannot be obtained by less restrictive rules'*[40]

The very broad scope of the definitions of overriding reasons or mandatory requirements is counter-balanced by the fact that a national restriction on the free movement of services must not merely be imposed for such a reason: it must furthermore be 'proportionate' and 'justified', i.e. indispensable[41], objectively necessary[42], an appropriate

---

35. Case 205/84, cited above, paragraph 54.

36. Case C-180/89, cited above, paragraph 18.

37. Case C-294/89, cited above, paragraph 26.

38. Case 205/84, cited above, paragraph 47.

39. Case C-154/89, cited above, *Commission v. France*, paragraph 15; Case C-180/89, cited above, paragraph 18; Case C-288/89, cited above, paragraph 13.

40. Case C-180/89, cited above, paragraph 18; Case C-154/89, cited above, paragraph 15; Case C-198/89, cited above, paragraph 19.

41. Case 252/83 *Commission v. Denmark* [1986] ECR 3713, paragraph 20; Case 205/84, cited above, paragraph 52.

42. Case 33/74, cited above, paragraph 14; Joined Cases 110 and 111/78, cited above,

means[43] of attaining the objective and non-excessive.

The Court had held that a restriction is excessive where the requirements of the State in which the service is provided go beyond what is necessary[44] for attaining the legitimate objectives. The restriction is excessive, for instance, if the same result can be obtained by less restrictive rules or rules that hinder trade less[45].

IV. CONCLUSIONS

Application of the principles established by the Court, which confirm the standpoints taken by the Commission[46], means that a Member State cannot normally prohibit the provision, in its territory, of a service lawfully provided in another Member State, even if the conditions in which it is provided are different in the country where the service provider is established.

In so far as the service in question suitably and satisfactorily fulfils the legitimate objective pursued by its own rules (public safety, public policy, etc.), a Member State cannot justify prohibiting the provision of a service in its territory by claiming that the way it fulfils the objective is different from that imposed on domestic service providers or service providers established in that Member State.

Any ban or restriction on the activities of a service provider established in another Member State must therefore be justified and not excessive.

---

paragraph 29; Case 205/84, cited above, paragraph 27; Case 252/83, cited above, paragraph 17; Case C-180/89, cited above, paragraph 17.

43. Joined Cases 62 and 63/81 *Seco v. Evi* [1982] ECR 223, paragraph 14.

44. Case 205/84, cited above, paragraph 33; Case C-76/90, cited above, paragraph 15; Case 96/85 (*Commission v. France*) [1986] ECR 1475, paragraph 11.

45. Case 33/74, cited above, paragraph 16; Case 252/83, cited above, paragraph 19; Case C-106/91, cited above, paragraph 31.

46. White Paper on completing the internal market, point 58.

15. COUNCIL DIRECTIVE 86/653/EEC

of 18 December 1986

on the coordination of the laws of the Member States relating to self-employed commercial agents

O.J. L 382/17 (Dec. 31, 1986)

THE COUNCIL OF THE EUROPEAN COMMUNITIES,

Having regard to the Treaty establishing the European Economic Community, and in particular Articles 57(2) and 100 thereof,

Having regard to the proposal from the Commission,[1]

Having regard to the opinion of the European Parliament,[2]

Having regard to the opinion of the Economic and Social Committee,[3]

Whereas the restrictions on the freedom of establishment and the freedom to provide services in respect of activities of intermediaries in commerce, industry and small craft industries were abolished by Directive 64/224/EEC;[4]

Whereas the differences in national laws concerning commercial representation substantially affect the conditions of competition and the carrying-on of that activity within the Community and are detrimental both to the protection available to commercial agents *vis-à-vis* their principals and to the security of commercial transactions; whereas moreover those differences are such as to inhibit substantially the conclusion and operation of commercial representation contracts where principal and commercial agent are established in different Member States;

Whereas trade in goods between Member States should be carried on under conditions which are similar to those of a single market, and this necessitates approximation of the legal systems of the Member States to the extent required for the proper functioning of the common market; whereas in this regard the rules concerning conflict of laws do not, in the matter of commercial representation, remove the inconsistencies referred to above, nor would they even if they were made uniform, and accordingly the proposed harmonization is necessary notwithstanding the existence of those rules;

Whereas in this regard the legal relationship between commercial agent and principal must be given priority;

Whereas it is appropriate to be guided by the principles of Article 117 of the Treaty and to maintain improvements already made, when harmonizing the laws of the Member States relating to commercial agents;

Whereas additional transitional periods should be allowed for certain Member States which have to make a particular effort to adapt their regulations, especially those concerning indemnity for termination of con-

---

1. OJ No. C 13, 18.1.1977, p. 2; OJ No. C 56, 2. 3. 1979, p. 5.
2. OJ No. C 239, 9.10.1978, p. 17.
3. OJ No. C 59, 8.3.1978, p. 31.
4. OJ No. 56, 4.4.1964, p. 869/64.

tract between the principal and the commercial agent, to the requirements of this Directive,

HAS ADOPTED THIS DIRECTIVE:

CHAPTER I
SCOPE
Article 1

1. The harmonization measures prescribed by this Directive shall apply to the laws, regulations and administrative provisions of the Member States governing the relations between commercial agents and their principals.

2. For the purposes of this Directive, 'commercial agent' shall mean a self-employed intermediary who has continuing authority to negotiate the sale or the purchase of goods on behalf of another person, hereinafter called the 'principal', or to negotiate and conclude such transactions on behalf of and in the name of that principal.

3. A commercial agent shall be understood within the meaning of this Directive as not including in particular:

—a person who, in his capacity as an officer, is empowered to enter into commitments binding on a company or association,

—a partner who is lawfully authorized to enter into commitments binding on his partners,

—a receiver, a receiver and manager, a liquidator or a trustee in bankruptcy.

Article 2

1. This Directive shall not apply to:

—commercial agents whose activities are unpaid,

—commercial agents when they operate on commodity exchanges or in the commodity market, or

—the body known as the Crown Agents for Overseas Governments and Administrations, as set up under the Crown Agents Act 1979 in the United Kingdom, or its subsidiaries.

2. Each of the Member States shall have the right to provide that the Directive shall not apply to those persons whose activities as commercial agents are considered secondary by the law of that Member State.

CHAPTER II
RIGHTS AND OBLIGATIONS
Article 3

1. In performing his activities, a commercial agent must look after his principal's interests and act dutifully and in good faith.

2. In particular, a commercial agent must:

(a) make proper efforts to negotiate and, where appropriate, conclude the transactions he is instructed to take care of;

(b) communicate to his principal all the necessary information available to him;

(c) comply with reasonable instructions given by his principal.

Article 4

1. In his relations with his commercial agent, a principal must act dutifully and in good faith.

2. A principal must in particular:

(a) provide his commercial agent with the necessary documentation relating to the goods concerned;

(b) obtain for his commercial agent the information necessary for the performance of the agency contract, and in particular notify the commercial agent within a reasonable period once he anticipates that the volume of commercial transactions will be significantly lower than that which the commercial agent could normally have expected.

3. A principal must, in addition, inform the commercial agent within a reasonable period of his acceptance, refusal, and of any non-execution of a commercial transaction which the commercial agent has procured for the principal.

Article 5

The parties may not derogate from the provisions of Articles 3 and 4.

CHAPTER III

REMUNERATION

Article 6

1. In the absence of any agreement on this matter between the parties, and without prejudice to the application of the compulsory provisions of the Member States concerning the level of remuneration, a commercial agent shall be entitled to the remuneration that commercial agents appointed for the goods forming the subject of his agency contract are customarily allowed in the place where he carries on his activities. If there is no such customary practice a commercial agent shall be entitled to reasonable remuneration taking into account all the aspects of the transaction.

2. Any part of the remuneration which varies with the number or value of business transactions shall be deemed to be commission within the meaning of this Directive.

3. Articles 7 to 12 shall not apply if the commercial agent is not remunerated wholly or in part by commission.

Article 7

1. A commercial agent shall be entitled to commission on commercial transactions concluded during the period covered by the agency contract:

(a) where the transaction has been concluded as a result of his action; or

(b) where the transaction is concluded with a third party whom he has previously acquired as a customer for transactions of the same kind.

2. A commercial agent shall also be entitled to commission on transactions concluded during the period covered by the agency contract:

—either where he is entrusted with a specific geographical area or group of customers,

—or where he has an exclusive right to a specific geographical area or group of customers,

and where the transaction has been entered into with a customer belonging to that area or group.

Member States shall include in their legislation one of the possibilities referred to in the above two indents.

Article 8

A commercial agent shall be entitled to commission on commercial transactions concluded after the agency contract has terminated:

(a) if the transaction is mainly attributable to the commercial agent's efforts during the period covered by the agency contract and if the transaction was entered into within a reasonable period after that contract terminated; or

(b) if, in accordance with the conditions mentioned in Article 7, the order of the third party reached the principal or the commercial agent before the agency contract terminated.

Article 9

A commercial agent shall not be entitled to the commission referred to in Article 7, if that commission is payable, pursuant to Article 8, to the previous commercial agent, unless it is equitable because of the circumstances for the commission to be shared between the commercial agents.

Article 10

1. The commission shall become due as soon as and to the extent that one of the following circumstances obtains:

(a) the principal has executed the transaction; or

(b) the principal should, according to his agreement with the third party, have executed the transaction; or

(c) the third party has executed the transaction.

2. The commission shall become due at the latest when the third party has executed his part of the transaction or should have done so if the principal had executed his part of the transaction, as he should have.

3. The commission shall be paid not later than on the last day of the month following the quarter in which it became due.

4. Agreements to derogate from paragraphs 2 and 3 to the detriment of the commercial agent shall not be permitted.

Article 11

1. The right to commission can be extinguished only if and to the extent that:

—it is established that the contract between the third party and the principal will not be executed, and

—that fact is due to a reason for which the principal is not to blame.

2. Any commission which the commercial agent has already received shall be refunded if the right to it is extinguished.

3. Agreements to derogate from paragraph 1 to the detriment of the commercial agent shall not be permitted.

Article 12

1. The principal shall supply his commercial agent with a statement of the commission due, not later than the last day of the month following the quarter in which the commission has become due. This statement shall set out the main components used in calculating the amount of commission.

2. A commercial agent shall be entitled to demand that he be provided with all the information, and in particular an extract from the books, which is available to his principal and which he needs in order to check the amount of the commission due to him.

3. Agreements to derogate from paragraphs 1 and 2 to the detriment of the commercial agent shall not be permitted.

4. This Directive shall not conflict with the internal provisions of Member States which recognize the right of a commercial agent to inspect a principal's books.

CHAPTER IV

CONCLUSION AND TERMINATION OF THE AGENCY CONTRACT

Article 13

1. Each party shall be entitled to receive from the other on request a signed written document setting out the terms of the agency contract including any terms subsequently agreed. Waiver of this right shall not be permitted.

2. Notwithstanding paragraph 1, a Member State may provide that an agency contract shall not be valid unless evidenced in writing.

Article 14

An agency contract for a fixed period which continues to be performed by both parties after that period has expired shall be deemed to be converted into an agency contract for an indefinite period.

Article 15

1. Where an agency contract is concluded for an indefinite period either party may terminate it by notice.

2. The period of notice shall be one month for the first year of the contract, two months for the second year commenced, and three months for the third year commenced and subsequent years. The parties may not agree on shorter periods of notice.

3. Member States may fix the period of notice at four months for the fourth year of the contract, five months for the fifth year and six months for the sixth and subsequent years. They may decide that the parties may not agree to shorter periods.

4. If the parties agree on longer periods than those laid down in paragraphs 2 and 3, the period of notice to be observed by the principal must not be shorter than that to be observed by the commercial agent.

5. Unless otherwise agreed by the parties, the end of the period of notice must coincide with the end of a calendar month.

6. The provisions of this Article shall apply to an agency contract for a fixed period where it is converted under Article 14 into an agency contract for an indefinite period, subject to the proviso that the earlier fixed period must be taken into account in the calculation of the period of notice.

Article 16

Nothing in this Directive shall affect the application of the law of the Member States where the latter provides for the immediate termination of the agency contract:

(a) because of the failure of one party to carry out all or part of his obligations;

(b) where exceptional circumstances arise.

Article 17

1. Member States shall take the measures necessary to ensure that the commercial agent is, after termination of the agency contract, indemnified in accordance with paragraph 2 or compensated for damage in accordance with paragraph 3.

2. (a) The commercial agent shall be entitled to an indemnity if and to the extent that:

— he has brought the principal new customers or has significantly increased the volume of business with existing customers and the principal continues to derive substantial benefits from the business with such customers, and

— the payment of this indemnity is equitable having regard to all the circumstances and, in particular, the commission lost by the commercial agent on the business transacted with such customers. Member States may provide for such circumstances also to include the application or otherwise of a restraint of trade clause, within the meaning of Article 20;

(b) The amount of the indemnity may not exceed a figure equivalent to an indemnity for one year calculated from the commercial agent's average annual remuneration over the preceding five years and if the contract goes back less than five years the indemnity shall be calculated on the average for the period in question;

(c) The grant of such an indemnity shall not prevent the commercial agent from seeking damages.

3. The commercial agent shall be entitled to compensation for the damage he suffers as a result of the termination of his relations with the principal.

Such damage shall be deemed to occur particularly when the termination takes place in circumstances:

— depriving the commercial agent of the commission which proper performance of the agency contract would have procured him whilst providing the principal with substantial benefits linked to the commercial agent's activities,

— and/or which have not enabled the commercial agent to amortize the costs and expenses that he had incurred for the performance of the agency contract on the principal's advice.

4. Entitlement to the indemnity as provided for in paragraph 2 or to compensation for damage as provided for under paragraph 3, shall also arise where the agency contract is terminated as a result of the commercial agent's death.

5. The commercial agent shall lose his entitlement to the indemnity in the instances provided for in paragraph 2 or to compensation for damage in the instances provided for in paragraph 3, if within one year following termination of the contract he has not notified the principal that he intends pursuing his entitlement.

6. The Commission shall submit to the Council, within eight years following the date of notification of this Directive, a report on the implementation of this Article, and shall if necessary submit to it proposals for amendments.

Article 18

The indemnity or compensation referred to in Article 17 shall not be payable:

(a) where the principal has terminated the agency contract because of default attributable to the commercial agent which would justify immediate termination of the agency contract under national law;

(b) where the commercial agent has terminated the agency contract, unless such termination is justified by circumstances attributable to the principal or on grounds of age, infirmity or illness of the commercial agent in consequence of which he cannot reasonably be required to continue his activities;

(c) where, with the agreement of the principal, the commercial agent assigns his rights and duties under the agency contract to another person.

Article 19

The parties may not derogate from Articles 17 and 18 to the detriment of the commercial agent before the agency contract expires.

Article 20

1. For the purposes of this Directive, an agreement restricting the business activities of a commercial agent following termination of the agency contract is hereinafter referred to as a restraint of trade clause.

2. A restraint of trade clause shall be valid only if and to the extent that:

(a) it is concluded in writing; and

(b) it relates to the geographical area or the group of customers and the geographical area entrusted to the commercial agent and to the kind of goods covered by his agency under the contract.

3. A restraint of trade clause shall be valid for not more than two years after termination of the agency contract.

4. This Article shall not affect provisions of national law which impose other restrictions on the validity or enforceability of restraint of trade clauses or which enable the courts to reduce the obligations on the parties resulting from such an agreement.

CHAPTER V

GENERAL AND FINAL PROVISIONS

Article 21

Nothing in this Directive shall require a Member State to provide for the disclosure of information where such disclosure would be contrary to public policy.

Article 22

1. Member States shall bring into force the provisions necessary to comply with this Directive before 1 January 1990. They shall forthwith inform the Commission thereof. Such provisions shall apply at least to

contracts concluded after their entry into force. They shall apply to contracts in operation by 1 January 1994 at the latest.

2. As from the notification of this Directive, Member States shall communicate to the Commission the main laws, regulations and administrative provisions which they adopt in the field governed by this Directive.

3. However, with regard to Ireland and the United Kingdom, 1 January 1990 referred to in paragraph 1 shall be replaced by 1 January 1994.

With regard to Italy, 1 January 1990 shall be replaced by 1 January 1993 in the case of the obligations deriving from Article 17.

Article 23

This Directive is addressed to the Member States.

16. COUNCIL DIRECTIVE 89/552/EEC

of 3 October 1989

on the coordination of certain provisions laid down by law, regulation or administrative action in Member States concerning the pursuit of television broadcasting activities

O.J. L 298/23 (Oct. 17, 1989)

THE COUNCIL OF THE EUROPEAN COMMUNITIES,

Having regard to the Treaty establishing the European Economic Community, and in particular Articles 57(2) and 66 thereof,

Having regard to the proposal from the Commission,[1]

In cooperation with the European Parliament,[2]

Having regard to the opinion of the Economic and Social Committee,[3]

Whereas the objectives of the Community as laid down in the Treaty include establishing an even closer union among the peoples of Europe, fostering closer relations between the States belonging to the Community, ensuring the economic and social progress of its countries by common action to eliminate the barriers which divide Europe, encouraging the constant improvement of the living conditions of its peoples as well as ensuring the preservation and strengthening of peace and liberty;

Whereas the Treaty provides for the establishment of a common market, including the abolition, as between Member States, of obstacles to freedom of movement for services and the institution of a system ensuring that competition in the common market is not distorted;

Whereas broadcasts transmitted across frontiers by means of various technologies are one of the ways of pursuing the objectives of the Community; whereas measures should be adopted to permit and ensure the transition from national markets to a common programme production and distribution market and to establish conditions of fair competition without prejudice to the public interest role to be discharged by the television broadcasting services;

* * *

Whereas television broadcasting constitutes, in normal circumstances, a service within the meaning of the Treaty;

Whereas the Treaty provides for free movement of all services normally provided against payment, without exclusion on grounds of their cultural or other content and without restriction of nationals of Member States established in a Community country other than that of the person for whom the services are intended;

1. OJ No. C 179, 17.7.1986, p. 4.
2. OJ No. C 49, 22.2.1988, p. 53, and OJ No. C 158, 26.6.1989.
3. OJ No. C 232, 31.8.1987, p. 29.

Whereas this right as applied to the broadcasting and distribution of television services is also a specific manifestation in Community law of a more general principle, namely the freedom of expression as enshrined in Article 10(1) of the Convention for the Protection of Human Rights and Fundamental Freedoms ratified by all Member States; whereas for this reason the issuing of directives on the broadcasting and distribution of television programmes must ensure their free movement in the light of the said Article and subject only to the limits set by paragraph 2 of that Article and by Article 56(1) of the Treaty;

Whereas the laws, regulations and administrative measures in Member States concerning the pursuit of activities as television broadcasters and cable operators contain disparities, some of which may impede the free movement of broadcasts within the Community and may distort competition within the common market;

Whereas all such restrictions on freedom to provide broadcasting services within the Community must be abolished under the Treaty;

Whereas such abolition must go hand in hand with coordination of the applicable laws; whereas this coordination must be aimed at facilitating the pursuit of the professional activities concerned and, more generally, the free movement of information and ideas within the Community;

Whereas it is consequently necessary and sufficient that all broadcasts comply with the law of Member State from which they emanate;

Whereas this Directive lays down the minimum rules needed to guarantee freedom of transmission in broadcasting; whereas, therefore, it does not affect the responsibility of the Member States and their authorities with regard to the organization—including the systems of licensing, administrative authorization or taxation—financing and the content of programmes; whereas the independence of cultural developments in the Member States and the preservation of cultural diversity in the Community therefore remain unaffected;

* * *

Whereas this Directive, being confined specifically to television broadcasting rules, is without prejudice to existing or future Community acts of harmonization, in particular to satisfy mandatory requirements concerning the protection of consumers and the fairness of commercial transactions and competition;

Whereas co-ordination is nevertheless needed to make it easier for persons and industries producing programmes having a cultural objective to take up and pursue their activities;

Whereas minimum requirements in respect of all public or private Community television programmes for European audio-visual productions have been a means of promoting production, independent production and distribution in the abovementioned industries and are complementary to other instruments which are already or will be proposed to favour the same objective;

Whereas it is therefore necessary to promote markets of sufficient size for television productions in the Member States to recover necessary investments not only by establishing common rules opening up national markets but also by envisaging for European productions where practicable and by appropriate means a majority proportion in television programmes of all Member States;

* * *

Whereas in order to ensure that the interests of consumers as television viewers are fully and properly protected, it is essential for television advertising to be subject to a certain number of minimum rules and standards and that the Member States must maintain the right to set more detailed or stricter rules and in certain circumstances to lay down different conditions for television broadcasters under their jurisdiction;

* * *

HAS ADOPTED THIS DIRECTIVE:

CHAPTER I
DEFINITIONS

Article 1

For the purpose of this Directive:

(a) 'television broadcasting' means the initial transmission by wire or over the air, including that by satellite, in unencoded or encoded form, of television programmes intended for reception by the public. It includes the communication of programmes between undertakings with a view to their being relayed to the public. It does not include communication services providing items of information or other messages on individual demand such as telecopying, electronic data banks and other similar services;

(b) 'television advertising' means any form of announcement broadcast in return for payment or for similar consideration by a public or private undertaking in connection with a trade, business, craft or profession in order to promote the supply of goods or services, including immovable property, or rights and obligations, in return for payment.

Except for the purposes of Article 18, this does not include direct offers to the public for the sale, purchase or rental of products or for the provision of services in return for payment;

(c) 'surreptitious advertising' means the representation in words or pictures of goods, services, the name, the trade mark or the activities of a producer of goods or a provider of services in programmes when such representation is intended by the broadcaster to serve advertising and might mislead the public as to its nature. Such representation is considered to be intentional in particular if it is done in return for payment or for similar consideration;

(d) 'sponsorship' means any contribution made by a public or private undertaking not engaged in television broadcasting activities or in the production of audio-visual works, to the financing of television programmes with a view to promoting its name, its trade mark, its image, its activities or its products.

CHAPTER II
GENERAL PROVISIONS

Article 2

1. Each Member State shall ensure that all television broadcasts transmitted

— by broadcasters under its jurisdiction, or

— by broadcasters who, while not being under the jurisdiction of any Member State, make use of a frequency or a satellite capacity granted by, or a satellite up-link situated in, that Member State,

comply with the law applicable to broadcasts intended for the public in that Member State.

2. Member States shall ensure freedom of reception and shall not restrict retransmission on their territory of television broadcasts from other Member States for reasons which fall within the fields coordinated by this Directive.

* * *

Article 3

1. Member States shall remain free to require television broadcasters under their jurisdiction to lay down more detailed or stricter rules in the areas covered by this Directive.

2. Member States shall, by appropriate means, ensure, within the framework of their legislation, that television broadcasters under their jurisdiction comply with the provisions of this Directive.

CHAPTER III
PROMOTION OF DISTRIBUTION AND PRODUCTION OF TELEVISION PROGRAMMES

Article 4

1. Member States shall ensure where practicable and by appropriate means, that broadcasters reserve for European works, within the meaning of Article 6, a majority proportion of their transmission time, excluding the time appointed to news, sports events, games, advertising and teletext services. This proportion, having regard to the broadcaster's informational, educational, cultural and entertainment responsibilities to its viewing public, should be achieved progressively, on the basis of suitable criteria.

2. Where the proportion laid down in paragraph 1 cannot be attained, it must not be lower than the average for 1988 in the Member State concerned.

However, in respect of the Hellenic Republic and the Portuguese Republic, the year 1988 shall be replaced by the year 1990.

3. From 3 October 1991, the Member States shall provide the Commission every two years with a report on the application of this Article and Article 5.

That report shall in particular include a statistical statement on the achievement of the proportion referred to in this Article and Article 5 for each of the television programmes falling within the jurisdiction of the Member State concerned, the reasons, in each case, for the failure to attain that proportion and the measures adopted or envisaged in order to achieve it.

The Commission shall inform the other Member States and the European Parliament of the reports, which shall be accompanied, where appropriate, by an opinion. * * *

4. The Council shall review the implementation of this Article on the basis of a report from the Commission accompanied by any proposals for revision that it may deem appropriate no later than the end of the fifth year from the adoption of the Directive.

* * *

Article 5

Member States shall ensure, where practicable and by appropriate means, that broadcasters reserve at least 10% of their transmission time, excluding the time appointed to news, sports events, games, advertising and teletext services, or alternately, at the discretion of the Member State, at least 10% of their programming budget, for European works created by producers who are independent of broadcasters. * * *

Article 6

1. Within the meaning of this chapter, 'European works' means the following:

   (a) works originating from Member States of the Community and, as regards television broadcasters falling within the jurisdiction of the Federal Republic of Germany, works from German territories where the Basic Law does not apply and fulfilling the conditions of paragraph 2;

   (b) works originating from European third States party to the European Convention on Transfrontier Television of the Council of Europe and fulfilling the conditions of paragraph 2;

   (c) works originating from other European third countries and fulfilling the conditions of paragraph 3.

2. The works referred to in paragraph 1(a) and (b) are works mainly made with authors and workers residing in one or more States referred to in paragraph 1(a) and (b) provided that they comply with one of the following three conditions:

   (a) they are made by one or more producers established in one or more of those States; or

(b) production of the works is supervised and actually controlled by one or more producers established in one or more of those States; or

(c) the contribution of co-producers of those States to the total co-production costs is preponderant and the co-production is not controlled by one or more producers established outside those States.

3. The works referred to in paragraph 1(c) are works made exclusively or in co-production with producers established in one or more Member State by producers established in one or more European third countries with which the Community will conclude agreements in accordance with the procedures of the Treaty, if those works are mainly made with authors and workers residing in one or more European States.

* * *

Article 7

Member States shall ensure that the television broadcasters under their jurisdiction do not broadcast any cinematographic work, unless otherwise agreed between its rights holders and the broadcaster, until two years have elapsed since the work was first shown in cinemas in one of the Member States of the Community; in the case of cinematographic works co-produced by the broadcaster, this period shall be one year.

Article 8

Where they consider it necessary for purposes of language policy, the Member States, whilst observing Community law, may as regards some or all programmes of television broadcasters under their jurisdiction, lay down more detailed or stricter rules in particular on the basis of language criteria.

Article 9

This chapter shall not apply to local television broadcasts not forming part of a national network.

CHAPTER IV

TELEVISION ADVERTISING AND SPONSORSHIP

Article 10

1. Television advertising shall be readily recognizable as such and kept quite separate from other parts of the programme service by optical and/or acoustic means.

2. Isolated advertising spots shall remain the exception.

3. Advertising shall not use subliminal techniques.

4. Surreptitious advertising shall be prohibited.

Article 11

1. Advertisements shall be inserted between programmes. Provided the conditions contained in paragraphs 2 to 5 of this Article are fulfilled,

advertisements may also be inserted during programmes in such a way that the integrity and value of the programme, taking into account natural breaks in and the duration and nature of the programme, and the rights of the rights holders are not prejudiced.

* * *

3. The transmission of audiovisual works such as feature films and films made for television (excluding series, serials, light entertainment programmes and documentaries), provided their programmed duration is more than 45 minutes, may be interrupted once for each complete period of 45 minutes. * * *

* * *

5. Advertisements shall not be inserted in any broadcast of a religious service. News and current affairs programmes, documentaries, religious programmes, and children's programmes, when their programmed duration is less than 30 minutes shall not be interrupted by advertisements. If their programmed duration is of 30 minutes or longer, the provisions of the previous paragraphs shall apply.

Article 12

Television advertising shall not:

(a) prejudice respect for human dignity;

(b) include any discrimination on grounds of race, sex or nationality;

(c) be offensive to religious or political beliefs;

(d) encourage behaviour prejudicial to health or to safety;

(e) encourage behaviour prejudicial to the protection of the environment.

Article 13

All forms of television advertising for cigarettes and other tobacco products shall be prohibited.

Article 14

Television advertising for medicinal products and medical treatment available only on prescription in the Member State within whose jurisdiction the broadcaster falls shall be prohibited.

Article 15

Television advertising for alcoholic beverages shall comply with the following criteria:

(a) it may not be aimed specifically at minors or, in particular, depict minors consuming these beverages;

(b) it shall not link the consumption of alcohol to enhanced physical performance or to driving;

(c) it shall not create the impression that the consumption of alcohol contributes towards social or sexual success;

(d) it shall not claim that alcohol has therapeutic qualities or that it is a stimulant, a sedative or a means of resolving personal conflicts;

(e) it shall not encourage immoderate consumption of alcohol or present abstinence or moderation in a negative light;

(f) it shall not place emphasis on high alcoholic content as being a positive quality of the beverages.

Article 16

Television advertising shall not cause moral or physical detriment to minors, and shall therefore comply with the following criteria for their protection:

(a) it shall not directly exhort minors to buy a product or a service by exploiting their inexperience or credulity;

(b) it shall not directly encourage minors to persuade their parents or others to purchase the goods or services being advertised;

(c) it shall not exploit the special trust minors place in parents, teachers or other persons;

(d) it shall not unreasonably show minors in dangerous situations.

Article 17

1. Sponsored television programmes shall meet the following requirements:

(a) the content and scheduling of sponsored programmes may in no circumstances be influenced by the sponsor in such a way as to affect the responsibility and editorial independence of the broadcaster in respect of programmes;

(b) they must be clearly identified as such by the name and/or logo of the sponsor at the beginning and/or the end of the programmes;

(c) they must not encourage the purchase or rental of the products or services of the sponsor or a third party, in particular by making special promotional references to those products or services.

2. Television programmes may not be sponsored by natural or legal persons whose principal activity is the manufacture or sale of products, or the provision of services, the advertising of which is prohibited by Article 13 or 14.

3. News and current affairs programmes may not be sponsored.

Article 18

1. The amount of advertising shall not exceed 15% of the daily transmission time. * * *

2. The amount of spot advertising within a given one-hour period shall not exceed 20%.

* * *

Article 19

Member States may lay down stricter rules than those in Article 18 for programming time and the procedures for television broadcasting for television broadcasters under their jurisdiction, so as to reconcile demand for televised advertising with the public interest, taking account in particular of:

(a) the role of television in providing information, education, culture and entertainment;

(b) the protection of pluralism of information and of the media.

* * *

CHAPTER V

PROTECTION OF MINORS

Article 22

Member States shall take appropriate measures to ensure that television broadcasts by broadcasters under their jurisdiction do not include programmes which might seriously impair the physical, mental or moral development of minors, in particular those that involve pornography or gratuitous violence. This provision shall extend to other programmes which are likely to impair the physical, mental or moral development of minors, except where it is ensured, by selecting the time of the broadcast or by any technical measure, that minors in the area of transmission will not normally hear or see such broadcasts.

Member States shall also ensure that broadcasts do not contain any incitement to hatred on grounds of race, sex, religion or nationality.

CHAPTER VI

RIGHT OF REPLY

Article 23

1. Without prejudice to other provisions adopted by the Member States under civil, administrative or criminal law, any natural or legal person, regardless of nationality, whose legitimate interests, in particular reputation and good name, have been damaged by an assertion of incorrect facts in a television programme must have a right of reply or equivalent remedies.

2. A right of reply or equivalent remedies shall exist in relation to all broadcasters under the jurisdiction of a Member State.

3. Member States shall adopt the measures needed to establish the right of reply or the equivalent remedies and shall determine the procedure to be followed for the exercise thereof. In particular, they shall ensure that

a sufficient time span is allowed and that the procedures are such that the right or equivalent remedies can be exercised appropriately by natural or legal persons resident or established in other Member States.

* * *

CHAPTER VII
FINAL PROVISIONS

* * *

Article 25

1. Member States shall bring into force the laws, regulations and administrative provisions necessary to comply with this Directive not later than 3 October 1991.

* * *

Article 26

Not later than the end of the fifth year after the date of adoption of this Directive and every two years thereafter, the Commission shall submit to the European Parliament, the Council, and the Economic and Social Committee a report on the application of this Directive and, if necessary, make further proposals to adapt it to developments in the field of television broadcasting.

Article 27

This Directive is addressed to the Member States.

[The initial text has been retained for pedagogical purposes. The directive was substantially amended by Directive 97/36 of the European Parliament and of the Council, O.J. L 202/60 (July 30, 1997). Its principal features are:

> 1) A more detailed coverage of jurisdiction in article 2, providing notably that a broadcaster comes under the jurisdiction of the State in which its head office is situated and its editorial decisions are taken, and setting out more refined rules for determining jurisdiction in case a broadcaster's editorial decisions are taken in a different State from that of the head office.

> 2) A new article 3a provides that Member States must ensure that "events ... of major importance for society" are not broadcast on an exclusive basis. Each State shall make a list of such events (presumably usually major sports attractions, such as Olympic or European-wide competitions).

> 3) Amendments to articles 10 and 11 require that teleshopping shall be readily recognizable and teleshopping spots shall be limited in duration and number during regular broadcasts.

4) An amendment to article 17 prohibits enterprises whose principal activity is the manufacture or sale of tobacco products from sponsoring television programs.

5) Article 22 was amended to clarify the manner in which minors are to be protected from programs that involve pornography, gratuitous violence, or other material harmful to their physical, mental or moral development. A new article 22b requires the Commission to study the need for technical devices enabling parents to filter out programs.]

17. FIRST COUNCIL DIRECTIVE 68/151/EEC

of 9 March 1968

on coordination of safeguards which, for the protection of the interests of members and others, are required by Member States of companies within the meaning of the second paragraph of Article 58 of the Treaty, with a view to making such safeguards equivalent throughout the Community

O.J. English Spec. Ed.1968-I, 41

THE COUNCIL OF THE EUROPEAN COMMUNITIES,

Having regard to the Treaty establishing the European Economic Community, and in particular Article 54(3)(g) thereof;

Having regard to the General Programme for the abolition of restrictions on freedom of establishment, and in particular Title VI thereof;

Having regard to the proposal from the Commission;

Having regard to the Opinion of the European Parliament;

Having regard to the Opinion of the Economic and Social Committee;

Whereas the co-ordination provided for in Article 54(3)(g) and in the General Programme for the abolition of restrictions on freedom of establishment is a matter of urgency, especially in regard to companies limited by shares or otherwise having limited liability, since the activities of such companies often extend beyond the frontiers of national territories;

* * *

HAS ADOPTED THIS DIRECTIVE:

Article 1

The co-ordination measures prescribed by this Directive shall apply to the laws, regulations and administrative provisions of the Member States relating to the following types of company:

— *In Germany:*

die Aktiengesellschaft, die Kommanditgesellschaft auf Aktien, die Gesellschaft mit beschränkter Haftung;

— *In Belgium:*

de naamloze vennootschap, la société anonyme,
de commanditaire vennootschap op aandelen, la société en commandite par actions,
de personen vennootschap met beperkte aansprakelijkheid; la société de personnes a responsabilité limitée;

— *In France:*

la société anonyme, la société en commandite par actions, la société a responsabilité limitée;

— *In Italy:*

società per azioni, società in accomandita per azioni, società a responsabilità limitata;

— *In Luxembourg:*

la société anonyme, la société en commandite par actions, la société a responsabilité limitée;

— *In the Netherlands:*

de naamloze vennootschap, de commanditaire vennootschap op aandelen.

[Amended by Treaties of Accession to add the stock corporation, limited liability company and limited partnership forms of Austria, Denmark, Finland, Greece, Ireland, Portugal, Spain, Sweden and the United Kingdom.]

SECTION 1

DISCLOSURE

Article 2

1. Member States shall take the measures required to ensure compulsory disclosure by companies of at least the following documents and particulars:

(a) The instrument of constitution, and the statutes if they are contained in a separate instrument;

(b) Any amendments to the instruments mentioned in (a), including any extension of the duration of the company;

(c) After every amendment of the instrument of constitution or of the statutes, the complete text of the instrument or statutes as amended to date;

(d) The appointment, termination of office and particulars of the persons who either as a body constituted pursuant to law or as members of any such body:

(i) are authorised to represent the company in dealings with third parties and in legal proceedings;

(ii) take part in the administration, supervision or control of the company.

It must appear from the disclosure whether the persons authorised to represent the company may do so alone or must act jointly;

(e) At least once a year, the amount of the capital subscribed, where the instrument of constitution or the statutes mention an authorised capital, unless any increase in the capital subscribed necessitates an amendment of the statutes;

(f) The balance sheet and the profit and loss account for each financial year. The document containing the balance sheet shall give particulars of the persons who are required by law to certify it.

[Modified by the Fourth Company Directive]

* * *

(g) Any transfer of the seat of the company;

(h) The winding up of the company;

(i) Any declaration of nullity of the company by the courts;

(j) The appointment of liquidators, particulars concerning them, and their respective powers, unless such powers are expressly and exclusively derived from law or from the statutes of the company;

(k) The termination of the liquidation and, in Member States where striking off the register entails legal consequences, the fact of any such striking off.

* * *

Article 3

1. In each Member State a file shall be opened in a central register, commercial register or companies register, for each of the companies registered therein.

2. All documents and particulars which must be disclosed in pursuance of Article 2 shall be kept in the file or entered in the register; the subject matter of the entries in the register must in every case appear in the file.

3. A copy of the whole or any part of the documents or particulars referred to in Article 2 must be obtainable by application in writing at a price not exceeding the administrative cost thereof.

Copies supplied shall be certified as 'true copies', unless the applicant dispenses with such certification.

4. Disclosure of the documents and particulars referred to in paragraph 2 shall be effected by publication in the national gazette appointed for that purpose by the Member State, either of the full or partial text, or by means of a reference to the document which has been deposited in the file or entered in the register.

* * *

Article 4

Member States shall prescribe that letters and order forms shall state the following particulars:

— the register in which the file mentioned in Article 3 is kept, together with the number of the company in that register;

— the legal form of the company, the location of its seat and, where appropriate, the fact that the company is being wound up.

Where in these documents mention is made of the capital of the company, the reference shall be to the capital subscribed and paid up.

Article 5

Each Member State shall determine by which persons the disclosure formalities are to be carried out.

Article 6

Member States shall provide for appropriate penalties in case of:

— failure to disclose the balance sheet and profit and loss account as required by Article 2(1)(f);

— omission from commercial documents of the compulsory particulars provided for in Article 4.

SECTION II

VALIDITY OF OBLIGATIONS ENTERED INTO BY A COMPANY

Article 7

If, before a company being formed has acquired legal personality, action has been carried out in its name and the company does not assume the obligations arising from such action, the persons who acted shall, without limit, be jointly and severally liable therefor, unless otherwise agreed.

* * *

Article 9

1. Acts done by the organs of the company shall be binding upon it even if those acts are not within the objects of the company, unless such acts exceed the powers that the law confers or allows to be conferred on those organs.

However, Member States may provide that the company shall not be bound where such acts are outside the objects of the company, if it proves that the third party knew that the act was outside those objects or could not in view of the circumstances have been unaware of it; disclosure of the statutes shall not of itself be sufficient proof thereof.

2. The limits on the powers of the organs of the company, arising under the statutes or from a decision of the competent organs, may never be relied on as against third parties, even if they have been disclosed.

* * *

SECTION III

NULLITY OF THE COMPANY

Article 10

In all Member States whose laws do not provide for preventive control, administrative or judicial, at the time of formation of a company, the instrument of constitution, the company statutes and any amendments to those documents shall be drawn up and certified in due legal form.

Article 11

The laws of the Member States may not provide for the nullity of companies otherwise than in accordance with the following provisions:

1. Nullity must be ordered by decision of a court of law;

2. Nullity may be ordered only on the following grounds:

   (a) that no instrument of constitution was executed or that the rules of preventive control or the requisite legal formalities were not complied with;

   (b) that the objects of the company are unlawful or contrary to public policy;

   (c) that the instrument of constitution or the statutes do not state the name of the company, the amount of the individual subscriptions of capital, the total amount of the capital subscribed or the objects of the company;

   (d) failure to comply with the provisions of the national law concerning the minimum amount of capital to be paid up;

   (e) the incapacity of all the founder members;

* * *

Article 12

* * *

2. Nullity shall entail the winding up of the company, as may dissolution.

* * *

SECTION IV

GENERAL PROVISIONS

* * *

Article 14

This Directive is addressed to the Member States.

18. SECOND COUNCIL DIRECTIVE 77/91/EEC

of 13 December 1976

on coordination of safeguards which, for the protection of the interests of members and others, are required by Member States of companies within the meaning of the second paragraph of Article 58 of the Treaty, in respect of the formation of public limited liability companies and the maintenance and alteration of their capital, with a view to making such safeguards equivalent

O.J. L. 26/1 (Jan. 31, 1977), as amended by Council Directive 92/101/EEC, O.J. L 347/64 (Nov. 28, 1992)

THE COUNCIL OF THE EUROPEAN COMMUNITIES,

Having regard to the Treaty establishing the European Economic Community, and in particular Article 54(3)(g) thereof,

Having regard to the proposal from the Commission,

Having regard to the opinion of the European Parliament,

Having regard to the opinion of the Economic and Social Committee,

Whereas the coordination provided for in Article 54(3)(g) and in the General Programme for the abolition of restrictions on freedom of establishment, which was begun by Directive 68/151/EEC, is especially important in relation to public limited liability companies, because their activities predominate in the economy of the Member States and frequently extend beyond their national boundaries;

Whereas in order to ensure minimum equivalent protection for both shareholders and creditors of public limited liability companies, the coordination of national provisions relating to their formation and to the maintenance, increase or reduction of their capital is particularly important;

* * *

Whereas Community provisions should be adopted for maintaining the capital, which constitutes the creditors' security, in particular by prohibiting any reduction thereof by distribution to shareholders where the latter are not entitled to it and by imposing limits on the company's right to acquire its own shares;

Whereas it is necessary, having regard to the objectives of Article 54(3)(g), that the Member States' laws relating to the increase or reduction of capital ensure that the principles of equal treatment of shareholders in the same position and of protection of creditors whose claims exist prior to the decision on reduction are observed and harmonized,

HAS ADOPTED THIS DIRECTIVE:

Article 1

1. The coordination measures prescribed by this Directive shall apply to the provisions laid down by law, regulation or administrative action in Member States relating to the following types of company:

— *in Belgium:*
la société anonyme / de naamloze vennootschap;
— *in Denmark:*
aktieselskabet;
— *in France:*
la société anonyme;
— *in Germany:*
die Aktiengesellschaft;
— *in Ireland:*
the public company limited by shares,
the public company limited by guarantee and having a share capital;
— *in Italy:*
la società per azioni;
— *in Luxembourg:*
la société anonyme;
— *in the Netherlands:*
de naamloze vennootschap;
— *in the United Kingdom:*
the public company limited by shares,
the public company limited by guarantee and having a share capital.

The name for any company of the above types shall comprise or be accompanied by a description which is distinct from the description required of other types of companies.

[Amended by Treaties of Accession to add the stock corporation forms in Austria, Finland, Greece, Portugal, Spain and Sweden.]

* * *

Article 2

The statutes or the instrument of incorporation of the company shall always give at least the following information:

(a) the type and name of the company;
(b) the objects of the company;
(c) — when the company has no authorized capital, the amount of the subscribed capital,
— when the company has an authorized capital, the amount thereof and also the amount of the capital subscribed at the time the company is incorporated or is authorized to commence business, and at the time of any change in the authorized capital, without prejudice to Article 2(1)(e) of Directive 68/151/EEC;
(d) in so far as they are not legally determined, the rules governing the number of and the procedure for appointing members of the bodies responsible for representing the company with regard to third parties, administration, management, supervision or control of the company and the allocation of powers among those bodies;
(e) the duration of the company, except where this is indefinite.

Article 3

The following information at least must appear in either the statutes or the instrument of incorporation or a separate document published in accordance with the procedure laid down in the laws of each Member State in accordance with Article 3 of Directive 68/151/EEC:

(a) the registered office;

(b) the nominal value of the shares subscribed and, at least once a year, the number thereof;

(c) the number of shares subscribed without stating the nominal value, where such shares may be issued under national law;

(d) the special conditions if any limiting the transfer of shares;

(e) where there are several classes of shares, the information under (b), (c) and (d) for each class and the rights attaching to the shares of each class;

(f) whether the shares are registered or bearer, where national law provides for both types, and any provisions relating to the conversion of such shares unless the procedure is laid down by law;

(g) the amount of the subscribed capital paid up at the time the company is incorporated or is authorized to commence business;

(h) the nominal value of the shares or, where there is not nominal value, the number of shares issued for a consideration other than in cash, together with the nature of the consideration and the name of the person providing this consideration;

(i) the identity of the natural or legal persons or companies or firms by whom or in whose name the statutes or the instrument of incorporation, or where the company was not formed at the same time, the drafts of these documents, have been signed;

(j) the total amount, or at least an estimate, of all the costs payable by the company or chargeable to it by reason of its formation and, where appropriate, before the company is authorized to commence business;

(k) any special advantage granted, at the time the company is formed or up to the time it receives authorization to commence business, to anyone who has taken part in the formation of the company or in transactions leading to the grant of such authorization.

* * *

Article 6

1. The laws of the Member States shall require that, in order that a company may be incorporated or obtain authorization to commence business, a minimum capital shall be subscribed the amount of which shall be not less than 25,000 [Euros].

* * *

Article 7

The subscribed capital may be formed only of assets capable of economic assessment. However, an undertaking to perform work or supply services may not form part of these assets.

Article 8

1. Shares may not be issued at a price lower than their nominal value, or, where there is no nominal value, their accountable par.

* * *

Article 9

1. Shares issued for a consideration must be paid up at the time the company is incorporated or is authorized to commence business at not less than 25% of their nominal value or, in the absence of a nominal value, their accountable par.

2. However, where shares are issued for a consideration other than in cash at the time the company is incorporated or is authorized to commence business, the consideration must be transferred in full within five years of that time.

Article 10

1. A report on any consideration other than in cash shall be drawn up before the company is incorporated or is authorized to commence business, by one or more independent experts appointed or approved by an administrative or judicial authority. Such experts may be natural persons as well as legal persons and companies or firms under the laws of each Member State.

2. The experts' report shall contain at least a description of each of the assets comprising the consideration as well as of the methods of valuation used and shall state whether the values arrived at by the application of these methods correspond at least to the number and nominal value or, where there is no nominal value, to the accountable par and, where appropriate, to the premium on the shares to be issued for them.

3. The expert's report shall be published in the manner laid down by the laws of each Member State, in accordance with Article 3 of Directive 68/151/EEC.

* * *

Article 15

1. (a) Except for cases of reductions of subscribed capital, no distribution to shareholders may be made when on the closing date of the last financial year the net assets as set out in the company's annual accounts are, or following such a distribution would become, lower than the amount of the subscribed capital plus those reserves which may not be distributed under the law or the statutes.

* * *

(c) The amount of a distribution to shareholders may not exceed the amount of the profits at the end of the last financial year plus any profits brought forward and sums drawn from reserves available for this purpose, less any losses brought forward and sums placed to reserve in accordance with the law or the statutes.

(d) The expression 'distribution' used in subparagraphs (a) and (c) includes in particular the payment of dividends and of interest relating to shares.

* * *

Article 17

1. In the case of a serious loss of the subscribed capital, a general meeting of shareholders must be called within the period laid down by the laws of the Member States, to consider whether the company should be wound up or any other measures taken.

2. The amount of a loss deemed to be serious within the meaning of paragraph 1 may not be set by the laws of Member States at a figure higher than half the subscribed capital.

Article 18

1. The shares of a company may not be subscribed for by the company itself.

* * *

Article 19

1. Where the laws of a Member State permit a company to acquire its own shares, either itself or through a person acting in his own name but on the company's behalf, they shall make such acquisitions subject to at least the following conditions:

(a) authorization shall be given by the general meeting, which shall determine the terms and conditions of such acquisitions, and in particular the maximum number of shares to be acquired, the duration of the period for which the authorization is given and which may not exceed 18 months, and, in the case of acquisition for value, the maximum and minimum consideration. Members of the administrative or management body shall be required to satisfy themselves that at the time when each authorized acquisition is effected the conditions referred to in subparagraphs (b), (c) and (d) are respected;

(b) the nominal value or, in the absence thereof, the accountable par of the acquired shares, including shares previously acquired by the company and held by it, and shares acquired by a person acting in his own name but on the company's behalf, may not exceed 10% of the subscribed capital;

(c) the acquisitions may not have the effect of reducing the net assets below the amount mentioned in Article 15(1)(a);

(d) only fully paid-up shares may be included in the transaction.

2. The laws of a Member State may provide for derogations from the first sentence of paragraph 1(a) where the acquisition of a company's own shares is necessary to prevent serious and imminent harm to the company.

* * *

3. Member States may decide not to apply the first sentence of paragraph 1(a) to shares acquired by either the company itself or by a person acting in his own name but on the company's behalf, for distribution to that company's employees or to the employees of an associate company. Such shares must be distributed within 12 months of their acquisition.

* * *

Article 21

Shares acquired in contravention of Articles 19 and 20 shall be disposed of within one year of their acquisition. Should they not be disposed of within that period, Article 20(3) shall apply.

Article 22

1. Where the laws of a Member State permit a company to acquire its own shares, either itself or through a person acting in his own name but on the company's behalf, they shall make the holding of these shares at all times subject to at least the following conditions:

(a) among the rights attaching to the shares, the right to vote attaching to the company's own shares shall in any event be suspended;

(b) if the shares are included among the assets shown in the balance sheet, a reserve of the same amount, unavailable for distribution, shall be included among the liabilities.

* * *

Article 23

1. A company may not advance funds, nor make loans, nor provide security, with a view to the acquisition of its shares by a third party.

2. Paragraph 1 shall not apply to transactions concluded by banks and other financial institutions in the normal course of business, nor to transactions effected with a view to the acquisition of shares by or for the company's employees or the employees of an associate company. However, these transactions may not have the effect of reducing the net assets below the amount specified in Article 15(1)(a).

* * *

Article 24a

1. (a) The subscription, acquisition or holding of shares in a public limited-liability company by another company within the meaning of Article 1 of Directive 68/151/EEC in which the public limited-liability company directly or indirectly holds a majority of the voting rights or on which it can directly or indirectly exercise a dominant influence shall be regarded as having been effected by the public limited-liability company itself;

(b) subparagraph (a) shall also apply where the other company is governed by the law of a third country and has a legal form comparable to those listed in Article I of Directive 68/151/EEC.

2. However, where the public limited-liability company holds a majority of the voting rights indirectly or can exercise a dominant influence indirectly Member States need not apply paragraph 1 if they provide for the suspension of the voting rights attached to the shares in the public limited-liability company held by the other company.

3. In the absence of coordination of national legislation on groups of companies, Member States may:

(a) define the cases in which a public limited-liability company shall be regarded as being able to exercise a dominant influence on another company; if a Member State exercises this option, its national law must in any event provide that a dominant influence can be exercised if a public limited-liability company:

—has the right to appoint or dismiss a majority of the members of the administrative organ, of the management organ or of the supervisory organ, and is at the same time a shareholder or member of the other company or

—is a shareholder or member of the other company and has sole control of a majority of the voting rights of its shareholders or members under an agreement concluded with other shareholders or members of that company.

Member States shall not be obliged to make provision for any cases other than those referred to in the first and second indents;

(b) define the cases in which a public limited-liability company shall be regarded as indirectly holding voting rights or as able indirectly to exercise a dominant influence;

(c) specify the circumstances in which a public limited-liability company shall be regarded as holding voting rights.

* * *

[Article 24a was introduced by Council Directive 92/101/EEC, O.J. L 347/64 (Nov. 28, 1992). The amendment's indication of certain exceptions and transitional provisions has been omitted.]

Article 25

1. Any increase in capital must be decided upon by the general meeting. Both this decision and the increase in the subscribed capital shall be published in the manner laid down by the laws of each Member State, in accordance with Article 3 of Directive 68/151/EEC.

2. Nevertheless, the statutes or instrument of incorporation or the general meeting, the decision of which must be published in accordance with the rules referred to in paragraph 1, may authorize an increase in the subscribed capital up to a maximum amount which they shall fix with due

regard for any maximum amount provided for by law. Where appropriate, the increase in the subscribed capital shall be decided on within the limits of the amount fixed, by the company body empowered to do so. The power of such body in this respect shall be for a maximum period of five years and may be renewed one or more times by the general meeting, each time for a period not exceeding five years.

3. Where there are several classes of shares, the decision by the general meeting concerning the increase in capital referred to in paragraph 1 or the authorization to increase the capital referred to in paragraph 2, shall be subject to a separate vote at least for each class of shareholder whose rights are affected by the transaction.

4. This Article shall apply to the issue of all securities which are convertible into shares or which carry the right to subscribe for shares, but not to the conversion of such securities, nor to the exercise of the right to subscribe.

Article 26

Shares issued for a consideration, in the course of an increase in subscribed capital, must be paid up to at least 25% of their nominal value or, in the absence of a nominal value, of their accountable par. Where provision is made for an issue premium, it must be paid in full.

Article 27

1. Where shares are issued for a consideration other than in cash in the course of an increase in the subscribed capital the consideration must be transferred in full within a period of five years from the decision to increase the subscribed capital.

2. The consideration referred to in paragraph 1 shall be the subject of a report drawn up before the increase in capital is made by one or more experts who are independent of the company and appointed or approved by an administrative or judicial authority. Such experts may be natural persons as well as legal persons and companies and firms under the laws of each Member State.

Article 10(2) and (3) shall apply.

* * *

Article 28

Where an increase in capital is not fully subscribed, the capital will be increased by the amount of the subscriptions received only if the conditions of the issue so provide.

Article 29

1. Whenever the capital is increased by consideration in cash, the shares must be offered on a pre-emptive basis to shareholders in proportion to the capital represented by their shares.

2. The laws of a Member State:

(a) need not apply paragraph 1 above to shares which carry a limited right to participate in distributions within the meaning of Article 15 and/or in the company's assets in the event of liquidation; or

(b) may permit, where the subscribed capital of a company having several classes of shares carrying different rights with regard to voting, or participation in distributions within the meaning of Article 15 or in assets in the event of liquidation, is increased by issuing new shares in only one of these classes, the right of pre-emption of shareholders of the other classes to be exercised only after the exercise of this right by the shareholders of the class in which the new shares are being issued.

* * *

4. The right of pre-emption may not be restricted or withdrawn by the statutes or instrument of incorporation. This may, however, be done by decision of the general meeting. The administrative or management body shall be required to present to such a meeting a written report indicating the reasons for restriction or withdrawal of the right of pre-emption, and justifying the proposed issue price. * * *

* * *

Article 30

Any reduction in the subscribed capital, except under a court order, must be subject at least to a decision of the general meeting acting in accordance with the rules for a quorum and a majority laid down in Article 40 without prejudice to Articles 36 and 37. * * *

Article 31

Where there are several classes of shares, the decision by the general meeting concerning a reduction in the subscribed capital shall be subject to a separate vote, at least for each class of shareholders whose rights are affected by the transaction.

* * *

Article 39

Where the laws of a Member State authorize companies to issue redeemable shares, they shall require that the following conditions, at least, are complied with for the redemption of such shares:

(a) redemption must be authorized by the company's statutes or instrument of incorporation before the redeemable shares are subscribed for;

(b) the shares must be fully paid up;

(c) the terms and the manner of redemption must be laid down in the company's statutes or instrument of incorporation;

(d) redemption can be only effected by using sums available for distribution in accordance with Article 15(1) or the proceeds of a new issue made with a view to effecting such redemption;

* * *

Article 40

1. The laws of the Member States shall provide that the decisions referred to in Articles 29(4) and (5), 30, 31, 35 and 38 must be taken at least by a majority of not less than two-thirds of the votes attaching to the securities or the subscribed capital represented.

2. The laws of the Member States may, however, lay down that a simple majority of the votes specified in paragraph 1 is sufficient when at least half the subscribed capital is represented.

Article 41

1. Member States may derogate from Article 9(1), Article 19(1)(a), first sentence, and (b) and from Articles 25, 26 and 29 to the extent that such derogations are necessary for the adoption or application of provisions designed to encourage the participation of employees, or other groups of persons defined by national law, in the capital of undertakings.

* * *

Article 42

For the purposes of the implementation of this Directive, the laws of the Member States shall ensure equal treatment to all shareholders who are in the same position.

* * *

Article 44

This Directive is addressed to the Member States.

19. THIRD COUNCIL DIRECTIVE 78/855/EEC

of 9 October 1978

based on Article 54(3)(g) of the Treaty concerning mergers of public limited liability companies

O.J.L. 295/36 (Oct. 20, 1978)

THE COUNCIL OF THE EUROPEAN COMMUNITIES,

Having regard to the Treaty establishing the European Economic Community, and in particular Article 54(3)(g) thereof,

Having regard to the proposal from the Commission,

Having regard to the opinion of the European Parliament,

Having regard to the opinion of the Economic and Social Committee,

* * *

Whereas the protection of the interests of members and third parties requires that the laws of the Member States relating to mergers of public limited liability companies be coordinated and that provision for mergers should be made in the laws of all the Member States;

Whereas in the context of such coordination it is particularly important that the shareholders of merging companies be kept adequately informed in as objective a manner as possible and that their rights be suitably protected;

Whereas the protection of employees' rights in the event of transfers of undertakings, businesses or parts of businesses is at present regulated by Directive 77/187/EEC[8];

Whereas creditors, including debenture holders, and persons having other claims on the merging companies must be protected so that the merger does not adversely affect their interests;

Whereas the disclosure requirements of Directive 68/151/EEC must be extended to include mergers so that third parties are kept adequately informed;

* * *

HAS ADOPTED THIS DIRECTIVE:

Article 1

Scope

1. The coordination measures laid down by this Directive shall apply to the laws, regulations and administrative provisions of the Member States relating to the following types of company:

— Germany:
die Aktiengesellschaft,

---

8. OJ No. L 61, 5. 3. 1977, p. 26.

— Belgium:
la société anonyme/de naamloze vennootschap,
— Denmark:
aktieselskaber,
— France:
la société anonyme,
— Ireland:
public companies limited by shares, and public companies limited by guarantee having a share capital,
— Italy:
la società per azioni,
— Luxembourg:
la société anonyme,
— the Netherlands:
de naamloze vennootschap,
— the United Kingdom:
public companies limited by shares, and public companies limited by guarantee having a share capital.

[Amended by Treaties of Accession to add the stock corporations of Austria, Finland, Greece Portugal, Spain and Sweden.]

* * *

CHAPTER I

REGULATION OF MERGER BY THE ACQUISITION OF ONE OR MORE COMPANIES BY ANOTHER AND OF MERGER BY THE FORMATION OF A NEW COMPANY

Article 2

The Member States shall, as regards companies governed by their national laws, make provision for rules governing merger by the acquisition of one or more companies by another and merger by the formation of a new company.

Article 3

1. For the purposes of this Directive, 'merger by acquisition' shall mean the operation whereby one or more companies are wound up without going into liquidation and transfer to another all their assets and liabilities in exchange for the issue to the shareholders of the company or companies being acquired of shares in the acquiring company and a cash payment, if any, not exceeding 10% of the nominal value of the shares so issued or, where they have no nominal value, of their accounting par value.

2. A Member State's laws may provide that merger by acquisition may also be effected where one or more of the companies being acquired is in liquidation, provided that this option is restricted to companies which have not yet begun to distribute their assets to their shareholders.

Article 4

1. For the purposes of this Directive, 'merger by the formation of a new company' shall mean the operation whereby several companies are

wound up without going into liquidation and transfer to a company that they set up all their assets and liabilities in exchange for the issue to their shareholders of shares in the new company and a cash payment, if any, not exceeding 10% of the nominal value of the shares so issued or, where they have no nominal value, of their accounting par value.

2. A Member State's laws may provide that merger by the formation of a new company may also be effected where one or more of the companies which are ceasing to exist is in liquidation, provided that this option is restricted to companies which have not yet begun to distribute their assets to their shareholders.

CHAPTER II
MERGER BY ACQUISITION

Article 5

1. The administrative or management bodies of the merging companies shall draw up draft terms of merger in writing.

2. Draft terms of merger shall specify at least:

(a) the type, name and registered office of each of the merging companies;

(b) the share exchange ratio and the amount of any cash payment;

(c) the terms relating to the allotment of shares in the acquiring company;

(d) the date from which the holding of such shares entitles the holders to participate in profits and any special conditions affecting that entitlement;

(e) the date from which the transactions of the company being acquired shall be treated for accounting purposes as being those of the acquiring company;

(f) the rights conferred by the acquiring company on the holders of shares to which special rights are attached and the holders of securities other than shares, or the measures proposed concerning them;

(g) any special advantage granted to the experts referred to in Article 10(1) and members of the merging companies' administrative, management, supervisory or controlling bodies.

Article 6

Draft terms of merger must be published in the manner prescribed by the laws of each Member State in accordance with Article 3 of Directive 68/151/EEC, for each of the merging companies, at least one month before the date fixed for the general meeting which is to decide thereon.

Article 7

1. A merger shall require at least the approval of the general meeting of each of the merging companies. The laws of the Member States shall

provide that this decision shall require a majority of not less than two thirds of the votes attaching either to the shares or to the subscribed capital represented.

The laws of a Member State may, however, provide that a simple majority of the votes specified in the first subparagraph shall be sufficient when at least half of the subscribed capital is represented. Moreover, where appropriate, the rules governing alterations to the memorandum and articles of association shall apply.

2. Where there is more than one class of shares, the decision concerning a merger shall be subject to a separate vote by at least each class of shareholders whose rights are affected by the transaction.

3. The decision shall cover both the approval of the draft terms of merger and any alterations to the memorandum and articles of association necessitated by the merger.

Article 8

The laws of a Member State need not require approval of the merger by the general meeting of the acquiring company if the following conditions are fulfilled:

(a) the publication provided for in Article 6 must be effected, for the acquiring company, at least one month before the date fixed for the general meeting of the company or companies being acquired which are to decide on the draft terms of merger;

(b) at least one month before the date specified in (a), all shareholders of the acquiring company must be entitled to inspect the documents specified in Article 11(1) at the registered office of the acquiring company;

(c) one or more shareholders of the acquiring company holding a minimum percentage of the subscribed capital must be entitled to require that a general meeting of the acquiring company be called to decide whether to approve the merger. This minimum percentage may not be fixed at more than 5%. The Member States may, however, provide for the exclusion of non-voting shares from this calculation.

Article 9

The administration or management bodies of each of the merging companies shall draw up a detailed written report explaining the draft terms of merger and setting out the legal and economic grounds for them, in particular the share exchange ratio.

The report shall also describe any special valuation difficulties which have arisen.

Article 10

1. One or more experts, acting on behalf of each of the merging companies but independent of them, appointed or approved by a judicial or administrative authority, shall examine the draft terms of merger and draw

up a written report to the shareholders. However, the laws of a Member State may provide for the appointment of one or more independent experts for all the merging companies, if such appointment is made by a judicial or administrative authority at the joint request of those companies. Such experts may, depending on the laws of each Member State, be natural or legal persons or companies or firms.

2. In the report mentioned in paragraph 1 the experts must in any case state whether in their opinion the share exchange ratio is fair and reasonable. Their statement must at least:

(a) indicate the method or methods used to arrive at the share exchange ratio proposed;

(b) state whether such method or methods are adequate in the case in question, indicate the values arrived at using each such method and give an opinion on the relative importance attributed to such methods in arriving at the value decided on.

The report shall also describe any special valuation difficulties which have arisen.

3. Each expert shall be entitled to obtain from the merging companies all relevant information and documents and to carry out all necessary investigations.

Article 11

1. All shareholders shall be entitled to inspect at least the following documents at the registered office at least one month before the date fixed for the general meeting which is to decide on the draft terms of merger:

(a) the draft terms of merger;

(b) the annual accounts and annual reports of the merging companies for the preceding three financial years;

(c) an accounting statement drawn up as at a date which must not be earlier than the first day of the third month preceding the date of the draft terms of merger, if the latest annual accounts relate to a financial year which ended more than six months before that date;

(d) the reports of the administrative or management bodies of the merging companies provided for in Article 9;

(e) the reports provided for in Article 10.

2. The accounting statement provided for in paragraph 1(c) shall be drawn up using the same methods and the same layout as the last annual balance sheet.

However, the laws of a Member State may provide that:

(a) it shall not be necessary to take a fresh physical inventory;

(b) the valuations shown in the last balance sheet shall be altered only to reflect entries in the books of account; the following shall nevertheless be taken into account:

—interim depreciation and provisions,

—material changes in actual value not shown in the books.

3. Every shareholder shall be entitled to obtain, on request and free of charge, full or, if so desired, partial copies of the documents referred to in paragraph 1.

Article 12

Protection of the rights of the employees of each of the merging companies shall be regulated in accordance with Directive 77/187/EEC.

Article 13

1. The laws of the Member States must provide for an adequate system of protection of the interests of creditors of the merging companies whose claims antedate the publication of the draft terms of merger and have not fallen due at the time of such publication.

2. To this end, the laws of the Member States shall at least provide that such creditors shall be entitled to obtain adequate safeguards where the financial situation of the merging companies makes such protection necessary and where those creditors do not already have such safeguards.

3. Such protection may be different for the creditors of the acquiring company and for those of the company being acquired.

Article 14

Without prejudice to the rules governing the collective exercise of their rights, Article 13 shall apply to the debenture holders of the merging companies, except where the merger has been approved by a meeting of the debenture holders, if such a meeting is provided for under national laws, or by the debenture holders individually.

Article 15

Holders of securities, other than shares, to which special rights are attached, must be given rights in the acquiring company at least equivalent to those they possessed in the company being acquired, unless the alteration of those rights has been approved by a meeting of the holders of such securities, if such a meeting is provided for under national laws, or by the holders of those securities individually, or unless the holders are entitled to have their securities repurchased by the acquiring company.

Article 16

1. Where the laws of a Member State do not provide for judicial or administrative preventive supervision of the legality of mergers, or where such supervision does not extend to all the legal acts required for a merger, the minutes of the general meetings which decide on the merger and, where appropriate, the merger contract subsequent to such general meetings shall be drawn up and certified in due legal form. In cases where the merger need not be approved by the general meetings of all the merging

companies, the draft terms of merger must be drawn up and certified in due legal form.

2. The notary or the authority competent to draw up and certify the document in due legal form must check and certify the existence and validity of the legal acts and formalities required of the company for which he or it is acting and of the draft terms of merger.

Article 17

The laws of the Member States shall determine the date on which a merger takes effect.

Article 18

1. A merger must be publicized in the manner prescribed by the laws of each Member State, in accordance with Article 3 of Directive 68/151/EEC, in respect of each of the merging companies.

2. The acquiring company may itself carry out the publication formalities relating to the company or companies being acquired.

Article 19

1. A merger shall have the following consequences *ipso jure* and simultaneously:

(a) the transfer, both as between the company being acquired and the acquiring company and as regards third parties, to the acquiring company of all the assets and liabilities of the company being acquired;

(b) the shareholders of the company being acquired become shareholders of the acquiring company;

(c) the company being acquired ceases to exist.

2. No shares in the acquiring company shall be exchanged for shares in the company being acquired held either:

(a) by the acquiring company itself or through a person acting in his own name but on its behalf;

or

(b) by the company being acquired itself or through a person acting in his own name but on its behalf.

* * *

Article 20

The laws of the Member States shall at least lay down rules governing the civil liability towards the shareholders of the company being acquired of the members of the administrative or management bodies of that company in respect of misconduct on the part of members of those bodies in preparing and implementing the merger.

Article 21

The laws of the Member States shall at least lay down rules governing the civil liability towards the shareholders of the company being acquired of the experts responsible for drawing up on behalf of that company the report referred to in Article 10(1) in respect of misconduct on the part of those experts in the performance of their duties.

Article 22

1. The laws of the Member States may lay down nullity rules for mergers in accordance with the following conditions only:

(a) nullity must be ordered in a court judgment;

(b) mergers which have taken effect pursuant to Article 17 may be declared void only if there has been no judicial or administrative preventive supervision of their legality, or if they have not been drawn up and certified in due legal form, or if it is shown that the decision of the general meeting is void or voidable under national law;

(c) nullification proceedings may not be initiated more than six months after the date on which the merger becomes effective as against the person alleging nullity or if the situation has been rectified;

(d) where it is possible to remedy a defect liable to render a merger void, the competent court shall grant the companies involved a period of time within which to rectify the situation;

(e) a judgment declaring a merger void shall be published in the manner prescribed by the laws of each Member State in accordance with Article 3 of Directive 68/151/EEC;

(f) where the laws of a Member State permit a third party to challenge such a judgment, he may do so only within six months of publication of the judgment in the manner prescribed by Directive 68/151/EEC;

(g) a judgment declaring a merger void shall not of itself affect the validity of obligations owed by or in relation to the acquiring company which arose before the judgment was published and after the date referred to in Article 17;

(h) companies which have been parties to a merger shall be jointly and severally liable in respect of the obligations of the acquiring company referred to in (g).

2. By way of derogation from paragraph 1(a), the laws of a Member State may also provide for the nullity of a merger to be ordered by an administrative authority if an appeal against such a decision lies to a court. Subparagraphs (b), (d), (e), (f), (g) and (h) shall apply by analogy to the administrative authority. Such nullification proceedings may not be initiated more than six months after the date referred to in Article 17.

3. The foregoing shall not affect the laws of the Member States on the nullity of a merger pronounced following any supervision other than judicial or administrative preventive supervision of legality.

CHAPTER III

MERGER BY FORMATION OF A NEW COMPANY

Article 23

1. Articles 5, 6, 7 and 9 to 22 shall apply, without prejudice to Articles 11 and 12 of Directive 68/151/EEC, to merger by formation of a new company. For this purpose, 'merging companies' and 'company being acquired' shall mean the companies which will cease to exist, and 'acquiring company' shall mean the new company.

2. Article 5(2)(a) shall also apply to the new company.

3. The draft terms of merger and, if they are contained in a separate document, the memorandum or draft memorandum of association and the articles or draft articles of association of the new company shall be approved at a general meeting of each of the companies that will cease to exist.

4. The Member States need not apply to the formation of a new company the rules governing the verification of any consideration other than cash which are laid down in Article 10 of Directive 77/91/EEC.

CHAPTER IV

ACQUISITION OF ONE COMPANY BY ANOTHER WHICH HOLDS 90% OR MORE OF ITS SHARES

Article 24

The Member States shall make provision, in respect of companies governed by their laws, for the operation whereby one or more companies are wound up without going into liquidation and transfer all their assets and liabilities to another company which is the holder of all their shares and other securities conferring the right to vote at general meetings. Such operations shall be regulated by the provisions of Chapter II, with the exception of Articles 5(2)(b), (c) and (d), 9, 10, 11(1)(d) and (e), 19(1)(b), 20 and 21.

Article 25

The Member States need not apply Article 7 to the operations specified in Article 24 if the following conditions at least are fulfilled:

(a) the publication provided for in Article 6 must be effected, as regards each company involved in the operation, at least one month before the operation takes effect;

(b) at least one month before the operation takes effect, all shareholders of the acquiring company must be entitled to inspect the documents specified in Article 11(1)(a), (b) and (c) at the company's registered office. Article 11(2) and (3) must apply;

(c) Article 8(c) must apply.

Article 26

The Member States may apply Articles 24 and 25 to operations whereby one or more companies are wound up without going into liquidation and transfer all their assets and liabilities to another company, if all the shares and other securities specified in Article 24 of the company or companies being acquired are held by the acquiring company and/or by persons holding those shares and securities in their own names but on behalf of that company.

Article 27

In cases of merger where one or more companies are acquired by another company which holds 90% or more, but not all, of the shares and other securities of each of those companies the holding of which confers the right to vote at general meetings, the Member States need not require approval of the merger by the general meeting of the acquiring company, provided that the following conditions at least are fulfilled:

(a) the publication provided for in Article 6 must be effected, as regards the acquiring company, at least one month before the date fixed for the general meeting of the company or companies being acquired which is to decide on the draft terms of merger;

(b) at least one month before the date specified in (a), all shareholders of the acquiring company must be entitled to inspect the documents specified in Article 11(1)(a), (b) and (c) at the company's registered office. Article 11(2) and (3) must apply;

(c) Article 8(c) must apply.

Article 28

The Member States need not apply Articles 9 to 11 to a merger within the meaning of Article 27 if the following conditions at least are fulfilled:

(a) the minority shareholders of the company being acquired must be entitled to have their shares acquired by the acquiring company;

(b) if they exercise that right, they must be entitled to receive consideration corresponding to the value of their shares;

(c) in the event of disagreement regarding such consideration, it must be possible for the value of the consideration to be determined by a court.

Article 29

The Member States may apply Articles 27 and 28 to operations whereby one or more companies are wound up without going into liquidation and transfer all their assets and liabilities to another company if 90% or more, but not all, of the shares and other securities referred to in Article 27 of the company or companies being acquired are held by that acquiring company and/or by persons holding those shares and securities in their own names but on behalf of that company.

CHAPTER V
OTHER OPERATIONS TREATED AS MERGERS

Article 30

Where in the case of one of the operations referred to in Article 2 the laws of a Member State permit a cash payment to exceed 10%, Chapters II and III and Articles 27, 28 and 29 shall apply.

Article 31

Where the laws of a Member State permit one of the operations referred to in Articles 2, 24 and 30, without all of the transferring companies thereby ceasing to exist, Chapter II, except for Article 19(1)(c), Chapter III or Chapter IV shall apply as appropriate.

CHAPTER VI
FINAL PROVISIONS

* * *

Article 33

This Directive is addressed to the Member States.

20. FOURTH COUNCIL DIRECTIVE 78/660/EEC

of 25 July 1978

based on Article 54(3)(g) of the Treaty on the annual accounts of certain types of companies

O.J. L 222/11 (Aug. 14, 1978), as amended by Council Directive 94/8/EC, O.J. L 82/33 (Mar. 25, 1994), and Council Directive 1999/60/EC, O.J. L 162/65 (June 26, 1999)

THE COUNCIL OF THE EUROPEAN COMMUNITIES,

Having regard to the Treaty establishing the European Economic Community, and in particular Article 54(3)(g) thereof,

Having regard to the proposal from the Commission,

Having regard to the opinion of the European Parliament,

Having regard to the opinion of the Economic and Social Committee,

Whereas the coordination of national provisions concerning the presentation and content of annual accounts and annual reports, the valuation methods used therein and their publication in respect of certain companies with limited liability is of special importance for the protection of members and third parties;

Whereas simultaneous coordination is necessary in these fields for these forms of company because, on the one hand, these companies' activities frequently extend beyond the frontiers of their national territories and, on the other, they offer no safeguards to third parties beyond the amounts of their net assets; * * *

Whereas it is necessary, moreover, to establish in the Community minimum equivalent legal requirements as regards the extent of the financial information that should be made available to the public by companies that are in competition with one another;

Whereas annual accounts must give a true and fair view of a company's assets and liabilities, financial position and profit or loss; whereas to this end a mandatory layout must be prescribed for the balance sheet and the profit and loss account and whereas the minimum content of the notes on the accounts and the annual report must be laid down; whereas, however, derogations may be granted for certain companies of minor economic or social importance;

Whereas the different methods for the valuation of assets and liabilities must be coordinated to the extent necessary to ensure that annual accounts disclose comparable and equivalent information;

Whereas the annual accounts of all companies to which this Directive applies must be published in accordance with Directive 68/151/EEC; whereas, however, certain derogations may likewise be granted in this area for small and medium-sized companies;

Whereas annual accounts must be audited by authorized persons whose minimum qualifications will be the subject of subsequent coordination; whereas only small companies may be relieved of this audit obligation;

Whereas, when a company belongs to a group, it is desirable that group accounts giving a true and fair view of the activities of the group as a whole be published; whereas, however, pending the entry into force of a Council Directive on consolidated accounts, derogations from certain provisions of this Directive are necessary;

Whereas, in order to meet the difficulties arising from the present position regarding legislation in certain Member States, the period allowed for the implementation of certain provisions of this Directive must be longer than the period generally laid down in such cases,

HAS ADOPTED THIS DIRECTIVE:

Article 1

1. The coordination measures prescribed by this Directive shall apply to the laws, regulations and administrative provisions of the Member States relating to the following types of companies:

— in Germany:
  die Aktiengesellschaft, die Kommanditgesellschaft auf Aktien, die Gesellschaft mit beschränkter Haftung;
— in Belgium:
  la société anonyme/de naamloze vennootschap, la société en commandite par actions/de commanditaire vennootschap op aandelen, la société de personnes à responsabilité limitée/de personenvennootschap met beperkte aansprakelijkheid;
— in Denmark:
  aktieselskaber, kommanditaktieselskaber, anpartsselskaber;
— in France:
  la société anonyme, la société en commandite par actions, la société à responsabilité limitée;
— in Ireland:
  public companies limited by shares or by guarantee, private companies limited by shares or by guarantee;
— in Italy:
  la società per azioni, la società in accomandita per azioni, la società a responsabilità limitata;
— in Luxembourg:
  la société anonyme, la société en commandite par actions, la société à responsabilité limitée;
— in the Netherlands:
  de naamloze vennootschap, de besloten vennootschap met beperkte aansprakelijkheid;
— in the United Kingdom:
  public companies limited by shares or by guarantee, private companies limited by shares or by guarantee.

[Amended by Treaties of Accession to list the stock corporation, limited liability company and limited partnership forms of Austria, Finland, Greece, Portugal, Spain and Sweden.]

2. Pending subsequent coordination, the Member States need not apply the provisions of this Directive to banks and other financial institutions or to insurance companies.

SECTION 1
GENERAL PROVISIONS

Article 2

1. The annual accounts shall comprise the balance sheet, the profit and loss account and the notes on the accounts. These documents shall constitute a composite whole.

2. They shall be drawn up clearly and in accordance with the provisions of this Directive.

3. The annual accounts shall give a true and fair view of the company's assets, liabilities, financial position and profit or loss.

4. Where the application of the provisions of this Directive would not be sufficient to give a true and fair view within the meaning of paragraph 3, additional information must be given.

5. Where in exceptional cases the application of a provision of this Directive is incompatible with the obligation laid down in paragraph 3, that provision must be departed from in order to give a true and fair view within the meaning of paragraph 3. Any such departure must be disclosed in the notes on the accounts together with an explanation of the reasons for it and a statement of its effect on the assets, liabilities, financial position and profit or loss. The Member States may define the exceptional cases in question and lay down the relevant special rules.

6. The Member States may authorize or require the disclosure in the annual accounts of other information as well as that which must be disclosed in accordance with this Directive.

SECTION 2
GENERAL PROVISIONS CONCERNING THE BALANCE SHEET AND THE PROFIT AND LOSS ACCOUNT

Article 3

The layout of the balance sheet and of the profit and loss account, particularly as regards the form adopted for their presentation, may not be changed from one financial year to the next. Departures from this principle shall be permitted in exceptional cases. Any such departure must be disclosed in the notes on the accounts together with an explanation of the reasons therefor.

Article 4

1. In the balance sheet and in the profit and loss account the items prescribed in Articles 9, 10 and 23 to 26 must be shown separately in the order indicated.

* * *

4. In respect of each balance sheet and profit and loss account item the figure relating to the corresponding item for the preceding financial year must be shown. The Member States may provide that, where these figures are not comparable, the figure for the preceding financial year must be adjusted. In any case, non-comparability and any adjustment of the figures must be disclosed in the notes on the accounts, with relevant comments.

5. Save where there is a corresponding item for the preceding financial year within the meaning of paragraph 4, a balance sheet or profit and loss account item for which there is no amount shall not be shown.

* * *

Article 6

The Member States may authorize or require adaptation of the layout of the balance sheet and profit and loss account in order to include the appropriation of profit or the treatment of loss.

Article 7

Any set-off between asset and liability items, or between income and expenditure items, shall be prohibited.

> [Omitted Articles 8–10 describe in detail the lay-out of items in the balance sheet.]

Article 11

The Member States may permit companies which on their balance sheet dates do not exceed the limits of two of the three following criteria:

—balance sheet total: [EUR 3,125,000]

—net turnover: [EUR 6,250,000]

—average number of employees during the financial year: 50

to draw up abridged balance sheets showing only [certain identified items] * * *.

> [Figures within brackets represent an amendment made by Directive 1999/60/EC to reflect the adoption of the Euro as a single currency. Member States that have not accepted the Euro must use equivalent amounts in their national currency.]

> [Omitted Articles 12–21 state rules for describing balance sheet items. Omitted Articles 22–26 describe in detail the lay-out of items in the profit and loss statement. Article 27 permits smaller companies to draw up abridged profit and loss statements. Omitted Articles 28–30 state rules for certain items.]

SECTION 7

VALUATION RULES

Article 31

1. The Member States shall ensure that the items shown in the annual accounts are valued in accordance with the following general principles:

(a) the company must be presumed to be carrying on its business as a going concern;

(b) the methods of valuation must be applied consistently from one financial year to another;

(c) valuation must be made on a prudent basis, and in particular:

(aa) only profits made at the balance sheet date may be included,

(bb) account must be taken of all foreseeable liabilities and potential losses arising in the course of the financial year concerned or of a previous one, even if such liabilities or losses become apparent only between the date of the balance sheet and the date on which it is drawn up,

(cc) account must be taken of all depreciation, whether the result of the financial year is a loss or a profit;

(d) account must be taken of income and charges relating to the financial year, irrespective of the date of receipt or payment of such income or charges;

(e) the components of asset and liability items must be valued separately;

(f) the opening balance sheet for each financial year must correspond to the closing balance sheet for the preceding financial year.

2. Departures from these general principles shall be permitted in exceptional cases. Any such departures must be disclosed in the notes on the accounts and the reasons for them given together with an assessment of their effect on the assets, liabilities, financial position and profit or loss.

Article 32

The items shown in the annual accounts shall be valued in accordance with Articles 34 to 42, which are based on the principle of purchase price or production cost.

* * *

Article 35

1. (a) Fixed assets must be valued at purchase price or production cost, without prejudice to (b) and (c) below.

(b) The purchase price or production cost of fixed assets with limited useful economic lives must be reduced by value adjustments calculated to write off the value of such assets systematically over their useful economic lives.

(c) (aa) Value adjustments may be made in respect of financial fixed assets, so that they are valued at the lower figure to be attributed to them at the balance sheet date.

(bb) Value adjustments must be made in respect of fixed assets, whether their useful economic lives are limited or not, so that they are valued at the lower figure to be attributed to them at the balance sheet date if it is expected that the reduction in their value will be permanent.

(cc) The value adjustments referred to in (aa) and (bb) must be charged to the profit and loss account and disclosed separately in the notes on the accounts if they have not been shown separately in the profit and loss account.

(dd) Valuation at the lower of the values provided for in (aa) and (bb) may not be continued if the reasons for which the value adjustments were made have ceased to apply.

(d) If fixed assets are the subject of exceptional value adjustments for taxation purposes alone, the amount of the adjustments and the reasons for making them shall be indicated in the notes on the accounts.

2. The purchase price shall be calculated by adding to the price paid the expenses incidental thereto.

3. (a) The production cost shall be calculated by adding to the purchasing price of the raw materials and consumables the costs directly attributable to the product in question.

(b) A reasonable proportion of the costs which are only indirectly attributable to the product in question may be added into the production costs to the extent that they relate to the period of production.

4. Interest on capital borrowed to finance the production of fixed assets may be included in the production costs to the extent that it relates to the period of production. In that event, the inclusion of such interest under 'Assets' must be disclosed in the notes on the accounts.

* * *

Article 37

1. Article 34 shall apply to costs of research and development. In exceptional cases, however, the Member States may permit derogations from Article 34(1)(a). In that case, they may also provide for derogations from Article 34(1)(b). Such derogations and the reasons for them must be disclosed in the notes on the accounts.

2. Article 34(1)(a) shall apply to goodwill. The Member States may, however, permit companies to write goodwill off systematically over a limited period exceeding five years provided that this period does not exceed the useful economic life of the asset and is disclosed in the notes on the accounts together with the supporting reasons therefor.

Article 38

Tangible fixed assets, raw materials and consumables which are constantly being replaced and the overall value of which is of secondary importance to the undertaking may be shown under 'Assets' at a fixed quantity and value, if the quantity, value and composition thereof do not vary materially.

Article 39

1. (a) Current assets must be valued at purchase price or production cost, without prejudice to (b) and (c) below.

(b) Value adjustments shall be made in respect of current assets with a view to showing them at the lower market value or, in particular circumstances, another lower value to be attributed to them at the balance sheet date.

(c) The Member States may permit exceptional value adjustments where, on the basis of a reasonable commercial assessment, these are necessary if the valuation of these items is not to be modified in the near future because of fluctuations in value. The amount of these value adjustments must be disclosed separately in the profit and loss account or in the notes on the accounts.

(d) Valuation at the lower value provided for in (b) and (c) may not be continued if the reasons for which the value adjustments were made have ceased to apply.

(e) If current assets are the subject of exceptional value adjustments for taxation purposes alone, the amount of the adjustments and the reasons for making them must be disclosed in the notes on the accounts.

2. The definitions of purchase price and of production cost given in Article 35(2) and (3) shall apply. The Member States may also apply Article 35(4). Distribution costs may not be included in production costs.

Article 40

1. The Member States may permit the purchase price or production cost of stocks of goods of the same category and all fungible items including investments to be calculated either on the basis of weighted average prices or by the 'first in, first out' (FIFO) method, the 'last in, first out' (LIFO) method, or some similar method.

* * *

Article 41

1. Where the amount repayable on account of any debt is greater than the amount received, the difference may be shown as an asset. It must be shown separately in the balance sheet or in the notes on the accounts.

2. The amount of this difference must be written off by a reasonable amount each year and completely written off no later than the time of repayment of the debt.

Article 42

Provisions for liabilities and charges may not exceed in amount the sums which are necessary.

The provisions shown in the balance sheet under 'Other provisions' must be disclosed in the notes on the accounts if they are material.

SECTION 8

CONTENTS OF THE NOTES ON THE ACCOUNTS

* * *

SECTION 9

CONTENTS OF THE ANNUAL REPORT

Article 46

1. The annual report must include at least a fair review of the development of the company's business and of its position.

2. The report shall also give an indication of:

(a) any important events that have occurred since the end of the financial year;

(b) the company's likely future development;

(c) activities in the field of research and development;

(d) the information concerning acquisitions of own shares prescribed by Article 22(2) of Directive 77/91/EEC.

SECTION 10

PUBLICATION

Article 47

1. The annual accounts, duly approved, and the annual report, together with the opinion submitted by the person responsible for auditing the accounts, shall be published as laid down by the laws of each Member State in accordance with Article 3 of Directive 68/151/EEC.

The laws of a Member State may, however, permit the annual report not to be published as stipulated above. In that case, it shall be made available to the public at the company's registered office in the Member State concerned. It must be possible to obtain a copy of all or part of any such report free of charge upon request.

2. By way of derogation from paragraph 1, the Member States may permit the companies referred to in Article 11 to publish:

(a) abridged balance sheets * * *.

In addition, the Member States may relieve such companies from the obligation to publish their profit and loss accounts and annual reports and the opinions of the persons responsible for auditing the accounts.

* * *

Article 48

Whenever the annual accounts and the annual report are published in full, they must be reproduced in the form and text on the basis of which the person responsible for auditing the accounts has drawn up his opinion. They must be accompanied by the full text of his report. If the person responsible for auditing the accounts has made any qualifications or refused to report upon the accounts, that fact must be disclosed and the reasons given.

* * *

SECTION 11

AUDITING

Article 51

1. (a) Companies must have their annual accounts audited by one or more persons authorized by national law to audit accounts.
   (b) The person or persons responsible for auditing the accounts must also verify that the annual report is consistent with the annual accounts for the same financial year.

2. The Member States may relieve the companies referred to in Article 11 from the obligation imposed by paragraph 1.

* * *

SECTION 12

FINAL PROVISIONS

Article 52

1. A Contact Committee shall be set up under the auspices of the Commission. Its function shall be:

(a) to facilitate, without prejudice to the provisions of Articles 169 and 170 of the Treaty, harmonized application of this Directive through regular meetings dealing in particular with practical problems arising in connection with its application;

(b) to advise the Commission, if necessary, on additions or amendments to this Directive.

2. The Contact Committee shall be composed of representatives of the Member States and representatives of the Commission. The chairman shall be a representative of the Commission. The Commission shall provide the secretariat.

3. The Committee shall be convened by the chairman either on his own initiative or at the request of one of its members.

* * *

21. COUNCIL REGULATION (EEC) 2137/85

of 25 July 1985

on the European Economic Interest Grouping (EEIG)

O.J. L 199/1 (July 31, 1985)

THE COUNCIL OF THE EUROPEAN COMMUNITIES,

Having regard to the Treaty establishing the European Economic Community, and in particular Article 235 thereof,

Having regard to the proposal from the Commission,[1]

Having regard to the opinion of the European Parliament,[2]

Having regard to the opinion of the Economic and Social Committee,[3]

Whereas a harmonious development of economic activities and a continuous and balanced expansion throughout the Community depend on the establishment and smooth functioning of a common market offering conditions analogous to those of a national market; whereas to bring about this single market and to increase its unity a legal framework which facilitates the adaptation of their activities to the economic conditions of the Community should be created for natural persons, companies, firms and other legal bodies in particular; whereas to that end it is necessary that those natural persons, companies, firms and other legal bodies should be able to cooperate effectively across frontiers;

Whereas cooperation of this nature can encounter legal, fiscal or psychological difficulties; whereas the creation of an appropriate Community legal instrument in the form of a European Economic Interest Grouping would contribute to the achievement of the abovementioned objectives and therefore proves necessary;

Whereas the Treaty does not provide the necessary powers for the creation of such a legal instrument;

Whereas a grouping's ability to adapt to economic conditions must be guaranteed by the considerable freedom for its members in their contractual relations and the internal organization of the grouping;

Whereas a grouping differs from a firm or company principally in its purpose, which is only to facilitate or develop the economic activities of its members to enable them to improve their own results; whereas, by reason of that ancillary nature, a grouping's activities must be related to the economic activities of its members but not replace them so that, to that extent, for example, a grouping may not itself, with regard to third parties, practise a profession, the concept of economic activities being interpreted in the widest sense;

Whereas access to grouping form must be made as widely available as possible to natural persons, companies, firms and other legal bodies, in

---

[1] OJ No. C 14, 15. 2. 1974, p. 30 and OJ No. C 103, 28. 4. 1978, p. 4.
[2] OJ No. C 163, 11. 7. 1977, p. 17.
[3] OJ No. C 108, 15. 5. 1975, p. 46.

keeping with the aims of this Regulation; whereas this Regulation shall not, however, prejudice the application at national level of legal rules and/or ethical codes concerning the conditions for the pursuit of business and professional activities;

* * *

Whereas this Regulation provides that the profits or losses resulting from the activities of a grouping shall be taxable only in the hands of its members; whereas it is understood that otherwise national tax laws apply, particularly as regards the apportionment of profits, tax procedures and any obligations imposed by national tax law;

Whereas in matters not covered by this Regulation the laws of the Member States and Community law are applicable, for example with regard to:

—social and labour laws,

—competition law,

—intellectual property law;

* * *

HAS ADOPTED THIS REGULATION:

Article 1

1. European Economic Interest Groupings shall be formed upon the terms, in the manner and with the effects laid down in this Regulation.

Accordingly, parties intending to form a grouping must conclude a contract and have the registration provided for in Article 6 carried out.

2. A grouping so formed shall, from the date of its registration as provided for in Article 6, have the capacity, in its own name, to have rights and obligations of all kinds, to make contracts or accomplish other legal acts, and to sue and be sued.

3. The Member States shall determine whether or not groupings registered at their registries, pursuant to Article 6, have legal personality.

Article 2

1. Subject to the provisions of this Regulation, the law applicable, on the one hand, to the contract for the formation of a grouping, except as regards matters relating to the status or capacity of natural persons and to the capacity of legal persons and, on the other hand, to the internal organization of a grouping shall be the internal law of the State in which the official address is situated, as laid down in the contract for the formation of the grouping.

2. Where a State comprises several territorial units, each of which has its own rules of law applicable to the matters referred to in paragraph 1, each territorial unit shall be considered as a State for the purposes of identifying the law applicable under this Article.

Article 3

1. The purpose of a grouping shall be to facilitate or develop the economic activities of its members and to improve or increase the results of those activities; its purpose is not to make profits for itself.

Its activity shall be related to the economic activities of its members and must not be more than ancillary to those activities.

2. Consequently, a grouping may not:

(a) exercise, directly or indirectly, a power of management or supervision over its members' own activities or over the activities of another undertaking, in particular in the fields of personnel, finance and investment;

(b) directly or indirectly, on any basis whatsoever, hold shares of any kind in a member undertaking; the holding of shares in another undertaking shall be possible only in so far as it is necessary for the achievement of the grouping's objects and if it is done on its members' behalf;

(c) employ more than 500 persons;

(d) be used by a company to make a loan to a director of a company, or any person connected with him, when the making of such loans is restricted or controlled under the Member States' laws governing companies. Nor must a grouping be used for the transfer of any property between a company and a director, or any person connected with him, except to the extent allowed by the Member States' laws governing companies. For the purposes of this provision the making of a loan includes entering into any transaction or arrangement of similar effect, and property includes moveable and immoveable property;

(e) be a member of another European Economic Interest Grouping.

Article 4

1. Only the following may be members of a grouping:

(a) companies or firms within the meaning of the second paragraph of Article 58 of the Treaty and other legal bodies governed by public or private law, which have been formed in accordance with the law of a Member State and which have their registered or statutory office and central administration in the Community; where, under the law of a Member State, a company, firm or other legal body is not obliged to have a registered or statutory office, it shall be sufficient for such a company, firm or other legal body to have its central administration in the Community;

(b) natural persons who carry on any industrial, commercial, craft or agricultural activity or who provide professional or other services in the Community.

2. A grouping must comprise at least:

(a) two companies, firms or other legal bodies, within the meaning of paragraph 1, which have their central administrations in different Member States, or

(b) two natural persons, within the meaning of paragraph 1, who carry on their principal activities in different Member States, or

(c) a company, firm or other legal body within the meaning of paragraph 1 and a natural person, of which the first has its central administration in one Member State and the second carries on his principal activity in another Member State.

3. A Member State may provide that groupings registered at its registries in accordance with Article 6 may have no more than 20 members. For this purpose, that Member State may provide that, in accordance with its laws, each member of a legal body formed under its laws, other than a registered company, shall be treated as a separate member of a grouping.

4. Any Member State may, on grounds of that State's public interest, prohibit or restrict participation in groupings by certain classes of natural persons, companies, firms, or other legal bodies.

Article 5

A contract for the formation of a grouping shall include at least:

(a) the name of the grouping preceded or followed either by the words 'European Economic Interest Grouping' or by the initials 'EEIG', unless those words or initials already form part of the name;

(b) the official address of the grouping;

(c) the objects for which the grouping is formed;

(d) the name, business name, legal form, permanent address or registered office, and the number and place of registration, if any, of each member of the grouping;

(e) the duration of the grouping, except where this is indefinite.

Article 6

A grouping shall be registered in the State in which it has its official address, at the registry designated pursuant to Article 39(1).

Article 7

A contract for the formation of a grouping shall be filed at the registry referred to in Article 6.

The following documents and particulars must also be filed at that registry:

(a) any amendment to the contract for the formation of a grouping, including any change in the composition of a grouping;

(b) notice of the setting up or closure of any establishment of the grouping;

(c) any judicial decision establishing or declaring the nullity of a grouping, in accordance with Article 15;

(d) notice of the appointment of the manager or managers of a grouping, their names and any other identification particulars required by the law of the Member State in which the register is kept, notification that they may act alone or must act jointly, and the termination of any manager's appointment;

(e) notice of a member's assignment of his participation in a grouping or a proportion thereof, in accordance with Article 22(1);

* * *

Article 8

The following must be published, as laid down in Article 39, in the gazette referred to in paragraph 1 of that Article:

(a) the particulars which must be included in the contract for the formation of a grouping, pursuant to Article 5, and any amendments thereto;

(b) the number, date and place of registration as well as notice of the termination of that registration;

(c) the documents and particulars referred to in Article 7(b) to (j).

* * *

Article 9

1. The documents and particulars which must be published pursuant to this Regulation may be relied on by a grouping as against third parties under the conditions laid down by the national law applicable pursuant to Article 3(5) and (7) of Council Directive 68/151/EEC of 9 March 1968 * * *.

* * *

Article 10

Any grouping establishment situated in a Member State other than that in which the official address is situated shall be registered in that State. For the purpose of such registration, a grouping shall file, at the appropriate registry in that Member State, copies of the documents which must be filed at the registry of the Member State in which the official address is situated, together, if necessary, with a translation which conforms with the practice of the registry where the establishment is registered.

Article 11

Notice that a grouping has been formed or that the liquidation of a grouping has been concluded stating the number, date and place of registration and the date, place and title of publication, shall be given in the *Official Journal of the European Communities* after it has been published in the gazette referred to in Article 39(1).

Article 12

The official address referred to in the contract for the formation of a grouping must be situated in the Community.

The official address must be fixed either:

(a) where the grouping has its central administration, or

(b) where one of the members of the grouping has its central administration or, in the case of a natural person, his principal activity, provided that the grouping carries on an activity there.

* * *

Article 16

1. The organs of a grouping shall be the members acting collectively and the manager or managers.

A contract for the formation of a grouping may provide for other organs; if it does it shall determine their powers.

2. The members of a grouping, acting as a body, may take any decision for the purpose of achieving the objects of the grouping.

Article 17

1. Each member shall have one vote. The contract for the formation of a grouping may, however, give more than one vote to certain members, provided that no one member holds a majority of the votes.

2. A unanimous decision by the members shall be required to:

(a) alter the objects of a grouping;

(b) alter the number of votes allotted to each member;

(c) alter the conditions for the taking of decisions;

(d) extend the duration of a grouping beyond any period fixed in the contract for the formation of the grouping;

(e) alter the contribution by every member or by some members to the grouping's financing;

(f) alter any other obligation of a member, unless otherwise provided by the contract for the formation of the grouping;

(g) make any alteration to the contract for the formation of the grouping not covered by this paragraph, unless otherwise provided by that contract.

3. Except where this Regulation provides that decisions must be taken unanimously, the contract for the formation of a grouping may prescribe the conditions for a quorum and for a majority, in accordance with which the decisions, or some of them, shall be taken. Unless otherwise provided for by the contract, decisions shall be taken unanimously.

4. On the initiative of a manager or at the request of a member, the manager or managers must arrange for the members to be consulted so that the latter can take a decision.

Article 18

Each member shall be entitled to obtain information from the manager or managers concerning the grouping's business and to inspect the grouping's books and business records.

Article 19

1. A grouping shall be managed by one or more natural persons appointed in the contract for the formation of the grouping or by decision of the members.

No person may be a manager of a grouping if:

—by virtue of the law applicable to him, or

—by virtue of the internal law of the State in which the grouping has its official address, or

—following a judicial or administrative decision made or recognized in a Member State

he may not belong to the administrative or management body of a company, may not manage an undertaking or may not act as manager of a European Economic Interest Grouping.

2. A Member State may, in the case of groupings registered at their registries pursuant to Article 6, provide that legal persons may be managers on condition that such legal persons designate one or more natural persons, whose particulars shall be the subject of the filing provisions of Article 7(d) to represent them.

If a Member State exercises this option, it must provide that the representative or representatives shall be liable as if they were themselves managers of the groupings concerned.

The restrictions imposed in paragraph 1 shall also apply to those representatives.

3. The contract for the formation of a grouping or, failing that, a unanimous decision by the members shall determine the conditions for the appointment and removal of the manager or managers and shall lay down their powers.

Article 20

1. Only the manager or, where there are two or more, each of the managers shall represent a grouping in respect of dealings with third parties.

Each of the managers shall bind the grouping as regards third parties when he acts on behalf of the grouping, even where his acts do not fall within the objects of the grouping, unless the grouping proves that the third party knew or could not, under the circumstances, have been unaware that the act fell outside the objects of the grouping; publication of the particulars referred to in Article 5(c) shall not of itself be proof thereof.

No limitation on the powers of the manager or managers, whether deriving from the contract for the formation of the grouping or from a decision by the members, may be relied on as against third parties even if it is published.

2. The contract for the formation of the grouping may provide that the grouping shall be validly bound only by two or more managers acting jointly. Such a clause may be relied on as against third parties in accordance with the conditions referred to in Article 9(1) only if it is published in accordance with Article 8.

Article 21

1. The profits resulting from a grouping's activities shall be deemed to be the profits of the members and shall be apportioned among them in the proportions laid down in the contract for the formation of the grouping or, in the absence of any such provision, in equal shares.

2. The members of a grouping shall contribute to the payment of the amount by which expenditure exceeds income in the proportions laid down in the contract for the formation of the grouping or, in the absence of any such provision, in equal shares.

Article 22

1. Any member of a grouping may assign his participation in the grouping, or a proportion thereof, either to another member or to a third party; the assignment shall not take effect without the unanimous authorization of the other members.

2. A member of a grouping may use his participation in the grouping as security only after the other members have given their unanimous authorization, unless otherwise laid down in the contract for the formation of the grouping. The holder of the security may not at any time become a member of the grouping by virtue of that security.

Article 23

No grouping may invite investment by the public.

Article 24

1. The members of a grouping shall have unlimited joint and several liability for its debts and other liabilities of whatever nature. National law shall determine the consequences of such liability.

2. Creditors may not proceed against a member for payment in respect of debts and other liabilities, in accordance with the conditions laid down in paragraph 1, before the liquidation of a grouping is concluded, unless they have first requested the grouping to pay and payment has not been made within an appropriate period.

Article 25

Letters, order forms and similar documents must indicate legibly:

(a) the name of the grouping preceded or followed either by the words 'European Economic Interest Grouping' or by the initials 'EEIG', unless those words or initials already occur in the name;

(b) the location of the registry referred to in Article 6, in which the grouping is registered, together with the number of the grouping's entry at the registry;

(c) the grouping's official address;

(d) where applicable, that the managers must act jointly;

* * *

Article 26

1. A decision to admit new members shall be taken unanimously by the members of the grouping.

2. Every new member shall be liable, in accordance with the conditions laid down in Article 24, for the grouping's debts and other liabilities, including those arising out of the grouping's activities before his admission.

He may, however, be exempted by a clause in the contract for the formation of the grouping or in the instrument of admission from the payment of debts and other liabilities which originated before his admission. Such a clause may be relied on as against third parties, under the conditions referred to in Article 9(1), only if it is published in accordance with Article 8.

Article 27

1. A member of a grouping may withdraw in accordance with the conditions laid down in the contract for the formation of a grouping or, in the absence of such conditions, with the unanimous agreement of the other members.

Any member of a grouping may, in addition, withdraw on just and proper grounds.

2. Any member of a grouping may be expelled for the reasons listed in the contract for the formation of the grouping and, in any case, if he seriously fails in his obligations or if he causes or threatens to cause serious disruption in the operation of the grouping.

Such expulsion may occur only by the decision of a court to which joint application has been made by a majority of the other members, unless otherwise provided by the contract for the formation of a grouping.

Article 28

1. A member of a grouping shall cease to belong to it on death or when he no longer complies with the conditions laid down in Article 4(1).

* * *

* * *

Article 31

1. A grouping may be wound up by a decision of its members ordering its winding up. Such a decision shall be taken unanimously, unless otherwise laid down in the contract for the formation of the grouping.

* * *

Article 35

1. The winding up of a grouping shall entail its liquidation.

2. The liquidation of a grouping and the conclusion of its liquidation shall be governed by national law.

* * *

Article 39

1. The Member States shall designate the registry or registries responsible for effecting the registration referred to in Articles 6 and 10 and shall lay down the rules governing registration. They shall prescribe the conditions under which the documents referred to in Articles 7 and 10 shall be filed. They shall ensure that the documents and particulars referred to in Article 8 are published in the appropriate official gazette of the Member State in which the grouping has its official address, and may prescribe the manner of publication of the documents and particulars referred to in Article 8(c).

The Member States shall also ensure that anyone may, at the appropriate registry pursuant to Article 6 or, where appropriate, Article 10, inspect the documents referred to in Article 7 and obtain, even by post, full or partial copies thereof.

The Member States may provide for the payment of fees in connection with the operations referred to in the preceding subparagraphs; those fees may not, however, exceed the administrative cost thereof.

* * *

Article 40

The profits or losses resulting from the activities of a grouping shall be taxable only in the hands of its members.

* * *

Article 43

This Regulation shall enter into force on the third day following its publication in the *Official Journal of the European Communities.*

It shall apply from 1 July 1989, with the exception of Articles 39, 41 and 42 which shall apply as from the entry into force of the Regulation.

This Regulation shall be binding in its entirety and directly applicable in all Member States.

22. COUNCIL DIRECTIVE 89/48/EEC

of 21 December 1988

on a general system for the recognition of higher-education diplomas awarded on completion of professional education and training of at least three years' duration

O.J. L 19/16 (Jan. 24, 1989)

THE COUNCIL OF THE EUROPEAN COMMUNITIES,

Having regard to the Treaty establishing the European Economic Community, and in particular Articles 49, 57(1) and 66 thereof,

Having regard to the proposal from the Commission,[1]

In cooperation with the European Parliament,[2]

Having regard to the opinion of the Economic and Social Committee,[3]

Whereas, pursuant to Article 3(c) of the Treaty the abolition, as between Member States, of obstacles to freedom of movement for persons and services constitutes one of the objectives of the Community; whereas, for nationals of the Member States, this means in particular the possibility of pursuing a profession, whether in a self-employed or employed capacity, in a Member State other than that in which they acquired their professional qualifications;

Whereas the provisions so far adopted by the Council, and pursuant to which Member States recognize mutually and for professional purposes higher-education diplomas issued within their territory, concern only a few professions; whereas the level and duration of the education and training governing access to those professions have been regulated in a similar fashion in all the Member States or have been the subject of the minimal harmonization needed to establish sectoral systems for the mutual recognition of diplomas;

Whereas, in order to provide a rapid response to the expectations of nationals of Community countries who hold higher-education diplomas awarded on completion of professional education and training issued in a Member State other than that in which they wish to pursue their profession, another method of recognition of such diplomas should also be put in place such as to enable those concerned to pursue all those professional activities which in a host Member State are dependent on the completion of post-secondary education and training, provided they hold such a diploma preparing them for those activities awarded on completion of a course of studies lasting at least three years and issued in another Member State;

Whereas this objective can be achieved by the introduction of a general system for the recognition of higher-education diplomas awarded on com-

1. OJ No. C 217, 28.8.1985, p. 3, and OJ No. C 143, 10.6.1986, p. 7.
2. OJ No. C 345, 31.12.1985, p. 80, and OJ No. C 309, 5.12.1988.
3. OJ No. C 75, 3.4.1986, p. 5.

pletion of professional education and training of at least three years' duration;

Whereas, for those professions for the pursuit of which the Community has not laid down the necessary minimum level of qualification, Member States reserve the option of fixing such a level with a view to guaranteeing the quality of services provided in their territory; whereas, however, they may not, without infringing their obligations laid down in Article 5 of the Treaty, require a national of a Member State to obtain those qualifications which in general they determine only by reference to diplomas issued under their own national education systems, where the person concerned has already acquired all or part of those qualifications in another Member State; whereas, as a result, any host Member State in which a profession is regulated is required to take account of qualifications acquired in another Member State and to determine whether those qualifications correspond to the qualifications which the Member State concerned requires;

* * *

Whereas the term 'regulated professional activity' should be defined so as to take account of differing national sociological situations; whereas the term should cover not only professional activities access to which is subject, in a Member State, to the possession of a diploma, but also professional activities, access to which is unrestricted when they are practised under a professional title reserved for the holders of certain qualifications; whereas the professional associations and organizations which confer such titles on their members and are recognized by the public authorities cannot invoke their private status to avoid application of the system provided for by this Directive;

* * *

Whereas an aptitude test may also be introduced in place of the adaptation period; whereas the effect of both will be to improve the existing situation with regard to the mutual recognition of diplomas between Member States and therefore to facilitate the free movement of persons within the Community; whereas their function is to assess the ability of the migrant, who is a person who has already received his professional training in another Member State, to adapt to this new professional environment; whereas, from the migrant's point of view, an aptitude test will have the advantage of reducing the length of the practice period; whereas, in principle, the choice between the adaptation period and the aptitude test should be made by the migrant; whereas, however, the nature of certain professions is such that Member States must be allowed to prescribe, under certain conditions, either the adaptation period or the test; whereas, in particular, the differences between the legal systems of the Member States, whilst they may vary in extent from one Member State to another, warrant special provisions since, as a rule, the education or training attested by the diploma, certificate or other evidence of formal qualifications in a field of law in the Member State of origin does not cover the legal knowledge required in the host Member State with respect to the corresponding legal field;

Whereas, moreover, the general system for the recognition of higher-education diplomas is intended neither to amend the rules, including those relating to professional ethics, applicable to any person pursuing a profession in the territory of a Member State nor to exclude migrants from the application of those rules; whereas that system is confined to laying down appropriate arrangements to ensure that migrants comply with the professional rules of the host Member State;

Whereas Articles 49, 57(1) and 66 of the Treaty empower the Community to adopt provisions necessary for the introduction and operation of such a system;

Whereas the general system for the recognition of higher-education diplomas is entirely without prejudice to the application of Article 48(4) and Article 55 of the Treaty;

Whereas such a system, by strengthening the right of a Community national to use his professional skills in any Member State, supplements and reinforces his right to acquire such skills wherever he wishes;

Whereas this system should be evaluated, after being in force for a certain time, to determine how efficiently it operates and in particular how it can be improved or its field of application extended,

HAS ADOPTED THIS DIRECTIVE:

Article 1

For the purposes of this Directive the following definitions shall apply:

(a) diploma: any diploma, certificate or other evidence of formal qualifications or any set of such diplomas, certificates or other evidence:

—which has been awarded by a competent authority in a Member State, designated in accordance with its own laws, regulations or administrative provisions,

—which shows that the holder has successfully completed a post-secondary course of at least three years' duration, or of an equivalent duration part-time, at a university or establishment of higher education or another establishment of similar level and, where appropriate, that he has successfully completed the professional training required in addition to the post-secondary course; and

—which shows that the holder has the professional qualifications required for the taking up or pursuit of a regulated profession in that Member State,

provided that the education and training attested by the diploma, certificate or other evidence of formal qualifications were received mainly in the Community, or the holder thereof has three years' professional experience certified by the Member State which recognized a third-country diploma, certificate or other evidence of formal qualifications.

* * *

(b) host Member State: any Member State in which a national of a Member State applies to pursue a profession subject to regulation in that Member State, other than the State in which he obtained his diploma or first pursued the profession in question;

(c) a regulated profession: the regulated professional activity or range of activities which constitute this profession in a Member State;

(d) regulated professional activity: a professional activity, in so far as the taking up or pursuit of such activity or one of its modes of pursuit in a Member State is subject, directly or indirectly by virtue of laws, regulations or administrative provisions, to the possession of a diploma.

* * *

A non-exhaustive list of associations or organizations which, when this Directive is adopted, satisfy the conditions of the second subparagraph is contained in the Annex. Whenever a Member State grants the recognition referred to in the second subparagraph to an association or organization, it shall inform the Commission thereof, which shall publish this information in the *Official Journal of the European Communities*.

(e) professional experience: the actual and lawful pursuit of the profession concerned in a Member State;

(f) adaptation period: the pursuit of a regulated profession in the host Member State under the responsibility of a qualified member of that profession, such period of supervised practice possibly being accompanied by further training. This period of supervised practice shall be the subject of an assessment. The detailed rules governing the adaptation period and its assessment as well as the status of a migrant person under supervision shall be laid down by the competent authority in the host Member States;

(g) aptitude test: a test limited to the professional knowledge of the applicant, made by the competent authorities of the host Member State with the aim of assessing the ability of the applicant to pursue a regulated profession in that Member State.

In order to permit this test to be carried out, the competent authorities shall draw up a list of subjects which, on the basis of a comparison of the education and training required in the Member State and that received by the applicant, are not covered by the diploma or other evidence of formal qualifications possessed by the applicant.

The aptitude test must take account of the fact that the applicant is a qualified professional in the Member State of origin or the Member State from which he comes. It shall cover subjects to be selected from those on the list, knowledge of which is essential in order to be able to exercise the profession in the host Member State. The test may also include knowledge of the professional rules applicable to the activities in question in the host Member State. The detailed application of the aptitude test shall be determined by the competent authorities of that State with due regard to the rules of Community law.

The status, in the host Member State, of the applicant who wishes to prepare himself for the aptitude test in that State shall be determined by the competent authorities in that State.

Article 2

This Directive shall apply to any national of a Member State wishing to pursue a regulated profession in a host Member State in a self-employed capacity or as an employed person.

This Directive shall not apply to professions which are the subject of a separate Directive establishing arrangements for the mutual recognition of diplomas by Member States.

Article 3

Where, in a host Member State, the taking up or pursuit of a regulated profession is subject to possession of a diploma, the competent authority may not, on the grounds of inadequate qualifications, refuse to authorize a national of a Member State to take up or pursue that profession on the same conditions as apply to its own nationals:

(a) if the applicant holds the diploma required in another Member State for the taking up or pursuit of the profession in question in its territory, such diploma having been awarded in a Member State;

* * *

Article 4

1. Notwithstanding Article 3, the host Member State may also require the applicant:

(a) to provide evidence of professional experience, where the duration of the education and training adduced in support of his application, as laid down in Article 3(a) and (b), is at least one year less than that required in the host Member State. In this event, the period of professional experience required:

—may not exceed twice the shortfall in duration of education and training where the shortfall relates to post-secondary studies and/or to a period of probationary practice carried out under the control of a supervising professional person and ending with an examination,

—may not exceed the shortfall where the shortfall relates to professional practice acquired with the assistance of a qualified member of the profession.

In the case of diplomas within the meaning of the last subparagraph of Article 1(a), the duration of education and training recognized as being of an equivalent level shall be determined as for the education and training defined in the first subparagraph of Article 1(a).

When applying these provisions, account must be taken of the professional experience referred to in Article 3(b).

At all events, the professional experience required may not exceed four years;

> (b) to complete an adaptation period not exceeding three years or take an aptitude test:
>
> —where the matters covered by the education and training he has received as laid down in Article 3(a) and (b), differ substantially from those covered by the diploma required in the host Member State, or
>
> —where, in the case referred to in Article 3(a), the profession regulated in the host Member State comprises one or more regulated professional activities which are not in the profession regulated in the Member State from which the applicant originates or comes and that difference corresponds to specific education and training required in the host Member State and covers matters which differ substantially from those covered by the diploma adduced by the applicant, or
>
> —where, in the case referred to in Article 3(b), the profession regulated in the host Member State comprises one or more regulated professional activities which are not in the profession pursued by the applicant in the Member State from which he originates or comes, and that difference corresponds to specific education and training required in the host Member State and covers matters which differ substantially from those covered by the evidence of formal qualifications adduced by the applicant.

Should the host Member State make use of this possibility, it must give the applicant the right to choose between an adaptation period and an aptitude test. By way of derogation from this principle, for professions whose practice requires precise knowledge of national law and in respect of which the provision of advice and/or assistance concerning national law is an essential and constant aspect of the professional activity, the host Member State may stipulate either an adaptation period or an aptitude test. Where the host Member State intends to introduce derogations for other professions as regards an applicant's right to choose, the procedure laid down in Article 10 shall apply.

2. However, the host Member State may not apply the provisions of paragraph 1(a) and (b) cumulatively.

Article 5

Without prejudice to Articles 3 and 4, a host Member State may allow the applicant, with a view to improving his possibilities of adapting to the professional environment in that State, to undergo there, on the basis of equivalence, that part of his professional education and training represented by professional practice, acquired with the assistance of a qualified member of the profession, which he has not undergone in his Member State of origin or the Member State from which he has come.

Article 6

1. Where the competent authority of a host Member State requires of persons wishing to take up a regulated profession proof that they are of good character or repute or that they have not been declared bankrupt, or suspends or prohibits the pursuit of that profession in the event of serious professional misconduct or a criminal offence, that State shall accept as sufficient evidence, in respect of nationals of Member States wishing to pursue that profession in its territory, the production of documents issued by competent authorities in the Member State of origin or the Member State from which the foreign national comes showing that those requirements are met.

* * *

2. Where the competent authority of a host Member State requires of nationals of that Member State wishing to take up or pursue a regulated profession a certificate of physical or mental health, that authority shall accept as sufficient evidence in this respect the production of the document required in the Member State of origin or the Member State from which the foreign national comes.

* * *

4. Where the competent authority of a host Member State requires nationals of that Member State wishing to take up or pursue a regulated profession to take an oath or make a solemn declaration and where the form of such oath or declaration cannot be used by nationals of other Member States, that authority shall ensure that an appropriate and equivalent form of oath or declaration is offered to the person concerned.

Article 7

1. The competent authorities of host Member States shall recognize the right of nationals of Member States who fulfil the conditions for the taking up and pursuit of a regulated profession in their territory to use the professional title of the host Member State corresponding to that profession.

2. The competent authorities of host Member States shall recognize the right of nationals of Member States who fulfil the conditions for the taking up and pursuit of a regulated profession in their territory to use their lawful academic title and, where appropriate, the abbreviation thereof deriving from their Member State of origin or the Member State from which they come, in the language of that State. Host Member States may require this title to be followed by the name and location of the establishment or examining board which awarded it.

* * *

Article 8

1. The host Member State shall accept as proof that the conditions laid down in Articles 3 and 4 are satisfied the certificates and documents issued by the competent authorities in the Member States, which the person concerned shall submit in support of his application to pursue the profession concerned.

2. The procedure for examining an application to pursue a regulated profession shall be completed as soon as possible and the outcome communicated in a reasoned decision of the competent authority in the host Member State not later than four months after presentation of all the documents relating to the person concerned. A remedy shall be available against this decision, or the absence thereof, before a court or tribunal in accordance with the provisions of national law.

Article 9

1. Member States shall designate, within the period provided for in Article 12, the competent authorities empowered to receive the applications and take the decisions referred to in this Directive.

They shall communicate this information to the other Member States and to the Commission.

2. Each Member State shall designate a person responsible for coordinating the activities of the authorities referred to in paragraph 1 and shall inform the other Member States and the Commission to that effect. His role shall be to promote uniform application of this Directive to all the professions concerned. A coordinating group shall be set up under the aegis of the Commission, composed of the coordinators appointed by each Member State or their deputies and chaired by a representative of the Commission.

The task of this group shall be:

—to facilitate the implementation of this Directive,

—to collect all useful information for its application in the Member States.

The group may be consulted by the Commission on any changes to the existing system that may be contemplated.

* * *

Article 10

1. If, pursuant to the third sentence of the second subparagraph of Article 4(1)(b), a Member State proposes not to grant applicants the right to choose between an adaptation period and an aptitude test in respect of a profession within the meaning of this Directive, it shall immediately communicate to the Commission the corresponding draft provision. It shall at the same time notify the Commission of the grounds which make the enactment of such a provision necessary.

* * *

Article 11

Following the expiry of the period provided for in Article 12, Member States shall communicate to the Commission, every two years, a report on the application of the system introduced.

In addition to general remarks, this report shall contain a statistical summary of the decisions taken and a description of the main problems arising from application of the Directive.

Article 12

Member States shall take the measures necessary to comply with this Directive within two years of its notification. They shall forthwith inform the Commission thereof.

Member States shall communicate to the Commission the texts of the main provisions of national law which they adopt in the field governed by this Directive.

Article 13

Five years at the latest following the date specified in Article 12, the Commission shall report to the European Parliament and the Council on the state of application of the general system for the recognition of higher-education diplomas awarded on completion of professional education and training of at least three years' duration.

After conducting all necessary consultations, the Commission shall, on this occasion, present its conclusions as to any changes that need to be made to the system as it stands. At the same time the Commission shall, where appropriate, submit proposals for improvements in the present system in the interest of further facilitating the freedom of movement, right of establishment and freedom to provide services of the persons covered by this Directive.

Article 14

This Directive is addressed to the Member States.

23. COUNCIL RECOMMENDATION 89/49/EEC

of 21 December 1988

concerning nationals of Member States who hold a diploma conferred in a third State

O.J. L 19/24 (Jan. 24, 1989)

THE COUNCIL OF THE EUROPEAN COMMUNITIES,

Approving Council Directive 89/48/EEC of 21 December 1988 on a general system for the recognition of higher-education diplomas awarded on completion of professional education and training of at least three years' duration;

Noting that this Directive refers only to diplomas, certificates and other evidence of formal qualifications awarded in Member States to nationals of Member States;

Anxious, however, to take account of the special position of nationals of Member States who hold diplomas, certificates or other evidence of formal qualifications awarded in third States and who are thus in a position comparable to one of those described in Article 3 of the Directive,

HEREBY RECOMMENDS:

that the Governments of the Member States should allow the persons referred to above to take up and pursue regulated professions within the Community by recognizing these diplomas, certificates and other evidence of formal qualifications in their territories.

24. COUNCIL DIRECTIVE 77/249/EEC

of 22 March 1977

to facilitate the effective exercise by lawyers of freedom to provide services

O.J. L 78/17 (Mar. 26, 1977)

THE COUNCIL OF THE EUROPEAN COMMUNITIES,

Having regard to the Treaty establishing the European Economic Community, and in particular Articles 57 and 66 thereof,

Having regard to the proposal from the Commission,

Having regard to the opinion of the European Parliament,

Having regard to the opinion of the Economic and Social Committee,

Whereas, pursuant to the Treaty, any restriction on the provision of services which is based on nationality or on conditions of residence has been prohibited since the end of the transitional period;

Whereas this Directive deals only with measures to facilitate the effective pursuit of the activities of lawyers by way of provision of services; whereas more detailed measures will be necessary to facilitate the effective exercise of the right of establishment;

Whereas if lawyers are to exercise effectively the freedom to provide services host Member States must recognize as lawyers those persons practising the profession in the various Member States;

Whereas, since this Directive solely concerns provision of services and does not contain provisions on the mutual recognition of diplomas, a person to whom the Directive applies must adopt the professional title used in the Member State in which he is established, hereinafter referred to as 'the Member State from which he comes',

HAS ADOPTED THIS DIRECTIVE:

Article 1

1. This Directive shall apply, within the limits and under the conditions laid down herein, to the activities of lawyers pursued by way of provision of services.

Notwithstanding anything contained in this Directive, Member States may reserve to prescribed categories of lawyers the preparation of formal documents for obtaining title to administer estates of deceased persons, and the drafting of formal documents creating or transferring interests in land.

2. 'Lawyer' means any person entitled to pursue his professional activities under one of the following designations:

Belgium:	Avocat—Advocaat
Denmark:	Advokat
Germany:	Rechtsanwalt
France:	Avocat

Ireland:	Barrister
	Solicitor
Italy:	Avvocato
Luxembourg:	Avocat-avoué
Netherlands:	Advocaat
United Kingdom:	Advocate
	Barrister
	Solicitor.

Article 2

Each Member State shall recognize as a lawyer for the purpose of pursuing the activities specified in Article 1(1) any person listed in paragraph 2 of that Article.

Article 3

A person referred to in Article 1 shall adopt the professional title used in the Member State from which he comes, expressed in the language or one of the languages, of that State, with an indication of the professional organization by which he is authorized to practise or the court of law before which he is entitled to practise pursuant to the laws of that State.

Article 4

1. Activities relating to the representation of a client in legal proceedings or before public authorities shall be pursued in each host Member State under the conditions laid down for lawyers established in that State, with the exception of any conditions requiring residence, or registration with a professional organization, in that State.

2. A lawyer pursuing these activities shall observe the rules of professional conduct of the host Member State, without prejudice to his obligations in the Member State from which he comes.

3. When these activities are pursued in the United Kingdom, 'rules of professional conduct of the host Member State' means the rules of professional conduct applicable to solicitors, where such activities are not reserved for barristers and advocates. Otherwise the rules of professional conduct applicable to the latter shall apply. However, barristers from Ireland shall always be subject to the rules of professional conduct applicable in the United Kingdom to barristers and advocates.

When these activities are pursued in Ireland 'rules of professional conduct of the host Member State' means, in so far as they govern the oral presentation of a case in court, the rules of professional conduct applicable to barristers. In all other cases the rules of professional conduct applicable to solicitors shall apply. However, barristers and advocates from the United Kingdom shall always be subject to the rules of professional conduct applicable in Ireland to barristers.

4. A lawyer pursuing activities other than those referred to in paragraph 1 shall remain subject to the conditions and rules of professional conduct of the Member State from which he comes without prejudice to

respect for the rules, whatever their source, which govern the profession in the host Member State, especially those concerning the incompatibility of the exercise of the activities of a lawyer with the exercise of other activities in that State, professional secrecy, relations with other lawyers, the prohibition on the same lawyer acting for parties with mutually conflicting interests, and publicity. The latter rules are applicable only if they are capable of being observed by a lawyer who is not established in the host Member State and to the extent to which their observance is objectively justified to ensure, in that State, the proper exercise of a lawyer's activities, the standing of the profession and respect for the rules concerning incompatibility.

Article 5

For the pursuit of activities relating to the representation of a client in legal proceedings, a Member State may require lawyers to whom Article 1 applies:

—to be introduced, in accordance with local rules or customs, to the presiding judge and, where appropriate, to the President of the relevant Bar in the host Member State;

—to work in conjunction with a lawyer who practises before the judicial authority in question and who would, where necessary, be answerable to that authority, or with an 'avoué' or 'procuratore' practising before it.

Article 6

Any Member State may exclude lawyers who are in the salaried employment of a public or private undertaking from pursuing activities relating to the representation of that undertaking in legal proceedings in so far as lawyers established in that State are not permitted to pursue those activities.

Article 7

1. The competent authority of the host Member State may request the person providing the services to establish his qualifications as a lawyer.

2. In the event of non-compliance with the obligations referred to in Article 4 and in force in the host Member State, the competent authority of the latter shall determine in accordance with its own rules and procedures the consequences of such non-compliance, and to this end may obtain any appropriate professional information concerning the person providing services. It shall notify the competent authority of the Member State from which the person comes of any decision taken. Such exchanges shall not affect the confidential nature of the information supplied.

* * *

Article 9

This Directive is addressed to the Member States.

25. DIRECTIVE 98/5/EC OF THE EUROPEAN PARLIAMENT AND OF THE COUNCIL

of 16 February 1998

to facilitate practice of the profession of lawyer on a permanent basis in a Member State other than that in which the qualification was obtained

O.J. L 77/36 (March 14, 1998)

THE EUROPEAN PARLIAMENT AND THE COUNCIL OF THE EUROPEAN UNION,

Having regard to the Treaty establishing the European Community, and in particular Article 49, Article 57(1) and the first and third sentences of Article 57(2) thereof,

Having regard to the proposal from the Commission,

Having regard to the Opinion of the Economic and Social Committee,

Acting in accordance with the procedure laid down in Article 189b of the Treaty,

(1) Whereas, pursuant to Article 7a of the Treaty, the internal market is to comprise an area without internal frontiers; whereas, pursuant to Article 3(c) of the Treaty, the abolition, as between Member States, of obstacles to freedom of movement for persons and services constitutes one of the objectives of the Community; whereas, for nationals of the Member States, this means among other things the possibility of practising a profession, whether in a self-employed or a salaried capacity, in a Member State other than that in which they obtained their professional qualifications;

(2) Whereas, pursuant to Council Directive 89/48/EEC of 21 December 1988 on a general system for the recognition of higher-education diplomas awarded on completion of professional education and training of at least three years' duration, a lawyer who is fully qualified in one Member State may already ask to have his diploma recognised with a view to establishing himself in another Member State in order to practise the profession of lawyer there under the professional title used in that State; whereas the objective of Directive 89/48/EEC is to ensure that a lawyer is integrated into the profession in the host Member State, and the Directive seeks neither to modify the rules regulating the profession in that State nor to remove such a lawyer from the ambit of those rules;

(3) Whereas while some lawyers may become quickly integrated into the profession in the host Member State, *inter alia* by passing an aptitude test as provided for in Directive 89/48/EEC, other fully qualified lawyers should be able to achieve such integration after a certain period of professional practice in the host Member State under their home-country professional titles or else continue to practise under their home-country professional titles;

(4) Whereas at the end of that period the lawyer should be able to integrate into the profession in the host Member States after verification that he possesses professional experience in that Member State;

(5) Whereas action along these lines is justified at Community level not only because, compared with the general system for the recognition of diplomas, it provides lawyers with an easier means whereby they can integrate into the profession in a host Member State, but also because, by enabling lawyers to practise under their home-country professional titles on a permanent basis in a host Member State, it meets the needs of consumers of legal services who, owing to the increasing trade flows resulting, in particular, from the internal market, seek advice when carrying out cross-border transactions in which international law, Community law and domestic laws often overlap;

(6) Whereas action is also justified at Community level because only a few Member States already permit in their territory the pursuit of activities of lawyers, otherwise than by way of provision of services, by lawyers from other Member States practising under their home-country professional titles; whereas, however, in the Member States where this possibility exists, the practical details concerning, for example, the area of activity and the obligation to register with the competent authorities differ considerably; whereas such a diversity of situations leads to inequalities and distortions in competition between lawyers from the Member States and constitutes an obstacle to freedom of movement; whereas only a directive laying down the conditions governing practice of the profession, otherwise than by way of provision of services, by lawyers practising under their home-country professional titles is capable of resolving these difficulties and of affording the same opportunities to lawyers and consumers of legal services in all Member States;

(7) Whereas, in keeping with its objective, this Directive does not lay down any rules concerning purely domestic situations, and where it does affect national rules regulating the legal profession it does so no more than is necessary to achieve its purpose effectively; whereas it is without prejudice in particular to national legislation governing access to and practice of the profession of lawyer under the professional title used in the host Member State;

(8) Whereas lawyers covered by the Directive should be required to register with the competent authority in the host Member State in order that that authority may ensure that they comply with the rules of professional conduct in force in that State; whereas the effect of such registration as regards the jurisdictions in which, and the levels and types of court before which, lawyers may practise is determined by the law applicable to lawyers in the host Member State;

(9) Whereas lawyers who are not integrated into the profession in the host Member State should practise in that State under their home-country professional titles so as to ensure that consumers are properly

informed and to distinguish between such lawyers and lawyers from the host Member State practising under the professional title used there;

(10) Whereas lawyers covered by this Directive should be permitted to give legal advice in particular on the law of their home Member States, on Community law, on international law and on the law of the host Member State; whereas this is already allowed as regards the provision of services under Council Directive 77/249/EEC of 22 March 1977 to facilitate the effective exercise by lawyers of freedom to provide services; whereas, however, provision should be made, as in Directive 77/249/EEC, for the option of excluding from the activities of lawyers practising under their home-country professional titles in the United Kingdom and Ireland the preparation of certain formal documents in the conveyancing and probate spheres; whereas this Directive in no way affects the provisions under which, in every Member State, certain activities are reserved for professions other than the legal profession; whereas the provision in Directive 77/249/EEC concerning the possibility of the host Member State to require a lawyer practising under his home-country professional title to work in conjunction with a local lawyer when representing or defending a client in legal proceedings should also be incorporated in this Directive; whereas that requirement must be interpreted in the light of the case law of the Court of Justice of the European Communities, in particular its judgment of 25 February 1988 in Case 427/85, Commission v. Germany;

(11) Whereas to ensure the smooth operation of the justice system Member States should be allowed, by means of specific rules, to reserve access to their highest courts to specialist lawyers, without hindering the integration of Member States' lawyers fulfilling the necessary requirements;

(12) Whereas a lawyer registered under his home-country professional title in the host Member State must remain registered with the competent authority in his home Member State if he is to retain his status of lawyer and be covered by this Directive; whereas for that reason close collaboration between the competent authorities is indispensable, in particular in connection with any disciplinary proceedings;

(13) Whereas lawyers covered by this Directive, whether salaried or self-employed in their home Member States, may practise as salaried lawyers in the host Member State, where that Member State offers that possibility to its own lawyers;

(14) Whereas the purpose pursued by this Directive in enabling lawyers to practise in another Member State under their home-country professional titles is also to make it easier for them to obtain the professional title of that host Member State; whereas under Articles 48 and 52 of the Treaty as interpreted by the Court of Justice the host Member State must take into consideration any professional experience gained in its territory; whereas after effectively and regularly pursuing in the host Member State an activity in the law of that State

including Community law for a period of three years, a lawyer may reasonably be assumed to have gained the aptitude necessary to become fully integrated into the legal profession there; whereas at the end of that period the lawyer who can, subject to verification, furnish evidence of his professional competence in the host Member State should be able to obtain the professional title of that Member State; whereas if the period of effective and regular professional activity of at least three years includes a shorter period of practice in the law of the host Member State, the authority shall also take into consideration any other knowledge of that State's law, which it may verify during an interview; whereas if evidence of fulfilment of these conditions is not provided, the decision taken by the competent authority of the host State not to grant the State's professional title under the facilitation arrangements linked to those conditions must be substantiated and subject to appeal under national law;

(15) Whereas, for economic and professional reasons, the growing tendency for lawyers in the Community to practise jointly, including in the form of associations, has become a reality; whereas the fact that lawyers belong to a grouping in their home Member State should not be used as a pretext to prevent or deter them from establishing themselves in the host Member State; whereas Member States should be allowed, however, to take appropriate measures with the legitimate aim of safe-guarding the profession's independence; whereas certain guarantees should be provided in those Member States which permit joint practice,

HAVE ADOPTED THIS DIRECTIVE:

Article 1

Object, scope and definitions

1. The purpose of this Directive is to facilitate practice of the profession of lawyer on a permanent basis in a self-employed or salaried capacity in a Member State other than that in which the professional qualification was obtained.

2. For the purposes of this Directive:

(a) *'lawyer'* means any person who is a national of a Member State and who is authorised to pursue his professional activities under one of the following professional titles:

Belgium	Avocat/Advocaat/Rechtsanwalt
Denmark	Advokat
Germany	Rechtsanwalt
Greece	Δικηγόρος
Spain	Abogado/Advocat/Avogado/Abokatu

France	Avocat
Ireland	Barrister/Solicitor
Italy	Avvocato
Luxembourg	Avocat
Netherlands	Advocaat
Austria	Rechtsanwalt
Portugal	Advogado
Finland	Asianajaja/Advokat
Sweden	Advokat
United Kingdom	Advocate/Barrister/Solicitor

(b) *'home Member State'* means the Member State in which a lawyer acquired the right to use one of the professional titles referred to in (a) before practising the profession of lawyer in another Member State;

(c) *'host Member State'* means the Member State in which a lawyer practises pursuant to this Directive;

(d) *'home-country professional title'* means the professional title used in the Member State in which a lawyer acquired the right to use that title before practising the profession of lawyer in the host Member State;

(e) *'grouping'* means any entity, with or without legal personality, formed under the law of a Member State, within which lawyers pursue their professional activities jointly under a joint name;

(f) *'relevant professional title'* or *'relevant profession'* means the professional title or profession governed by the competent authority with whom a lawyer has registered under Article 3, and *'competent authority'* means that authority.

3. This Directive shall apply both to lawyers practising in a self-employed capacity and to lawyers practising in a salarial capacity in the home Member State and, subject to Article 8, in the host Member State.

4. Practice of the profession of lawyer within the meaning of this Directive shall not include the provision of services, which is covered by Directive 77/249/EEC.

Article 2

Right to practise under the home-country professional title

Any lawyer shall be entitled to pursue on a permanent basis, in any other Member State under his home-country professional title, the activities specified in Article 5.

Integration into the profession of lawyer in the host Member State shall be subject to Article 10.

Article 3

Registration with the competent authority

1. A lawyer who wishes to practise in a Member State other than that in which he obtained his professional qualification shall register with the competent authority in that State.

2. The competent authority in the host Member State shall register the lawyer upon presentation of a certificate attesting to his registration with the competent authority in the home Member State. It may require that, when presented by the competent authority of the home Member State, the certificate be not more than three months old. It shall inform the competent authority in the home Member State of the registration.

3. For the purpose of applying paragraph 1:

— in the United Kingdom and Ireland, lawyers practising under a professional title other than those used in the United Kingdom or Ireland shall register either with the authority responsible for the profession of barrister or advocate or with the authority responsible for the profession of solicitor,

— in the United Kingdom, the authority responsible for a barrister from Ireland shall be that responsible for the profession of barrister or advocate, and the authority responsible for a solicitor from Ireland shall be that responsible for the profession of solicitor,

— in Ireland, the authority responsible for a barrister or an advocate from the United Kingdom shall be that responsible for the profession of barrister, and the authority responsible for a solicitor from the United Kingdom shall be that responsible for the profession of solicitor.

4. Where the relevant competent authority in a host Member State publishes the names of lawyers registered with it, it shall also publish the names of lawyers registered pursuant to this Directive.

Article 4

Practice under the home-country professional title

1. A lawyer practising in a host Member State under his home-country professional title shall do so under that title, which must be expressed in the official language or one of the official languages of his

home Member State, in an intelligible manner and in such a way as to avoid confusion with the professional title of the host Member State.

2. For the purpose of applying paragraph 1, a host Member State may require a lawyer practising under his home-country professional title to indicate the professional body of which he is a member in his home Member State or the judicial authority before which he is entitled to practise pursuant to the laws of his home Member State. A host Member State may also require a lawyer practising under his home-country professional title to include a reference to his registration with the competent authority in that State.

Article 5

Area of activity

1. Subject to paragraphs 2 and 3, a lawyer practising under his home-country professional title carries on the same professional activities as a lawyer practising under the relevant professional title used in the host Member State and may, *inter alia*, give advice on the law of his home Member State, on Community law, on international law and on the law of the host Member State. He shall in any event comply with the rules of procedure applicable in the national courts.

2. Member States which authorise in their territory a prescribed category of lawyers to prepare deeds for obtaining title to administer estates of deceased persons and for creating or transferring interests in land which, in other Member States, are reserved for professions other than that of lawyer may exclude from such activities lawyers practising under a home-country professional title conferred in one of the latter Member States.

3. For the pursuit of activities relating to the representation or defence of a client in legal proceedings and insofar as the law of the host Member State reserves such activities to lawyers practising under the professional title of that State, the latter may require lawyers practising under their home-country professional titles to work in conjunction with a lawyer who practises before the judicial authority in question and who would, where necessary, be answerable to that authority or with an 'avoue' practising before it.

Nevertheless, in order to ensure the smooth operation of the justice system, Member States may lay down specific rules for access to supreme courts, such as the use of specialist lawyers.

Article 6

Rules of professional conduct applicable

1. Irrespective of the rules of professional conduct to which he is subject in his home Member State, a lawyer practising under his home-country professional title shall be subject to the same rules of professional

conduct as lawyers practising under the relevant professional title of the host Member State in respect of all the activities he pursues in its territory.

2. Lawyers practising under their home-country professional titles shall be granted appropriate representation in the professional associations of the host Member State. Such representation shall involve at least the right to vote in elections to those associations' governing bodies.

3. The host Member State may require a lawyer practising under his home-country professional title either to take out professional indemnity insurance or to become a member of a professional guarantee fund in accordance with the rules which that State lays down for professional activities pursued in its territory. Nevertheless, a lawyer practising under his home-country professional title shall be exempted from that requirement if he can prove that he is covered by insurance taken out or a guarantee provided in accordance with the rules of his home Member State, insofar as such insurance or guarantee is equivalent in terms of the conditions and extent of cover. Where the equivalence is only partial, the competent authority in the host Member State may require that additional insurance or an additional guarantee be contracted to cover the elements which are not already covered by the insurance or guarantee contracted in accordance with the rules of the home Member State.

Article 7

Disciplinary proceedings

1. In the event of failure by a lawyer practising under his home-country professional title to fulfil the obligations in force in the host Member State, the rules of procedure, penalties and remedies provided for in the host Member State shall apply.

2. Before initiating disciplinary proceedings against a lawyer practising under his home-country professional title, the competent authority in the host Member State shall inform the competent authority in the home Member State as soon as possible, furnishing it with all the relevant details.

The first subparagraph shall apply *mutatis mutandis* where disciplinary proceedings are initiated by the competent authority of the home Member State, which shall inform the competent authority of the host Member State(s) accordingly.

3. Without prejudice to the decision-making power of the competent authority in the host Member State, that authority shall cooperate throughout the disciplinary proceedings with the competent authority in the home Member State. In particular, the host Member State shall take the measures necessary to ensure that the competent authority in the home Member State can make submissions to the bodies responsible for hearing any appeal.

4. The competent authority in the home Member State shall decide what action to take, under its own procedural and substantive rules, in the

light of a decision of the competent authority in the host Member State concerning a lawyer practising under his home-country professional title.

5. Although it is not a prerequisite for the decision of the competent authority in the host Member State, the temporary or permanent withdrawal by the competent authority in the home Member State of the authorisation to practise the profession shall automatically lead to the lawyer concerned being temporarily or permanently prohibited from practising under his home-country professional title in the host Member State.

Article 8

Salaried practice

A lawyer registered in a host Member State under his home-country professional title may practise as a salaried lawyer in the employ of another lawyer, an association or firm of lawyers, or a public or private enterprise to the extent that the host Member State so permits for lawyers registered under the professional title used in that State.

Article 9

Statement of reasons and remedies

Decisions not to effect the registration referred to in Article 3 or to cancel such registration and decisions imposing disciplinary measures shall state the reasons on which they are based.

A remedy shall be available against such decisions before a court or tribunal in accordance with the provisions of domestic law.

Article 10

Like treatment as a lawyer of the host Member State

1. A lawyer practising under his home-country professional title who has effectively and regularly pursued for a period of at least three years an activity in the host Member State in the law of that State including Community law shall, with a view to gaining admission to the profession of lawyer in the host Member State, be exempted from the conditions set out in Article 4(1)(b) of Directive 89/48/EEC, *'Effective and regular pursuit'* means actual exercise of the activity without any interruption other than that resulting from the events of everyday life.

It shall be for the lawyer concerned to furnish the competent authority in the host Member State with proof of such effective regular pursuit for a period of at least three years of an activity in the law of the host Member State. To that end:

(a) the lawyer shall provide the competent authority in the host Member State with any relevant information and documentation, notably on the number of matters he has dealt with and their nature;

(b) the competent authority of the host Member State may verify the effective and regular nature of the activity pursued and may, if need be, request the lawyer to provide, orally or in writing, clarification of or further details on the information and documentation mentioned in point (a).

Reasons shall be given for a decision by the competent authority in the host Member State not to grant an exemption where proof is not provided that the requirements laid down in the first subparagraph have been fulfilled, and the decision shall be subject to appeal under domestic law.

2. A lawyer practising under his home-country professional title in a host Member State may, at any time, apply to have his diploma recognised in accordance with Directive 89/48/EEC with a view to gaining admission to the profession of lawyer in the host Member State and practising it under the professional title corresponding to the profession in that Member State.

3. A lawyer practising under his home-country professional title who has effectively and regularly pursued a professional activity in the host Member State for a period of at least three years but for a lesser period in the law of that Member State may obtain from the competent authority of that State admission to the profession of lawyer in the host Member State and the right to practise it under the professional title corresponding to the profession in that Member State, without having to meet the conditions referred to in Article 4(1)(b) of Directive 89/48/EEC, under the conditions and in accordance with the procedures set out below:

(a) The competent authority of the host Member State shall take into account the effective and regular professional activity pursued during the abovementioned period and any knowledge and professional experience of the law of the host Member State, and any attendance at lectures or seminars on the law of the host Member State, including the rules regulating professional practice and conduct.

(b) The lawyer shall provide the competent authority of the host Member State with any relevant information and documentation, in particular on the matters he has dealt with. Assessment of the lawyer's effective and regular activity in the host Member State and assessment of his capacity to continue the activity he has pursued there shall be carried out by means of an interview with the competent authority of the host Member State in order to verify the regular and effective nature of the activity pursued.

Reasons shall be given for a decision by the competent authority in the host Member State not to grant authorisation where proof is not provided that the requirements laid down in the first subparagraph have been fulfilled, and the decision shall be subject to appeal under domestic law.

4. The competent authority of the host Member State may, by reasoned decision subject to appeal under domestic law, refuse to allow the lawyer the benefit of the provisions of this Article if it considers that this would be against public policy, in particular because of disciplinary proceedings, complaints or incidents of any kind.

5. The representatives of the competent authority entrusted with consideration of the application shall preserve the confidentiality of any information received.

6. A lawyer who gains admission to the profession of lawyer in the host Member State in accordance with paragraphs 1, 2 and 3 shall be entitled to use his home-country professional title, expressed in the official language or one of the official languages of his home Member State, alongside the professional title corresponding to the profession of lawyer in the host Member State.

Article 11

Joint practice

Where joint practise is authorised in respect of lawyers carrying on their activities under the relevant professional title in the host Member State, the following provisions shall apply in respect of lawyers wishing to carry on activities under that title or registering with the competent authority:

(1) One or more lawyers who belong to the same grouping in their home Member State and who practise under their home-country professional title in a host Member State may pursue their professional activities in a branch or agency of their grouping in the host Member State. However, where the fundamental rules governing that grouping in the home Member State are incompatible with the fundamental rules laid down by law, regulation or administrative action in the host Member State, the latter rules shall prevail insofar as compliance therewith is justified by the public interest in protecting clients and third parties.

(2) Each Member State shall afford two or more lawyers from the same grouping or the same home Member State who practise in its territory under their home-country professional titles access to a form of joint practice. If the host Member State gives its lawyers a choice between several forms of joint practice, those same forms shall also be made available to the aforementioned lawyers. The manner in which such lawyers practise jointly in the host Member State shall be governed by the laws, regulations and administrative provisions of that State.

(3) The host Member State shall take the measures necessary to permit joint practice also between:

(a) several lawyers from different Member States practising under their home-country professional titles;

(b) one or more lawyers covered by point (a) and one or more lawyers from the host Member State.

The manner in which such lawyers practice jointly in the host Member State shall be governed by the laws, regulations and administrative provisions of that State.

(4) A lawyer who wishes to practise under his home-country professional title shall inform the competent authority in the host Member State of the fact that he is a member of a grouping in his home Member State and furnish any relevant information on that grouping.

(5) Notwithstanding points 1 to 4, a host Member State, insofar as it prohibits lawyers practising under its own relevant professional title from practising the profession of lawyer within a grouping in which some persons are not members of the profession, may refuse to allow a lawyer registered under his home-country professional title to practice in its territory in his capacity as a member of his grouping. The grouping is deemed to include persons who are not members of the profession if

— the capital of the grouping is held entirely or partly, or

— the name under which it practises is used, or

— the decision-making power in that grouping is exercised, *de facto* or *de jure*,

by persons who do not have the status of lawyer within the meaning of Article 1(2).

Where the fundamental rules governing a grouping of lawyers in the home Member State are incompatible with the rules in force in the host Member State or with the provisions of the first subparagraph, the host Member State may oppose the opening of a branch or agency within its territory without the restrictions laid down in point (1).

Article 12

Name of the grouping

Whatever the manner in which lawyers practise under their home-country professional titles in the host Member State, they may employ the name of any grouping to which they belong in their home Member State.

The host Member State may require that, in addition to the name referred to in the first subparagraph, mention be made of the legal form of the grouping in the home Member State and/or of the names of any members of the grouping practising in the host Member State.

Article 13

Cooperation between the competent authorities in the home and host Member States and confidentiality

In order to facilitate the application of this Directive and to prevent its provisions from being misapplied for the sole purpose of circumventing the rules applicable in the host Member State, the competent authority in the host Member State and the competent authority in the home Member State shall collaborate closely and afford each other mutual assistance.

They shall preserve the confidentiality of the information they exchange.

Article 14

Designation of the competent authorities

Member States shall designate the competent authorities empowered to receive the applications and to take the decisions referred to in this Directive by 14 March 2000. They shall communicate this information to the other Member States and to the Commission.

Article 15

Report by the Commission

Ten years at the latest from the entry into force of this Directive, the Commission shall report to the European Parliament and to the Council on progress in the implementation of the Directive.

After having held all the necessary consultations, it shall on that occasion present its conclusions and any amendments which could be made to the existing system.

Article 16

Implementation

1. Member States shall bring into force the laws, regulations and administrative provisions necessary to comply with this Directive by 14 March 2000. They shall forthwith inform the Commission thereof.

26. COUNCIL DIRECTIVE 89/104/EEC

of 21 December 1988

to approximate the laws of the Member States relating to trade marks

O.J. L 40/1 (Feb. 11, 1989)

THE COUNCIL OF THE EUROPEAN COMMUNITIES,

Having regard to the Treaty establishing the European Economic Community, and in particular Article 100a thereof,

Having regard to the proposal from the Commission[1],

In cooperation with the European Parliament[2],

Having regard to the opinion of the Economic and Social Committee[3],

Whereas the trade mark laws at present applicable in the Member States contain disparities which may impede the free movement of goods and freedom to provide services and may distort competition within the common market; whereas it is therefore necessary, in view of the establishment and functioning of the internal market, to approximate the laws of Member States;

Whereas it is important not to disregard the solutions and advantages which the Community trade mark system may afford to undertakings wishing to acquire trade marks;

Whereas it does not appear to be necessary at present to undertake full-scale approximation of the trade mark laws of the Member States and it will be sufficient if approximation is limited to those national provisions of law which most directly affect the functioning of the internal market;

Whereas the Directive does not deprive the Member States of the right to continue to protect trade marks acquired through use but takes them into account only in regard to the relationship between them and trade marks acquired by registration;

Whereas Member States also remain free to fix the provisions of procedure concerning the registration, the revocation and the invalidity of trade marks acquired by registration; whereas they can, for example, determine the form of trade mark registration and invalidity procedures, decide whether earlier rights should be invoked either in the registration procedure or in the invalidity procedure or in both and, if they allow earlier rights to be invoked in the registration procedure, have an opposition procedure or an *ex officio* examination procedure or both; whereas Member States remain free to determine the effects of revocation or invalidity of trade marks;

1. OJ No. C 351, 31.12.1980, p. 1 and OJ No. C 351, 31.12.1985, p. 4.
2. OJ No. C 307, 14.11.1983, p. 66 and OJ No C 309, 5.12.1988.
3. OJ No. C 310, 30.11.1981, p. 22.

Whereas this Directive does not exclude the application to trade marks of provisions of law of the Member States other than trade mark law, such as the provisions relating to unfair competition, civil liability or consumer protection;

Whereas attainment of the objectives at which this approximation of laws is aiming requires that the conditions for obtaining and continuing to hold a registered trade mark are, in general, identical in all Member States; whereas, to this end, it is necessary to list examples of signs which may constitute a trade mark, provided that such signs are capable of distinguishing the goods or services of one undertaking from those of other undertakings; whereas the grounds for refusal or invalidity concerning the trade mark itself, for example, the absence of any distinctive character, or concerning conflicts between the trade mark and earlier rights, are to be listed in an exhaustive manner, even if some of these grounds are listed as an option for the Member States which will therefore be able to maintain or introduce those grounds in their legislation; whereas Member States will be able to maintain or introduce into their legislation grounds of refusal or invalidity linked to conditions for obtaining and continuing to hold a trade mark for which there is no provision of approximation, concerning, for example, the eligibility for the grant of a trade mark, the renewal of the trade mark or rules on fees, or related to the non-compliance with procedural rules;

Whereas in order to reduce the total number of trade marks registered and protected in the Community and, consequently, the number of conflicts which arise between them, it is essential to require that registered trade marks must actually be used or, if not used, be subject to revocation; whereas it is necessary to provide that a trade mark cannot be invalidated on the basis of the existence of a non-used earlier trade mark, while the Member States remain free to apply the same principle in respect of the registration of a trade mark or to provide that a trade mark may not be successfully invoked in infringement proceedings if it is established as a result of a plea that the trade mark could be revoked; whereas in all these cases it is up to the Member States to establish the applicable rules of procedure;

Whereas it is fundamental, in order to facilitate the free circulation of goods and services, to ensure that henceforth registered trade marks enjoy the same protection under the legal systems of all the Member States; whereas this should however not prevent the Member States from granting at their option extensive protection to those trade marks which have a reputation;

Whereas the protection afforded by the registered trade mark, the function of which is in particular to guarantee the trade mark as an indication of origin, is absolute in the case of identity between the mark and the sign and goods or services; whereas the protection applies also in case of similarity between the mark and the sign and the goods or services; whereas it is indispensable to give an interpretation of the concept of similarity in relation to the likelihood of confusion; whereas the likelihood of confusion, the appreciation of which depends on numerous elements and, in particular, on the recognition of the trade mark on the market, of the association which can be made with the used or registered sign, of the degree of similarity between the trade mark and the sign and between the goods or services identified, constitutes the specific condition for such protection; whereas the ways in which likelihood of confusion may be established, and in particular the onus of proof, are a matter for national procedural rules which are not prejudiced by the Directive;

Whereas it is important, for reasons of legal certainty and without inequitably prejudicing the interests of a proprietor of an earlier trade mark, to provide that the latter may no longer request a declaration of invalidity nor may he oppose the use of a trade mark subsequent to his own of which he has knowingly tolerated the use for a substantial length of time, unless the application for the subsequent trade mark was made in bad faith;

Whereas all Member States of the Community are bound by the Paris Convention for the Protection of Industrial Property; whereas it is necessary that the provisions of this Directive are entirely consistent with those of the Paris Convention; whereas the obligations of the Member States resulting from this Convention are not affected by this Directive; whereas, where appropriate, the second subparagraph of Article 234 of the Treaty is applicable,

HAS ADOPTED THIS DIRECTIVE:

Article 1

Scope

This Directive shall apply to every trade mark in respect of goods or services which is the subject of registration or of an application in a Member State for registration as an individual trade mark, a collective mark or a guarantee or certification mark, or which is the subject of a registration or an application for registration in the Benelux Trade Mark Office or of an international registration having effect in a Member State.

Article 2

Signs of which a trade mark may consist

A trade mark may consist of any sign capable of being represented graphically, particularly words, including personal names, designs, letters, numerals, the shape of goods or of their packaging, provided that such signs are capable of distinguishing the goods or services of one undertaking from those of other undertakings.

Article 3

Grounds for refusal or invalidity

1. The following shall not be registered or if registered shall be liable to be declared invalid:

(a) signs which cannot constitute a trade mark;

(b) trade marks which are devoid of any distinctive character;

(c) trade marks which consist exclusively of signs or indications which may serve, in trade, to designate the kind, quality, quantity, intended purpose, value, geographical origin, or the time of production of the goods or of rendering of the service, or other characteristics of the goods or service;

(d) trade marks which consist exclusively of signs or indications which have become customary in the current language or in the *bona fide* and established practices of the trade;

(e) signs which consist exclusively of:

—the shape which results from the nature of the goods themselves, or

—the shape of goods which is necessary to obtain a technical result, or

—the shape which gives substantial value to the goods;

(f) trade marks which are contrary to public policy or to accepted principles of morality;

(g) trade marks which are of such a nature as to deceive the public, for instance as to the nature, quality or geographical origin of the goods or service;

(h) trade marks which have not been authorized by the competent authorities and are to be refused or invalidated pursuant to Article 6 *ter* of the Paris Convention for the Protection of Industrial Property, hereinafter referred to as the 'Paris Convention'.

2. Any Member State may provide that a trade mark shall not be registered or, if registered, shall be liable to be declared invalid where and to the extent that:

(a) the use of that trade mark may be prohibited pursuant to provisions of law other than trade mark law of the Member State concerned or of the Community;

(b) the trade mark covers a sign of high symbolic value, in particular a religious symbol;

(c) the trade mark includes badges, emblems and escutcheons other than those covered by Article 6 *ter* of the Paris Convention and which are of public interest, unless the consent of the appropriate authorities to its registration has been given in conformity with the legislation of the Member State;

(d) the application for registration of the trade mark was made in bad faith by the applicant.

3. A trade mark shall not be refused registration or be declared invalid in accordance with paragraph 1(b), (c) or (d) if, before the date of application for registration and following the use which has been made of it, it has acquired a distinctive character. Any Member State may in addition provide that this provision shall also apply where the distinctive

character was acquired after the date of application for registration or after the date of registration.

4. Any Member State may provide that, by derogation from the preceding paragraphs, the grounds of refusal of registration or invalidity in force in that State prior to the date on which the provisions necessary to comply with this Directive enter into force, shall apply to trade marks for which application has been made prior to that date.

Article 4

Further grounds for refusal or invalidity concerning conflicts with earlier rights

1. A trade mark shall not be registered or, if registered, shall be liable to be declared invalid:

(a) if it is identical with an earlier trade mark, and the goods or services for which the trade mark is applied for or is registered are identical with the goods or services for which the earlier trade mark is protected;

(b) if because of its identity with, or similarity to, the earlier trade mark and the identity or similarity of the goods or services covered by the trade marks, there exists a likelihood of confusion on the part of the public, which includes the likelihood of association with the earlier trade mark.

2. 'Earlier trade marks' within the meaning of paragraph 1 means:

(a) trade marks of the following kinds with a date of application for registration which is earlier than the date of application for registration of the trade mark, taking account, where appropriate, of the priorities claimed in respect of those trade marks:

(i) Community trade marks;
(ii) trade marks registered in the Member State or, in the case of Belgium, Luxembourg or the Netherlands, at the Benelux Trade Mark Office;
(iii) trade marks registered under international arrangements which have effect in the Member State;

(b) Community trade marks which validly claim seniority, in accordance with the Regulation on the Community trade mark, from a trade mark referred to in (a)(ii) and (iii), even when the latter trade mark has been surrendered or allowed to lapse;

(c) applications for the trade marks referred to in (a) and (b), subject to their registration;

(d) trade marks which, on the date of application for registration of the trade mark, or, where appropriate, of the priority claimed in respect of the application for registration of the trade mark, are well known in a Member State, in the sense in which the words 'well known' are used in Article 6 *bis* of the Paris Convention;

3. A trade mark shall furthermore not be registered or, if registered, shall be liable to be declared invalid if it is identical with, or similar to, an earlier Community trade mark within the meaning of paragraph 2 and is to be, or has been, registered for goods or services which are not similar to those for which the earlier Community trade mark is registered, where the earlier Community trade mark has a reputation in the Community and where the use of the later trade mark without due cause would take unfair advantage of, or be detrimental to, the distinctive character or the repute of the earlier Community trade mark.

4. Any Member State may furthermore provide that a trade mark shall not be registered or, if registered, shall be liable to be declared invalid where, and to the extent that:

(a) the trade mark is identical with, or similar to, an earlier national trade mark within the meaning of paragraph 2 and is to be, or has been, registered for goods or services which are not similar to those for which the earlier trade mark is registered, where the earlier trade mark has a reputation in the Member State concerned and where the use of the later trade mark without due cause would take unfair advantage of, or be detrimental to, the distinctive character or the repute of the earlier trade mark;

(b) rights to a non-registered trade mark or to another sign used in the course of trade were acquired prior to the date of application for registration of the subsequent trade mark, or the date of the priority claimed for the application for registration of the subsequent trade mark and that non-registered trade mark or other sign confers on its proprietor the right to prohibit the use of a subsequent trade mark;

(c) the use of the trade mark may be prohibited by virtue of an earlier right other than the rights referred to in paragraphs 2 and 4(b) and in particular:

(i) a right to a name;
(ii) a right of personal portrayal;
(iii) a copyright;
(iv) an industrial property right;

(d) the trade mark is identical with, or similar to, an earlier collective trade mark conferring a right which expired within a period of a maximum of three years preceding application;

(e) the trade mark is identical with, or similar to, an earlier guarantee or certification mark conferring a right which expired within a period preceding application the length of which is fixed by the Member State;

(f) the trade mark is identical with, or similar to, an earlier trade mark which was registered for identical or similar goods or services and conferred on them a right which has expired for failure to renew within a period of a maximum of two years preceding application, unless the proprietor of the earlier trade mark gave his agreement for the registration of the later mark or did not use his trade mark;

(g) the trade mark is liable to be confused with a mark which was in use abroad on the filing date of the application and which is still in use there, provided that at the date of the application the applicant was acting in bad faith.

5. The Member States may permit that in appropriate circumstances registration need not be refused or the trade mark need not be declared invalid where the proprietor of the earlier trade mark or other earlier right consents to the registration of the later trade mark.

6. Any Member State may provide that, by derogation from paragraphs 1 to 5, the grounds for refusal of registration or invalidity in force in that State prior to the date on which the provisions necessary to comply with this Directive enter into force, shall apply to trade marks for which application has been made prior to that date.

Article 5

Rights conferred by a trade mark

1. The registered trade mark shall confer on the proprietor exclusive rights therein. The proprietor shall be entitled to prevent all third parties not having his consent from using in the course of trade:

(a) any sign which is identical with the trade mark in relation to goods or services which are identical with those for which the trade mark is registered;

(b) any sign where, because of its identity with, or similarity to, the trade mark and the identity or similarity of the goods or services covered by the trade mark and the sign, there exists a likelihood of confusion on the part of the public, which includes the likelihood of association between the sign and the trade mark.

2. Any Member State may also provide that the proprietor shall be entitled to prevent all third parties not having his consent from using in the course of trade any sign which is identical with, or similar to, the trade mark in relation to goods or services which are not similar to those for which the trade mark is registered, where the latter has a reputation in the Member State and where use of that sign without due cause takes unfair advantage of, or is detrimental to, the distinctive character or the repute of the trade mark.

3. The following, *inter alia,* may be prohibited under paragraphs 1 and 2:

(a) affixing the sign to the goods or to the packaging thereof;

(b) offering the goods, or putting them on the market or stocking them for those purposes under that sign, or offering or supplying services thereunder;

(c) importing or exporting the goods under the sign;

(d) using the sign on business papers and in advertising.

4. Where, under the law of the Member State, the use of a sign under the conditions referred to in 1(b) or 2 could not be prohibited before the date on which the provisions necessary to comply with this Directive entered into force in the Member State concerned, the rights conferred by the trade mark may not be relied on to prevent the continued use of the sign.

5. Paragraphs 1 to 4 shall not affect provisions in any Member State relating to the protection against the use of a sign other than for the purposes of distinguishing goods or services, where use of that sign without due cause takes unfair advantage of, or is detrimental to, the distinctive character or the repute of the trade mark.

Article 6

Limitation of the effects of a trade mark

1. The trade mark shall not entitle the proprietor to prohibit a third party from using, in the course of trade,

(a) his own name or address;

(b) indications concerning the kind, quality, quantity, intended purpose, value, geographical origin, the time of production of goods or of rendering of the service, or other characteristics of goods or services;

(c) the trade mark where it is necessary to indicate the intended purpose of a product or service, in particular as accessories or spare parts;

provided he uses them in accordance with honest practices in industrial or commercial matters.

2. The trade mark shall not entitle the proprietor to prohibit a third party from using, in the course of trade, an earlier right which only applies in a particular locality if that right is recognized by the laws of the Member State in question and within the limits of the territory in which it is recognized.

Article 7

Exhaustion of the rights conferred by a trade mark

1. The trade mark shall not entitle the proprietor to prohibit its use in relation to goods which have been put on the market in the Community under that trade mark by the proprietor or with his consent.

2. Paragraph 1 shall not apply where there exist legitimate reasons for the proprietor to oppose further commercialization of the goods, especially where the condition of the goods is changed or impaired after they have been put on the market.

Article 8

Licensing

1. A trade mark may be licensed for some or all of the goods or services for which it is registered and for the whole or part of the Member State concerned. A license may be exclusive or non-exclusive.

2. The proprietor of a trade mark may invoke the rights conferred by that trade mark against a licensee who contravenes any provision in his licensing contract with regard to its duration, the form covered by the registration in which the trade mark may be used, the scope of the goods or services for which the licence is granted, the territory in which the trade mark may be affixed, or the quality of the goods manufactured or of the services provided by the licensee.

Article 9

Limitation in consequence of acquiescence

1. Where, in a Member State, the proprietor of an earlier trade mark as referred to in Article 4(2) has acquiesced, for a period of five successive years, in the use of a later trade mark registered in that Member State while being aware of such use, he shall no longer be entitled on the basis of the earlier trade mark either to apply for a declaration that the later trade mark is invalid or to oppose the use of the later trade mark in respect of the goods or services for which the later trade mark has been used, unless registration of the later trade mark was applied for in bad faith.

2. Any Member State may provide that paragraph 1 shall apply *mutatis mutandis* to the proprietor of an earlier trade mark referred to in Article 4(4)(a) or an other earlier right referred to in Article 4(4)(b) or (c).

3. In the cases referred to in paragraphs 1 and 2, the proprietor of a later registered trade mark shall not be entitled to oppose the use of the earlier right, even though that right may no longer be invoked against the later trade mark.

Article 10

Use of trade marks

1. If, within a period of five years following the date of the completion of the registration procedure, the proprietor has not put the trade mark to genuine use in the Member State in connection with the goods or services in respect of which it is registered, or if such use has been suspended during an uninterrupted period of five years, the trade mark shall be subject to the sanctions provided for in this Directive, unless there are proper reasons for non-use.

2. The following shall also constitute use within the meaning of paragraph 1:

(a) use of the trade mark in a form differing in elements which do not alter the distinctive character of the mark in the form in which it was registered;

(b) affixing of the trade mark to goods or to the packaging thereof in the Member State concerned solely for export purposes.

3. Use of the trade mark with the consent of the proprietor or by any person who has authority to use a collective mark or a guarantee or certification mark shall be deemed to constitute use by the proprietor.

4. In relation to trade marks registered before the date on which the provisions necessary to comply with this Directive enter into force in the Member State concerned:

(a) where a provision in force prior to that date attaches sanctions to non-use of a trade mark during an uninterrupted period, the relevant period of five years mentioned in paragraph 1 shall be deemed to have begun to run at the same time as any period of non-use which is already running at that date;

(b) where there is no use provision in force prior to that date, the periods of five years mentioned in paragraph 1 shall be deemed to run from that date at the earliest.

Article 11

Sanctions for non-use of a trade mark in legal or administrative proceedings

1. A trade mark may not be declared invalid on the ground that there is an earlier conflicting trade mark if the latter does not fulfil the requirements of use set out in Article 10(1), (2) and (3) or in Article 10(4), as the case may be.

2. Any Member State may provide that registration of a trade mark may not be refused on the ground that there is an earlier conflicting trade mark if the latter does not fulfil the requirements of use set out in Article 10(1), (2) and (3) or in Article 10(4), as the case may be.

3. Without prejudice to the application of Article 12, where a counter-claim for revocation is made, any Member State may provide that a trade mark may not be successfully invoked in infringement proceedings if it is established as a result of a plea that the trade mark could be revoked pursuant to Article 12(1).

4. If the earlier trade mark has been used in relation to part only of the goods or services for which it is registered, it shall, for purposes of applying paragraphs 1, 2 and 3, be deemed to be registered in respect only of that part of the goods or services.

Article 12

Grounds for revocation

1. A trade mark shall be liable to revocation if, within a continuous period of five years, it has not been put to genuine use in the Member State

in connection with the goods or services in respect of which it is registered, and there are no proper reasons for non-use; however, no person may claim that the proprietor's rights in a trade mark should be revoked where, during the interval between expiry of the five-year period and filing of the application for revocation, genuine use of the trade mark has been started or resumed; the commencement or resumption of use within a period of three months preceding the filing of the application for revocation which began at the earliest on expiry of the continuous period of five years of non-use, shall, however, be disregarded where preparations for the commencement or resumption occur only after the proprietor becomes aware that the application for revocation may be filed.

2. A trade mark shall also be liable to revocation if, after the date on which it was registered,

(a) in consequence of acts or inactivity of the proprietor, it has become the common name in the trade for a product or service in respect of which it is registered;

(b) in consequence of the use made of it by the proprietor of the trade mark or with his consent in respect of the goods or services for which it is registered, it is liable to mislead the public, particularly as to the nature, quality or geographical origin of those goods or services.

Article 13

Grounds for refusal or revocation or invalidity relating to only some of the goods or services

Where grounds for refusal of registration or for revocation or invalidity of a trade mark exist in respect of only some of the goods or services for which that trade mark has been applied for or registered, refusal of registration or revocation or invalidity shall cover those goods or services only.

Article 14

Establishment *a posteriori* of invalidity or revocation of a trade mark

Where the seniority of an earlier trade mark which has been surrendered or allowed to lapse, is claimed for a Community trade mark, the invalidity or revocation of the earlier trade mark may be established *a posteriori*.

Article 15

Special provisions in respect of collective marks, guarantee marks and certification marks

1. Without prejudice to Article 4, Member States whose laws authorize the registration of collective marks or of guarantee or certification marks may provide that such marks shall not be registered, or shall be

revoked or declared invalid, on grounds additional to those specified in Articles 3 and 12 where the function of those marks so requires.

2. By way of derogation from Article 3(1)(c), Member States may provide that signs or indications which may serve, in trade, to designate the geographical origin of the goods or services may constitute collective, guarantee or certification marks. Such a mark does not entitle the proprietor to prohibit a third party from using in the course of trade such signs or indications, provided he uses them in accordance with honest practices in industrial or commercial matters; in particular, such a mark may not be invoked against a third party who is entitled to use a geographical name.

Article 16

National provisions to be adopted pursuant to this Directive

1. The Member States shall bring into force the laws, regulations and administrative provisions necessary to comply with this Directive not later than 28 December 1991. They shall immediately inform the Commission thereof.

2. Acting on a proposal from the Commission, the Council, acting by qualified majority, may defer the date referred to in paragraph 1 until 31 December 1992 at the latest.

3. Member States shall communicate to the Commission the text of the main provisions of national law which they adopt in the field governed by this Directive.

Article 17

Addressees

This Directive is addressed to the Member States.

Part IV

COMPETITION POLICY

INTRODUCTION

The primary documents for the study of competition law are the Treaty, especially Articles 81 through 87, and the Merger Regulation, included herein as document 7. For an understanding of Article 81 and its implementation, it is important to know, also, which agreements are entitled to nearly automatic exemption, as provided by block exemption regulations. Three block exemption regulations are included in this supplement, as documents 4–6.

There are numerous other documents that the student of competition law may want to consult, including notices, regulations and lengthy guidelines. The most important documents are either included herein or simply noted in the text of the casebook, usually with a citation to the Commission's web site. This introduction will describe the documents we have chosen to include, and will refer to several others.

The first document, Regulation 17, is a procedural regulation that implements Articles 81 and 82 of the Treaty. It gives the Commission the necessary powers to enforce Articles 81 and 82—the power to get information, to grant clearances and exemptions, and to impose fines and other remedies. Also it establishes the procedures for notification of agreements that fall within Article 81(1). The procedures for notification and approval set out in Regulation 17 are undergoing major change. A proposal for modernisation would abolish the notification requirements and procedures for agreements, decisions and concerted practices, and give exemption powers to Member States as well as the Commission, subject to controls by the Commission.

Document 2 is the Commission Notice on Agreements of Minor Importance, also called the De Minimis Notice. This notice identifies the categories of agreements that do not appreciably restrict competition and therefore are not caught by Article 81(1).

Document 3 is the Commission Notice on the Definition of the Relevant Market. In all antitrust and merger cases, unless there is a hard core violation such as price fixing, the relevant market must be defined at a first stage of analysis. This notice gives analytical guidance on how to define the relevant market.

Documents 4, 5 and 6 are regulations that establish block exemptions. If the agreement falls within the confines of the block exemption, it need not be notified, and it has an automatic exemption unless the Commission withdraws the benefits of the legislation. Document 4 is the important block exemption for vertical agreements; that is, agreements between suppliers and buyers in a chain of production or distribution. This regulation, No. 2790/1999, replaces a more regulatory regime. In general, absent a hard core violation, it provides a block exemption for agreements where the parties' market share does not exceed 30%. Analysis of vertical agreements should include a study of both the vertical block exemption regulation and the Guidelines on Vertical Restraints, O.J. C 291/1 (Oct. 13, 2000), which may be found at http://europa.eu.int/comm/competition/antitrust/legislation. Click on Vertical agreements.

Document 5 is Regulation 2658/2000, providing a block exemption for specialisation agreements where market share does not exceed 20%. Specialisation may be unilateral (where one participant gives up the supply of certain products or services in favor of another), reciprocal specialisation, or specialisation pursuant to joint production. Document 6, Regulation 2659/2000, provides a block exemption for categories of research and development agreements, to encourage R & D where it is unlikely to harm competition. Where the parties are competitors, to fall within the regulation, their combined market share must not exceed 25%.

The most important block exemption regulations not included in this volume are those for technology transfer agreements and car distribution. The existing regulation for technology transfer agreements is Regulation 240/96, O.J. L 31/2 (Jan. 31, 1996). This regulation is in the process of revision. The revision is expected to provide a wider exemption, in the spirit of the block exemption for vertical agreements. The documents regarding review of the regulation may be found at http://europa.eu.int/comm/competition/antitrust/others/.

For automobiles, the expiring block exemption regulation addresses the problem of divergent prices in different Member States. Regulation 1475/95, O.J. L 145/25 (June 29, 1995). This special sector block exemption is likely to be replaced. Current review documents may be found at http://europa.eu.int/comm/competition/antitrust/others/; go to Car Sector.

Perhaps the most important regulation in the field of competition law is the Merger Regulation, No. 4064/89, as last amended in 1997. This regulation, unlike the others, is primary law. It governs what concentrations are compatible or not with the common market. The Merger Regulation contains both procedural and substantive provisions, and is the basis for a significant portion of the work of the Competition Directorate. There are a number of related forms and notices that give guidance on filing procedures and substantive interpretation. These related documents may be found at http://europa.eu.int/comm/competition/mergers/legislation.

Also helpful are various other guidelines and notices of the Commission. In addition to the vertical restraints guidelines, noted above, are the guidelines on horizontal (competitor) cooperation agreements, O.J. C 3/2 (Jan. 6, 2001) (see web page for antitrust legislation, above), and the Commission Notice on Ancillary Restraints, O.J. C 188/5 (July 4, 2001), which is applicable both to mergers and agreements. (See web page for merger legislation, above.)

Footnotes are omitted from some of the documents.

Table of Contents

Part IV. COMPETITION POLICY

	Page
Introduction	471

Doc.
1. Council Regulation 17/62 implementing Articles 81 and 82 (ex 85 and 86) . 474
2. Commission Notice on Agreements on Minor Importance which do not appreciably restrict competition under Article 81(1) 486
3. Commission Notice on the Definition of the Relevant Market 491
4. Commission Regulation 2790/1999 on the application of Article 81(3) to Vertical Agreements—block exemption 504
5. Commission Regulation 2658/2000 on the application of Article 81(3) to Specialisation Agreements—block exemption 514
6. Commission Regulation 2659/2000 on the application of Article 81(3) to Research and Development Agreements—block exemption 521
7. Council Regulation 4064/1989 on the control of concentrations—Merger Regulation 531

1. COUNCIL REGULATION NO. 17/62*

First Regulation implementing Articles 81 and 82 (ex 85 and 86) of the Treaty

O.J. P 13/204 (Feb. 21, 1962), as last amended June 10, 1999

[All article numbers refer to the numbers prior to the renumbering by the Treaty of Amsterdam.]

THE COUNCIL OF THE EUROPEAN ECONOMIC COMMUNITY,

Having regard to the Treaty establishing the European Economic Community, and in particular Article 87 thereof;

Having regard to the proposal from the Commission;

Having regard to the Opinion of the Economic and Social Committee;

Having regard to the Opinion of the European Parliament;

(1) Whereas, in order to establish a system ensuring that competition shall not be distorted in the common market, it is necessary to provide for balanced application of Articles 85 and 86 in a uniform manner in the Member States;

(2) Whereas in establishing the rules for applying Article 85(3) account must be taken of the need to ensure effective supervision and to simplify administration to the greatest possible extent;

(3) Whereas it is accordingly necessary to make it obligatory, as a general principle, for undertakings which seek application of Article 85(3) to notify to the Commission their agreements, decisions and concerted practices;

(4) Whereas, on the one hand, such agreements, decisions and concerted practices are probably very numerous and cannot therefore all be examined at the same time and, on the other hand, some of them have special features which may make them less prejudicial to the development of the common market;

(5) Whereas there is consequently a need to make more flexible arrangements for the time being in respect of certain categories of agreement, decision and concerted practice without prejudging their validity under Article 85;

(6) Whereas it may be in the interest of undertakings to know whether any agreements, decisions or practices to which they are party, or propose

---

* Editors' note: This regulation is in the process of revision in connection with a plan to modernise the process for vetting agreements that fall within Article 81(1). If the proposal for modernisation is adopted, the notification process will be abolished and Member State courts and authorities will have power, along with the Commission and subject to controls by the Commission, to grant exemptions under Article 81(3). For the modernisation proposal, see Proposal for a Council Regulation on the implementation of the rules on competition laid down in Articles 81 and 82 of the Treaty, COM (2000) 582 final. The proposal may be found at http://europa.eu.int/comm/competition/antitrust/others/. Go to Reform of regulation 17.

to become party, may lead to action on the part of the Commission pursuant to Article 85 (1) or Article 86;

(7) Whereas, in order to secure uniform application of Articles 85 and 86 in the common market, rules must be made under which the Commission, acting in close and constant liaison with the competent authorities of the Member States, may take the requisite measures for applying those Articles;

(8) Whereas for this purpose the Commission must have the co-operation of the competent authorities of the Member States and be empowered, throughout the common market, to require such information to be supplied and to undertake such investigations as are necessary to bring to light any agreement, decision or concerted practice prohibited by Article 85(1) or any abuse of a dominant position prohibited by Article 86:

(9) Whereas, in order to carry out its duty of ensuring that the provisions of the Treaty are applied, the Commission must be empowered to address to undertakings or associations of undertakings recommendations and decisions for the purpose of bringing to an end infringements of Articles 85 and 86;

(10) Whereas compliance with Articles 85 and 86 and the fulfilment of obligations imposed on undertakings and associations of undertakings under this Regulation must be enforceable by means of fines and periodic penalty payments;

(11) Whereas undertakings concerned must be accorded the right to be heard by the Commission, third parties whose interests may be affected by a decision must be given the opportunity of submitting their comments beforehand, and it must be ensured that wide publicity is given to decisions taken;

(12) Whereas all decisions taken by the Commission under this Regulation are subject to review by the Court of Justice under the conditions specified in the Treaty; whereas it is moreover desirable to confer upon the Court of Justice, pursuant to Article 172, unlimited jurisdiction in respect of decisions under which the Commission imposes fines or periodic penalty payments;

(13) Whereas this Regulation may enter into force without prejudice to any other provisions that may hereafter be adopted pursuant to Article 87;

HAS ADOPTED THIS REGULATION:

Article 1

Basic provision

Without prejudice to Articles 6, 7 and 23 of this Regulation, agreements, decisions and concerted practices of the kind described in Article 85(1) of the Treaty and the abuse of a dominant position in the market, within the meaning of Article 86 of the Treaty, shall be prohibited, no prior decision to that effect being required.

Article 2

Negative clearance

Upon application by the undertakings or associations of undertakings concerned, the Commission may certify that, on the basis of the facts in its possession, there are no grounds under Article 85(1) or Article 86 of the Treaty for action on its part in respect of an agreement, decision or practice.

Article 3

Termination of infringements

1. Where the Commission, upon application or upon its own initiative, finds that there is infringement of Article 85 or Article 86 [now 81 and 82] of the Treaty, it may by decision require the undertakings or associations of undertakings concerned to bring such infringement to an end.

2. Those entitled to make application are:

(a) Member States;

(b) natural or legal persons who claim a legitimate interest.

3. Without prejudice to the other provisions of this Regulation, the Commission may, before taking a decision under paragraph 1, address to the undertakings or associations of undertakings concerned recommendations for termination of the infringement.

Article 4

Notification of new agreements, decisions and practices

1. Agreements, decisions and concerted practices of the kind described in Article 85(1) of the Treaty which come into existence after the entry into force of this Regulation and in respect of which the parties seek application of Article 85(3) must be notified to the Commission. Until they have been notified, no decision in application of Article 85(3) may be taken.

2. Paragraph 1 shall not apply to agreements, decisions and concerted practices where:

(1) the only parties thereto are undertakings from one Member State and the agreements, decisions or practices do not relate either to imports or to exports between Member States;

(2) (a) the agreements or concerted practices are entered into by two or more undertakings, each operating, for the purposes of the agreement, at a different level of the production or distribution chain, and relate to the conditions under which the parties may purchase, sell or resell certain goods or services; [or]

(b) not more than two undertakings are party thereto, and the agreements only impose restrictions on the exercise of the rights of the assignee or user of industrial property rights, in particular patents, utility models, designs or trade marks, or of the person entitled under a contract to the assignment, or grant, of the right to use a method of manufacture or knowledge relating to the use and to the application of industrial processes;

(3) they have as their sole object:

(a) the development or uniform application of standards or types; or

(b) joint research and development;

(c) specialisation in the manufacture of products, including agreements necessary for achieving this:

— where the products which are the subject of specialisation do not, in a substantial part of the common market, represent more than 15% of the volume of business done in identical products or those considered by consumers to be similar by reason of their characteristics, price and use, and

— where the total annual turnover of the participating undertakings does not exceed 200 million unit of account.

These agreements, decisions and practices may be notified to the Commission.

Article 5

Notification of agreements, decisions and practices existing at date of entry into force of regulation

[omitted]

Article 6

Decisions pursuant to Article 85(3)

1. Whenever the Commission takes a decision pursuant to Article 85(3) of the Treaty, it shall specify therein the date from which the decision shall take effect. Such a date shall not be earlier than the date of notification.

2. The second sentence of paragraph 1 shall not apply to agreements, decisions or concerted practices falling within Article 4(2) and Article 5(2), nor to those falling within Article 5(1) which have been notified within the time limit specified in Article 5(1).

Article 7

Special provisions for agreements, decisions and practices existing at date of entry into force of regulation

[omitted]

Article 8

Duration and revocation of decisions under Article 85(3)

1. A decision in application of Article 85(3) of the Treaty shall be issued for a specified period and conditions and obligations may be attached thereto.

2. A decision may on application be renewed if the requirements of Article 85(3) of the Treaty continue to be satisfied.

3. The Commission may revoke or amend its decision or prohibit specified acts by the parties:

(a) where there has been a change in any of the facts which were basic to the making of the decision;

(b) where the parties commit a breach of any obligation attached to the decision;

(c) where the decision is based on incorrect information or was induced by deceit;

(d) where the parties abuse the exemption from the provisions of Article 85(1) of the Treaty granted to them by the decision.

In cases to which subparagraphs (b), (c) or (d) apply, the decision may be revoked with retroactive effect.

Article 9

Powers

1. Subject to review of its decision by the Court of Justice, the Commission shall have sole power to declare Article 85(1) inapplicable pursuant to Article 85(3) of the Treaty.

2. The Commission shall have power to apply Article 85(1) and Article 86 of the Treaty; this power may be exercised notwithstanding that the time limits specified in Article 5(1) and in Article 7(2) relating to notification have not expired.

3. As long as the Commission has not initiated any procedure under Articles 2, 3 or 6, the authorities of the Member States shall remain competent to apply Article 85(1) and Article 86 in accordance with Article 88 of the Treaty; they shall remain competent in this respect notwithstanding that the time limits specified in Article 5(1) and in Article 7(2) relating to notification have not expired.

Article 10

Liaison with the authorities of the Member States

1. The Commission shall forthwith transmit to the competent authorities of the Member States a copy of the applications and notifications together with copies of the most important documents lodged with the Commission for the purpose of establishing the existence of infringements

of Articles 85 or 86 of the Treaty or of obtaining negative clearance or a decision in application of Article 85(3).

2. The Commission shall carry out the procedure set out in paragraph 1 in close and constant liaison with the competent authorities of the Member States; such authorities shall have the right to express their views upon that procedure.

3. An Advisory Committee on Restrictive Practices and Monopolies shall be consulted prior to the taking of any decision following upon a procedure under paragraph 1, and of any decision concerning the renewal, amendment or revocation of a decision pursuant to Article 85(3) of the Treaty.

4. The Advisory Committee shall be composed of officials competent in the matter of restrictive practices and monopolies. Each Member State shall appoint an official to represent it who, if prevented from attending, may be replaced by another official.

5. The consultation shall take place at a joint meeting convened by the Commission; such a meeting shall be held not earlier than fourteen days after dispatch of the notice convening it. The notice shall, in respect of each case to be examined, be accompanied by a summary of the case together with an indication of the most important documents, and a preliminary draft decision.

6. The Advisory Committee may deliver an opinion notwithstanding that some of its members or their alternates are not present. A report of the outcome of the consultative proceedings shall be annexed to the draft decision. It shall not be made public.

Article 11

Requests for information

1. In carrying out the duties assigned to it by Article 89 and by provisions adopted under Article 87 of the Treaty, the Commission may obtain all necessary information from the Governments and competent authorities of the Member States and from undertakings and associations of undertakings.

2. When sending a request for information to an undertaking or association of undertakings, the Commission shall at the same time forward a copy of the request to the competent authority of the Member State in whose territory the seat of the undertaking or association of undertakings is situated.

3. In its request the Commission shall state the legal basis and the purpose of the request and also the penalties provided for in Article 15(1)(b) for supplying incorrect information.

4. The owners of the undertakings or their representatives and, in the case of legal persons, companies or firms, or of associations having no legal personality, the persons authorised to represent them by law or by their constitution shall supply the information requested.

5. Where an undertaking or association of undertakings does not supply the information requested within the time limit fixed by the Commission, or supplies incomplete information, the Commission shall by decision require the information to be supplied. The decision shall specify what information is required, fix an appropriate time limit within which it is to be supplied and indicate the penalties provided for in Article 15(1)(b) and Article 16(1)(c) and the right to have the decision reviewed by the Court of Justice.

6. The Commission shall at the same time forward a copy of its decision to the competent authority of the Member State in whose territory the seat of the undertaking or association of undertakings is situated.

Article 12

Inquiry into sectors of the economy

1. If in any sector of the economy the trend of trade between Member States, price movements, inflexibility of prices or other circumstances suggest that in the economic sector concerned competition is being restricted or distorted within the common market, the Commission may decide to conduct a general inquiry into that economic sector and in the course thereof may request undertakings in the sector concerned to supply the information necessary for giving effect to the principles formulated in Articles 85 and 86 of the Treaty and for carrying out the duties entrusted to the Commission.

2. The Commission may in particular request every undertaking or association of undertakings in the economic sector concerned to communicate to it all agreements, decisions and concerted practices which are exempt from notification by virtue of Article 4(2) and Article 5(2).

3. When making inquiries pursuant to paragraph 2, the Commission shall also request undertakings or groups of undertakings whose size suggests that they occupy a dominant position within the common market or a substantial part thereof to supply to the Commission such particulars of the structure of the undertakings and of their behaviour as are requisite to an appraisal of their position in the light of Article 86 of the Treaty.

4. Article 10(3) to (6) and Articles 11, 13 and 14 shall apply correspondingly.

Article 13

Investigations by the authorities of the Member States

1. At the request of the Commission, the competent authorities of the Member States shall undertake the investigations which the Commission considers to be necessary under Article 14(1), or which it has ordered by decision pursuant to Article 14(3). The officials of the competent authorities of the Member States responsible for conducting these investigations shall exercise their powers upon production of an authorisation in writing issued by the competent authority of the Member State in whose territory

the investigation is to be made. Such authorisation shall specify the subject matter and purpose of the investigation.

2. If so requested by the Commission or by the competent authority of the Member State in whose territory the investigation is to be made, the officials of the Commission may assist the officials of such authorities in carrying out their duties.

Article 14

Investigating powers of the Commission

1. In carrying out the duties assigned to it by Article 89 and by provisions adopted under Article 87 of the Treaty, the Commission may undertake all necessary investigations into undertakings and associations of undertakings. To this end the officials authorised by the Commission are empowered:

(a) to examine the books and other business records;

(b) to take copies of or extracts from the books and business records;

(c) to ask for oral explanations on the spot;

(d) to enter any premises; land and means of transport of undertakings.

2. The officials of the Commission authorised for the purpose of these investigations shall exercise their powers upon production of an authorisation in writing specifying the subject matter and purpose of the investigation and the penalties provided for in Article 15(1)(c) in cases where production of the required books or other business records is incomplete. In good time before the investigation, the Commission shall inform the competent authority of the Member State in whose territory the same is to be made of the investigation and of the identity of the authorised officials.

3. Undertakings and associations of undertakings shall submit to investigations ordered by decision of the Commission. The decision shall specify the subject matter and purpose of the investigation, appoint the date on which it is to begin and indicate the penalties provided for in Article 15(1)(c) and Article 16(1)(d) and the right to have the decision reviewed by the Court of Justice.

4. The Commission shall take decisions referred to in paragraph 3 after consultation with the competent authority of the Member State in whose territory the investigation is to be made.

5. Officials of the competent authority of the Member State in whose territory the investigation is to be made may, at the request of such authority or of the Commission, assist the officials of the Commission in carrying out their duties.

6. Where an undertaking opposes an investigation ordered pursuant to this Article, the Member State concerned shall afford the necessary assistance to the officials authorised by the Commission to enable them to

make their investigation. Member States shall, after consultation with the Commission, take the necessary measures to this end before 1 October 1962.

Article 15

Fines

1. The Commission may by decision impose on undertakings or associations of undertakings fines of 100 to 5000 units of account where, intentionally or negligently:

(a) they supply incorrect or misleading information in an application pursuant to Article 2 or in a notification pursuant to Articles 4 or 5; or

(b) they supply incorrect information in response to a request made pursuant to Article 11(3) or (5) or to Article 12, or do not supply information within the time limit fixed by a decision taken under Article 11(5); or

(c) they produce the required books or other business records in incomplete form during investigations under Article 13 or 14, or refuse to submit to an investigation ordered by decision issued in implementation of Article 14(3).

2. The Commission may by decision impose on undertakings or associations of undertakings fines of 1000 to 1 000 000 units of account, or a sum in excess thereof but not exceeding 10% of the turnover in the preceding business year of each of the undertakings participating in the infringement where, either intentionally or negligently:

(a) they infringe Article 85(1) or Article 86 of the Treaty; or

(b) they commit a breach of any obligation imposed pursuant to Article 8(1).

In fixing the amount of the fine, regard shall be had both to the gravity and to the duration of the infringement.

3. Article 10(3) to (6) shall apply.

4. Decisions taken pursuant to paragraphs 1 and 2 shall not be of a criminal law nature.

5. The fines provided for in paragraph 2(a) shall not be imposed in respect of acts taking place:

(a) after notification to the Commission and before its decision in application of Article 85(3) of the Treaty, provided they fall within the limits of the activity described in the notification;

(b) before notification and in the course of agreements, decisions or concerted practices in existence at the date of entry into force of this Regulation, provided that notification was effected within the time limits specified in Article 5(1) and Article 7(2).

6. Paragraph 5 shall not have effect where the Commission has informed the undertakings concerned that after preliminary examination it is of opinion that Article 85(1) of the Treaty applies and that application of Article 85(3) is not justified.

Article 16

Periodic penalty payments

1. The Commission may by decision impose on undertakings or associations of undertakings periodic penalty payments of 50 to 1000 units of account per day, calculated from the date appointed by the decision, in order to compel them:

(a) to put an end to an infringement of Article 85 or 86 of the Treaty, in accordance with a decision taken pursuant to Article 3 of this Regulation;

(b) to refrain from any act prohibited under Article 8(3);

(c) to supply complete and correct information which it has requested by decision taken pursuant to Article 11(5);

(d) to submit to an investigation which it has ordered by decision taken pursuant to Article 14(3).

2. Where the undertakings or associations of undertakings have satisfied the obligation which it was the purpose of the periodic penalty payment to enforce, the Commission may fix the total amount of the periodic penalty payment at a lower figure than that which would arise under the original decision.

3. Article 10(3) to (6) shall apply.

Article 17

Review by the Court of Justice

The Court of Justice shall have unlimited jurisdiction within the meaning of Article 172 of the Treaty to review decisions whereby the Commission has fixed a fine or periodic penalty payment; it may cancel, reduce or increase the fine or periodic penalty payment imposed.

Article 18

Unit of account [now EURO]

For the purposes of applying Articles 15 to 17 the unit of account shall be that adopted in drawing up the budget of the Community in accordance with Articles 207 and 209 of the Treaty.

Article 19

Hearing of the parties and of third persons

1. Before taking decisions as provided for in Articles 2, 3, 6, 7, 8, 15 and 16, the Commission shall give the undertakings or associations of

undertakings concerned the opportunity of being heard on the matters to which the Commission has taken objection.

2. If the Commission or the competent authorities of the Member States consider it necessary, they may also hear other natural or legal persons. Applications to be heard on the part of such persons shall, where they show a sufficient interest, be granted.

3. Where the Commission intends to give negative clearance pursuant to Article 2 or take a decision in application of Article 85(3) of the Treaty, it shall publish a summary of the relevant application or notification and invite all interested third parties to submit their observations within a time limit which it shall fix being not less than one month. Publication shall have regard to the legitimate interest of undertakings in the protection of their business secrets.

Article 20

Professional secrecy

1. Information acquired as a result of the application of Articles 11, 12, 13 and 14 shall be used only for the purpose of the relevant requestor investigation.

2. Without prejudice to the provisions of Articles 19 and 21, the Commission and the competent authorities of the Member States, their officials and other servants shall not disclose information acquired by them as a result of the application of this Regulation and of the kind covered by the obligation of professional secrecy.

3. The provisions of paragraphs 1 and 2 shall not prevent publication of general information or surveys which do not contain information relating to particular undertakings or associations of undertakings.

Article 21

Publication of decisions

1. The Commission shall publish the decisions which it takes pursuant to Articles 2, 3, 6, 7 and 8.

2. The publication shall state the names of the parties and the main content of the decision; it shall have regard to the legitimate interest of undertakings in the protection of their business secrets.

Article 22

Special provisions

1. The Commission shall submit to the Council proposals for making certain categories of agreement, decision and concerted practice falling within Article 4(2) or Article 5(2) compulsorily notifiable under Article 4 or 5.

2. Within one year from the date of entry into force of this Regulation, the Council shall examine, on a proposal from the Commission, what

special provisions might be made for exempting from the provisions of this Regulation agreements, decisions and concerted practices falling within Article 4(2) or Article 5(2).

Article 23

Transitional provisions applicable to decisions of authorities of the Member States

1. Agreements, decisions and concerted practices of the kind described in Article 85(1) of the Treaty to which, before the entry into force of this Regulation, the competent authority of a Member State has declared Article 85(1) to be inapplicable pursuant to Article 85(3) shall not be subject to compulsory notification under Article 5. The decision of the competent authority of the Member State shall be deemed to be a decision within the meaning of Article 6; it shall cease to be valid upon expiration of the period fixed by such authority but in any event not more than three years after the entry into force of this Regulation. Article 8(3) shall apply.

2. Applications for renewal of decisions of the kind described in paragraph 1 shall be decided upon by the Commission in accordance with Article 8(2).

Article 24

Implementing provisions

The Commission shall have power to adopt implementing provisions concerning the form, content and other details of applications pursuant to Articles 2 and 3 and of notifications pursuant to Articles 4 and 5, and concerning hearings pursuant to Article 19(1) and (2).

Article 25

Special provisions regarding dates of notification and fines for agreements, decisions and concerted practices to which Article 85 of the Treaty applies by virtue of accession

[omitted]

This Regulation shall be binding in its entirety and directly applicable in all Member States.

2. COMMISSION NOTICE ON AGREEMENTS OF MINOR IMPORTANCE WHICH DO NOT APPRECIABLY RESTRICT COMPETITION UNDER ARTICLE 81(1)

(DE MINIMIS NOTICE)[1]

O.J. C 368/07 (Dec. 22, 2001)

I

1. Article 81(1) prohibits agreements between undertakings which may affect trade between Member States and which have as their object or effect the prevention, restriction or distortion of competition within the common market. The Court of Justice of the European Communities has clarified that this provision is not applicable where the impact of the agreement on intra-Community trade or on competition is not appreciable.

2. In this notice the Commission quantifies, with the help of market share thresholds, what is not an appreciable restriction of competition under Article 81 of the EC Treaty. This negative definition of appreciability does not imply that agreements between undertakings which exceed the thresholds set out in this notice appreciably restrict competition. Such agreements may still have only a negligible effect on competition and may therefore not be prohibited by Article 81(1).[2]

3. Agreements may in addition not fall under Article 81(1) because they are not capable of appreciably affecting trade between Member States. This notice does not deal with this issue. It does not quantify what does not constitute an appreciable effect on trade. It is however acknowledged that agreements between small and medium-sized undertakings, as defined in the Annex to Commission Recommendation 96/280/EC,[3] are rarely capable of appreciably affecting trade between Member States. Small and medium-sized undertakings are currently defined in that recommendation as undertakings which have fewer than 250 employees and have either an annual turnover not exceeding EUR 40 million or an annual balance-sheet total not exceeding EUR 27 million.

4. In cases covered by this notice the Commission will not institute proceedings either upon application or on its own initiative. Where undertakings assume in good faith that an agreement is covered by this notice, the Commission will not impose fines. Although not binding on them, this

---

1. This notice replaces the notice on agreements of minor importance published in OJ C 372, 9.12.1997.

2. See, for instance, the judgment of the Court of Justice in Joined Cases C-215/96 and C-216/96 *Bagnasco (Carlos) v Banca Popolare di Novara and Casa di Risparmio di Genova e Imperia* (1999) ECR I-135, points 34-35. This notice is also without prejudice to the principles for assessment under Article 81(1) as expressed in the Commission notice 'Guidelines on the applicability of Article 81 of the EC Treaty to horizontal cooperation agreements', OJ C 3, 6.1.2001, in particular points 17-31 inclusive, and in the Commission notice 'Guidelines on vertical restraints', OJ C 291, 13.10.2000, in particular points 5-20 inclusive.

3. OJ L 107, 30.4.1996, p. 4. This recommendation will be revised. It is envisaged to increase the annual turnover threshold from EUR 40 million to EUR 50 million and the annual balance-sheet total threshold from EUR 27 million to EUR 43 million.

notice also intends to give guidance to the courts and authorities of the Member States in their application of Article 81.

5. This notice also applies to decisions by associations of undertakings and to concerted practices.

6. This notice is without prejudice to any interpretation of Article 81 which may be given by the Court of Justice or the Court of First Instance of the European Communities.

II

7. The Commission holds the view that agreements between undertakings which affect trade between Member States do not appreciably restrict competition within the meaning of
Article 81(1):

> (a) if the aggregate market share held by the parties to the agreement does not exceed 10% on any of the relevant markets affected by the agreement, where the agreement is made between undertakings which are actual or potential competitors on any of these markets (agreements between competitors);[4] or
>
> (b) if the market share held by each of the parties to the agreement does not exceed 15% on any of the relevant markets affected by the agreement, where the agreement is made between undertakings which are not actual or potential competitors on any of these markets (agreements between non-competitors).

In cases where it is difficult to classify the agreement as either an agreement between competitors or an agreement between non-competitors the 10% threshold is applicable.

8. Where in a relevant market competition is restricted by the cumulative effect of agreements for the sale of goods or services entered into by different suppliers or distributors (cumulative foreclosure effect of parallel networks of agreements having similar effects on the market), the market share thresholds under point 7 are reduced to 5%, both for agreements between competitors and for agreements between non-competitors. Individual suppliers or distributors with a market share not exceeding 5% are in general not considered to contribute significantly to a cumulative foreclo-

---

4. On what are actual or potential competitors, see the Commission notice Guidelines on the applicability of Article 81 of the EC Treaty to horizontal cooperation agreements, OJ C 3, 6.1.2001, paragraph 9. A firm is treated as an actual competitor if it is either active on the same relevant market or if, in the absence of the agreement, it is able to switch production to the relevant products and market them in the short term without incurring significant additional costs or risks in response to a small and permanent increase in relative prices (immediate supply-side substitutability). A firm is treated as a potential competitor if there is evidence that, absent the agreement, this firm could and would be likely to undertake the necessary additional investments or other necessary switching costs so that it could enter the relevant market in response to a small and permanent increase in relative prices.

sure effect.[5] A cumulative foreclosure effect is unlikely to exist if less than 30% of the relevant market is covered by parallel (networks of) agreements having similar effects.

9. The Commission also holds the view that agreements are not restrictive of competition if the market shares do not exceed the thresholds of respectively 10%, 15% and 5% set out in point 7 and 8 during two successive calendar years by more than 2 percentage points.

10. In order to calculate the market share, it is necessary to determine the relevant market. This consists of the relevant product market and the relevant geographic market. When defining the relevant market, reference should be had to the notice on the definition of the relevant market for the purposes of Community competition law.[6] The market shares are to be calculated on the basis of sales value data or, where appropriate, purchase value data. If value data are not available, estimates based on other reliable market information, including volume data, may be used.

11. Points 7, 8 and 9 do not apply to agreements containing any of the following hardcore restrictions:

(1) as regards agreements between competitors as defined in point 7, restrictions which, directly or indirectly, in isolation or in combination with other factors under the control of the parties, have as their object:[7]

   (a) the fixing of prices when selling the products to third parties;

   (b) the limitation of output or sales;

   (c) the allocation of markets or customers;

(2) as regards agreements between non-competitors as defined in point 7, restrictions which, directly or indirectly, in isolation or in combination with other factors under the control of the parties, have as their object:

   (a) the restriction of the buyer's ability to determine its sale price, without prejudice to the possibility of the supplier imposing a maximum sale price or recommending a sale price, provided that they do not amount to a fixed or minimum sale price as a result of pressure from, or incentives offered by, any of the parties;

   (b) the restriction of the territory into which, or of the customers to whom, the buyer may sell the contract goods or services, except the following restrictions which are not hardcore:

---

5. See also the Commission notice 'Guidelines on vertical restraints,' OJ C 291, 13.10.2000, in particular paragraphs 73, 142, 143 and 189. While in the guidelines on vertical restraints in relation to certain restrictions reference is made not only to the total but also to the tied market share of a particular supplier or buyer, in this notice all market share thresholds refer to total market shares.

6. OJ C 372, 9.12.1997, p. 5.

7. Without prejudice to situations of joint production with or without joint distribution as defined in Article 5, paragraph 2, of Commission Regulation (EC) No 2658/2000 and Article 5, paragraph 2, of Commission Regulation (EC) No 2659/2000, OJ L 304, 5.12.2000, pp. 3 and 7 respectively.

— the restriction of active sales into the exclusive territory or to an exclusive customer group reserved to the supplier or allocated by the supplier to another buyer, where such a restriction does not limit sales by the customers of the buyer,

— the restriction of sales to end users by a buyer operating at the wholesale level of trade,

— the restriction of sales to unauthorised distributors by the members of a selective distribution system, and

— the restriction of the buyer's ability to sell components, supplied for the purposes of incorporation, to customers who would use them to manufacture the same type of goods as those produced by the supplier;

(c) the restriction of active or passive sales to end users by members of a selective distribution system operating at the retail level of trade, without prejudice to the possibility of prohibiting a member of the system from operating out of an unauthorised place of establishment;

(d) the restriction of cross-supplies between distributors within a selective distribution system, including between distributors operating at different levels of trade;

(e) the restriction agreed between a supplier of components and a buyer who incorporates those components, which limits the supplier's ability to sell the components as spare parts to end users or to repairers or other service providers not entrusted by the buyer with the repair or servicing of its goods;

(3) as regards agreements between competitors as defined in point 7, where the competitors operate, for the purposes of the agreement, at a different level of the production or distribution chain, any of the hardcore restrictions listed in paragraph (1) and (2) above.

12. (1) For the purposes of this notice, the terms 'undertaking', 'party to the agreement', 'distributor', 'supplier' and 'buyer' shall include their respective connected undertakings.

(2) 'Connected undertakings' are:

(a) undertakings in which a party to the agreement, directly or indirectly:

— has the power to exercise more than half the voting rights, or

— has the power to appoint more than half the members of the supervisory board, board of management or bodies legally representing the undertaking, or has the right to manage the undertaking's affairs;

(b) undertakings which directly or indirectly have, over a party to the agreement, the rights or powers listed in (a);

(c) undertakings in which an undertaking referred to in (b) has, directly or indirectly, the rights or powers listed in (a);

(d) undertakings in which a party to the agreement together with one or more of the undertakings referred to in (a), (b) or (c), or in which two or more of the latter undertakings, jointly have the rights or powers listed in (a);

(e) undertakings in which the rights or the powers listed in (a) are jointly held by:

— parties to the agreement or their respective connected undertakings referred to in (a) to (d), or

— one or more of the parties to the agreement or one or more of their connected undertakings referred to in (a) to (d) and one or more third parties.

(3) For the purposes of paragraph 2(e), the market share held by these jointly held undertakings shall be apportioned equally to each undertaking having the rights or the powers listed in paragraph 2(a).

3. COMMISSION NOTICE ON THE DEFINITION OF THE RELEVANT MARKET

O.J. C 372/5 (Dec. 9, 1997)

I. INTRODUCTION

The purpose of this notice is to provide guidance as to how the Commission applies the concept of relevant product and geographic market in its ongoing enforcement of Community competition law, in particular the application of Regulations 17/62 and 4064/89, their equivalents in other sectoral applications such as transport, coal and steel, and agriculture, and the relevant provisions of the EEA agreement.[1] Throughout this notice, references to Articles 85 and 86 [now 81 and 82] of the Treaty and to merger control are to be understood as referring to the equivalent provisions in the EEA agreement and the ECSC Treaty.

Market definition is a tool to identify and define the boundaries of competition between firms. It allows to establish the framework within which competition policy is applied by the Commission. The main purpose of market definition is to identify in a systematic way the competitive constraints that the undertakings involved[2] face. The objective of defining a market in both its product and geographic dimension is to identify those actual competitors of the undertakings involved that are capable of constraining their behaviour and of preventing them from behaving independently of an effective competitive pressure. It is from this perspective, that the market definition makes it possible, inter alia, to calculate market shares that would convey meaningful information regarding market power for the purposes of assessing dominance or for the purposes of applying Article 85.

It follows from the above, that the concept of relevant market is different from other concepts of market often used in other contexts. For instance, companies often use the term market to refer to the area where it sells its products or to refer broadly to the industry or sector where it belongs

The definition of the relevant market in both its product and geographic dimensions often has a decisive influence on the assessment of a competition case. By rendering public the procedures the Commission follows when considering market definition and by indicating the criteria and evidence on which it relies to reach a decision, the Commission expects to increase the transparency of its policy and decision making in the area of competition policy.

Increased transparency will also result in companies and their advisors being able to better anticipate the possibility that the Commission would raise competition concerns in an individual case. Companies could, therefore, take such a possibility into account in their own internal decision making when contemplating for instance, acquisitions, the creation of joint ventures or the establishment of certain agreements. It is also intended that companies are in a better position to understand what sort of information the Commission considers relevant for the purposes of market definition.

The Commission's interpretation of the notion of relevant market is without prejudice to the interpretation which may be given by the Court of Justice or the Court of First Instance of the European Communities.

II. DEFINITION OF RELEVANT MARKET

Definition of relevant product and relevant geographic market.

The regulations based on Articles 85 and 86 of the Treaty, in particular in section 6 of Form A/B with respect to Regulation 17, as well as in section 6 of Form CO with respect to regulation 4064/89 on the control of concentrations of a Community dimension have laid down the following definitions. Relevant product markets are defined as follows:

"A relevant product market comprises all those products and/or services which are regarded as interchangeable or substitutable by the consumer, by reason of the products' characteristics, their prices and their intended use."

Relevant geographic markets are defined as follows:

"The relevant geographic market comprises the area in which the undertakings concerned are involved in the supply and demand of products or services, in which the conditions of competition are sufficiently homogeneous and which can be distinguished from neighbouring areas because the conditions of competition are appreciably different in those areas".

The relevant market within which to assess a given competition issue is therefore established by the combination of the product and geographic markets. The Commission interprets the definitions at paragraphs 7 and 8 (which reflect the jurisprudence of the Court of Justice and the Court of First Instance as well as its own decisional practice) according to the orientations defined in this Notice.

Concept of relevant market and objectives of Community competition policy.

The concept of relevant market is closely related to the objectives pursued under Community competition policy. For example under the Community's merger control, the objective in controlling structural changes in the supply of a product/service is to prevent the creation or reinforcement of a dominant position as a result of which effective competition would be significantly impeded in a substantial part of the common market. Under the Community's competition policy, a dominant position is such that a firm or group of firms would be in a position to behave to an appreciable extent independently of its competitors, customers and ultimately of its consumers.[3] Such a position would usually arise when a firm or group of firms would account for a large share of the supply in any given market, provided that other factors analysed in the assessment (such as entry barriers, capacity of reaction of customers, etc.) point in the same direction.

The same approach is followed by the Commission in its application of Article 86 of the Treaty to firms that enjoy a single or collective dominant position. Under Regulation 17 the Commission has the power to investigate and bring to an end abuses of such a dominant position, which must also be defined by reference to the relevant market. Markets may also need to be defined in the application of Article 85 of the Treaty, in particular, in determining whether an appreciable restriction of competition exists or in establishing if the condition under Article 85(3)(b) for an exemption from the application of Article 85(1) is met.

The criteria to define the relevant market are applied generally for the analysis of certain behaviours in the market and for the analysis of structural changes in the supply of products. This methodology, though, might lead to different results depending on the nature of the competition issue being examined. For instance, the scope of the geographic market might be different when analysing a concentration, where the analysis is essentially prospective, than when analysing past behaviour. The different time horizon considered in each case might lead to the result that different geographic markets are defined for the same products depending on whether the Commission is examining a change in the structure of supply, such as a concentration or a cooperative joint venture, or issues relating to certain past behaviour.

Basic principles for market definition.

Competitive constraints

Firms are subject to three main sources of competitive constraints: demand substitutability, supply substitutability and potential competition. From an economic point of view, for the definition of the relevant market, demand substitution constitutes the most immediate and effective disciplinary force on the suppliers of a given product, in particular in relation to their pricing decisions. A firm or a group of firms cannot have a significant impact on the prevailing conditions of sale, such as prices, if its customers are in a position to switch easily to available substitute products or to suppliers located elsewhere. Basically, the exercise of market definition consists in identifying the effective alternative sources of supply for the customers of the undertakings involved, both in terms of products/services and geographic location of suppliers.

The competitive constraints arising from supply side substitutability other then those described in para 20–23 and from potential competition are in general less immediate and in any case require an analysis of additional factors. As a result such constraints are taken into account at the assessment stage of competition analysis.

Demand substitution

The assessment of demand substitution entails a determination of the range of products which are viewed as substitutes by the consumer. One way of making this determination can be viewed, as a thought experiment, postulating a hypothetical small, non-transitory change in relative prices and evaluating the likely reactions of customers to that increase. The exercise of market definition focuses on prices for operational and practical purposes, and more precisely on demand substitution arising from small, permanent changes in relative prices. This concept can provide clear indications as to the evidence that is relevant to define markets.

Conceptually, this approach implies that starting from the type of products that the undertakings involved sell and the area in which they sell them, additional products and areas will be included into or excluded from the market definition depending on whether competition from these other products and areas affect or restrain sufficiently the pricing of the parties' products in the short term.

The question to be answered is whether the parties' customers would switch to readily available substitutes or to suppliers located elsewhere in response to an hypothetical small (in the range 5%–10%), permanent relative price increase in the products and areas being considered. If substitution would be enough to make the price increase unprofitable because of the resulting loss of sales, additional substitutes and areas are included in the relevant market. This would be done until the set of products and geographic areas is such that small, permanent increases in relative prices would be profitable. The equivalent analysis is applicable in cases concerning the concentration of buying power, where the starting point would then be the supplier and the price test allows to identify the alternative distribution channels or outlets for the supplier's products. In the application of these principles, careful account should be taken of certain particular situations as described under paragraphs 56 and 58.

A practical example of this test can be provided by its application to a merger of, for instance, soft drink bottlers. An issue to examine in such a case would be to decide whether different flavours of soft drinks belong to the same market. In practice, the question to address would be if consumers of flavour A would switch to other flavours when confronted with a permanent price increase of 5% to 10% for flavour A. If a sufficient number of consumers would switch to, say, flavour B, to such an extent that the price increase for flavour A would not be profitable due to the resulting loss of sales, then the market would comprise at least flavours A and B. The process would have to be extended in addition to other available flavours until a set of products is identified for which a price rise would not induce a sufficient substitution in demand.

Generally, and in particular for the analysis of merger cases, the price to take into account will be the prevailing market price. This might not be the case where the prevailing price has been determined in the absence of sufficient competition. In particular for investigation of abuses of dominant positions, the fact that the prevailing price might already have been substantially increased will be taken into account.

Supply substitution

Supply-side substitutability may also be taken into account when defining markets in those situations in which its effects are equivalent to those of demand substitution in terms of effectiveness and immediacy. This requires that suppliers be able to switch production to the relevant products and market them in the short term[4] without incurring significant additional costs or risks in response to small and permanent changes in relative prices. When these conditions are met, the additional production that is put on the market will have a disciplinary effect on the competitive behaviour of the companies involved. Such an impact in terms of effectiveness and immediacy is equivalent to the demand substitution effect.

These situations typically arise when companies market a wide range of qualities or grades of one product; even if for a given final customer or group of consumers, the different qualities are not substitutable, the different qualities will be grouped into one product market provided that most of the suppliers are able to offer and sell the various qualities under the conditions of immediacy and absence of significant increase in costs described above. In such cases, the relevant product market will encompass all products that are substitutable in demand and supply, and the current sales of those products will be summed to calculate the total value or volume of the market. The same reasoning may lead to group different geographic areas.

A practical example of the approach to supply side substitutability when defining product markets is to be found in the case of paper. Paper is usually supplied in a range of different qualities, from standard writing paper to high quality papers to be used for instance to publish art books. From a demand point of view, different qualities of paper cannot be used for a specific use, i.e. an art book or a high quality publication cannot be based on lower quality papers. However, paper plants are prepared to manufacture the different qualities, and production can be adjusted with negligible costs and in a short time frame. In the absence of particular difficulties in distribution, paper manufacturers are able therefore to compete for orders of the various qualities, in particular if orders are passed with a sufficient lead time to allow to modify production plans. Under such circumstances, the Commission would not define a separate market for each quality of paper and respective usage. The various qualities of paper are included in the relevant market, and their sales added up to estimate total market value and volume.

When supply side substitutability would imply the need to adjust significantly existing tangible and intangible assets, additional investments, strategic decisions or time delays, it will not be considered at the stage of market definition. Examples where supply side substitution did not lead the Commission to enlarge the market are offered in the area of consumer products, in particular for branded beverages. Although bottling plants may in principle bottle different beverages, there are costs and lead times involved (in terms of advertising, product testing and distribution) before the products can actually be sold. In these cases, the effects of supply side substitutability and other forms of potential competition would then be examined at a later stage.

Potential competition

The third source of competitive constraint, potential competition, is not taken into account when defining markets, since the conditions under which potential competition will actually represent an effective competitive constraint depend on the analysis of specific factors and circumstances related to the conditions of entry. If required, this analysis is only carried out at a subsequent stage, in general once the position of the companies involved in the relevant market has already been ascertained, and such position is indicative of concerns from a competition point of view.

III. EVIDENCE RELIED UPON TO DEFINE RELEVANT MARKETS

The process of defining the relevant market in practice

Product dimension

There is a range of evidence permitting to assess the extent to which substitution would take place. In individual cases, certain types of evidence will be determinant, depending very much on the characteristics and specificity of the industry and products or services that are being examined. The same type of evidence may be of no importance in other cases. In most cases, a decision will have to be based on the consideration of a number of criteria and different items of evidence. The Commission follows an open approach to empirical evidence, aimed at making an effective use of all available information which may be relevant in individual cases. The Commission does not follow a rigid hierarchy of different sources of information or types of evidence.

The process of defining relevant markets may be summarised as follows: on the basis of the preliminary information available or information submitted by the undertakings involved, the Commission will usually be in a position to broadly establish the possible relevant markets within which, for instance a concentration or a restriction of competition has to be assessed. In general, and for all practical purposes when handling individual cases, the question will usually be to decide on a few alternative possible relevant markets. For instance, with respect to the product market, the issue will often be to establish whether product A and product B belong or do not belong to the same product market. It is often the case that the inclusion of product B would be enough to remove any competition concerns.

In such situations it is not necessary to consider whether the market also includes additional products and reach a definitive conclusion on the precise product market. If under the conceivable alternative market definitions the operation in question does not raise competition concerns, the question of market definition will be left open, reducing thereby the burden on companies to supply information.

Geographic dimension

The Commission's approach to geographic market definition might be summarised as follows: it will take a preliminary view of the scope of the geographic market on the basis of broad indications regarding the distribution of market shares of the parties and their competitors as well as a preliminary analysis of pricing and price differences at national and EU or EEA level. This initial view is used basically as a working hypothesis to focus the Commission's enquiries for the purposes of arriving at a precise geographic market definition.

The reasons behind any particular configuration of prices and market shares need to be explored. Companies might enjoy high market shares in their domestic markets just because of the weight of the past, and conversely, a homogeneous presence of companies throughout the EEA might be consistent with national or regional geographic markets. The initial working hypothesis will therefore be checked against an analysis of demand characteristics (importance of national or local preferences, current patterns of purchases of customers, product differentiation/brands, other) in order to establish whether companies in different areas do really constitute an actual alternative source of supply for consumers. The theoretical experiment is again based on substitution arising from changes in relative prices, and the question to answer is again whether the customers of the parties would switch their orders to companies located elsewhere in the short term and at a negligible cost.

If necessary, a further check on supply factors will be carried out to ensure that those companies located in distinct areas do not face impediments to develop their sales on competitive terms throughout the whole geographic market. This analysis will include an examination of requirements for a local presence in order to sell in that area, the conditions of access to distribution channels, costs associated with setting up a distribution network, and the existence or absence of regulatory barriers arising from public procurement, price regulations, quotas and tariffs limiting trade or production, technical standards, monopolies, freedom of establishment, requirements for administrative authorisations, packaging regulations, etc ... In short, the Commission will identify possible obstacles and barriers isolating companies located in a given area from the competitive pressure of companies located outside that area, so as to determine the precise degree of market interpenetration at national, European or global level.

The actual pattern and evolution of trade flows offers useful supplementary indications as to the economic importance of each demand or supply factors mentioned above, and the extent to which they may or may not constitute actual barriers creating different geographic markets. The analysis of trade flows will generally address the question of transport costs and the extent to which these may hinder trade between different areas, having regard to plant location, costs of production and relative price levels.

Market integration in the European Union

Finally, the Commission also takes into account the continuing process of market integration in particular in the European Union when defining geographic markets, especially in the area of concentrations and structural joint ventures. The measures adopted and implemented in the internal market programme to remove barriers to trade and further integrate the community markets cannot be ignored when assessing the effects on competition of a concentration or a structural joint venture. A situation where national markets have been artificially isolated from each other because of the existence of legislative barriers that have now been removed, will generally lead to a cautious assessment of past evidence regarding prices, market shares or trade patterns. A process of market integration that would, in the short term, lead to wider geographic markets may therefore be taken into consideration when defining the geographic market for the purposes of assessing concentrations and joint ventures.

The process of gathering evidence

When a precise market definition is deemed necessary, the Commission will often contact the main customers and the main companies in the industry to enquire into their views about the boundaries of product and geographic markets and to obtain the necessary factual evidence to reach a conclusion. The Commission might also contact the relevant professional associations, and where appropriate, companies active in upstream markets, so as to be able to define, insofar as necessary, separate product and geographic markets, for different levels of production or distribution of the products/services in question. It might also request additional information to the undertakings involved.

Where appropriate, the Commission services will address written requests for information to the market players mentioned above. These requests will usually include questions relating to the perceptions of companies about reactions to hypothetical price increases and their views of the boundaries of the relevant market. They will also include requests to provide the factual information the Commission deems necessary to reach a conclusion on the extent of the relevant market. The Commission services might also discuss with marketing directors or other officers of those companies to gain a better understanding on how negotiations between suppliers and customers take place and better understand issues relating to the definition of the relevant market. Where appropriate, they might also carry out visits or inspections to the premises of the parties, their customers and/or their competitors, in order to better understand how products are manufactured and sold.

The type of evidence relevant to reach a conclusion as to the product market can be categorised as follows.

Evidence to define markets—Product dimension

An analysis of the product characteristics and its intended use allows the Commission, in a first step, to limit the field of investigation of possible substitutes. However, product characteristics and intended use are insufficient to conclude whether two products are demand substitutes. Functional interchangeability or similarity in characteristics may not provide in themselves sufficient criteria because the responsiveness of customers to relative price changes may be determined by other considerations also. For example, there may be different competitive constraints in the original equipment market for car components and in spare parts, thereby leading to a distinction of two relevant markets. Conversely, differences in product characteristics are not in themselves sufficient to exclude demand substitutability, since this will depend to a large extent on how customers value different characteristics.

The type of evidence the Commission considers relevant to assess whether two products are demand substitutes can be categorised as follows:

Evidence of substitution in the recent past. In certain cases, it is possible to analyse evidence relating to recent past events or shocks in the market that offer actual examples of substitution between two products. When available, this sort of information will normally be fundamental for market definition. If there have been changes in relative prices in the past (all else being equal), the reactions in terms of quantities demanded will be determinant in establishing substitutability. Launches of new products in the past can also offer useful information, when it is possible to precisely analyse which products lost sales to the new product.

There are a number of quantitative tests that have specifically been designed for the purpose of delineating markets. These tests consist of various econometric and statistical approaches: estimates of elasticities and cross-price elasticities[5] for the demand of a product, tests based on similarity of price movements over time, the analysis of causality between price series and similarity of price levels and/or their convergence. The Commission takes into account the available quantitative evidence capable of withstanding rigorous scrutiny for the purposes of establishing patterns of substitution in the past.

Views of customers and competitors. The Commission often contacts the main customers and competitors of the companies involved in its enquiries, to gather their views on the boundaries of the product market as well as most of the factual information it requires to reach a conclusion on the scope of the market. Reasoned answers of customers and competitors as to what would happen if relative prices for the candidate products would increase in the candidate geographic area by a small amount (for instance of 5%–10%) are taken into account when they are sufficiently backed by factual evidence.

Consumer preferences. In cases of consumer goods, it might be difficult for the Commission to gather the direct views of end consumers about substitute products. Marketing studies that companies have commissioned in the past and that are used by companies in their own decision making as to pricing of their products and/or marketing actions may provide useful information for the Commission's delineation of the relevant market. Consumer surveys on usage patterns and attitudes, data from consumer's purchasing patterns, the views expressed by retailers and more generally, market research studies submitted by the parties and their competitors are taken into account to establish whether an economically significant proportion of consumers consider two products as substitutable, taking also into account the importance of brands for the products in question. The methodology followed in consumer surveys carried out ad-hoc by the undertakings involved or their competitors for the purposes of a merger procedure or a procedure under Regulation 17 will usually be scrutinized with utmost care. Unlike pre-existing studies, they have not been prepared in the normal course of business for the adoption of business decisions.

Barriers and costs associated with switching demand to potential substitutes. There are a number of barriers and costs that might prevent the Commission from considering two prima facie demand substitutes as belonging to one single product market. It is not possible to provide an exhaustive list of all the possible barriers to substitution and of switching costs. These barriers or obstacles might have a wide range of origins, and in its decisions, the Commission has been confronted with regulatory barriers or other forms of State intervention, constraints arising in downstream markets, need to incur specific capital investment or loss in current output in order to switch to alternative inputs, the location of customers, specific investment in production process, learning and human capital investment, retooling costs or other investments, uncertainty about quality and reputation of unknown suppliers, and others.

Different categories of customers and price discrimination. The extent of the product market might be narrowed in the presence of distinct groups of customers. A distinct group of customers for the relevant product may constitute a narrower, distinct market when such group could be subject to price discrimination. This will usually be the case when two conditions are met: a) it is possible to identify clearly which group an individual customer belongs to at the moment of selling the relevant products to him, and b) trade among customers or arbitrage by third parties should not be feasible.

Evidence to define markets—Geographic dimension

The type of evidence the Commission considers relevant to reach a conclusion as to the geographic market can be categorised as follows:

Past evidence of diversion of orders to other areas. In certain cases, evidence on changes in prices between different areas and consequent reactions by customers might be available. Generally, the same quantitative tests used for product market definition might as well be used in geographic market definition, bearing in mind that international comparisons of prices might be more complex due to a number of factors such as exchange rate movements, taxation and product differentiation.

Basic demand characteristics. The nature of demand for the relevant product may in itself determine the scope of the geographical market. Factors such as national preferences or preferences for national brands, language, culture and life style, and the need for a local presence have a strong potential to limit the geographic scope of competition.

Views of customers and competitors. Where appropriate, the Commission will contact the main customers and competitors of the parties in its enquiries, to gather their views on the boundaries of the geographic market as well as most of the factual information it requires to reach a conclusion on the scope of the market when they are sufficiently backed by factual evidence.

Current geographic pattern of purchases. An examination of the customers' current geographic pattern of purchases provides useful evidence as to the possible scope of the geographic market. When customers purchase from companies located anywhere in the EU or the EEA on similar terms, or they procure their supplies through effective tendering procedures in which companies from anywhere in the EU or the EEA do submit bids, the geographic market will be usually considered to be Community-wide.

Trade flows/pattern of shipments. When the number of customers is so large that it is not possible to obtain through them a clear picture of geographic purchasing patterns, information on trade flows might be used alternatively, provided that the trade statistics are available with a sufficient degree of detail for the relevant products. Trade flows, and above all, the rational behind trade flows provide useful insights and information for the purpose of establishing the scope of the geographic market but are not in themselves conclusive.

Barriers and switching costs associated to divert orders to companies located in other areas. The absence of transborder purchases or trade flows, for instance, does not necessarily mean that the market is at most national in scope. Still, barriers isolating the national market have to identified before concluding that the relevant geographic market in such a case is national. Perhaps the clearest obstacle for a customer to divert its orders to other areas is the impact of transport costs and transport restrictions arising from legislation or from the nature of the relevant products. The impact of transport costs will usually limit the scope of the geographic market for bulky, low value products, bearing in mind that a transport disadvantage might also be compensated by a comparative advantage in other costs (labour costs or raw materials). Access to distribution in a given area, regulatory barriers still existing in certain sectors, quotas and custom tariffs might also constitute barriers isolating a geographic area from the competitive pressure of companies located outside that area. Significant switching costs in procuring supplies from companies located in other countries constitute additional sources of such barriers.

On the basis of the evidence gathered, the Commission will then define a geographic market that could range from a local dimension to a global one, and there are examples of both local and global markets in past decisions of the Commission.

The paragraphs above describe the different factors which might be relevant to define markets. This does not imply that in each individual case it will be necessary to obtain evidence and assess each of these factors. Often in practice the evidence provided by a subset of these factors will be sufficient to reach a conclusion, as shown in the past decisional practice of the Commission.

IV. CALCULATION OF MARKET SHARES

The definition of the relevant market in both its product and geographic dimensions allows to identify the suppliers and the customers/consumers active on that market. On that basis, a total market size and market shares for each supplier can be calculated on the basis of their sales of the relevant products on the relevant area. In practice, the total market size and market shares are often available from market sources, i.e. companies' estimates, studies commissioned to industry consultants and/or trade associations. When this is not the case, or also when available estimates are not reliable, the Commission will usually ask each supplier in the relevant market to provide its own sales in order to calculate total market size and market shares.

If sales are usually the reference to calculate market shares, there are nevertheless other indications that, depending on the specific products or industry in question, can offer useful information such as, in particular, capacity, the number of players in bidding markets, units of fleet as in aerospace, or the reserves held in the case of sectors such as mining.

As a rule of thumb, both volume sales and value sales provide useful information. In cases of differentiated products, sales in value and their associated market share will usually be considered to better reflect the relative position and strength of each supplier.

V. ADDITIONAL CONSIDERATIONS

There are certain areas where the application of the principles above has to be undertaken with care. This is the case when considering primary and secondary markets, in particular, when the behaviour of undertakings at a point in time has to be analysed under Article 86. The method to define markets in these cases is the same, i.e. to assess the responses of customers based on their purchasing decisions to relative price changes, but taking into account as well constraints on substitution imposed by conditions in the connected markets. A narrow definition of market for secondary products, for instance, spare parts, may result when compatibility with the primary product is important. Problems of finding compatible secondary products together with the existence of high prices and a long life time of the primary products may render relative price increases of secondary products profitable. A different market definition may result if significant substitution between secondary products is possible or if the characteristics of the primary products make quick and direct consumer responses to relative price increases of the secondary products feasible.

In certain cases, the existence of chains of substitution might lead to the definition of a relevant market where products or areas at the extreme of the market are not directly substitutable. An example might be provided by the geographic dimension of a product with significant transport costs. In such cases, deliveries from a given plant are limited to a certain area around each plant by the impact of transport costs. In principle, such area could constitute the relevant geographic market. However, if the distribution of plants is such that there are considerable overlaps between the areas around different plants, it is possible that the pricing of those products will be constrained by a chain substitution effect, and lead to define a broader geographic market. The same reasoning may apply if product B is a demand substitute for products A and C. Even if products A and C are not direct demand substitutes they might be found to be in the same relevant product market since their respective pricing might be constrained by substitution to B.

From a practical perspective, the concept of chains of substitution has to be corroborated by actual evidence, for instance related to price interdependence at the extremes of the chains of substitution, in order to lead to an extension of the relevant market in an individual case. Price levels at the extremes of the chains would have to be as well of the same magnitude.

---

[1] The focus of assessment in state aid cases is the aid recipient and the industry/sector concerned rather than identification of competitive constraints faced by the aid recipient. When consideration of market power and therefore of the relevant market are raised in any particular case, elements of the approach outlined here might serve as a basis for the assessment of state aid cases.

[2] For the purposes of this notice, the undertakings involved will be in the case of a concentration the parties to the concentration. In investigations under Article 86 of the Treaty, the undertaking being investigated or the complainants. For investigations under Article 85, the parties to the agreement.

[3] Definition given by the Court of Justice in Hoffmann La Roche (Court of Justice 13.02.1979, case 85/76), and confirmed in subsequent judgements.

[4] I.e. the period which does not imply a significant adjustment of existing tangible and intangible assets (see para. 23).

[5] Own price elasticity of demand for product X is a measure of the responsiveness of demand for X to percentage change in its own price. Cross-price elasticity between products X and Y is the responsiveness of demand for product X to percentage change in the price of product Y.

4. VERTICAL AGREEMENTS—BLOCK EXEMPTION

Commission Regulation 2790/1999 on the application of Article 81(3)

O.J. L 336/21 (Dec. 29, 1999)

THE COMMISSION OF THE EUROPEAN COMMUNITIES,

Having regard to the Treaty establishing the European Community,

Having regard to Council Regulation No 19/65/EEC of 2 March 1965 on the application of Article 85(3) of the Treaty to certain categories of agreements and concerted practices, as last amended by Regulation (EC) No 1215/1999, and in particular Article 1 thereof,

Having published a draft of this Regulation,

Having consulted the Advisory Committee on Restrictive Practices and Dominant Positions,

Whereas:

(1) Regulation No 19/65/EEC empowers the Commission to apply Article 81(3) of the Treaty (formerly Article 85(3)) by regulation to certain categories of vertical agreements and corresponding concerted practices falling within Article 81(1).

(2) Experience acquired to date makes it possible to define a category of vertical agreements which can be regarded as normally satisfying the conditions laid down in Article 81(3).

(3) This category includes vertical agreements for the purchase or sale of goods or services where these agreements are concluded between non-competing undertakings, between certain competitors or by certain associations of retailers of goods; it also includes vertical agreements containing ancillary provisions on the assignment or use of intellectual property rights; for the purposes of this Regulation, the term "vertical agreements" includes the corresponding concerted practices.

(4) For the application of Article 81(3) by regulation, it is not necessary to define those vertical agreements which are capable of falling within Article 81(1); in the individual assessment of agreements under Article 81(1), account has to be taken of several factors, and in particular the market structure on the supply and purchase side.

(5) The benefit of the block exemption should be limited to vertical agreements for which it can be assumed with sufficient certainty that they satisfy the conditions of Article 81(3).

(6) Vertical agreements of the category defined in this Regulation can improve economic efficiency within a chain of production or distribution by facilitating better coordination between the participating undertakings; in particular, they can lead to a reduction in the transaction and distribution costs of the parties and to an optimisation of their sales and investment levels.

(7) The likelihood that such efficiency-enhancing effects will outweigh any anti-competitive effects due to restrictions contained in vertical agreements depends on the degree of market power of the undertakings concerned and, therefore, on the extent to which those undertakings face competition from other suppliers of goods or services regarded by the buyer as interchangeable or substitutable for one another, by reason of the products' characteristics, their prices and their intended use.

(8) It can be presumed that, where the share of the relevant market accounted for by the supplier does not exceed 30%, vertical agreements which do not contain certain types of severely anti-competitive restraints generally lead to an improvement in production or distribution and allow consumers a fair share of the resulting benefits; in the case of vertical agreements containing exclusive supply obligations, it is the market share of the buyer which is relevant in determining the overall effects of such vertical agreements on the market.

(9) Above the market share threshold of 30%, there can be no presumption that vertical agreements falling within the scope of Article 81(1) will usually give rise to objective advantages of such a character and size as to compensate for the disadvantages which they create for competition.

(10) This Regulation should not exempt vertical agreements containing restrictions which are not indispensable to the attainment of the positive effects mentioned above; in particular, vertical agreements containing certain types of severely anti-competitive restraints such as minimum and fixed resale-prices, as well as certain types of territorial protection, should be excluded from the benefit of the block exemption established by this Regulation irrespective of the market share of the undertakings concerned.

(11) In order to ensure access to or to prevent collusion on the relevant market, certain conditions are to be attached to the block exemption; to this end, the exemption of non-compete obligations should be limited to obligations which do not exceed a definite duration; for the same reasons, any direct or indirect obligation causing the members of a selective distribution system not to sell the brands of particular competing suppliers should be excluded from the benefit of this Regulation.

(12) The market-share limitation, the non-exemption of certain vertical agreements and the conditions provided for in this Regulation normally ensure that the agreements to which the block exemption applies do not enable the participating undertakings to eliminate competition in respect of a substantial part of the products in question.

(13) In particular cases in which the agreements falling under this Regulation nevertheless have effects incompatible with Article 81(3), the Commission may withdraw the benefit of the block exemption; this may occur in particular where the buyer has significant market power in the relevant market in which it resells the goods or provides the services or where parallel networks of vertical agreements have similar effects which significantly restrict access to a relevant market or competition therein;

such cumulative effects may for example arise in the case of selective distribution or non-compete obligations.

(14) Regulation No 19/65/EEC empowers the competent authorities of Member States to withdraw the benefit of the block exemption in respect of vertical agreements having effects incompatible with the conditions laid down in Article 81(3), where such effects are felt in their respective territory, or in a part thereof, and where such territory has the characteristics of a distinct geographic market; Member States should ensure that the exercise of this power of withdrawal does not prejudice the uniform application throughout the common market of the Community competition rules or the full effect of the measures adopted in implementation of those rules.

(15) In order to strengthen supervision of parallel networks of vertical agreements which have similar restrictive effects and which cover more than 50% of a given market, the Commission may declare this Regulation inapplicable to vertical agreements containing specific restraints relating to the market concerned, thereby restoring the full application of Article 81 to such agreements.

(16) This Regulation is without prejudice to the application of Article 82.

(17) In accordance with the principle of the primacy of Community law, no measure taken pursuant to national laws on competition should prejudice the uniform application throughout the common market of the Community competition rules or the full effect of any measures adopted in implementation of those rules, including this Regulation,

HAS ADOPTED THIS REGULATION:

Article 1

[Definitions]

For the purposes of this Regulation:

(a) "competing undertakings" means actual or potential suppliers in the same product market; the, product market includes goods or services which are regarded by the buyer as interchangeable with or substitutable for the contract goods or services, by reason of the products' characteristics, their prices and their intended use;

(b) "non-compete obligation" means any direct or indirect obligation causing the buyer not to manufacture, purchase, sell or resell goods or services which compete with the contract goods or services, or any direct or indirect obligation on the buyer to purchase from the supplier or from another undertaking designated by the supplier more than 80% of the buyer's total purchases of the contract goods or services and their substitutes on the relevant market, calculated on the basis of the value of its purchases in the preceding calendar year;

(c) "exclusive supply obligation" means any direct or indirect obligation causing the supplier to sell the goods or services specified in the agreement only to one buyer inside the Community for the purposes of a specific use or for resale;

(d) "Selective distribution system" means a distribution system where the supplier undertakes to sell the contract goods or services, either directly or indirectly, only to distributors selected on the basis of specified criteria and where these distributors undertake not to sell such goods or services to unauthorised distributors;

(e) "intellectual property rights" includes industrial property rights, copyright and neighbouring rights;

(f) "know-how" means a package of non-patented practical information, resulting from experience and testing by the supplier, which is secret, substantial and identified: in this context, "secret" means that the know-how, as a body or in the precise configuration and assembly of its components, is not generally known or easily accessible; "substantial" means that the know-how includes information which is indispensable to the buyer for the use, sale or resale of the contract goods or services; "identified" means that the know-how must be described in a sufficiently comprehensive manner so as to make it possible to verify that it fulfils the criteria of secrecy and substantiality;

(g) "buyer" includes an undertaking which, under an agreement falling within Article 81(1) of the Treaty, sells goods or services on behalf of another undertaking.

Article 2

[Exemption]

1. Pursuant to Article 81(3) of the Treaty and subject to the provisions of this Regulation, it is hereby declared that Article 81(1) shall not apply to agreements or concerted practices entered into between two or more undertakings each of which operates, for the purposes of the agreement, at a different level of the production or distribution chain, and relating to the conditions under which the parties may purchase, sell or resell certain goods or services ("vertical agreements").

This exemption shall apply to the extent that such agreements contain restrictions of competition falling within the scope of Article 81(1) ("vertical restraints").

2. The exemption provided for in paragraph 1 shall apply to vertical agreements entered into between an association of undertakings and its members, or between such an association and its suppliers, only if all its members are retailers of goods and if no individual member of the association, together with its connected undertakings, has a total annual turnover exceeding EUR 50 million; vertical agreements entered into by such associations shall be covered by this Regulation without prejudice to the application of Article 81 to horizontal agreements concluded between the members of the association or decisions adopted by the association.

3. The exemption provided for in paragraph 1 shall apply to vertical agreements containing provisions which relate to the assignment to the

buyer or use by the buyer of intellectual property rights, provided that those provisions do not constitute the primary object of such agreements and are directly related to the use, sale or resale of goods or services by the buyer or its customers. The exemption applies on condition that, in relation to the contract goods or services, those provisions do not contain restrictions of competition having the same object or effect as vertical restraints which are not exempted under this Regulation.

4. The exemption provided for in paragraph 1 shall not apply to vertical agreements entered into between competing undertakings; however, it shall apply where competing undertakings enter into a non-reciprocal vertical agreement and:

(a) the buyer has a total annual turnover not exceeding EUR 100 million, or

(b) the supplier is a manufacturer and a distributor of goods, while the buyer is a distributor not manufacturing goods competing with the contract goods, or

(c) the supplier is a provider of services at several levels of trade, while the buyer does not provide competing services at the level of trade where it purchases the contract services.

5. This Regulation shall not apply to vertical agreements the subject matter of which falls within the scope of any other block exemption regulation.

Article 3

[Market share condition]

1. Subject to paragraph 2 of this Article, the exemption provided for in Article 2 shall apply on condition that the market share held by the supplier does not exceed 30% of the relevant market on which it sells the contract goods or services.

2. In the case of vertical agreements containing exclusive supply obligations, the exemption provided for in Article 2 shall apply on condition that the market share held by the buyer does not exceed 30% of the relevant market on which it purchases the contract goods or services.

Article 4

[Inapplicability to hard core restraints]

The exemption provided for in Article 2 shall not apply to vertical agreements which, directly or indirectly, in isolation or in combination with other factors under the control of the parties, have as their object:

(a) the restriction of the buyer's ability to determine its sale price, without prejudice to the possibility of the supplier's imposing a maximum sale price or recommending a sale price, provided that they do not amount to a fixed or minimum sale price as a result of pressure from, or incentives offered by, any of the parties;

(b) the restriction of the territory into which, or of the customers to whom, the buyer may sell the contract goods or services, except:

— the restriction of active sales into the exclusive territory or to an exclusive customer group reserved to the supplier or allocated by the supplier to another buyer, where such a restriction does not limit sales by the customers of the buyer,

— the restriction of sales to end users by a buyer operating at the wholesale level of trade,

— the restriction of sales to unauthorised distributors by the members of a selective distribution system, and

— the restriction of the buyer's ability to sell components, supplied for the purposes of incorporation, to customers who would use them to manufacture the same type of Goods as those produced by the supplier;

(c) the restriction of active or passive sales to end users by members of a selective distribution system operating at the retail level of trade, without prejudice to the possibility of prohibiting a member of the system from operating out of an unauthorised place of establishment;

(d) the restriction of cross-supplies between distributors within a selective distribution system, including between distributors operating at different level of trade;

(e) the restriction agreed between a supplier of components and a buyer who incorporates those components, which limits the supplier to selling the components as spare parts to end-users or to repairers or other service providers not entrusted by the buyer with the repair or servicing of its goods.

Article 5

[Obligations not covered]

The exemption provided for in Article 2 shall not apply to any of the following obligations contained in vertical agreements:

(a) any direct or indirect non-compete obligation, the duration of which is indefinite or exceeds five years. A non-compete obligation which is tacitly renewable beyond a period of five years is to be deemed to have been concluded for an indefinite duration. However, the time limitation of five years shall not apply where the contract goods or services are sold by the buyer from premises and land owned by the supplier or leased by the supplier from third parties not connected with the buyer, provided that the duration of the non-compete obligation does not exceed the period of occupancy of the premises and land by the buyer;

(b) any direct or indirect obligation causing the buyer, after termination of the agreement, not to manufacture, purchase, sell or resell goods or services, unless such obligation:

— relates to goods or services which compete with the contract goods or services, and

— is limited to the premises and land from which the buyer has operated during the contract period, and

— is indispensable to protect know-how transferred by the supplier to the buyer, and provided that the duration of such non-compete obligation is limited to a period of one year after termination of the agreement; this obligation is without prejudice to the possibility of imposing a restriction which is unlimited in time on the use and disclosure of know-how which has not entered the public domain;

(c) any direct or indirect obligation causing the members of a selective distribution system not to sell the brands of particular competing suppliers.

Article 6

[Withdrawal by Commission]

The Commission may withdraw the benefit of this Regulation, pursuant to Article 7(1) of Regulation No 19/65/EEC, where it finds in any particular case that vertical agreements to which this Regulation applies nevertheless have effects which are incompatible with the conditions laid down in Article 81(3) of the Treaty, and in particular where access to the relevant market or competition therein is significantly restricted by the cumulative effect of parallel networks of similar vertical restraints implemented by competing suppliers or buyers.

Article 7

[Withdrawal by Member State]

Where in any particular case vertical agreements to which the exemption provided for in Article 2 applies have effects incompatible with the conditions laid down in Article 81(3) of the Treaty in the territory of a Member State, or in a part thereof, which has all the characteristics of a distinct geographic market, the competent authority of that Member State may withdraw the benefit of application of this Regulation in respect of that territory, under the same conditions as provided in Article 6.

Article 8

[Parallel networks]

1. Pursuant to Article 1 a of Regulation No 19/65/EEC, the Commission may by regulation declare that, where parallel networks of similar vertical restraints cover more than 50% of a relevant market, this Regulation shall not apply to vertical agreements containing specific restraints relating to that market.

2. A regulation pursuant to paragraph 1 shall not become applicable earlier than six months following its adoption.

Article 9

[Application of the market share threshold]

1. The market share of 30% provided for in Article 3(1) shall be calculated on the basis of the market sales value of the contract goods or services and other goods or services sold by the supplier, which are regarded as interchangeable or substitutable by the buyer, by reason of the products' characteristics, their prices and their intended use; if market sales value data are not available, estimates based on other reliable market information, including market sales volumes, may be used to establish the market share of the undertaking concerned. For the purposes of Article 3(2), it is either the market purchase value or estimates thereof which shall be used to calculate the market share.

2. For the purposes of applying the market share, threshold provided for in Article 3 the following rules shall apply:

(a) the market share shall be calculated on the basis of data relating to the preceding calendar year;

(b) the market share shall include any goods or services supplied to integrated distributors for the purposes of sale;

(c) if the market share is initially not more than 30% but subsequently rises above that level without exceeding 35%, the exemption provided for in Article 2 shall continue to apply for a period of two consecutive calendar years following the year in which the 30% market share threshold was first exceeded;

(d) if the market share is initially not more than 30% but subsequently rises above 35%, the exemption provided for in Article 2 shall continue to apply for one calendar year following the year in which the level of 35% was first exceeded;

(e) the benefit of points (c) and (d) may not be combined so as to exceed a period of two calendar years.

Article 10

[Calculation]

1. For the purpose of calculating total annual turnover within the meaning of Article 2(2) and (4), the turnover achieved during the previous financial year by the relevant party to the vertical agreement and the turnover achieved by its connected undertakings in respect of all goods and services, excluding all taxes and other duties, shall be added together. For this purpose, no account shall be taken of dealings between the party to the vertical agreement and its connected undertakings or between its connected undertakings.

2. The exemption provided for in Article 2 shall remain applicable where, for any period of two consecutive financial years, the total annual turnover threshold is exceeded by no more than 10%.

Article 11

[Connected undertakings]

1. For the purposes of this Regulation, the terms "undertaking", "supplier" and "buyer" shall include their respective connected undertakings.

2. "Connected undertakings" are:

(a) undertakings in which a party to the agreement, directly or indirectly:

— has the power to exercise more than half the voting rights, or

— has the power to appoint more than half the members of the supervisory board, board of management or bodies legally representing the undertaking, or

— has the right to manage the undertaking's affairs;

(b) undertakings which directly or indirectly have, over a party to the agreement, the rights or powers listed in (a);

(c) undertakings in which an undertaking referred to in (b) has, directly or indirectly, the rights or powers listed in (a);

(d) undertakings in which a party to the agreement together with one or more of the undertakings referred to in (a), (b) or (c), or in which two or more of the latter undertakings, jointly have the rights or powers listed in (a);

(e) undertakings in which the rights or the powers listed in (a) are jointly held by:

— parties to the agreement or their respective connected undertakings referred to in (a) to (d), or

— one or more of the parties to the agreement or one or more of their connected undertakings referred to in (a) to (d) and one or more third parties.

3. For the purposes of Article 3, the market share held by the undertakings referred to in paragraph 2(e) of this Article shall be apportioned equally to each undertaking having the rights or the powers listed in paragraph 2(a).

Article 12

[Transitional period]

1. The exemptions provided for in Commission Regulations (EEC) No 1983/83, (EEC) No 1984/83 and (EEC) No 4087/88 shall continue to apply until 31 May 2000.

2. The prohibition laid down in Article 81(1) of the EC Treaty shall not apply during the period from 1 June 2000 to 31 December 2001 in respect of agreements already in force on 31 May 2000 which do not satisfy the conditions for exemption provided for in this Regulation but which

satisfy the conditions for exemption provided for in Regulations (EEC) No 1983/83, (EEC) No 1984/83 or (EEC) No 4087/88.

Article 13

[Period of validity]

This Regulation shall enter into force on 1 January 2000. It shall apply from 1 June 2000, except for Article 12(1) which shall apply from 1 January 2000. This Regulation shall expire on 31 May 2010.

This Regulation shall be binding in its entirety and directly applicable in all Member States.

5. SPECIALISATION—BLOCK EXEMPTION

Commission Regulation 2658/2000 on the application of Article 81(3)

O.J. L 304/3 (Dec. 5, 2000)

THE COMMISSION OF THE EUROPEAN COMMUNITIES,

Having regard to the Treaty establishing the European Community,

Having regard to Council Regulation (EEC) No 2821/71 of 20 December 1971 on the application of Article 85(3) of the Treaty to categories of agreements, decisions and concerted practices, as last amended by the Act of Accession of Austria, Finland and Sweden, and in particular Article 1(1)(c) thereof,

Having published a draft of this Regulation,

Having consulted the Advisory Committee on Restrictive Practices and Dominant Positions,

Whereas:

(1) Regulation (EEC) No 2821/71 empowers the Commission to apply Article 81(3) (formerly Article 85(3)) of the Treaty by regulation to certain categories of agreements, decisions and concerted practices falling within the scope of Article 81(1) which have as their object specialisation, including agreements necessary for achieving it.

(2) Pursuant to Regulation (EEC) No 2821/71, in particular, the Commission has adopted Regulation (EEC) No 417/85 of 19 December 1984 on the application of Article 85(3) of the Treaty to categories of specialisation agreements, as last amended by Regulation (EC) No 2236/97. Regulation (EEC) No 417/85 expires on 31 December 2000.

(3) A new regulation should meet the two requirements of ensuring effective protection of competition and providing adequate legal security for undertakings. The pursuit of these objectives should take account of the need to simplify administrative supervision and the legislative framework to as great an extent as possible.

Below a certain level of market power it can, for the application of Article 81(3), in general be presumed that the positive effects of specialisation agreements will outweigh any negative effects on competition.

(4) Regulation (EEC) No 2821/71 requires the exempting regulation of the Commission to define the categories of agreements, decisions and concerted practices to which it applies, to specify the restrictions or clauses which may, or may not, appear in the agreements, decisions and concerted practices, and to specify the clauses which must be contained in the agreements, decisions and concerted practices or the other conditions which must be satisfied.

(5) It is appropriate to move away from the approach of listing exempted clauses and to place greater emphasis on defining the categories of agreements which are exempted up to a certain level of market power and on specifying the restrictions or clauses which are not to be contained

in such agreements. This is consistent with an economics-based approach which assesses the impact of agreements on the relevant market.

(6) For the application of Article 81(3) by regulation, it is not necessary to define those agreements which are capable of falling within Article 81(1). In the individual assessment of agreements under Article 81(1), account has to be taken of several factors, and in particular the market structure on the relevant market.

(7) The benefit of the block exemption should be limited to those agreements for which it can be assumed with sufficient certainty that they satisfy the conditions of Article 81(3).

(8) Agreements on specialisation in production generally contribute to improving the production or distribution of goods, because the undertakings concerned can concentrate on the manufacture of certain products and thus operate more efficiently and supply the products more cheaply. Agreements on specialisation in the provision of services can also be said to generally give rise to similar improvements. It is likely that, given effective competition, consumers will receive a fair share of the resulting benefit.

(9) Such advantages can arise equally from agreements whereby one participant gives up the manufacture of certain products or provision of certain services in favour of another participant ("unilateral specialisation"), from agreements whereby each participant gives up the manufacture of certain products or provision of certain services in favour of another participant ("reciprocal specialisation") and from agreements whereby the participants undertake to jointly manufacture certain products or provide certain services ("joint production").

(10) As unilateral specialisation agreements between non-competitors may benefit from the block exemption provided by Commission Regulation (EC) No 2790/1999 of 22 December 1999 on the application of Article 81(3) of the Treaty to categories of vertical agreements and concerted practices, the application of the present Regulation to unilateral specialisation agreements should be limited to agreements between competitors.

(11) All other agreements entered into between undertakings relating to the conditions under which they specialise in the production of goods and/or services should fall within the scope of this Regulation. The block exemption should also apply to provisions contained in specialisation agreements which do not constitute the primary object of such agreements, but are directly related to and necessary for their implementation, and to certain related purchasing and marketing arrangements.

(12) To ensure that the benefits of specialisation will materialise without one party leaving the market downstream of production, unilateral and reciprocal specialisation agreements should only be covered by this Regulation where they provide for supply and purchase obligations. These obligations may, but do not have to, be of an exclusive nature.

(13) It can be presumed that, where the participating undertakings' share of the relevant market does not exceed 20%, specialisation agreements as defined in this Regulation will, as a general rule, give rise to

economic benefits in the form of economies of scale or scope or better production technologies, while allowing consumers a fair share of the resulting benefits.

(14) This Regulation should not exempt agreements containing restrictions which are not indispensable to attain the positive effects mentioned above. In principle certain severe anti-competitive restraints relating to the fixing of prices charged to third parties, limitation of output or sales, and allocation of markets or customers should be excluded from the benefit of the block exemption established by this Regulation irrespective of the market share of the undertakings concerned.

(15) The market share limitation, the non-exemption of certain agreements and the conditions provided for in this Regulation normally ensure that the agreements to which the block exemption applies do not enable the participating undertakings to eliminate competition in respect of a substantial part of the products or services in question.

(16) In particular cases in which the agreements falling under this Regulation nevertheless have effects incompatible with Article 81(3) of the Treaty, the Commission may withdraw the benefit of the block exemption.

(17) In order to facilitate the conclusion of specialisation agreements, which can have a bearing on the structure of the participating undertakings, the period of validity of this Regulation should be fixed at 10 years.

(18) This Regulation is without prejudice to the application of Article 82 of the Treaty.

(19) In accordance with the principle of the primacy of Community law, no measure taken pursuant to national laws on competition should prejudice the uniform application throughout the common market of the Community competition rules or the full effect of any measures adopted in implementation of those rules, including this Regulation,

HAS ADOPTED THIS REGULATION:

Article 1

Exemption

1. Pursuant to Article 81(3) of the Treaty and subject to the provisions of this Regulation, it is hereby declared that Article 81(1) shall not apply to the following agreements entered into between two or more undertakings (hereinafter referred to as "the parties") which relate to the conditions under which those undertakings specialise in the production of products (hereinafter referred to as "specialisation agreements"):

(a) unilateral specialisation agreements, by virtue of which one party agrees to cease production of certain products or to refrain from producing those products and to purchase them from a competing undertaking, while the competing undertaking agrees to produce and supply those products; or

(b) reciprocal specialisation agreements, by virtue of which two or more parties on a reciprocal basis agree to cease or refrain from producing certain but different products and to purchase these products from the other parties, who agree to supply them; or

(c) joint production agreements, by virtue of which two or more parties agree to produce certain products jointly.

This exemption shall apply to the extent that such specialisation agreements contain restrictions of competition falling within the scope of Article 81(1) of the Treaty.

2. The exemption provided for in paragraph 1 shall also apply to provisions contained in specialisation agreements, which do not constitute the primary object of such agreements, but are directly related to and necessary for their implementation, such as those concerning the assignment or use of intellectual property rights.

The first subparagraph does, however, not apply to provisions which have the same object as the restrictions of competition enumerated in Article 5(1).

Article 2

Definitions

For the purposes of this Regulation:

1. "Agreement" means an agreement, a decision of an association of undertakings or a concerted practice.

2. "Participating undertakings" means undertakings party to the agreement and their respective connected undertakings.

3. "Connected undertakings" means:

(a) undertakings in which a party to the agreement, directly or indirectly:

(i) has the power to exercise more than half the voting rights, or

(ii) has the power to appoint more than half the members of the supervisory board, board of management or bodies legally representing the undertaking, or

(iii) has the right to manage the undertaking's affairs;

(b) undertakings which directly or indirectly have, over a party to the agreement, the rights or powers listed in (a);

(c) undertakings in which an undertaking referred to in (b) has, directly or indirectly, the rights or powers listed in (a);

(d) undertakings in which a party to the agreement together with one or more of the undertakings referred to in (a), (b) or (c), or in which two or more of the latter undertakings, jointly have the rights or powers listed in (a);

(e) undertakings in which the rights or the powers listed in (a) are jointly held by: (i) parties to the agreement or their respective connected undertakings referred to in (a) to (d), or (ii) one or more of the parties to the agreement or one or more of their connected undertakings referred to in (a) to (d) and one or more third parties.

4. "Product" means a good and/or a service, including both intermediary goods and/or services and final goods and/or services, with the exception of distribution and rental services.

5. "Production" means the manufacture of goods or the provision of services and includes production by way of subcontracting.

6. "Relevant market" means the relevant product and geographic market(s) to which the products, which are the subject matter of a specialisation agreement, belong.

7. "Competing undertaking" means an undertaking that is active on the relevant market (an actual competitor) or an undertaking that would, on realistic grounds, undertake the necessary additional investments or other necessary switching costs so that it could enter the relevant market in response to a small and permanent increase in relative prices (a potential competitor).

8. "Exclusive supply obligation" means an obligation not to supply a competing undertaking other than a party to the agreement with the product to which the specialisation agreement relates.

9. "Exclusive purchase obligation" means an obligation to purchase the product to which the specialisation agreement relates only from the party which agrees to supply it.

Article 3

Purchasing and marketing arrangements

The exemption provided for in Article 1 shall also apply where:

(a) the parties accept an exclusive purchase and/or exclusive supply obligation in the context of a unilateral or reciprocal specialisation agreement or a joint production agreement, or

(b) the parties do not sell the products which are the object of the specialisation agreement independently but provide for joint distribution or agree to appoint a third party distributor on an exclusive or non-exclusive basis in the context of a joint production agreement provided that the third party is not a competing undertaking.

Article 4

Market share threshold

The exemption provided for in Article 1 shall apply on condition that the combined market share of the participating undertakings does not exceed 20% of the relevant market.

Article 5

Agreements not covered by the exemption

1. The exemption provided for in Article 1 shall not apply to agreements which, directly or indirectly, in isolation or in combination with other factors under the control of the parties, have as their object:

(a) the fixing of prices when selling the products to third parties;

(b) the limitation of output or sales; or

(c) the allocation of markets or customers.

2. Paragraph 1 shall not apply to:

(a) provisions on the agreed amount of products in the context of unilateral or reciprocal specialisation agreements or the setting of the capacity and production volume of a production joint venture in the context of a joint production agreement;

(b) the setting of sales targets and the fixing of prices that a production joint venture charges to its immediate customers in the context of point (b) of Article 3.

Article 6

Application of the market share threshold

1. For the purposes of applying the market share threshold provided for in Article 4 the following rules shall apply:

(a) the market share shall be calculated on the basis of the market sales value; if market sales value data are not available, estimates based on other reliable market information, including market sales volumes, may be used to establish the market share of the undertaking concerned;

(b) the market share shall be calculated on the basis of data relating to the preceding calendar year;

(c) the market share held by the undertakings referred to in point 3(e) of Article 2 shall be apportioned equally to each undertaking having the rights or the powers listed in point 3(a) of Article 2.

2. If the market share referred to in Article 4 is initially not more than 20% but subsequently rises above this level without exceeding 25%, the exemption provided for in Article 1 shall continue to apply for a period of two consecutive calendar years following the year in which the 20% threshold was first exceeded.

3. If the market share referred to in Article 4 is initially not more than 20% but subsequently rises above 25%, the exemption provided for in Article 1 shall continue to apply for one calendar year following the year in which the level of 25% was first exceeded.

4. The benefit of paragraphs 2 and 3 may not be combined so as to exceed a period of two calendar years.

Article 7

Withdrawal

The Commission may withdraw the benefit of this Regulation, pursuant to Article 7 of Regulation (EEC) No 2821/71, where, either on its own initiative or at the request of a Member State or of a natural or legal person claiming a legitimate interest, it finds in a particular case that an agreement to which the exemption provided for in Article 1 applies nevertheless has effects which are incompatible with the conditions laid down in Article 81(3) of the Treaty, and in particular where:

(a) the agreement is not yielding significant results in terms of rationalisation or consumers are not receiving a fair share of the resulting benefit, or

(b) the products which are the subject of the specialisation are not subject in the common market or a substantial part thereof to effective competition from identical products or products considered by users to be equivalent in view of their characteristics, price and intended use.

Article 8

Transitional period

The prohibition laid down in Article 81(1) of the Treaty shall not apply during the period from 1 January 2001 to 30 June 2002 in respect of agreements already in force on 31 December 2000 which do not satisfy the conditions for exemption provided for in this Regulation but which satisfy the conditions for exemption provided for in Regulation (EEC) No 417/85.

Article 9

Period of validity

This Regulation shall enter into force on 1 January 2001.

It shall expire on 31 December 2010.

This Regulation shall be binding in its entirety and directly applicable in all Member States.

6. RESEARCH AND DEVELOPMENT AGREEMENTS—BLOCK EXEMPTION

Commission Regulation 2659/2000 on the application of Article 81(3)

O.J. L 304/7 (Dec. 5, 2000)

THE COMMISSION OF THE EUROPEAN COMMUNITIES,

Having regard to the Treaty establishing the European Community,

Having regard to Council Regulation (EEC) No 2821/71 of 20 December 1971 on application of Article 85(3) of the Treaty to categories of agreements, decisions and concerted practices, as last amended by the Act of Accession of Austria, Finland and Sweden, and in particular Article 1(1)(b) thereof,

Having published a draft of this Regulation,

Having consulted the Advisory Committee on Restrictive Practices and Dominant Positions,

Whereas:

(1) Regulation (EEC) No 2821/71 empowers the Commission to apply Article 81(3) (formerly Article 85(3)) of the Treaty by regulation to certain categories of agreements, decisions and concerted practices falling within the scope of Article 81(1) which have as their object the research and development of products or processes up to the stage of industrial application, and exploitation of the results, including provisions regarding intellectual property rights.

(2) Article 163(2) of the Treaty calls upon the Community to encourage undertakings, including small and medium-sized undertakings, in their research and technological development activities of high quality, and to support their efforts to cooperate with one another. Pursuant to Council Decision 1999/65/EC of 22 December 1998 concerning the rules for the participation of undertakings, research centres and universities and for the dissemination of research results for the implementation of the fifth framework programme of the European Community (1998–2002) and Commission Regulation (EC) No 996/1999 on the implementation of Decision 1999/65/EC, indirect research and technological development (RTD) actions supported under the fifth framework programme of the Community are required to be carried out cooperatively.

(3) Agreements on the joint execution of research work or the joint development of the results of the research, up to but not including the stage of industrial application, generally do not fall within the scope of Article 81(1) of the Treaty. In certain circumstances, however, such as where the parties agree not to carry out other research and development in the same field, thereby forgoing the opportunity of gaining competitive advantages over the other parties, such agreements may fall within Article 81(1) and should therefore be included within the scope of this Regulation.

(4) Pursuant to Regulation (EEC) No 2821/71, the Commission has, in particular, adopted Regulation (EEC) No 418/85 of 19 December 1984 on the application of Article 85(3) of the Treaty to categories of research and development agreements, as last amended by Regulation (EC) No 2236/97. Regulation (EEC) No 418/85 expires on 31 December 2000.

(5) A new regulation should meet the two requirements of ensuring effective protection of competition and providing adequate legal security for undertakings. The pursuit of these objectives should take account of the need to simplify administrative supervision and the legislative framework to as great an extent possible. Below a certain level of market power it can, for the application of Article 81(3), in general be presumed that the positive effects of research and development agreements will outweigh any negative effects on competition.

(6) Regulation (EEC) No 2821/71 requires the exempting regulation of the Commission to define the categories of agreements, decisions and concerted practices to which it applies, to specify the restrictions or clauses which may, or may not, appear in the agreements, decisions and concerted practices, and to specify the clauses which must be contained in the agreements, decisions and concerted practices or the other conditions which must be satisfied.

(7) It is appropriate to move away from the approach of listing exempted clauses and to place greater emphasis on defining the categories of agreements which are exempted up to a certain level of market power and on specifying the restrictions or clauses which are not to be contained in such agreements. This is consistent with an economics based approach which assesses the impact of agreements on the relevant market.

(8) For the application of Article 81(3) by regulation, it is not necessary to define those agreements which are capable of falling within Article 81(1). In the individual assessment of agreements under Article 81(1), account has to be taken of several factors, and in particular the market structure on the relevant market.

(9) The benefit of the block exemption should be limited to those agreements for which it can be assumed with sufficient certainty that they satisfy the conditions of Article 81(3).

(10) Cooperation in research and development and in the exploitation of the results generally promotes technical and economic progress by increasing the dissemination of know-how between the parties and avoiding duplication of research and development work, by stimulating new advances through the exchange of complementary know-how, and by rationalising the manufacture of the products or application of the processes arising out of the research and development.

(11) The joint exploitation of results can be considered as the natural consequence of joint research and development. It can take different forms such as manufacture, the exploitation of intellectual property rights that substantially contribute to technical or economic progress, or the marketing of new products.

(12) Consumers can generally be expected to benefit from the increased volume and effectiveness of research and development through the introduction of new or improved products or services or the reduction of prices brought about by new or improved processes.

(13) In order to attain the benefits and objectives of joint research and development the benefit of this Regulation should also apply to provisions contained in research and development agreements which do not constitute the primary object of such agreements, but are directly related to and necessary for their implementation.

(14) In order to justify the exemption, the joint exploitation should relate to products or processes for which the use of the results of the research and development is decisive, and each of the parties is given the opportunity of exploiting any results that interest it. However, where academic bodies, research institutes or undertakings which supply research and development as a commercial service without normally being active in the exploitation of results participate in research and development, they may agree to use the results of research and development solely for the purpose of further research. Similarly, non-competitors may agree to limit their right to exploitation to one or more technical fields of application to facilitate cooperation between parties with complementary skills.

(15) The exemption granted under this Regulation should be limited to research and development agreements which do not afford the undertakings the possibility of eliminating competition in respect of a substantial part of the products or services in question. It is necessary to exclude from the block exemption agreements between competitors whose combined share of products or services capable of being improved or replaced by the results of the research and development exceeds a certain level at the time the agreement is entered into.

(16) In order to guarantee the maintenance of effective competition during joint exploitation of the results, provision should be made for the block exemption to cease to apply if the parties' combined share of the market for the products arising out of the joint research and development becomes too great. The exemption should continue to apply, irrespective of the parties' market shares, for a certain period after the commencement of joint exploitation, so as to await stabilisation of their market shares, particularly after the introduction of an entirely new product, and to guarantee a minimum period of return on the investments involved.

(17) This Regulation should not exempt agreements containing restrictions which are not indispensable to attain the positive effects mentioned above. In principle certain severe anti-competitive restraints such as limitations on the freedom of parties to carry out research and development in a field unconnected to the agreement, the fixing of prices charged to third parties, limitations on output or sales, allocation of markets or customers, and limitations on effecting passive sales for the contract products in territories reserved for other parties should be excluded from the benefit of the block exemption established by this Regulation irrespective of the market share of the undertakings concerned.

(18) The market share limitation, the non-exemption of certain agreements, and the conditions provided for in this Regulation normally ensure that the agreements to which the block exemption applies do not enable the participating undertakings to eliminate competition in respect of a substantial part of the products or services in question.

(19) In particular cases in which the agreements falling under this Regulation nevertheless have effects incompatible with Article 81(3) of the Treaty, the Commission may withdraw the benefit of the block exemption.

(20) Agreements between undertakings which are not competing manufacturers of products capable of being improved or replaced by the results of the research and development will only eliminate effective competition in research and development in exceptional circumstances. It is therefore appropriate to enable such agreements to benefit from the block exemption irrespective of market share and to address such exceptional cases by way of withdrawal of its benefit.

(21) As research and development agreements are often of a long-term nature, especially where the cooperation extends to the exploitation of the results, the period of validity of this Regulation should be fixed at 10 years.

(22) This Regulation is without prejudice to the application of Article 82 of the Treaty.

(23) In accordance with the principle of the primacy of Community law, no measure taken pursuant to national laws on competition should prejudice the uniform application throughout the common market of the Community competition rules or the full effect of any measures adopted in implementation of those rules, including this Regulation,

HAS ADOPTED THIS REGULATION:

Article 1

Exemption

1. Pursuant to Article 81(3) of the Treaty and subject to the provisions of this Regulation, it is hereby declared that Article 81(1) shall not apply to agreements entered into between two or more undertakings (hereinafter referred to as "the parties") which relate to the conditions under which those undertakings pursue:

(a) joint research and development of products or processes and joint exploitation of the results of that research and development;

(b) joint exploitation of the results of research and development of products or processes jointly carried out pursuant to a prior agreement between the same parties; or

(c) joint research and development of products or processes excluding joint exploitation of the results.

This exemption shall apply to the extent that such agreements (hereinafter referred to as "research and development agreements") contain restrictions of competition falling within the scope of Article 81(1).

2. The exemption provided for in paragraph 1 shall also apply to provisions contained in research and development agreements which do not constitute the primary object of such agreements, but are directly related to and necessary for their implementation, such as an obligation not to carry out, independently or together with third parties, research and development in the field to which the agreement relates or in a closely connected field during the execution of the agreement.

The first subparagraph does, however, not apply to provisions which have the same object as the restrictions of competition enumerated in Article 5(1).

Article 2

Definitions

For the purposes of this Regulation:

1. "agreement" means an agreement, a decision of an association of undertakings or a concerted practice;

2. "participating undertakings" means undertakings party to the research and development agreement and their respective connected undertakings;

3. "connected undertakings" means:

(a) undertakings in which a party to the research and development agreement, directly or indirectly:

(i) has the power to exercise more than half the voting rights,

(ii) has the power to appoint more than half the members of the supervisory board, board of management or bodies legally representing the undertaking, or

(iii) has the right to manage the undertaking's affairs;

(b) undertakings which directly or indirectly have, over a party to the research and development agreement, the rights or powers listed in (a);

(c) undertakings in which an undertaking referred to in (b) has, directly or indirectly, the rights or powers listed in (a);

(d) undertakings in which a party to the research and development agreement together with one or more of the undertakings referred to in (a), (b) or (c), or in which two or more of the latter undertakings, jointly have the rights or powers listed in (a);

(e) undertakings in which the rights or the powers listed in (a) are jointly held by:

(i) parties to the research and development agreement or their respective connected undertakings referred to in (a) to (d), or

(ii) one or more of the parties to the research and development agreement or one or more of their connected undertakings referred to in (a) to (d) and one or more third parties;

4. "research and development" means the acquisition of know-how relating to products or processes and the carrying out of theoretical analysis, systematic study or experimentation, including experimental production, technical testing of products or processes, the establishment of the necessary facilities and the obtaining of intellectual property rights for the results;

5. "product" means a good and/or a service, including both intermediary goods and/or services and final goods and/or services;

6. "contract process" means a technology or process arising out of the joint research and development;

7. "contract product" means a product arising out of the joint research and development or manufactured or provided applying the contract processes;

8. "exploitation of the results" means the production or distribution of the contract products or the application of the contract processes or the assignment or licensing of intellectual property rights or the communication of know-how required for such manufacture or application;

9. "intellectual property rights" includes industrial property rights, copyright and neighbouring rights;

10. "know-how" means a package of non-patented practical information, resulting from experience and testing, which is secret, substantial and identified: in this context, "secret" means that the know-how is not generally known or easily accessible; "substantial" means that the know-how includes information which is indispensable for the manufacture of the contract products or the application of the contract processes; "identified" means that the know-how is described in a sufficiently comprehensive manner so as to make it possible to verify that it fulfils the criteria of secrecy and substantiality;

11. research and development, or exploitation of the results, are carried out "jointly" where the work involved is:

(a) carried out by a joint team, organisation or undertaking,

(b) jointly entrusted to a third party, or

(c) allocated between the parties by way of specialisation in research, development, production or distribution;

12. "competing undertaking" means an undertaking that is supplying a product capable of being improved or replaced by the contract product (an actual competitor) or an undertaking that would, on realistic grounds, undertake the necessary additional investments or other necessary switching costs so that it could supply such a product in response to a small and permanent increase in relative prices (a potential competitor);

13. "relevant market for the contract products" means the relevant product and geographic market(s) to which the contract products belong.

Article 3

Conditions for exemption

1. The exemption provided for in Article 1 shall apply subject to the conditions set out in paragraphs 2 to 5.

2. All the parties must have access to the results of the joint research and development for the purposes of further research or exploitation. However, research institutes, academic bodies, or undertakings which supply research and development as a commercial service without normally being active in the exploitation of results may agree to confine their use of the results for the purposes of further research.

3. Without prejudice to paragraph 2, where the research and development agreement provides only for joint research and development, each party must be free independently to exploit the results of the joint research and development and any pre-existing know-how necessary for the purposes of such exploitation. Such right to exploitation may be limited to one or more technical fields of application, where the parties are not competing undertakings at the time the research and development agreement is entered into.

4. Any joint exploitation must relate to results which are protected by intellectual property rights or constitute know-how, which substantially contribute to technical or economic progress and the results must be decisive for the manufacture of the contract products or the application of the contract processes.

5. Undertakings charged with manufacture by way of specialisation in production must be required to fulfil orders for supplies from all the parties, except where the research and development agreement also provides for joint distribution.

Article 4

Market share threshold and duration of exemption

1. Where the participating undertakings are not competing undertakings, the exemption provided for in Article 1 shall apply for the duration of the research and development. Where the results are jointly exploited, the exemption shall continue to apply for seven years from the time the contract products are first put on the market within the common market.

2. Where two or more of the participating undertakings are competing undertakings, the exemption provided for in Article 1 shall apply for the period referred to in paragraph 1 only if, at the time the research and development agreement is entered into, the combined market share of the participating undertakings does not exceed 25% of the relevant market for the products capable of being improved or replaced by the contract products.

3. After the end of the period referred to in paragraph 1, the exemption shall continue to apply as long as the combined market share of the

participating undertakings does not exceed 25% of the relevant market for the contract products.

Article 5

Agreements not covered by the exemption

1. The exemption provided for in Article 1 shall not apply to research and development agreements which, directly or indirectly, in isolation or in combination with other factors under the control of the parties, have as their object:

(a) the restriction of the freedom of the participating undertakings to carry out research and development independently or in cooperation with third parties in a field unconnected with that to which the research and development relates or, after its completion, in the field to which it relates or in a connected field;

(b) the prohibition to challenge after completion of the research and development the validity of intellectual property rights which the parties hold in the common market and which are relevant to the research and development or, after the expiry of the research and development agreement, the validity of intellectual property rights which the parties hold in the common market and which protect the results of the research and development, without prejudice to the possibility to provide for termination of the research and development agreement in the event of one of the parties challenging the validity of such intellectual property rights;

(c) the limitation of output or sales;

(d) the fixing of prices when selling the contract product to third parties;

(e) the restriction of the customers that the participating undertakings may serve, after the end of seven years from the time the contract products are first put on the market within the common market;

(f) the prohibition to make passive sales of the contract products in territories reserved for other parties;

(g) the prohibition to put the contract products on the market or to pursue an active sales policy for them in territories within the common market that are reserved for other parties after the end of seven years from the time the contract products are first put on the market within the common market;

(h) the requirement not to grant licences to third parties to manufacture the contract products or to apply the contract processes where the exploitation by at least one of the parties of the results of the joint research and development is not provided for or does not take place;

(i) the requirement to refuse to meet demand from users or resellers in their respective territories who would market the contract products in other territories within the common market; or

(j) the requirement to make it difficult for users or resellers to obtain the contract products from other resellers within the common market, and in particular to exercise intellectual property rights or take measures so as to prevent users or resellers from obtaining, or from putting on the market within the common market, products which have been lawfully put on the market within the Community by another party or with its consent.

2. Paragraph 1 shall not apply to:

(a) the setting of production targets where the exploitation of the results includes the joint production of the contract products;

(b) the setting of sales targets and the fixing of prices charged to immediate customers where the exploitation of the results includes the joint distribution of the contract products.

Article 6

Application of the market share threshold

1. For the purposes of applying the market share threshold provided for in Article 4 the following rules shall apply:

(a) the market share shall be calculated on the basis of the market sales value; if market sales value data are not available, estimates based on other reliable market information, including market sales volumes, may be used to establish the market share of the undertaking concerned;

(b) the market share shall be calculated on the basis of data relating to the preceding calendar year;

(c) the market share held by the undertakings referred to in point 3(e) of Article 2 shall be apportioned equally to each undertaking having the rights or the powers listed in point 3(a) of Article 2.

2. If the market share referred to in Article 4(3) is initially not more than 25% but subsequently rises above this level without exceeding 30%, the exemption provided for in Article 1 shall continue to apply for a period of two consecutive calendar years following the year in which the 25% threshold was first exceeded.

3. If the market share referred to in Article 4(3) is initially not more than 25% but subsequently rises above 30%, the exemption provided for in Article 1 shall continue to apply for one calendar year following the year in which the level of 30% was first exceeded.

4. The benefit of paragraphs 2 and 3 may not be combined so as to exceed a period of two calendar years.

Article 7

Withdrawal

The Commission may withdraw the benefit of this Regulation, pursuant to Article 7 of Regulation (EEC) No 2821/71, where, either on its own initiative or at the request of a Member State or of a natural or legal person claiming a legitimate interest, it finds in a particular case that a research and development agreement to which the exemption provided for in Article 1 applies nevertheless has effects which are incompatible with the conditions laid down in Article 81(3) of the Treaty, and in particular where:

(a) the existence of the research and development agreement substantially restricts the scope for third parties to carry out research and development in the relevant field because of the limited research capacity available elsewhere;

(b) because of the particular structure of supply, the existence of the research and development agreement substantially restricts the access of third parties to the market for the contract products;

(c) without any objectively valid reason, the parties do not exploit the results of the joint research and development;

(d) the contract products are not subject in the whole or a substantial part of the common market to effective competition from identical products or products considered by users as equivalent in view of their characteristics, price and intended use;

(e) the existence of the research and development agreement would eliminate effective competition in research and development on a particular market.

Article 8

Transitional period

The prohibition laid down in Article 81(1) of the Treaty shall not apply during the period from 1 January 2001 to 30 June 2002 in respect of agreements already in force on 31 December 2000 which do not satisfy the conditions for exemption provided for in this Regulation but which satisfy the conditions for exemption provided for in Regulation (EEC) No 418/85.

Article 9

Period of validity

This Regulation shall enter into force on 1 January 2001. It shall expire on 31 December 2010.

This Regulation shall be binding in its entirety and directly applicable in all Member States.

7. THE MERGER REGULATION

Council Regulation 4064/1989 on the control of concentrations

O.J. L 395/1 (Dec. 12, 1989), amended as of 1997, O.J. L 180/1
(July 9, 1997), corrigendum O.J. L 40/17
(Feb. 13, 1998)

THE COUNCIL OF THE EUROPEAN COMMUNITIES,

Having regard to the Treaty establishing the European Economic Community, and in particular Articles 87 and 235 thereof,*

Having regard to the proposal from the Commission,

Having regard to the opinion of the European Parliament,

Having regard to the opinion of the Economic and Social Committee,

(1) Whereas, for the achievement of the aims of the Treaty establishing the European Economic Community, Article 3(f) gives the Community the objective of instituting 'a system ensuring that competition in the common market is not distorted';

(2) Whereas this system is essential for the achievement of the internal market by 1992 and its further development;

(3) Whereas the dismantling of internal frontiers is resulting and will continue to result in major corporate re-organizations in the Community, particularly in the form of concentrations;

(4) Whereas such a development must be welcomed as being in line with the requirements of dynamic competition and capable of increasing the competitiveness of European industry, improving the conditions of growth and raising the standard of living in the Community;

(5) Whereas, however, it must be ensured that the process of reorganization does not result in lasting damage to competition; whereas Community law must therefore include provisions governing those concentrations which may significantly impede effective competition in the common market or in a substantial part of it;

(6) Whereas Articles 85 and 86, while applicable, according to the case-law of the Court of Justice, to certain concentrations, are not, however, sufficient to cover all operations which may prove to be incompatible with the system of undistorted competition envisaged in the Treaty;

(7) Whereas a new legal instrument should therefore be created in the form of a Regulation to permit effective monitoring of all concentrations from the point of view of their effect on the structure of competition in the Community and to be the only instrument applicable to such concentrations;

(8) Whereas this Regulation should therefore be based not only on Article 87 but, principally, on Article 235 of the Treaty, under which the

---

* Editors' note: The recitals have not been amended and therefore refer to the former Treaty numbers.

Community may give itself the additional powers of action necessary for the attainment of its objectives, and also with regard to concentrations on the markets for agricultural products listed in Annex II to the Treaty;

(9) Whereas the provisions to be adopted in this Regulation should apply to significant structural changes the impact of which on the market goes beyond the national borders of any one Member State;

(10) Whereas the scope of application of this Regulation should therefore be defined according to the geographical area of activity of the undertakings concerned and be limited by quantitative thresholds in order to cover those concentrations which have a Community dimension; whereas, at the end of an initial phase of the implementation of this Regulation, these thresholds should be reviewed in the light of the experience gained;

(11) Whereas a concentration with a Community dimension exists where the aggregate turnover of the undertakings concerned exceeds given levels worldwide and throughout the Community and where at least two of the undertakings concerned have their sole or main fields of activities in different Member States or where, although the undertakings in question act mainly in one and the same Member State, at least one of them has substantial operations in at least one other Member State; whereas that is also the case where the concentrations are effected by undertakings which do not have their principal fields of activities in the Community but which have substantial operations there;

(12) Whereas the arrangements to be introduced for the control of concentrations should, without prejudice to Article 90(2) of the Treaty, respect the principle of non-discrimination between the public and the private sectors; whereas, in the public sector, calculation of the turnover of an undertaking concerned in a concentration needs, therefore, to take account of undertakings making up an economic unit with an independent power of decision, irrespective of the way in which their capital is held or of the rules of administrative supervision applicable to them;

(13) Whereas it is necessary to establish whether concentrations with a Community dimension are compatible or not with the common market from the point of view of the need to preserve and develop effective competition in the common market; whereas, in so doing, the Commission must place its appraisal within the general framework of the achievement of the fundamental objectives referred to in Article 2 of the Treaty, including that of strengthening the Community's economic and social cohesion, referred to in Article 130a;

(14) Whereas this Regulation should establish the principle that a concentration with a Community dimension which creates or strengthens a position as result of which effective competition in the common market or in a substantial part of it is significantly impeded is to be declared incompatible with the common market;

(15) Whereas concentrations which, by reason of the limited market share of the undertakings concerned, are not liable to impede effective competition may be presumed to be compatible with the common market;

whereas, without prejudice to Articles 85 and 86 of the Treaty, an indication to this effect exists, in particular, where the market share of the undertakings concerned does not exceed 25% either in the common market or in a substantial part of it;

(16) Whereas the Commission should have the task of taking all the decisions necessary to establish whether or not concentrations of a Community dimension are compatible with the common market, as well as decisions designed to restore effective competition;

(17) Whereas to ensure effective control undertakings should be obliged to give prior notification of concentrations with a Community dimension and provision should be made for the suspension of concentrations for a limited period, and for the possibility of extending or waiving a suspension where necessary; whereas in the interests of legal certainty the validity of transactions must nevertheless be protected as much as necessary;

(18) Whereas a period within which the Commission must initiate a proceeding in respect of a notified concentration and a period within which it must give a final decision on the compatibility or incompatibility with the common market of a notified concentration should be laid down;

(19) Whereas the undertakings concerned must be accorded the right to be heard by the Commission as soon as a proceeding has been initiated; whereas the members of management and supervisory organs and recognized workers' representatives in the undertakings concerned, together with third parties showing a legitimate interest, must also be given the opportunity to be heard;

(20) Whereas the Commission should act in close and constant liaison with the competent authorities of the Member States from which it obtains comments and information;

(21) Whereas, for the purposes of this Regulation, and in accordance with the case-law of the Court of Justice, the Commission must be afforded the assistance of the Member States and must also be empowered to require information to be given and to carry out the necessary investigations in order to appraise concentrations;

(22) Whereas compliance with this Regulation must be enforceable by means of fines and periodic penalty payments; whereas the Court of Justice should be given unlimited jurisdiction in that regard pursuant to Article 172 of the Treaty;

(23) Whereas it is appropriate to define the concept of concentration in such a manner as to cover only operations bringing about a durable change in the structure of the undertakings concerned; whereas it is therefore necessary to exclude from the scope of this Regulation those operations which have as their object or effect the coordination of the competitive behaviour of independent undertakings, since such operations fall to be examined under the appropriate provisions of Regulations implementing Article 85 or Article 86 of the Treaty; whereas it is appropriate to make this distinction specifically in the case of the creation of joint ventures;

(24) Whereas there is no coordination of competitive behaviour within the meaning of this Regulation where two or more undertakings agree to acquire jointly control of one or more other undertakings with the object and effect of sharing amongst themselves such undertakings or their assets;

(25) Whereas the application of this Regulation is not excluded where the undertakings concerned accept restrictions directly related and necessary to the implementation of the concentration;

(26) Whereas the Commission should be given exclusive competence to apply this Regulation, subject to review by the Court of Justice;

(27) Whereas the Member States may not apply their national legislation on competition to concentrations with a Community dimension, unless the Regulation makes provision therefor; whereas the relevant powers of national authorities should be limited to cases where, failing intervention by the Commission, effective competition is likely to be significantly impeded within the territory of a Member State and where the competition interests of that Member State cannot be sufficiently protected otherwise than by this Regulation; whereas the Member States concerned must act promptly in such cases; whereas this Regulation cannot, because of the diversity of national law, fix a single deadline for the adoption of remedies;

(28) Whereas, furthermore, the exclusive application of this Regulation to concentrations with a Community dimension is without prejudice to Article 223 of the Treaty, and does not prevent the Member States' taking appropriate measures to protect legitimate interests other than those pursued by this Regulation, provided that such measures are compatible with the general principles and other provisions of Community law;

(29) Whereas concentrations not referred to in this Regulation come, in principle, within the jurisdiction of the Member States; whereas, however, the Commission should have the power to act, at the request of a Member State concerned, in cases where effective competition would be significantly impeded within that Member State's territory;

(30) Whereas the conditions in which concentrations involving Community undertakings are carried out in non-member countries should be observed, and provision should be made for the possibility of the Council's giving the Commission an appropriate mandate for negotiation with a view to obtaining non-discriminatory treatment for Community undertakings;

(31) Whereas this Regulation in no way detracts from the collective rights of workers as recognized in the undertakings concerned,

HAS ADOPTED THIS REGULATION:

Article 1

Scope

1. Without prejudice to Article 22, this Regulation shall apply to all concentrations with a Community dimension as defined in paragraphs 2 and 3.

2. For the purposes of this Regulation, a concentration has a Community dimension where:

(a) the combined aggregate worldwide turnover of all the undertakings concerned is more than ECU 5000 million; and

(b) the aggregate Community-wide turnover of each of at least two of the undertakings concerned is more than ECU 250 million, unless each of the undertakings concerned achieves more than two-thirds of its aggregate Community-wide turnover within one and the same Member State.

3. For the purposes of this Regulation, a concentration that does not meet the thresholds laid down in paragraph 2 has a Community dimension where:

(a) the combined aggregate worldwide turnover of all the undertakings concerned is more than ECU 2500 million;

(b) in each of at least three Member States, the combined aggregate turnover of all the undertakings concerned is more than ECU 100 million;

(c) in each of at least three Member States included for the purpose of point (b), the aggregate turnover of each of at least two of the undertakings concerned is more than ECU 25 million; and

(d) the aggregate Community-wide turnover of each of at least two of the undertakings concerned is more than ECU 100 million;

unless each of the undertakings concerned achieves more than two-thirds of its aggregate Community-wide turnover within one and the same Member State.

4. Before 1 July 2000 the Commission shall report to the Council on the operation of the thresholds and criteria set out in paragraphs 2 and 3.

5. Following the report referred to in paragraph 4 and on a proposal from the Commission, the Council, acting by a qualified majority, may revise the thresholds and criteria mentioned in paragraph 3.

Article 2

Appraisal of concentrations

1. Concentrations within the scope of this Regulation shall be appraised in accordance with the following provisions with a view to establishing whether or not they are compatible with the common market. In making this appraisal, the Commission shall take into account:

(a) the need to maintain and develop effective competition within the common market in view of, among other things, the structure of all the markets concerned and the actual or potential competition from undertakings located either within or without the Community;

(b) the market position of the undertakings concerned and their economic and financial power, the alternatives available to suppliers and users, their access to supplies or markets, any legal or other barriers to entry, supply and demand trends for the relevant goods and services, the interests of the intermediate and ultimate consumers, and the development of technical and economic progress provided that it is to consumers' advantage and does not form an obstacle to competition.

2. A concentration which does not create or strengthen a dominant position as a result of which effective competition would be significantly impeded in the common market or in a substantial part of it shall be declared compatible with the common market.

3. A concentration which creates or strengthens a dominant position as a result of which effective competition would be significantly impeded in the common market or in a substantial part of it shall be declared incompatible with the common market.

4. To the extent that the creation of a joint venture constituting a concentration pursuant to Article 3 has as its object or effect the coordination of the competitive behaviour of undertakings that remain independent, such coordination shall be appraised in accordance with the criteria of Article 85(1) and (3) of the Treaty, with a view to establishing whether or not the operation is compatible with the common market.

In making this appraisal, the Commission shall take into account in particular:

— whether two or more parent companies retain to a significant extent activities in the same market as the joint venture or in a market which is downstream or upstream from that of the joint venture or in a neighbouring market closely related to this market;

— whether the coordination which is the direct consequence of the creation of the joint venture affords the undertakings concerned the possibility of eliminating competition in respect of a substantial part of the products or services in question.

Article 3

Definition of concentration

1. A concentration shall be deemed to arise where:

   (a) two or more previously independent undertakings merge, or

   (b) — one or more persons already controlling at least one undertaking, or

   — one or more undertakings

acquire, whether by purchase of securities or assets, by contract or by any other means, direct or indirect control of the whole or parts of one or more other undertakings.

2. The creation of a joint venture performing on a lasting basis all the functions of an autonomous economic entity, shall constitute a concentration within the meaning of paragraph 1(b).

3. For the purposes of this Regulation, control shall be constituted by rights, contracts or any other means which, either separately or in combi-

nation and having regard to the considerations of fact or law involved, confer the possibility of exercising decisive influence on an undertaking, in particular by:

(a) ownership or the right to use all or part of the assets of an undertaking;

(b) rights or contracts which confer decisive influence on the composition, voting or decisions of the organs of an undertaking.

4. Control is acquired by persons or undertakings which:

(a) are holders of the rights or entitled to rights under the contracts concerned, or

(b) while not being holders of such rights or entitled to rights under such contracts, have the power to exercise the rights deriving therefrom.

5. A concentration shall not be deemed to arise where:

(a) credit institutions or other financial institutions or insurance companies, the normal activities of which include transactions and dealing in securities for their own account or for the account of others, hold on a temporary basis securities which they have acquired in an undertaking with a view to reselling them, provided that they do not exercise voting rights in respect of those securities with a view to determining the competitive behaviour of that undertaking or provided that they exercise such voting rights only with a view to preparing the disposal of all or part of that undertaking or of its assets or the disposal of those securities and that any such disposal takes place within one year of the date of acquisition; that period may be extended by the Commission on request where such institutions or companies can show that the disposal was not reasonably possible within the period set;

(b) control is acquired by an office-holder according to the law of a Member State relating to liquidation, winding up, insolvency, cessation of payments, compositions or analogous proceedings;

(c) the operations referred to in paragraph 1(b) are carried out by the financial holding companies referred to in Article 5(3) of the Fourth Council Directive 78/660/EEC of 25 July 1978 on the annual accounts of certain types of companies, as last amended by Directive 84/569/EEC, provided however that the voting rights in respect of the holding are exercised, in particular in relation to the appointment of members of the management and supervisory bodies of the undertakings in which they have holdings, only to maintain the full value of those investments and not to determine directly or indirectly the competitive conduct of those undertakings.

Article 4

Prior notification of concentrations

1. Concentrations with a Community dimension defined in this Regulation shall be notified to the Commission not more than one week after

the conclusion of the agreement, or the announcement of the public bid, or the acquisition of a controlling interest. That week shall begin when the first of those events occurs.

2. A concentration which consists of a merger within the meaning of Article 3(1)(a) or in the acquisition of joint control within the meaning of Article 3(1)(b) shall be notified jointly by the parties to the merger or by those acquiring joint control as the case may be. In all other cases, the notification shall be effected by the person or undertaking acquiring control of the whole or parts of one or more undertakings.

3. Where the Commission finds that a notified concentration falls within the scope of this Regulation, it shall publish the fact of the notification, at the same time indicating the names of the parties, the nature of the concentration and the economic sectors involved. The Commission shall take account of the legitimate interest of undertakings in the protection of their business secrets.

Article 5

Calculation of turnover

1. Aggregate turnover within the meaning of Article 1(2) shall comprise the amounts derived by the undertakings concerned in the preceding financial year from the sale of products and the provision of services falling within the undertakings' ordinary activities after deduction of sales rebates and of value added tax and other taxes directly related to turnover. The aggregate turnover of an undertaking concerned shall not include the sale of products or the provision of services between any of the undertakings referred to in paragraph 4.

Turnover, in the Community or in a Member State, shall comprise products sold and services provided to undertakings or consumers, in the Community or in that Member State as the case may be.

2. By way of derogation from paragraph 1, where the concentration consists in the acquisition of parts, whether or not constituted as legal entities, of one or more undertakings, only the turnover relating to the parts which are the subject of the transaction shall be taken into account with regard to the seller or sellers.

However, two or more transactions within the meaning of the first subparagraph which take place within a two-year period between the same persons or undertakings shall be treated as one and the same concentration arising on the date of the last transaction.

3. In place of turnover the following shall be used:

(a) for credit institutions and other financial institutions, as regards Article 1(2) and (3), the sum of the following income items as defined in Council Directive 86/635/EEC of 8 December 1986 on the annual accounts and consolidated accounts of banks and other financial institutions, after deduction of value added tax and other taxes directly related to those items, where appropriate:

(i) interest income and similar income;

(ii) income from securities:

— income from shares and other variable yield securities,

— income from participating interests,

— income from shares in affiliated undertakings;

(iii) commissions receivable;

(iv) net profit on financial operations;

(v) other operating income.

The turnover of a credit or financial institution in the Community or in a Member State shall comprise the income items, as defined above, which are received by the branch or division of that institution established in the Community or in the Member State in question, as the case may be.

(b) for insurance undertakings, the value of gross premiums written which shall comprise all amounts received and receivable in respect of insurance contracts issued by or on behalf of the insurance undertakings, including also outgoing reinsurance premiums, and after deduction of taxes and parafiscal contributions or levies charged by reference to the amounts of individual premiums or the total volume of premiums; as regards Article 1(2)(b) and (3)(b), (c) and (d) and the final part of Article 1(2) and (3), gross premiums received from Community residents and from residents of one Member State respectively shall be taken into account.

4. Without prejudice to paragraph 2, the aggregate turnover of an undertaking concerned within the meaning of Article 1(2) and 3 shall be calculated by adding together the respective turnovers of the following:

(a) the undertaking concerned;

(b) those undertakings in which the undertaking concerned, directly or indirectly;

— owns more than half the capital or business assets, or

— has the power to exercise more than half the voting rights, or

— has the power to appoint more than half the members of the supervisory board, the administrative board or bodies legally representing the undertakings, or

— has the right to manage the undertakings' affairs;

(c) those undertakings which have in an undertaking concerned the rights or powers listed in (b);

(d) those undertakings in which an undertaking as referred to in (c) has the rights or powers listed in (b);

(e) those undertakings in which two or more undertakings as referred to in (a) to (d) jointly have the rights or powers listed in (b).

5. Where undertakings concerned by the concentration jointly have the rights or powers listed in paragraph 4(b), in calculating the aggregate

turnover of the undertakings concerned for the purposes of Article 1(2) and (3):

(a) no account shall be taken of the turnover resulting from the sale of products or the provision of services between the joint undertaking and each of the undertakings concerned or any other undertaking connected with any one of them, as set out in paragraph 4(b) to (e);

(b) account shall be taken of the turnover resulting from the sale of products and the provision of services between the joint undertaking and any third undertakings. This turnover shall be apportioned equally amongst the undertakings concerned.

Article 6

Examination of the notification and initiation of proceedings

1. The Commission shall examine the notification as soon as it is received.

(a) Where it concludes that the concentration notified does not fall within the scope of this Regulation, it shall record that finding by means of a decision.

(b) Where it finds that the concentration notified, although falling within the scope of this Regulation, does not raise serious doubts as to its compatibility with the common market, it shall decide not to oppose it and shall declare that it is compatible with the common market.

The decision declaring the concentration compatible shall also cover restrictions directly related and necessary to the implementation of the concentration.

(c) Without prejudice to paragraph 2, where the Commission finds that the concentration notified falls within the scope of this Regulation and raises serious doubts as to its compatibility with the common market, it shall decide to initiate proceedings.

2. Where the Commission finds that, following modification by the undertakings concerned, a notified concentration no longer raises serious doubts within the meaning of paragraph 1(c), it may decide to declare the concentration compatible with the common market pursuant to paragraph 1(b).

The Commission may attach to its decision under paragraph 1(b) conditions and obligations intended to ensure that the undertakings concerned comply with the commitments they have entered into vis-à-vis the Commission with a view to rendering the concentration compatible with the common market.

3. The Commission may revoke the decision it has taken pursuant to paragraph 1(a) or (b) where:

(a) the decision is based on incorrect information for which one of the undertakings is responsible or where it has been obtained by deceit, or

(b) the undertakings concerned commit a breach of an obligation attached to the decision.

4. In the cases referred to in paragraph 3, the Commission may take a decision under paragraph 1, without being bound by the deadlines referred to in Article 10(1).

5. The Commission shall notify its decision to the undertakings concerned and the competent authorities of the Member States without delay.

Article 7

Suspension of concentrations

1. A concentration as defined in Article 1 shall not be put into effect either before its notification or until it has been declared compatible with the common market pursuant to a decision under Article 6(1)(b) or Article 8(2) or on the basis of a presumption according to Article 10(6).

3. Paragraph 1 shall not prevent the implementation of a public bid which has been notified to the Commission in accordance with Article 4(1), provided that the acquirer does not exercise the voting rights attached to the securities in question or does so only to maintain the full value of those investments and on the basis of a derogation granted by the Commission under paragraph 4.

4. The Commission may, on request, grant a derogation from the obligations imposed in paragraph 1 or 3. The request to grant a derogation must be reasoned. In deciding on the request, the Commission shall take into account inter alia the effects of the suspension on one or more undertakings concerned by a concentration or on a third party and the threat to competition posed by the concentration. That derogation may be made subject to conditions and obligations in order to ensure conditions of effective competition. A derogation may be applied for and granted at any time, even before notification or after the transaction.

5. The validity of any transaction carried out in contravention of paragraph 1 shall be dependent on a decision pursuant to Article 6(1)(b) or 8(2) or (3) or on a presumption pursuant to Article 10(6).

This Article shall, however, have no effect on the validity of transactions in securities including those convertible into other securities admitted to trading on a market which is regulated and supervised by authorities recognized by public bodies, operates regularly and is accessible directly or indirectly to the public, unless the buyer and seller knew or ought to have known that the transaction was carried out in contravention of paragraph 1.

Article 8

Powers of decision of the Commission

1. Without prejudice to Article 9, all proceedings initiated pursuant to Article 6(1)(c) shall be closed by means of a decision as provided for in paragraphs 2 to 5.

2. Where the Commission finds that, following modification by the undertakings concerned if necessary, a notified concentration fulfils the criterion laid down in Article 2(2) and, in the cases referred to in Article 2(4), the criteria laid down in Article 85(3) of the Treaty, it shall issue a decision declaring the concentration compatible with the common market.

It may attach to its decision conditions and obligations intended to ensure that the undertakings concerned comply with the commitments they have entered into vis-à-vis the Commission with a view to rendering the concentration compatible with the common market. The decision declaring the concentration compatible with the common market shall also cover restrictions directly related and necessary to the implementation of the concentration.

3. Where the Commission finds that a concentration fulfils the criterion defined in Article 2(3) or, in the cases referred to in Article 2(4), does not fulfil the criteria laid down in Article 85(3) of the Treaty, it shall issue a decision declaring that the concentration is incompatible with the common market.

4. Where a concentration has already been implemented, the Commission may, in a decision pursuant to paragraph 3 or by separate decision, require the undertakings or assets brought together to be separated or the cessation of joint control or any other action that may be appropriate in order to restore conditions of effective competition.

5. The Commission may revoke the decision it has taken pursuant to paragraph 2 where:

(a) the declaration of compatibility is based on incorrect information for which one of the undertakings is responsible or where it has been obtained by deceit, or

(b) the undertakings concerned commit a breach of an obligation attached to the decision.

6. In the cases referred to in paragraph 5, the Commission may take a decision pursuant to paragraph 3, without being bound by the deadline referred to in Article 10(3).

Article 9

Referral to the competent authorities of the Member States

1. The Commission may, by means of a decision notified without delay to the undertakings concerned and the competent authorities of the other Member States, refer a notified concentration to the competent authorities of the Member State concerned in the following circumstances.

2. Within three weeks of the date of receipt of the copy of the notification a Member State may inform the Commission, which shall inform the undertakings concerned, that:

(a) a concentration threatens to create or to strengthen a dominant position as a result of which effective competition will be significantly impeded on a market within that Member State, which presents all the characteristics of a distinct market, or

(b) a concentration affects competition on a market within that Member State, which presents all the characteristics of a distinct market and which does not constitute a substantial part of the common market.

3. If the Commission considers that, having regard to the market for the products or services in question and the geographical reference market within the meaning of paragraph 7, there is such a distinct market and that such a threat exists, either:

(a) it shall itself deal with the case in order to maintain or restore effective competition on the market concerned, or

(b) it shall refer the whole or part of the case to the competent authorities of the Member State concerned with a view to the application of that State's national competition law.

If, however, the Commission considers that such a distinct market or threat does not exist it shall adopt a decision to that effect which it shall address to the Member State concerned.

In cases where a Member State informs the Commission that a concentration affects competition in a distinct market within its territory that does not form a substantial part of the common market, the Commission shall refer the whole or part of the case relating to the distinct market concerned, if it considers that such a distinct market is affected.

4. A decision to refer or not to refer pursuant to paragraph 3 shall be taken where:

(a) as a general rule within the six-week period provided for in Article 10(1), second subparagraph, where the Commission, pursuant to Article 6(1)(b), has not initiated proceedings, or

(b) within three months at most of the notification of the concentration concerned where the Commission has initiated proceedings under Article 6(1)(c), without taking the preparatory steps in order to adopt the necessary measures under to Article 8(2), second subparagraph, (3) or (4) to maintain or restore effective competition on the market concerned.

5. If within the three months referred to in paragraph 4(b) the Commission, despite a reminder from the Member State concerned, has not taken a decision on referral in accordance with paragraph 3 nor has taken the preparatory steps referred to in paragraph 4(b), it shall be deemed to have taken a decision to refer the case to the Member State concerned in accordance with paragraph 3(b).

6. The publication of any report or the announcement of the findings of the examination of the concentration by the competent authority of the Member State concerned shall be effected not more than four months after the Commission's referral.

7. The geographical reference market shall consist of the area in which the undertakings concerned are involved in the supply and demand of products or services, in which the conditions of competition are sufficiently homogeneous and which can be distinguished from neighbouring areas because, in particular, conditions of competition are appreciably different in those areas. This assessment should take account in particular of the nature and characteristics of the products or services concerned, of the existence of entry barriers or of consumer preferences, of appreciable differences of the undertakings' market shares between the area concerned and neighbouring areas or of substantial price differences.

8. In applying the provisions of this Article, the Member State concerned may take only the measures strictly necessary to safeguard or restore effective competition on the market concerned.

9. In accordance with the relevant provisions of the Treaty, any Member State may appeal to the Court of Justice, and in particular request the application of Article 186, for the purpose of applying its national competition law.

10. This Article may be re-examined at the same time as the thresholds referred to in Article 1.

Article 10

Time limits for initiating proceedings and for decisions

1. The decisions referred to in Article 6(1) must be taken within one month at most. That period shall begin on the day following that of the receipt of a notification or, if the information to be supplied with the notification is incomplete, on the day following that of the receipt of the complete information.

That period shall be increased to six weeks if the Commission receives a request from a Member State in accordance with Article 9(2), or where, after notification of a concentration, the undertakings concerned submit commitments pursuant to Article 6(2), which are intended by the parties to form the basis for a decision pursuant to Article 6(1)(b).

2. Decisions taken pursuant to Article 8(2) concerning notified concentrations must be taken as soon as it appears that the serious doubts referred to in Article 6(1)(c) have been removed, particularly as a result of modifications made by the undertakings concerned, and at the latest by the deadline laid down in paragraph 3.

3. Without prejudice to Article 8(6), decisions taken pursuant to Article 8 (3) concerning notified concentrations must be taken within not more than four months of the date on which proceedings are initiated.

4. The periods set by paragraphs 1 and 3 shall exceptionally be suspended where, owing to circumstances for which one of the undertakings involved in the concentration is responsible, the Commission has had to request information by decision pursuant to Article 11 or to order an investigation by decision pursuant to Article 13.

5. Where the Court of Justice gives a Judgement which annuls the whole or part of a Commission decision taken under this Regulation, the periods laid down in this Regulation shall start again from the date of the Judgement.

6. Where the Commission has not taken a decision in accordance with Article 6(1)(b) or (c) or Article 8(2) or (3) within the deadlines set in paragraphs 1 and 3 respectively, the concentration shall be deemed to have been declared compatible with the common market, without prejudice to Article 9.

Article 11

Requests for information

1. In carrying out the duties assigned to it by this Regulation, the Commission may obtain all necessary information from the Governments and competent authorities of the Member States, from the persons referred to in Article 3(1)(b), and from undertakings and associations of undertakings.

2. When sending a request for information to a person, an undertaking or an association of undertakings, the Commission shall at the same time send a copy of the request to the competent authority of the Member State within the territory of which the residence of the person or the seat of the undertaking or association of undertakings is situated.

3. In its request the Commission shall state the legal basis and the purpose of the request and also the penalties provided for in Article 14(1)(c) for supplying incorrect information.

4. The information requested shall be provided, in the case of undertakings, by their owners or their representatives and, in the case of legal persons, companies or firms, or of associations having no legal personality, by the persons authorized to represent them by law or by their statutes.

5. Where a person, an undertaking or an association of undertakings does not provide the information requested within the period fixed by the Commission or provides incomplete information, the Commission shall by decision require the information to be provided. The decision shall specify what information is required, fix an appropriate period within which it is to be supplied and state the penalties provided for in Articles 14(1)(c) and 15(1)(a) and the right to have the decision reviewed by the Court of Justice.

6. The Commission shall at the same time send a copy of its decision to the competent authority of the Member State within the territory of which the residence of the person or the seat of the undertaking or association of undertakings is situated.

Article 12

Investigations by the authorities of the Member States

1. At the request of the Commission, the competent authorities of the Member States shall undertake the investigations which the Commission

considers to be necessary under Article 13(1), or which it has ordered by decision pursuant to Article 13(3). The officials of the competent authorities of the Member States responsible for conducting those investigations shall exercise their powers upon production of an authorization in writing issued by the competent authority of the Member State within the territory of which the investigation is to be carried out. Such authorization shall specify the subject matter and purpose of the investigation.

2. If so requested by the Commission or by the competent authority of the Member State within the territory of which the investigation is to be carried out, officials of the Commission may assist the officials of that authority in carrying out their duties.

Article 13

Investigative powers of the Commission

1. In carrying out the duties assigned to it by this Regulation, the Commission may undertake all necessary investigations into undertakings and associations of undertakings. To that end the officials authorized by the Commission shall be empowered:

(a) to examine the books and other business records;

(b) to take or demand copies of or extracts from the books and business records;

(c) to ask for oral explanations on the spot;

(d) to enter any premises, land and means of transport of undertakings.

2. The officials of the Commission authorized to carry out the investigations shall exercise their powers on production of an authorization in writing specifying the subject matter and purpose of the investigation and the penalties provided for in Article 14(1)(d) in cases where production of the required books or other business records is incomplete. In good time before the investigation, the Commission shall inform, in writing, the competent authority of the Member State within the territory of which the investigation is to be carried out of the investigation and of the identities of the authorized officials.

3. Undertakings and associations of undertakings shall submit to investigations ordered by decision of the Commission. The decision shall specify the subject matter and purpose of the investigation, appoint the date on which it shall begin and state the penalties provided for in Articles 14(1)(d) and 15(1)(b) and the right to have the decision reviewed by the Court of Justice.

4. The Commission shall in good time and in writing inform the competent authority of the Member State within the territory of which the investigation is to be carried out of its intention of taking a decision pursuant to paragraph 3. It shall hear the competent authority before taking its decision.

5. Officials of the competent authority of the Member State within the territory of which the investigation is to be carried out may, at the request of that authority or of the Commission, assist the officials of the Commission in carrying out their duties.

6. Where an undertaking or association of undertakings opposes an investigation ordered pursuant to this Article, the Member State concerned shall afford the necessary assistance to the officials authorized by the Commission to enable them to carry out their investigation. To this end the Member States shall, after consulting the Commission, take the necessary measures within one year of the entry into force of this Regulation.

Article 14

Fines

1. The Commission may by decision impose on the persons referred to in Article 3(1)(b), undertakings or associations of undertakings fines of from ECU 1000 to 50,000 where intentionally or negligently:

(a) they fail to notify a concentration in accordance with Article 4;

(b) they supply incorrect or misleading information in a notification pursuant to Article 4;

(c) they supply incorrect information in response to a request made pursuant to Article 11 or fail to supply information within the period fixed by a decision taken pursuant to Article 11;

(d) they produce the required books or other business records in incomplete form during investigations under Article 12 or 13, or refuse to submit to an investigation ordered by decision taken pursuant to Article 13.

2. The Commission may by decision impose fines not exceeding 10% of the aggregate turnover of the undertakings concerned within the meaning of Article 5 on the persons or undertakings concerned where, either intentionally or negligently, they;

(a) fail to comply with an obligation imposed by decision pursuant to Article 7(4) or 8(2), second subparagraph;

(b) put into effect a concentration in breach of Article 7(1) or disregard a decision taken pursuant to Article 7(2);

(c) put into effect a concentration declared incompatible with the common market by decision pursuant to Article 8(3) or do not take the measures ordered by decision pursuant to Article 8(4).

3. In setting the amount of a fine, regard shall be had to the nature and gravity of the infringement.

4. Decisions taken pursuant to paragraphs 1 and 2 shall not be of criminal law nature.

Article 15

Periodic penalty payments

1. The Commission may by decision impose on the persons referred to in Article 3(1)(b), undertakings or associations of undertakings concerned

periodic penalty payments of up to ECU 25000 for each day of delay calculated from the date set in the decision, in order to compel them:

(a) to supply complete and correct information which it has requested by decision pursuant to Article 11;

(b) to submit to an investigation which it has ordered by decision pursuant to Article 13.

2. The Commission may by decision impose on the persons referred to in Article 3(1)(b) or on undertakings periodic penalty payments of up to ECU 100 000 for each day of delay calculated from the date set in the decision, in order to compel them:

(a) to comply with an obligation imposed by decision pursuant to Article 7(4) or Article 8(2), second subparagraph, or

(b) to apply the measures ordered by decision pursuant to Article 8(4).

3. Where the persons referred to in Article 3(1)(b), undertakings or associations of undertakings have satisfied the obligation which it was the purpose of the periodic penalty payment to enforce, the Commission may set the total amount of the periodic penalty payments at a lower figure than that which would arise under the original decision.

Article 16

Review by the Court of Justice

The Court of Justice shall have unlimited jurisdiction within the meaning of Article 172 of the Treaty to review decisions whereby the Commission has fixed a fine or periodic penalty payments; it may cancel, reduce or increase the fine or periodic penalty payments imposed.

Article 17

Professional secrecy

1. Information acquired as a result of the application of Articles 11, 12, 13 and 18 shall be used only for the purposes of the relevant request, investigation or hearing.

2. Without prejudice to Articles 4(3), 18 and 20, the Commission and the competent authorities of the Member States, their officials and other servants shall not disclose information they have acquired through the application of this Regulation of the kind covered by the obligation of professional secrecy.

3. Paragraphs 1 and 2 shall not prevent publication of general information or of surveys which do not contain information relating to particular undertakings or associations of undertakings.

Article 18

Hearing of the parties and of third persons

1. Before taking any decision provided for in Article 7(4), Article 8(2), second subparagraph, and (3) to (5), and Articles 14 and 15, the Commis-

sion shall give the persons, undertakings and associations of undertakings concerned the opportunity, at every stage of the procedure up to the consultation of the Advisory Committee, of making known their views on the objections against them.

2. By way of derogation from paragraph 1, a decision to grant a derogation from suspension as referred to in Article 7(4) may be taken provisionally, without the persons, undertakings or associations of undertakings concerned being given the opportunity to make known their views beforehand, provided that the Commission gives them that opportunity as soon as possible after having taken its decision.

3. The Commission shall base its decision only on objections on which the parties have been able to submit their observations. The rights of the defence shall be fully respected in the proceedings. Access to the file shall be open at least to the parties directly involved, subject to the legitimate interest of undertakings in the protection of their business secrets.

4. Insofar as the Commission or the competent authorities of the Member States deem it necessary, they may also hear other natural or legal persons. Natural or legal persons showing a sufficient interest and especially members of the administrative or management bodies of the undertakings concerned or the recognized representatives of their employees shall be entitled, upon application, to be heard.

Article 19

Liaison with the authorities of the Member States

1. The Commission shall transmit to the competent authorities of the Member States copies of notifications within three working days and, as soon as possible, copies of the most important documents lodged with or issued by the Commission pursuant to this Regulation. Such documents shall include commitments which are intended by the parties to form the basis for a decision pursuant to Articles 6(1)(b) or 8(2).

2. The Commission shall carry out the procedures set out in this Regulation in close and constant liaison with the competent authorities of the Member States, which may express their views upon those procedures. For the purposes of Article 9 it shall obtain information from the competent authority of the Member State as referred to in paragraph 2 of that Article and give it the opportunity to make known its views at every stage of the procedure up to the adoption of a decision pursuant to paragraph 3 of that Article; to that end it shall give it access to the file.

3. An Advisory Committee on concentrations shall be consulted before any decision is taken pursuant to Articles 8(2) to (5), 14 or 15, or any provisions are adopted pursuant to Article 23.

4. The Advisory Committee shall consist of representatives of the authorities of the Member States. Each Member State shall appoint one or two representatives; if unable to attend, they may be replaced by other representatives. At least one of the representatives of a Member State shall be competent in matters of restrictive practices and dominant positions.

5. Consultation shall take place at a joint meeting convened at the invitation of and chaired by the Commission. A summary of the case, together with an indication of the most important documents and a preliminary draft of the decision to be taken for each case considered, shall be sent with the invitation. The meeting shall take place not less than 14 days after the invitation has been sent. The Commission may in exceptional cases shorten that period as appropriate in order to avoid serious harm to one or more of the undertakings concerned by a concentration.

6. The Advisory Committee shall deliver an opinion on the Commission's draft decision, if necessary by taking a vote. The Advisory Committee may deliver an opinion even if some members are absent and unrepresented. The opinion shall be delivered in writing and appended to the draft decision. The Commission shall take the utmost account of the opinion delivered by the Committee. It shall inform the Committee of the manner in which its opinion has been taken into account.

7. The Advisory Committee may recommend publication of the opinion. The Commission may carry out such publication. The decision to publish shall take due account of the legitimate interest of undertakings in the protection of their business secrets and of the interest of the undertakings concerned in such publication's taking place.

Article 20

Publication of decisions

1. The Commission shall publish the decisions which it takes pursuant to Article 8(2) to (5) in the Official Journal of the European Communities.

2. The publication shall state the names of the parties and the main content of the decision; it shall have regard to the legitimate interest of undertakings in the protection of their business secrets.

Article 21

Jurisdiction

1. Subject to review by the Court of Justice, the Commission shall have sole jurisdiction to take the decisions provided for in this Regulation.

2. No Member State shall apply its national legislation on competition to any concentration that has a Community dimension.

The first subparagraph shall be without prejudice to any Member State's power to carry out any enquiries necessary for the application of Article 9(2) or after referral, pursuant to Article 9(3), first subparagraph, indent (b), or (5), to take the measures strictly necessary for the application of Article 9(8).

3. Notwithstanding paragraphs 1 and 2, Member States may take appropriate measures to protect legitimate interests other than those taken into consideration by this Regulation and compatible with the general principles and other provisions of Community law.

Public security, plurality of the media and prudential rules shall be regarded as legitimate interests within the meaning of the first subparagraph.

Any other public interest must be communicated to the Commission by the Member State concerned and shall be recognized by the Commission after an assessment of its compatibility with the general principles and other provisions of Community law before the measures referred to above may be taken. The Commission shall inform the Member State concerned of its decision within one month of that communication.

Article 22

Application of the Regulation

1. This Regulation alone shall apply to concentrations as defined in Article 3, and Regulations No 17, (EEC) No 1017/68, (EEC) No 4056/86 and (EEC) No 3975/87 shall not apply, except in relation to joint ventures that do not have a Community dimension and which have as their object or effect the coordination of the competitive behaviour of undertakings that remain independent.

3. If the Commission finds, at the request of a Member State or at the joint request of two or more Member States, that a concentration as defined in Article 3 that has no Community dimension within the meaning of Article 1 creates or strengthens a dominant position as a result of which effective competition would be significantly impeded within the territory of the Member State or States making the joint request, it may, insofar as that concentration affects trade between Member States, adopt the decisions provided for in Article 8(2), second subparagraph, (3) and (4).

4. Articles 2(1)(a) and (b), 5, 6, 8 and 10 to 20 shall apply to a request made pursuant to paragraph 3. Article 7 shall apply to the extent that the concentration has not been put into effect on the date on which the Commission informs the parties that a request has been made.

The period within which proceedings may be initiated pursuant to Article 10(1) shall begin on the day following that of the receipt of the request from the Member State or States concerned. The request must be made within one month at most of the date on which the concentration was made known to the Member State or to all Member States making a joint request or effected. This period shall begin on the date of the first of those events.

5. Pursuant to paragraph 3 the Commission shall take only the measures strictly necessary to maintain or restore effective competition within the territory of the Member State or States at the request of which it intervenes.

Article 23

Implementing provisions

The Commission shall have the power to adopt implementing provisions concerning the form, content and other details of notifications pursuant to Article 4, time limits pursuant to Articles 7, 9, 10 and 22 and hearings pursuant to Article 18.

The Commission shall have the power to lay down the procedure and time limits for the submission of commitments pursuant to Articles 6(2) and 8(2).

Article 24

Relations with non-member countries

1. The Member States shall inform the Commission of any general difficulties encountered by their undertakings with concentrations as defined in Article 3 in a non-member country.

2. Initially not more than one year after the entry into force of this Regulation and thereafter periodically the Commission shall draw up a report examining the treatment accorded to Community undertakings, in the terms referred to in paragraphs 3 and 4, as regards concentrations in non-member countries. The Commission shall submit those reports to the Council, together with any recommendations.

3. Whenever it appears to the Commission, either on the basis of the reports referred to in paragraph 2 or on the basis of other information, that a non-member country does not grant Community undertakings treatment comparable to that granted by the Community to undertakings from that non-member country, the Commission may submit proposals to the Council for an appropriate mandate for negotiation with a view to obtaining comparable treatment for Community undertakings.

4. Measures taken under this Article shall comply with the obligations of the Community or of the Member States, without prejudice to Article 234 of the Treaty, under international agreements, whether bilateral or multilateral.

Article 25

Entry into force

1. This Regulation shall enter into force on 21 September 1990.

2. This Regulation shall not apply to any concentration which was the subject of an agreement or announcement or where control was acquired within the meaning of Article 4(1) before the date of this Regulation's entry into force and it shall not in any circumstances apply to any concentration in respect of which proceedings were initiated before that date by a Member State's authority with responsibility for competition.

3. As regards concentrations to which this Regulation applies by virtue of accession, the date of accession shall be substituted for the date of entry into force of this Regulation. The provision of paragraph 2, second alternative, applies in the same way to proceedings initiated by a competition authority of the new Member States or by the EFTA Surveillance Authority.

This Regulation shall be binding in its entirety and directly applicable in all Member States.

Part V

EXTERNAL RELATIONS AND COMMERCIAL POLICY

INTRODUCTION

We have selected only a few documents for Part V. In the case of Chapter 27 on the external relations powers of the EU, the relevant documents are the EC Treaty and the Treaty on European Union, all of which are reproduced in the documents section for Part I.

Although there are many agreements documenting the EU's relationship with the various countries of the world, space considerations preclude including any of them. Citations to the major agreements are given in Chapters 28 and 29.

With respect to customs law, the basic subject of Chapter 30, the Community adopted a Community Customs Code on October 12, 1992, effective as of January 1, 1994. Council Regulation (EEC) No. 2913/92 of 12 October 1992 establishing the Community Customs Code, O.J. L 302/1 (Oct. 19, 1992). The Code deals comprehensively with customs law issues, except for classification and tariff rates, which remain covered by the Taric. We excerpt those provisions dealing with origin and valuation. It is worth noting that the these provisions are largely unchanged from the previous separate regulations on origin and valuation that are the subject of several cases in the casebook.

In connection with Chapter 31, we have included three important documents. The first document is the Community regulation on antidumping procedures. Council Regulation (EC) No. 384/96 of 22 December 1995 on protection against dumped imports from countries not members of the European Community, O.J. L 56/1 (Mar. 6, 1996).

The second document connected to Chapter 31 is the Community regulation on protection against subsidized imports. Council Regulation (EC) No. 2026/97 of 6 October 1997 on protection against subsidized imports from countries not members of the European Community, O.J. L 288/1 (Oct. 21, 1997). Prior to 1995, the subsidy rules were included in the antidumping regulation. Since the procedures for investigating and applying antidumping and countervailing duties are quite similar, we excerpt only selected parts of the subsidy regulation, particularly those dealing with the definition and calculation of subsidies.

The third document associated with Chapter 31 is the new Trade Barriers Regulation, which is based on the 1984 new commercial policy instrument dealing with illicit commercial practices. Council Regulation (EC) No. 3286/94 of 22 December 1994 laying down Community procedures in the field of the common commercial policy in order to ensure the exercise of the Community's rights under international trade rules, in particular those established under the auspices of the World Trade Organization, O.J. L 349/71 (Dec. 31, 1994). This regulation and its predecessor were adopted in part in response to the use by the United States of so-called Section 301 of the Trade Act of 1974 (actually now sections 301–310), 19 U.S.C. secs. 2411–2420.

Table of Contents

PART V. EXTERNAL RELATIONS AND COMMERCIAL POLICY

Doc. Page

Introduction. 553

1. Council Regulation (EEC) No. 2913/92 of 12 October 1992 establishing the Community Customs Code. 555
2. Council Regulation (EC) No. 384/96 of 22 December 1995 on protection against dumped imports from countries not members of the European Community. 565
3. Council Regulation (EC) No 2026/97 of 6 October 1997 on protection against subsidized imports from countries not members of the European Community. 597
4. Council Regulation (EC) No. 3286/94 of 22 December 1994 laying down Community procedures in the field of the common commercial policy in order to ensure the exercise of the Community's rights under international trade rules, in particular those established under the auspices of the World Trade Organization. 608

1. COUNCIL REGULATION (EEC) NO. 2913/92

of 12 October 1992

establishing the Community Customs Code (as amended)

O.J. L 302/1 (Oct. 19, 1992)

THE COUNCIL OF THE EUROPEAN COMMUNITIES,

Having regard to the Treaty establishing the European Economic Community, and in particular Articles [26, 95 and 133] thereof,

* * *

HAS ADOPTED THIS REGULATION:

* * *

TITLE II

FACTORS ON THE BASIS OF WHICH IMPORT DUTIES OR EXPORT DUTIES AND THE OTHER MEASURES PRESCRIBED IN RESPECT OF TRADE IN GOODS ARE APPLIED

CHAPTER 1

CUSTOMS TARIFF OF THE EUROPEAN COMMUNITIES AND TARIFF CLASSIFICATION OF GOODS

Article 20

1. Duties legally owned where a customs debt is incurred shall be based on the Customs Tariff of the European Communities.

2. The other measures prescribed by Community provisions governing specific fields relating to trade in goods shall, where appropriate, be applied according to the tariff classification of those goods.

3. The Customs Tariff of the European Communities shall comprise:

(a) the combined nomenclature of goods;

(b) any other nomenclature which is wholly or partly based on the combined nomenclature or which adds any subdivisions to it, and which is established by Community provisions governing specific fields with a view to the application of tariff measures relating to trade in goods;

(c) the rates and other items of charge normally applicable to goods covered by the combined nomenclature as regards:

(i) customs duties; and

(ii) import charges laid down under the common agricultural policy or under the specific arrangements applicable to certain goods resulting from the processing of agricultural products.

(d) the preferential tariff measures contained in agreements which the Community has concluded with certain countries or groups of countries and which provide for the granting of preferential tariff treatment;

(e) preferential tariff measures adopted unilaterally by the Community in respect of certain countries, groups of countries or territories;

(f) autonomous suspensive measures providing for a reduction in or relief from import duties chargeable on certain goods;

(g) other tariff measures provided for by other Community legislation.

4. Without prejudice to the rules on flat-rate charges, the measures referred to in paragraph 3(d), (e) and (f) shall apply at the declarant's request instead of those provided for in subparagraph (c) where the goods concerned fulfil the conditions laid down by those first-mentioned measures. An application may be made after the event provided that the relevant conditions are fulfilled.

5. Where application of the measures referred to in paragraph 3(d), (e) and (f) is restricted to a certain volume of imports, it shall cease:

(a) In the case of tariff quotas, as soon as the stipulated limit on the volume of imports is reached;

(b) in the case of tariff ceilings, by ruling of the Commission.

6. The tariff classification of goods shall be the determination, according to the rules in force, of:

(a) the subheading of the combined nomenclature or the subheading of any other nomenclature referred to in paragraph 3(b); or

(b) the subheading of any other nomenclature which is wholly or partly based on the combined nomenclature or which adds any subdivisions to it, and which is established by Community provisions governing specific fields with a view to the application of measures other than tariff measures relating to trade in goods,

under which the aforesaid goods are to be classified.

Article 21

1. The favourable tariff treatment from which certain goods may benefit by reason of their nature or end-use shall be subject to conditions laid down in accordance with the Committee procedure. Where an authorization is required Articles 86 and 87 shall apply.

2. For the purposes of paragraph 1, the expression "favourable tariff treatment" means a reduction in or suspension of an import duty as referred to in Article 4(10), even within the framework of a tariff quota.

CHAPTER 2
ORIGIN OF GOODS

Section 1

Non-preferential origin

Article 22

Articles 23 to 26 define the non-preferential origin of goods for the purposes of:

(a) applying the Customs Tariff of the European Communities with the exception of the measures referred to in Article 20(3)(d) and (e);

(b) applying measures other than tariff measures established by Community provisions governing specific fields relating to trade in goods;

(c) the preparation and issue of certificates of origin.

Article 23

1. Goods originating in a country shall be those wholly obtained or produced in that country.

2. The expression "goods wholly obtained in a country" means:

(a) mineral products extracted within that country;

(b) vegetable products harvested therein;

(c) live animals born and raised therein;

(d) products derived from live animals raised therein;

(e) products of hunting or fishing carried on therein;

(f) products of sea-fishing and other products taken from the sea outside a country's territorial sea by vessels registered or recorded in the country concerned and flying the flag of that country;

(g) goods obtained or produced on board factory ships from the products referred to in subparagraph (f) originating in that country, provided that such factory ships are registered or recorded in that country and fly its flag;

(h) products taken from the seabed or subsoil beneath the seabed outside the territorial sea provided that that country has exclusive rights to exploit that seabed or subsoil;

(i) waste and scrap products derived from manufacturing operations and used articles, if they were collected therein and are fit only for the recovery of raw materials;

(j) goods which are produced therein exclusively from goods referred to in subparagraphs (a) to (i) or from their derivatives, at any stage of production.

3. For the purposes of paragraph 2 the expression "country" covers that country's territorial sea.

Article 24

Goods whose production involved more than one country shall be deemed to originate in the country where they underwent their last, substantial, economically justified processing or working in an undertaking equipped for that purpose and resulting in the manufacture of a new product or representing an important stage of manufacture.

Article 25

Any processing or working in respect of which it is established, or in respect of which the facts as ascertained justify the presumption, that its sole object was to circumvent the provisions applicable in the Community to goods from specific countries shall under no circumstances be deemed to confer on the goods thus produced the origin of the country where it is carried out within the meaning of Article 24.

Article 26

1. Customs legislation or other Community legislation governing specific fields may provide that a document must be produced as proof of the origin of goods.

2. Notwithstanding the production of that document, the customs authorities may, in the event of serious doubts, require any additional proof to ensure that the indication of origin does comply with the rules laid down by the relevant Community legislation.

Section 2

Preferential Origin of Goods

Article 27

The rules on preferential origin shall lay down the conditions governing acquisition of origin which goods must fulfil in order to benefit from the measures referred to in Article 20(3)(d) or (e).

Those rules shall:

(a) in the case of goods covered by the agreements referred to in Article 20(3)(d), be determined in those agreements;

(b) in the case of goods benefitting from the preferential tariff measures referred to in Article 20(3)(e), be determined in accordance with the Committee procedure.

CHAPTER 3

VALUE OF GOODS FOR CUSTOMS PURPOSES

Article 28

The provisions of this Chapter shall determine the customs value for the purposes of applying the Customs Tariff of the European Communities and non-tariff measures laid down by Community provisions governing specific fields relating to trade in goods.

Article 29

1. The customs value of imported goods shall be the transaction value, that is, the price actually paid or payable for the goods when sold for export to the customs territory of the Community, adjusted, where necessary, in accordance with Articles 32 and 33, provided:

(a) that there are no restrictions as to the disposal or use of the goods by the buyer, other than restrictions which:

(i) are imposed or required by a law or by the public authorities in the Community;

(ii) limit the geographical area in which the goods may be resold; or

(iii) do not substantially affect the value of the goods;

(b) that the sale or price is not subject to some condition or consideration for which a value cannot be determined with respect to the goods being valued;

(c) that no part of the proceeds of any subsequent resale, disposal or use of the goods by the buyer will accrue directly or indirectly to the seller, unless an appropriate adjustment can be made in accordance with Article 32; and

(d) that the buyer and seller are not related, or, where the buyer and seller are related, that the transaction value is acceptable for customs purposes under paragraph 2.

2. (a) In determining whether the transaction value is acceptable for the purposes of paragraph 1, the fact that the buyer and the seller are related shall not in itself be sufficient grounds for regarding the transaction value as unacceptable. Where necessary, the circumstances surrounding the sale shall be examined and the transaction value shall be accepted provided that the relationship did not influence the price. If, in the light of information provided by the declarant or otherwise, the customs authorities have grounds for considering that the relationship influenced the price, they shall communicate their grounds to the declarant and he shall be given a reasonable opportunity to respond. If the declarant so requests, the communication of the grounds shall be in writing.

(b) In a sale between related persons, the transaction value shall be accepted and the goods valued in accordance with paragraph 1 wherever the declarant demonstrates that such value closely approximates to one of the following occurring at or about the same time:

(i) the transaction value in sales, between buyers and sellers who are not related in any particular case, of identical or similar goods for export to the Community;

(ii) the customs value of identical or similar goods, as determined under Article 30(2)(c);

(iii) the customs value of identical or similar goods, as determined under Article 30(2)(d).

In applying the foregoing tests, due account shall be taken of demonstrated differences in commercial levels, quantity levels, the elements enumerated in Article 32 and costs incurred by the seller in sales in which he and the buyer are not related and where such costs are not incurred by the seller in sales in which he and the buyer are related.

(c) The tests set forth in subparagraph (b) are to be used at the initiative of the declarant and only for comparison purposes. Substitute values may not be established under the said paragraph.

3. (a) The price actually paid or payable is the total payment made or to be made by the buyer to or for the benefit of the seller for the imported goods and includes all payments made or to be made as a condition of sale of the imported goods by the buyer to the seller or by the buyer to a third party to satisfy an obligation of the seller. The payment need not necessarily take the form of a transfer of money. Payment may be made by way of letters of credit or negotiable instrument and may be made directly or indirectly.

(b) Activities, including marketing activities, undertaken by the buyer on his own account, other than those for which an adjustment is provided in Article 32, are not considered to be an indirect payment to the seller, even though they might be regarded as of benefit to the seller or have been undertaken by agreement with the seller, and their cost shall not be added to the price actually paid or payable in determining the customs value of imported goods.

Article 30

1. Where the customs value cannot be determined under Article 29, it is to be determined by proceeding sequentially through subparagraphs (a), (b), (c) and (d) of paragraph 2 to the first subparagraph under which it can be determined, subject to the proviso that the order of application of subparagraphs (c) and (d) shall be reversed if the declarant so requests; it is only when such value cannot be determined under a particular subparagraph that the provisions of the next subparagraph in a sequence established by virtue of this paragraph can be applied.

2. The customs value as determined under this Article shall be:

(a) the transaction value of identical goods sold for export to the Community and exported at or about the same time as the goods being valued;

(b) the transaction value of similar goods sold for export to the Community and exported at or about the same time as the goods being valued;

(c) the value based on the unit price at which the imported goods for identical or similar imported goods are sold within the Community in the greatest aggregate quantity to persons not related to the sellers;

(d) the computed value, consisting of the sum of:

(i) the cost or value of materials and fabrication or other processing employed in producing the imported goods;

(ii) an amount for profit and general expenses equal to that usually reflected in sales of goods of the same class or kind as the goods being valued which are made by producers in the country of exportation for export to the Community;

(iii) the cost or value of the items referred to in Article 32(1)(e).

3. Any further conditions and rules for the application of paragraph 2 above shall be determined in accordance with the committee procedure.

Article 31

1. Where the customs value of imported goods cannot be determined under Articles 29 or 30, it shall be determined, on the basis of data available in the Community, using reasonable means consistent with the principles and general provisions of:

(a) the Agreement on Implementation of Article VII of the General Agreement on Tariffs and Trade of 1994;

(b) Article VII of the General Agreement on Tariffs and Trade of 1994;

(c) the provisions of this Chapter.

2. No customs value shall be determined under paragraph 1 on the basis of:

(a) the selling price in the Community of goods produced in the Community;

(b) a system which provides for the acceptance for customs purposes of the higher of two alternative values;

(c) the price of goods on the domestic market of the country of exportation;

(d) the cost of production, other than computed values which have been determined for identical or similar goods in accordance with Article 30(2)(d);

(e) prices for export to a country not forming part of the customs territory of the Community;

(f) minimum customs values; or

(g) arbitrary or fictitious values.

Article 32

1. In determining the customs value under Article 29, there shall be added to the price actually paid or payable for the imported goods:

(a) the following, to the extent that they are incurred by the buyer but are not included in the price actually paid or payable for the goods:

(i) commissions and brokerage, except buying commissions;

(ii) the cost of containers which are treated as being one, for customs purposes, with the goods in question;

(iii) the cost of packing, whether for labour or materials;

(b) the value, apportioned as appropriate, of the following goods and services where supplied directly or indirectly by the buyer free-of-charge or at reduced cost for use in connection with the production and sale for export of the imported goods, to the extent that such value has not been included in the price actually paid or payable:

(i) materials, components, parts and similar items incorporated in the imported goods;

(ii) tools, dyes, moulds and similar items used in the production of imported goods;

(iii) materials consumed in the production of the imported goods;

(iv) engineering, development, artwork, design work, and plans and sketches undertaken elsewhere than in the Community and necessary for the production of the imported goods;

(c) royalties and licence fees related to the goods being valued that the buyer must pay, either directly or indirectly, as a condition of sale of the goods being valued, to the extent that such royalties and fees are not included in the price actually paid or payable;

(d) the value of any part of the proceeds of any subsequent resale, disposal or use of the imported goods that accrues directly or indirectly to the seller;

(e) (i) the cost of transport and insurance of the imported goods; and

(ii) loading and handling of charges associated with the transport of the imported goods to the place of introduction into the customs territory of the Community.

2. Additions to the price actually paid or payable shall be made under this Article only on the basis of objective and quantifiable data.

3. No additions shall be made to the price actually paid or payable in determining the customs value except as provided in this Article.

4. In this Chapter, the term "buying commissions" means fees paid by an importer to his agent for the service of representing him in the purchase of the goods being valued.

5. Notwithstanding paragraph 1(c):

(a) charges for the right to reproduce the imported goods in the Community shall not be added to the price actually paid or payable for the imported goods in determining the customs value; and

(b) payments made by the buyer for the right to distribute or resell the imported goods shall not be added to the price actually paid or payable for the imported goods if such payments are not a condition of the sale for export to the Community of the goods.

Article 33

1. Provided that they are shown separately from the price actually paid or payable, the following shall not be included in the customs value:

(a) charges for the transport of goods after their arrival at the place of introduction into the customs territory of the Community;

(b) charges for construction, erection, assembly, maintenance or technical assistance, undertaken after importation of imported goods such as industrial plant, machinery or equipment;

(c) charges for interest under a financing arrangement entered into by the buyer and relating to the purchase of imported goods, irrespective of whether the finance is provided by the seller or another person, provided that the financing arrangement has been made in writing and where required, the buyer can demonstrate that:

(i) such goods are actually sold at the price declared as the price actually paid or payable; and

(ii) the claimed rate of interest does not exceed the level for such transactions prevailing in the country where, and at the time when, the finance was provided;

(d) charges for the right to reproduce imported goods in the Community;

(e) buying commissions;

(f) import duties or other charges payable in the Community by reason of the importation or sale of the goods.

Article 34

Specific rules may be laid down in accordance with the procedure of the committee to determine the customs value of carrier media for use in data processing equipment and bearing data or instructions.

Article 35

Where factors used to determine the customs value of goods are expressed in a currency other than that of the member State where the valuation is made, the rate of exchange to be used shall be that duly published by the authorities competent in the matter.

Such rate shall reflect as effectively as possible the current value of such currency in commercial transactions in terms of the currency of such member State and shall apply during such period as may be determined in accordance with the procedure of the committee.

Where such a rate does not exist, the rate of exchange to be used shall be determined in accordance with the procedure of the committee.

Article 36

1. The provisions of this chapter shall be without prejudice to the specific provisions regarding the determination of the value for customs purposes of goods released for free circulation after being assigned a different customs-approved treatment or use.

2. By way of derogation from Articles 29, 30 and 31, the customs value of perishable goods usually delivered on consignment may, at the

request of the declarant, be determined under simplified rules drawn up for the whole Community in accordance with the committee procedure.

* * *

TITLE IV

CUSTOMS—APPROVED TREATMENT OR USE

* * *

CHAPTER 2

CUSTOMS PROCEDURES

* * *

Section 2

Release for Free Circulation

Article 79

Release for free circulation shall confer on non-Community goods the customs status of Community goods.

It shall entail application of commercial policy measures, completion of the other formalities laid down in respect of the importation of goods and the charging of any duties legally due.

2. COUNCIL REGULATION (EC) NO. 384/96

of 22 December 1995

on protection against dumped imports from countries not members of the European Community (as amended)

O.J. L 56/1 (Mar. 6, 1996)

THE COUNCIL OF THE EUROPEAN UNION,

Having regard to the Treaty establishing the European Community, and in particular Article 133 thereof,

Having regard to the Regulations establishing the common organization of agricultural markets and the Regulations adopted pursuant to Article 308 of the Treaty applicable to goods manufactured from agricultural products, and in particular the provisions of those Regulations which allow for derogation from the general principle that protective measures at frontiers may be replaced solely by the measures provided for in those Regulations,

* * *

1. Whereas, by Regulation (EC) No. 2423/88, the Council adopted common rules for protection against dumped or subsidized imports from countries which are not members of the European Community;

2. Whereas those rules were adopted in accordance with existing international obligations, in particular those arising from Article VI of the General Agreement on Tariffs and Trade (hereinafter referred to as "GATT"), from the Agreement on Implementation of Article VI of the GATT (1979 Anti-Dumping Code) and from the Agreement on Interpretation and Application of Articles VI, XVI and XXIII of the GATT (Code on Subsidies and Countervailing Duties);

3. Whereas the multilateral trade negotiations concluded in 1994 have led to new agreements on the implementation of Article VI of GATT and it is therefore appropriate to amend the Community rules in the light of these new Agreements; whereas is it also desirable, in the light of the different nature of the new rules for dumping and subsidies respectively, to have a separate body of Community rules in each of those two areas; whereas, consequently, the new rules on protection against subsidies and countervailing duties are contained in a separate Regulation;

4. Whereas, in applying the rules it is essential, in order to maintain the balance of rights and obligations which the GATT Agreement establishes, that the Community take account of how they are interpreted by the Community's major trading partners;

5. Whereas the new agreement on dumping, namely, the Agreement on Implementation of Article VI of the General Agreement on Tariffs and Trade 1994 (hereinafter referred to as "the 1994 Anti-Dumping Agreement"), contains new and detailed rules, relating in particular to the

calculation of dumping, procedures for initiating and pursuing an investigation, including the establishment and treatment of the facts, the imposition of provisional measures, the imposition and collection of anti-dumping duties, the duration and review of anti-dumping measures and the public disclosure of information relating to anti-dumping investigations; whereas, in view of the extent of the changes and to ensure a proper and transparent application of the new rules, the language of the new agreements should be brought into Community legislation as far as possible;

* * *

20. Whereas the 1994 Anti–Dumping Agreement does not contain provisions regarding the circumvention of anti-dumping measures, though a separate GATT Ministerial Decision recognizes circumvention as a problem and has referred it to the GATT Anti–Dumping Committee for resolution; whereas given the failure of the multilateral negotiations so far and pending the outcome of the referral to the GATT Anti–Dumping Committee, it is necessary to introduce new provisions into Community legislation to deal with practices, including mere assembly of goods in the Community or a third country, which have as their main aim the circumvention of anti-dumping measures;

* * *

HAS ADOPTED THIS REGULATION:

Article 1

Principles

1. An anti-dumping duty may be applied to any dumped product whose release for free circulation in the Community causes injury.

2. A product is to be considered as being dumped if its export price to the Community is less than a comparable price for the like product, in the ordinary course of trade, as established for the exporting country.

3. The exporting country shall normally be the country of origin. However, it may be an intermediate country, except where, for example, the products are merely transhipped through that country, or the products concerned are not produced in that country, or there is no comparable price for them in that country.

4. For the purpose of this Regulation, the term "like product" shall be interpreted to mean a product which is identical, that is to say, alike in all respects, to the product under consideration, or in the absence of such a product, another product which although not alike in all respects, has characteristics closely resembling those of the product under consideration.

Article 2

Determination of dumping

A. NORMAL VALUE

1. The normal value shall normally be based on the prices paid or payable, in the ordinary course of trade, by independent customers in the exporting country.

However, where the exporter in the exporting country does not produce or does not sell the like product, the normal value may be established on the basis of prices of other sellers or producers.

Prices between parties which appear to be associated or to have a compensatory arrangement with each other may not be considered to be in the ordinary course of trade and may not be used to establish normal value unless it is determined that they are unaffected by the relationship.

2. Sales of the like product intended for domestic consumption shall normally be used to determine normal value if such sales volume constitutes 5 per cent or more of the sales volume of the product under consideration to the Community. However, a lower volume of sales may be used when, for example, the prices charged are considered representative for the market concerned.

3. When there are no or insufficient sales of the like product in the ordinary course of trade, or where because of the particular market situation such sales do not permit a proper comparison, the normal value of the like product shall be calculated on the basis of the cost of production in the country of origin plus a reasonable amount for selling, general and administrative costs and for profits, or on the basis of the export prices, in the ordinary course of trade, to an appropriate third country, provided that those prices are representative.

4. Sales of the like product in the domestic market of the exporting country, or export sales to a third country, at prices below unit production costs (fixed and variable) plus selling, general and administrative costs may be treated as not being in the ordinary course of trade by reasons of price, and may be disregarded in determining normal value, only if is determined that such sales are made within an extended period in substantial quantities, and are at prices which do not provide for the recovery of all costs within a reasonable period of time.

If prices which are below costs at the time of sale are above weighted average costs for the period of investigation, such prices shall be considered to provide for recovery of costs within a reasonable period of time.

The extended period of time shall normally be one year but shall in no case be less than six months, and sales below unit cost shall be considered to be made in substantial quantities within such a period when it is established that the weighted average selling price is below the weighted average unit cost, or that the volume of sales below unit cost is not less than 20 per cent of sales being used to determine normal value.

5. Costs shall normally be calculated on the basis of records kept by the party under investigation, provided that such records are in accordance with the generally accepted accounting principles of the country concerned and that it is shown that the records reasonably reflect the costs associated with the production and sale of the product under consideration.

Consideration shall be given to evidence submitted on the proper allocation of costs, provided that it is shown that such allocations have been historically utilized. In the absence of a more appropriate method, preference shall be given to the allocation of costs on the basis of turnover. Unless already reflected in the cost allocations under this subparagraph, costs shall be adjusted appropriately for those non-recurring items of cost which benefit future and/or current production.

Where the costs for part of the period for cost recovery are affected by the use of new production facilities requiring substantial additional investment and by low capacity utilization rates, which are the result of start-up operations which take place within or during part of the investigation period, the average costs for the start-up phase shall be those applicable, under the above-mentioned allocation rules, at the end of such a phase, and shall be included at that level, for the period concerned, in the weighted average costs referred to in the second sub-paragraph of paragraph 4. The length of a start-up phase shall be determined in relation to the circumstances of the producer or exporter concerned, but shall not exceed an appropriate initial portion of the period for cost recovery. For this adjustment to costs applicable during the investigation period, information relating to a start-up phase which extends beyond that period shall be taken into account where it is submitted prior to verification visits and within three months of the initiation of the investigation.

6. The amounts for selling, for general and administrative costs and for profits shall be based on actual data pertaining to production and sales, in the ordinary course of trade, of the like product, by the exporter or producer under investigation. When such amounts cannot be determined on this basis, the amounts may be determined on the basis of:

(a) the weighted average of the actual amounts determined for other exporters or producers subject to investigation in respect of production and sales of the like product in the domestic market of the country of origin;

(b) the actual amounts applicable to production and sales, in the ordinary course of trade, of the same general category of products for the exporter or producer in question in the domestic market of the country of origin;

(c) any other reasonable method, provided that the amount for profit so established shall not exceed the profit normally realized by other exporters or producers on sales of products of the same general category in the domestic market of the country of origin.

7. (a) In the case of imports from non-market economy countries[1], normal value shall be determined on the basis of the price or constructed value in a market economy third country, or the price from such a third country to other countries, including the Community, or where those are not possible, on any other reasonable basis, including the price actually paid or payable in the Community for the like product, duly adjusted if necessary to include a reasonable profit margin.

1. Including Albania, Armenia, Azerbaijan, Belarus, Georgia, North Korea, Kyrgyzstan, Moldova, Mongolia, Tajikistan, Turkmenistan, Uzbekistan.

An appropriate market economy third country shall be selected in a not unreasonable manner, due account being taken of any reliable information made available at the time of selection. Account shall also be taken of time limits; where appropriate, a market economy third country which is subject to the same investigation shall be used.

The parties to the investigation shall be informed shortly after its initiation of the market economy third country envisaged and shall be given 10 days to comment.

(b) In anti-dumping investigations concerning imports from the Russian Federation, the People's Republic of China, the Ukraine, Vietnam and Kazakhstan and any non-market-economy country which is a member of the WTO at the date of the initiation of the investigation, normal value will be determined in accordance with paragraphs 1 to 6, if it is shown, on the basis of properly substantiated claims by one or more producers subject to the investigation and in accordance with the criteria and procedures set out in subparagraph (c) that market economy conditions prevail for this producer or producers in respect of the manufacture and sale of the like product concerned. When this is not the case, the rules set out under subparagraph (a) shall apply.

(c) A claim under subparagraph (b) must be made in writing and contain sufficient evidence that the producer operates under market economy conditions, that is if:

— decisions of firms regarding prices, costs and inputs, including for instance raw materials, cost of technology and labour, output, sales and investment, are made in response to market signals reflecting supply and demand, and without significant State interference in this regard, and costs of major inputs substantially reflect market values,

— firms have one clear set of basic accounting records which are independently audited in line with international accounting standards and are applied for all purposes,

— the production costs and financial situation of firms are not subject to significant distortions carried over from the former non-market economy system, in particular in relation to depreciation of assets, other write-offs, barter trade and payment via compensation of debts,

— the firms concerned are subject to bankruptcy and property laws which guarantee legal certainty and stability for the operation of firms, and

— exchange rate conversions are carried out at the market rate.

A determination whether the producer meets the abovementioned criteria shall be made within three months of the initiation of the investigation, after specific consultation of the Advisory Committee and after the Community industry has been given an opportunity to comment. This determination shall remain in force throughout the investigation.

B. EXPORT PRICE

8. The export price shall be the price actually paid or payable for the product when sold for export from the exporting country to the Community.

9. In cases where there is no export price or where it appears that the export price is unreliable because of an association or a compensatory arrangement between the exporter and the importer or a third party, the export price may be constructed on the basis of the price at which the imported products are first resold to an independent buyer, or, if products are not resold to an independent buyer, or are not resold in the condition in which they were imported, on any reasonable basis.

In these cases, adjustment for all costs, including duties and taxes, incurred between importation and resale, and for profits accruing, shall be made so as to establish a reliable export price, at the Community frontier level.

The items for which adjustment shall be made shall include those normally borne by an importer but paid by any party, either inside or outside the Community, which appears to be associated or to have a compensatory arrangement with the importer or exporter, including usual transport, insurance, handling, loading and ancillary costs; customs duties, any anti-dumping duties, and other taxes payable in the importing country by reason of the importation or sale of the goods; and a reasonable margin for selling, general and administrative costs and profit.

C. COMPARISON

10. A fair comparison shall be made between the export price and the normal value. This comparison shall be made at the same level of trade and in respect of sales made at as nearly as possible the same time and with due account taken of other differences which affect price comparability. Where the normal value and the export price as established are not on such a comparable basis due allowance, in the form of adjustments, shall be made in each case, on its merits, for differences in factors which are claimed, and demonstrated, to affect prices and price comparability. Any duplication when making adjustments shall be avoided, in particular in relation to discounts, rebates, quantities and level of trade. When the specified conditions are met, the factors for which adjustment can be made are listed as follows:

(a) *Physical characteristics*

An adjustment shall be made for differences in the physical characteristics of the product concerned. The amount of the adjustment shall correspond to a reasonable estimate of the market value of the difference.

(b) *Import charges and indirect taxes*

An adjustment shall be made to normal value for an amount corresponding to any import charges or indirect taxes borne by the like product and by materials physically incorporated therein, when intended for consumption in the exporting country and not collected or refunded in respect of the product exported to the Community.

(c) *Discounts, rebates and quantities*

An adjustment shall be made for differences in discounts and rebates, including those given for differences in quantities, if these are properly quantified and are directly linked to the sales under consideration. An adjustment may also be made for deferred discounts and rebates if the claim is based on consistent practice in prior periods, including compliance with the conditions required to qualify for the discount or rebates.

(d) *Level of trade*

(i) An adjustment for differences in levels of trade, including any differences which may arise in OEM (Original Equipment Manufacturer) sales, shall be made where, in relation to the distribution chain in both markets, it is shown that the export price, including a constructed export price, is at a different level of trade from the normal value and the difference has affected price comparability which is demonstrated by consistent and distinct differences in functions and prices of the seller for the different levels of trade in the domestic market of the exporting country. The amount of the adjustment shall be based on the market value of the difference.

(ii) However, in circumstances not envisaged under (i), when an existing difference in level of trade cannot be quantified because of the absence of the relevant levels on the domestic market of the exporting countries, or where certain functions are shown clearly to relate to levels of trade other than the one which is to be used in the comparison, a special adjustment may be granted.

(e) *Transport, insurance, handling, loading and ancillary costs*

An adjustment shall be made for differences in the directly related costs incurred for conveying the product concerned from the premises of the exporter to an independent buyer, where such costs are included in the prices charged. Those costs shall include transport, insurance, handling, loading and ancillary costs.

(f) *Packing*

An adjustment shall be made for differences in the directly related packing costs for the product concerned.

(g) *Credit*

An adjustment shall be made for differences in the cost of any credit granted for the sales under consideration, provided that it is a factor taken into account in the determination of the prices charged.

(h) *After-sales costs*

An adjustment shall be made for differences in the direct costs of providing warranties, guarantees, technical assistance and services, as provided for by law and/or in the sales contract.

(i) *Commissions*

An adjustment shall be made for differences in commissions paid in respect of the sales under consideration.

(j) *Currency conversions*

When the price comparison requires a conversion of currencies, such conversion shall be made using the rate of exchange on the date of sale, except that when a sale of foreign currency on forward markets is directly linked to the export sale involved, the rate of exchange in the forward sale shall be used.

Normally, the date of sale shall be the date of invoice but the date of contract, purchase order or order confirmation may be used if these more appropriately establish the material terms of sale. Fluctuations in exchange rates shall be ignored and exporters shall be granted 60 days to reflect a sustained movement in exchange rates during the investigation period.

(k) *Other factors*

An adjustment may also be made for differences in other factors not provided for under subparagraphs (a) to (j) if it is demonstrated that they affect price comparability as required under this paragraph, in particular that customers consistently pay different prices on the domestic market because of the difference in such factors.

D. DUMPING MARGIN

11. Subject to the relevant provisions governing fair comparison, the existence of margins of dumping during the investigation period shall normally be established on the basis of a comparison of a weighted average normal value with a weighted average of prices of all export transactions to the Community, or by a comparison of individual normal values and individual export prices to the Community on a transaction-to-transaction basis. However, a normal value established on a weighted average basis may be compared to prices of all individual export transactions to the Community, if there is a pattern of export prices which differs significantly among different purchasers, regions or time periods, and if the methods specified in the first sentence of this paragraph would not reflect the full degree of dumping being practised. This paragraph shall not preclude the use of sampling in accordance with Article 17.

12. The dumping margin shall be the amount by which the normal value exceeds the export price. Where dumping margins vary, a weighted average dumping margin may be established.

Article 3

Determination of injury

1. Pursuant to this Regulation, the term "injury" shall unless otherwise specified, be taken to mean material injury to the Community industry, threat of material injury to the Community industry or material retardation of the establishment of such an industry and shall be interpreted in accordance with the provisions of this Article.

2. A determination of injury shall be based on positive evidence and shall involve an objective examination of both (a) the volume of the dumped imports and the effect of the dumped imports on prices in the Community market for like products; and (b) the consequent impact of those imports on the Community industry.

3. With regard to the volume of the dumped imports, consideration shall be given to whether there has been a significant increase in dumped imports, either in absolute terms or relative to production or consumption in the Community. With regard to the effect of the dumped imports on prices, consideration shall be given to whether there has been significant price undercutting by the dumped imports as compared with the price of a like product of the Community industry, or whether the effect of such imports is otherwise to depress prices to a significant degree or prevent price increases, which would otherwise have occurred, to a significant degree. No one or more of these factors can necessarily give decisive guidance.

4. Where imports of a product from more than one country are simultaneously subject to anti-dumping investigations, the effects of such imports shall be cumulatively assessed only if it is determined that (a) the margin of dumping established in relation to the imports from each country is more than *de minimis* as defined in Article 9(3) and that the volume of imports from each country is not negligible; and (b) a cumulative assessment of the effects of the imports is appropriate in light of the conditions of competition between imported products and the conditions of competition between the imported products and the like Community product.

5. The examination of the impact of the dumped imports on the Community industry concerned shall include an evaluation of all relevant economic factors and indices having a bearing on the state of the industry, including the fact that an industry is still in the process of recovering from the effects of past dumping or subsidization, the magnitude of the actual margin of dumping, actual and potential decline in sales, profits, output, market share, productivity, return on investments, utilization of capacity; factors affecting Community prices; actual and potential negative effects on cash flow, inventories, employment, wages, growth, ability to raise capital or investments. This list is not exhaustive, nor can any one or more of these factors necessarily give decisive guidance.

6. It must be demonstrated, from all the relevant evidence presented in relation to paragraph 2, that the dumped imports are causing injury within the meaning of this Regulation. Specifically, this shall entail a demonstration that the volume and/or price levels identified pursuant to paragraph 3 are responsible for an impact on the Community industry as provided for in paragraph 5, and that this impact exists to a degree which enables it to be classified as material.

7. Known factors other than the dumped imports which at the same time are injuring the Community industry shall also be examined to ensure that injury caused by these other factors is not attributed to the dumped imports under paragraph 6. Factors which may be considered in this

respect include the volume and prices of imports not sold at dumping prices, contraction in demand or changes in the patterns of consumption, restrictive trade practices of, and competition between, third country and Community producers, developments in technology and the export performance and productivity of the Community industry.

8. The effect of the dumped imports shall be assessed in relation to the production of the Community industry of the like product when available data permit the separate identification of that production on the basis of such criteria as the production process, producers' sales and profits. If such separate identification of that production is not possible, the effect of the dumped imports shall be assessed by examination of the production of the narrowest group or range of products which includes the like product, for which the necessary information can be provided.

9. A determination of a threat of material injury shall be based on facts and not merely on allegation, conjecture or remote possibility. The change in circumstances which would create a situation in which the dumping would cause injury must be clearly foreseen and imminent.

In making a determination regarding the existence of a threat of material injury, consideration should be given to such factors as:

(a) a significant rate of increase of dumped imports into the Community market indicating the likelihood of substantially increased imports;

(b) sufficient freely disposable capacity of the exporter or an imminent and substantial increase in such capacity indicating the likelihood of substantially increased dumped exports to the Community, account being taken of the availability of other export markets to absorb any additional exports;

(c) whether imports are entering at prices that would, to a significant degree, depress prices or prevent price increases which otherwise would have occurred, and would probably increase demand for further imports; and

(d) inventories of the product being investigated.

No one of the factors listed above by itself can necessarily give decisive guidance but the totality of the factors considered must lead to the conclusion that further dumped exports are imminent and that, unless protective action is taken, material injury will occur.

Article 4

Definition of Community industry

1. For the purposes of this Regulation, the term "Community industry" shall be interpreted as referring to the Community producers as a whole of the like products or to those of them whose collective output of the products constitutes a major proportion, as defined in Article 5(4), of the total Community production of those products, except that:

(a) when producers are related to the exporters or importers or are themselves importers of the allegedly dumped product, the term "Community industry" may be interpreted as referring to the rest of the producers;

(b) in exceptional circumstances the territory of the Community may, for the production in question, be divided into two or more competitive markets and the producers within each market may be regarded as a separate industry if (i) the producers within such a market sell all or almost all or their production of the product in question in that market; and (ii) the demand in that market is not to any substantial degree supplied by producers of the product in question located elsewhere in the Community. In such circumstances, injury may be found to exist even where a major portion of the total Community industry is not injured, provided there is a concentration of dumped imports into such an isolated market and provided further that the dumped imports are causing injury to the producers of all or almost all of the production within such a market.

2. For the purpose of paragraph 1, producers shall be considered to be related to exporters or importers only if (a) one of them directly or indirectly controls the other; or (b) both of them are directly or indirectly controlled by a third person; or (c) together they directly or indirectly control a third person provided that there are grounds for believing or suspecting that the effect of the relationship is such as to cause the producer concerned to behave differently from non-related producers. For the purpose of this paragraph, one shall be deemed to control another when the former is legally or operationally in a position to exercise restraint or direction over the latter.

3. Where the Community industry has been interpreted as referring to the producers in a certain region, the exporters shall be given an opportunity to offer undertakings pursuant to Article 8 in respect of the region concerned. In such cases, when evaluating the Community interest of the measures, special account shall be taken of the interest of the region. If an adequate undertaking is not offered promptly or the situations set out in Article 8(9) and (10) apply, a provisional or definitive duty may be imposed in respect of the Community as a whole. In such cases, the duties may, if practicable, be limited to specific producers or exporters.

4. The provisions of Article 3(8) shall be applicable to this Article.

Article 5

Initiation of proceedings

1. Except as provided for in paragraph 6, an investigation to determine the existence, degree and effect of any alleged dumping shall be initiated upon a written complaint by any natural or legal person, or any association not having legal personality, acting on behalf of the Community industry.

The complaint may be submitted to the Commission, or to a Member State, which shall forward it to the Commission. The Commission shall send Member States a copy of any complaint it receives. the complaint shall be deemed to have been lodged on the first working day following its delivery to the Commission by registered mail or the issuing of an acknowledgement of receipt by the Commission.

Where, in the absence of any complaint, a Member State is in possession of sufficient evidence of dumping and of resultant injury to the Community industry, it shall immediately communicate such evidence to the Commission.

2. A complaint under paragraph 1 shall include evidence of dumping, injury and a causal link between the allegedly dumped imports and the alleged injury. The complaint shall contain such information as is reasonably available to the complainant on the following:

(a) identity of the complainant and a description of the volume and value of the Community production of the like product by the complainant. Where a written complaint is made on behalf of the Community industry, the complaint shall identify the industry on behalf of which the complaint is made by a list of all known Community producers of the like product (or associations of Community producers of the like product) and, to the extent possible, a description of the volume and value of Community production of the like product accounted for by such producers;

(b) a complete description of the allegedly dumped product, the names of the country or countries of origin or export in question, the identity of each known exporter or foreign producer and a list of known persons importing the product in question;

(c) information on prices at which the product in question is sold when destined for consumption in the domestic markets of the country or countries of origin or export (or, where appropriate, information on the prices at which the product is sold from the country or countries of origin or export to a third country or countries or on the constructed value of the product) and information on export prices or, where appropriate, on the prices at which the product is first resold to an independent buyer in the Community;

(d) information on changes in the volume of the allegedly dumped imports, the effect of those imports on prices of the like product on the Community market and the consequent impact of the imports on the community industry, as demonstrated by relevant factors and indices having a bearing on the state of the community industry, such as those listed in Article 3(3) and (5).

3. The Commission shall, as far as possible, examine the accuracy and adequacy of the evidence provided in the complaint to determine whether there is sufficient evidence to justify the initiation of an investigation.

4. An investigation shall not be initiated pursuant to paragraph 1 unless it has been determined, on the basis of an examination as to the

degree of support for, or opposition to, the complaint expressed by Community producers of the like product, that the complaint has been made by or on behalf of the Community industry. The complaint shall be considered to have been made by or on behalf of the Community industry if it is supported by those Community producers whose collective output constitutes more than 50% of the total production of the like product produced by that portion of the Community industry expressing either support for or opposition to the complaint. However, no investigation shall be initiated when Community producers expressly supporting the complaint account for less than 25% of total production of the like product produced by the Community industry.

5. The authorities shall avoid, unless a decision has been made to initiate an investigation, any publicizing of the complaint seeking the initiation of an investigation. However, after receipt of a properly documented complaint and before proceeding to initiate an investigation, the government of the exporting country concerned shall be notified.

6. If in special circumstances, it is decided to initiate an investigation without having received a written complaint by or on behalf of the Community industry for the initiation of such investigation, this shall be done on the basis of sufficient evidence of dumping, injury and a causal link, as described in paragraph 2, to justify such initiation.

7. The evidence of both dumping and injury shall be considered simultaneously in the decision on whether or not to initiate an investigation. A complaint shall be rejected where there is insufficient evidence of either dumping or of injury to justify proceeding with the case. Proceedings shall not be initiated against countries whose imports represent a market share of below 1%, unless such countries collectively account for 3% or more of Community consumption.

8. The complaint may be withdrawn prior to initiation, in which case it shall be considered not to have been lodged.

9. Where, after consultation, it is apparent that there is sufficient evidence to justify initiating a proceeding, the Commission shall do so within 45 days of the lodging of the complaint and shall publish a notice in the *Official Journal of the European Communities*. Where insufficient evidence has been presented, the complainant shall, after consultation, be so informed within 45 days of the date on which the complaint is lodged with the Commission.

10. The notice of initiation of the proceedings shall announce the initiation of an investigation, indicate the product and countries concerned, give a summary of the information received, and provide that all relevant information is to be communicated to the Commission; it shall state the periods within which interested parties may make themselves known, present their views in writing and submit information if such views and information are to be taken into account during the investigation; it shall also state the period within which interested parties may apply to be heard by the Commission in accordance with Article 6(5).

11. The Commission shall advise the exporters, importers and representative associations of importers or exporters known to it to be concerned, as well as representatives of the exporting country and the complainants, of the initiation of the proceedings and, with due regard to the protection of confidential information, provide the full text of the written complaint received pursuant to paragraph 1 to the known exporters and to the authorities of the exporting country, and make it available upon request to other interested parties involved. Where the number of exporters involved is particularly high, the full text of the written complaint may instead be provided only to the authorities of the exporting country or to the relevant trade association.

12. An anti-dumping investigation shall not hinder the procedures of customs clearance.

Article 6

The investigation

1. Following the initiation of the proceeding, the Commission, acting in cooperation with the Member States, shall commence an investigation at Community level. Such investigation shall cover both dumping and injury and these shall be investigated simultaneously. For the purpose of a representative finding, an investigation period shall be selected which, in the case of dumping shall, normally, cover a period of not less than six months immediately prior to the initiation of the proceeding. Information relating to a period subsequent to the investigation period shall, normally, not be taken into account.

2. Parties receiving questionnaires used in an anti-dumping investigation shall be given at least 30 days to reply. The time limit for exporters shall be counted from the date of receipt of the questionnaire, which for this purpose shall be deemed to have been received one week from the day on which it was sent to the exporter or transmitted to the appropriate diplomatic representative of the exporting country. An extension to the 30 day period may be granted, due account being taken of the time limits of the investigation, provided that the party shows due cause for such extension, in terms of its particular circumstances.

3. The Commission may request Member States to supply information, and Member States shall take whatever steps are necessary in order to give effect to such requests. They shall send to the Commission the information requested together with the results of all inspections, checks or investigations carried out. Where this information is of general interest or where its transmission has been requested by a Member State, the Commission shall forward it to the Member States, provided it is not confidential, in which case a non-confidential summary shall be forwarded.

4. The Commission may request Member States to carry out all necessary checks and inspections, particularly amongst importers, traders and Community producers, and to carry out investigations in third countries, provided that the firms concerned give their consent and that the

government of the country in question has been officially notified and raises no objection. Member States shall take whatever steps are necessary in order to give effect to such requests from the Commission. Officials of the Commission shall be authorized, if the Commission or a Member State so requests, to assist the officials of Member States in carrying out their duties.

5. The interested parties which have made themselves known in accordance with Article 5(10) shall be heard if they have, within the period prescribed in the notice published in the *Official Journal of the European Communities*, made a written request for a hearing showing that they are an interested party likely to be affected by the result of the proceeding and that there are particular reasons why they should be heard.

6. Opportunities shall, on request, be provided for the importers, exporters, representatives of the government of the exporting country and the complainants, which have made themselves known in accordance with Article 5(10), to meet those parties with adverse interests, so that opposing views may be presented and rebuttal arguments offered. Provision of such opportunities must take account of the need to preserve confidentiality and of the convenience to the parties. There shall be no obligation on any party to attend a meeting, and failure to do so shall not be prejudicial to that party's case. Oral information provided under this paragraph shall be taken into account in so far as it is subsequently confirmed in writing.

7. The complainants, importers and exporters and their representative associations, users and consumer organizations, which have made themselves known in accordance with Article 5(10), as well as the representatives of the exporting country may, upon written request, inspect all information made available by any party to an investigation, as distinct from internal documents prepared by the authorities of the Community or its Member States, which is relevant to the presentation of their cases and not confidential within the meaning of Article 19, and that it is used in the investigation. Such parties may respond to such information and their comments shall be taken into consideration, wherever they are sufficiently substantiated in the response.

8. Except in the circumstances provided for in Article 18, the information which is supplied by interested parties and upon which findings are based shall be examined for accuracy as far as possible.

9. For proceedings initiated pursuant to Article 5(9), an investigation shall, whenever possible, be concluded within one year. In any event, such investigations shall in all cases be concluded within 15 months of initiation, in accordance with the findings made pursuant to Article 8 for undertakings or the findings made pursuant to Article 9 for definitive action.

Article 7

Provisional measures

1. Provisional duties may be imposed if proceedings have been initiated in accordance with Article 5, if a notice has been given to that effect

and interested parties have been given adequate opportunities to submit information and make comments in accordance with Article 5(10), if a provisional affirmative determination has been made of dumping and consequent injury to the Community industry, and if the Community interest calls for intervention to prevent such injury. The provisional duties shall be imposed no earlier than 60 days from the initiation of the proceedings but not later than nine months from the initiation of the proceedings.

2. The amount of the provisional anti-dumping duty shall not exceed the margin of dumping as provisionally established, but it should be less than the margin if such lesser duty would be adequate to remove the injury to the Community industry.

3. Provisional duties shall be secured by a guarantee, and the release of the products concerned for free circulation in the Community shall be conditional upon the provision of such guarantee.

4. The Commission shall take provisional action after consultation or, in cases of extreme urgency, after informing the Member States. In this latter case, consultations shall take place 10 days, at the latest, after notification to the Member States of the action taken by the Commission.

5. Where a Member State requests immediate intervention by the Commission and where the conditions in paragraph 1 are met, the Commission shall within a maximum of five working days of receipt of the request, decide whether a provisional anti-dumping duty shall be imposed.

6. The Commission shall forthwith inform the Council and the Member States of any decision taken under paragraphs 1 to 5. The Council, acting by a qualified majority, may decide differently.

7. Provisional duties may be imposed for six months and extended for a further three months or they may be imposed for nine months. However, they may only be extended, or imposed for a nine-month period, where exporters representing a significant percentage of the trade involved so request or do not object upon notification by the Commission.

Article 8

Undertakings

1. Investigations may be terminated without the imposition of provisional or definitive duties upon receipt of satisfactory voluntary undertakings from any exporter to revise its prices or to cease exports to the area in question at dumped prices, so that the Commission, after consultation, is satisfied that the injurious effect of the dumping is eliminated. Price increases under such undertakings shall not be higher than necessary to eliminate the margin of dumping and they should be less than the margin of dumping if such increases would be adequate to remove the injury to the Community industry.

2. Undertakings may be suggested by the Commission, but no exporter shall be obliged to enter into such an undertaking. The fact that

exporters do not offer such undertakings, or do not accept an invitation to do so, shall in no way prejudice consideration of the case. However, it may be determined that a threat of injury is more likely to be realized if the dumped imports continue. Undertakings shall not be sought or accepted from exporters unless a provisional affirmative determination of dumping and injury caused by such dumping has been made. Save in exceptional circumstances, undertakings may not be offered later than the end of the period during which representations may be made pursuant to Article 20(5).

3. Undertakings offered need not be accepted if their acceptance is considered impractical, if such as where the number of actual or potential exporters is too great, or for other reasons, including reasons of general policy.

The exporter concerned may be provided with the reasons for which it is proposed to reject the offer of an undertaking and may be given an opportunity to make comments thereon. The reasons for rejection shall be set out in the definitive decision.

4. Parties which offer an undertaking shall be required to provide a non-confidential version of such undertaking, so that it may be made available to interested parties to the investigation.

5. Where undertakings are, after consultation, accepted and where there is no objection raised within the Advisory Committee, the investigation shall be terminated. In all other cases, the Commission shall submit to the Council forthwith a report on the results of the consultation, together with a proposal that the investigation be terminated. The investigation shall be deemed terminated if, within one month, the Council, acting by a qualified majority, has not decided otherwise.

6. If the undertakings are accepted, the investigation of dumping and injury shall normally be completed. In such a case, if a negative determination of dumping or injury is made, the undertaking shall automatically lapse, except in cases where such a determination is due in large part to the existence of an undertaking. In such cases it may be required that an undertaking be maintained for a reasonable period. In the event that an affirmative determination of dumping and injury is made, the undertaking shall continue consistent with its terms and the provisions of this Regulation.

7. The Commission shall require any exporter from which an undertaking has been accepted to provide, periodically, information relevant to the fulfilment of such undertaking, and to permit verification of pertinent data. Non-compliance with such requirements shall be construed as a breach of the undertaking.

8. Where undertakings are accepted from certain exporters during the course of an investigation, they shall, for the purpose of Article 11, be deemed to take effect from the date on which the investigation is concluded for the exporting country.

9. In case of breach or withdrawal of undertakings by any party, a definitive duty shall be imposed in accordance with Article 9, on the basis of the facts established within the context of the investigation which led to the undertaking, provided that such investigation was concluded with a final determination as to dumping and injury and that the exporter concerned has, except where he himself has withdrawn the undertaking, been given an opportunity to comment.

10. A provisional duty may, after consultation, be imposed in accordance with Article 7 on the basis of the best information available, where there is reason to believe that an undertaking is being breached, or in case of breach or withdrawal of an undertaking where the investigation which led to the undertaking has not been concluded.

Article 9

Termination without measures; imposition of definitive duties

1. Where the complaint is withdrawn, the proceeding may be terminated unless such termination would not be in the Community interest.

2. Where, after consultation, protective measures are unnecessary and there is no objection raised within the Advisory Committee, the investigation or proceeding shall be terminated. In all other cases, the Commission shall submit to the Council forthwith a report on the results of the consultation, together with a proposal that the proceeding be terminated. The proceeding shall be deemed terminated if, within one month, the Council, acting by a qualified majority, has not decided otherwise.

3. For a proceeding initiated pursuant to Article 5(9), injury shall normally be regarded as negligible where the imports concerned represent less than the volumes set out in Article 5(7). For the same proceeding, there shall be immediate termination where it is determined that the margin of dumping is less than 2%, expressed as a percentage of the export price, provided that it is only the investigation that shall be terminated where the margin is below 2% for individual exporters and they shall remain subject to the proceeding and may be reinvestigated in any subsequent review carried out for the country concerned pursuant to Article 11.

4. Where the facts as finally established show that there is dumping and injury caused thereby, and the Community interest calls for intervention in accordance with Article 21, a definitive anti-dumping duty shall be imposed by the Council, acting by simple majority on a proposal submitted by the Commission after consultation of the Advisory Committee. Where provisional duties are in force, a proposal for definitive action shall be submitted to the Council not later than one month before the expiry of such duties. The amount of the anti-dumping duty shall not exceed the margin of dumping established but it should be less than the margin if such lesser duty would be adequate to remove the injury to the Community industry.

5. An anti-dumping duty shall be imposed in the appropriate amounts in each case, on a non-discriminatory basis on imports of a product from all

sources found to be dumped and causing injury, except as to imports from those sources from which undertakings under the terms of this Regulation have been accepted. The Regulation imposing the duty shall specify the duty for each supplier or, if that is impracticable, and as a general rule in the cases referred to in Article 2(7), the supplying country concerned.

6. When the Commission has limited its examination in accordance with Article 17, any anti-dumping duty applied to imports from exporters or producers which have made themselves known in accordance with Article 17 but were not included in the examination shall not exceed the weighted average margin of dumping established for the parties in the sample. For the purpose of this paragraph, the Commission shall disregard any zero and *de minimis* margins, and margins established in the circumstances referred to in Article 18. Individual duties shall be applied to imports from any exporter or producer which is granted individual treatment, as provided for in Article 17.

Article 10

Retroactivity

1. Provisional measures and definitive anti-dumping duties shall only be applied to products which enter free circulation after the time when the decision taken pursuant to Articles 7(1) or 9(4), as the case may be, enters into force, subject to the exceptions set out in this Regulation.

2. Where a provisional duty has been applied and the facts as finally established show that there is dumping and injury, the Council shall decide, irrespective of whether a definitive anti-dumping duty is to be imposed, what proportion of the provisional duty is to be definitively collected. For this purpose, "injury" shall not include material retardation of the establishment of a Community industry, nor threat of material injury, except where it is found that this would, in the absence of provisional measures, have developed into material injury. In all other cases involving such threat or retardation, any provisional amounts shall be released and definitive duties can only be imposed from the date that a final determination of threat or material retardation is made.

3. If the definitive anti-dumping duty is higher than the provisional duty, the difference shall not be collected. If the definitive duty is lower than the provisional duty, the duty shall be recalculated. Where a final determination is negative, the provisional duty shall not be confirmed.

4. A definitive anti-dumping duty may be levied on products which were entered for consumption not more than 90 days prior to the date of application of provisional measures but not prior to the initiation of the investigation, provided that imports have been registered in accordance with Article 14(5), the Commission has allowed the importers concerned an opportunity to comment, and:

    (a) there is, for the product in question, a history of dumping over an extended period, or the importer was aware of, or should have been aware of, the dumping as regards the extent of the dumping and the injury alleged or found; and

(b) in addition to the level of imports which caused injury during the investigation period, there is a further substantial rise in imports which, in the light of its timing and volume and other circumstances, is likely to seriously undermine the remedial effect of the definitive anti-dumping duty to be applied.

5. In cases of breach or withdrawal of undertakings, definitive duties may be levied on goods entered for free circulation not more than 90 days before the application of provisional measures, provided that imports have been registered in accordance with Article 14(5), and that any such retroactive assessment shall not apply to imports entered before the breach or withdrawal of the undertaking.

Article 11

Duration, reviews and refunds

1. An anti-dumping measure shall remain in force only as long as, and to the extent that, it is necessary to counteract the dumping which is causing injury.

2. A definitive anti-dumping measure shall expire five years from its imposition or five years from the date of the conclusion of the most recent review which has covered both dumping and injury, unless it is determined in a review that the expiry would be likely to lead to a continuation or recurrence of dumping and injury. Such an expiry review shall be initiated on the initiative of the Commission, or upon request made by or on behalf of Community producers, and the measure shall remain in force pending the outcome of such review.

An expiry review shall be initiated where the request contains sufficient evidence that the expiry of the measures would be likely to result in a continuation or recurrence of dumping and injury. Such a likelihood may, for example, be indicated by evidence of continued dumping and injury or evidence that the removal of injury is partly or solely due to the existence of measures or evidence that the circumstances of the exporters, or market conditions, are such that they would indicate the likelihood of further injurious dumping.

In carrying out investigations under this paragraph, the exporters, importers, the representatives of the exporting country and the Community producers shall be provided with the opportunity to amplify, rebut or comment on the matters set out in the review request, and conclusions shall be reached with due account taken of all relevant and duly documented evidence presented in relation to the question as to whether the expiry of measures would be likely, or unlikely, to lead to the continuation or recurrence of dumping and injury.

A notice of impending expiry shall be published in the *Official Journal of the European Communities* at an appropriate time in the final year of the period of application of the measures as defined in this paragraph. Thereafter, the Community producers shall, no later than three months before the end of the five-year period, be entitled to lodge a review request in accordance with the second sub-paragraph. A notice announcing the actual expiry of measures pursuant to this paragraph shall also be published.

3. The need for the continued imposition of measures may also be reviewed, where warranted, on the initiative of the Commission or at the request of a Member State or, provided that a reasonable period of time of at least one year has elapsed since the imposition of the definitive measure, upon a request by any exporter or importer or by the Community producers which contains sufficient evidence substantiating the need for such an interim review.

An interim review shall be initiated where the request contains sufficient evidence that the continued imposition of the measure is no longer necessary to offset dumping and/or that the injury would be unlikely to continue or recur if the measure were removed or varied, or that the existing measure is not, or is no longer, sufficient to counteract the dumping which is causing injury.

In carrying out investigations pursuant to this paragraph, the Commission may, *inter alia*, consider whether the circumstances with regard to dumping and injury have changed significantly, or whether existing measures are achieving the intended results in removing the injury previously established under Article 3. In these respects, account shall be taken in the final determination of all relevant and duly documented evidence.

4. A review shall also be carried out for the purpose of determining individual margins of dumping for new exporters in the exporting country in question which have not exported the product during the period of investigation on which the measures were based.

The review shall be initiated where a new exporter or producer can show that it is not related to any of the exporters or producers in the exporting country which are subject to the anti-dumping measures on the product, and that it has actually exported to the Community following the above-mentioned investigation period, or where it can demonstrate that it has entered into an irrevocable contractual obligation to export a significant quantity to the Community.

A review for a new exporter shall be initiated, and carried out on an accelerated basis, after consultation of the Advisory Committee and after the Community producers have been given an opportunity to comment. The Commission Regulation initiating a review shall repeal the duty in force with regard to the new exporter concerned by amending the Regulation which has imposed such duty, and by making imports subject to registration in accordance with Article 14(5) in order to ensure that, should the review result in a determination of dumping in respect of such an exporter, anti-dumping duties can be levied retroactively to the date of the initiation of the review.

The provisions of this paragraph shall not apply where duties have been imposed under Article 9(6).

5. The relevant provisions of this Regulation with regard to procedures and the conduct of investigations, excluding those relating to time limits, shall apply to any review carried out pursuant to paragraphs 2, 3 and 4. Any such review shall be carried out expeditiously and shall normally be concluded within 12 months of the date of initiation of the review.

6. Reviews pursuant to this Article shall be initiated by the Commission after consultation of the Advisory Committee. Where warranted by reviews, measures shall be repealed or maintained pursuant to paragraph 2, or repealed, maintained or amended pursuant to paragraphs 3 and 4, by the Community institution responsible for their introduction. Where measures are repealed for individual exporters, but not for the country as a whole, such exporters shall remain subject to the proceeding and may, automatically, be reinvestigated in any subsequent review carried out for that country pursuant to this Article.

7. Where a review of measures pursuant to paragraph 3 is in progress at the end of the period of application of measures as defined in paragraph 2, such review shall also cover the circumstances set out in paragraph 2.

8. Notwithstanding paragraph 2, an importer may request reimbursement of duties collected where it is shown that the dumping margin, on the basis of which duties were paid, has been eliminated, or reduced to a level which is below the level of the duty in force.

In requesting a refund of anti-dumping duties, the importer shall submit an application to the Commission. The application shall be submitted via the Member State of the territory in which the products were released for free circulation, within six months of the date on which the amount of the definitive duties to be levied was duly determined by the competent authorities or the date on which a decision was made definitively to collect the amounts secured by way of provisional duty. Member States shall forward the request to the Commission forthwith.

An application for refund shall only be considered to be duly supported by evidence where it contains precise information on the amount of refund of anti-dumping duties claimed and all customs documentation relating to the calculation and payment of such amount. It shall also include evidence, for a representative period, of normal values and export prices to the Community for the exporter or producer to which the duty applies. In cases where the importer is not associated with the exporter or producer concerned and such information is not immediately available, or where the exporter or producer is unwilling to release it to the importer, the application shall contain a statement from the exporter or producer that the dumping margin has been reduced or eliminated as specified in this Article, and that the relevant supporting evidence will be provided to the Commission. Where such evidence is not forthcoming from the exporter or producer within a reasonable period of time the application shall be rejected.

The Commission shall, after consultation of the Advisory Committee, decide whether and to what extent the application should be granted, or it may decide at any time to initiate an interim review, whereupon the information and findings from such review carried out in accordance with the provisions applicable for such reviews, shall be used to determine whether and to what extent a refund is justified. Refunds of duties shall normally take place within 12 months, and in no circumstances more than 18 months after the date on which a request for a refund, duly supported by evidence, has been made by an importer of the product subject to the anti-dumping duty. The payment of any refund authorized should normally be made by Member States within 90 days of the above-mentioned decision.

9. In all review or refund investigations carried out pursuant to this Article, the Commission shall, provided that circumstances have not changed, apply the same methodology as in the investigation which led to the duty, with due account being taken of Article 2, and in particular paragraphs 11 and 12 thereof, and of Article 17.

10. In any investigation carried out pursuant to this Article, the Commission shall examine the reliability of export prices in accordance with Article 2. However, where it is decided to construct the export price in accordance with Article 2(9), it shall calculate it with no deduction for the amount of anti-dumping duties paid when conclusive evidence is provided that the duty is duly reflected in resale prices and the subsequent selling prices in the Community.

Article 12

1. Where the Community industry submits sufficient information showing that measures have led to no movement, or insufficient movement, in resale prices or subsequent selling prices in the Community, the investigation may, after consultation, be reopened to examine whether the measure has had effects on the above-mentioned prices.

2. During a reinvestigation pursuant to this Article, exporters, importers and Community producers shall be provided with an opportunity to clarify the situation with regard to resale prices and subsequent selling prices: if it is concluded that the measure should have led to movements in such prices, then, in order to remove the injury previously established in accordance with Article 3, export prices shall be reassessed in accordance with Article 2 and dumping margins shall be recalculated to take account of the reassessed export prices. Where it is considered that a lack of movement in the prices in the Community is due to a fall in export prices which has occurred prior to or following the imposition of measures, dumping margins may be recalculated to take account of such lower export prices.

3. Where a reinvestigation pursuant to this Article shows increased dumping the measures in force shall be amended by the Council, by simple majority on a proposal from the Commission, in accordance with the new findings on export prices.

4. The relevant provisions of Articles 5 and 6 shall apply to any review carried out pursuant to this Article, except that such review shall be carried out expeditiously and shall normally be concluded within six months of the date of initiation of the reinvestigation.

5. Alleged changes in normal value shall only be taken into account under this Article where complete information on revised normal values, duly substantiated by evidence, is made available to the Commission within the time limits set out in the notice of initiation of an investigation. Where an investigation involves a re-examination of normal values, imports may be made subject to registration in accordance with Article 14(5) pending the outcome of the reinvestigation.

Article 13

Circumvention

1. Anti-dumping duties imposed pursuant to this Regulation may be extended to imports from third countries of like products, or parts thereof, when circumvention of the measures in force is taking place. Circumvention shall be defined as a change in the pattern of trade between third countries and the Community which stems from a practice, process or work for which there is insufficient due cause or economic justification other than the imposition of the duty, and where there is evidence that the remedial effects of the duty are being undermined in terms of the prices and/or quantities of the like products and there is evidence of dumping in relation to the normal values previously established for the like or similar products.

2. An assembly operation in the Community or a third country shall be considered to circumvent the measures in force where:

(a) the operation started or substantially increased since, or just prior to, the initiation of the anti-dumping investigation and the parts concerned are from the country subject to measures; and

(b) the parts constitute 60% or more of the total value of the parts of the assembled product, except that in no case shall circumvention be considered to be taking place where the value added to the parts brought in, during the assembly or completion operation, is greater than 25% of the manufacturing cost, and

(c) the remedial effects of the duty are being undermined in terms of the prices and/or quantities of the assembled like product and there is evidence of dumping in relation to the normal values previously established for the like or similar products.

3. Investigations shall be initiated pursuant to this Article where the request contains sufficient evidence regarding the factors set out in paragraph 1. Initiations shall be made, after consultation of the Advisory Committee, by Commission Regulation which shall also instruct the customs authorities to make imports subject to registration in accordance with Article 14(5) or to request guarantees. Investigations shall be carried out by the Commission, which may be assisted by customs authorities and shall be concluded within nine months. When the facts as finally ascertained justify the extension of measures, this shall be done by the Council, acting by simple majority and on a proposal from the Commission, from the date on which registration was imposed pursuant to Article 14(5) or on which

guarantees were requested. The relevant procedural provision of this Regulation with regard to initiations and the conduct of investigations shall apply pursuant to this Article.

4. Products shall not be subject to registration pursuant to Article 14(5) or measures where they are accompanied by a customs certificate declaring that the importation of the goods does not constitute circumvention. These certificates may be issued to importers, upon written application following authorization by decision of the Commission after consultation of the Advisory Committee or decision of the Council imposing measures and they shall remain valid for the period, and under the conditions, set down therein.

5. Nothing in this Article shall preclude the normal application of the provisions in force concerning customs duties.

Article 14

General provisions

1. Provisional or definitive anti-dumping duties shall be imposed by Regulation, and collected by Member States in the form, at the rate specified and according to the other criteria laid down in the Regulation imposing such duties. Such duties shall also be collected independently of the customs duties, taxes and other charges normally imposed on imports. No product shall be subject to both anti-dumping and countervailing duties for the purpose of dealing with one and the same situation arising from dumping or from export subsidization.

2. Regulations imposing provisional or definite anti-dumping duties, and Regulations or Decisions accepting undertakings or terminating investigations or proceedings, shall be published in the *Official Journal of the European Communities*. Such Regulations or Decisions shall contain in particular and with due regard to the protection of confidential information, the names of the exporters, if possible, or of the countries involved, a description of the product and a summary of the material facts and considerations relevant to the dumping and injury determinations. In each case, a copy of the Regulation or Decision shall be sent to known interested parties. The provisions of this paragraph shall apply *mutatis mutandis* to reviews.

3. Special provisions, in particular with regard to the common definition of the concept of origin, as contained in Council Regulation (EEC) No. 2913/92[2], may be adopted pursuant to this Regulation.

4. In the community interest, measures imposed pursuant to this Regulation may, after consultation of the Advisory Committee, be suspended by a decision of the Commission for a period of nine months. The suspension may be extended for a further period, not exceeding one year, if the Council so decides, acting by simple majority on a proposal from the Commission. Measures may only be suspended where market conditions

---

2. OJ No. L 302, 19.10.1992, p. 1.

have temporarily changed to an extent that injury would be unlikely to resume as a result of the suspension, and provided that the Community industry has been given an opportunity to comment and these comments have been taken into account. Measures may, at any time and after consultation, be reinstated if the reason for suspension is no longer applicable.

5. The Commission may, after consultation of the Advisory Committee, direct the customs authorities to take the appropriate steps to register imports, so that measures may subsequently be applied against those imports from the date of such registration. Imports may be made subject to registration following a request from the Community industry which contains sufficient evidence to justify such action. Registration shall be introduced by Regulation which shall specify the purpose of the action and, if appropriate, the estimated amount of possible future liability. Imports shall not be made subject to registration for a period longer than nine months.

6. Member States shall report to the Commission every month, on the import trade in products subject to investigation and to measures, and on the amount of duties collected pursuant to this Regulation.

Article 15

Consultations

1. Any consultations provided for in this Regulation shall take place within an Advisory Committee, which shall consist of representatives of each Member State, with a representative of the Commission as chairman. Consultations shall be held immediately at the request of a Member State or on the initiative of the Commission and in any even within a period of time which allows the time limits set by this Regulation to be adhered to.

2. The Committee shall meet when convened by its chairman. He shall provide the Member States, as promptly as possible, with all relevant information.

3. Where necessary, consultation may be in writing only; in that event, the Commission shall notify the Member States and shall specify a period within which they shall be entitled to express their opinions or to request an oral consultation which the chairman shall arrange, provided that such oral consultation can be held within a period of time which allows the time limits set by this Regulation to be adhered to.

4. Consultation shall cover, in particular:

   (a) the existence of dumping and the methods of establishing the dumping margin;

   (b) the existence and extent of injury;

   (c) the causal link between the dumped imports and injury;

   (d) the measures which, in the circumstances, are appropriate to prevent or remedy the injury caused by dumping and the ways and means of putting such measures into effect.

Article 16

Verification visits

1. The Commission shall, where it considers it appropriate, carry out visits to examine the records of importers, exporters, traders, agents, producers, trade associations and organizations and to verify information provided on dumping and injury. In the absence of a proper and timely reply, a verification visit may not be carried out.

2. The Commission may carry out investigations in third countries as required, provided that it obtains the agreement of the firms concerned, that it notifies the representatives of the government of the country in question and that the latter does not object to the investigation. As soon as the agreement of the firms concerned has been obtained the Commission should notify the authorities of the exporting country of the names and addresses of the firms to be visited and the dates agreed.

3. The firms concerned shall be advised of the nature of the information to be verified during verification visits and of any further information which needs to be provided during such visits, though this should not preclude requests made during the verification for further details to be provided in the light of information obtained.

4. In investigations carried out pursuant to paragraphs 1, 2 and 3, the Commission shall be assisted by officials of those Member States who so request.

Article 17

Sampling

1. In cases where the number of complainants, exporters or importers, types of product or transactions is large, the investigation may be limited to a reasonable number of parties, products or transactions by using samples which are statistically valid on the basis of information available at the time of the selection, or to the largest representative volume of production, sales or exports which can reasonably be investigated within the time available.

2. The final selection of parties, types of products or transactions made under these sampling provisions shall rest with the Commission, though preference shall be given to choosing a sample in consultation with, and with the consent of, the parties concerned, provided such parties make themselves known and make sufficient information available, within three weeks of initiation of the investigation, to enable a representative sample to be chosen.

3. In cases where the examination has been limited in accordance with this Article, an individual margin of dumping shall, nevertheless, be calculated for any exporter or producer not initially selected who submits the necessary information within the time limits provided for in this Regulation, except where the number of exporters or producers is so large

that individual examinations would be unduly burdensome and would prevent completion of the investigation in good time.

4. Where it is decided to sample and there is a degree of non-cooperation by some or all of the parties selected which is likely to materially affect the outcome of the investigation, a new sample may be selected. However, if a material degree of non-cooperation persists or there is insufficient time to select a new sample, the relevant provisions of Article 18 shall apply.

Article 18

Non-cooperation

1. In cases in which any interested party refuses access to, or otherwise does not provide, necessary information within the time limits provided in this Regulation, or significantly impedes the investigation, provisional or final findings, affirmative or negative, may be made on the basis of the facts available. Where it is found that any interested party has supplied false or misleading information, the information shall be disregarded and use may be made of facts available. Interested parties should be made aware of the consequences of non-cooperation.

2. Failure to give a computerized response shall not be deemed to constitute non-cooperation, provided that the interested party shows that presenting the response as requested would result in an unreasonable extra burden or unreasonable additional cost.

3. Where the information submitted by an interested party is not ideal in all respects it should nevertheless not be disregarded, provided that any deficiencies are not such as to cause undue difficulty in arriving at a reasonably accurate finding and that the information is appropriately submitted in good time and is verifiable, and that the party has acted to the best of its ability.

4. If evidence or information is not accepted, the supplying party shall be informed forthwith of the reasons therefor and shall be granted an opportunity to provide further explanations within the time limit specified. If the explanations are considered unsatisfactory, the reasons for rejection of such evidence or information shall be disclosed and given in published findings.

5. If determinations, including those regarding normal value, are based on the provisions of paragraph 1, including the information supplied in the complaint, it shall, where practicable and with due regard to the time limits of the investigation, be checked by reference to information from other independent sources which may be available, such as published price lists, official import statistics and customs returns, or information obtained from other interested parties during the investigation.

6. If an interested party does not cooperate, or cooperates only partially, so that relevant information is thereby withheld, the result may be less favourable to the party than if it had cooperated.

Article 19

Confidentiality

1. Any information which is by nature confidential, (for example, because its disclosure would be of significant competitive advantage to a competitor or would have a significantly adverse effect upon a person supplying the information or upon a person from whom he has acquired the information) or which is provided on a confidential basis by parties to an investigation shall, if good cause is shown, be treated as such by the authorities.

2. Interested parties providing confidential information shall be required to furnish non-confidential summaries thereof. Those summaries shall be in sufficient detail to permit a reasonable understanding of the substance of the information submitted in confidence. In exceptional circumstances, such parties may indicate that such information is not susceptible of summary. In such exceptional circumstances, a statement of the reasons why summarization is not possible must be provided.

3. If it is considered that a request for confidentiality is not warranted and if the supplier of the information is either unwilling to make the information available or to authorize its disclosure in generalized or summary form, such information may be disregarded unless it can be satisfactorily demonstrated from appropriate sources that the information is correct. Requests for confidentiality shall not be arbitrarily rejected.

4. This Article shall not preclude the disclosure of general information by the Community authorities and in particular of the reasons on which decisions taken pursuant to this Regulation are based, or disclosure of the evidence relied on by the Community authorities in so far as is necessary to explain those reasons in court proceedings. Such disclosure must take into account the legitimate interests of the parties concerned that their business secrets should not be divulged.

5. The Council, the Commission and Member States or the officials of any of these, shall not reveal any information received pursuant to this Regulation for which confidential treatment has been requested by its supplier, without specific permission from the supplier. Exchanges of information between the Commission and Member States, or any information relating to consultations made pursuant to Article 15, or any internal documents prepared by the authorities of the Community or its Member States, shall not be divulged except as specifically provided for in this Regulation.

6. Information received pursuant to this Regulation shall be used only for the purpose for which it was requested.

Article 20

Disclosure

1. The complainants, importers and exporters and their representative associations, and representatives of the exporting country, may request

disclosure of the details underlying the essential facts and considerations on the basis of which provisional measures have been imposed. Requests for such disclosure shall be made in writing immediately following the imposition of provisional measures, and the disclosure shall be made in writing as soon as possible thereafter.

2. The parties mentioned in paragraph 1 may request final disclosure of the essential facts and considerations on the basis of which it is intended to recommend the imposition of definitive measures, or the termination of an investigation or proceedings without the imposition of measures, particular attention being paid to the disclosure of any facts or considerations which are different from those used for any provisional measures.

3. Requests for final disclosure, as defined in paragraph 2, shall be addressed to the Commission in writing and be received, in cases where a provisional duty has been applied, not later than one month after publication of the imposition of that duty. Where a provisional duty has not been applied, parties shall be provided with an opportunity to request final disclosure within time limits set by the Commission.

4. Final disclosure shall be given in writing. It shall be made, due regard being had to the protection of confidential information, as soon as possible and, normally, not later than one month prior to a definitive decision or the submission by the Commission of any proposal for final action pursuant to Article 9. Where the Commission is not in a position to disclose certain facts or considerations at that time, these shall be disclosed as soon as possible thereafter. Disclosure shall not prejudice any subsequent decision which may be taken by the Commission or the Council but where such decision is based on any different facts and considerations, these shall be disclosed as soon as possible.

5. Representations made after final disclosure is given shall be taken into consideration only if received within a period to be set by the Commission in each case, which shall be at least ten days, due consideration being given to the urgency of the matter.

Article 21

Community interest

1. A determination as to whether the Community interest calls for intervention shall be based on an appreciation of all the various interests taken as a whole including the interests of the domestic industry and users and consumers; and a determination pursuant to this Article shall only be made where all parties have been given the opportunity to make their views known pursuant to paragraph 2. In such an examination, the need to eliminate the trade distorting effects of injurious dumping and to restore effective competition shall be given special consideration. Measures, as determined on the basis of the dumping and injury found, may not be applied where the authorities, on the basis of all the information submitted, can clearly conclude that it is not in the Community interest to apply such measures.

2. In order to provide a sound basis on which the authorities can take account of all views and information in the decision as to whether or not the imposition of measures is in the Community interest, the complainants, importers and their representative associations, representative users and representative consumer organizations may, within the time limits specified in the notice of initiation of the anti-dumping investigation, make themselves known and provide information to the Commission. Such information, or appropriate summaries thereof, shall be made available to the other parties specified in this Article, and they shall be entitled to respond to such information.

3. The parties which have acted in conformity with paragraph 2 may request a hearing. Such requests shall be granted when they are submitted within the time limits set in paragraph 2, and when they set out the reasons, in terms of the Community interest, why the parties should be heard.

4. The parties which have acted in conformity with paragraph 2 may provide comments on the application of any provisional duties imposed. Such comments shall be received within one month of the application of such measures if they are to be taken into account and they, or appropriate summaries thereof, shall be made available to other parties who shall be entitled to respond to such comments.

5. The commission shall examine the information which is properly submitted and the extent to which it is representative and the results of such analysis, together with an opinion on its merits, shall be transmitted to the Advisory Committee. The balance of views expressed in the Committee shall be taken into account by the Commission in any proposal made pursuant to Article 9.

6. The parties which have acted in conformity with paragraph 2 may request the facts and considerations on which final decisions are likely to be taken to be made available to them. Such information shall be made available to the extent possible and without prejudice to any subsequent decision taken by the Commission or the Council.

7. Information shall only be taken into account where it is supported by actual evidence which substantiates its validity.

Article 22

Final provisions

This Regulation shall not preclude the application of:

(a) any special rules laid down in agreements concluded between the Community and third countries;

(b) the Community Regulations in the agricultural sector and Council Regulations (EC) No. 3448/93, (EEC) No. 2730/75 and (EEC) No. 2783/75; this Regulation shall operate by way of complement to those Regulations and in derogation from any provisions thereof which preclude the application of anti-dumping duties;

(c) special measures, provided that such action does not run counter to obligations pursuant to the GATT.

Article 23

Repeal of existing legislation and transitional measures

* * *

Article 24

Entry into force

This Regulation shall enter into force on the day of its publication in the *Official Journal of the European Communities*.

However, the time limits provided for in Articles 5(9), 6(9) and 7(1) shall apply to complaints lodged under Article 5(9) as from 1 September 1995 and investigations initiated pursuant to such complaints.

This Regulation shall be binding in its entirety and directly applicable in all Member States.

3. COUNCIL REGULATION (EC) NO. 2026/97

of 6 October 1997

on protection against subsidized imports from countries not members of the European Community

O.J. L 288/1 (Oct. 21, 1997)

THE COUNCIL OF THE EUROPEAN UNION,

* * *

HAS ADOPTED THIS REGULATION:

Article 1

Principles

1. A countervailing duty may be imposed for the purpose of offsetting any subsidy granted, directly or indirectly, for the manufacture, production, export or transport of any product whose release for free circulation in the Community causes injury.

2. For the purpose of this Regulation, a product is considered to be subsidized if it benefits from a countervailable subsidy as defined in Articles 2 and 3.

3. Such subsidy may be granted by the government of the country of origin of the imported product, or by the government of an intermediate country from which the product is exported to the Community, known for the purpose of this Regulation as 'the country of export'. The term 'government' is defined, for the purposes of this Regulation as a government or any public body within the territory of the country of origin or export.

4. Notwithstanding paragraphs 1, 2 and 3, where products are not directly imported from the country of origin but are exported to the Community from an intermediate country, the provisions of this Regulation shall be fully applicable and the transaction or transactions shall, where appropriate, be regarded as having taken place between the country of origin and the Community.

5. For the purpose of this Regulation the term 'like product' shall be interpreted to mean a product which is identical, that is to say, alike in all respects, to the product under consideration, or in the absence of such a product, another product which although not alike in all respects, has characteristics closely resembling those of the product under consideration.

Article 2

Definition of a subsidy

A subsidy shall be deemed to exist if:

1. (a) there is a financial contribution by a government in the country of origin or export, that is to say, where:

(i) a government practice involves a direct transfer of funds (for example, grants, loans, equity infusion), potential direct transfers of funds or liabilities (for example, loan guarantees);

(ii) government revenue that is otherwise due is forgone or not collected (for example, fiscal incentives such as tax credits); in this regard, the exemption of an exported product from duties or taxes borne by the like product when destined for domestic consumption, or the remission of such duties or taxes in amounts not in excess of those which have been accrued, shall not be deemed to be a subsidy, provided that such an exemption is granted in accordance with the provisions of Annexes I to III;

(iii) a government provides goods or services other than general infrastructure, or purchases goods;

(iv) a government:

— makes payments to a funding mechanism,

or

— entrusts or directs a private body to carry out one or more of the type of functions illustrated in points (i), (ii) and (iii) which would normally be vested in the government, and the practice, in no real sense, differs from practices normally followed by governments;

or

(b) there is any form of income or price support within the meaning of Article XVI of the GATT 1994; and

2. a benefit is thereby conferred.

Article 3

Countervailable subsidies

1. Subsidies shall be subject to countervailing measures only if they are specific, as defined in paragraphs 2, 3 and 4.

2. In order to determine whether a subsidy is specific to an enterprise or industry or group of enterprises or industries (hereinafter referred to as 'certain enterprises') within the jurisdiction of the granting authority, the following principles shall apply:

(a) where the granting authority, or the legislation pursuant to which the granting authority operates, explicitly limits access to a subsidy to certain enterprises, such subsidy shall be specific;

(b) where the granting authority, or the legislation pursuant to which the granting authority operates, establishes objective criteria or conditions governing the eligibility for, and the amount of, a subsidy, specificity shall not exist, provided that the eligibility is automatic and that such criteria and conditions are strictly adhered to.

For the purpose of this Article, objective criteria or conditions mean criteria or conditions which are neutral, which do not favour certain enterprises over others, and which are economic in nature and horizontal in application, such as number of employees or size of enterprise.

The criteria or conditions must be clearly set out by law, regulation, or other official document, so as to be capable of verification;

(c) if, notwithstanding any appearance of non-specificity resulting from the application of the principles laid down in subparagraphs (a) and (b), there are reasons to believe that the subsidy may in fact be specific, other factors may be considered. Such factors are: use of a subsidy programme by a limited number of certain enterprises; predominant use by certain enterprises; the granting of disproportionately large amounts of subsidy to certain enterprises; and the manner in which discretion has been exercised by the granting authority in the decision to grant a subsidy. In this regard, information on the frequency with which applications for a subsidy are refused or approved and the reasons for such decisions shall, in particular, be considered.

In applying the first subparagraph, account shall be taken of the extent of diversification of economic activities within the jurisdiction of the granting authority, as well as of the length of time during which the subsidy programme has been in operation.

3. A subsidy which is limited to certain enterprises located within a designated geographical region within the jurisdiction of the granting authority shall be specific. The setting or changing of generally applicable tax rates by all levels of government entitled to do so shall not be deemed to be a specific subsidy for the purposes of this Regulation.

4. Notwithstanding paragraphs 2 and 3, the following subsidies shall be deemed to be specific:

(a) subsidies contingent, in law or in fact, whether solely or as one of several other conditions, upon export performance, including those illustrated in Annex I.

Subsidies shall be considered to be contingent in fact upon export performance when the facts demonstrate that the granting of a subsidy, without having been made legally contingent upon export performance, is in fact tied to actual or anticipated exportation or export earnings. The mere fact that a subsidy is accorded to enterprises which export shall not for that reason alone be considered to be an export subsidy within the meaning of this provision;

(b) subsidies contingent, whether solely or as one of several other conditions, upon the use of domestic over imported goods.

5. Any determination of specificity under the provisions of this Article shall be clearly substantiated on the basis of positive evidence.

Article 4

Non-countervailable subsidies

1. The following subsidies shall not be subjected to countervailing measures:

(a) subsidies which are not specific within the meaning of Article 3 (2) and (3);

(b) subsidies which are specific, within the meaning of Article 3 (2) and (3), but which meet the conditions provided for in paragraphs 2, 3 or 4 of this Article;

(c) the element of subsidy which may exist in any of the measures listed in Annex IV.

2. Subsidies for research activities conducted by firms or by higher education or research establishments on a contract basis with firms shall not be subject to countervailing measures, if the subsidies cover not more than 75% of the costs of industrial research or 50% of the costs of pre-competitive development activity, and provided that such subsidies are limited exclusively to:

(a) personnel costs (researchers, technicians and other supporting staff employed exclusively in the research activity);

(b) costs of instruments, equipment, land and buildings used exclusively and permanently (except when disposed of on a commercial basis) for the research activity;

(c) costs of consultancy and equivalent services used exclusively for the research activity, including bought-in research, technical knowledge, patents, etc.;

(d) additional overhead costs incurred directly as a result of the research activity;

(e) other running costs (such as those of materials, supplies and the like), incurred directly as a result of the research activity.

The first subparagraph shall not apply to civil aircraft (as defined in the 1979 Agreement on Trade in Civil Aircraft, as amended, or in any later Agreement amending or replacing such Agreement).

For the purpose of the first subparagraph:

(a) the allowable levels of non-countervailable subsidy shall be established by reference to the total eligible costs incurred over the duration of an individual project.

In the case of programmes which span both 'industrial research' and 'pre-competitive development activity', the allowable level of non-countervailable subsidy shall not exceed the simple average of the allowable levels of non-countervailable subsidy applicable to the above two categories, calculated on the basis of all eligible costs as set forth in points (a) to (e) of the first subparagraph;

(b) the term "industrial research' means planned search or critical investigation aimed at discovery of new knowledge, with the objective that such knowledge may be useful in developing new products, processor services, or in bringing about a significant improvement to existing products, processes or services;

(c) the term 'pre-competitive development activity' means the translation of industrial research findings into a plan, blueprint or design for new, modified or improved products, processes or services, whether intended for sale or for use, including the creation of a first prototype which would not be capable of commercial use. It may further include the conceptual formulation and design of products, processes or services alternatives and initial demonstration or pilot projects, provided that these same projects cannot be converted or used for industrial application or commercial exploitation. It does not include routine or periodic alterations to existing products, production lines, manufacturing process, services, and other ongoing operations even though those alterations may represent improvements.

3. Subsidies to disadvantaged regions within the territory of the country of origin and/or export, given pursuant to a general framework of regional development, which would be non-specific if the criteria laid down in Article 3(2) and (3) were applied to each eligible region concerned, shall not be subject to countervailing measures, provided that:

(a) each disadvantaged region is a clearly designated contiguous geographical area with a definable economic and administrative identity;

(b) the region is regarded as disadvantaged on the basis of neutral and objective criteria, indicating that the region's difficulties arise out of more than temporary circumstances; such criteria must be clearly spelled out by law, regulation, or other official document, so as to be capable of verification;

(c) the criteria mentioned under (b) include a measurement of economic development which shall be based on at least one of the following factors:

— either income per capita, or household income per capita, or GDP per capita, which must not be above 85% of the average for the territory of the country of origin or export concerned,

— unemployment rate, which must be at least 110% of the average for the territory of the country of origin or export concerned;

as measured over a three-year period; such measurement, however, may be a composite one and may include other factors.

For the purpose of the first subparagraph:

(a) a 'general framework of regional development' means that regional subsidy programmes are part of an internally consistent and generally applicable regional development policy and that regional development subsidies are not granted in isolated geographical points having no, or virtually no, influence on the development of a region;

(b) 'neutral and objective criteria' means criteria which do not favour certain regions beyond what is appropriate for the elimination or reduction of regional disparities within the framework of the regional development policy. In this regard, regional subsidy programmes shall include ceilings on the amount of subsidy which can be granted to each subsidized project. Such ceilings must be differentiated according to the different levels of development of eligible regions and must be expressed in terms of investment costs or the cost of job creation. Within such ceilings, the distribution of subsidy shall be sufficiently broad and even to avoid the predominant use of a subsidy by, or the granting of disproportionately large amounts of subsidy to, certain enterprises.

This provision shall be applied in the light of the criteria set out in Article 3(2) and (3).

4. Subsidies to promote adaptation of existing facilities to new environmental requirements imposed by law and/or regulation which result in greater constraints and financial burden on firms shall not be subject to countervailing measures, provided that the subsidy:

(a) is a one-off non-recurring measure; and

(b) is limited to 20% of the cost of adaptation; and

(c) does not cover the cost of replacing and operating the subsidized investment, which must be fully borne by the firms; and

(d) is directly linked to and proportionate to a firm's planned reduction of nuisances and pollution, and does not cover any manufacturing cost savings which may be achieved; and

(e) is available to all firms which can adopt the new equipment and/or production processes.

For the purpose of the first subparagraph the term 'existing facilities' means facilities having been in operation for at least two years at the time when new environmental requirements are imposed.

Article 5

Calculation of the amount of the countervailable subsidy

The amount of countervailable subsidies, for the purposes of this Regulation, shall be calculated in terms of the benefit conferred on the recipient which is found to exist during the investigation period for subsidization. Normally this period shall be the most recent accounting year of the beneficiary, but may be any other period of at least six months prior to the initiation of the investigation for which reliable financial and other relevant data are available.

Article 6

Calculation of benefit to the recipient

As regards the calculation of benefit to the recipient, the following rules shall apply:

(a) government provision of equity capital shall not be considered to confer a benefit, unless the investment can be regarded as inconsistent with the usual investment practice (including for the provision of risk capital) of private investors in the territory of the country of origin and/or export;

(b) a loan by a government shall not be considered to confer a benefit, unless there is a difference between the amount that the firm receiving the loan pays on the government loan and the amount that the firm would pay for a comparable commercial loan which the firm could actually obtain on the market. In that event the benefit shall be the difference between these two amounts;

(c) a loan guarantee by a government shall not be considered to confer a benefit, unless there is a difference between the amount that the firm receiving the guarantee pays on a loan guaranteed by the government and the amount that the firm would pay for a comparable commercial loan in the absence of the government guarantee. In this case the benefit shall be the difference between these two amounts, adjusted for any differences in fees;

(d) the provision of goods or services or purchase of goods by a government shall not be considered to confer a benefit, unless the provision is made for less than adequate remuneration or the purchase is made for more than adequate remuneration. The adequacy of remuneration shall be determined in relation to prevailing market conditions for the product or service in question in the country of provision or purchase (including price, quality, availability, marketability, transportation and other conditions of purchase or sale).

Article 7

General provisions on calculation

1. The amount of the countervailable subsidies shall be determined per unit of the subsidized product exported to the Community.

In establishing this amount the following elements may be deducted from the total subsidy:

(a) any application fee, or other costs necessarily incurred in order to qualify for, or to obtain, the subsidy;

(b) export taxes, duties or other charges levied on the export of the product to the Community specifically intended to offset the subsidy.

Where an interested party claims a deduction, it must prove that the claim is justified.

2. Where the subsidy is not granted by reference to the quantities manufactured, produced, exported or transported, the amount of countervailable subsidy shall be determined by allocating the value of the total subsidy, as appropriate, over the level of production, sales or exports of the products concerned during the investigation period for subsidization.

3. Where the subsidy can be linked to the acquisition or future acquisition of fixed assets, the amount of the countervailable subsidy shall be calculated by spreading the subsidy across a period which reflects the

normal depreciation of such assets in the industry concerned. The amount so calculated which is attributable to the investigation period, including that which derives from fixed assets acquired before this period, shall be allocated as described in paragraph 2.

Where the assets are non-depreciating, the subsidy shall be valued as an interest-free loan, and be treated in accordance with Article 6(b).

4. Where a subsidy cannot be linked to the acquisition of fixed assets, the amount of the benefit received during the investigation period shall in principle be attributed to this period, and allocated as described in paragraph 2, unless special circumstances arise justifying attribution over a different period.

* * *

ANNEX I

ILLUSTRATIVE LIST OF EXPORT SUBSIDIES

(a) The provision by governments of direct subsidies to a firm or an industry contingent upon export performance.

(b) Currency retention schemes or any similar practices which involve a bonus on exports.

(c) Internal transport and freight charges on export shipments, provided or mandated by governments, on terms more favourable than for domestic shipments.

(d) The provision by governments or their agencies either directly or indirectly through government-mandated schemes, of imported or domestic products or services for use in the production of exported goods, on terms or conditions more favourable than for provision of like or directly competitive products or services for use in the production of goods for domestic consumption, if (in the case of products) such terms or conditions are more favourable than those commercially available[3] on world markets to their exporters.

(e) The full or partial exemption, remission, or deferral specifically related to exports, of direct taxes[4] or social welfare charges paid or payable

---

3. The term 'commercially available' means that the choice between domestic and imported products is unrestricted and depends only on commercial considerations.

4. For the purpose of this Regulation:
— the term 'direct taxes' shall mean taxes on wages, profits, interests, rents, royalties, and all other forms of income, and taxes on the ownership of real property,
— the term 'import charges' shall mean tariffs, duties, and other fiscal charges not elsewhere enumerated in this note that are levied on imports,
— the term 'indirect taxes' shall mean sales, excise, turnover, value added, franchise, stamp, transfer, inventory and equipment taxes, border taxes and all taxes other than direct taxes and import charges,
— 'prior-stage' indirect taxes are those levied on goods or services used directly or indirectly in making the product,
— 'cumulative' indirect taxes are multi-staged taxes levied where there is no mechanism for subsequent crediting of the tax if the goods or services subject to tax at one stage of production are used in a succeeding state of production,
— 'remission' of taxes includes the refund or rebate of taxes,

by industrial or commercial enterprises.[5]

(f) The allowance of special deductions directly related to exports or export performance, over and above those granted in respect of production for domestic consumption, in the calculation of the base on which direct taxes are charged.

(g) The exemption or remission, in respect of the production and distribution of exported products, of indirect taxes[6] in excess of those levied in respect of the production and distribution of like products when sold for domestic consumption.

(h) The exemption, remission or deferral of prior-stage cumulative indirect taxes[7] on goods or services used in the production of exported products in excess of the exemption, remission or deferral of like prior-stage cumulative indirect taxes on goods or services used in the production of like products when sold for domestic consumption; provided, however, that prior-stage cumulative indirect taxes may be exempted, remitted or deferred on exported products even when not exempted, remitted or deferred on like products when sold for domestic consumption, if the prior-stage cumulative indirect taxes are levied on inputs that are consumed in the production of the exported product (making normal allowance for waste.[8] This item shall be interpreted in accordance with the guidelines on consumption of inputs in the production process contained in Annex II.

(i) The remission or drawback of import charges[9] in excess of those levied on imported inputs that are consumed in the production of the exported product (making normal allowance for waste); provided, however, that in particular cases a firm may use a quantity of home market inputs equal to, and having the same quality and characteristics as, the imported inputs as a substitute for them in order to benefit from this provision if the import and the corresponding export operations both occur within a reasonable time period, not to exceed two years. This item shall be interpreted in accordance with the guidelines on consumption of inputs in the production process contained in Annex II and the guidelines in the determination of substitution drawback systems as export subsidies contained in Annex III.

(j) The provision by governments (or special institutions controlled by governments) of export credit guarantee or insurance programmes, of insurance or guarantee programmes against increases in the cost of exported products or of exchange risk programmes, at premium rates which are inadequate to cover the long-term operating costs and losses of the programmes.

— 'remission or drawback' includes the full or partial exemption or deferral of import charges.

5. Deferral may not amount to an export subsidy where, for example, appropriate interest charges are collected.

6. See note 4 supra.

7. See note 4 supra.

8. Paragraph (h) does not apply to value-added tax systems and border-tax adjustment in lieu thereof; the problem of the excessive remission of value-added taxes is exclusively covered by paragraph (g).

9. See note 4 supra.

(k) The grant by governments (or special institutions controlled by and/or acting under the authority of governments) of export credits at rates below those which they actually have to pay for the funds so employed (or would have to pay if they borrowed on international capital markets in order to obtain funds of the same maturity and other credit terms and denominated in the same currency as the export credit), or the payment by them of all or part of the costs incurred by exporters or financial institutions in obtaining credits, insofar as they are used to secure a material advantage in the field of export credit terms.

Provided, however, that if a Member of the WTO is a party to an international undertaking on official export credits to which at least 12 original such Members are parties as of 1 January 1979 (or a successor undertaking which has been adopted by those original Members), or if in practice a Member of the WTO applies the interest rates provisions of the relevant undertaking, an export credit practice which is in conformity with those provisions shall not be considered an export subsidy.

(*l*) Any other charge on the public account constituting an export subsidy in the sense of Article XVI of GATT 1994.

[The following articles are omitted. In most cases, the provision is similar to the article dealing with the same subject in the Anti–Dumping Regulation.]

Article 8 **Determination of Injury**
Article 9 **Definition of Community Industry**
Article 10 **Initiation of Proceedings**
Article 11 **The Investigation**
Article 12 **Provisional Measures**
Article 13 **Undertakings**
Article 14 **Termination Without Measures**
Article 15 **Imposition of Definitive Duties**
Article 16 **Retroactivity**
Article 17 **Duration**
Article 18 **Expiry Reviews**
Article 19 **Interim Reviews**
Article 20 **Accelerated Reviews**
Article 21 **Refunds**
Article 22 **General Provisions on Reviews and Refunds**
Article 23 **Circumvention**
Article 24 **General Provisions**
Article 25 **Consultations**
Article 26 **Verification Visits**
Article 27 **Sampling**
Article 28 **Non-cooperation**
Article 29 **Confidentiality**
Article 30 **Disclosure**
Article 31 **Community Interests**
Article 32 **Relationships Between Countervailing Duty Measures and Multilateral Remedies**

Article 33 **Final Provisions**
Article 34 **Repeal of Existing Legislation**
Article 35 **Entry Into Force**
Annexes

4. COUNCIL REGULATION (EC) NO. 3286/94

of 22 December 1994

laying down Community procedures in the field of the common commercial policy in order to ensure the exercise of the Community's rights under international trade rules, in particular those established under the auspices of the World Trade Organization

O.J. L 349/71 (Dec. 31, 1994)

The Council of the European Union,

* * *

Whereas the abovementioned Community procedures should be based on a legal mechanism under Community law which would be fully transparent, and would ensure that the decision to invoke the Community's rights under international trade rules is taken on the basis of accurate factual information and legal analysis;

* * *

Whereas it is appropriate to confirm that the Community must act in compliance with its international obligations and, where such obligations result from agreements, maintain the balance of rights and obligations which it is the purpose of those agreements to establish;

Whereas it is also appropriate to confirm that any measures taken under the procedures in question should also be in conformity with the Community's international obligations, as well as being without prejudice to other measures in cases not covered by this Regulation which might be adopted directly pursuant to Article 133 of the Treaty;

* * *

Has Adopted This Regulation:

Article 1

Aims

This Regulation establishes Community procedures in the field of the common commercial policy in order to ensure the exercise of the Community's rights under international trade rules, in particular those established under the auspices of the World Trade Organization which, subject to compliance with existing international obligations and procedures, are aimed at:

(a) responding to obstacles to trade that have an effect on the market of the Community, with a view to removing the injury resulting therefrom;

(b) responding to obstacles to trade that have an effect on the market of a third country, with a view to removing the adverse trade effects resulting therefrom.

These procedures shall be applied in particular to the initiation and subsequent conduct and termination of international dispute settlement procedures in the area of common commercial policy.

Article 2

Definitions

1. For the purposes of this Regulation, 'obstacles to trade' shall be any trade practice adopted or maintained by a third country in respect of which international trade rules establish a right of action. Such a right of action exists when international trade rules either prohibit a practice outright, or give another party affected by the practice a right to seek elimination of the effect of the practice in question.

2. For the purposes of this Regulation and subject to paragraph 8, 'the Community's rights' shall be those international trade rights of which it may avail itself under international trade rules. In this context, 'international trade rules' are primarily those established under the auspices of the WTO and laid down in the Annexes to the WTO Agreement, but they can also be those laid down in any other agreement to which the Community is a party and which sets out rules applicable to trade between the Community and third countries.

3. For the purposes of this Regulation, 'injury' shall be any material injury which an obstacle to trade causes or threatens to cause, in respect of a product or service, to a Community industry on the market of the Community.

4. For the purposes of this Regulation, 'adverse trade effects' shall be those which an obstacle to trade causes or threatens to cause, in respect of a product or service, to Community enterprises on the market of any third country, and which have a material impact on the economy of the Community or of a region of the Community, or on a sector of economic activity therein. The fact that the complainant suffers from such adverse effects shall not be considered sufficient to justify, on its own, that the Community institutions proceed with any action.

5. The term 'Community industry' shall be taken to mean all Community producers or providers, respectively:

(a) of products or services identical or similar to the product or service which is the subject of an obstacle to trade, or

(b) of products or services competing directly with that product or service, or

(c) who are consumers or processors of the product or consumers or users of the service which is the subject of an obstacle to trade, or all those producers or providers whose combined output constitutes a major proportion of total Community production of the products or services in question; however:

(a) when producers or providers are related to the exporters or importers or are themselves importers of the product or service alleged to be the subject of obstacles to trade, the term 'Community industry' may be interpreted as referring to the rest of the producers or providers;

(b) in particular circumstances, the producers or providers within a region of the Community may be regarded as the Community industry if their collective output constitutes the major proportion of the output of the product or service in question in the Member State or Member States within which the region is located provided that the effect of the obstacle to trade is concentrated in that Member State or those Member States.

6. The term 'Community enterprise' shall be taken to mean a company or firm formed in accordance with the law of a Member State and having its registered office, central administration or principal place of business within the Community, directly concerned by the production of goods or the provision of services which are the subject of the obstacle to trade.

7. For the purposes of this Regulation, the notion of 'providers of services' in the context of both the term 'Community industry' as defined in paragraph 5, and the term 'Community enterprises' as defined in paragraph 6, is without prejudice to the non-commercial nature which the provision of any particular service may have according to the legislation or regulation of a Member State.

8. For the purposes of this Regulation, the term 'services' shall be taken to mean those services in respect of which international agreements can be concluded by the Community on the basis of Article 133 of the Treaty.

Article 3

Complaint on behalf of the Community industry

1. Any natural or legal person, or any association not having legal personality, acting on behalf of a Community industry which considers that it has suffered injury as a result of obstacles to trade that have an effect on the market of the Community may lodge a written complaint.

2. The complaint must contain sufficient evidence of the existence of the obstacles to trade and of the injury resulting therefrom. Evidence of injury must be given on the basis of the illustrative list of factors indicated in Article 10, where applicable.

Article 4

Complaint on behalf of Community enterprises

1. Any Community enterprise, or any association, having or not legal personality, acting on behalf of one or more Community enterprises, which

considers that such Community enterprises have suffered adverse trade effects as a result of obstacles to trade that have an effect on the market of a third country may lodge a written complaint. Such complaint, however, shall only be admissible if the obstacle to trade alleged therein is the subject of a right of action established under international trade rules laid down in a multilateral or plurilateral trade agreement.

2. The complaint must contain sufficient evidence of the existence of the obstacles to trade and of the adverse trade effects, resulting therefrom. Evidence of adverse trade effects must be given on the basis of the illustrative list of factors indicated in Article 10, where applicable.

Article 5

Complaint procedures

1. The complaint shall be submitted to the Commission, which shall send a copy thereof to the Member States.

2. The complaint may be withdrawn, in which case the procedure may be terminated unless such termination would not be in the interests of the Community.

3. Where it becomes apparent after consultation that the complaint does not provide sufficient evidence to justify initiating an investigation, then the complainant shall be so informed.

4. The Commission shall take a decision as soon as possible on the opening of a Community examination procedure following any complaint made in accordance with Articles 3 or 4; the decision shall normally be taken within 45 days of the lodging of the complaint; this period may be suspended at the request, or with the agreement, of the complainant, in order to allow the provision of complementary information which may be needed to fully assess the validity of the complainant's case.

Article 6

Referral by a Member State

1. Any Member State may ask the Commission to initiate the procedures referred to in Article 1.

2. It shall supply the Commission with sufficient evidence to support its request, as regards obstacles to trade and of any effects resulting therefrom. Where evidence of injury or of adverse trade effects is appropriate, is must be given on the basis of the illustrative list of factors indicated in Article 10, where applicable.

3. The Commission shall notify the other Member States of the requests without delay.

4. Where it becomes apparent after consultation that the request does not provide sufficient evidence to justify initiating an investigation, then the Member State shall be so informed.

5. The Commission shall take a decision as soon as possible on the opening of a Community examination procedure following any referral by a Member State made in accordance with Article 6; the decision shall normally be taken with 45 days of the referral; this period may be suspended at the request, or with the agreement, of the referring Member State, in order to allow the provision of complementary information which may be needed to fully assess the validity of the case presented by the referring Member State.

Article 7

Consultation procedure

1. For the purpose of consultations pursuant to this Regulation, an Advisory Committee, hereinafter referred to as 'the Committee', is hereby set up and shall consist of representatives of each Member State, with a representative of the Commission as chairman.

2. Consultations shall be held immediately at the request of a Member State or on the initiative of the Commission, and in any event within a time frame which allows the time limits set by this Regulation to be respected. The chairman of the Committee shall provide the Member States, as promptly as possible, with all relevant information in his possession. The Commission shall also refer such information to the committee established by Article 133 of the Treaty so that it can consider any wider implications for the common commercial policy.

3. The Committee shall meet when convened by its chairman.

4. Where necessary, consultations may be in writing. In such case the Commission shall notify in writing the Member States who, within a period of eight working days from such notification, shall be entitled to express their opinions in writing or to request oral consultations which the chairman shall arrange, provided that such oral consultations can be held within a time frame which allows the time limits set by this Regulation to be respected.

Article 8

Community examination procedure

1. Where, after consultation, it is apparent to the Commission that there is sufficient evidence to justify initiating an examination procedure and that it is necessary in the interest of the Community, the Commission shall act as follows:

(a) it shall announce the initiation of an examination procedure in the Official Journal of the European Communities; such announcement shall indicate the product or service and countries concerned, give a summary of the information received, and provide that all relevant information is to be communicated to the Commission; it shall state the period within which interested parties may apply to be heard orally by the Commission in accordance with paragraph 5;

(b) it shall officially notify the representatives of the country or countries which are the subject of the procedure, with whom, where appropriate, consultations may be held;

(c) it shall conduct the examination at Community level, acting in cooperation with the Member States.

2. (a) If necessary the Commission shall seek all the information it deems necessary and attempt to check this information with the importers, traders, agents, producers, trade associations and organizations, provided that the undertakings or organizations concerned give their consent.

(b) Where necessary, the Commission shall carry out investigations in the territory of third countries, provided that the governments of the countries have been officially notified and raise no objection within a reasonable period.

(c) The Commission shall be assisted in its investigation by officials of the Member State in whose territory the checks are carried out, provided that the Member State in question so requests.

3. Member States shall supply the Commission, upon request, with all information necessary for the examination, in accordance with the detailed arrangements laid down by the Commission.

4. (a) The complainants and the exporters and importers concerned, as well as the representatives of the country or countries concerned, may inspect all information made available to the Commission except for internal documents for the use of the Commission and the administrations, provided that such information is relevant to the protection of their interests and not confidential within the meaning of Article 9 and that it is used by the Commission in its examination procedure. The persons concerned shall address a reasoned request in writing to the Commission, indicating the information required.

(b) The complainants and the exporters and importers concerned and the representatives of the country or countries concerned may ask to be informed of the principal facts and considerations resulting from the examination procedure.

5. The Commission may hear the parties concerned. It shall hear them if they have, within the period prescribed in the notice published in the Official Journal of the European Communities, made a written request for a hearing showing that they are a party primarily concerned by the result of the procedure.

6. Furthermore, the Commission shall, on request, give the parties primarily concerned an opportunity to meet, so that opposing views may be presented and any rebuttal argument put forward. In providing this opportunity the Commission shall take account of the wishes of the parties and of the need to preserve confidentiality. There shall be no obligation on any party to attend a meeting and failure to do so shall not be prejudicial to that party's case.

7. When the information requested by the Commission is not supplied within a reasonable time or where the investigation is significantly impeded, findings may be made on the basis of the facts available.

8. When it has concluded its examination the Commission shall report to the Committee. The report should normally be presented within five months of the announcement of initiation of the procedure, unless the complexity of the examination is such that the Commission extends the period to seven months.

Article 9

Confidentiality

1. Information received pursuant to this Regulation shall be used only for the purpose for which it was requested.

2. (a) Neither the Council, nor the Commission, nor Member States, nor the officials of any of these, shall reveal any information of a confidential nature received pursuant to this Regulation, or any information provided on a confidential basis by a party to an examination procedure, without specific permission from the party submitting such information.

(b) Each request for confidential treatment shall indicate why the information is confidential and shall be accompanied by a non-confidential summary of the information or a statement of the reasons why the information is not susceptible of such summary.

3. Information will normally be considered to be confidential if its disclosure is likely to have a significantly adverse effect upon the supplier or the source of such information.

4. However, if it appears that a request for confidentiality is not warranted and if the supplier is either unwilling to make the information public or to authorize its disclosure in generalized or summary form, the information in question may be disregarded.

5. This Article shall not preclude the disclosure of general information by the Community authorities and in particular of the reasons on which decisions taken pursuant to this Regulation are based. Such disclosure must take into account the legitimate interest of the parties concerned that their business secrets should not be divulged.

Article 10

Evidence

1. An examination of injury shall involve where applicable the following factors:

(a) the volume of Community imports or exports concerned, notably where there has been a significant increase or decrease, either in absolute terms or relative to production or consumption on the market in question;

(b) the prices of the Community industry's competitors, in particular in order to determine whether there has been, either in the Community or on third country markets, significant undercutting of the prices of the Community industry;

(c) the consequent impact on the Community industry and as indicated by trends in certain economic factors such as: production, utilization of capacity, stocks, sales, market share, prices (that is depression of prices or prevention of price increases which would normally have occurred), profits, return on capital, investment, employment.

2. Where a threat of injury is alleged, the Commission shall also examine whether it is clearly foreseeable that a particular situation is likely to develop into actual injury. In this regard, account may also be taken of factors such as:

(a) the rate of increase of exports to the market where the competition with Community products is taking place;

(b) export capacity in the country of origin or export, which is already in existence or will be operational in the foreseeable future, and the likelihood that the exports resulting from that capacity will be to the market referred to in point (a).

3. Injury caused by other factors which, either individually or in combination, are also adversely affecting Community industry must not be attributed to the practices under consideration.

4. Where adverse trade effects are alleged, the Commission shall examine the impact of such adverse effects on the economy of the Community or of a region of the Community, or on a sector of economic activity therein. To this effect, the Commission may take into account, where relevant, factors of the type listed in paragraphs 1 and 2. Adverse trade effects may arise, inter alia, in situations in which trade flows concerning a product or service are prevented, impeded or diverted as a result of any obstacle to trade, or from situations in which obstacles to trade have materially affected the supply or inputs (e. g. parts and components or raw materials) to Community enterprises. Where a threat of adverse trade effects is alleged, the Commission shall also examine whether it is clearly foreseeable that a particular situation is likely to develop into actual adverse trade effects.

5. The Commission shall also, in examining evidence of adverse trade effects, have regard to the provisions, principles or practice which govern the right of action under relevant international rules referred to in Article 2(1).

6. The Commission shall further examine any other relevant evidence contained in the complaint or in the referral. In this respect, the list of factors and the indications given in paragraphs 1 to 5 are not exhaustive, nor can one or several of such factors and indications necessarily give decisive guidance as to the existence of injury or of adverse trade effects.

Article 11

Termination and suspension of the procedure

1. When it is found as a result of the examination procedure that the interests of the Community do not require any action to be taken, the procedure shall be terminated in accordance with Article 14.

2. (a) When, after an examination procedure, the third country or countries concerned take(s) measures which are considered satisfactory, and therefore no action by the Community is required, the procedure may be suspended in accordance with the provisions of Article 14.

(b) The Commission shall supervise the application of these measures, where appropriate on the basis of information supplied at intervals, which it may request from the third countries concerned and check as necessary.

(c) Where the measures taken by the third country or countries concerned have been rescinded, suspended or improperly implemented or where the Commission has grounds for believing this to be the case or, finally, where a request for information made by the Commission as provided for by point (b) has not been granted, the Commission shall inform the Member States, and where necessary and justified by the results of the investigation and the new facts available any measures shall be taken in accordance with Article 13(3).

3. Where, either after an examination procedure, or at any time before, during and after an international dispute settlement procedure, it appears that the most appropriate means to resolve a dispute arising from an obstacle to trade is the conclusion of an agreement with the third country or countries concerned, which may change the substantive rights of the Community and of the third country or countries concerned, the procedure shall be suspended according to the provisions of Article 14, and negotiations shall be carried out according to the provisions of Article 13 3 of the Treaty.

Article 12

Adoption of commercial policy measures

1. Where it is found (as a result of the examination procedure, unless the factual and legal situation is such that an examination procedure may not be required) that action is necessary in the interests of the Community in order to ensure the exercise of the Community's rights under international trade rules, with a view to removing the injury or the adverse trade effects resulting from obstacles to trade adopted or maintained by third countries, the appropriate measures shall be determined in accordance with the procedure set out in Article 13.

2. Where the Community's international obligations require the prior discharge of an international procedure for consultation or for the settlement of disputes, the measures referred to in paragraph 3 shall only be decided on after that procedure has been terminated, and taking account of

the results of the procedure. In particular, where the Community has requested an international dispute settlement body to indicate and authorize the measures which are appropriate for the implementation of the results of an international dispute settlement procedure, the Community commercial policy measures which may be needed in consequence of such authorization shall be in accordance with the recommendation of such international dispute settlement body.

3. Any commercial policy measures may be taken which are compatible with existing international obligations and procedures, notably:

(a) suspension or withdrawal of any concession resulting from commercial policy negotiations;

(b) the raising of existing customs duties or the introduction of any other charge on imports;

(c) the introduction of quantitative restrictions or any other measures modifying import or export conditions or otherwise affecting trade with the third country concerned.

4. The corresponding decisions shall state the reasons on which they are based and shall be published in the Official Journal of the European Communities. Publication shall also be deemed to constitute notification to the countries and parties primarily concerned.

Article 13

Decision-making procedures

1. The decisions referred to in Article 11(1) and (2)(a) shall be adopted in accordance with the provisions of Article 14.

2. Where the Community, as a result of a complaint pursuant to Articles 3 or 4, or of a referral pursuant to Article 6, follows formal international consultation or dispute settlement procedures, decisions relating to the initiation, conduct or termination of such procedures shall be taken in accordance with Article 14.

3. Where the Community, having acted in accordance with Article 12 (2), has to take a decision on the measures of commercial policy to be adopted pursuant to Article 11(2)(c) or pursuant to Article 12 the Council shall act, in accordance with Article 133 of the Treaty, by a qualified majority, not later than 30 working days after receiving the proposal.

Article 14

Committee procedure

1. Should reference be made to the procedure provided for in this Article, the matter shall be brought before the Committee by its chairman.

2. The Commission representative shall submit to the Committee a draft of the decision to be taken. The Committee shall discuss the matter within a period to be fixed by the chairman, depending on the urgency of the matter.

3. The Commission shall adopt a decision which it shall communicate to the Member States and which shall apply after a period of 10 days if during this period no Member State has referred the matter to the Council.

4. The Council may, at the request of a Member State and acting by a qualified majority revise the Commission's decision.

5. The Commission's decision shall apply after a period of 30 days if the Council has not given a ruling within this period, calculated from the day on which the matter was referred to the Council.

Article 15

General provisions

1. This Regulation shall not apply in cases covered by other existing rules in the common commercial policy field. It shall operate by way of complement to:

(a) the rules establishing the common organization of agricultural markets and their implementing provisions, and

(b) the specific rules adopted pursuant to Article 308 of the Treaty, applicable to goods processed from agricultural products.

It shall be without prejudice to other measures which may be taken pursuant to Article 133 of the Treaty, as well as to Community procedures for dealing with matters concerning obstacles to trade raised by Member States in the committee established by Article 133 of the Treaty.

2. Regulation (EEC) No. 2641/84 is hereby repealed. References to the repealed Regulation shall be construed as references to this Regulation where appropriate.

Article 16

Entry into force

This Regulation shall enter into force on 1 January 1995. It shall apply to proceedings initiated after that date as well as to proceedings pending at that date and in relation to which Community examination procedures have been completed.

Part VI

FREE MOVEMENT OF CAPITAL AND ECONOMIC AND MONETARY UNION

Doc.

Table of Contents

1. Council Directive 88/361 for the implementation of Article 67 [free movement of capital]. 620
2. Council Directive 79/279 coordinating the conditions for the admission of securities to official stock exchange listing. 624
3. Council Directive 82/121 on information to be published by companies the shares of which have been admitted to official stock-exchange listing. 637
4. Council Directive 89/592 coordinating regulations on insider dealing. 641
5. First Council Directive 77/780 on the coordination of laws, regulations and administrative provisions relating to the taking up and pursuit of the business of credit institutions. 646
6. Second Council Directive 89/646 on the coordination of laws relating to the business of credit institutions. 652
7. Council Regulation 974/98 on the introduction of the Euro, O.J. L 139/1 (May 11, 1998). 671
8. Council Regulation 1103/97 on certain provisions related to the introduction of the Euro, O.J. L 162/1 (June 19, 1997). 678

1. COUNCIL DIRECTIVE 88/361/EEC

of 24 June 1988

for the implementation of Article 67 of the Treaty

O.J. L 178/5 (July 8, 1988)

The Council of the European Communities,

Having regard to the Treaty establishing the European Economic Community, and in particular Articles 69 and 70(1) thereof,

Having regard to the proposal from the Commission, submitted following consultation with the Monetary Committee,

Having regard to the opinion of the European Parliament,

Whereas Article 8a of the Treaty stipulates that the internal market shall comprise an area without internal frontiers in which the free movement of capital is ensured, without prejudice to the other provisions of the Treaty;

* * *

Whereas advantage should be taken of the period adopted for bringing this Directive into effect in order to enable the Commission to submit proposals designed to eliminate or reduce risks of distortion, tax evasion and tax avoidance resulting from the diversity of national systems for taxation and to permit the Council to take a position on such proposals;

Whereas, in accordance with Article 70(1) of the Treaty, the Community shall endeavour to attain the highest possible degree of liberalization in respect of the movement of capital between its residents and those of third countries;

* * *

Has Adopted This Directive:

Article 1

1. Without prejudice to the following provisions, Member States shall abolish restrictions on movements of capital taking place between persons resident in Member States. To facilitate application of this Directive, capital movements shall be classified in accordance with the Nomenclature in Annex I.

2. Transfers in respect of capital movements shall be made on the same exchange rate conditions as those governing payments relating to current transactions.

Article 2

Member States shall notify the Committee of Governors of the Central Banks, the Monetary Committee and the Commission, by the date of their entry into force at the latest, of measures to regulate bank liquidity which have a specific impact on capital transactions carried out by credit institutions with non-residents.

Such measures shall be confined to what is necessary for the purposes of domestic monetary regulation. The Monetary Committee and the Committee of Governors of the Central Banks shall provide the Commission with opinions on this subject.

Article 3

1. Where short-term capital movements of exceptional magnitude impose severe strains on foreign-exchange markets and lead to serious disturbances in the conduct of a Member State's monetary and exchange rate policies, being reflected in particular in substantial variations in domestic liquidity, the Commission may, after consulting the Monetary Committee and the Committee of Governors of the Central Banks, authorize that Member State to take, in respect of the capital movements listed in Annex II, protective measures the conditions and details of which the Commission shall determine.

2. The Member State concerned may itself take the protective measures referred to above, on grounds of urgency, should these measures be necessary. The Commission and the other Member States shall be informed of such measures by the date of their entry into force at the latest. The Commission, after consulting the Monetary Committee and the Committee of Governors of the Central Banks, shall decide whether the Member State concerned may continue to apply these measures or whether it should amend or abolish them.

3. The decisions taken by the Commission under paragraphs 1 and 2 may be revoked or amended by the Council acting by a qualified majority.

4. The period of application of protective measures taken pursuant to this Article shall not exceed six months.

5. Before 31 December 1992, the Council shall examine, on the basis of a report from the Commission, after delivery of an opinion by the Monetary Committee and the Committee of Governors of the Central Banks, whether the provisions of this Article remain appropriate, as regards their principle and details, to the requirements which they were amended to satisfy.

Article 4

This Directive shall be without prejudice to the right of Member States to take all requisite measures to prevent infringements of their laws and regulations, *inter alia* in the field of taxation and prudential supervision of financial institutions, or to lay down procedures for the declaration of capital movements for purposes of administrative or statistical information.

Application of those measures and procedures may not have the effect of impeding capital movements carried out in accordance with Community law.

* * *

Article 6

1. Member States shall take the measures necessary to comply with this Directive no later than 1 July 1990. They shall forthwith inform the Commission thereof. They shall also make known, by the date of their entry into force at the latest, any new measure or any amendment made to the provisions governing the capital movements listed in Annex I.

2. The Kingdom of Spain and the Portuguese Republic, without prejudice for these two Member States to Articles 61 to 66 and 222 to 232 of the 1985 Act of Accession, and the Hellenic Republic and Ireland may temporarily continue to apply restrictions to the capital movements listed in Annex IV, subject to the conditions and time limits laid down in that Annex.

If, before expiry of the time limit set for the liberalization of the capital movements referred to in Lists III and IV of Annex IV, the Portuguese Republic or the Hellenic Republic considers that it is unable to proceed with liberalization, in particular because of difficulties as regards its balance of payments or because the national financial system is insufficiently adapted, the Commission, at the request of one or other of these Member States, shall in collaboration with the Monetary Committee, review the economic and financial situation of the Member State concerned. On the basis of the outcome of this review, the Commission shall propose to the Council an extension of the time limit set for liberalization of all or part of the capital movements referred to. This extension may not exceed three years. The Council shall act in accordance with the procedure laid down in Article 69 of the Treaty.

3. The Kingdom of Belgium and the Grand Duchy of Luxembourg may temporarily continue to operate the dual exchange market under the conditions and for the periods laid down in Annex V.

4. Existing national legislation regulating purchases of secondary residences may be upheld until the Council adopts further provisions in this area in accordance with Article 69 of the Treaty. This provision does not affect the applicability of other provisions of Community law.

5. The Commission shall submit to the Council, by 31 December 1988, proposals aimed at eliminating or reducing risks or distortion, tax evasion and tax avoidance linked to the diversity of national systems for the taxation of savings and for controlling the application of these systems.

The Council shall take a position on these Commission proposals by 30 June 1989. Any tax provisions of a Community nature shall, in accordance with the Treaty, be adopted unanimously.

Article 7

1. In their treatment of transfers in respect of movements of capital to or from third countries, the Member States shall endeavour to attain the same degree of liberalization as that which applies to operations with residents of other Member States, subject to the other provisions of this Directive.

The provisions of the preceding subparagraph shall not prejudice the application to third countries of domestic rules or Community law, particularly any reciprocal conditions, concerning operations involving establishment, the provisions of financial services and the admission of securities to capital markets.

2. Where large-scale short-term capital movements to or from third countries seriously disturb the domestic or external monetary or financial situation of the Member States, or of a number of them, or cause serious strains in exchange relations within the Community or between the Community and third countries, Member States shall consult with one another on any measure to be taken to counteract such difficulties. This consultation shall take place within the Committee of Governors of the Central Banks and the Monetary Committee on the initiative of the Commission or of any Member State.

Article 8

At least once a year the Monetary Committee shall examine the situation regarding free movement of capital as it results from the application of this Directive. The examination shall cover measures concerning the domestic regulation of credit and financial and monetary markets which could have a specific impact on international capital movements and on all other aspects of this Directive. The Committee shall report to the Commission on the outcome of this examination.

Article 9

The First Directive of 11 May 1960 and Directive 72/156/EEC shall be repealed with effect from 1 July 1990.

Article 10

This Directive is addressed to the Member States.

2. COUNCIL DIRECTIVE 79/279/EEC

of 5 March 1979

coordinating the conditions for the admission of securities to official stock exchange listing

O.J. L 66/21 (Mar. 16, 1979)

THE COUNCIL OF THE EUROPEAN COMMUNITIES,

Having regard to the Treaty establishing the European Economic Community, and in particular Articles 54(3)(g) and 100 thereof,

Having regard to the proposal from the Commission,

Having regard to the opinion of the European Parliament,

Having regard to the opinion of the Economic and Social Committee,

Whereas the coordination of the conditions for the admission of securities to official listing on stock exchanges situated or operating in the Member States is likely to provide equivalent protection for investors at Community level, because of the more uniform guarantees offered to investors in the various Member States; whereas it will facilitate both the admission to official stock exchange listing, in each such State, of securities from other Member States and the listing of any given security on a number of stock exchanges in the Community; whereas it will accordingly make for greater interpenetration of national securities markets and therefore contribute to the prospect of establishing a European capital market;

Whereas such coordination must therefore apply to securities, independently of the legal status of their issuers, and must therefore also apply to securities issued by non-member States or their regional or local authorities or international public bodies; whereas this Directive therefore covers entities not covered by the second paragraph of Article 58 of the Treaty and goes beyond the scope of Article 54(3)(g) while directly affecting the establishment and functioning of the common market within the meaning of Article 100;

Whereas there should be the possibility of a right to apply to the courts against decisions by the competent national authorities in respect of the application of this Directive, although such right to apply must not be allowed to restrict the discretion of these authorities;

Whereas, initially, this coordination should be sufficiently flexible to enable account to be taken of present differences in the structures of securities markets in the Member States and to enable the Member States to take account of any specific situations with which they may be confronted;

Whereas, for this reason, coordination should first be limited to the establishment of minimum conditions for the admission of securities to official listing on stock exchanges situated or operating in the Member States, without however giving issuers any right to listing;

Whereas, this partial coordination of the conditions for admission to official listing constitutes a first step towards subsequent closer alignment of the rules of Member States in this field,

HAS ADOPTED THIS DIRECTIVE:

SECTION I
GENERAL PROVISIONS

Article 1

1. This Directive concerns securities which are admitted to official listing or are the subject of an application for admission to official listing on a stock exchange situated or operating within a Member State.

2. Member States may decide not to apply this Directive to:

— units issued by collective investment undertakings other than the closed-end type,

— securities issued by a Member State or its regional or local authorities.

* * *

Article 3

Member States shall ensure that:

— securities may not be admitted to official listing on any stock exchange situated or operating within their territory unless the conditions laid down by this Directive are satisfied, and that

— issuers of securities admitted to such official listing, whether admission takes place before or after the date on which this Directive is implemented, are subject to the obligations provided for by this Directive.

Article 4

1. The admission of securities to official listing shall be subject to the conditions set out in Schedules A and B to this Directive, relating to shares and debt securities respectively.

2. The issuers of securities admitted to official listing must fulfil the obligations set out in Schedules C and D to this Directive, relating to shares and debt securities respectively.

3. Certificates representing shares may be admitted to official listing only if the issuer of the shares represented fulfils the conditions set out in I(1) to I(3) of Schedule A and the obligations set out in Schedule C and if the certificates fulfil the conditions set out in II(1) to II(6) of Schedule A.

Article 5

1. Subject to the prohibitions provided for in Article 6 and in Schedules A and B, the Member States may make the admission of securities to official listing subject to more stringent conditions than those set out in Schedules A and B or to additional conditions, provided that these more stringent and additional conditions apply generally for all issuers or for

individual classes of issuers and that they have been published before application for admission of such securities is made.

2. Member States may make the issuers of securities admitted to official listing subject to more stringent obligations than those set out in Schedules C and D or to additional obligations, provided that these more stringent and additional obligations apply generally for all issuers or for individual classes of issuer.

3. Member States may, under the same conditions as those laid down in Article 7, authorize derogations from the additional or more stringent conditions and obligations referred to in paragraphs 1 and 2 hereof.

4. [Essentially replaced by Directive 82/121.]

Article 6

Member States may not make the admission to official listing of securities issued by companies or other legal persons which are nationals of another Member State subject to the condition that the securities must already have been admitted to official listing on a stock exchange situated or operating in one of the Member States.

Article 7

Any derogations from the conditions for the admission of securities to official listing which may be authorized in accordance with Schedules A and B must apply generally for all issuers where the circumstances justifying them are similar.

* * *

SECTION II

AUTHORITIES COMPETENT TO ADMIT SECURITIES TO OFFICIAL LISTING

Article 9

1. Member States shall designate the national authority or authorities competent to decide on the admission of securities to official listing on a stock exchange situated or operating within their territories and shall ensure that this Directive is applied. They shall inform the Commission accordingly, indicating, if appropriate, how duties have been allocated.

2. Member States shall ensure that the competent authorities have such powers as may be necessary for the exercise of their duties.

3. Without prejudice to the other powers conferred upon them, the competent authorities may reject an application for the admission of a security to official listing if, in their opinion, the issuer's situation is such that admission would be detrimental to investors' interests.

Article 10

By way of derogation from Article 5, Member States may, solely in the interests of protecting the investors, give the competent authorities power to make the admission of a security to official listing subject to any special condition which the competent authorities consider appropriate and of which they have explicitly informed the applicant.

Article 11

The competent authorities may refuse to admit to official listing a security already officially listed in another Member State where the issuer fails to comply with the obligations resulting from admission in that Member State.

Article 12

Without prejudice to any other action or penalties which they may contemplate in the event of failure on the part of the issuer to comply with the obligations resulting from admission to official listing, the competent authorities may make public the fact that an issuer is failing to comply with those obligations.

Article 13

1. An issuer whose securities are admitted to official listing shall provide the competent authorities with all the information which the latter consider appropriate in order to protect investors or ensure the smooth operation of the market.

2. Where protection of investors or the smooth operation of the market so requires, an issuer may be required by the competent authorities to publish such information in such a form and within such time limits as they consider appropriate. Should the issuer fail to comply with such requirement, the competent authorities may themselves publish such information after having heard the issuer.

Article 14

1. The competent authorities may decide to suspend the listing of a security where the smooth operation of the market is, or may be, temporarily jeopardized or where protection of investors so requires.

2. The competent authorities may decide that the listing of the security be discontinued where they are satisfied that, owing to special circumstances, normal regular dealings in a security are no longer possible.

Article 15

1. Member States shall ensure decisions of the competent authorities refusing the admission of a security to official listing or discontinuing such a listing shall be subject to the right to apply to the courts.

2. An applicant shall be notified of a decision regarding his application for admission to official listing within six months of receipt of the application or, should the competent authority require any further information within that period, within six months of the applicant's supplying such information.

3. Failure to give a decision within the time limit specified in paragraph 2 shall be deemed a rejection of the application. Such rejection shall give rise to the right to apply to the courts provided for in paragraph 1.

Article 16

Where an application for admission to official listing relates to certificates representing shares, the application shall be considered only if the competent authorities are of the opinion that the issuer of the certificates is offering adequate safeguards for the protection of investors.

SECTION III

PUBLICATION OF THE INFORMATION TO BE MADE AVAILABLE TO THE PUBLIC

Article 17

1. The information which issuers of a security admitted to official listing in a Member State are required to make available to the public in accordance with the requirements of Schedules C and D shall be published in one or more newspapers distributed throughout the Member State or distributed widely therein or shall be made available to the public either in writing in places indicated by announcements to be published in one or more newspapers distributed throughout the Member State or widely distributed therein or by other equivalent means approved by the competent authorities. The issuers must simultaneously send such information to the competent authorities.

2. The information referred to in paragraph 1 shall be published in the official language or languages, or in one of the official languages or in another language provided that in the Member State in question the official language or languages or such other language is or are customary in the sphere of finance and accepted by the competent authorities.

SECTION IV

COOPERATION BETWEEN MEMBER STATES

Article 18

1. The competent authorities shall cooperate wherever necessary for the purpose of carrying out their duties and shall exchange any information required for that purpose.

2. Where applications are to be made simultaneously or within short intervals of one another for admission of the same securities to official listing on stock exchanges situated or operating in more than one Member State, or where an application for admission is made in respect of a security already listed on a stock exchange in another Member State, the competent authorities shall communicate with each other and make such arrangements as may be necessary to expedite the procedure and simplify as far as

possible the formalities and any additional conditions required for admission of the security concerned.

* * *

Article 19

1. Member States shall provide that all persons employed or formerly employed by the competent authorities shall be bound by professional secrecy. This means that any confidential information received in the course of their duties may not be divulged to any person or authority except by virtue of provisions laid down by law.

* * *

SECTION V

CONTACT COMMITTEE

Article 20

1. A Contact Committee (hereinafter called 'the Committee') shall be set up alongside the Commission. Its function shall be:

(a) without prejudice to Articles 169 and 170 of the EEC Treaty to facilitate the harmonized implementation of this Directive through regular consultations on any practical problems arising from its application and on which exchanges of view are deemed useful;

(b) to facilitate the establishment of a concerted attitude between the Member States on the more stringent or additional conditions and obligations which, pursuant to Article 5 of this Directive, they may lay down at national level;

(c) to advise the Commission, if necessary, on any supplements or amendments to be made to this Directive or on any adjustments to be made in accordance with Article 21.

2. It shall not be the function of the Committee to appraise the merits of decisions taken by the competent authorities in individual cases.

3. The Committee shall be composed of persons appointed by the Member States and of representatives of the Commission. The chairman shall be a representative of the Commission. Secretarial services shall be provided by the Commission.

4. Meetings of the Committee shall be convened by its chairman, either on his own initiative or at the request of one Member State delegation. The Committee shall draw up its rules of procedure.

* * *

SECTION VI

FINAL PROVISIONS

* * *

Article 23

This Directive is addressed to the Member States.

ANNEX

SCHEDULE A

CONDITIONS FOR THE ADMISSION OF SHARES TO OFFICIAL LISTING ON A STOCK EXCHANGE

I. Conditions relating to companies for the shares of which admission to official listing is sought

1. *Legal position of the company*

The legal position of the company must be in conformity with the laws and regulations to which it is subject, as regards both its formation and its operation under its statutes.

2. *Minimum size of the company*

The foreseeable market capitalization of the shares for which admission to official listing is sought or, if this cannot be assessed, the company's capital and reserves, including profit or loss, from the last financial year, must be at least one million European [currency] units.

However, Member States may provide for admission to official listing, even when this condition is not fulfilled, provided that the competent authorities are satisfied that there will be an adequate market for the shares concerned.

A higher foreseeable market capitalization or higher capital and reserves may be required by a Member State for admission to official listing only if another regulated, regularly operating, recognized open market exists in that State and the requirements for it are equal to or less than those referred to in the first paragraph.

The condition set out in the first paragraph shall not be applicable for the admission to official listing of a further block of shares of the same class as those already admitted.

* * *

3. *A company's period of existence*

A company must have published or filed its annual accounts in accordance with national law for the three financial years preceding the application for official listing. By way of exception, the competent authorities may derogate from this condition where such derogation is desirable in the interests of the company or of investors and where the competent authorities are satisfied that investors have the necessary information available to be able to arrive at an informed judgment on the company and the shares for which admission to official listing is sought.

II. Conditions relating to the shares for which admission to official listing is sought

1. *Legal position of the shares*

The legal position of the shares must be in conformity with the laws and regulations to which they are subject.

2. *Negotiability of the shares*

The shares must be freely negotiable.

* * *

3. *Public issue preceding admission to official listing*

Where public issue precedes admission to official listing, the first listing may be made only after the end of the period during which subscription applications may be submitted.

4. *Distribution of shares*

A sufficient number of shares must be distributed to the public in one or more Member States not later than the time of admission.

This condition shall not apply where shares are to be distributed to the public through the stock exchange. In that event, admission to official listing may be granted only if the competent authorities are satisfied that a sufficient number of shares will be distributed through the stock exchange within a short period.

Where admission to official listing is sought for a further block of shares of the same class, the competent authorities may assess whether a sufficient number of shares has been distributed to the public in relation to all the shares issued and not only in relation to this further block.

However, by way of derogation from the first paragraph, if the shares are admitted to official listing in one or more non-Member States, the competent authorities may provide for their admission to official listing if a sufficient number of shares is distributed to the public in the non-Member State or States where they are listed.

A sufficient number of shares shall be deemed to have been distributed either when the shares in respect of which application for admission has been made are in the hands of the public to the extent of a least 25% of the subscribed capital represented by the class of shares concerned or when, in view of the large number of shares of the same class and the extent of their distribution to the public, the market will operate properly with a lower percentage.

5. *Listing of shares of the same class*

The application for admission to official listing must cover all the shares of the same class already issued.

However, Member States may provide that this condition shall not apply to applications for admission not covering all the shares of the same class already issued where the shares of that class for which admission is not sought belong to blocks serving to maintain control of the company or are not negotiable for a certain time under agreements, provided that the public is informed of such situations and that there is no danger of such situations prejudicing the interests of the holders of the shares for which admission to official listing is sought.

6. *Physical form of shares*

For the admission to official listing of shares issued by companies which are nationals of another Member State and which shares have a physical form it is necessary and sufficient that their physical form comply with the standards laid down in that other Member State. * * *

The physical form of shares issued by companies which are nationals of a non-member State must afford sufficient safeguard for the protection of the investors.

7. *Shares issued by companies from a non-member State*

If the shares issued by a company which is a national of a non-member State are not listed in either the country of origin or in the country in which the major proportion of the shares is held, they may not be admitted to official listing unless the competent authorities are satisfied that the absence of a listing in the country of origin or in the country in which the major proportion is held is not due to the need to protect investors.

SCHEDULE B

CONDITIONS FOR THE ADMISSION OF DEBT SECURITIES TO OFFICIAL LISTING ON A STOCK EXCHANGE

A. ADMISSION TO OFFICIAL LISTING OF DEBT SECURITIES ISSUED BY AN UNDERTAKING

I. Conditions relating to undertakings for the debt securities of which admission to official listing is sought

Legal position of the undertaking

The legal position of the undertaking must be in conformity with the laws and regulations to which it is subject, as regards both its formation and its operation under its statutes.

II. Conditions relating to the debt securities for which admission to official listing is sought

1. *Legal position of the debt securities*

The legal position of the debt securities must be in conformity with the laws and regulations to which they are subject.

2. *Negotiability of the debt securities*

The debt securities must be freely negotiable.

* * *

3. *Public issue preceding admission to official listing*

Where public issue precedes admission to official listing, the first listing may be made only after the end of the period during which subscription applications may be submitted. * * *

4. Listing of debt securities ranking pari passu

The application for admission to official listing must cover all debt securities ranking *pari passu*.

5. Physical form of debt securities

For the admission to official listing of debt securities issued by undertakings which are nationals of another Member State and which debt securities have a physical form, it is necessary and sufficient that their physical form comply with the standards laid down in that other Member State. * * *

III. Other conditions

1. Minimum amount of the loan

The amount of the loan may not be less than 200,000 European [currency] units * * *. Member States may, however, provide for admission to official listing even when this condition is not fulfilled, where the competent authorities are satisfied that there will be a sufficient market for the debt securities concerned.

* * *

2. Convertible or exchangeable debentures, and debentures with warrants

Convertible or exchangeable debentures and debentures with warrants may be admitted to official listing only if the related shares are already listed on the same stock exchange or on another regulated, regularly operating, recognized open market or are so admitted simultaneously.

* * *

B. ADMISSION TO OFFICIAL LISTING OF DEBT SECURITIES ISSUED BY A STATE, ITS REGIONAL OR LOCAL AUTHORITIES OR A PUBLIC INTERNATIONAL BODY

[Essentially the same provisions as A.II(2)–(5) supra.]

SCHEDULE C

OBLIGATIONS OF COMPANIES WHOSE SHARES ARE ADMITTED TO OFFICIAL LISTING ON A STOCK EXCHANGE

1. Listing of newly issued shares of the same class

Without prejudice to the second paragraph of II(5) of Schedule A, in the case of a new public issue of shares of the same class as those already officially listed, the company shall be required, where the new shares are not automatically admitted, to apply for their admission to the same listing, either not more than a year after their issue or when they become freely negotiable.

2. *Treatment of shareholders*

(a) The company shall ensure equal treatment for all shareholders who are in the same position.

(b) The company must ensure, at least in each Member State in which its shares are listed, that all the necessary facilities and information are available to enable shareholders to exercise their rights. In particular, it must:

— inform shareholders of the holding of meetings and enable them to exercise their right to vote,

— publish notices or distribute circulars concerning the allocation and payment of dividends, the issue of new shares including allotment, subscription, renunciation and conversion arrangements,

— designate as its agent a financial institution through which shareholders may exercise their financial rights, unless the company itself provides financial services.

3. *Amendment of the instrument of incorporation or the statutes*

(a) A company planning an amendment to its instrument of incorporation or its statutes must communicate a draft thereof to the competent authorities of the Member States in which its shares are listed.

(b) That draft must be communicated to the competent authorities no later than the calling of the general meeting which is to decide on the proposed amendment.

4. *Annual accounts and annual report*

(a) The company must make available to the public, as soon as possible, its most recent annual accounts and its last annual report.

(b) If the company prepares both annual own and annual consolidated accounts, it must make them available to the public. * * *

(c) If the annual accounts and reports do not comply with the provisions of Council Directives concerning companies' accounts and if they do not give a true and fair view of the company's assets and liabilities, financial position and profit or loss, more detailed and/or additional information must be provided.

5. *Additional information*

(a) The company must inform the public as soon as possible of any major new developments in its sphere of activity which are not public knowledge and which may, by virtue of their effect on its assets and liabilities or financial position or on the general course of its business, lead to substantial movements in the prices of its shares. [Supplemented by Directive 82/121.]

The competent authorities may, however, exempt the company from this requirement, if the disclosure of particular information is such as to prejudice the legitimate interests of the company.

(b) The company must inform the public without delay of any changes in the rights attaching to the various classes of shares.

(c) The company must inform the public of any changes in the structure (shareholders and breakdown of holdings) of the major holdings in its capital as compared with information previously published on that subject as soon as such changes come to its notice. [Replaced by Directive 88/627.]

6. *Equivalence of information*

(a) A company whose shares are officially listed on stock exchanges situated or operating in different Member States must ensure that equivalent information is made available to the market at each of these exchanges.

(b) A company whose shares are officially listed on stock exchanges situated or operating in one or more Member States and in one or more non-member States must make available to the markets of the Member State or States in which its shares are listed information which is at least equivalent to that which it makes available to the markets of the non-member State or States in question, if such information may be of importance for the evaluation of the shares.

SCHEDULE D

OBLIGATIONS OF ISSUERS WHOSE DEBT SECURITIES ARE ADMITTED TO OFFICIAL LISTING ON A STOCK EXCHANGE

A. DEBT SECURITIES ISSUED BY AN UNDERTAKING

1. *Treatment of holders of debt securities*

(a) The undertaking must ensure that all holders of debt securities ranking *pari passu* are given equal treatment in respect of all the rights attaching to those debt securities.

* * *

(b) The undertaking must ensure that at least in each Member State where its debt securities are officially listed all the facilities and information necessary to enable holders to exercise their rights are available. In particular, it must:

— publish notices or distribute circulars concerning the holding of meetings of holders of debt securities, the payment of interest, the exercise of any conversion, exchange, subscription or renunciation rights, and repayment,

— designate as its agent a financial institution through which holders of debt securities may exercise their financial rights, unless the undertaking itself provides financial services.

2. *Amendment of the instrument of incorporation or the statutes*

(a) An undertaking planning an amendment to its instrument of incorporation or its statutes affecting the rights of holders of debt securities must forward a draft thereof to the competent authorities of the Member States in which its debt securities are listed.

(b) That draft must be communicated to the competent authorities no later than the calling of the meeting of the body which is to decide on the proposed amendment.

3. *Annual accounts and annual report*

[Identical to Schedule C.(4).]

* * *

4. *Additional information*

(a) The undertaking must inform the public as soon as possible of any major new developments in its sphere of activity which are not public knowledge and which may significantly affect its ability to meet its commitments.

The competent authorities may, however, exempt the undertaking from this obligation at its request if the disclosure of particular information would be such as to prejudice the legitimate interests of the undertaking.

(b) The undertaking must inform the public without delay of any change in the rights of holders of debt securities resulting in particular from a change in loan terms or in interest rates.

(c) The undertaking must inform the public without delay of new loan issues and in particular of any guarantee or security in respect thereof.

(d) Where the debt securities officially listed are convertible or exchangeable debentures, or debentures with warrants, the undertaking must inform the public without delay of any changes in the rights attaching to the various classes of shares to which they relate.

5. *Equivalence of information*

[Identical to Schedule C.(6).]

* * *

B. DEBT SECURITIES ISSUED BY A STATE OR ITS REGIONAL OR LOCAL AUTHORITIES OR BY A PUBLIC INTERNATIONAL BODY

[Essentially the same as A.(1) and (5) supra.]

* * *

[This directive, the following Directive 82/121 and several supplemental directives, have been consolidated without substantial amendment, in Directive 2001/34/EC of the European Parliament and of the Council, O.J. L 184/66 (July 6, 2001).]

3. COUNCIL DIRECTIVE 82/121/EEC

of 15 February 1982

on information to be published on a regular basis by companies the shares of which have been admitted to official stock-exchange listing

O.J. L 48/26 (Feb. 20, 1982)

THE COUNCIL OF THE EUROPEAN COMMUNITIES,

Having regard to the Treaty establishing the European Economic Community, and in particular Articles 54(3)(g) and 100 thereof,

Having regard to the proposal from the Commission,

Having regard to the opinion of the European Parliament,

Having regard to the opinion of the Economic and Social Committee,

* * *

Whereas, in the case of securities admitted to official stock-exchange listing, the protection of investors requires that the latter be supplied with appropriate regular information throughout the entire period during which the securities are listed; whereas coordination of requirements for this regular information has similar objectives to those envisaged for the listing particulars, namely to improve such protection and to make it more equivalent, to facilitate the listing of these securities on more than one stock exchange in the Community, and in so doing to contribute towards the establishment of a genuine Community capital market by permitting a fuller interpenetration of securities markets;

Whereas, under Council Directive 79/279/EEC of 5 March 1979 coordinating the conditions for the admission of securities to official stock-exchange listing, listed companies must as soon as possible make available to investors their annual accounts and report giving information on the company for the whole of the financial year; whereas the fourth Directive 78/660/EEC has coordinated the laws, regulations and administrative provisions of the Member States concerning the annual accounts of certain types of companies;

Whereas companies should also, at least once during each financial year, make available to investors reports on their activities; whereas this Directive can, consequently, be confined to coordinating the content and distribution of a single report covering the first six months of the financial year;

* * *

Whereas the half-yearly report must enable investors to make an informed appraisal of the general development of the company's activities during the period covered by the report; whereas, however, this report need contain only the essential details on the financial position and general progress of the business of the company in question;

* * *

Whereas, so as to ensure the effective protection of investors and the proper operation of stock exchanges, the rules relating to regular information to be published by companies, the shares of which are admitted to official stock-exchange listing within the Community, should apply not only to companies from Member States, but also to companies from non-member countries

HAS ADOPTED THIS DIRECTIVE:

SECTION 1
GENERAL PROVISIONS AND SCOPE

Article 1

1. This Directive shall apply to companies the shares of which are admitted to official listing on a stock exchange situated or operating in a Member State, whether the admission is of the shares themselves or of certificates representing them and whether such admission precedes or follows the date on which this Directive enters into force.

2. This Directive shall not, however, apply to investment companies other than those of the closed-end type.

* * *

Article 2

The Member States shall ensure that the companies publish half-yearly reports on their activities and profits and losses during the first six months of each financial year.

Article 3

The Member States may subject companies to obligations more stringent than those provided for by this Directive or to additional obligations, provided that they apply generally to all companies or to all companies of a given class.

SECTION II
PUBLICATION AND CONTENTS OF THE HALF–YEARLY REPORT

Article 4

1. The half-yearly report shall be published within four months of the end of the relevant six-month period.

2. In exceptional, duly substantiated cases, the competent authorities shall be permitted to extend the time limit for publication.

Article 5

1. The half-yearly report shall consist of figures and an explanatory statement relating to the company's activities and profits and losses during the relevant six-month period.

2. The figures, presented in table form shall indicate at least:

— the net turnover, and

— the profit or loss before or after deduction of tax.

These terms shall have the same meanings as in the Council Directives on company accounts.

3. The Member States may allow the competent authorities to authorize companies, exceptionally and on a case-by-case basis, to supply estimated figures for profits and losses, provided that the shares of each such company are listed officially in only one Member State. The use of this procedure must be indicated by the company in its report and must not mislead investors.

4. Where the company has paid or proposes to pay an interim dividend, the figures must indicate the profit or loss after tax for the six-month period and the interim dividend paid or proposed.

5. Against each figure there must be shown the figure for the corresponding period in the preceding financial year.

6. The explanatory statement must include any significant information enabling investors to make an informed assessment of the trend of the company's activities and profits or losses together with an indication of any special factor which has influenced those activities and those profits or losses during the period in question, and enable a comparison to be made with the corresponding period of the preceding financial year.

It must also, as far as possible, refer to the company's likely future development in the current financial year.

7. Where the figures provided for in paragraph 2 are unsuited to the company's activities, the competent authorities shall ensure that appropriate adjustments are made.

Article 6

Where a company publishes consolidated accounts it may publish its half-yearly report in either consolidated or unconsolidated form. However, the Member States may allow the competent authorities, where the latter consider that the form not adopted would have contained additional material information, to require the company to publish such information.

Article 7

1. The half-yearly report must be published in the Member State or Member States where the shares are admitted to official listing by insertion in one or more newspapers distributed throughout the State or widely distributed therein or in the national gazette, or shall be made available to the public either in writing in places indicated by announcement to be published in one or more newspapers distributed throughout the State or widely distributed therein, or by other equivalent means approved by the competent authorities.

* * *

3. The company shall send a copy of its half-yearly report simultaneously to the competent authorities of each Member State in which its shares are admitted to official listing. It shall do so not later than the time when the half-yearly report is published for the first time in a Member State.

Article 8

Where the accounting information has been audited by the official auditor of the company's accounts, that auditor's report and any qualifications he may have shall be reproduced in full.

SECTION III
POWERS OF THE COMPETENT AUTHORITIES

Article 9

1. Member States shall appoint one or more competent authorities and shall notify the Commission of the appointment of such authorities, giving details of any division of powers among them. Member States shall also ensure that this Directive is applied.

2. The Member States shall ensure that the competent authorities have the necessary powers to carry out their task.

* * *

SECTION IV
COOPERATION BETWEEN MEMBER STATES

Article 10

1. The competent authorities shall cooperate whenever necessary for the purpose of carrying out their duties and shall exchange any information required for that purpose.

2. Where a half-yearly report has to be published in more than one Member State, the competent authorities of these Member States shall, by way of derogation from Article 3, use their best endeavours to accept as a single text the text which meets the requirements of the Member State in which the company's shares were admitted to official listing for the first time or the text which most closely approximates to that text.

* * *

Article 13

This Directive is addressed to the Member States.

Article 27

This Directive is addressed to the Member States.

[This directive, the preceding Directive 79/279 and several supplemental directives, have been consolidated without substantial amendment in Directive 2001/34/EC of the European Parliament and of the Council, O.J. L 184/66 (July 6, 2001).]

4. COUNCIL DIRECTIVE 89/592/EEC

of 13 November 1989

coordinating regulations on insider dealing

O.J. L 334/30 (Nov. 18, 1989)

THE COUNCIL OF THE EUROPEAN COMMUNITIES,

Having regard to the Treaty establishing the European Economic Community, and in particular Article 100a thereof,

Having regard to the proposal from the Commission,[1]

In cooperation with the European Parliament,[2]

Having regard to the opinion of the Economic and Social Committee,[3]

Whereas Article 100a(1) of the Treaty states that the Council shall adopt the measures for the approximation of the provisions laid down by law, regulation or administrative action in Member States which have as their object the establishment and functioning of the internal market;

Whereas the secondary market in transferable securities plays an important role in the financing of economic agents;

Whereas, for that market to be able to play its role effectively, every measure should be taken to ensure that market operates smoothly;

Whereas the smooth operation of that market depends to a large extent on the confidence it inspires in investors;

Whereas the factors on which such confidence depends include the assurance afforded to investors that they are placed on an equal footing and that they will be protected against the improper use of inside information;

Whereas, by benefiting certain investors as compared with others, insider dealing is likely to undermine that confidence and may therefore prejudice the smooth operation of the market;

Whereas the necessary measures should therefore be taken to combat insider dealing;

Whereas in some Member States there are no rules or regulations prohibiting insider dealing and whereas the rules or regulations that do exist differ considerably from one Member State to another;

Whereas it is therefore advisable to adopt coordinated rules at a Community level in this field;

Whereas such coordinated rules also have the advantage of making it possible, through cooperation by the competent authorities, to combat transfrontier insider dealing more effectively;

* * *

---

1. OJ No. C 153, 11.6.1987, p. 8 and OJ No. C 277, 27.10.1988, p. 13.
2. OJ No. C 187, 18.7.1987, p. 93.
3. OJ No. C 35, 8.2.1989, p. 22.

Whereas estimates developed from publicly available data cannot be regarded as inside information and whereas, therefore, any transaction carried out on the basis of such estimates does not constitute insider dealing within the meaning of this Directive;

* * *

HAS ADOPTED THIS DIRECTIVE:

Article 1

For the purposes of this Directive:

1. 'inside information' shall mean information which has not been made public of a precise nature relating to one or several issuers of transferable securities or to one or several transferable securities, which, if it were made public, would be likely to have a significant effect on the price of the transferable security or securities in question;

2. 'transferable securities' shall mean:

(a) shares and debt securities, as well as securities equivalent to shares and debt securities;

(b) contracts or rights to subscribe for, acquire or dispose of securities referred to in (a);

(c) futures contracts, options and financial futures in respect of securities referred to in (a);

(d) index contracts in respect of securities referred to in (a),

when admitted to trading on a market which is regulated and supervised by authorities recognized by public bodies, operates regularly and is accessible directly or indirectly to the public.

Article 2

1. Each Member State shall prohibit any person who:

— by virtue of his membership of the administrative, management or supervisory bodies of the issuer,

— by virtue of his holding in the capital of the issuer, or

— because he has access to such information by virtue of the exercise of his employment, profession or duties,

possesses inside information from taking advantage of that information with full knowledge of the facts by acquiring or disposing of for his own account or for the account of a third party, either directly or indirectly, transferable securities of the issuer or issuers to which that information relates.

2. Where the person referred to in paragraph 1 is a company or other type of legal person, the prohibition laid down in that paragraph shall apply to the natural persons who take part in the decision to carry out the transaction for the account of the legal person concerned.

3. The prohibition laid down in paragraph 1 shall apply to any acquisition or disposal of transferable securities effected through a professional intermediary.

Each Member State may provide that this prohibition shall not apply to acquisitions or disposals of transferable securities effected without the involvement of a professional intermediary outside a market as defined in Article 1(2) *in fine*.

4. This Directive shall not apply to transactions carried out in pursuit of monetary, exchange-rate or public debt-management policies by a sovereign State, by its central bank or any other body designated to that effect by the State, or by any person acting on their behalf. Member States may extend this exemption to their federated States or similar local authorities in respect of the management of their public debt.

Article 3

Each Member State shall prohibit any person subject to the prohibition laid down in Article 2 who possesses inside information from:

(a) disclosing that inside information to any third party unless such disclosure is made in the normal course of the exercise of his employment, profession or duties;

(b) recommending or procuring a third party, on the basis of that inside information, to acquire or dispose of transferable securities admitted to trading on its securities markets as referred to in Article 1(2) *in fine*.

Article 4

Each Member State shall also impose the prohibition provided for in Article 2 on any person other than those referred to in that Article who with full knowledge of the facts possesses inside information, the direct or indirect source of which could not be other than a person referred to in Article 2.

Article 5

Each Member State shall apply the prohibitions provided for in Articles 2, 3 and 4, at least to actions undertaken within its territory to the extent that the transferable securities concerned are admitted to trading on a market of a Member State. In any event, each Member State shall regard a transaction as carried out within its territory if it is carried out on a market, as defined in Article 1(2) *in fine*, situated or operating within that territory.

Article 6

Each Member State may adopt provisions more stringent than those laid down by this Directive or additional provisions, provided that such provisions are applied generally. In particular it may extend the scope of the prohibition laid down in Article 2 and impose on persons referred to in Article 4 the prohibitions laid down in Article 3.

Article 7

The provisions of Schedule C.5(a) of the Annex to Directive 79/279/EEC shall also apply to companies and undertakings the transferable securities of which, whatever their nature, are admitted to trading on a market as referred to in Article 1(2) *in fine* of this Directive.

Article 8

1. Each Member State shall designate the administrative authority or authorities competent, if necessary in collaboration with other authorities to ensure that the provisions adopted pursuant to this Directive are applied. It shall so inform the Commission which shall transmit that information to all Member States.

2. The competent authorities must be given all supervisory and investigatory powers that are necessary for the exercise of their functions, where appropriate in collaboration with other authorities.

Article 9

Each Member State shall provide that all persons employed or formerly employed by the competent authorities referred to in Article 8 shall be bound by professional secrecy. Information covered by professional secrecy may not be divulged to any person or authority except by virtue of provisions laid down by law.

Article 10

1. The competent authorities in the Member States shall cooperate with each other whenever necessary for the purpose of carrying out their duties, making use of the powers mentioned in Article 8(2). To this end, and notwithstanding Article 9, they shall exchange any information required for that purpose, including information relating to actions prohibited, under the options given to Member States by Article 5 and by the second sentence of Article 6, only by the Member State requesting cooperation. Information thus exchanged shall be covered by the obligation of professional secrecy to which the persons employed or formerly employed by the competent authorities receiving the information are subject.

2. The competent authorities may refuse to act on a request for information:

(a) where communication of the information might adversely affect the sovereignty, security or public policy of the State addressed;

(b) where judicial proceedings have already been initiated in respect of the same actions and against the same persons before the authorities of the State addressed or where final judgment has already been passed on such persons for the same actions by the competent authorities of the State addressed.

3. Without prejudice to the obligations to which they are subject in judicial proceedings under criminal law, the authorities which receive information pursuant to paragraph 1 may use it only for the exercise of

their functions within the meaning of Article 8(1) and in the context of administrative or judicial proceedings specifically relating to the exercise of those functions. However, where the competent authority communicating information consents thereto, the authority receiving the information may use it for other purposes or forward it to other States' competent authorities.

Article 11

The Community may, in conformity with the Treaty, conclude agreements with non-member countries on the matters governed by this Directive.

Article 12

The Contact Committee set up by Article 20 of Directive 79/279/EEC shall also have as its function:

(a) to permit regular consultation on any practical problems which arise from the application of this Directive and on which exchanges of view are deemed useful;

(b) to advise the Commission, if necessary, on any additions or amendments to be made to this Directive.

Article 13

Each Member State shall determine the penalties to be applied for infringement of the measures taken pursuant to this Directive. The penalties shall be sufficient to promote compliance with those measures.

Article 14

1. Member States shall take the measures necessary to comply with this Directive before 1 June 1992. They shall forthwith inform the Commission thereof.

2. Member States shall communicate to the Commission the provisions of national law which they adopt in the field governed by this Directive.

Article 15

This Directive is addressed to the Member States.

[The Commission proposed substantial amendments in a draft directive, COM (2001) 281 final, on May 30, 2001.]

5. FIRST COUNCIL DIRECTIVE 77/780/EEC

of 12 December 1977

on the coordination of laws, regulations and administrative provisions relating to the taking up and pursuit of the business of credit institutions

O.J. L 322/30 (Dec. 17, 1977)

THE COUNCIL OF THE EUROPEAN COMMUNITIES,

Having regard to the Treaty establishing the European Economic Community, and in particular Article 57 thereof,

Having regard to the proposal from the Commission,

Having regard to the opinion of the European Parliament,

Having regard to the opinion of the Economic and Social Committee,

* * *

Whereas, in order to make it easier to take up and pursue the business of credit institutions, it is necessary to eliminate the most obstructive differences between the laws of the Member States as regards the rules to which these institutions are subject;

Whereas, however, given the extent of these differences, the conditions required for a common market for credit institutions cannot be created by means of a single Directive; whereas it is therefore necessary to proceed by successive stages; whereas the result of this process should be to provide for overall supervision of a credit institution operating in several Member States by the competent authorities in the Member State where it has its head office, in consultation, as appropriate, with the competent authorities of the other Member States concerned;

Whereas measures to coordinate credit institutions must, both in order to protect savings and to create equal conditions of competition between these institutions, apply to all of them; whereas due regard must be had, where applicable, to the objective differences in their statutes and their proper aims as laid down by national laws;

Whereas the scope of those measures should therefore be as broad as possible, covering all institutions whose business is to receive repayable funds from the public whether in the form of deposits or in other forms such as the continuing issue of bonds and other comparable securities and to grant credits for their own account; whereas exceptions must be provided for in the case of certain credit institutions to which this Directive cannot apply;

* * *

Whereas the rules governing branches of credit institutions having their head office outside the Community should be analogous in all Member States; whereas it is important at the present time to provide that such rules may not be more favourable than those for branches of institutions from another Member State; whereas it should be specified that the

Community may conclude agreements with third countries providing for the application of rules which accord such branches the same treatment throughout its territory, account being taken of the principle of reciprocity;

* * *

HAS ADOPTED THIS DIRECTIVE

TITLE 1

DEFINITIONS AND SCOPE

Article 1

For the purposes of this Directive

— 'credit institution' means an undertaking whose business is to receive deposits or other repayable funds from the public and to grant credits for its own account,

— 'authorization' means an instrument issued in any form by the authorities by which the right to carry on the business of a credit institution is granted,

— 'branch' means a place of business which forms a legally dependent part of a credit institution and which conducts directly all or some of the operations inherent in the business of credit institutions; any number of branches set up in the same Member State by a credit institution having its head office in another Member State shall be regarded as a single branch, without prejudice to Article 4(1),

— 'own funds' means the credit institution's own capital, including items which may be treated as capital under national rules.

Article 2

1. This Directive shall apply to the taking up and pursuit of the business of credit institutions.

2. It shall not apply to:

— the central banks of Member States.

— post office giro institutions.

[— listed savings banks and credit unions in each of the Member States.]

TITLE II

CREDIT INSTITUTIONS HAVING THEIR HEAD OFFICE IN A MEMBER STATE AND THEIR BRANCHES IN OTHER MEMBER STATES

Article 3

[Essentially replaced by the Second Directive.]

1. Member States shall require credit institutions subject to this Directive to obtain authorization before commencing their activities. They shall lay down the requirements for such authorization subject to para-

graphs 2, 3 and 4 and notify them to both the Commission and the Advisory Committee.

2. Without prejudice to other conditions of general application laid down by national laws, the competent authorities shall grant authorization only when the following conditions are complied with:

— the credit institution must possess separate own funds,

— the credit institution must possess adequate minimum own funds,

— there shall be at least two persons who effectively direct the business of the credit institution.

Moreover, the authorities concerned shall not grant authorization if the persons referred to in the third indent of the first subparagraph are not of sufficiently good repute or lack sufficient experience to perform such duties.

3. (a) The provisions referred to in paragraphs 1 and 2 may not require the application for authorization to be examined in terms of the economic needs of the market.

* * *

4. Member States shall also require applications for authorization to be accompanied by a programme of operations setting out *inter alia* the types of business envisaged and the structural organization of the institution.

* * *

7. Every authorization shall be notified to the Commission. Each credit institution shall be entered in a list which the Commission shall publish in the *Official Journal of the European Communities* and shall keep up to date.

Article 4

[Repealed by the Second Directive.]

1. Member States may make the commencement of business in their territory by branches of credit institutions covered by this Directive which have their head office in another Member State subject to authorization according to the law and procedure applicable to credit institutions established on their territory.

2. However, authorization may not be refused to a branch of a credit institution on the sole ground that it is established in another Member State in a legal form which is not allowed in the case of a credit institution carrying out similar activities in the host country. * * *

Article 5

For the purpose of exercising their activities, credit institutions to which this Directive applies may, notwithstanding any provisions concerning the use of the words 'bank', 'saving bank' or other banking names which may exist in the host Member State, use throughout the territory of the Community the same name as they use in the Member States in which their head office is situated. In the event of there being any danger of confusion, the host Member State may, for the purposes of clarification, require that the name be accompanied by certain explanatory particulars.

Article 6

[Replaced by Directives 89/299/EEC and 89/647/ EEC.]

1. Pending subsequent coordination, the competent authorities shall, for the purposes of observation and, if necessary, in addition to such coefficients as may be applied by them, establish ratios between the various assets and/or liabilities of credit institutions with a view to monitoring their solvency and liquidity and the other measures which may serve to ensure that savings are protected.

* * *

Article 7

[Amended by Second Directive.]

1. The competent authorities of the Member States concerned shall collaborate closely in order to supervise the activities of credit institutions operating, in particular by having established branches there, in one or more Member States other than that in which their head offices are situated. They shall supply one another with all information concerning the management and ownership of such credit institutions that is likely to facilitate their supervision and the examination of the conditions for their authorization and all information likely to facilitate the monitoring of their liquidity and solvency.

* * *

Article 8

[Modified by Second Directive.]

1. The competent authorities may withdraw the authorization issued to a credit institution subject to this Directive or to a branch authorized under Article 4 only where such an institution or branch:

(a) does not make use of the authorization within 12 months, expressly renounces the authorization or has ceased to engage in business for more than six months, if the Member State concerned has made no provision for the authorization to lapse in such cases;

(b) has obtained the authorization through false statements or any other irregular means;

(c) no longer fulfils the conditions under which authorization was granted, with the exception of those in respect of own funds;

(d) no longer possesses sufficient own funds or can no longer be relied upon to fulfil its obligations towards its creditors, and in particular no longer provides security for the assets entrusted to it;

(e) falls within one of the other cases where national law provides for withdrawal of authorization.

2. In addition, the authorization issued to a branch under Article 4 shall be withdrawn if the competent authority of the country in which the credit institution which established the branch has its head office has withdrawn authorization from that institution.

* * *

5. Reasons must be given for any withdrawal of authorization and those concerned informed thereof; such withdrawal shall be notified to the Commission.

TITLE III

BRANCHES OF CREDIT INSTITUTIONS HAVING THEIR HEAD OFFICES OUTSIDE THE COMMUNITY

Article 9

1. Member States shall not apply to branches of credit institutions having their head office outside the Community, when commencing or carrying on their business, provisions which result in more favourable treatment than that accorded to branches of credit institutions having their head office in the Community.

2. The competent authorities shall notify the Commission and the Advisory Committee of all authorizations for branches granted to credit institutions having their head office outside the Community.

3. Without prejudice to paragraph 1, the Community may, through agreements concluded in accordance with the Treaty with one or more third countries, agree to apply provisions which, on the basis of the principle of reciprocity, accord to branches of a credit institution having its head office outside the Community identical treatment throughout the territory of the Community.

TITLE IV

GENERAL AND TRANSITIONAL PROVISIONS

Article 10

1. Credit institutions subject to this Directive, which took up their business in accordance with the provisions of the Member States in which they have their head offices before the entry into force of the provisions implementing this Directive shall be deemed to be authorized. They shall be subject to the provisions of this Directive concerning the carrying on of the business of credit institutions and to the requirements set out in the first and third indents of the first subparagraph and in the second subparagraph of Article 3(2).

* * *

Article 11

1. An 'Advisory Committee of the Competent Authorities of the Member States of the European Economic Community' shall be set up alongside the Commission.

2. The tasks of the Advisory Committee shall be to assist the Commission in ensuring the proper implementation of both this Directive and Council Directive 73/183/EEC of 28 June 1973 on the abolition of restrictions on freedom of establishment and freedom to provide services in respect of self-employed activities of banks and other financial institutions in so far as it relates to credit institutions. Further it shall carry out the other tasks prescribed by this Directive and shall assist the Commission in the preparation of new proposals to the Council concerning further coordination in the sphere of credit institutions.

3. The Advisory Committee shall not concern itself with concrete problems relating to individual credit institutions.

4. The Advisory Committee shall be composed of not more than three representatives from each Member State and from the Commission. These representatives may be accompanied by advisers * * * subject to the prior agreement of the Committee. The Committee may also invite qualified persons and experts to participate in its meetings. The secretariat shall be provided by the Commission.

* * *

Article 13

Member States shall ensure that decisions taken in respect of a credit institution in pursuance of laws, regulations and administrative provisions adopted in accordance with this Directive may be subject to the right to apply to the courts. The same shall apply where no decision is taken within six months of its submission in respect of an application for authorization which contains all the information required under the provisions in force.

TITLE V

FINAL PROVISIONS

* * *

Article 15

This Directive is addressed to the Member States.

6. SECOND COUNCIL DIRECTIVE 89/646/EEC

of 15 December 1989

on the coordination of laws, regulations and administrative provisions relating to the taking up and pursuit of the business of credit institutions and amending Directive 77/780/EEC

O.J. L 386/1 (Dec. 30, 1989)

THE COUNCIL OF THE EUROPEAN COMMUNITIES,

Having regard to the Treaty establishing the European Economic Community, and in particular the first and third sentences of Article 57(2) thereof,

Having regard to the proposal from the Commission,[1]

In cooperation with the European Parliament,[2]

Having regard to the opinion of the Economic and Social Committee,[3]

Whereas this Directive is to constitute the essential instrument for the achievement of the internal market, a course determined by the Single European Act and set out in timetable form in the Commission's White Paper, from the point of view of both the freedom of establishment and the freedom to provide financial services, in the field of credit institutions;

Whereas this Directive will join the body of Community legislation already enacted, in particular the first Council Directive 77/780/EEC of 12 December 1977, Council Directive 83/350/EEC of 13 June 1983 on the supervision of credit institutions on a consolidated basis,[6] Council Directive 86/635/EEC of 8 December 1986 on the annual and consolidated accounts of banks and other financial institutions[7] and Council Directive 89/299/EEC of 17 April 1989 on the own funds of credit institutions;[8]

Whereas the Commission has adopted recommendations 87/62/EEC on large exposures of credit institutions[9] and 87/63/EEC concerning the introduction of deposit-guarantee schemes;[10]

Whereas the approach which has been adopted is to achieve only the essential harmonization necessary and sufficient to secure the mutual recognition of authorization and of prudential supervision systems, making possible the granting of a single licence recognized throughout the Community and the application of the principle of home Member State prudential supervision;

Whereas, in this context, this Directive can be implemented only simultaneously with specific Community legislation dealing with the addi-

1. OJ No C 84, 31.3.1988, p. 1.
2. OJ No C 96, 17.4.1989, p. 33.
3. OJ No C 318, 17.12.1988, p. 42.
6. OJ No L 193, 18.7.1983, p. 18.
7. OJ No L 372, 31.12.1986, p. 1.
8. OJ No L 124, 5.5.1989, p. 16.
9. OJ No L 33, 4.2.1987, p. 10.
10. OJ No L 33, 4.2.1987, p. 16.

tional harmonization of technical matters relating to own funds and solvency ratios;

Whereas, moreover, the harmonization of the conditions relating to the reorganization and winding-up of credit institutions is also proceeding;

Whereas the arrangements necessary for the supervision of the liquidity, market, interest-rate and foreign-exchange risks run by credit institutions will also have to be harmonized;

Whereas the principles of mutual recognition and of home Member State control require the competent authorities of each Member State not to grant authorization or to withdraw it where factors such as the activities programme, the geographical distribution or the activities actually carried on make it quite clear that a credit institution has opted for the legal system of one Member State for the purpose of evading the stricter standards in force in another Member State in which it intends to carry on or carries on the greater part of its activities; whereas, for the purposes of this Directive, a credit institution shall be deemed to be situated in the Member State in which it has its registered office; whereas the Member States must require that the head office be situated in the same Member State as the registered office;

Whereas the home Member State may also establish rules stricter than those laid down in Articles 4, 5, 11, 12 and 16 for institutions authorized by its competent authorities;

Whereas responsibility for supervising the financial soundness of a credit institution, and in particular its solvency, will rest with the competent authorities of its home Member State; whereas the host Member State's competent authorities will retain responsibility for the supervision of liquidity and monetary policy; whereas the supervision of market risk must be the subject of close cooperation between the competent authorities of the home and host Member States;

Whereas the harmonization of certain financial and investment services will be effected, where the need exists, by specific Community instruments, with the intention, in particular, of protecting consumers and investors; whereas the Commission has proposed measures for the harmonization of mortgage credit in order, *inter alia,* to allow mutual recognition of the financial techniques peculiar to that sphere;

Whereas, by virtue of mutual recognition, the approach chosen permits credit institutions authorized in their home Member States to carry on, throughout the Community, any or all of the activities listed in the Annex by establishing branches or by providing services;

Whereas the carrying-on of activities not listed in the Annex shall enjoy the right of establishment and the freedom to provide services under the general provisions of the Treaty;

Whereas it is appropriate, however, to extend mutual recognition to the activities listed in the Annex when they are carried on by financial institutions which are subsidiaries of credit institutions, provided that such subsidiaries are covered by the consolidated supervision of their parent undertakings and meet certain strict conditions;

Whereas the host Member State may, in connection with the exercise of the right of establishment and the freedom to provide services, require compliance with specific provisions of its own national laws or regulations on the part of institutions not authorized as credit institutions in their home Member States and with regard to activities not listed in the Annex provided that, on the one hand, such provisions are compatible with Community law and are intended to protect the general good and that, on the other hand, such institutions or such activities are not subject to equivalent rules under the legislation or regulations of their home Member States;

Whereas the Member States must ensure that there are no obstacles to carrying on activities receiving mutual recognition in the same manner as in the home Member State, as long as the latter do not conflict with legal provisions protecting the general good in the host Member State;

Whereas the abolition of the authorization requirement with respect to the branches of Community credit institutions once the harmonization in progress has been completed necessitates the abolition of endowment capital; whereas Article 6(2) constitutes a first transitional step in this direction, but does not, however, affect the Kingdom of Spain or the Portuguese Republic, as provided for in the Act concerning the conditions of those States' accession to the Community;

Whereas there is a necessary link between the objective of this Directive and the liberalization of capital movements being brought about by other Community legislation; whereas in any case the measures regarding the liberalization of banking services must be in harmony with the measures liberalizing capital movements; whereas where the Member States may, by virtue of Council Directive 88/361/EEC of 24 June 1988 for the implementation of Article 67 of the Treaty,[1] invoke safeguard clauses in respect of capital movements, they may suspend the provision of banking services to the extent necessary for the implementation of the abovementioned safeguard clauses;

Whereas the procedures established in Directive 77/780/EEC, in particular with regard to the authorization of branches of credit institutions authorized in third countries, will continue to apply to such institutions; whereas those branches will not enjoy the freedom to provide services under the second paragraph of Article 59 of the Treaty or the freedom of establishment in Member States other than those in which they are established; whereas, however, requests for the authorization of subsidiaries or of the acquisition of holdings made by undertakings governed by the laws of third countries are subject to a procedure intended to ensure that Community credit institutions receive reciprocal treatment in the third countries in question;

1. OJ No L 178, 8.7.1988, p. 5.

Whereas the authorizations granted to credit institutions by the competent national authorities pursuant to this Directive will have Community-wide, and no longer merely nationwide, application, and whereas existing reciprocity clauses will henceforth have no effect; whereas a flexible procedure is therefore needed to make it possible to assess reciprocity on a Community basis; whereas the aim of this procedure is not to close the Community's financial markets but rather, as the Community intends to keep its financial markets open to the rest of the world, to improve the liberalization of the global financial markets in other third countries; whereas, to that end, this Directive provides for procedures for negotiating with third countries and, as a last resort, for the possibility of taking measures involving the suspension of new applications for authorization or the restriction of new authorizations;

Whereas the smooth operation of the internal banking market will require not only legal rules but also close and regular cooperation between the competent authorities of the Member States; whereas for the consideration of problems concerning individual credit institutions the Contact Committee set up between the banking supervisory authorities, referred to in the final recital of Directive 77/780/EEC, remains the most appropriate forum; whereas that Committee is a suitable body for the mutual exchange of information provided for in Article 7 of that Directive;

Whereas that mutual information procedure will not in any case replace the bilateral collaboration established by Article 7 of Directive 77/780/EEC; whereas the competent host Member State authorities can, without prejudice to their powers of control proper, continue either, in an emergency, on their own initiative or following the initiative of the competent home Member State authorities to verify that the activities of a credit institution established within their territories comply with the relevant laws and with the principles of sound administrative and accounting procedures and adequate internal control;

Whereas technical modifications to the detailed rules laid down in this Directive may from time to time be necessary to take account of new developments in the banking sector; whereas the Commission shall accordingly make such modifications as are necessary, after consulting the Banking Advisory Committee, within the limits of the implementing powers conferred on the Commission by the Treaty; whereas that Committee shall act as a 'Regulatory' Committee, according to the rules of procedure laid down in Article 2, procedure III, variant (b), of Council Decision 87/373/EEC of 13 July 1987 laying down the procedures for the exercise of implementing powers conferred on the Commission,[1]

HAS ADOPTED THIS DIRECTIVE:

TITLE I
DEFINITIONS AND SCOPE
Article 1

For the purpose of this Directive:

1. 'credit institution' shall mean a credit institution as defined in the first indent of Article 1 of Directive 77/780/EEC;

---

1. OJ No L 197, 18.7.1987, p. 33.

2. 'authorization' shall mean authorization as defined in the second indent of Article 1 of Directive 77/780/EEC;

3. 'branch' shall mean a place of business which forms a legally dependent part of a credit institution and which carries out directly all or some of the transactions inherent in the business of credit institutions; any number of places of business set up in the same Member State by a credit institution with headquarters in another Member State shall be regarded as a single branch;

4. 'own funds' shall mean own funds as defined in Directive 89/299/EEC;

5. 'competent authorities' shall mean competent authorities as defined in Article 1 of Directive 83/350/EEC;

6. 'financial institution' shall mean an undertaking other than a credit institution the principal activity of which is to acquire holdings or to carry on one or more of the activities listed in points 2 to 12 in the Annex;

7. 'home Member State' shall mean the Member State in which a credit institution has been authorized in accordance with Article 3 of Directive 77/780/EEC;

8. 'host Member State' shall mean the Member State in which a credit institution has a branch or in which it provides services;

9. 'control' shall mean the relationship between a parent undertaking and a subsidiary, as defined in Article 1 of Directive 83/349/EEC,[2] or a similar relationship between any natural or legal person and an undertaking;

10. 'qualifying holding' shall mean a direct or indirect holding in an undertaking which represents 10% or more of the capital or of the voting rights or which makes it possible to exercise a significant influence over the management of the undertaking in which a holding subsists.

For the purposes of this definition, in the context of Articles 5 and 11 and of the other levels of holding referred to in Article 11, the voting rights referred to in Article 7 of Directive 88/627/EEC,[3] shall be taken into consideration;

11. 'initial capital' shall mean capital as defined in Article 2(1)(1) and (2) of Directive 89/299/EEC;

12. 'parent undertaking' shall mean a parent undertaking as defined in Articles 1 and 2 of Directive 83/349/EEC;

13. 'subsidiary' shall mean a subsidiary undertaking as defined in Articles 1 and 2 of Directive 83/349/EEC; any subsidiary of a subsidiary undertaking shall also be regarded as a subsidiary of the parent undertaking which is at the head of those undertakings;

2. OJ No L 193, 18.7.1983, p. 1.   3. OJ No L 348, 17.12.1988, p. 62.

14. 'solvency ratio' shall mean the solvency coefficient of credit institutions calculated in accordance with Directive 89/647/EEC[1].

Article 2

1. This Directive shall apply to all credit institutions.

2. It shall not apply to the institutions referred to in Article 2(2) of Directive 77/780/EEC.

* * *

Article 3

The Member States shall prohibit persons or undertakings that are not credit institutions from carrying on the business of taking deposits or other repayable funds from the public. This prohibition shall not apply to the taking of deposits or other funds repayable by a Member State or by a Member State's regional or local authorities or by public international bodies of which one or more Member States are members or to cases expressly covered by national or Community legislation, provided that those activities are subject to regulations and controls intended to protect depositors and investors and applicable to those cases.

TITLE II

HARMONIZATION OF AUTHORIZATION CONDITIONS

Article 4

1. The competent authorities shall not grant authorization in cases where initial capital is less than ECU 5 million.

2. The Member States shall, however, have the option of granting authorization to particular categories of credit institutions the initial capital of which is less than that prescribed in paragraph 1. In such cases:

(a) the initial capital shall not be less than ECU 1 million * * *.

Article 5

The competent authorities shall not grant authorization for the taking-up of the business of credit institutions before they have been informed of the identities of the shareholders or members, whether direct or indirect, natural or legal persons, that have qualifying holdings, and of the amounts of those holdings.

The competent authorities shall refuse authorization if, taking into account the need to ensure the sound and prudent management of a credit institution, they are not satisfied as to the suitability of the abovementioned shareholders or members.

Article 6

1. Host Member States may no longer require authorization, as provided for in Article 4 of Directive 77/780/EEC, or endowment capital for

---

1. OJ L 386, 30.12.1989, p. 14.

branches of credit institutions authorized in other Member States. The establishment and supervision of such branches shall be effected as prescribed in Articles 13, 19 and 21 of this Directive.

2. Until the entry into force of the provisions implementing paragraph 1, host Member States may not, as a condition of the authorization of branches of credit institutions, authorized in other Member States, require initial endowment capital exceeding 50% of the initial capital required by national rules for the authorization of credit institutions of the same nature.

3. Credit institutions shall be entitled to the free use of the funds no longer required pursuant to paragraphs 1 and 2.

Article 7

There must be prior consultation with the competent authorities of the other Member State involved on the authorization of a credit institution which is:

— a subsidiary of a credit institution authorized in another Member State, or

— a subsidiary of the parent undertaking of a credit institution authorized in another Member State, or

— controlled by the same persons, whether natural or legal, as control a credit institution authorized in another Member State.

TITLE III
RELATIONS WITH THIRD COUNTRIES

Article 8

The competent authorities of the Member States shall inform the Commission:

> (a) of any authorization of a direct or indirect subsidiary one or more parent undertakings of which are governed by the laws of a third country. The Commission shall inform the Banking Advisory Committee accordingly;
>
> (b) whenever such a parent undertaking acquires a holding in a Community credit institution such that the latter would become its subsidiary. The Commission shall inform the Banking Advisory Committee accordingly.

When authorization is granted to the direct or indirect subsidiary of one or more parent undertakings governed by the law of third countries, the structure of the group shall be specified in the notification which the competent authorities shall address to the Commission in accordance with Article 3(7) of Directive 77/780/EEC.

Article 9

1. The Member States shall inform the Commission of any general difficulties encountered by their credit institutions in establishing themselves or carrying on banking activities in a third country.

2. Initially no later than six months before the application of this Directive and thereafter periodically, the Commission shall draw up a report examining the treatment accorded to Community credit institutions in third countries, in the terms referred to in paragraphs 3 and 4, as regards establishment and the carrying-on of banking activities, and the acquisition of holdings in third-country credit institutions. The Commission shall submit those reports to the Council, together with any appropriate proposals.

3. Whenever it appears to the Commission, either on the basis of the reports referred to in paragraph 2 or on the basis of other information, that a third country is not granting Community credit institutions effective market access comparable to that granted by the Community to credit institutions from that third country, the Commission may submit proposals to the Council for the appropriate mandate for negotiation with a view to obtaining comparable competitive opportunities for Community credit institutions. The Council shall decide by a qualified majority.

4. Whenever it appears to the Commission, either on the basis of the reports referred to in paragraph 2 or on the basis of other information that Community credit institutions in a third country do not receive national treatment offering the same competitive opportunities as are available to domestic credit institutions and the conditions of effective market access are not fulfilled, the Commission may initiate negotiations in order to remedy the situation.

In the circumstances described in the first subparagraph, it may also be decided at any time, and in addition to initiating negotiations, in accordance with the procedure laid down in Article 22(2), that the competent authorities of the Member States must limit or suspend their decisions regarding requests pending at the moment of the decision or future requests for authorizations and the acquisition of holdings by direct or indirect parent undertakings governed by the laws of the third country in question. The duration of the measures referred to may not exceed three months.

Before the end of that three-month period, and in the light of the results of the negotiations, the Council may, acting on a proposal from the Commission, decide by a qualified majority whether the measures shall be continued.

Such limitations or suspension may not apply to the setting up of subsidiaries by credit institutions or their subsidiaries duly authorized in the Community, or to the acquisition of holdings in Community credit institutions by such institutions or subsidiaries.

5. Whenever it appears to the Commission that one of the situations described in paragraphs 3 and 4 obtains, the Member States shall inform it at its request:

(a) of any request for the authorization of a direct or indirect subsidiary one or more parent undertakings of which are governed by the laws of the third country in question;

(b) whenever they are informed in accordance with Article 11 that such an undertaking proposes to acquire a holding in a Community credit institution such that the latter would become its subsidiary.

This obligation to provide information shall lapse whenever an agreement is reached with the third country referred to in paragraph 3 or 4 or when the measures referred to in the second and third subparagraphs of paragraph 4 cease to apply.

6. Measures taken pursuant to this Article shall comply with the Community's obligations under any international agreements, bilateral or multilateral, governing the taking-up and pursuit of the business of credit institutions.

TITLE IV

HARMONIZATION OF THE CONDITIONS GOVERNING PURSUIT OF THE BUSINESS OF CREDIT INSTITUTIONS

Article 10

1. A credit institution's own funds may not fall below the amount of initial capital required pursuant to Article 4 at the time of its authorization.

* * *

Article 11

1. The Member States shall require any natural or legal person who proposes to acquire, directly or indirectly a qualifying holding in a credit institution first to inform the competent authorities, telling them of the size of the intended holding. Such a person must likewise inform the competent authorities if he proposes to increase his qualifying holding so that the proportion of the voting rights or of the capital held by him would reach or exceed 20%, 33% or 50% or so that the credit institution would become his subsidiary.

Without prejudice to the provisions of paragraph 2 the competent authorities shall have a maximum of three months from the date of the notification provided for in the first subparagraph to oppose such a plan if, in view of the need to ensure sound and prudent management of the credit institution, they are not satisfied as to the suitability of the person referred to in the first subparagraph. If they do not oppose the plan referred to in the first subparagraph, they may fix a maximum period for its implementation.

2. If the acquirer of the holdings referred to in paragraph 1 is a credit institution authorized in another Member State or the parent undertaking of a credit institution authorized in another Member State or a natural or legal person controlling a credit institution authorized in another Member State and if, as a result of that acquisition, the institution in which the acquirer proposes to acquire a holding would become a subsidiary or subject

to the control of the acquirer, the assessment of the acquisition must be the subject of the prior consultation referred to in Article 7.

3. The Member States shall require any natural or legal person who proposes to dispose, directly or indirectly, of a qualifying holding in a credit institution first to inform the competent authorities, telling them of the size of his intended holding. Such a person must likewise inform the competent authorities if he proposes to reduce his qualifying holding so that the proportion of the voting rights or of the capital held by him would fall below 20%, 33% or 50% or so that the credit institution would cease to be his subsidiary.

4. On becoming aware of them, credit institutions shall inform the competent authorities of any acquisitions or disposals of holdings in their capital that cause holdings to exceed or fall below one of the thresholds referred to in paragraphs 1 and 3.

They shall also, at least once a year, inform them of the names of shareholders and members possessing qualifying holdings and the sizes of such holdings as shown, for example, by the information received at the annual general meetings of shareholders and members or as a result of compliance with the regulations relating to companies listed on stock exchanges.

5. The Member States shall require that, where the influence exercised by the persons referred to in paragraph 1 is likely to operate to the detriment of the prudent and sound management of the institution, the competent authorities shall take appropriate measures to put an end to that situation. Such measures may consist for example in injunctions, sanctions against directors and managers, or the suspension of the exercise of the voting rights attaching to the shares held by the shareholders or members in question.

Similar measures shall apply to natural or legal persons failing to comply with the obligation to provide prior information, as laid down in paragraph 1. If a holding is acquired despite the opposition of the competent authorities, the Member States shall, regardless of any other sanctions to be adopted, provide either for exercise of the corresponding voting rights to be suspended, or for the nullity of votes cast or for the possibility of their annulment.

Article 12

1. No credit institution may have a qualifying holding the amount of which exceeds 15% of its own funds in an undertaking which is neither a credit institution, nor a financial institution, nor an undertaking carrying on an activity referred to in the second subparagraph of Article 43(2)(f) of Directive 86/635/EEC.

2. The total amount of a credit institution's qualifying holdings in undertakings other than credit institutions, financial institutions or undertakings carrying on activities referred to in the second subparagraph of

Article 43(2)(f) of Directive 86/635/EEC may not exceed 60% of its own funds.

3. The Member States need not apply the limits laid down in paragraphs 1 and 2 to holdings in insurance companies as defined in Directive 73/239/EEC,[1] as last amended by Directive 88/357/EEC,[2] and Directive 79/267/EEC,[3] as last amended by the Act of Accession of 1985.

4. Shares held temporarily during a financial reconstruction or rescue operation or during the normal course of underwriting or in an institution's own name on behalf of others shall not be counted as qualifying holdings for the purpose of calculating the limits laid down in paragraphs 1 and 2.

* * *

7. Credit institutions which, on the date of entry into force of the provisions implementing this Directive, exceed the limits laid down in paragraphs 1 and 2 shall have a period of 10 years from that date in which to comply with them.

* * *

Article 13

1. The prudential supervision of a credit institution, including that of the activities it carries on in accordance with Article 18, shall be the responsibility of the competent authorities of the home Member State, without prejudice to those provisions of this Directive which give responsibility to the authorities of the host Member State.

2. Home Member State competent authorities shall require that every credit institution have sound administrative and accounting procedures and adequate internal control mechanisms.

3. Paragraphs 1 and 2 shall not prevent supervision on a consolidated basis pursuant to Directive 83/350/EEC.

Article 14

1. In Article 7(1) of Directive 77/780/EEC, the end of the second sentence is hereby replaced by the following: 'and all information likely to facilitate the monitoring of such institutions, in particular with regard to liquidity, solvency, deposit guarantees, the limiting of large exposures, administrative and accounting procedures and internal control mechanisms'.

2. Host Member States shall retain responsibility in cooperation with the competent authorities of the home Member State for the supervision of the liquidity of the branches of credit institutions pending further coordination. Without prejudice to the measures necessary for the reinforcement of the European Monetary System, host Member States shall retain complete responsibility for the measures resulting from the implementation of their

1. OJ No L 228, 16.8.1973, p. 3.
2. OJ No L 172, 4.7.1988, p. 1.
3. OJ No L 63, 13.3.1979, p. 1.

monetary policies. Such measures may not provide for discriminatory or restrictive treatment based on the fact that a credit institution is authorized in another Member State.

3. Without prejudice to further coordination of the measures designed to supervise the risks arising out of open positions on markets, where such risks result from transactions carried out on the financial markets of other Member States, the competent authorities of the latter shall collaborate with the competent authorities of the home Member State to ensure that the institutions concerned take steps to cover those risks.

Article 15

1. Host Member States shall provide that, where a credit institution authorized in another Member State carries on its activities through a branch, the competent authorities of the home Member State may, after having first informed the competent authorities of the host Member State, carry out themselves or through the intermediary of persons they appoint for that purpose on-the-spot verification of the information referred to in Article 7(1) of Directive 77/780/EEC.

2. The competent authorities of the home Member State may also, for purposes of the verification of branches, have recourse to one of the other procedures laid down in Article 5(4) of Directive 83/350/EEC.

3. This Article shall not affect the right of the competent authorities of the host Member State to carry out, in the discharge of their responsibilities under this Directive, on-the-spot verifications of branches established within their territory.

Article 16

Article 12 of Directive 77/780/EEC is hereby replaced by the following:

Article 12

1. The Member States shall provide that all persons working or who have worked for the competent authorities, as well as auditors or experts acting on behalf of the competent authorities, shall be bound by the obligation of professional secrecy. This means that no confidential information which they may receive in the course of their duties may be divulged to any person or authority whatsoever, except in summary or collective form, such that individual institutions cannot be identified, without prejudice to cases covered by criminal law.

Nevertheless, where a credit institution has been declared bankrupt or is being compulsorily wound up, confidential information which does not concern third parties involved in attempts to rescue that credit institution may be divulged in civil or commercial proceedings.

2. Paragraph 1 shall not prevent the competent authorities of the various Member States from exchanging information in accordance with the Directives applicable to credit institutions. That information shall be subject to the conditions of professional secrecy indicated in paragraph 1.

3. Member States may conclude cooperation agreements, providing for exchanges of information, with the competent authorities of third countries only if the information disclosed is subject to guarantees of professional secrecy at least equivalent to those referred to in this Article.

* * *

Article 17

Without prejudice to the procedures for the withdrawal of authorizations and the provisions of criminal law, the Member States shall provide that their respective competent authorities may, as against credit institutions or those who effectively control the business of credit institutions which breach laws, regulations or administrative provisions concerning the supervision or pursuit of their activities, adopt or impose in respect of them penalties or measures aimed specifically at ending observed breaches or the causes of such breaches.

TITLE V

PROVISIONS RELATING TO THE FREEDOM OF ESTABLISHMENT AND THE FREEDOM TO PROVIDE SERVICES

Article 18

1. The Member States shall provide that the activities listed in the Annex may be carried on within their territories, in accordance with Articles 19 to 21, either by the establishment of a branch or by way of the provision of services, by any credit institution authorized and supervised by the competent authorities of another Member State, in accordance with this Directive, provided that such activities are covered by the authorization.

2. The Member States shall also provide that the activities listed in the Annex may be carried on within their territories, in accordance with Articles 19 to 21, either by the establishment of a branch or by way of the provision of services, by any financial institution from another Member State, whether a subsidiary of a credit institution or the jointly-owned subsidiary of two or more credit institutions, the memorandum and articles of association of which permit the carrying on of those activities and which fulfils each of the following conditions:

— the parent undertaking or undertakings must be authorized as credit institutions in the Member State by the law of which the subsidiary is governed,

— the activities in question must actually be carried on within the territory of the same Member State,

— the parent undertaking or undertakings must hold 90% or more of the voting rights attaching to shares in the capital of the subsidiary,

— the parent undertaking or undertakings must satisfy the competent authorities regarding the prudent management of the subsidiary and must have declared, with the consent of the relevant home Member State competent authorities, that they jointly and severally guarantee the commitments entered into by the subsidiary,

— the subsidiary must be effectively included, for the activities in question in particular, in the consolidated supervision of the parent undertaking, or of each of the parent undertakings, in accordance with Directive 83/350/EEC, in particular for the calculation of the solvency ratio, for the control of large exposures and for purposes of the limitation of holdings provided for in Article 12 of this Directive.

Compliance with these conditions must be verified by the competent authorities of the home Member State and the latter must supply the subsidiary with a certificate of compliance which must form part of the notification referred to in Articles 19 and 20.

* * *

Article 19

1. A credit institution wishing to establish a branch within the territory of another Member State shall notify the competent authorities of its home Member State.

2. The Member State shall require every credit institution wishing to establish a branch in another Member State to provide the following information when effecting the notification referred to in paragraph 1:

(a) the Member State within the territory of which it plans to establish a branch;

(b) a programme of operations setting out inter alia the types of business envisaged and the structural organization of the branch;

(c) the address in the host Member State from which documents may be obtained;

(d) the names of those responsible for the management of the branch.

3. Unless the competent authorities of the home Member State have reason to doubt the adequacy of the administrative structure or the financial situation of the credit institution, taking into account the activities envisaged, they shall within three months of receipt of the information referred to in paragraph 2 communicate that information to the competent authorities of the host Member State and shall inform the institution concerned accordingly.

The home Member State competent authorities shall also communicate the amount of own funds and the solvency ratio of the credit institution and, pending subsequent coordination, details of any deposit-guarantee scheme which is intended to ensure the protection of depositors in the branch.

Where the competent authorities of the home Member State refuse to communicate the information referred to in paragraph 2 to the competent authorities of the host Member State, they shall give reasons for their refusal to the institution concerned within three months of receipt of all the information. That refusal or failure to reply shall be subject to a right to apply to the courts in the home Member State.

4. Before the branch of a credit institution commences its activities the competent authorities of the host Member State shall, within two months of receiving the information mentioned in paragraph 3, prepare for the supervision of the credit institution in accordance with Article 21 and if necessary indicate the conditions under which, in the interest of the general good, those activities must be carried on in the host Member State.

5. On receipt of a communication from the competent authorities of the host Member State, or in the event of the expiry of the period provided for in paragraph 4 without receipt of any communication from the latter, the branch may be established and commence its activities.

6. In the event of a change in any of the particulars communicated pursuant to paragraph 2(b), (c) or (d) or in the deposit-guarantee scheme referred to in paragraph 3 a credit institution shall give written notice of the change in question to the competent authorities of the home and host Member States at least one month before making the change so as to enable the competent authorities of the home Member State to take a decision pursuant to paragraph 3 and the competent authorities of the host Member State to take a decision on the change pursuant to paragraph 4.

Article 20

1. Any credit institution wishing to exercise the freedom to provide services by carrying on its activities within the territory of another Member State for the first time shall notify the competent authorities of the home Member State of the activities on the list in the Annex which it intends to carry on.

2. The competent authorities of the home Member State shall, within one month of receipt of the notification mentioned in paragraph 1, send that notification to the competent authorities of the host Member State.

Article 21

1. Host Member States may, for statistical purposes, require that all credit institutions having branches within their territories shall report periodically on their activities in those host Member States to the competent authorities of those host Member States.

In discharging the responsibilities imposed on them in Article 14(2) and (3), host Member States may require that branches of credit institutions from other Member States provide the same information as they require from national credit institutions for that purpose.

2. Where the competent authorities of a host Member State ascertain that an institution having a branch or providing services within its territo-

ry is not complying with the legal provisions adopted in that State pursuant to the provisions of this Directive involving powers of the host Member State competent authorities, those authorities shall require the institution concerned to put an end to that irregular situation.

3. If the institution concerned fails to take the necessary steps, the competent authorities of the host Member State shall inform the competent authorities of the home Member State accordingly. The competent authorities of the home Member State shall, at the earliest opportunity, take all appropriate measures to ensure that the institution concerned puts an end to that irregular situation. The nature of those measures shall be communicated to the competent authorities of the host Member State.

4. If, despite the measures taken by the home Member State or because such measures prove inadequate or are not available in the Member State in question, the institution persists in violating the legal rules referred to in paragraph 2 in force in the host Member State, the latter State may, after informing the competent authorities of the home Member State, take appropriate measures to prevent or to punish further irregularities and, insofar as is necessary, to prevent that institution from initiating further transactions within its territory. The Member States shall ensure that within their territories it is possible to serve the legal documents necessary for these measures on credit institutions.

5. The foregoing provisions shall not affect the power of host Member States to take appropriate measures to prevent or to punish irregularities committed within their territories which are contrary to the legal rules they have adopted in the interest of the general good. This shall include the possibility of preventing offending institutions from initiating any further transactions within their territories.

6. Any measure adopted pursuant to paragraphs 3, 4 and 5 involving penalties or restrictions on the exercise of the freedom to provide services must be properly justified and communicated to the institution concerned. Every such measure shall be subject to a right of appeal to the courts in the Member State the authorities of which adopted it.

7. Before following the procedure provided for in paragraphs 2 to 4, the competent authorities of the host Member State may, in emergencies, take any precautionary measures necessary to protect the interests of depositors, investors and others to whom services are provided. The Commission and the competent authorities of the other Member States concerned must be informed of such measures at the earliest opportunity.

The Commission may, after consulting the competent authorities of the Member States concerned, decide that the Member State in question must amend or abolish those measures.

8. Host Member States may exercise the powers conferred on them under this Directive by taking appropriate measures to prevent or to punish irregularities committed within their territories. This shall include the possibility of preventing institutions from initiating further transactions within their territories.

9. In the event of the withdrawal of authorization the competent authorities of the host Member State shall be informed and shall take appropriate measures to prevent the institution concerned from initiating further transactions within its territory and to safeguard the interests of depositors. Every two years the Commission shall submit a report on such cases to the Banking Advisory Committee.

10. The Member States shall inform the Commission of the number and type of cases in which there has been a refusal pursuant to Article 19 or in which measures have been taken in accordance with paragraph 4. Every two years the Commission shall submit a report on such cases to the Banking Advisory Committee.

11. Nothing this Article shall prevent credit institutions with head offices in other Member States from advertising their services through all available means of communication in the host Member State, subject to any rules governing the form and the content of such advertising adopted in the interest of the general good.

TITLE VI

FINAL PROVISIONS

Article 22

1. The technical adaptations to be made to this Directive * * * shall be adopted in accordance with the procedure laid down in paragraph 2 * * *.

2. The Commission shall be assisted by a committee composed of representatives of the Member States and chaired by a representative of the Commission.

The Commission representative shall submit to the committee a draft of the measures to be taken. The committee shall deliver its opinion on the draft within a time limit which the chairman may lay down according to the urgency of the matter. The opinion shall be delivered by the majority laid down in Article 148(2) of the Treaty in the case of decisions which the Council is required to adopt on a proposal from the Commission. The votes of the representatives of the Member States in the committee shall be weighted in the manner set out in that Article. The chairman shall not vote.

The Commission shall adopt the measures envisaged if they are in accordance with the opinion of the committee.

If the measures envisaged are not in accordance with the opinion of the committee, or if no opinion is delivered, the Commission shall, without delay, submit to the Council a proposal concerning the measures to be taken. The Council shall act by a qualified majority.

If the Council does not act within three months of the referral to it the Commission shall adopt the measures proposed, unless the Council has decided against those measures by a simple majority.

Article 23

1. Branches which have commenced their activities, in accordance with the provisions in force in their host Member States, before the entry into force of the provisions adopted in implementation of this Directive shall be presumed to have been subject to the procedure laid down in Article 19(1) to (5). They shall be governed, from the date of that entry into force, by Articles 15, 18, 19(6) and 21. They shall benefit pursuant to Article 6(3).

2. Article 20 shall not affect rights acquired by credit institutions providing services before the entry into force of the provisions adopted in implementation of this Directive.

Article 24

1. Subject to paragraph 2, the Member States shall bring into force the laws, regulations and administrative provisions necessary for them to comply with this Directive by the later of the two dates laid down for the adoption of measures to comply with Directives 89/299/EEC and 89/647/EEC and at the latest by 1 January 1993. They shall forthwith inform the Commission thereof.

2. The Member States shall adopt the measures necessary for them to comply with Article 6(2) by 1 January 1990.

* * *

Article 25

This Directive is addressed to the Member States.

ANNEX

LIST OF ACTIVITIES SUBJECT TO MUTUAL RECOGNITION

1. Acceptance of deposits and other repayable funds from the public.
2. Lending [1].
3. Financial leasing.
4. Money transmission services.
5. Issuing and administering means of payment (e.g. credit cards, travellers' cheques and bankers' drafts).
6. Guarantees and commitments.
7. Trading for own account or for account of customers in:
   (1) money market instruments (cheques, bills, CDs, etc.);
   (b) foreign exchange;
   (c) financial futures and options;
   (d) exchange and interest rate instruments;
   (e) transferable securities.
8. Participation in share issues and the provision of services related to such issues.

[1] Including *inter alia*:
— consumer credit,
— mortgage credit,
— factoring, with or without recourse,
— financing of commercial transactions (including forfeiting).

9. Advice to undertakings on capital structure, industrial strategy and related questions and advice and services relating to mergers and the purchase of undertakings.
10. Money broking.
11. Portfolio management and advice.
12. Safekeeping and administration of securities.
13. Credit reference services.
14. Safe custody services.

[The First and Second Banking Directives have been codified, but without substantive change, together with several supplemental directives, in Directive 2000/12 of the European Parliament and of the Council, O.J. L 126/1 (May 26, 2000).]

7. COUNCIL REGULATION (EC) NO. 974/98

of 3 May 1998

on the introduction of the euro

O.J. L. 139/1 (May 11, 1998)

THE COUNCIL OF THE EUROPEAN UNION,

Having regard to the Treaty establishing the European Community, and in particular Article 109l(4), third sentence thereof,

Having regard to the proposal from the Commission,

Having regard to the opinion of the European Monetary Institute,

Having regard to the opinion of the European Parliament,

* * *

(2) Whereas, at the meeting of the European Council in Madrid on 15 and 16 December 1995, the decision was taken that the term 'ecu' used by the Treaty to refer to the European currency unit is a generic term; whereas the governments of the 15 Member States have reached the common agreement that this decision is the agreed and definitive interpretation of the relevant Treaty provisions; whereas the name given to the European currency shall be the 'euro'; whereas the euro as the currency of the participating Member States shall be divided into one hundred sub-units with the name 'cent'; whereas the definition of the name 'cent' does not prevent the use of variants of this term in common usage in the Member States; whereas the European Council furthermore considered that the name of the single currency must be the same in all the official languages of the European Union, taking into account the existence of different alphabets;

(3) Whereas the Council when acting in accordance with the third sentence of Article 109(4) of the Treaty shall take the measures necessary for the rapid introduction of the euro other than the adoption of the conversion rates;

(4) Whereas whenever under Article 109k(2) of the Treaty a Member State becomes a participating Member State, the Council shall according to Article 109l(5) of the Treaty take the other measures necessary for the rapid introduction of the euro as the single currency of this Member State;

(5) Whereas according to the first sentence of Article 109l(4) of the Treaty the Council shall at the starting date of the third stage adopt the conversion rates at which the currencies of the participating Member States shall be irrevocably fixed and at which irrevocably fixed rate the euro shall be substituted for these currencies;

(6) Whereas given the absence of exchange rate risk either between the euro unit and the national currency units or between these national currency units, legislative provisions should be interpreted accordingly;

(7) Whereas the term 'contract' used for the definition of legal instruments is meant to include all types of contracts, irrespective of the way in which they are concluded;

(8) Whereas in order to prepare a smooth changeover to the euro a transitional period is needed between the substitution of the euro for the currencies of the participating Member States and the introduction of euro banknotes and coins; whereas during this period the national currency units will be defined as sub-divisions of the euro; whereas thereby a legal equivalence is established between the euro unit and the national currency units;

(9) Whereas in accordance with Article 109g of the Treaty and with Regulation (EC) No 1103/97, the euro will replace the ECU as from 1 January 1999 as the unit of account of the institutions of the European Communities; whereas the euro should also be the unit of account of the European Central Bank (ECB) and of the central banks of the participating Member States; whereas, in line with the Madrid conclusions, monetary policy operations will be carried out in the euro unit by the European System of Central Banks (ESCB), whereas this does not prevent national central banks from keeping accounts in their national currency unit during the transitional period, in particular for their staff and for public administrations;

(10) Whereas each participating Member State may allow the full use of the euro unit in its territory during the transitional period;

(11) Whereas during the transitional period contracts, national laws and other legal instruments can be drawn up validly in the euro unit or in the national currency unit; whereas during this period, nothing in this Regulation should affect the validity of any reference to a national currency unit in any legal instrument;

(12) Whereas, unless agreed otherwise, economic agents have to respect the denomination of a legal instrument in the performance of all acts to be carried out under that instrument;

(13) Whereas the euro unit and the national currency units are units of the same currency; whereas it should be ensured that payments inside a participating Member State by crediting an account can be made either in the euro unit or the respective national currency unit; * * *

(14) Whereas in accordance with the conclusions reached by the European Council at its meeting held in Madrid, new tradeable public debt will be issued in the euro unit by the participating Member States as from 1 January 1999; whereas it is desirable to allow issuers of debt to redenominate outstanding debt in the euro unit; * * * whereas it is desirable to allow Member States to take appropriate measures for changing the unit of account of the operating procedures of organized markets.

(15) Whereas further action at the Community level may also be necessary to clarify the effect of the introduction of the euro on the application of existing provisions of Community law, in particular concerning netting, set-off and techniques of similar effect;

(16) Whereas any obligation to use the euro unit can only be imposed on the basis of Community legislation; whereas in transactions with the public sector participating Member States may allow the use of the euro unit; whereas in accordance with the reference scenario decided by the European Council at its meeting held in Madrid, the Community legislation laying down the time frame for the generalization of the use of the euro unit might leave some freedom to individual Member States;

(17) Whereas in accordance with Article 105a of the Treaty the Council may adopt measures to harmonize the denominations and technical specifications of all coins;

(18) Whereas banknotes and coins need adequate protection against counterfeiting;

(19) Whereas banknotes and coins denominated in the national currency units lose their status of legal tender at the latest six months after the end of the transitional period; * * *

* * *

(23) Whereas, in accordance with Article 109l(4) of the Treaty, the single currency will be introduced only in the Member States without a derogation;

(24) Whereas this Regulation, therefore, shall be applicable pursuant to Article 189 of the Treaty, subject to Protocols 11 and 12 and Article 109k(1),

HAS ADOPTED THIS REGULATION:

PART I

DEFINITIONS

Article 1

For the purpose of this Regulation:

— 'participating Member States' shall mean Belgium, Germany, Spain, France, Ireland, Italy, Luxembourg, Netherlands, Austria, Portugal and Finland,

— 'legal instruments' shall mean legislative and statutory provisions, acts of administration, judicial decisions, contracts, unilateral legal acts, payment instruments other than banknotes and coins, and other instruments with legal effect,

— 'conversion rate' shall mean the irrevocably fixed conversion rate adopted for the currency of each participating Member State by the Council according to the first sentence of Article 109l(4) of the Treaty,

— 'euro unit' shall mean the currency unit as referred to in the second sentence of Article 2,

— 'national currency units' shall mean the units of the currencies of participating Member States, as those units are defined on the day before the start of the third stage of economic and monetary union,

— 'transitional period' shall mean the period beginning on 1 January 1999 and ending on 31 December 2001,

— 'redenominate' shall mean changing the unit in which the amount of outstanding debt is stated from a national currency unit to the euro unit, as defined in Article 2, but which does not have through the act of redenomination the effect of altering any other term of the debt, this being a matter subject to relevant national law.

PART II

SUBSTITUTION OF THE EURO FOR THE CURRENCIES OF THE PARTICIPATING MEMBER STATES

Article 2

As from 1 January 1999 the currency of the participating Member States shall be the euro. The currency unit shall be one euro. One euro shall be divided into one hundred cent.

Article 3

The euro shall be substituted for the currency of each participating Member State at the conversion rate.

Article 4

The euro shall be the unit of account of the European Central Bank (ECB) and of the central banks of the participating Member States.

PART III

TRANSITIONAL PROVISIONS

Article 5

Articles 6, 7, 8 and 9 shall apply during the transitional period.

Article 6

1. The euro shall also be divided into the national currency units according to the conversion rates. Any subdivision thereof shall be maintained. Subject to the provisions of this Regulation the monetary law of the participating Member States shall continue to apply.

2. Where in a legal instrument reference is made to a national currency unit, this reference shall be as valid as if reference were made to the euro unit according to the conversion rates.

Article 7

The substitution of the euro for the currency of each participating Member State shall not in itself have the effect of altering the denomination of legal instruments in existence on the date of substitution.

Article 8

1. Acts to be performed under legal instruments stipulating the use of or denominated in a national currency unit shall be performed in that national currency unit. Acts to be performed under legal instruments stipulating the use of or denominated in the euro unit shall be performed in that unit.

2. The provisions of paragraph 1 are subject to anything which parties may have agreed.

3. Notwithstanding the provisions of paragraph 1, any amount denominated either in the euro unit or in the national currency unit of a given participating Member State and payable within that Member State by crediting an account of the creditor, can be paid by the debtor either in the euro unit or in that national currency unit. The amount shall be credited to the account of the creditor in the denomination of his account, with any conversion being effected at the conversion rates.

4. Notwithstanding the provisions of paragraph 1, each participating Member State may take measures which may be necessary in order to:

— redenominate in the euro unit outstanding debt issued by that Member State's general government, as defined in the European system of integrated accounts, denominated in its national currency unit and issued under its own law. If a Member State has taken such a measure, issuers may redenominate in the euro unit debt denominated in that Member State's national currency unit unless redenomination is expressly excluded by the terms of the contract; this provision shall apply to debt issued by the general government of a Member State as well as to bonds and other forms of securitised debt negotiable in the capital markets, and to money market instruments, issued by other debtors,

— enable the change of the unit of account of their operating procedures from a national currency unit to the euro unit by:

   (a) markets for the regular exchange, clearing and settlement of any instrument listed in section B of the Annex to Council Directive 93/22/EEC of 10 May 1993 on investment services in the securities field and of commodities; and

   (b) systems for the regular exchange, clearing and settlement of payments.

5. Provisions other than those of paragraph 4 imposing the use of the euro unit may only be adopted by the participating Member States in accordance with any timeframe laid down by Community legislation.

6. National legal provisions of participating Member States which permit or impose netting, set-off or techniques with similar effects shall apply to monetary obligations, irrespective of their currency denomination, if that denomination is in the euro unit or in a national currency unit, with any conversion being effected at the conversion rates.

Article 9

Banknotes and coins denominated in a national currency unit shall retain their status as legal tender within their territorial limits as of the day before the entry into force of this Regulation.

PART IV

EURO BANKNOTES AND COINS

Article 10

As from 1 January 2002, the ECB and the central banks of the participating Member States shall put into circulation banknotes denominated in euro. Without prejudice to Article 15, these banknotes denominated in euro shall be the only banknotes which have the status of legal tender in all the Member States.

Article 11

As from 1 January 2002, the participating Member States shall issue coins denominated in euro or in cent and complying with the denominations and technical specifications which the Council may lay down in accordance with the second sentence of Article 105a(2) of the Treaty. Without prejudice to Article 15, these coins shall be the only coins which have the status of legal tender in all these Member States. Except for the issuing authority and for those persons specifically designated by the national legislation of the issuing Member State, no party shall be obliged to accept more than 50 coins in any single payment.

Article 12

Participating Member States shall ensure adequate sanctions against counterfeiting and falsification of euro banknotes and coins.

PART V

FINAL PROVISIONS

Article 13

Articles 14, 15 and 16 shall apply as from the end of the transitional period.

Article 14

Where in legal instruments existing at the end of the transitional period reference is made to the national currency units, these references shall be read as references to the euro unit according to the respective conversion rates. The rounding rules laid down in Regulation (EC) No 1103/97 shall apply.

Article 15

1. Banknotes and coins denominated in a national currency unit as referred to in Article 6(1) shall remain legal tender within their territorial

limits until six months after the end of the transitional period at the latest; this period may be shortened by national law.

2. Each participating Member State may, for a period of up to six months after the end of the transitional period, lay down rules for the use of the banknotes and coins denominated in its national currency unit as referred to in Article 6(1) and take any measures necessary to facilitate their withdrawal.

Article 16

In accordance with the laws or practices of participating Member States, the respective issuers of banknotes and coins shall continue to accept, against euro at the conversion rate, the banknotes and coins previously issued by them.

PART VI
ENTRY INTO FORCE

Article 17

This regulation shall enter into force on 1 January 1999.

8. COUNCIL REGULATION (EC) NO. 1103/97

of 17 June 1997

on certain provisions relating to the introduction of the euro

O.J. L 162/1 (June 19, 1997)

THE COUNCIL OF THE EUROPEAN UNION,

Having regard to the Treaty establishing the European Community, and in particular Article 235 thereof,

Having regard to the proposal of the Commission,

Having regard to the opinion of the European Parliament,

Having regard to the opinion of the European Monetary Institute,

(1) Whereas, at its meeting held in Madrid on 15 and 16 December 1995, the European Council confirmed that the third stage of Economic and Monetary Union will start on 1 January 1999 as laid down in Article 109j(4) of the Treaty; whereas the Member States which will adopt the euro as the single currency in accordance with the Treaty will be defined for the purposes of this Regulation as the 'participating Member States';

(2) Whereas, at the meeting of the European Council in Madrid, the decision was taken that the term 'ECU' used by the Treaty to refer to the European currency unit is a generic term; whereas the Governments of the fifteen Member States have achieved the common agreement that this decision is the agreed and definitive interpretation of the relevant Treaty provisions; whereas the name given to the European currency shall be the 'euro'; whereas the euro as the currency of the participating Member States will be divided into one hundred sub-units with the name 'cent'; whereas the European Council furthermore considered that the name of the single currency must be the same in all the official languages of the European Union, taking into account the existence of different alphabets;

(3) Whereas a Regulation on the introduction of the euro will be adopted by the Council on the basis of the third sentence of Article 109l(4) of the Treaty as soon as the participating Member States are known in order to define the legal framework of the euro; whereas the Council, when acting at the starting date of the third stage in accordance with the first sentence of Article 109l(4) of the Treaty, shall adopt the irrevocably fixed conversion rates;

(4) Whereas it is necessary, in the course of the operation of the common market and for the changeover to the single currency, to provide legal certainty for citizens and firms in all Member States on certain provisions relating to the introduction of the euro well before the entry into the third stage; whereas this legal certainty at an early stage will allow preparations by citizens and firms to proceed under good conditions;

(5) Whereas the third sentence of Article 109l(4) of the Treaty, which allows the Council, acting with the unanimity of participating Member

States, to take other measures necessary for the rapid introduction of the single currency is available as a legal basis only when it has been confirmed, in accordance with Article 109j(4) of the Treaty, which Member States fulfil the necessary conditions for the adoption of a single currency; whereas it is therefore necessary to have recourse to Article 235 of the Treaty as a legal basis for those provisions where there is an urgent need for legal certainty; whereas therefore this Regulation and the aforesaid Regulation on the introduction of the euro will together provide the legal framework for the euro, the principles of which legal framework were agreed by the European Council in Madrid; whereas the introduction of the euro concerns day-to-day operations of the whole population in participating Member States; whereas measures other than those in this Regulation and in the Regulation which will be adopted under the third sentence of Article 109l(4) of the Treaty should be examined to ensure a balanced changeover, in particular for consumers;

(6) Whereas the ECU as referred to in Article 109g of the Treaty and as defined in Council Regulation (EC) No 3320/94 of 22 December 1994 on the consolidation of the existing Community legislation on the definition of the ECU following the entry into force of the Treaty on European Union will cease to be defined as a basket of component currencies on 1 January 1999 and the euro will become a currency in its own right; whereas the decision of the Council regarding the adoption of the conversion rates shall not in itself modify the external value of the ECU; whereas this means that one ECU in its composition as a basket of component currencies will become one euro; whereas Regulation (EC) No 3320/94 therefore becomes obsolete and should be repealed; whereas for references in legal instruments to the ECU, parties shall be presumed to have agreed to refer to the ECU as referred to in Article 109g of the Treaty and as defined in the aforesaid Regulation; whereas such presumption should be rebuttable taking into account the intentions of the parties;

(7) Whereas it is a generally accepted principle of law that the continuity of contracts and other legal instruments is not affected by the introduction of a new currency; whereas the principle of freedom of contract has to be respected; whereas the principle of continuity should be compatible with anything which parties might have agreed with reference to the introduction of the euro; whereas, in order to reinforce legal certainty and clarity, it is appropriate explicitly to confirm that the principle of continuity of contracts and other legal instruments shall apply between the former national currencies and the euro and between the ECU as referred to in Article 109g of the Treaty and as defined in Regulation (EC) No 3320/94 and the euro; whereas this implies, in particular, that in the case of fixed interest rate instruments the introduction of the euro does not alter the nominal interest rate payable by the debtor; whereas the provisions on continuity can fulfil their objective to provide legal certainty and transparency to economic

agents, in particular for consumers, only if they enter into force as soon as possible;

(8) Whereas the introduction of the euro constitutes a change in the monetary law of each participating Member State; whereas the recognition of the monetary law of a State is a universally accepted principle; whereas the explicit confirmation of the principle of continuity should lead to the recognition of continuity of contracts and other legal instruments in the jurisdictions of third countries;

(9) Whereas the term 'contract' used for the definition of legal instruments is meant to include all types of contracts, irrespective of the way in which they are concluded;

(10) Whereas the Council, when acting in accordance with the first sentence of Article 109l(4) of the Treaty, shall define the conversion rates of the euro in terms of each of the national currencies of the participating Member States; whereas these conversion rates should be used for any conversion between the euro and the national currency units or between the national currency units;

* * *

HAS ADOPTED THIS REGULATION:

Article 1

For the purpose of this Regulation:

— 'legal instruments' shall mean legislative and statutory provisions, acts of administration, judicial decisions, contracts, unilateral legal acts, payment instruments other than banknotes and coins, and other instruments with legal effect,

— 'participating Member States' shall mean those Member States which adopt the single currency in accordance with the Treaty,

— 'conversion rates' shall mean the irrevocably fixed conversion rates which the Council adopts in accordance with the first sentence of Article 109l(4) of the Treaty,

— 'national currency units' shall mean the units of the currencies of participating Member States, as those units are defined on the day before the start of the third stage of Economic and Monetary Union,

— 'euro unit' shall mean the unit of the single currency as defined in the Regulation on the introduction of the euro which will enter into force at the starting date of the third stage of Economic and Monetary Union.

Article 2

1. Every reference in a legal instrument to the ECU, as referred to in Article 109g of the Treaty and as defined in Regulation (EC) No 3320/94, shall be replaced by a reference to the euro at a rate of one euro to one ECU. References in a legal instrument to the ECU without such a definition shall be presumed, such presumption being rebuttable taking into account the intentions of the parties, to be references to the ECU as

referred to in Article 109g of the Treaty and as defined in Regulation (EC) No 3320/94.

2. Regulation (EC) No 3320/94 is hereby repealed.

3. This Article shall apply as from 1 January 1999 in accordance with the decision pursuant to Article 109j(4) of the Treaty.

Article 3

The introduction of the euro shall not have the effect of altering any term of a legal instrument or of discharging or excusing performance under any legal instrument, nor give a party the right unilaterally to alter or terminate such an instrument. This provision is subject to anything which parties may have agreed.

Article 4

1. The conversion rates shall be adopted as one euro expressed in terms of each of the national currencies of the participating Member States. They shall be adopted with six significant figures.

2. The conversion rates shall not be rounded or truncated when making conversions.

3. The conversion rates shall be used for conversions either way between the euro unit and the national currency units. Inverse rates derived from the conversion rates shall not be used.

4. Monetary amounts to be converted from one national currency unit into another shall first be converted into a monetary amount expressed in the euro unit, which amount may be rounded to not less than three decimals and shall then be converted into the other national currency unit. No alternative method of calculation may be used unless it produces the same results.

Article 5

Monetary amounts to be paid or accounted for when a rounding takes place after a conversion into the euro unit pursuant to Article 4 shall be rounded up or down to the nearest cent. Monetary amounts to be paid or accounted for which are converted into a national currency unit shall be rounded up or down to the nearest sub-unit or in the absence of a sub-unit to the nearest unit, or according to national law or practice to a multiple or fraction of the sub-unit or unit of the national currency unit. If the application of the conversion rate gives a result which is exactly half-way, the sum shall be rounded up.

Article 6

This Regulation shall enter into force on the day following that of its publication in the *Official Journal of the European Communities*.

*

Part VII

SPECIFIC COMMUNITY POLICIES

INTRODUCTION

Part VII of the casebook examines several major Community policies and fields of action. Out of the vast number of regulations and directives adopted to implement those policies, we have selected certain key representative documents.

In the field of the environment (Chapter 34), we have reprinted Directive 85/337 on the assessment of the effects of certain public and private projects on the environment. This directive is the subject of one of the principal cases in the chapter and is also quite important because of the possibility that it gives private parties to aid in the enforcement of Community environmental rules. There are numerous other Community environmental directives, but space precludes their inclusion.

As for consumer protection, we have reproduced the three basic directives on the topics that we discuss in detail in Chapter 35—Directive 84/450 on misleading advertising (as amended to deal with comparative advertising); Directive 93/13 on unfair terms in consumer contracts; and Directive 85/374 on products liability. Other important directives are cited in the text of Chapter 35.

In the case of social policy, the subject of Chapter 36, we have excerpted the directives on (i) collective redundancies, (ii) safeguarding employees rights in business transfers, (iii) protecting employees in insolvencies, (iv) pregnant workers, (v) working time and (vi) information of employees of conditions of employment. Document 8 is the very important Community Charter on the Fundamental Social Rights of Workers.

In connection with Chapter 37 on equal treatment, we have included the principal directives on equal pay and equal treatment as between men and women, which are considered in some detail in the casebook, where the directive and the caselaw of the Court of Justice are examined. In this connection the directive on the burden of proof in sex discrimination cases (Document 15) is also included. Additionally, the directive on implementing the equal treatment principle irrespective of race or ethnic origin (Document 16) and the general framework directive on equal treatment in employment matters (Document 17) are reproduced.

Finally, for Chapter 38, we have included the three documents that are the focus of that chapter—The Brussels Convention on Jurisdiction and the Enforcement of Judgments in Civil and Commercial Matters and related Protocol authorizing the Court of Justice to interpret the Convention, as well as the December 2000 Council Regulation that effectively replaces the Convention for the Member States (except Denmark).

Table of Contents

PART VII. SPECIFIC COMMUNITY POLICIES

Doc.		Page
1.	Council Directive 85/337/EEC on the assessment of the effects of certain public and private projects on the environment	686
2.	Council Directive 84/450/EEC relating to the approximation of the laws, regulations and administrative provisions of the Member States concerning misleading advertising	702
3.	Council Directive 93/13/EEC on unfair terms in consumer contracts	708
4.	Council Directive 85/374/EEC on the approximation of the laws, regulations and administrative provisions of the Member States concerning liability for defective products	716
5.	Council Directive 98/59 on the approximation of the laws relating to collective redundancies	723
6.	Council Directive 2001/23 on the approximation of the laws relating to the safeguarding of employees' rights in the event of transfers of undertakings, businesses or parts of businesses	728
7.	Council Directive 80/987 on the approximation of the laws relating to the protection of employees in the event of the insolvency of their employer	735
8.	Community Charter of the Fundamental Social Rights of Workers	739
9.	Council Directive 92/85 on measures to encourage improvements in the safety and health at work of pregnant workers and workers who have recently given birth or are breastfeeding	746
10.	Council Directive 93/104 concerning certain aspects of the organization of working time	754
11.	Council Directive 91/533 on an employer's obligation to inform employees of the conditions applicable to the contract or employment relationship	764
12.	Council Directive 75/117 on the approximation of the laws relating to the principle of equal pay for men and women	770
13.	Council Directive 76/207 on the implementation of the principle of equal treatment for men and women as regards access to employment, vocational training and promotion, and working conditions	773
14.	Council Directive 79/7 on the progressive implementation of the principle of equal treatment for men and women in matters of social security	777
15.	Council Directive 97/80 on burden of proof in sex discrimination cases	780
16.	Council Directive 2000/43 on equal treatment irrespective of racial or ethnic origin	785

17.	Council Directive 2000/78 establishing general framework for equal treatment in employment and occupation	795
18.	1968 Brussels Convention on Jurisdiction and the Enforcement of Judgments in Civil and Commercial Matters	808
19.	Protocol on the Interpretation by the Court of Justice of the Convention on Jurisdiction and the Enforcement of Judgments in Civil and Commercial Matters	824
20.	Council Regulation 44/2001 of 22 December 2000 on Jurisdiction and the Recognition and Enforcement of Judgments in Civil and Commercial Matters	826

1. COUNCIL DIRECTIVE 85/337/EEC

of 27 June 1985

on the assessment of the effects of certain public and private projects on the environment

O.J. L 175/40 (July 5, 1985), amended by
Council Directive 97/11/EC of 3 March 1997

O.J. L 73/5 (March 14, 1997)

THE COUNCIL OF THE EUROPEAN COMMUNITIES,

Having regard to the Treaty establishing the European Economic Community, and in particular Articles 100 and 235 thereof,

* * *

Whereas the 1973 and 1977 action programmes of the European Communities on the environment, as well as the 1983 action programme, the main outlines of which have been approved by the Council of the European Communities and the representatives of the Governments of the Member States, stress that the best environmental policy consists in preventing the creation of pollution or nuisances at source, rather than subsequently trying to counteract their effects; whereas they affirm the need to take effects on the environment into account at the earliest possible stage in all the technical planning and decision-making processes; whereas to that end, they provide for the implementation of procedures to evaluate such effects;

Whereas the disparities between the laws in force in the various Member States with regard to the assessment of the environmental effects of public and private projects may create unfavorable competitive conditions and thereby directly affect the functioning of the common market; whereas, therefore, it is necessary to approximate national laws in this field pursuant to Article 100 of the Treaty;

Whereas, in addition, it is necessary to achieve one of the Community's objectives in the sphere of the protection of the environment and the quality of life;

Whereas, since the Treaty has not provided the powers required for this end, recourse should be had to Article 235 of the Treaty;

Whereas general principles for the assessment of environmental effects should be introduced with a view to supplementing and coordinating development consent procedures governing public and private projects likely to have a major effect on the environment;

Whereas development consent for public and private projects which are likely to have significant effects on the environment should be granted only after prior assessment of the likely significant environmental effects of these projects has been carried out; whereas this assessment must be conducted on the basis of the appropriate information supplied by the developer, which may be supplemented by the authorities and by the people who may be concerned by the project in question;

Whereas the principles of the assessment of environmental effects should be harmonized, in particular with reference to the projects which should be subject to assessment, the main obligations of the developers and the content of the assessment;

Whereas projects belonging to certain types have significant effects on the environment and these projects must as a rule be subject to systematic assessment;

Whereas projects of other types may not have significant effects on the environment in every case and whereas these projects should be assessed where the Member States consider that their characteristics so require;

Whereas, for projects which are subject to assessment, a certain minimal amount of information must be supplied, concerning the project and its effects;

Whereas the effects of a project on the environment must be assessed in order to take account of concerns to protect human health, to contribute by means of a better environment to the quality of life, to ensure maintenance of the diversity of species and to maintain the reproductive capacity of the ecosystem as a basic resource for life;

Whereas, however, this Directive should not be applied to projects the details of which are adopted by a specific act of national legislation, since the objectives of this Directive, including that of supplying information, are achieved through the legislative process;

Whereas, furthermore, it may be appropriate in exceptional cases to exempt a specific project from the assessment procedures laid down by this Directive, subject to appropriate information being supplied to the Commission,

HAS ADOPTED THIS DIRECTIVE:

Article 1

1. This Directive shall apply to the assessment of the environmental effects of those public and private projects which are likely to have significant effects on the environment.

2. For the purposes of this Directive:

'project' means:

— the execution of construction works or of other installations or schemes,

— other interventions in the natural surroundings and landscape including those involving the extraction of mineral resources;

'developer' means:

the applicant for authorization for a private project or the public authority which initiates a project;

'development consent' means:

the decision of the competent authority or authorities which entitles the developer to proceed with the project.

3. The competent authority or authorities shall be that or those which the Member States designate as responsible for performing the duties arising from this Directive.

4. Projects serving national defence purposes are not covered by this Directive.

5. This Directive shall not apply to projects the details of which are adopted by a specific act of national legislation, since the objectives of this Directive, including that of supplying information, are achieved through the legislative process.

Article 2

1. Member States shall adopt all measures necessary to ensure that, before consent is given, projects likely to have significant effects on the environment by virtue, *inter alia*, of their nature, size or location are made subject to a requirement for development consent and an assessment with regard to their effects. These projects are defined in Article 4.

2. The environmental impact assessment may be integrated into the existing procedures for consent to projects in the Member States, or, failing this, into other procedures or into procedures to be established to comply with the aims of this Directive.

2a. Member States may provide for a single procedure in order to fulfil the requirements of this Directive and the requirements of Council Directive 96/61/EC of 24 September 1996 on integrated pollution prevention and control.

3. Without prejudice to Article 7, Member States may, in exceptional cases, exempt a specific project in whole or in part from the provisions laid down in this Directive. In this event, the Member States shall:

   (a) consider whether another form of assessment would be appropriate and whether the information thus collected should be made available to the public;

   (b) make available to the public concerned the information relating to the exemption and the reasons for granting it;

   (c) inform the Commission, prior to granting consent, of the reasons justifying the exemption granted, and provide it with the information made available, where applicable, to their own nationals.

The Commission shall immediately forward the documents received to the other Member States. The Commission shall report annually to the Council on the application of this paragraph.

Article 3

The environmental impact assessment shall identify, describe and assess in an appropriate manner, in the light of each individual case and in accordance with Articles 4 to 11, the direct and indirect effects of a project on the following factors:

— human beings, fauna and flora;

— soil, water, air, climate and the landscape;

— material assets and the cultural heritage;

— the interaction between the factors mentioned in the first, second and third indents.

Article 4

1. Subject to Article 2 (3), projects listed in Annex I shall be made subject to an assessment in accordance with Articles 5 to 10.

2. Subject to Article 2 (3), for projects listed in Annex II, the Member States shall determine through:

(a) a case-by-case examination,

or

(b) thresholds or criteria set by the Member State

whether the project shall be made subject to an assessment in accordance with Articles 5 to 10.

Member States may decide to apply both procedures referred to in (a) and (b).

3. When a case-by-case examination is carried out or thresholds or criteria are set for the purpose of paragraph 2, the relevant selection criteria set out in Annex III shall be taken into account.

4. Member States shall ensure that the determination made by the competent authorities under paragraph 2 is made available to the public.

Article 5

1. In the case of projects which, pursuant to Article 4, must be subjected to an environmental impact assessment in accordance with Articles 5 to 10, Member States shall adopt the necessary measures to ensure that the developer supplies in an appropriate form the information specified in Annex IV inasmuch as:

(a) the Member States consider that the information is relevant to a given stage of the consent procedure and to the specific characteristics of a particular project or type of project and of the environmental features likely to be affected;

(b) the Member States consider that a developer may reasonably be required to compile this information having regard *inter alia* to current knowledge and methods of assessment.

2. Member States shall take the necessary measures to ensure that, if the developer so requests before submitting an application for development consent, the competent authority shall give an opinion on the information to be supplied by the developer in accordance with paragraph 1. The competent authority shall consult the developer and authorities referred to

in Article 6 (1) before it gives its opinion. The fact that the authority has given an opinion under this paragraph shall not preclude it from subsequently requiring the developer to submit further information. Member States may require the competent authorities to give such an opinion, irrespective of whether the developer so requests.

3. The information to be provided by the developer in accordance with paragraph 1 shall include at least:

— a description of the project comprising information on the site, design and size of the project,

— a description of the measures envisaged in order to avoid, reduce and, if possible, remedy significant adverse effects,

— the data required to identify and assess the main effects which the project is likely to have on the environment,

— an outline of the main alternatives studied by the developer and an indication of the main reasons for his choice, taking into account the environmental effects,

— a non-technical summary of the information mentioned in the previous indents.

4. Member States shall, if necessary, ensure that any authorities holding relevant information, with particular reference to Article 3, shall make this information available to the developer.

Article 6

1. Member States shall take the measures necessary to ensure that the authorities likely to be concerned by the project by reason of their specific environmental responsibilities are given an opportunity to express their opinion on the information supplied by the developer and on the request for development consent. To this end, Member States shall designate the authorities to be consulted, either in general terms or on a case-by-case basis. The information gathered pursuant to Article 5 shall be forwarded to those authorities. Detailed arrangements for consultation shall be laid down by the Member States.

2. Member States shall ensure that any request for development consent and any information gathered pursuant to Article 5 are made available to the public within a reasonable time in order to give the public concerned the opportunity to express an opinion before the development consent is granted.

3. The detailed arrangements for such information and consultation shall be determined by the Member States, which may in particular, depending on the particular characteristics of the projects or sites concerned:

— determine the public concerned,

— specify the places where the information can be consulted,

— specify the way in which the public may be informed, for example by bill-posting within a certain radius, publication in local newspapers, organization of exhibitions with plans, drawings, tables, graphs, models,

— determine the manner in which the public is to be consulted, for example, by written submissions, by public enquiry,

— fix appropriate time limits for the various stages of the procedure in order to ensure that a decision is taken within a reasonable period.

Article 7

1. Where a Member State is aware that a project is likely to have significant effects on the environment in another Member State or where a Member State likely to be significantly affected so requests, the Member State in whose territory the project is intended to be carried out shall send to the affected Member State as soon as possible and no later than when informing its own public, inter alia:

(a) a description of the project, together with any available information on its possible transboundary impact;

(b) information on the nature of the decision which may be taken, and shall give the other Member State a reasonable time in which to indicate whether it wishes to participate in the Environmental Impact Assessment procedure, and may include the information referred to in paragraph 2.

2. If a Member State which receives information pursuant to paragraph 1 indicates that it intends to participate in the Environmental Impact Assessment procedure, the Member State in whose territory the project is intended to be carried out shall, if it has not already done so, send to the affected Member State the information gathered pursuant to Article 5 and relevant information regarding the said procedure, including the request for development consent.

3. The Member States concerned, each insofar as it is concerned, shall also:

(a) arrange for the information referred to in paragraphs 1 and 2 to be made available, within a reasonable time, to the authorities referred to in Article 6 (1) and the public concerned in the territory of the Member State likely to be significantly affected; and

(b) ensure that those authorities and the public concerned are given an opportunity, before development consent for the project is granted, to forward their opinion within a reasonable time on the information supplied to the competent authority in the Member State in whose territory the project is intended to be carried out.

4. The Member States concerned shall enter into consultations regarding, *inter alia*, the potential transboundary effects of the project and the measures envisaged to reduce or eliminate such effects and shall agree on a reasonable time frame for the duration of the consultation period.

5. The detailed arrangements for implementing the provisions of this Article may be determined by the Member States concerned.

Article 8

The results of consultations and the information gathered pursuant to Articles 5, 6 and 7 must be taken into consideration in the development consent procedure.

Article 9

1. When a decision to grant or refuse development consent has been taken, the competent authority or authorities shall inform the public thereof in accordance with the appropriate procedures and shall make available to the public the following information:

— the content of the decision and any conditions attached thereto,

— the main reasons and considerations on which the decision is based,

— a description, where necessary, of the main measures to avoid, reduce and, if possible, offset the major adverse effects.

2. The competent authority or authorities shall inform any Member State which has been consulted pursuant to Article 7, forwarding to it the information referred to in paragraph 1.

Article 10

The provisions of this Directive shall not affect the obligation on the competent authorities to respect the limitations imposed by national regulations and administrative provisions and accepted legal practices with regard to commercial and industrial confidentiality, including intellectual property, and the safeguarding of the public interest. Where Article 7 applies, the transmission of information to another Member State and the receipt of information by another Member State shall be subject to the limitations in force in the Member State in which the project is proposed.

Article 11

1. The Member States and the Commission shall exchange information on the experience gained in applying this Directive.

2. In particular, Member States shall inform the Commission of any criteria and/or thresholds adopted for the selection of the projects in question, in accordance with Article 4 (2).

3. Five years after notification of this Directive, the Commission shall send the European Parliament and the Council a report on its application and effectiveness. The report shall be based on the aforementioned exchange of information.

4. On the basis of this exchange of information, the Commission shall submit to the Council additional proposals, should this be necessary, with a view to this Directive's being applied in a sufficiently coordinated manner.

Article 12

1. Member States shall take the measures necessary to comply with this Directive within three years of its notification.

2. Member States shall communicate to the Commission the texts of the provisions of national law which they adopt in the field covered by this Directive.

Article 14

This Directive is addressed to the Member States.

ANNEX I

PROJECTS SUBJECT TO ARTICLE 4(1)

1. Crude-oil refineries (excluding undertakings manufacturing only lubricants from crude oil) and installations for the gasification and liquefaction of 500 tonnes or more of coal or bituminous shale per day.

2. — Thermal power stations and other combustion installations with a heat output of 300 megawatts or more, and
— nuclear power stations and other nuclear reactors including the dismantling or decommissioning of such power stations or reactors (except research installations for the production and conversion of fissionable and fertile materials, whose maximum power does not exceed 1 kilowatt continuous thermal load).

3. (a) Installations for the reprocessing of irradiated nuclear fuel.

(b) Installations designed:

— for the production or enrichment of nuclear fuel,
— for the processing of irradiated nuclear fuel or high-level radioactive waste,
— for the final disposal of irradiated nuclear fuel,
— solely for the final disposal of radioactive waste,
— solely for the storage (planned for more than 10 years) of irradiated nuclear fuels or radioactive waste in a different site than the production site.

4. —Integrated works for the initial smelting of cast-iron and steel;
— Installations for the production of non-ferrous crude metals from ore, concentrates or secondary raw materials by metallurgical, chemical or electrolytic processes.

5. Installations for the extraction of asbestos and for the processing and transformation of asbestos and products containing asbestos: for asbestos-cement products, with an annual production of more than 20,000 tonnes of finished products, for friction material, with an annual production of more than 50 tonnes of finished products, and for other uses of asbestos, utilization of more than 200 tonnes per year.

6. Integrated chemical installations, i.e. those installations for the manufacture on an industrial scale of substances using chemical conversion processes, in which several units are juxtaposed and are functionally linked to one another and which are:

(i) for the production of basic organic chemicals;

(ii) for the production of basic inorganic chemicals;

(iii) for the production of phosphorous-, nitrogen- or potassium-based fertilizers (simple or compound fertilizers);

(iv) for the production of basic plant health products and of biocides;

(v) for the production of basic pharmaceutical products using a chemical or biological process;

(vi) for the production of explosives.

7. (a) Construction of lines for long-distance railway traffic and of airports with a basic runway length of 2,100 m or more;

(b) Construction of motorways and express roads;

(c) Construction of a new road of four or more lanes, or realignment and/or widening of an existing road of two lanes or less so as to provide four or more lanes, where such new road, or realigned and/or widened section of road would be 10 km or more in a continuous length.

8. (a) Inland waterways and ports for inland-waterway traffic which permit the passage of vessels of over 1,350 tonnes;

(b) Trading ports, piers for loading and unloading connected to land and outside ports (excluding ferry piers) which can take vessels of over 1,350 tonnes.

9. Waste disposal installations for the incineration, chemical treatment as defined in Annex IIA to Directive 75/442/EEC under heading D9, or landfill of hazardous waste (i.e. waste to which Directive 91/689/EEC applies).

10. Waste disposal installations for the incineration or chemical treatment as defined in Annex IIA to Directive 75/442/EEC under heading D9 of nonhazardous waste with a capacity exceeding 100 tonnes per day.

11. Groundwater abstraction or artificial groundwater recharge schemes where the annual volume of water abstracted or recharged is equivalent to or exceeds 10 million cubic metres.

12. (a) Works for the transfer of water resources between river basins where this transfer aims at preventing possible shortages of water and where the amount of water transferred exceeds 100 million cubic metres/year;

(b) In all other cases, works for the transfer of water resources between river basins where the multi-annual average flow of the basin of abstraction exceeds 2 000 million cubic metres/year and where the amount of water transferred exceeds 5% of this flow.

In both cases transfers of piped drinking water are excluded.

13. Waste water treatment plants with a capacity exceeding 150,000 population equivalent as defined in Article 2 point (6) of Directive 91/271/EEC.

14. Extraction of petroleum and natural gas for commercial purposes where the amount extracted exceeds 500 tonnes/day in the case of petroleum and 500,000 m3/day in the case of gas.

15. Dams and other installations designed for the holding back or permanent storage of water, where a new or additional amount of water held back or stored exceeds 10 million cubic metres.

16. Pipelines for the transport of gas, oil or chemicals with a diameter of more than 800 mm and a length of more than 40 km.

17. Installations for the intensive rearing of poultry or pigs with more than:

(a) 85,000 places for broilers, 60,000 places for hens;

(b) 3,000 places for production pigs (over 30 kg); or

(c) 900 places for sows.

18. Industrial plants for the

(a) production of pulp from timber or similar fibrous materials;

(b) production of paper and board with a production capacity exceeding 200 tonnes per day.

19. Quarries and open-cast mining where the surface of the site exceeds 25 hectares, or peat extraction, where the surface of the site exceeds 150 hectares.

20. Construction of overhead electrical power lines with a voltage of 220 kV or more and a length of more than 15 km.

21. Installations for storage of petroleum, petrochemical, or chemical products with a capacity of 200,000 tonnes or more.

ANNEX II

PROJECTS SUBJECT TO ARTICLE 4(2)

1. **Agriculture, silviculture and aquaculture**

(a) Projects for the restructuring of rural land holdings;

(b) Projects for the use of uncultivated land or semi-natural areas for intensive agricultural purposes;

(c) Water management projects for agriculture, including irrigation and land drainage projects;

(d) Initial afforestation and deforestation for the purposes of conversion to another type of land use;

(e) Intensive livestock installations (projects not included in Annex I);

(f) Intensive fish farming;

(g) Reclamation of land from the sea.

2. **Extractive industry**

(a) Quarries, open-cast mining and peat extraction (projects not included in Annex I);

(b) Underground mining;

(c) Extraction of minerals by marine or fluvial dredging;

(d) Deep drillings, in particular:

— geothermal drilling,

— drilling for the storage of nuclear waste material,

— drilling for water supplies,

with the exception of drillings for investigating the stability of the soil;

(e) Surface industrial installations for the extraction of coal, petroleum, natural gas and ores, as well as bituminous shale.

3. **Energy industry**

(a) Industrial installations for the production of electricity, steam and hot water (projects not included in Annex I);

(b) Industrial installations for carrying gas, steam and hot water; transmission of electrical energy by overhead cables (projects not included in Annex I);

(c) Surface storage of natural gas;

(d) Underground storage of combustible gases;

(e) Surface storage of fossil fuels;

(f) Industrial briquetting of coal and lignite;

(g) Installations for the processing and storage of radioactive waste (unless included in Annex I);

(h) Installations for hydroelectric energy production;

(i) Installations for the harnessing of wind power for energy production (wind farms).

4. **Production and processing of metals**

(a) Installations for the production of pig iron or steel (primary or secondary fusion) including continuous casting;

(b) Installations for the processing of ferrous metals:

   (i) hot-rolling mills;

   (ii) smitheries with hammers;

   (iii) application of protective fused metal coats;

(c) Ferrous metal foundries;

(d) Installations for the smelting, including the alloyage, of non-ferrous metals, excluding precious metals, including recovered products (refining, foundry casting, etc.);

(e) Installations for surface treatment of metals and plastic materials using an electrolytic or chemical process;

(f) Manufacture and assembly of motor vehicles and manufacture of motor vehicle engines;

(g) Shipyards;

(h) Installations for the construction and repair of aircraft;

(i) Manufacture of railway equipment;

(j) Swaging by explosives;

(k) Installations for the roasting and sintering of metallic ores.

5. **Mineral industry**

(a) Coke ovens (dry coal distillation);

(b) Installations for the manufacture of cement;

(c) Installations for the production of asbestos and the manufacture of asbestos-products (projects not included in Annex I);

(d) Installations for the manufacture of glass including glass fibre;

(e) Installations for smelting mineral substances including the production of mineral fibres;

(f) Manufacture of ceramic products by burning, in particular roofing tiles, bricks, refractory bricks, tiles, stoneware or porcelain.

6. **Chemical industry (Projects not included in Annex I)**

(a) Treatment of intermediate products and production of chemicals;

(b) Production of pesticides and pharmaceutical products, paint and varnishes, elastomers and peroxides;

(c) Storage facilities for petroleum, petrochemical and chemical products.

7. **Food industry**

(a) Manufacture of vegetable and animal oils and fats;

(b) Packing and canning of animal and vegetable products;

(c) Manufacture of dairy products;

(d) Brewing and malting;

(e) Confectionery and syrup manufacture;

(f) Installations for the slaughter of animals;

(g) Industrial starch manufacturing installations;

(h) Fish-meal and fish-oil factories;

(i) Sugar factories.

8. **Textile, leather, wood and paper industries**

(a) Industrial plants for the production of paper and board (projects not included in Annex I);

(b) Plants for the pretreatment (operations such as washing, bleaching, mercerization) or dyeing of fibres or textiles;

(c) Plants for the tanning of hides and skins;

(d) Cellulose-processing and production installations.

9. **Rubber industry**

Manufacture and treatment of elastomer-based products.

10. **Infrastructure projects**

(a) Industrial estate development projects;

(b) Urban development projects, including the construction of shopping centres and car parks;

(c) Construction of railways and intermodal transshipment facilities, and of intermodal terminals (projects not included in Annex I);

(d) Construction of airfields (projects not included in Annex I);

(e) Construction of roads, harbours and port installations, including fishing harbours (projects not included in Annex I);

(f) Inland-waterway construction not included in Annex I, canalization and flood-relief works;

(g) Dams and other installations designed to hold water or store it on a long-term basis (projects not included in Annex I);

(h) Tramways, elevated and underground railways, suspended lines or similar lines of a particular type, used exclusively or mainly for passenger transport;

(i) Oil and gas pipeline installations (projects not included in Annex I);

(j) Installations of long-distance aqueducts;

(k) Coastal work to combat erosion and maritime works capable of altering the coast through the construction, for example, of dykes, moles, jetties and other sea defence works, excluding the maintenance and reconstruction of such works;

(*l*) Groundwater abstraction and artificial groundwater recharge schemes not included in Annex I;

(m) Works for the transfer of water resources between river basins not included in Annex I.

11. **Other projects**

(a) Permanent racing and test tracks for motorized vehicles;

(b) Installations for the disposal of waste (projects not included in Annex I);

(c) Waste-water treatment plants (projects not included in Annex I);

(d) Sludge-deposition sites;

(e) Storage of scrap iron, including scrap vehicles;

(f) Test benches for engines, turbines or reactors;

(g) Installations for the manufacture of artificial mineral fibres;

(h) Installations for the recovery or destruction of explosive substances;

(i) Knackers' yards.

a **Tourism and leisure**

(a) Ski-runs, ski-lifts and cable-cars and associated developments;

(b) Marinas;

(c) Holiday villages and hotel complexes outside urban areas and associated developments;

(d) Permanent camp sites and caravan sites;

(e) Theme parks.

13. — Any change or extension of projects listed in Annex I or Annex II, already authorized, executed or in the process of being executed, which may have significant adverse effects on the environment;

— Projects in Annex I, undertaken exclusively or mainly for the development and testing of new methods or products and not used for more than two years.

ANNEX III

SELECTION CRITERIA REFERRED TO IN ARTICLE 4(3)

1. **Characteristics of projects**

The characteristics of projects must be considered having regard, in particular, to:

— the size of the project,

— the cumulation with other projects,

— the use of natural resources,

— the production of waste,

— pollution and nuisances,

— the risk of accidents, having regard in particular to substances or technologies used.

2. **Location of projects**

The environmental sensitivity of geographical areas likely to be affected by projects must be considered, having regard, in particular, to:

— the existing land use,

— the relative abundance, quality and regenerative capacity of natural resources in the area,

— the absorption capacity of the natural environment, paying particular attention to the following areas:

   (a) wetlands;

   (b) coastal zones;

   (c) mountain and forest areas;

   (d) nature reserves and parks;

(e) areas classified or protected under Member States' legislation; special protection areas designated by Member States pursuant to Directive 79/409/EEC and 92/43/EEC;

(f) areas in which the environmental quality standards laid down in Community legislation have already been exceeded;

(g) densely populated areas;

(h) landscapes of historical, cultural or archaeological significance.

3. **Characteristics of the potential impact**

The potential significant effects of projects must be considered in relation to criteria set out under 1 and 2 above, and having regard in particular to:

— the extent of the impact (geographical area and size of the affected population),

— the transfrontier nature of the impact,

— the magnitude and complexity of the impact,

— the probability of the impact,

— the duration, frequency and reversibility of the impact.

ANNEX IV

INFORMATION REFERRED TO IN ARTICLE 5(1)

1. Description of the project, including in particular:

— a description of the physical characteristics of the whole project and the land-use requirements during the construction and operational phases,

— a description of the main characteristics of the production processes, for instance, nature and quantity of the materials used,

— an estimate, by type and quantity, of expected residues and emissions (water, air and soil pollution, noise, vibration, light, heat, radiation, etc.) resulting from the operation of the proposed project.

2. An outline of the main alternatives studied by the developer and an indication of the main reasons for this choice, taking into account the environmental effects.

3. A description of the aspects of the environment likely to be significantly affected by the proposed project, including, in particular, population, fauna, flora, soil, water, air, climatic factors, material assets, including the architectural and archaeological heritage, landscape and the inter-relationship between the above factors.

4. A description (1) of the likely significant effects of the proposed project on the environment resulting from:

— the existence of the project,

— the use of natural resources,

— the emission of pollutants, the creation of nuisances and the elimination of waste,

and the description by the developer of the forecasting methods used to assess the effects on the environment.

5. A description of the measures envisaged to prevent, reduce and where possible offset any significant adverse effects on the environment.

6. A non-technical summary of the information provided under the above headings.

7. An indication of any difficulties (technical deficiencies or lack of know-how) encountered by the developer in compiling the required information.

2. COUNCIL DIRECTIVE 84/450/EEC

of 10 September 1984

relating to the approximation of the laws, regulations and administrative provisions of the Member States concerning misleading advertising

O.J. L 250/17 (Sept. 19,1984), amended by

O.J. L 290/18 (Oct. 23, 1997)

THE COUNCIL OF THE EUROPEAN COMMUNITIES,

Having regard to the Treaty establishing the European Economic Community, and in particular Article 100 thereof,

* * *

Whereas the laws against misleading advertising now in force in the Member States differ widely; whereas, since advertising reaches beyond the frontiers of individual Member States, it has a direct effect on the establishment and the functioning of the common market;

Whereas misleading advertising can lead to distortion of competition within the common market;

Whereas advertising, whether or not it induces a contract, affects the economic welfare of consumers;

Whereas misleading advertising may cause a consumer to take decisions prejudicial to him when acquiring goods or other property, or using services, and the differences between the laws of the Member States not only lead, in many cases, to inadequate levels of consumer protection, but also hinder the execution of advertising campaigns beyond national boundaries and thus affect the free circulation of goods and provision of services;

Whereas the second programme of the European Economic Community fora consumer protection and information policy (4) provides for appropriate action for the protection of consumers against misleading and unfair advertising;

Whereas it is in the interest of the public in general, as well as that of consumers and all those who, in competition with one another, carry on a trade, business, craft or profession, in the common market, to harmonize in the first instance national provisions against misleading advertising and that, at a second stage, unfair advertising and, as far as necessary, comparative advertising should be dealt with, on the basis of appropriate Commission proposals;

Whereas minimum and objective criteria for determining whether advertising is misleading should be established for this purpose;

Whereas the laws to be adopted by Member States against misleading advertising must be adequate and effective;

Whereas persons or organizations regarded under national law as having a legitimate interest in the matter must have facilities for initiating proceedings against misleading advertising, either before a court or before an administrative authority which is competent to decide upon complaints or to initiate appropriate legal proceedings;

Whereas it should be for each Member State to decide whether to enable the courts or administrative authorities to require prior recourse to other established means of dealing with the complaint;

Whereas the courts or administrative authorities must have powers enabling them to order or obtain the cessation of misleading advertising;

Whereas in certain cases it may be desirable to prohibit misleading advertising even before it is published; whereas, however, this in no way implies that Member States are under an obligation to introduce rules requiring the systematic prior vetting of advertising;

Whereas provision should be made for accelerated procedures under which measures with interim or definitive effect can be taken;

Whereas it may be desirable to order the publication of decisions made by courts or administrative authorities or of corrective statements in order to eliminate any continuing effects of misleading advertising;

Whereas administrative authorities must be impartial and the exercise of their powers must be subject to judicial review;

Whereas the voluntary control exercised by self-regulatory bodies to eliminate misleading advertising may avoid recourse to administrative or judicial action and ought therefore to be encouraged;

Whereas the advertiser should be able to prove, by appropriate means, the material accuracy of the factual claims he makes in his advertising, and may in appropriate cases be required to do so by the court or administrative authority;

Whereas this Directive must not preclude Member States from retaining or adopting provisions with a view to ensuring more extensive protection of consumers, persons carrying on a trade, business, craft or profession, and the general public,

HAS ADOPTED THIS DIRECTIVE:

Article 1

The purpose of this Directive is to protect consumers, persons carrying on a trade or business or practicing a craft or profession and the interests of the public in general against misleading advertising and the unfair consequences thereof and to lay down the conditions under which comparative advertising is permitted.

Article 2

For the purposes of this Directive:

1. 'advertising' means the making of a representation in any form in connection with a trade, business, craft or profession in order to promote the supply of goods or services, including immovable property, rights and obligations;

2. 'misleading advertising' means any advertising which in any way, including its presentation, deceives or is likely to deceive the persons to whom it is addressed or whom it reaches and which, by reason of its deceptive nature, is likely to affect their economic behaviour or which, for those reasons, injures or is likely to injure a competitor;

2a. 'comparative advertising' means any advertising which explicitly or by implication identifies a competitor or goods or services offered by a competitor;

3. 'person' means any natural or legal person.

Article 3

In determining whether advertising is misleading, account shall be taken of all its features, and in particular of any information it contains concerning:

(a) the characteristics of goods or services, such as their availability, nature, execution, composition, method and date of manufacture or provision, fitness for purpose, uses, quantity, specification, geographical or commercial origin or the results to be expected from their use, or the results and material features of tests or checks carried out on the goods or services;

(b) the price or the manner in which the price is calculated, and the conditions on which the goods are supplied or the services provided;

(c) the nature, attributes and rights of the advertiser, such as his identity and assets, his qualifications and ownership of industrial, commercial or intellectual property rights or his awards and distinctions.

Article 3a

1. Comparative advertising shall, as far as the comparison is concerned, be permitted when the following conditions are met:

(a) it is not misleading according to Articles 2 (2), 3 and 7 (1);

(b) it compares goods or services meeting the same needs or intended for the same purpose;

(c) it objectively compares one or more material, relevant, verifiable and representative features of those goods and services, which may include price;

(d) it does not create confusion in the market place between the advertiser and a competitor or between the advertiser's trade marks, trade names, other distinguishing marks, goods or services and those of a competitor;

(e) it does not discredit or denigrate the trade marks, trade names, other distinguishing marks, goods, services, activities, or circumstances of a competitor;

(f) for products with designation of origin, it relates in each case to products with the same designation;

(g) it does not take unfair advantage of the reputation of a trade mark, trade name or other distinguishing marks of a competitor or of the designation of origin of competing products;

(h) it does not present goods or services as imitations or replicas of goods or services bearing a protected trade mark or trade name.

2. Any comparison referring to a special offer shall indicate in a clear and unequivocal way the date on which the offer ends or, where appropriate, that the special offer is subject to the availability of the goods and services, and, where the special offer has not yet begun, the date of the start of the period during which the special price or other specific conditions shall apply.

Article 4

1. Member States shall ensure that adequate and effective means exist to combat misleading advertising and for the compliance with the provisions on comparative advertising in the interests of consumers as well as competitors and the general public.

Such means shall include legal provisions under which persons or organizations regarded under national law as having a legitimate interest in prohibiting misleading advertising or regulating comparative advertising may:

(a) take legal action against such advertising; and/or

(b) bring such advertising before an administrative authority competent either to decide on complaints or to initiate appropriate legal proceedings.

It shall be for each Member State to decide which of these facilities shall be available and whether to enable the courts or administrative authorities to require prior recourse to other established means of dealing with complaints, including those referred to in Article 5.

2. Under the legal provisions referred to in paragraph 1, Member States shall confer upon the courts or administrative authorities powers enabling them, in cases where they deem such measures to be necessary taking into account all the interests involved and in particular the public interest:

— to order the cessation of, or to institute appropriate legal proceedings for an order for the cessation of, misleading advertising or unpermitted comparative advertising, or

— if the misleading advertising or unpermitted comparative advertising has not yet been published but publication is imminent, to order the prohibition of, or to institute appropriate legal proceedings for an order for the prohibition of, such publication,

even without proof of actual loss or damage or of intention or negligence on the part of the advertiser.

Member States shall also make provision for the measures referred to in the first subparagraph to be taken under an accelerated procedure:

— either with interim effect, or

— with definitive effect,

on the understanding that it is for each Member State to decide which of the two options to select.

Furthermore, Member States may confer upon the courts or administrative authorities powers enabling them, with a view to eliminating the continuing effects of misleading advertising or unpermitted comparative advertising, the cessation of which has been ordered by a final decision:

— to require publication of that decision in full or in part and in such form as they deem adequate,

— to require in addition the publication of a corrective statement.

3. The administrative authorities referred to in paragraph 1 must:

(a) be composed so as not to cast doubt on their impartiality;

(b) have adequate powers, where they decide on complaints, to monitor and enforce the observance of their decisions effectively;

(c) normally give reasons for their decisions.

Where the powers referred to in paragraph 2 are exercised exclusively by an administrative authority, reasons for its decisions shall always be given. Furthermore in this case, provision must be made for procedures whereby improper or unreasonable exercise of its powers by the administrative authority or improper or unreasonable failure to exercise the said powers can be the subject of judicial review.

Article 5

This Directive does not exclude the voluntary control, which Member States may encourage, of misleading or comparative advertising by self-regulatory bodies and recourse to such bodies by the persons or organizations referred to in Article 4 if proceedings before such bodies are in addition to the court or administrative proceedings referred to in that Article.

Article 6

Member States shall confer upon the courts or administrative authorities powers enabling them in the civil or administrative proceedings provided for in Article 4:

(a) to require the advertiser to furnish evidence as to the accuracy of factual claims in advertising if, taking into account the legitimate interest of the advertiser and any other party to the proceedings, such a requirement appears appropriate on the basis of the circumstances of the particular case and in the case of comparative advertising to require the advertiser to furnish such evidence in a short period of time; and

(b) to consider factual claims as inaccurate if the evidence demanded in accordance with (a) is not furnished or is deemed insufficient by the court or administrative authority.

Article 7

1. This Directive shall not preclude Member States from retaining or adopting provisions with a view to ensuring more extensive protection, with regard to misleading advertising, for consumers, persons carrying on a trade, business, craft or profession, and the general public.

2. Paragraph 1 shall not apply to comparative advertising as far as the comparison is concerned.

3. The provisions of this Directive shall apply without prejudice to Community provisions on advertising for specific products and/or services or to restrictions or prohibitions on advertising in particular media.

4. The provisions of this Directive concerning comparative advertising shall not oblige Member States which, in compliance with the provisions of the Treaty, maintain or introduce advertising bans regarding certain goods or services, whether imposed directly or by a body or organization responsible, under the law of the Member States, for regulating the exercise of a commercial, industrial, craft or professional activity, to permit comparative advertising regarding those goods or services. Where these bans are limited to particular media, the Directive shall apply to the media not covered by these bans.

5. Nothing in this Directive shall prevent Member States from, in compliance with the provisions of the Treaty, maintaining or introducing bans or limitations on the use of comparisons in the advertising of professional services, whether imposed directly or by a body or organization responsible, under the law of the Member States, for regulating the exercise of a professional activity.

Article 8

Member States shall bring into force the measures necessary to comply with this Directive by 1 October 1986 at the latest. They shall forthwith inform the Commission thereof. Member States shall communicate to the Commission the text of all provisions of national law which they adopt in the field covered by this Directive.

Article 9

This Directive is addressed to the Member States.

3. COUNCIL DIRECTIVE 93/13/EEC

of 5 April, 1993

on unfair terms in consumer contracts

O.J. L 95/29 (Apr. 21, 1993)

The Council of the European Communities,

Having regard to the Treaty establishing the European Economic Community, and in particular Article 100 A thereof,

* * *

Whereas it is necessary to adopt measures with the aim of progressively establishing the internal market before 31 December 1992; whereas the internal market comprises an area without internal frontiers in which goods, persons, services and capital move freely;

Whereas the laws of Member States relating to the terms of contract between the seller of goods or supplier of services, on the one hand, and the consumer of them, on the other hand, show many disparities, with the result that the national markets for the sale of goods and services to consumers differ from each other and that distortions of competition may arise amongst the sellers and suppliers, notably when they sell and supply in other Member States;

Whereas, in particular, the laws of Member States relating to unfair terms in consumer contracts show marked divergences;

Whereas it is the responsibility of the Member States to ensure that contracts concluded with consumers do not contain unfair terms;

Whereas, generally speaking, consumers do not know the rules of law which, in Member States other than their own, govern contracts for the sale of goods or services; whereas this lack of awareness may deter them from direct transactions for the purchase of goods or services in another Member State;

Whereas, in order to facilitate the establishment of the internal market and to safeguard the citizen in his role as consumer when acquiring goods and services under contracts which are governed by the laws of Member States other than his own, it is essential to remove unfair terms from those contracts;

Whereas sellers of goods and suppliers of services will thereby be helped in their task of selling goods and supplying services, both at home and throughout the internal market; whereas competition will thus be stimulated, so contributing to increased choice for Community citizens as consumers;

Whereas the two Community programmes for a consumer protection and information policy underlined the importance of safeguarding consumers in the matter of unfair terms of contract; whereas this protection ought to be provided by laws and regulations which are either harmonized at Community level or adopted directly at that level;

Whereas in accordance with the principle laid down under the heading 'Protection of the economic interests of the consumers', as stated in those programmes: 'acquirers of goods and services should be protected against the abuse of power by the seller or supplier, in particular against one-sided standard contracts and the unfair exclusion of essential rights in contracts';

Whereas more effective protection of the consumer can be achieved by adopting uniform rules of law in the matter of unfair terms; whereas those rules should apply to all contracts concluded between sellers or suppliers and consumers; whereas as a result *inter alia* contracts relating to employment, contracts relating to succession rights, contracts relating to rights under family law and contracts relating to the incorporation and organization of companies or partnership agreements must be excluded from this Directive;

Whereas the consumer must receive equal protection under contracts concluded by word of mouth and written contracts regardless, in the latter case, of whether the terms of the contract are contained in one or more documents;

Whereas, however, as they now stand, national laws allow only partial harmonization to be envisaged; whereas, in particular, only contractual terms which have not been individually negotiated are covered by this Directive; whereas Member States should have the option, with due regard for the Treaty, to afford consumers a higher level of protection through national provisions that are more stringent than those of this Directive;

Whereas the statutory or regulatory provisions of the Member States which directly or indirectly determine the terms of consumer contracts are presumed not to contain unfair terms; whereas, therefore, it does not appear to be necessary to subject the terms which reflect mandatory statutory or regulatory provisions and the principles or provisions of international conventions to which the Member States or the Community are party; whereas in that respect the wording 'mandatory statutory or regulatory provisions' in Article 1(2) also covers rules which, according to the law, shall apply between the contracting parties provided that no other arrangements have been established;

Whereas Member States must however ensure that unfair terms are not included, particularly because this Directive also applies to trades, business or professions of a public nature;

Whereas it is necessary to fix in a general way the criteria for assessing the unfair character of contract terms;

Whereas the assessment, according to the general criteria chosen, of the unfair character of terms, in particular in sale or supply activities of a public nature providing collective services which take account of solidarity among users, must be supplemented by a means of making an overall evaluation of the different interests involved; whereas this constitutes the requirement of good faith; whereas, in making an assessment of good faith, particular regard shall be had to the strength of the bargaining positions of the parties, whether the consumer had an inducement to agree to the term and whether the goods or services were sold or supplied to the special order of the consumer; whereas the requirement of good faith may be satisfied by the seller or supplier where he deals fairly and equitably with the other party whose legitimate interests he has to take into account;

Whereas, for the purposes of this Directive, the annexed list of terms can be of indicative value only and, because of the cause of the minimal character of the Directive, the scope of these terms may be the subject of amplification or more restrictive editing by the Member States in their national laws;

Whereas the nature of goods or services should have an influence on assessing the unfairness of contractual terms;

Whereas, for the purposes of this Directive, assessment of unfair character shall not be made of terms which describe the main subject matter of the contract nor the quality/price ratio of the goods or services supplied; whereas the main subject matter of the contract and the price/quality ratio may nevertheless be taken into account in assessing the fairness of other terms; whereas it follows, *inter alia,* that in insurance contracts, the terms which clearly define or circumscribe the insured risk and the insurer's liability shall not be subject to such assessment since these restrictions are taken into account in calculating the premium paid by the consumer;

Whereas contracts should be drafted in plain, intelligible language, the consumer should actually be given an opportunity to examine all the terms and. if in doubt, the interpretation most favourable to the consumer should prevail;

Whereas Member States should ensure that unfair terms are not used in contracts concluded with consumers by a seller or supplier and that if, nevertheless, such terms are so used, they will not bind the consumer, and the contract will continue to bind the parties upon those terms if it is capable of continuing in existence without the unfair provisions;

Whereas there is a risk that, in certain cases, the consumer may be deprived of protection under this Directive by designating the law of a non-Member country as the law applicable to the contract; whereas provisions should therefore be included in this Directive designed to avert this risk;

Whereas persons or organizations, if regarded under the law of a Member State as having a legitimate interest in the matter, must have facilities for initiating proceedings concerning terms of contract drawn up for general use in contracts concluded with consumers, and in particular unfair terms, either before a court or before an administrative authority competent to decide upon complaints or to initiate appropriate legal proceedings; whereas this possibility does not, however, entail prior verification of the general conditions obtaining in individual economic sectors;

Whereas the courts or administrative authorities of the Member States must have at their disposal adequate and effective means of preventing the continued application of unfair terms in consumer contracts,

Has Adopted This Directive:

Article 1

1. The purpose of this Directive is to approximate the laws, regulations and administrative provisions of the Member States relating to unfair terms in contracts concluded between a seller or supplier and a consumer.

2. The contractual terms which reflect mandatory statutory or regulatory provisions and the provisions or principles of international conventions to which the Member States or the Community are party, particularly in the transport area, shall not be subject to the provisions of this Directive.

Article 2

For the purposes of this Directive:

(a) 'unfair terms' means the contractual terms defined in Article 3;

(b) 'consumer' means any natural person who, in contracts covered by this Directive, is acting for purposes which are outside his trade, business or profession;

(c) 'seller or supplier' means any natural or legal person who, in contracts covered by this Directive, is acting for purposes relating to his trade, business or profession, whether publicly owned or privately owned.

Article 3

1. A contractual term which has not been individually negotiated shall be regarded as unfair if, contrary to the requirement of good faith, it causes a significant imbalance in the parties' rights and obligations arising under the contract, to the detriment of the consumer.

2. A term shall always be regarded as not individually negotiated where it has been drafted in advance and the consumer has therefore not been able to influence the substance of the term, particularly in the context of a pre-formulated standard contract.

The fact that certain aspects of a term or one specific term have been individually negotiated shall not exclude the application of this Article to the rest of a contract if an overall assessment of the contract indicates that it is nevertheless a pre-formulated standard contract.

Where any seller or supplier claims that a standard term has been individually negotiated, the burden of proof in this respect shall be incumbent on him.

3. The Annex shall contain an indicative and non-exhaustive list of the terms which may be regarded as unfair.

Article 4

1. Without prejudice to Article 7, the unfairness of a contractual term shall be assessed, taking into account the nature of the goods or services for which the contract was concluded and by referring, at the time of conclu-

sion of the contract, to all the circumstances attending the conclusion of the contract and to all the other terms of the contract or of another contract on which it is dependent.

2. Assessment of the unfair nature of the terms shall relate neither to the definition of the main subject matter of the contract nor to the adequacy of the price and remuneration, on the one hand, as against the services or goods supplied in exchange, on the other, in so far as these terms are in plain intelligible language.

Article 5

In the case of contracts where all or certain terms offered to the consumer are in writing, these terms must always be drafted in plain, intelligible language. Where there is doubt about the meaning of a term, the interpretation most favourable to the consumer shall prevail. This rule on interpretation shall not apply in the context of the procedures laid down in Article 7 (2).

Article 6

1. Member States shall lay down that unfair terms used in a contract concluded with a consumer by a seller or supplier shall, as provided for under their national law, not be binding on the consumer and that the contract shall continue to bind the parties upon those terms if it is capable of continuing in existence without the unfair terms.

2. Member States shall take the necessary measures to ensure that the consumer does not lose the protection granted by this Directive by virtue of the choice of the law of a non-Member country as the law applicable to the contract if the latter has a close connection with the territory of the Member States.

Article 7

1. Member States shall ensure that, in the interests of consumers and of competitors, adequate and effective means exist to prevent the continued use of unfair terms in contracts concluded with consumers by sellers or suppliers.

2. The means referred to in paragraph 1 shall include provisions whereby persons or organizations, having a legitimate interest under national law in protecting consumers, may take action according to the national law concerned before the courts or before competent administrative bodies for a decision as to whether contractual terms drawn up for general use are unfair, so that they can apply appropriate and effective means to prevent the continued use of such terms.

3. With due regard for national laws, the legal remedies referred to in paragraph 2 may be directed separately or jointly against a number of sellers or suppliers from the same economic sector or their associations which use or recommend the use of the same general contractual terms or similar terms.

Article 8

Member States may adopt or retain the most stringent provisions compatible with the Treaty in the area covered by this Directive, to ensure a maximum degree of protection for the consumer.

Article 9

The Commission shall present a report to the European Parliament and to the Council concerning the application of this Directive five years at the latest after the date in Article 10(1).

Article 10

1. Member States shall bring into force the laws, regulations and administrative provisions necessary to comply with this Directive no later than 31 December 1994. They shall forthwith inform the Commission thereof.

These provisions shall be applicable to all contracts concluded after 31 December 1994.

2. When Member States adopt these measures, they shall contain a reference to this Directive or shall be accompanied by such reference on the occasion of their official publication. The methods of making such a reference shall be laid down by the Member States.

3. Member States shall communicate the main provisions of national law which they adopt in the field covered by this Directive to the Commission.

Article 11

This Directive is addressed to the Member States.

ANNEX

TERMS REFERRED TO IN ARTICLE 3(3)

1. Terms which have the object or effect of:

(a) excluding or limiting the legal liability of a seller or supplier in the event of the death of a consumer or personal injury to the latter resulting from an act or omission of that seller or supplier;

(b) inappropriately excluding or limiting the legal rights of the consumer *vis-à-vis* the seller or supplier or another party in the event of total or partial non-performance or inadequate performance by the seller or supplier of any of the contractual obligations, including the option of offsetting a debt owed to the seller or supplier against any claim which the consumer may have against him;

(c) making an agreement binding on the consumer whereas provision of services by the seller or supplier is subject to a condition whose realization depends on his own will alone;

(d) permitting the seller or supplier to retain sums paid by the consumer where the latter decides not to conclude or perform the contract, without providing for the consumer to receive compensation of an equivalent amount from the seller or supplier where the latter is the party cancelling the contract;

(e) requiring any consumer who fails to fulfil his obligation to pay a disproportionately high sum in compensation;

(f) authorizing the seller or supplier to dissolve the contract on a discretionary basis where the same facility is not granted to the consumer, or permitting the seller or supplier to retain the sums paid for services not yet supplied by him where it is the seller or supplier himself who dissolves the contract;

(g) enabling the seller or supplier to terminate a contract of indeterminate duration without reasonable notice except where there are serious grounds for doing so;

(h) automatically extending a contract of fixed duration where the consumer does not indicate otherwise, when the deadline fixed for the consumer to express this desire not to extend the contract is unreasonably early;

(i) irrevocably binding the consumer to terms with which he had no real opportunity of becoming acquainted before the conclusion of the contracts;

(j) enabling the seller or supplier to alter the terms of the contract unilaterally without a valid reason which is specified in the contract;

(k) enabling the seller or supplier to alter unilaterally without a valid reason any characteristics of the product or service to be provided;

(*l*) providing for the price or goods to be determined at the time of delivery or allowing a seller of goods or supplier of services to increase their price without in both cases giving the consumer the corresponding right to cancel the contract if the final price is too high in relation to the price agreed when the contract was concluded;

(m) giving the seller or supplier the right to determine whether the goods or services supplied are in conformity with the contract, or giving him the exclusive right to interpret any term of the contract;

(n) limiting the seller's or supplier's obligation to respect commitments undertaken by his agents or making his commitments subject to compliance with a particular formality;

(o) obliging the consumer to fulfil all his obligations where the seller or supplier does not perform his;

(p) giving the seller or supplier the possibility or transferring his rights and obligations under the contract, where this may serve to reduce the guarantees for the consumer, without the latter's agreement;

(q) excluding or hindering the consumer's right to take legal action or exercise any other legal remedy, particularly by requiring the consumer to take disputes exclusively to arbitration not covered by legal provisions, unduly restricting the evidence available to him or imposing on him a burden of proof which, according to the applicable law, should lie with another party to the contract.

2. Scope of subparagraphs (g), (j) and (*l*)

(a) Subparagraph (g) is without hindrance to terms by which a supplier of financial services reserves the right to terminate unilaterally a contract of indeterminate duration without notice where there is a valid reason, provided that the supplier is required to inform the other contracting party or parties thereof immediately.

(b) Subparagraph (j) is without hindrance to terms under which a supplier of financial services reserves the right to alter the rate of interest payable by the consumer or due to the latter, or the amount of other charges for financial services without notice where there is a valid reason, provided that the supplier is required to inform the other contracting party or parties thereof at the earliest opportunity and that the latter are free to dissolve the contract immediately.

Subparagraph (j) is also without hindrance to terms under which a seller or supplier reserves the right to alter unilaterally the conditions of a contract of indeterminate duration, provided that he is required to inform the consumer with reasonable notice and that the consumer is free to dissolve the contract.

(c) Subparagraphs (g), (j) and (*l*) do not apply to:

— transactions in transferable securities, financial instruments and other products or services where the price is linked to fluctuations in a stock exchange quotation or index or a financial market rate that the seller or supplier does not control;

— contracts for the purchase or sale of foreign currency, traveller's cheques or international money orders denominated in foreign currency;

(d) Subparagraph (*l*) is without hindrance to price-indexation clauses, where lawful, provided that the method by which prices vary is explicitly described.

4. COUNCIL DIRECTIVE 85/374/EEC

of 25 July 1985

on the approximation of the laws, regulations and administrative provisions of the Member States concerning liability for defective products

O.J. L 210/29 (Aug. 7, 1985), amended by

European Parliament and Council Directive 1999/34/EC of May 10, 1999
O.J. L 141 (June 4, 1999)

THE COUNCIL OF THE EUROPEAN COMMUNITIES,

Having regard to the Treaty establishing the European Economic Community, and in particular Article 100 thereof,

* * *

Whereas approximation of the laws of the Member States concerning the liability of the producer for damage caused by the defectiveness of his products is necessary because the existing divergences may distort competition and affect the movement of goods within the common market and entail a differing degree of protection of the consumer against damage caused by a defective product to his health or property;

Whereas liability without fault on the part of the producer is the sole means of adequately solving the problem, peculiar to our age of increasing technicality, of a fair apportionment of the risks inherent in modern technological production;

* * *

Whereas, in situations where several persons are liable for the same damage, the protection of the consumer requires that the injured person should be able to claim full compensation for the damage from any one of them;

Whereas, to protect the physical well-being and property of the consumer, the defectiveness of the product should be determined by reference not to its fitness for use but to the lack of the safety which the public at large is entitled to expect; whereas the safety is assessed by excluding any misuse of the product not reasonable under the circumstances;

Whereas a fair apportionment of risk between the injured person and the producer implies that the producer should be able to free himself from liability if he furnishes proof as to the existence of certain exonerating circumstances;

Whereas the protection of the consumer requires that the liability of the producer remains unaffected by acts or omissions of other persons having contributed to cause the damage; whereas, however, the contributory negligence of the injured person may be taken into account to reduce or disallow such liability;

Whereas the protection of the consumer requires compensation for death and personal injury as well as compensation for damage to property;

whereas the latter should nevertheless be limited to goods for private use or consumption and be subject to a deduction of a lower threshold of a fixed amount in order to avoid litigation in an excessive number of cases; whereas this Directive should not prejudice compensation for pain and suffering and other non-material damages payable, where appropriate, under the law applicable to the case;

Whereas a uniform period of limitation for the bringing of action for compensation is in the interests both of the injured person and of the producer;

Whereas products age in the course of time, higher safety standards are developed and the state of science and technology progresses; whereas, therefore, it would not be reasonable to make the producer liable for an unlimited period for the defectiveness of his product; whereas, therefore, liability should expire after a reasonable length of time, without prejudice to claims pending at law;

Whereas, to achieve effective protection of consumers, no contractual derogation should be permitted as regards the liability of the producer in relation to the injured person;

Whereas under the legal systems of the Member States an injured party may have a claim for damages based on grounds of contractual liability or on grounds of non-contractual liability other than that provided for in this Directive; in so far as these provisions also serve to attain the objective of effective protection of consumers, they should remain unaffected by this Directive; whereas, in so far as effective protection of consumers in the sector of pharmaceutical products is already also attained in a Member State under a special liability system, claims based on this system should similarly remain possible;

Whereas, to the extent that liability for nuclear injury or damage is already covered in all Member States by adequate special rules, it has been possible to exclude damage of this type from the scope of this Directive;

Whereas, since the exclusion of primary agricultural products and game from the scope of this Directive may be felt, in certain Member States, in view of what is expected for the protection of consumers, to restrict unduly such protection, it should be possible for a Member State to extend liability to such products;

Whereas, for similar reasons, the possibility offered to a producer to free himself from liability if he proves that the state of scientific and technical knowledge at the time when he put the product into circulation was not such as to enable the existence of a defect to be discovered may be felt in certain Member States to restrict unduly the protection of the consumer; whereas it should therefore be possible for a Member State to maintain in its legislation or to provide by new legislation that this exonerating circumstance is not admitted; whereas, in the case of new legislation, making use of this derogation should, however, be subject to a Community stand-still procedure, in order to raise, if possible, the level of protection in a uniform manner throughout the Community;

Whereas, taking into account the legal traditions in most of the Member States, it is inappropriate to set any financial ceiling on the producer's liability without fault; whereas, in so far as there are, however, differing traditions, it seems possible to admit that a Member State may derogate from the principle of unlimited liability by providing a limit for the total liability of the producer for damage resulting from a death or personal injury and caused by identical items with the same defect, provided that this limit is established at a level sufficiently high to guarantee adequate protection of the consumer and the correct functioning of the common market;

Whereas the harmonization resulting from this cannot be total at the present stage, but opens the way towards greater harmonization; whereas it is therefore necessary that the Council receive at regular intervals, reports from the Commission on the application of this Directive, accompanied, as the case may be, by appropriate proposals;

Whereas it is particularly important in this respect that a re-examination be carried out of those parts of the Directive relating to the derogations open to the Member States, at the expiry of a period of sufficient length to gather practical experience on the effects of these derogations on the protection of consumers and on the functioning of the common market,

HAS ADOPTED THIS DIRECTIVE:

Article 1

The producer shall be liable for damage caused by a defect in his product.

Article 2

For the purpose of this Directive 'product' means all movables, even if incorporated into another movable or into an immovable. 'Product' includes electricity.

Article 3

1. 'Producer' means the manufacturer of a finished product, the producer of any raw material or the manufacturer of a component part and any person who, by putting his name, trade mark or other distinguishing feature on the product presents himself as its producer.

2. Without prejudice to the liability of the producer, any person who imports into the Community a product for sale, hire, leasing or any form of distribution in the course of his business shall be deemed to be a producer within the meaning of this Directive and shall be responsible as a producer.

3. Where the producer of the product cannot be identified, each supplier of the product shall be treated as its producer unless he informs the injured person, within a reasonable time, of the identity of the producer or of the person who supplied him with the product. The same shall apply, in the case of an imported product, if this product does not indicate the

identity of the importer referred to in paragraph 2, even if the name of the producer is indicated.

Article 4

The injured person shall be required to prove the damage, the defect and the causal relationship between defect and damage.

Article 5

Where, as a result of the provisions of this Directive, two or more persons are liable for the same damage, they shall be liable jointly and severally, without prejudice to the provisions of national law concerning the rights of contribution or recourse.

Article 6

1. A product is defective when it does not provide the safety which a person is entitled to expect, taking all circumstances into account, including:

   (a) the presentation of the product;

   (b) the use to which it could reasonably be expected that the product would be put;

   (c) the time when the product was put into circulation.

2. A product shall not be considered defective for the sole reason that a better product is subsequently put into circulation.

Article 7

The producer shall not be liable as a result of this Directive if he proves:

   (a) that he did not put the product into circulation; or

   (b) that, having regard to the circumstances, it is probable that the defect which caused the damage did not exist at the time when the product was put into circulation by him or that this defect came into being afterwards; or

   (c) that the product was neither manufactured by him for sale or any form of distribution for economic purpose nor manufactured or distributed by him in the course of his business; or

   (d) that the defect is due to compliance of the product with mandatory regulations issued by the public authorities; or

   (e) that the state of scientific and technical knowledge at the time when he put the product into circulation was not such as to enable the existence of the defect to be discovered; or

   (f) in the case of a manufacturer of a component, that the defect is attributable to the design of the product in which the component has been fitted or to the instructions given by the manufacturer of the product.

Article 8

1. Without prejudice to the provisions of national law concerning the right of contribution or recourse, the liability of the producer shall not be reduced when the damage is caused both by a defect in product and by the act or omission of a third party.

2. The liability of the producer may be reduced or disallowed when, having regard to all the circumstances, the damage is caused both by a defect in the product and by the fault of the injured person or any person for whom the injured person is responsible.

Article 9

For the purpose of Article 1, 'damage' means:

(a) damage caused by death or by personal injuries;

(b) damage to, or destruction of, any item of property other than the defective product itself, with a lower threshold of 500 ECU, provided that the item of property:

(i) is of a type ordinarily intended for private use or consumption, and

(ii) was used by the injured person mainly for his own private use or consumption.

This Article shall be without prejudice to national provisions relating to non-material damage.

Article 10

1. Member States shall provide in their legislation that a limitation period of three years shall apply to proceedings for the recovery of damages as provided for in this Directive. The limitation period shall begin to run from the day on which the plaintiff became aware, or should reasonably have become aware, of the damage, the defect and the identity of the producer.

2. The laws of Member States regulating suspension or interruption of the limitation period shall not be affected by this Directive.

Article 11

Member States shall provide in their legislation that the rights conferred upon the injured person pursuant to this Directive shall be extinguished upon the expiry of a period of 10 years from the date on which the producer put into circulation the actual product which caused the damage, unless the injured person has in the meantime instituted proceedings against the producer.

Article 12

The liability of the producer arising from this Directive may not, in relation to the injured person, be limited or excluded by a provision limiting his liability or exempting him from liability.

Article 13

This Directive shall not affect any rights which an injured person may have according to the rules of the law of contractual or non-contractual liability or a special liability system existing at the moment when this Directive is notified.

Article 14

This Directive shall not apply to injury or damage arising from nuclear accidents and covered by international conventions ratified by the Member States.

Article 15

1. Each Member State may:

(a) [deleted];

(b) by way of derogation from Article 7(e), maintain or, subject to the procedure set out in paragraph 2 of this Article, provide in this legislation that the producer shall be liable even if he proves that the state of scientific and technical knowledge at the time when he put the product into circulation was not such as to enable the existence of a defect to be discovered.

2. A Member State wishing to introduce the measure specified in paragraph 1(b) shall communicate the text of the proposed measure to the Commission. The Commission shall inform the other Member States thereof.

The Member State concerned shall hold the proposed measure in abeyance for nine months after the Commission is informed and provided that in the meantime the Commission has not submitted to the Council a proposal amending this Directive on the relevant matter. However, if within three months of receiving the said information, the Commission does not advise the Member State concerned that it intends submitting such a proposal to the Council, the Member State may take the proposed measure immediately.

If the Commission does submit to the Council such a proposal amending this Directive within the aforementioned nine months, the Member State concerned shall hold the proposed measure in abeyance for a further period of 18 months from the date on which the proposal is submitted.

3. Ten years after the date of notification of this Directive, the Commission shall submit to the Council a report on the effect that rulings by the courts as to the application of Article 7(e) and of paragraph 1(b) of this Article have on consumer protection and the functioning of the common market. In the light of this report the Council, acting on a proposal from the Commission and pursuant to the terms of Article 100 of the Treaty, shall decide whether to repeal Article 7(e).

Article 16

1. Any Member State may provide that a producer's total liability for damage resulting from a death or personal injury and caused by identical items with the same defect shall be limited to an amount which may not be less than 70 million ECU.

2. Ten years after the date of notification of this Directive, the Commission shall submit to the Council a report on the effect on consumer protection and the functioning of the common market of the implementation of the financial limit on liability by those Member States which have used the option provided for in paragraph 1. In the light of this report the Council, acting on a proposal from the Commission and pursuant to the terms of Article 100 of the Treaty, shall decide whether to repeal paragraph 1.

Article 17

This Directive shall not apply to products put into circulation before the date on which the provisions referred to in Article 19 enter into force.

Article 18

1. For the purposes of this Directive, the ECU shall be that defined by Regulation (EEC) No 3180/78, as amended by Regulation (EEC) No 2626/84. The equivalent in national currency shall initially be calculated at the rate obtaining on the date of adoption of this Directive.

2. Every five years the Council, acting on a proposal from the Commission, shall examine and, if need be, revise the amounts in this Directive, in the light of economic and monetary trends in the Community.

Article 19

1. Member States shall bring into force, not later than three years from the date of notification of this Directive [July 30, 1985], the laws, regulations and administrative provisions necessary to comply with this Directive. They shall forthwith inform the Commission thereof.

2. The procedure set out in Article 15(2) shall apply from the date of notification of this Directive.

Article 20

Member States shall communicate to the Commission the texts of the main provisions of national law which they subsequently adopt in the field governed by this Directive.

Article 21

Every five years the Commission shall present a report to the Council on the application of this Directive and, if necessary, shall submit appropriate proposals to it.

Article 22

This Directive is addressed to the Member States.

5. COUNCIL DIRECTIVE 98/59/EC

of 20 July 1998

on the approximation of the laws of the Member States relating to collective redundancies

O.J. L 225/16 (Aug. 12, 1998)

THE COUNCIL OF THE EUROPEAN UNION,

Having regard to the Treaty establishing the European Community, and in particular Article 100 thereof,

Having regard to the proposal from the Commission,

Having regard to the opinion of the European Parliament,

Having regard to the opinion of the Economic and Social Committee,

(1) Whereas for reasons of clarity and rationality Council Directive 75/129/EEC of 17 February 1975 on the approximation of the laws of the Member States relating to collective redundancies should be consolidated;

(2) Whereas it is important that greater protection should be afforded to workers in the event of collective redundancies while taking into account the need for balanced economic and social development within the Community;

(3) Whereas, despite increasing convergence, differences still remain between the provisions in force in the Member States concerning the practical arrangements and procedures for such redundancies and the measures designed to alleviate the consequences of redundancy for workers;

(4) Whereas these differences can have a direct effect on the functioning of the internal market;

(5) Whereas the Council resolution of 21 January 1974 concerning a social action programme made provision for a directive on the approximation of Member States' legislation on collective redundancies;

(6) Whereas the Community Charter of the fundamental social rights of workers, adopted at the European Council meeting held in Strasbourg on 9 December 1989 by the Heads of State or Government of 11 Member States, states,

> '7. The completion of the internal market must lead to an improvement in the living and working conditions of workers in the European Community (. . .).
>
> The improvement must cover, where necessary, the development of certain aspects of employment regulations such as procedures for collective redundancies and those regarding bankruptcies.
>
> (. . .)

17. Information, consultation and participation for workers must be developed along appropriate lines, taking account of the practices in force in the various Member States.'

* * *

(8) Whereas, in order to calculate the number of redundancies provided for in the definition of collective redundancies within the meaning of this Directive, other forms of termination of employment contracts on the initiative of the employer should be equated to redundancies, provided that there are at least five redundancies;

(9) Whereas it should be stipulated that this Directive applies in principle also to collective redundancies resulting where the establishment's activities are terminated as a result of a judicial decision;

(10) Whereas the Member States should be given the option of stipulating that workers' representatives may call on experts on grounds of the technical complexity of the matters which are likely to be the subject of the informing and consulting;

(11) Whereas it is necessary to ensure that employers' obligations as regards information, consultation and notification apply independently of whether the decision on collective redundancies emanates from the employer or from an undertaking which controls that employer;

(12) Whereas Member States should ensure that workers' representatives and/or workers have at their disposal administrative and/or judicial procedures in order to ensure that the obligations laid down in this Directive are fulfilled;

* * *

HAS ADOPTED THIS DIRECTIVE:

SECTION I

Definitions and scope

Article 1

1. For the purposes of this Directive:

(a) 'collective redundancies' means dismissals effected by an employer for one or more reasons not related to the individual workers concerned where, according to the choice of the Member States, the number of redundancies is:

(i) either, over a period of 30 days:

— at least 10 in establishments normally employing more than 20 and less than 100 workers,

— at least 10% of the number of workers in establishments normally employing at least 100 but less than 300 workers,

— at least 30 in establishments normally employing 300 workers or more,

(ii) or, over a period of 90 days, at least 20, whatever the number of workers normally employed in the establishments in question;

(b) 'workers' representatives' means the workers' representatives provided for by the laws or practices of the Member States.

For the purpose of calculating the number of redundancies provided for in the first subparagraph of point (a), terminations of an employment contract which occur on the employer's initiative for one or more reasons not related to the individual workers concerned shall be assimilated to redundancies, provided that there are at least five redundancies. [Added in 1998.]

2. This Directive shall not apply to:

(a) collective redundancies effected under contracts of employment concluded for limited periods of time or for specific tasks except where such redundancies take place prior to the date of expiry or the completion of such contracts;

(b) workers employed by public administrative bodies or by establishments governed by public law (or, in Member States where this concept is unknown, by equivalent bodies);

(c) the crews of seagoing vessels.

SECTION II

Information and consultation

Article 2

1. Where an employer is contemplating collective redundancies, he shall begin consultations with the workers' representatives in good time with a view to reaching an agreement.

2. These consultations shall, at least, cover ways and means of avoiding collective redundancies or reducing the number of workers affected, and of mitigating the consequences by recourse to accompanying social measures aimed, *inter alia*, at aid for redeploying or retraining workers made redundant.

Member States may provide that the workers' representative may call on the services of experts in accordance with national legislation and/or practice. [Added in 1998.]

3. To enable workers' representatives to make constructive proposals, the employers shall in good time during the course of the consultations:

(a) supply them with all relevant information and

(b) in any event notify them in writing of:

(i) the reasons for the projected redundancies;

(ii) the number of [sic "and"?] categories of workers to be made redundant;

(iii) the number and categories of workers normally employed;

(iv) the period over which the projected redundancies are to be effected;

(v) the criteria proposed for the selection of the workers to be made redundant in so far as national legislation and/or practice confers the power therefor upon the employer;

(vi) the method for calculating any redundancy payments other than those arising out of national legislation and/or practice.

[Paras. (v) and (vi) added in 1992.]

The employer shall forward to the competent public authority a copy of, at least, the elements of the written communication which are provided for in the first subparagraph, point (b), subpoints (i) to (v).

4. The obligations laid down in paragraphs 1, 2 and 3 shall apply irrespective of whether the decision regarding collective redundancies is being taken by the employer or by an undertaking controlling the employer.

In considering alleged breaches of the information, consultation and notification requirements laid down by this Directive, account shall not be taken of any defence on the part of the employer on the ground that the necessary information has not been provided to the employer by the undertaking which took the decision leading to collective redundancies. [Para. 4 added in 1992.]

SECTION III

Procedure for collective redundancies

Article 3

1. Employers shall notify the competent public authority in writing of any projected collective redundancies.

However, Member States may provide that in the case of planned collective redundancies arising from termination of the establishment's activities as a result of a judicial decision, the employer shall be obliged to notify the competent public authority in writing only if the latter so requests. [Added in 1998.]

This notification shall contain all relevant information concerning the projected collective redundancies and the consultations with workers' representatives provided for in Article 2, and particularly the reasons for the redundancies, the number of workers to be made redundant, the number of workers normally employed and the period over which the redundancies are to be effected.

2. Employers shall forward to the workers' representatives a copy of the notification provided for in paragraph 1. The workers' representatives may send any comments they may have to the competent public authority.

Article 4

1. Projected collective redundancies notified to the competent public authority shall take effect not earlier than 30 days after the notification

referred to in Article 3(1) without prejudice to any provisions governing individual rights with regard to notice of dismissal.

Member States may grant the competent public authority the power to reduce the period provided for in the preceding subparagraph.

2. The period provided for in paragraph 1 shall be used by the competent public authority to seek solutions to the problems raised by the projected collective redundancies.

3. Where the initial period provided for in paragraph 1 is shorter than 60 days, Member States may grant the competent public authority the power to extend the initial period to 60 days following notification where the problems raised by the projected collective redundancies are not likely to be solved within the initial period.

Member States may grant the competent public authority wider powers of extension.

The employer must be informed of the extension and the grounds for it before expiry of the initial period provided for in paragraph 1.

4. Member States need not apply this Article to collective redundancies arising from termination of the establishment's activities where this is the result of a judicial decision. [Para. 4 added in 1998.]

SECTION IV

Final provisions

Article 5

This Directive shall not affect the right of Member States to apply or to introduce laws, regulations or administrative provisions which are more favourable to workers or to promote or to allow the application of collective agreements more favourable to workers.

Article 6

Member States shall ensure that judicial and/or administrative procedures for the enforcement of obligations under this Directive are available to the workers' representatives and/or workers. [Added in 1992.]

Article 7

Member States shall forward to the Commission the text of any fundamental provisions of national law already adopted or being adopted in the area governed by this Directive.

Article 8

[Repealed directives.]

Article 9

This Directive shall enter into force on the 20th day following its publication in the *Official Journal of the European Communities*.

Article 10

This Directive is addressed to the Member States.

6. COUNCIL DIRECTIVE 2001/23/EC

of 12 March 2001

on the approximation of the laws of the Member States relating to the safeguarding of employees' rights in the event of transfers of undertakings, businesses or parts of undertakings or businesses

O.J. L 82/16 (Mar. 22, 2001)

THE COUNCIL OF THE EUROPEAN UNION,

Having regard to the Treaty establishing the European Community, and in particular Article 94 thereof,

Having regard to the proposal from the Commission,

Having regard to the opinion of the European Parliament,

Having regard to the opinion of the Economic and Social Committee,

Whereas:

(1) Council Directive 77/187/EEC of 14 February 1977 on the approximation of the laws of the Member States relating to the safeguarding of employees' rights in the event of transfers of undertakings, businesses or parts of undertakings or businesses has been substantially amended. In the interests of clarity and rationality, it should therefore be codified.

(2) Economic trends are bringing in their wake, at both national and Community level, changes in the structure of undertakings, through transfers of undertakings, businesses or parts of undertakings or businesses to other employers as a result of legal transfers or mergers.

(3) It is necessary to provide for the protection of employees in the event of a change of employer, in particular, to ensure that their rights are safeguarded.

(4) Differences still remain in the Member States as regards the extent of the protection of employees in this respect and these differences should be reduced.

(5) The Community Charter of the Fundamental Social Rights of Workers adopted on 9 December 1989 ("Social Charter") states, in points 7, 17 and 18 in particular that: 'The completion of the internal market must lead to an improvement in the living and working conditions of workers in the European Community. The improvement must cover, where necessary, the development of certain aspects of employment regulations such as procedures for collective redundancies and those regarding bankruptcies. Information, consultation and participation for workers must be developed along appropriate lines, taking account of the practice in force in the various Member States. Such information, consultation and participation must be implemented in due time, particularly in connection with restructuring operations in undertakings or in cases of mergers having an impact on the employment of workers'.

(6) In 1977 the Council adopted Directive 77/187/EEC to promote the harmonization of the relevant national laws ensuring the safeguarding of the rights of employees and requiring transferors and transferees to inform and consult employees' representatives in good time.

(7) That Directive was subsequently amended in the light of the impact of the internal market, the legislative tendencies of the Member States with regard to the rescue of undertakings in economic difficulties, the case-law of the Court of Justice of the European Communities, Council Directive 75/129/EEC of 17 February 1975 on the approximation of the laws of the Member States relating to collective redundancies and the legislation already in force in most Member States.

(8) Considerations of legal security and transparency required that the legal concept of transfer be clarified in the light of the case-law of the Court of Justice. Such clarification has not altered the scope of Directive 77/187/EEC as interpreted by the Court of Justice.

(9) The Social Charter recognizes the importance of the fight against all forms of discrimination, especially based on sex, colour, race, opinion and creed.

* * *

HAS ADOPTED THIS DIRECTIVE:

CHAPTER I

Scope and definitions

Article 1

1. (a) This Directive shall apply to any transfer of an undertaking, business, or part of an undertaking or business to another employer as a result of a legal transfer or merger.

   (b) Subject to subparagraph (a) and the following provisions of this Article, there is a transfer within the meaning of this Directive where there is a transfer of an economic entity which retains its identity, meaning an organised grouping of resources which has the objective of pursuing an economic activity, whether or not that activity is central or ancillary. [Added in 1998 and amended in 2001.]

   (c) This Directive shall apply to public and private undertakings engaged in economic activities whether or not they are operating for gain. An administrative reorganization of public administrative authorities, or the transfer of administrative functions between public administrative authorities, is not a transfer within the meaning of this Directive. [First sentence added in 1998; second in 2001.]

2. This Directive shall apply where and in so far as the undertaking, business or part of the undertaking or business to be transferred is situated within the territorial scope of the Treaty.

3. This Directive shall not apply to seagoing vessels.

Article 2

1. For the purposes of this Directive:

(a) 'transferor' shall mean any natural or legal person who, by reason of a transfer within the meaning of Article 1(1), ceases to be the employer in respect of the undertaking, business or part of the undertaking or business;

(b) 'transferee' shall mean any natural or legal person who, by reason of a transfer within the meaning of Article 1(1), becomes the employer in respect of the undertaking, business or part of the undertaking or business;

(c) 'representatives of employees' and related expressions shall mean the representatives of the employees provided for by the laws or practices of the Member States;

(d) 'employee' shall mean any person who, in the Member State concerned, is protected as an employee under national employment law. [Added in 2001.]

2. This Directive shall be without prejudice to national law as regards the definition of contract of employment or employment relationship.

However, Member States shall not exclude from the scope of this Directive contracts of employment or employment relationships solely because:

(a) of the number of working hours performed or to be performed,

(b) they are employment relationships governed by a fixed-duration contract of employment within the meaning of Article 1(1) of Council Directive 91/383/EEC of 25 June 1991 supplementing the measures to encourage improvements in the safety and health at work of workers with a fixed-duration employment relationship or a temporary employment relationship [1], or

(c) they are temporary employment relationships within the meaning of Article 1(2) of Directive 91/383/EEC, and the undertaking, business or part of the undertaking or business transferred is, or is part of, the temporary employment business which is the employer.

[Para. 2 added in 1998].

CHAPTER II

Safeguarding of employees' rights

Article 3

1. The transferor's rights and obligations arising from a contract of employment or from an employment relationship existing on the date of a transfer shall, by reason of such transfer, be transferred to the transferee.

1. OJ L 206, 29.7.1991, p. 19.

Member States may provide that, after the date of transfer, the transferor and the transferee shall be jointly and severally liable in respect of obligations which arose before the date of transfer from a contract of employment or an employment relationship existing on the date of the transfer. [Added in 1998 and amended in 2001.]

2. Member States may adopt appropriate measures to ensure that the transferor notifies the transferee of all the rights and obligations which will be transferred to the transferee under this Article, so far as those rights and obligations are or ought to have been known to the transferor at the time of the transfer. A failure by the transferor to notify the transferee of any such right or obligation shall not affect the transfer of that right or obligation and the rights of any employees against the transferee and/or transferor in respect of that right or obligation. [Added in 2001.]

3. Following the transfer, the transferee shall continue to observe the terms and conditions agreed in any collective agreement on the same terms applicable to the transferor under that agreement, until the date of termination or expiry of the collective agreement or the entry into force or application of another collective agreement.

Member States may limit the period for observing such terms and conditions with the proviso that it shall not be less than one year.

4. (a) Unless Member States provide otherwise, paragraphs 1 and 3 shall not apply in relation to employees' rights to old-age, invalidity or survivors' benefits under supplementary company or intercompany pension schemes outside the statutory social security schemes in Member States.

(b) Even where they do not provide in accordance with subparagraph (a) that paragraphs 1 and 3 apply in relation to such rights, Member States shall adopt the measures necessary to protect the interests of employees and of persons no longer employed in the transferor's business at the time of the transfer in respect of rights conferring on them immediate or prospective entitlement to old age benefits, including survivors' benefits, under supplementary schemes referred to in subparagraph (a).

[Para. 4 as amended in 1998.]

Article 4

1. The transfer of the undertaking, business or part of the undertaking or business shall not in itself constitute grounds for dismissal by the transferor or the transferee. This provision shall not stand in the way of dismissals that may take place for economic, technical or organisational reasons entailing changes in the workforce.

Member States may provide that the first subparagraph shall not apply to certain specific categories of employees who are not covered by the laws or practice of the Member States in respect of protection against dismissal.

2. If the contract of employment or the employment relationship is terminated because the transfer involves a substantial change in working

conditions to the detriment of the employee, the employer shall be regarded as having been responsible for termination of the contract of employment or of the employment relationship.

Article 5

1. Unless Member States provide otherwise, Articles 3 and 4 shall not apply to any transfer of an undertaking, business or part of an undertaking or business where the transferor is the subject of bankruptcy proceedings or any analogous insolvency proceedings which have been instituted with a view to the liquidation of the assets of the transferor and are under the supervision of a competent public authority (which may be an insolvency practitioner authorized by a competent public authority). [Added in 1998 and amended in 2001.]

* * *

Article 6

1. If the undertaking, business or part of an undertaking or business preserves its autonomy, the status and function of the representatives or of the representation of the employees affected by the transfer shall be preserved on the same terms and subject to the same conditions as existed before the date of the transfer by virtue of law, regulation, administrative provision or agreement, provided that the conditions necessary for the constitution of the employee's representation are fulfilled.

* * *

CHAPTER III

Information and consultation

Article 7

1. The transferor and transferee shall be required to inform the representatives of their respective employees affected by the transfer of the following:

— the date or proposed date of the transfer,

— the reasons for the transfer,

— the legal, economic and social implications of the transfer for the employees,

— any measures envisaged in relation to the employees.

The transferor must give such information to the representatives of his employees in good time, before the transfer is carried out.

The transferee must give such information to the representatives of his employees in good time, and in any event before his employees are directly affected by the transfer as regards their conditions of work and employment.

2. Where the transferor or the transferee envisages measures in relation to his employees, he shall consult the representatives of his

employees in good time on such measures with a view to reaching an agreement.

* * *

4. The obligations laid down in this Article shall apply irrespective of whether the decision resulting in the transfer is taken by the employer or an undertaking controlling the employer.

In considering alleged breaches of the information and consultation requirements laid down by this Directive, the argument that such a breach occurred because the information was not provided by an undertaking controlling the employer shall not be accepted as an excuse.

[Para. 4 added in 1998.]

5. Member States may limit the obligations laid down in paragraphs 1, 2 and 3 to undertakings or businesses which, in terms of the number of employees, meet the conditions for the election or nomination of a collegiate body representing the employees.

6. Member States shall provide that, where there are no representatives of the employees in an undertaking or business through no fault of their own, the employees concerned must be informed in advance of:

— the date or proposed date of the transfer,

— the reason for the transfer,

— the legal, economic and social implications of the transfer for the employees,

— any measures envisaged in relation to the employees.

CHAPTER IV

Final provisions

Article 8

This Directive shall not affect the right of Member States to apply or introduce laws, regulations or administrative provisions which are more favourable to employees or to promote or permit collective agreements or agreements between social partners more favourable to employees.

Article 9

Member States shall introduce into their national legal systems such measures as are necessary to enable all employees and representatives of employees who consider themselves wronged by failure to comply with the obligations arising from this Directive to pursue their claims by judicial process after possible recourse to other competent authorities. [Added in 1998.]

Article 10

The Commission shall submit to the Council an analysis of the effect of the provisions of this Directive before 17 July 2006. It shall propose any amendment which may seem necessary.

Article 11

Member States shall communicate to the Commission the texts of the laws, regulations and administrative provisions which they adopt in the field covered by this Directive.

Article 12

[Repealed directives.]

Article 13

This Directive shall enter into force on the 20th day following its publication in the *Official Journal of the European Communities*.

Article 14

This Directive is addressed to the Member States.

7. COUNCIL DIRECTIVE 80/987/EEC

of 20 October 1980

on the approximation of the laws of the Member States relating to the protection of employees in the event of the insolvency of their employer

O.J. L 283/23 (Oct. 28, 1980)

THE COUNCIL OF THE EUROPEAN COMMUNITIES,

Having regard to the Treaty establishing the European Economic Community, and in particular Article 100 thereof,

Having regard to the proposal from the Commission,

Having regard to the opinion of the European Parliament,

Having regard to the opinion of the Economic and Social Committee,

Whereas it is necessary to provide for the protection of employees in the event of the insolvency of their employer, in particular in order to guarantee payment of their outstanding claims, while taking account of the need for balanced economic and social development in the Community;

Whereas differences still remain between the Member States as regards the extent of the protection of employees in this respect; whereas efforts should be directed towards reducing these differences, which can have a direct effect on the functioning of the common market;

Whereas the approximation of laws in this field should, therefore, be promoted while the improvement within the meaning of Article 117 of the Treaty is maintained;

* * *

HAS ADOPTED THIS DIRECTIVE:

SECTION I

SCOPE AND DEFINITIONS

Article 1

1. This Directive shall apply to employees' claims arising from contracts of employment or employment relationships and existing against employers who are in a state of insolvency within the meaning of Article 2(1).

2. Member States may, by way of exception, exclude claims by certain categories of employee from the scope of this Directive, by virtue of the special nature of the employee's contract of employment or employment relationship or of the existence of other forms of guarantee offering the employee protection equivalent to that resulting from this Directive.

The categories of employee referred to in the first subparagraph are listed in the Annex.

* * *

Article 2

1. For the purposes of this Directive, an employer shall be deemed to be in a state of insolvency:

(a) where a request has been made for the opening of proceedings involving the employer's assets, as provided for under the laws, regulations and administrative provisions of the Member State concerned, to satisfy collectively the claims of creditors and which make it possible to take into consideration the claims referred to in Article 1(1), and

(b) where the authority which is competent pursuant to the said laws, regulations and administrative provisions has:

— either decided to open the proceedings,

— or established that the employer's undertaking or business has been definitively closed down and that the available assets are insufficient to warrant the opening of the proceedings.

2. This Directive is without prejudice to national law as regards the definition of the terms 'employee', 'employer', 'pay', 'right conferring immediate entitlement' and 'right conferring prospective entitlement'.

SECTION II
PROVISIONS CONCERNING GUARANTEE INSTITUTIONS

Article 3

1. Member States shall take the measures necessary to ensure that guarantee institutions guarantee, subject to Article 4, payment of employees' outstanding claims resulting from contracts of employment or employment relationships and relating to pay for the period prior to a given date.

2. At the choice of the Member States, the date referred to in paragraph 1 shall be:

— either that of the onset of the employer's insolvency;

— or that of the notice of dismissal issued to the employee concerned on account of the employer's insolvency;

— or that of the onset of the employer's insolvency or that on which the contract of employment or the employment relationship with the employee concerned was discontinued on account of the employer's insolvency.

Article 4

1. Member States shall have the option to limit the liability of guarantee institutions, referred to in Article 3.

2. When Member States exercise the option referred to in paragraph 1, they shall:

— in the case referred to in Article 3(2), first indent, ensure the payment of outstanding claims relating to pay for the last three months of the contract of employment or employment relationship occurring within a period of six months preceding the date of the onset of the employer's insolvency;

— in the case referred to in Article 3(2), second indent, ensure the payment of outstanding claims relating to pay for the last three months of the contract of employment or employment relationship preceding the date of the notice of dismissal issued to the employee on account of the employer's insolvency;

— in the case referred to in Article 3(2), third indent, ensure the payment of outstanding claims relating to pay for the last 18 months of the contract of employment or employment relationship preceding the date of the onset of the employer's insolvency or the date on which the contract of employment or the employment relationship with the employee was discontinued on account of the employer's insolvency. In this case, Member States may limit the liability to make payment to pay corresponding to a period of eight weeks or to several shorter periods totalling eight weeks.

3. However, in order to avoid the payment of sums going beyond the social objective of this Directive, Member States may set a ceiling to the liability for employees' outstanding claims.

When Member States exercise this option, they shall inform the Commission of the methods used to set the ceiling.

Article 5

Member States shall lay down detailed rules for the organization, financing and operation of the guarantee institutions, complying with the following principles in particular:

(a) the assets of the institutions shall be independent of the employers' operating capital and be inaccessible to proceedings for insolvency;

(b) employers shall contribute to financing, unless it is fully covered by the public authorities;

(c) the institutions' liabilities shall not depend on whether or not obligations to contribute to financing have been fulfilled.

SECTION III

PROVISIONS CONCERNING SOCIAL SECURITY

Article 6

Member States may stipulate that Articles 3, 4 and 5 shall not apply to contributions due under national statutory social security schemes or under supplementary company or inter-company pension schemes outside the national statutory social security schemes.

Article 7

Member States shall take the measures necessary to ensure that non-payment of compulsory contributions due from the employer, before the onset of his insolvency, to their insurance institutions under national statutory social security schemes does not adversely affect employees' benefit entitlement in respect of these insurance institutions inasmuch as the employees' contributions were deducted at source from the remuneration paid.

Article 8

Member States shall ensure that the necessary measures are taken to protect the interests of employees and of persons having already left the employer's undertaking or business at the date of the onset of the employer's insolvency in respect of rights conferring on them immediate or prospective entitlement to old-age benefits, including survivors' benefits, under supplementary company or inter-company pension schemes outside the national statutory social security schemes.

SECTION IV

General and final provisions

Article 9

This Directive shall not affect the option of Member States to apply or introduce laws, regulations or administrative provisions which are more favourable to employees.

Article 10

This Directive shall not affect the option of Member States:

(a) to take the measures necessary to avoid abuses;

(b) to refuse or reduce the liability referred to in Article 3 or the guarantee obligation referred to in Article 7 if it appears that fulfilment of the obligation is unjustifiable because of the existence of special links between the employee and the employer and of common interests resulting in collusion between them.

Article 11

1. Member States shall bring into force the laws, regulations and administrative provisions necessary to comply with this Directive within 36 months of its notification. They shall forthwith inform the Commission thereof.

* * *

Article 12

Within 18 months of the expiry of the period of 36 months laid down in Article 11(1), Member States shall forward all relevant information to the Commission in order to enable it to draw up a report on the application of this Directive for submission to the Council.

Article 13

This Directive is addressed to the Member States.

8. COMMUNITY CHARTER OF THE FUNDAMENTAL SOCIAL RIGHTS OF WORKERS

[Adopted by all of the Member States other than the United Kingdom at a European Council meeting in Strassbourg on December 9–10, 1989. The UK's Labor government, elected in May 1997, endorsed the Charter, making its adoption unanimous.]

Whereas, under the terms of Article 117 of the EEC Treaty, the Member States have agreed on the need to promote improved living and working conditions for workers so as to make possible their harmonization while the improvement is being maintained;

Whereas following on from the conclusions of the European Councils of Hanover and Rhodes the European Council of Madrid considered that, in the context of the establishment of the single European market, the same importance must be attached to the social aspects as to the economic aspects and whereas, therefore, they must be developed in a balanced manner;

Having regard to the Resolutions of the European Parliament of 15 March 1989 and 14 September 1989 and to the Opinion of the Economic and Social Committee of 22 February 1989;

Whereas the completion of the internal market is the most effective means of creating employment and ensuring maximum well-being in the Community; whereas employment development and creation must be given first priority in the completion of the internal market; whereas it is for the Community to take up the challenges of the future with regard to economic competitiveness, taking into account, in particular, regional imbalances;

Whereas the social consensus contributes to the strengthening of the competitiveness of undertakings and of the economy as a whole and to the creation of employment; whereas in this respect it is an essential condition for ensuring sustained economic development;

Whereas the completion of the internal market must favour the approximation of improvements in living and working conditions, as well as economic and social cohesion within the European Community, while avoiding distortions of competition;

Whereas the completion of the internal market must offer improvements in the social field for workers of the European Community, especially in terms of freedom of movement, living and working conditions, health and safety at work, social protection, education and training;

Whereas, in order to ensure equal treatment, it is important to combat every form of discrimination, including discrimination on grounds of sex, colour, race, opinions and beliefs, and whereas, in a spirit of solidarity, it is important to combat social exclusion;

Whereas it is for Member States to guarantee that workers from non-member countries and members of their families who are legally resident in a Member State of the European Community are able to enjoy, as regards their living and working conditions, treatment comparable to that enjoyed by workers who are nationals of the Member State concerned;

Whereas inspiration should be drawn from the Conventions of the International Labour Organization and from the European Social Charter of the Council of Europe;

Whereas the Treaty, as amended by the Single European Act, contains provisions laying down the powers of the Community relating, inter alia, to the freedom of movement of workers (Articles 7, 48–51), to the right of establishment (Articles 52–58), to the social field under the conditions laid down in Articles 117–122—in particular as regards the improvement of health and safety in the working environment (Article 118a), the development of the dialogue between management and labour at European level (Article 118b), equal pay for men and women for equal work (Article 119)— to the general principles for implementing a common vocational training policy (Article 128), to economic and social cohesion (Article 130a to 130e) and, more generally, to the approximation of legislation (Articles 100, 100a and 235); whereas the implementation of the Charter must not entail an extension of the Community's powers as defined by the Treaties;

Whereas the aim of the present Charter is on the one hand to consolidate the progress made in the social field, through action by the Member States, the two sides of industry and the Community;

Whereas its aim is on the other hand to declare solemnly that the implementation of the Single European Act must take full account of the social dimension of the Community and that it is necessary in this context to ensure at appropriate levels the development of the social rights of workers of the European Community, especially employed workers and self-employed persons;

Whereas, in accordance with the conclusions of the Madrid European Council, the respective roles of Community rules, national legislation and collective agreements must be clearly established;

Whereas, by virtue of the principle of subsidiarity, responsibility for the initiatives to be taken with regard to the implementation of these social rights lies with the Member States or their constituent parts and, within the limits of its powers, with the European Community; whereas such implementation may take the form of laws, collective agreements or existing practices at the various appropriate levels and whereas it requires in many spheres the active involvement of the two sides of industry;

Whereas the solemn proclamation of fundamental social rights at European Community level may not, when implemented, provide grounds for any retrogression compared with the situation currently existing in each Member State,

HAVE ADOPTED THE FOLLOWING DECLARATION CONSTITUTING THE "COMMUNITY CHARTER OF THE FUNDAMENTAL SOCIAL RIGHTS OF WORKERS":

TITLE I

FUNDAMENTAL SOCIAL RIGHTS OF WORKERS

FREEDOM OF MOVEMENT

1. Every worker of the European Community shall have the right to freedom of movement throughout the territory of the Community, subject

to restrictions justified on grounds of public order, public safety or public health.

2. The right to freedom of movement shall enable any worker to engage in any occupation or profession in the Community in accordance with the principles of equal treatment as regards access to employment, working conditions and social protection in the host country.

3. The right of freedom of movement shall also imply:

— harmonization of conditions of residence in all Member States, particularly those concerning family reunification;

— elimination of obstacles arising from the non-recognition of diplomas or equivalent occupational qualifications;

— improvement of the living and working conditions of frontier workers.

EMPLOYMENT AND REMUNERATION

4. Every individual shall be free to choose and engage in an occupation according to the regulations governing each occupation.

5. All employment shall be fairly remunerated.

To this effect, in accordance with arrangements applying in each country:

— workers shall be assured of an equitable wage, i.e. a wage sufficient to enable them to have a decent standard of living;

— workers subject to terms of employment other than an open-ended full time contract shall receive an equitable reference wage;

— wages may be withheld, seized or transferred only in accordance with the provisions of national law; such provisions should entail measures enabling the worker concerned to continue to enjoy the necessary means of subsistence for himself and his family.

6. Every individual must be able to have access to public placement services free of charge.

IMPROVEMENT OF LIVING AND WORKING CONDITIONS

7. The completion of the internal market must lead to an improvement in the living and working conditions of workers in the European Community. This process must result from an approximation of these conditions while the improvement is being maintained, as regards in particular the duration and organization of working time and forms of employment other than open-ended contracts, such as fixed-term contracts, part-time working, temporary work and seasonal work.

The improvement must cover, where necessary, the development of certain aspects of employment regulations such as procedures for collective redundancies and those regarding bankruptcies.

8. Every worker of the European Community shall have a right to a weekly rest period and to annual paid leave, the duration of which must be

harmonized in accordance with national practices while the improvement is being maintained.

9. The conditions of employment of every worker of the European Community shall be stipulated in laws, in a collective agreement or in a contract of employment, according to arrangements applying in each country.

SOCIAL PROTECTION

According to the arrangements applying in each country:

10. Every worker of the European Community shall have a right to adequate social protection and shall, whatever his status and whatever the size of the undertaking in which he is employed, enjoy an adequate level of social security benefits.

Persons who have been unable either to enter or re-enter the labour market and have no means of subsistence must be able to receive sufficient resources and social assistance in keeping with their particular situation.

FREEDOM OF ASSOCIATION AND COLLECTIVE BARGAINING

11. Employers and workers of the European Community shall have the right of association in order to constitute professional organizations or trade unions of their choice for the defence of their economic and social interests.

Every employer and every worker shall have the freedom to join or not to join such organizations without any personal or occupational damage being thereby suffered by him.

12. Employers or employers' organizations, on the one hand, and workers' organizations, on the other, shall have the right to negotiate and conclude collective agreements under the conditions laid down by national legislation and practice.

The dialogue between the two sides of industry at European level which must be developed, may, if the parties deem it desirable, result in contractual relations, in particular at inter-occupational and sectoral level.

13. The right to resort to collective action in the event of a conflict of interests shall include the right to strike, subject to the obligations arising under national regulations and collective agreements.

In order to facilitate the settlement of industrial disputes the establishment and utilization at the appropriate levels of conciliation, mediation and arbitration procedures should be encouraged in accordance with national practice.

14. The internal legal order of the Member States shall determine under which conditions and to what extent the rights provided for in Articles 11 to 13 apply to the armed forces, the police and the civil service.

VOCATIONAL TRAINING

15. Every worker of the European Community must be able to have access to vocational training and to receive such training throughout his

working life. In the conditions governing access to such training there may be no discrimination on grounds of nationality.

The competent public authorities, undertakings or the two sides of industry, each within their own sphere of competence, should set up continuing and permanent training systems enabling every person to undergo retraining more especially through leave for training purposes, to improve his skills or to acquire new skills, particularly in the light of technical developments.

EQUAL TREATMENT FOR MEN AND WOMEN

16. Equal treatment for men and women must be assured. Equal opportunities for men and women must be developed.

To this end, action should be intensified wherever necessary to ensure the implementation of the principle of equality between men and women as regards in particular access to employment, remuneration, working conditions, social protection, education, vocational training and career development.

Measures should also be developed enabling men and women to reconcile their occupational and family obligations.

INFORMATION, CONSULTATION AND PARTICIPATION FOR WORKERS

17. Information, consultation and participation for workers must be developed along appropriate lines, taking account of the practices in force in the various Member States.

This shall apply especially in companies or groups of companies having establishments or companies in several Member States of the European Community.

18. Such information, consultation and participation must be implemented in due time, particularly in the following cases:

— when technological changes which, from the point of view of working conditions and work organization, have major implications for the work force are introduced into undertakings;

— in connection with restructuring operations in undertakings or in cases of mergers having an impact on the employment of workers;

— in cases of collective redundancy procedures;

— when transfrontier workers in particular are affected by employment policies pursued by the undertaking where they are employed.

HEALTH PROTECTION AND SAFETY AT THE WORKPLACE

19. Every worker must enjoy satisfactory health and safety conditions in his working environment. Appropriate measures must be taken in order to achieve further harmonization of conditions in this area while maintaining the improvements made.

These measures shall take account, in particular, of the need for the training, information, consultation and balanced participation of workers as regards the risks incurred and the steps taken to eliminate or reduce them.

The provisions regarding implementation of the internal market shall help to ensure such protection.

PROTECTION OF CHILDREN AND ADOLESCENTS

20. Without prejudice to such rules as may be more favourable to young people, in particular those ensuring their preparation for work through vocational training, and subject to derogations limited to certain light work, the minimum employment age must not be lower than the minimum school-leaving age and, in any case, not lower than 15 years.

21. Young people who are in gainful employment must receive equitable remuneration in accordance with national practice.

22. Appropriate measures must be taken to adjust labour regulations applicable to young workers so that their specific needs regarding development, vocational training and access to employment are met.

The duration of work must, in particular, be limited—without it being possible to circumvent this limitation through recourse to overtime—and night work prohibited in the case of workers of under eighteen years of age, save in the case of certain jobs laid down in national legislation or regulations.

23. Following the end of compulsory education, young people must be entitled to receive initial vocational training of a sufficient duration to enable them to adapt to the requirements of their future working life; for young workers, such training should take place during working hours.

ELDERLY PERSONS

According to the arrangements applying in each country:

24. Every worker of the European Community must, at the time of retirement, be able to enjoy resources affording him or her a decent standard of living.

25. Every person who has reached retirement age but who is not entitled to a pension or who does not have other means of subsistence, must be entitled to sufficient resources and to medical and social assistance specifically suited to his needs.

DISABLED PERSONS

26. All disabled persons, whatever the origin and nature of their disablement, must be entitled to additional concrete measures aimed at improving their social and professional integration.

These measures must concern, in particular, according to the capacities of the beneficiaries, vocational training, ergonomics, accessibility, mobility, means of transport and housing.

TITLE II

IMPLEMENTATION OF THE CHARTER

27. It is more particularly the responsibility of the Member States, in accordance with the national practices, notably through legislative measures or collective agreements, to guarantee the fundamental social rights in this Charter and to implement the social measures indispensable to the smooth operation of the internal market as part of a strategy of economic and social cohesion.

28. The European Council invites the Commission to submit as soon as possible initiatives which fall within its powers, as provided for in the Treaties, with a view to the adoption of legal instruments for the effective implementation, as and when the internal market is completed, of those rights which come within the Community's area of competence.

29. The Commission shall establish each year, during the last three months, a report on the application of the Charter by the Member States and by the European Community.

30. The report of the Commission shall be forwarded to the European Council, the European Parliament and the Economic and Social Committee.

9. COUNCIL DIRECTIVE 92/85/EEC

of 19 Oct. 1992

on the introduction of measures to encourage improvements in the safety and health at work of pregnant workers and workers who have recently given birth or are breastfeeding

O.J. L 348/1 (Nov. 28, 1992)

THE COUNCIL OF THE EUROPEAN COMMUNITIES,

Having regard to the Treaty establishing the European Economic Community, and in particular Article 118a thereof,

Having regard to the proposal from the Commission, drawn up after consultation with the Advisory Committee on Safety, Hygiene and Health Protection at work[1]

In cooperation with the European Parliament[2],

Having regard to the opinion of the Economic and Social Committee[3],

Whereas Article 118a of the Treaty provides that the Council shall adopt, by means of directives, minimum requirements for encouraging improvements, especially in the working environment, to protect the safety and health of workers;

Whereas this Directive does not justify any reduction in levels of protection already achieved in individual Member States, the Member States being committed, under the Treaty, to encouraging improvements in conditions in this area and to harmonizing conditions while maintaining the improvements made;

Whereas, under the terms of Article 118 a of the Treaty, the said directives are to avoid imposing administrative, financial and legal constraints in a way which would hold back the creation and development of small and medium-sized undertakings;

Whereas, pursuant to Decision 74/325/EEC[4], as last amended by the 1985 Act of Accession, the Advisory Committee on Safety, Hygiene and Health Protection at Work is consulted by the Commission on the drafting of proposals in this field;

Whereas the Community Charter of the fundamental social rights of workers, adopted at the Strasbourg European Council on 9 December 1989 by the Heads of State or Government of 11 Member States, lays down, in paragraph 19 in particular, that:

'Every worker must enjoy satisfactory health and safety conditions in his working environment. Appropriate measures must be taken in

---

1. OJ No C 281, 9.11.190, p. 3; and OJ No C 25.1.2. 1991, p. 9.
2. OJ No C 19, 28.1.1991, p. 177; and OJ No C 150, 15.6.1992, p. 99.
3. OJ No C 41, 18.2.1991, p. 29.
4. OJ No L 185, 9.7.1974, p. 15.

order to achieve further harmonization of conditions in this area while maintaining the improvements made;'

Whereas the Commission, in its action programme for the implementation of the Community Charter of the fundamental social rights of workers, has included among its aims the adoption by the Council of a Directive on the protection of pregnant women at work;

Whereas Article 15 of Council Directive 89/391/EEC of 12 June 1989 on the introduction of measures to encourage improvements in the safety and health of workers at work[5] provides that particularly sensitive risk groups must be protected against the dangers which specifically affect them;

Whereas pregnant workers, workers who have recently given birth or who are breastfeeding must be considered a specific risk group in many respects, and measures must be taken with regard to their safety and health;

Whereas the protection of the safety and health of pregnant workers, workers who have recently given birth or workers who are breastfeeding should not treat women on the labour market unfavourably nor work to the detriment of directives concerning equal treatment for men and women;

Whereas some types of activities may pose a specific risk, for pregnant workers, workers who have recently given birth or workers who are breastfeeding, of exposure to dangerous agents, processes or working conditions; whereas such risks must therefore be assessed and the result of such assessment communicated to female workers and/or their representatives;

Whereas, further, should the result of this assessment reveal the existence of a risk to the safety or health of the female worker, provision must be made for such worker to be protected;

Whereas pregnant workers and workers who are breastfeeding must not engage in activities which have been assessed as revealing a risk of exposure, jeopardizing safety and health, to certain particularly dangerous agents or working conditions;

Whereas provision should be made for pregnant workers, workers who have recently given birth or workers who are breastfeeding not to be required to work at night where such provision is necessary from the point of view of their safety and health;

Whereas the vulnerability of pregnant workers, workers who have recently given birth or who are breastfeeding makes it necessary for them to be granted the right to maternity leave of at least 14 continuous weeks, allocated before and/or after confinement, and renders necessary the compulsory nature of maternity leave of at least two weeks, allocated before and/or after confinement;

Whereas the risk of dismissal for reasons associated with their condition may have harmful effects on the physical and mental state of pregnant

---

5. OJ No L 183, 29.6.1989, p. 1.

workers, workers who have recently given birth or who are breastfeeding; whereas provision should be made for such dismissal to be prohibited;

Whereas measures for the organization of work concerning the protection of the health of pregnant workers, workers who have recently given birth or workers who are breastfeeding would serve no purpose unless accompanied by the maintenance of rights linked to the employment contract, including maintenance of payment and/or entitlement to an adequate allowance;

Whereas, moreover, provision concerning maternity leave would also serve no purpose unless accompanied by the maintenance of rights linked to the employment contract and or entitlement to an adequate allowance;

Whereas the concept of an adequate allowance in the case of maternity leave must be regarded as a technical point of reference with a view to fixing the minimum level of protection and should in no circumstances be interpreted as suggesting an analogy between pregnancy and illness,

HAS ADOPTED THIS DIRECTIVE:

SECTION I
PURPOSE AND DEFINITIONS

Article 1

Purpose

1. The purpose of this Directive, which is the tenth individual Directive within the meaning of Article 16(1) of Directive 89/391/EEC, is to implement measures to encourage improvements in the safety and health at work of pregnant workers and workers who have recently given birth or who are breastfeeding.

2. The provisions of Directive 89/391/EEC, except for Article 2(2) thereof, shall apply in full to the whole area covered by paragraph 1, without prejudice to any more stringent and/or specific provisions contained in this Directive.

3. This Directive may not have the effect of reducing the level of protection afforded to pregnant workers, workers who have recently given birth or who are breastfeeding as compared with the situation which exists in each Member State on the date on which this Directive is adopted.

Article 2

Definitions

For the purposes of this Directive:

(a) *pregnant worker* shall mean a pregnant worker who informs her employer of her condition, in accordance with national legislation and/or national practice;

(b) *worker who has recently given birth* shall mean a worker who has recently given birth within the meaning of national legislation and/or national practice and who informs her employer of her condition, in accordance with that legislation and/or practice;

(c) *worker who is breastfeeding* shall mean a worker who is breastfeeding within the meaning of national legislation and/or national practice and who informs her employer of her condition, in accordance with that legislation and/or practice.

SECTION II
GENERAL PROVISIONS

Article 3

Guidelines

1. In consultation with the Member States and assisted by the Advisory Committee on Safety, Hygiene and Health Protection at Work, the Commission shall draw up guidelines on the assessment of the chemical, physical and biological agents and industrial processes considered hazardous for the safety or health of workers within the meaning of Article 2.

The guidelines referred to in the first subparagraph shall also cover movements and postures, mental and physical fatigue and other types of physical and mental stress connected with the work done by workers within the meaning of Article 2.

2. The purpose of the guidelines referred to in paragraph 1 is to serve as a basis for the assessment referred to in Article 4(1).

To this end, Member States shall bring these guidelines to the attention of all employers and all female workers and/or their representatives in the respective Member State.

Article 4

Assessment and information

1. For all activities liable to involve a specific risk of exposure to the agents, processes or working conditions of which a non-exhaustive list is given in Annex 1, the employer shall assess the nature, degree and duration of exposure, in the undertaking and/or establishment concerned, of workers within the meaning of Article 2, either directly or by way of the protective and preventive services referred to in Article 7 of Directive 89/391/EEC, in order to:

— assess any risks to the safety or health and any possible effect on the pregnancies or breastfeeding of workers within the meaning of Article 2,

— decide what measures should be taken.

2. Without prejudice to Article 10 of Directive 89/391/EEC, workers within the meaning of Article 2 and workers likely to be in one of the situations referred to in Article 2 in the undertaking and/or establishment concerned and/or their representatives shall be informed of the results of the assessment referred to in paragraph 1 and of all measures to be taken concerning health and safety at work.

Article 5

Action further to the results of the assessment

1. Without prejudice to Article 6 of Directive 89/391/EEC, if the results of the assessment referred to in Article 4(1) reveal a risk to the safety or health or an effect on the pregnancy or breastfeeding of a worker within the meaning of Article 2, the employer shall take the necessary measures to ensure that, by temporarily adjusting the working conditions and/or the working hours of the worker concerned, the exposure of that worker to such risks is avoided.

2. If the adjustment of her working conditions and/or working hours is not technically and/or objectively feasible, or cannot reasonably be required on duly substantiated grounds, the employer shall take the necessary measures to move the worker concerned to another job.

3. If moving her to another job is not technically and/or objectively feasible or cannot reasonably be required on duly substantiated grounds, the worker concerned shall be granted leave in accordance with national legislation and/or national practice for the whole of the period necessary to protect her safety or health.

4. The provisions of this Article shall apply *mutatis mutandis* to the case where a worker pursuing an activity which is forbidden pursuant to Article 6 becomes pregnant or starts breastfeeding and informs her employer thereof.

Article 6

Cases in which exposure is prohibited

In addition to the general provisions concerning the protection of workers, in particular those relating to the limit values for occupational exposure:

> 1. pregnant workers within the meaning of Article 2(a) may under no circumstances be obliged to perform duties for which the assessment has revealed a risk of exposure, which would jeopardize safety or health, to the agents and working conditions listed in Annex II, Section A;
>
> 2. workers who are breastfeeding, within the meaning of Article 2(c), may under no circumstances be obliged to perform duties for which the assessment has revealed a risk of exposure, which would jeopardize safety or health, to the agents and working conditions listed in Annex II, Section B.

Article 7

Night work

1. Member States shall take the necessary measures to ensure that workers referred to in Article 2 are not obliged to perform night work during their pregnancy and for a period following childbirth which shall be determined by the national authority competent for safety and health, subject to submission, in accordance with the procedures laid down by the

Member States, of a medical certificate stating that this is necessary for the safety or health of the worker concerned.

2. The measures referred to in paragraph 1 must entail the possibility, in accordance with national legislation and/or national practice, of:

(a) transfer to daytime work; or

(b) leave from work or extension of maternity leave where such a transfer is not technically and/or objectively feasible or cannot reasonably be required on duly substantiated grounds.

Article 8

Maternity leave

1. Member States shall take the necessary measures to ensure that workers within the meaning of Article 2 are entitled to a continuous period of maternity leave of a least 14 weeks allocated before and/or after confinement in accordance with national legislation and/or practice.

2. The maternity leave stipulated in paragraph 1 must include compulsory maternity leave of at least two weeks allocated before and/or after confinement in accordance with national legislation and/or practice.

Article 9

Time off for ante-natal examinations

Member States shall take the necessary measures to ensure that pregnant workers within the meaning of Article 2(a) are entitled to in accordance with national legislation and/or practice, time off, without loss of pay, in order to attend ante-natal examinations, if such examinations have to take place during working hours.

Article 10

Prohibition of dismissal

In order to guarantee workers, within the meaning of Article 2, the exercise of their health and safety protection rights as recognized under this Article, it shall be provided that:

1. Member States shall take the necessary measures to prohibit the dismissal of workers, within the meaning of Article 2, during the period from the beginning of their pregnancy to the end of the maternity leave referred to in Article 8(1), save in exceptional cases not connected with their condition which are permitted under national legislation and/or practice and, where applicable, provided that the competent authority has given its consent;

2. if a worker, within the meaning of Article 2, is dismissed during the period referred to in point 1, the employer must cite duly substantiated grounds for her dismissal in writing;

3. Member States shall take the necessary measures to protect workers, within the meaning of Article 2, from consequences of dismissal which is unlawful by virtue of point 1.

Article 11

Employment rights

In order to guarantee workers within the meaning of Article 2 the exercise of their health and safety protection rights, as recognized in this Article, it shall be provided that:

1. in the cases referred to in Articles 5, 6 and 7, the employment rights relating to the employment contract, including the maintenance of a payment to, and/or entitlement to an adequate allowance for, workers within the meaning of Article 2, must be ensured in accordance with national legislation and/or national practice;

2. in the case referred to in Article 8, the following must be ensured:

   (a) the rights connected with the employment contract of workers within the meaning of Article 2, other than those referred to in point (b) below;

   (b) maintenance of a payment to, and/or entitlement to an adequate allowance for, workers within the meaning of Article 2;

3. the allowance referred to in point 2(b) shall be deemed adequate if it guarantees income at least equivalent to that which the worker concerned would receive in the event of a break in her activities on grounds connected with her state of health. subject to any ceiling laid down under national legislation;

4. Member States may make entitlement to pay or the allowance referred to in points 1 and 2(b) conditional upon the worker concerned fulfilling the conditions of eligibility for such benefits laid down under national legislation.

These conditions may under no circumstances provide for periods of previous employment in excess of 12 months immediately prior to the presumed date of confinement.

Article 12

Defence of rights

Member States shall introduce into their national legal systems such measures as are necessary to enable all workers who should (sic. "consider"?) themselves wronged by failure to comply with the obligations arising from this Directive to pursue their claims by judicial process (and/or, in accordance with national laws and/or practices) by recourse to other competent authorities.

Article 13

Amendments to the Annexes

1. Strictly technical adjustments to Annex I as a result of technical progress, changes in international regulations or specifications and new

findings in the area covered by this Directive shall be adopted in accordance with the procedure laid down in Article 17 of Directive 89/391/EEC.

2. Annex II may be amended only in accordance with the procedure laid down in Article 118a of the Treaty.

Article 14

Final provisions

1. Member States shall bring into force the laws, regulations and administrative provisions necessary to comply with this Directive not later than two years after the adoption thereof or ensure, at the latest two years after adoption of this Directive, that the two sides of industry introduce the requisite provisions by means of collective agreements, with Member States being required to make all the necessary provisions to enable them at all times to guarantee the results laid down by this Directive. They shall forthwith inform the Commission thereof.

2. When Member States adopt the measures referred to in paragraph 1, they shall contain a reference of this Directive or shall be accompanied by such reference on the occasion of their official publication. The methods of making such a reference shall be laid down by the Member States.

3. Member States shall communicate to the Commission the texts of the essential provisions of national law which they have already adopted or adopt in the field governed by this Directive.

4. Member States shall report to the Commission every five years on the practical implementation of the provisions of this Directive, indicating the points of view of the two sides of industry.

However, Member States shall report for the first time to the Commission on the practical implementation of the provisions of this Directive, indicating the points of view of the two sides of industry, four years after its adoption.

The Commission shall inform the European Parliament, the Council, the Economic and Social Committee and the Advisory Committee on Safety, Hygiene and Health Protection at Work.

5. The Commission shall periodically submit to the European Parliament, the Council and the Economic and Social Committee a report on the implementation of this Directive, taking into account paragraphs 1, 2 and 3.

6. The Council will re-examine this Directive, on the basis of an assessment carried out on the basis of the reports referred to in the second subparagraph of paragraph 4 and, should the need arise, of a proposal, to be submitted by the Commission at the latest five years after adoption of the Directive.

Article 15

This Directive is addressed to the Member States.

10. COUNCIL DIRECTIVE 93/104/EC

of 23 November 1993

concerning certain aspects of the organization of working time

O.J. L 307/1 (Dec. 13, 1993)

THE COUNCIL OF THE EUROPEAN UNION,

Having regard to the Treaty establishing the European Community, and in particular Article 118a thereof,

Having regard to the proposal from the Commission,

In cooperation with the European Parliament,

Having regard to the opinion of the Economic and Social Committee,

Whereas Article 118a of the Treaty provides that the Council shall adopt, by means of directives, minimum requirements for encouraging improvements, especially in the working environment, to ensure a better level of protection of the safety and health of workers;

Whereas, under the terms of that Article, those directives are to avoid imposing administrative, financial and legal constraints in a way which would hold back the creation and development of small and medium-sized undertakings;

Whereas the provisions of Council Directive 89/391/EEC of 12 June 1989 on the introduction of measures to encourage improvements in the safety and health of workers at work (4) are fully applicable to the areas covered by this Directive without prejudice to more stringent and/or specific provisions contained therein;

Whereas the Community Charter of the Fundamental Social Rights of Workers, adopted at the meeting of the European Council held at Strasbourg on 9 December 1989 by the Heads of State or of Government of 11 Member States, and in particular points 7, first subparagraph, 8 and 19, first subparagraph, thereof, declared that:

> "7. The completion of the internal market must lead to an improvement in the living and working conditions of workers in the European Community. This process must result from an approximation of these conditions while the improvement is being maintained, as regards in particular the duration and organization of working time and forms of employment other than open-ended contracts, such as fixed-term contracts, part-time working, temporary work and seasonal work.
>
> 8. Every worker in the European Community shall have a right to a weekly rest period and to annual paid leave, the duration of which must be progressively harmonized in accordance with national practices.
>
> 19. Every worker must enjoy satisfactory health and safety conditions in his working environment. Appropriate measures must be

taken in order to achieve further harmonization of conditions in this area while maintaining the improvements made.";

Whereas the improvement of workers' safety, hygiene and health at work is an objective which should not be subordinated to purely economic considerations;

Whereas this Directive is a practical contribution towards creating the social dimension of the internal market;

Whereas laying down minimum requirements with regard to the organization of working time is likely to improve the working conditions of workers in the Community;

Whereas, in order to ensure the safety and health of Community workers, the latter must be granted minimum daily, weekly and annual periods of rest and adequate breaks; whereas it is also necessary in this context to place a maximum limit on weekly working hours;

Whereas account should be taken of the principles of the International Labour Organization with regard to the organization of working time, including those relating to night work;

Whereas, with respect to the weekly rest period, due account should be taken of the diversity of cultural, ethnic, religious and other factors in the Member States; whereas, in particular, it is ultimately for each Member State to decide whether Sunday should be included in the weekly rest period, and if so to what extent;

Whereas research has shown that the human body is more sensitive at night to environmental disturbances and also to certain burdensome forms of work organization and that long periods of night work can be detrimental to the health of workers and can endanger safety at the workplace;

Whereas there is a need to limit the duration of periods of night work, including overtime, and to provide for employers who regularly use night workers to bring this information to the attention of the competent authorities if they so request;

Whereas it is important that night workers should be entitled to a free health assessment prior to their assignment and thereafter at regular intervals and that whenever possible they should be transferred to day work for which they are suited if they suffer from health problems;

* * *

Whereas, given the specific nature of the work concerned, it may be necessary to adopt separate measures with regard to the organization of working time in certain sectors or activities which are excluded from the scope of this Directive;

Whereas, in view of the question likely to be raised by the organization of working time within an undertaking, it appears desirable to provide for flexibility in the application of certain provisions of this Directive, whilst ensuring compliance with the principles of protecting the safety and health of workers;

Whereas it is necessary to provide that certain provisions may be subject to derogations implemented, according to the case, by the Member States or the two sides of industry; whereas, as a general rule, in the event of a derogation, the workers concerned must be given equivalent compensatory rest periods,

HAS ADOPTED THIS DIRECTIVE:

SECTION I
SCOPE AND DEFINITIONS

Article 1

Purpose and scope

1. This Directive lays down minimum safety and health requirements for the organization of working time.

2. This Directive applies to:

(a) minimum periods of daily rest, weekly rest and annual leave, to breaks and maximum weekly working time; and

(b) certain aspects of night work, shift work and patterns of work.

3. This Directive shall apply to all sectors of activity, both public and private, within the meaning of Article 2 of Directive 89/391/EEC, without prejudice to Article 17 of this Directive, with the exception of air, rail, road, sea, inland waterway and lake transport, sea fishing, other work at sea and the activities of doctors in training;

4. The provisions of Directive 89/391/EEC are fully applicable to the matters referred to in paragraph 2, without prejudice to more stringent and/or specific provisions contained in this Directive.

Article 2

Definitions

For the purposes of this Directive, the following definitions shall apply:

1. working time shall mean any period during which the worker is working, at the employer's disposal and carrying out his activity or duties, in accordance with national laws and/or practice;

2. rest period shall mean any period which is not working time;

3. night time shall mean any period of not less than seven hours, as defined by national law, and which must include in any case the period between midnight and 5 a.m.;

4. night worker shall mean:

(a) on the one hand, any worker, who, during night time, works at least three hours of his daily working time as a normal course; and (b) on the other hand, any worker who is likely during night time to work a certain proportion of his annual working time, as defined at the choice of the Member State concerned:

(i) by national legislation, following consultation with the two sides of industry; or

(ii) by collective agreements or agreements concluded between the two sides of industry at national or regional level;

5. shift work shall mean any method of organizing work in shifts whereby workers succeed each other at the same work stations according to a certain pattern, including a rotating pattern, and which may be continuous or discontinuous, entailing the need for workers to work at different times over a given period of days or weeks;

6. shift worker shall mean any worker whose work schedule is part of shift work.

SECTION II

MINIMUM REST PERIODS—OTHER ASPECTS OF THE ORGANIZATION OF WORKING TIME

Article 3

Daily rest

Member States shall take the measures necessary to ensure that every worker is entitled to a minimum daily rest period of 11 consecutive hours per 24–hour period.

Article 4

Breaks

Member States shall take the measures necessary to ensure that, where the working day is longer than six hours, every worker is entitled to a rest break, the details of which, including duration and the terms on which it is granted, shall be laid down in collective agreements or agreements between the two sides of industry or, failing that, by national legislation.

Article 5

Weekly rest period

Member States shall take the measures necessary to ensure that, per each seven-day period, every worker is entitled to a minimum uninterrupted rest period of 24 hours plus the 11 hours' daily rest referred to in Article 3.

The minimum rest period referred to in the first subparagraph shall in principle include Sunday.

If objective, technical or work organization conditions so justify, a minimum rest period of 24 hours may be applied.

Article 6

Maximum weekly working time

Member States shall take the measures necessary to ensure that, in keeping with the need to protect the safety and health of workers:

1. the period of weekly working time is limited by means of laws, regulations or administrative provisions or by collective agreements or agreements between the two sides of industry;

2. the average working time for each seven-day period, including overtime, does not exceed 48 hours.

Article 7

Annual leave

1. Member States shall take the measures necessary to ensure that every worker is entitled to paid annual leave of at least four weeks in accordance with the conditions for entitlement to, and granting of, such leave laid down by national legislation and/or practice.

2. The minimum period of paid annual leave may not be replaced by an allowance in lieu, except where the employment relationship is terminated.

SECTION III

NIGHT WORK—SHIFT WORK—PATTERNS OF WORK

Article 8

Length of night work

Member States shall take the measures necessary to ensure that:

1. normal hours of work for night workers do not exceed an average of eight hours in any 24–hour period;

2. night workers whose work involves special hazards or heavy physical or mental strain do not work more than eight hours in any period of 24 hours during which they perform night work.

For the purposes of the aforementioned, work involving special hazards or heavy physical or mental strain shall be defined by national legislation and/or practice or by collective agreements or agreements concluded between the two sides of industry, taking account of the specific effects and hazards of night work.

Article 9

Health assessment and transfer of night workers to day work

1. Member States shall take the measures necessary to ensure that:

   (a) night workers are entitled to a free health assessment before their assignment and thereafter at regular intervals;

   (b) night workers suffering from health problems recognized as being connected with the fact that they perform night work are transferred whenever possible to day work to which they are suited.

2. The free health assessment referred to in paragraph 1(a) must comply with medical confidentiality.

3. The free health assessment referred to in paragraph 1(a) may be conducted within the national health system.

Article 10

Guarantees for night-time working

Member States may make the work of certain categories of night workers subject to certain guarantees, under conditions laid down by national legislation and/or practice, in the case of workers who incur risks to their safety or health linked to night-time working.

Article 11

Notification of regular use of night workers

Member States shall take the measures necessary to ensure that an employer who regularly uses night workers brings this information to the attention of the competent authorities if they so request.

Article 12

Safety and health protection

Member States shall take the measures necessary to ensure that:

1. night workers and shift workers have safety and health protection appropriate to the nature of their work;

2. appropriate protection and prevention services or facilities with regard to the safety and health of night workers and shift workers are equivalent to those applicable to other workers and are available at all times.

Article 13

Pattern of work

Member States shall take the measures necessary to ensure that an employer who intends to organize work according to a certain pattern takes account of the general principle of adapting work to the worker, with a view, in particular, to alleviating monotonous work and work at a predetermined work-rate, depending on the type of activity, and of safety and health requirements, especially as regards breaks during working time.

SECTION IV

MISCELLANEOUS PROVISIONS

Article 14

More specific Community provisions

The provisions of this Directive shall not apply where other Community instruments contain more specific requirements concerning certain occupations or occupational activities.

Article 15

More favourable provisions

This Directive shall not affect Member States' right to apply or introduce laws, regulations or administrative provisions more favourable to the protection of the safety and health of workers or to facilitate or permit the application of collective agreements or agreements concluded between the two sides of industry which are more favourable to the protection of the safety and health of workers.

Article 16

Reference periods

* * *

Article 17

Derogations

1. With due regard for the general principles of the protection of the safety and health of workers, Member States may derogate from Article 3, 4, 5, 6, 8 or 16 when, on account of the specific characteristics of the activity concerned, the duration of the working time is not measured and/or predetermined or can be determined by the workers themselves, and particularly in the case of:

    (a) managing executives or other persons with autonomous decision-taking powers;

    (b) family workers; or

    (c) workers officiating at religious ceremonies in churches and religious communities.

2. Derogations may be adopted by means of laws, regulations or administrative provisions or by means of collective agreements or agreements between the two sides of industry provided that the workers concerned are afforded equivalent periods of compensatory rest or that, in exceptional cases in which it is not possible, for objective reasons, to grant such equivalent periods of compensatory rest, the workers concerned are afforded appropriate protection:

2.1. from Articles 3, 4, 5, 8 and 16:

    (a) in the case of activities where the worker's place of work and his place of residence are distant from one another or where the worker's different places of work are distant from one another;

    (b) in the case of security and surveillance activities requiring a permanent presence in order to protect property and persons, particularly security guards and caretakers or security firms;

    (c) in the case of activities involving the need for continuity of service or production, particularly:

(i) services relating to the reception, treatment and/or care provided by hospitals or similar establishments, residential institutions and prisons;

(ii) dock or airport workers;

(iii) press, radio, television, cinematographic production, postal and telecommunications services, ambulance, fire and civil protection services;

(iv) gas, water and electricity production, transmission and distribution, household refuse collection and incineration plants;

(v) industries in which work cannot be interrupted on technical grounds;

(vi) research and development activities;

(vii) agriculture;

(d) where there is a foreseeable surge of activity, particularly in:

(i) agriculture;

(ii) tourism;

(iii) postal services;

2.2. from Articles 3, 4, 5, 8 and 16:

(a) in the circumstances described in Article 5(4) of Directive 89/391/EEC;

(b) in cases of accident or imminent risk of accident;

2.3. from Articles 3 and 5:

(a) in the case of shift work activities, each time the worker changes shift and cannot take daily and/or weekly rest periods between the end of one shift and the start of the next one;

(b) in the case of activities involving periods of work split up over the day, particularly those of cleaning staff.

* * *

Article 18

Final provisions

1. (a) Member States shall adopt the laws, regulations and administrative provisions necessary to comply with this Directive by 23 November 1996, or shall ensure by that date that the two sides of industry establish the necessary measures by agreement, with Member States being obliged to take any necessary steps to enable them to guarantee at all times that the provisions laid down by this Directive are fulfilled.

(b) (i) However, a Member State shall have the option not to apply Article 6, while respecting the general principles of the protection of the safety and health of workers, and provided it takes the necessary measures to ensure that:

— no employer requires a worker to work more than 48 hours over a seven-day period, calculated as an average for the reference period referred to in point 2 of Article 16, unless he has first obtained the worker's agreement to perform such work,

— no worker is subjected to any detriment by his employer because he is not willing to give his agreement to perform such work,

— the employer keeps up-to-date records of all workers who carry out such work,

— the records are placed at the disposal of the competent authorities, which may, for reasons connected with the safety and/or health of workers, prohibit or restrict the possibility of exceeding the maximum weekly working hours,

— the employer provides the competent authorities at their request with information on cases in which agreement has been given by workers to perform work exceeding 48 hours over a period of seven days, calculated as an average for the reference period referred to in point 2 of Article 16.

Before the expiry of a period of seven years from the date referred to in (a), the Council shall, on the basis of a Commission proposal accompanied by an appraisal report, re-examine the provisions of this point (i) and decide on what action to take.

(ii) Similarly, Member States shall have the option, as regards the application of Article 7, of making use of a transitional period of not more than three years from the date referred to in (a), provided that during that transitional period:

— every worker receives three weeks' paid annual leave in accordance with the conditions for the entitlement to, and granting of, such leave laid down by national legislation and/or practice, and

— the three-week period of paid annual leave may not be replaced by an allowance in lieu, except where the employment relationship is terminated.

(c) Member States shall forthwith inform the Commission thereof.

* * *

3. Without prejudice to the right of Member States to develop, in the light of changing circumstances, different legislative, regulatory or contractual provisions in the field of working time, as long as the minimum requirements provided for in this Directive are complied with, implementation of this Directive shall not constitute valid grounds for reducing the general level of protection afforded to workers.

4. Member States shall communicate to the Commission the texts of the provisions of national law already adopted or being adopted in the field governed by this Directive.

5. Member States shall report to the Commission every five years on the practical implementation of the provisions of this Directive, indicating the viewpoints of the two sides of industry.

[This directive was amended by Directive 2000/34/EC of the European Parliament and of the Council, O.J. L 195/41 (Aug. 1, 2000), in order to cover almost all of the sectors of workers omitted initially, i.e., workers in road, air, sea and rail transport, workers in offshore facilities (such as oil rigs), and doctors while in training. Certain specific derogations were provided for these sectors.]

11. COUNCIL DIRECTIVE 91/533/EEC

of 14 October 1991

on an employer's obligation to inform employees of the conditions applicable to the contract or employment relationship

O.J. L 288/32 (Oct. 18, 1991)

THE COUNCIL OF THE EUROPEAN COMMUNITIES,

Having regard to the Treaty establishing the European Economic Community, and in particular Article 100 thereof,

Having regard to the proposal from the Commission,[6]

Having regard to the opinion of the European Parliament,[7]

Having regard to the opinion of the Economic and Social Committee,[8]

Whereas the development, in the Member States, of new forms of work has led to an increase in the number of types of employment relationship;

Whereas, faced with this development, certain Member States have considered it necessary to subject employment relationships to formal requirements; whereas these provisions are designed to provide employees with improved protection against possible infringements of their rights and to create greater transparency on the labour market;

Whereas the relevant legislation of the Member States differs considerably on such fundamental points as the requirement to inform employees in writing of the main terms of the contract or employment relationship;

Whereas differences in the legislation of Member States may have a direct effect on the operation of the common market;

Whereas Article 117 of the Treaty provides for the Member States to agree upon the need to promote improved working conditions and an improved standard of living for workers, so as to make possible their harmonization while the improvement is being maintained;

Whereas point 9 of the Community Charter of Fundamental Social Rights for Workers, adopted at the Strasbourg European Council on 9 December 1989 by the Heads of State and Government of 11 Member States, states:

'The conditions of employment of every worker of the European Community shall be stipulated in laws, a collective agreement or a contract of employment, according to arrangements applying in each country.';

Whereas it is necessary to establish at Community level the general requirement that every employee must be provided with a document containing information on the essential elements of his contract or employment relationship;

---

6. OJ No C 24, 31.1.1991, p. 3.
7. OJ No C 240, 16.9.1991, p. 21.
8. OJ No C 159, 17.6.1991, p. 32.

Whereas, in view of the need to maintain a certain degree of flexibility in employment relationships, Member States should be able to exclude certain limited cases of employment relationship from this Directive's scope of application;

* * *

Whereas, in order to protect the interests of employees with regard to obtaining a document, any change in the main terms of the contract or employment relationship must be communicated to them in writing;

* * *

HAS ADOPTED THIS DIRECTIVE:

Article 1

Scope

1. This Directive shall apply to every paid employee having a contract or employment relationship defined by the law in force in a Member State and/or governed by the law in force in a Member State.

2. Member States may provide that this Directive shall not apply to employees having a contract or employment relationship:

(a) — with a total duration not exceeding one month, and/or

— with a working week not exceeding eight hours; or

(b) of a casual and/or specific nature provided, in these cases, that its non-application is justified by objective considerations.

Article 2

Obligation to provide information

1. An employer shall be obliged to notify an employee to whom this Directive applies, hereinafter referred to as 'the employee', of the essential aspects of the contract or employment relationship.

2. The information referred to in paragraph 1 shall cover at least the following:

(a) the identities of the parties;

(b) the place of work; where there is no fixed or main place of work, the principle that the employee is employed at various places and the registered place of business or, where appropriate, the domicile of the employer;

(c)(i) the title, grade, nature or category of the work for which the employee is employed; or

(ii) a brief specification or description of the work;

(d) the date of commencement of the contract or employment relationship;

(e) in the case of a temporary contract or employment relationship, the expected duration thereof;

(f) the amount of paid leave to which the employee is entitled or, where this cannot be indicated when the information is given, the procedures for allocating and determining such leave;

(g) the length of the periods of notice to be observed by the employer and the employee should their contract or employment relationship be terminated or, where this cannot be indicated when the information is given, the method for determining such periods of notice;

(h) the initial basic amount, the other component elements and the frequency of payment of the remuneration to which the employee is entitled;

(i) the length of the employee's normal working day or week;

(j) where appropriate;

(i) the collective agreements governing the employee's conditions of work;

or

(ii) in the case of collective agreements concluded outside the business by special joint bodies or institutions, the name of the competent body or joint institution within which the agreements were concluded.

3. The information referred to in paragraph 2(f), (g), (h) and (i) may, where appropriate, be given in the form of a reference to the laws, regulations and administrative or statutory provisions or collective agreements governing those particular points.

Article 3

Means of information

1. The information referred to in Article 2(2) may be given to the employee, not later than two months after the commencement of employment, in the form of:

(a) a written contract of employment; and/or

(b) a letter of engagement; and/or

(c) one or more other written documents, where one of these documents contains at least all the information referred to in Article 2(2)(a), (b), (c), (d), (h) and (i).

2. Where none of the documents referred to in paragraph 1 is handed over to the employee within the prescribed period, the employer shall be obliged to give the employee, not later than two months after the commencement of employment, a written declaration signed by the employer and containing at least the information referred to in Article 2(2).

Where the document(s) referred to in paragraph 1 contain only part of the information required, the written declaration provided for in the first subparagraph of this paragraph shall cover the remaining information.

3. Where the contract or employment relationship comes to an end before expiry of a period of two months as from the date of the start of work, the information provided for in Article 2 and in this Article must be made available to the employee by the end of this period at the latest.

Article 4

Expatriate employees

1. Where an employee is required to work in a country or countries other than the Member State whose law and/or practice governs the contract or employment relationship, the document(s) referred to in Article 3 must be in his/her possession before his/her departure and must include at least the following additional information:

(a) the duration of the employment abroad;

(b) the currency to be used for the payment of remuneration;

(c) where appropriate, the benefits in cash or kind attendant on the employment abroad;

(d) where appropriate, the conditions governing the employee's repatriation.

2. The information referred to in paragraph 1(b) and (c) may, where appropriate, be given in the form of a reference to the laws, regulations and administrative or statutory provisions or collective agreements governing those particular points.

3. Paragraphs 1 and 2 shall not apply if the duration of the employment outside the country whose law and/or practice governs the contract or employment relationship is one month or less.

Article 5

Modification of aspects of the contract or employment relationship

1. Any change in the details referred to in Articles 2(2) and 4(1) must be the subject of a written document to be given by the employer to the employee at the earliest opportunity and not later than one month after the date of entry into effect of the change in question.

2. The written document referred to in paragraph 1 shall not be compulsory in the event of a change in the laws, regulations and administrative or statutory provisions or collective agreements cited in the documents referred to in Article 3, supplemented, where appropriate, pursuant to Article 4(1).

Article 6

Form and proof of the existence of a contract or employment relationship and procedural rules

This Directive shall be without prejudice to national law and practice concerning:

— the form of the contract or employment relationship,

— proof as regards the existence and content of a contract or employment relationship,

— the relevant procedural rules.

Article 7

More favourable provisions

This Directive shall not affect Member States' prerogative to apply or to introduce laws, regulations or administrative provisions which are more favourable to employees or to encourage or permit the application of agreements which are more favourable to employees.

Article 8

Defence of rights

1. Member States shall introduce into their national legal systems such measures as are necessary to enable all employees who consider themselves wronged by failure to comply with the obligations arising from this Directive to pursue their claims by judicial process after possible recourse to other competent authorities.

2. Member States may provide that access to the means of redress referred to in paragraph 1 are subject to the notification of the employer by the employee and the failure by the employer to reply within 15 days of notification.

However, the formality of prior notification may in no case be required in the cases referred to in Article 4, neither for workers with a temporary contract or employment relationship, nor for employees not covered by a collective agreement or by collective agreements relating to the employment relationship.

Article 9

Final provisions

1. Member States shall adopt the laws, regulations and administrative provisions necessary to comply with this Directive no later than 30 June 1993 or shall ensure by that date that the employers' and workers' representatives introduce the required provisions by way of agreement, the Member States being obliged to take the necessary steps enabling them at all times to guarantee the results imposed by this Directive.

They shall forthwith inform the Commission thereof.

2. Member States shall take the necessary measures to ensure that, in the case of employment relationships in existence upon entry into force of the provisions that they adopt, the employer gives the employee, on request, within two months of receiving that request, any of the documents referred to in Article 3, supplemented, where appropriate, pursuant to Article 4(1).

3. When Member States adopt the measures referred to in paragraph 1, such measures shall contain a reference to this Directive or shall be accompanied by such reference on the occasion of their official publication. The methods of making such a reference shall be laid down by the Member States.

4. Member States shall forthwith inform the Commission of the measures they take to implement this Directive.

Article 10

This Directive is addressed to the Member States.

12. EQUAL PAY DIRECTIVE

Council Directive 75/117/EEC of 10 February 1975

on the approximation of the laws of the Member States relating to the application of the principle of equal pay for men and women

O.J. L 45/19 (Feb. 19, 1975)

THE COUNCIL OF THE EUROPEAN COMMUNITIES,

Having regard to the Treaty establishing the European Economic Community, and in particular Article 100 thereof;

Having regard to the proposal from the Commission;

Having regard to the Opinion of the European Parliament;

Having regard to the Opinion of the Economic and Social Committee;

Whereas implementation of the principle that men and women should receive equal pay contained in Article 119 of the Treaty is an integral part of the establishment and functioning of the common market;

Whereas it is primarily the responsibility of the Member States to ensure the application of this principle by means of appropriate laws, regulations and administrative provisions;

Whereas the Council resolution of 21 January 1974 concerning a social action programme, aimed at making it possible to harmonize living and working conditions while the improvement is being maintained and at achieving a balanced social and economic development of the Community, recognized that priority should be given to action taken on behalf of women as regards access to employment and vocational training and advancement, and as regards working conditions, including pay;

Whereas it is desirable to reinforce the basic laws by standards aimed at facilitating the practical application of the principle of equality in such a way that all employees in the Community can be protected in these matters;

Whereas differences continue to exist in the various Member States despite the efforts made to apply the resolution of the conference of the Member States of 30 December 1961 on equal pay for men and women and whereas, therefore, the national provisions should be approximated as regards application of the principle of equal pay,

HAS ADOPTED THIS DIRECTIVE:

Article 1

The principle of equal pay for men and women outlined in Article 119 of the Treaty, hereinafter called 'principle of equal pay', means, for the same work or for work to which equal value is attributed, the elimination of all discrimination on grounds of sex with regard to all aspects and conditions of remuneration.

In particular, where a job classification system is used for determining pay, it must be based on the same criteria for both men and women and so drawn up as to exclude any discrimination on grounds of sex.

Article 2

Member States shall introduce into their national legal systems such measures as are necessary to enable all employees who consider themselves wronged by failure to apply the principle of equal pay to pursue their claims by judicial process after possible recourse to other competent authorities.

Article 3

Member States shall abolish all discrimination between men and women arising from laws, regulations or administrative provisions which is contrary to the principle of equal pay.

Article 4

Member States shall take the necessary measures to ensure that provisions appearing in collective agreements, wage scales, wage agreements or individual contracts of employment which are contrary to the principle of equal pay shall be, or may be declared, null and void or may be amended.

Article 5

Member States shall take the necessary measures to protect employees against dismissal by the employer as a reaction to a complaint within the undertaking or to any legal proceedings aimed at enforcing compliance with the principle of equal pay.

Article 6

Member States shall, in accordance with their national circumstances and legal systems, take the measures necessary to ensure that the principle of equal pay is applied. They shall see that effective means are available to take care that this principle is observed.

Article 7

Member States shall take care that the provisions adopted pursuant to this Directive, together with the relevant provisions already in force, are brought to the attention of employees by all appropriate means, for example at their place of employment.

Article 8

1. Member States shall put into force the laws, regulations and administrative provisions necessary in order to comply with this Directive within one year of its notification and shall immediately inform the Commission thereof.

2. Member States shall communicate to the Commission the texts of the laws, regulations and administrative provisions which they adopt in the field covered by this Directive.

Article 9

Within two years of the expiry of the one-year period referred to in Article 8, Member States shall forward all necessary information to the Commission to enable it to draw up a report on the application of the Directive for submission to the Council.

Article 10

This Directive is addressed to the Member States.

13. EQUAL TREATMENT DIRECTIVE

Council Directive 76/207/EEC of 9 February 1976

on the implementation of the principle of equal treatment for men and women as regards access to employment, vocational training and promotion, and working conditions

O.J. L 39/40 (Feb. 14, 1976)*

THE COUNCIL OF THE EUROPEAN COMMUNITIES,

Having regard to the Treaty establishing the European Economic Community, and in particular Article 235 thereof,

Having regard to the proposal from the Commission,

Having regard to the opinion of the European Parliament,

Having regard to the opinion of the Economic and Social Committee,

Whereas the Council, in its resolution of 21 January 1974 concerning a social action programme, included among the priorities action for the purpose of achieving equality between men and women as regards access to employment and vocational training and promotion and as regards working conditions, including pay; * * *

Whereas Community action to achieve the principle of equal treatment for men and women in respect of access to employment and vocational training and promotion and in respect of other working conditions also appears to be necessary; whereas, equal treatment for male and female workers constitutes one of the objectives of the Community, in so far as the harmonization of living and working conditions while maintaining their improvement are inter alia to be furthered; whereas the Treaty does not confer the necessary specific powers for this purpose;

Whereas the definition and progressive implementation of the principle of equal treatment in matters of social security should be ensured by means of subsequent instruments,

HAS ADOPTED THIS DIRECTIVE:

Article 1

1. The purpose of this Directive is to put into effect in the Member States the principle of equal treatment for men and women as regards access to employment, including promotion, and to vocational training and as regards working conditions and, on the conditions referred to in paragraph 2, social security. This principle is hereinafter referred to as 'the principle of equal treatment.'

---

* Editors' note: A proposal to amend Directive 76/207 would, among other things: 1) add an article stating that sexual harassment constitutes discrimination on grounds of sex, 2) define "indirect discrimination" based on Article 13, 3) specify to what extent genuine occupational qualifications allow differences in treatment, 4) require States to provide the right of a woman who has given birth to return to her job or an equivalent post, and 5) enhance judicial protection of victims. Commission proposal of 7 June 2000.

2. With a view to ensuring the progressive implementation of the principle of equal treatment in matters of social security, the Council, acting on a proposal from the Commission, will adopt provisions defining its substance, its scope and the arrangements for its application.

Article 2

1. For the purposes of the following provisions, the principle of equal treatment shall mean that there shall be no discrimination whatsoever on grounds of sex either directly or indirectly by reference in particular to marital or family status.

2. This Directive shall be without prejudice to the right of Member States to exclude from its field of application those occupational activities and, where appropriate, the training leading thereto, for which, by reason of their nature or the context in which they are carried out, the sex of the worker constitutes a determining factor.

3. This Directive shall be without prejudice to provisions concerning the protection of women, particularly as regards pregnancy and maternity.

4. This Directive shall be without prejudice to measures to promote equal opportunity for men and women, in particular by removing existing inequalities which affect women's opportunities in the areas referred to in Article 1(1).

Article 3

1. Application of the principle of equal treatment means that there shall be no discrimination whatsoever on grounds of sex in the conditions, including selection criteria, for access to all jobs or posts, whatever the sector or branch of activity, and to all levels of the occupational hierarchy.

2. To this end, Member States shall take the measures necessary to ensure that:

(a) any laws, regulations and administrative provisions contrary to the principle of equal treatment shall be abolished;

(b) any provisions contrary to the principle of equal treatment which are included in collective agreements, individual contracts of employment, internal rules of undertakings or in rules governing the independent occupations and professions shall be, or may be declared, null and void or may be amended;

(c) those laws, regulations and administrative provisions contrary to the principle of equal treatment when the concern for protection which originally inspired them is no longer well founded shall be revised; and that where similar provisions are included in collective agreements labour and management shall be requested to undertake the desired revision.

Article 4

Application of the principle of equal treatment with regard to access to all types and to all levels, of vocational guidance, vocational training, advanced vocational training and retraining, means that Member States shall take all necessary measures to ensure that:

(a) any laws, regulations and administrative provisions contrary to the principle of equal treatment shall be abolished;

(b) any provisions contrary to the principle of equal treatment which are included in collective agreements, individual contracts of employment, internal rules of undertakings or in rules governing the independent occupations and professions shall be, or may be declared, null and void or may be amended;

(c) without prejudice to the freedom granted in certain Member States to certain private training establishments, vocational guidance, vocational training, advanced vocational training and retraining shall be accessible on the basis of the same criteria and at the same levels without any discrimination on grounds of sex.

Article 5

1. Application of the principle of equal treatment with regard to working conditions, including the conditions governing dismissal, means that men and women shall be guaranteed the same conditions without discrimination on grounds of sex.

2. To this end, Member States shall take the measures necessary to ensure that:

(a) any laws, regulations and administrative provisions contrary to the principle of equal treatment shall be abolished;

(b) any provisions contrary to the principle of equal treatment which are included in collective agreements, individual contracts of employment, internal rules of undertakings or in rules governing the independent occupations and professions shall be, or may be declared, null and void or may be amended;

(c) those laws, regulations and administrative provisions contrary to the principle of equal treatment when the concern for protection which originally inspired them is no longer well founded shall be revised; and that where similar provisions are included in collective agreements labour and management shall be requested to undertake the desired revision.

Article 6

Member States shall introduce into their national legal systems such measures as are necessary to enable all persons who consider themselves wronged by failure to apply to them the principle of equal treatment within the meaning of Articles 3, 4 and 5 to pursue their claims by judicial process after possible recourse to other competent authorities.

Article 7

Member States shall take the necessary measures to protect employees against dismissal by the employer as a reaction to a complaint within the undertaking or to any legal proceedings aimed at enforcing compliance with the principle of equal treatment.

Article 8

Member States shall take care that the provisions adopted pursuant to this Directive, together with the relevant provisions already in force, are brought to the attention of employees by all appropriate means, for example at their place of employment.

Article 9

1. Member States shall put into force the laws, regulations and administrative provisions necessary in order to comply with this Directive within 30 months of its notification and shall immediately inform the Commission thereof.

However, as regards the first part of Article 3(2)(c) and the first part of Article 5(2)(c), Member States shall carry out a first examination and if necessary a first revision of the laws, regulations and administrative provisions referred to therein within four years of notification of this Directive.

2. Member States shall periodically assess the occupational activities referred to in Article 2(2) in order to decide, in the light of social developments, whether there is justification for maintaining the exclusions concerned. They shall notify the Commission of the results of this assessment.

3. Member States shall also communicate to the Commission the texts of laws, regulations and administrative provisions which they adopt in the field covered by this Directive.

Article 10

Within two years following expiry of the 30-month period laid down in the first subparagraph of Article 9(1), Member States shall forward all necessary information to the Commission to enable it to draw up a report on the application of this Directive for submission to the Council.

Article 11

This Directive is addressed to the Member States.

14. EQUAL TREATMENT IN SOCIAL SECURITY

Council Directive 79/7/EEC of 19 December 1978
on the progressive implementation of the principle of equal treatment for men and women in matters of social security

O.J. L 6/24 (Jan. 10, 1979)

THE COUNCIL OF THE EUROPEAN COMMUNITIES,

Having regard to the Treaty establishing the European Economic Community, and in particular Article 235 thereof,

Having regard to the proposal from the Commission,

Having regard to the opinion of the European Parliament,

Having regard to the opinion of the Economic and Social Committee,

Whereas Article 1(2) of Council Directive 76/207/EEC of 9 February 1976 on the implementation of the principle of equal treatment for men and women as regards access to employment, vocational training and promotion, and working conditions provides that, with a view to ensuring the progressive implementation of the principle of equal treatment in matters of social security, the Council, acting on a proposal from the Commission, will adopt provisions defining its substance, its scope and the arrangements for its application; whereas the Treaty does not confer the specific powers required for this purpose;

Whereas the principle of equal treatment in matters of social security should be implemented in the first place in the statutory schemes which provide protection against the risks of sickness, invalidity, old age, accidents at work, occupational diseases and unemployment, and in social assistance in so far as it is intended to supplement or replace the above-mentioned schemes;

Whereas the implementation of the principle of equal treatment in matters of social security does not prejudice the provisions relating to the protection of women on the ground of maternity; whereas, in this respect, Member States may adopt specific provisions for women to remove existing instances of unequal treatment,

HAS ADOPTED THIS DIRECTIVE:

Article 1

The purpose of this Directive is the progressive implementation, in the field of social security and other elements of social protection provided for in Article 3, of the principle of equal treatment for men and women in matters of social security, hereinafter referred to as 'the principle of equal treatment'.

Article 2

This Directive shall apply to the working population—including self-employed persons, workers and self-employed persons whose activity is interrupted by illness, accident or involuntary unemployment and persons seeking employment—and to retired or invalided workers and self-employed persons.

Article 3

1. This Directive shall apply to:

(a) statutory schemes which provide protection against the following risks:

— sickness,

— invalidity,

— old age,

— accidents at work and occupational diseases,

— unemployment

(b) social assistance, in so far as it is intended to supplement or replace the schemes referred to in (a).

2. This Directive shall not apply to the provisions concerning survivors' benefits nor to those concerning family benefits, except in the case of family benefits granted by way of increases of benefits due in respect of the risks referred to in paragraph 1(a).

3. With a view to ensuring implementation of the principle of equal treatment in occupational schemes, the Council, acting on a proposal from the Commission, will adopt provisions defining its substance, its scope and the arrangements for its application.

Article 4

1. The principle of equal treatment means that there shall be no discrimination whatsoever on ground of sex either directly, or indirectly by reference in particular to marital or family status, in particular as concerns:

— the scope of the schemes and the conditions of access thereto,

— the obligation to contribute and the calculation of contributions,

— the calculation of benefits including increases due in respect of a spouse and for dependents and the conditions governing the duration and retention of entitlement to benefits.

2. The principle of equal treatment shall be without prejudice to the provisions relating to the protection of women on the grounds of maternity.

Article 5

Member States shall take the measures necessary to ensure that any laws, regulations and administrative provisions contrary to the principle of equal treatment are abolished.

Article 6

Member States shall introduce into their national legal systems such measures as are necessary to enable all persons who consider themselves wronged by failure to apply the principle of equal treatment to pursue their claims by judicial process, possibly after recourse to other competent authorities.

Article 7

1. This Directive shall be without prejudice to the right of Member States to exclude from its scope:

(a) the determination of pensionable age for the purposes of granting old-age and retirement pensions and the possible consequences thereof for other benefits;

(b) advantages in respect of old-age pension schemes granted to persons who have brought up children; the acquisition of benefit entitlements following periods of interruption of employment due to the bringing up of children;

(c) the granting of old-age or invalidity benefit entitlements by virtue of the derived entitlements of a wife;

(d) the granting of increases of long-term invalidity, old-age, accidents at work and occupational disease benefits for a dependent wife;

(e) the consequences of the exercise, before the adoption of this Directive, of a right of option not to acquire rights or incur obligations under a statutory scheme.

2. Member States shall periodically examine matters excluded under paragraph 1 in order to ascertain, in the light of social developments in the matter concerned, whether there is justification for maintaining the exclusions concerned.

Article 8

1. Member States shall bring into force the laws, regulations and administrative provisions necessary to comply with this Directive within six years of its notification. They shall immediately inform the Commission thereof.

2. Member States shall communicate to the Commission the text of laws, regulations and administrative provisions which they adopt in the field covered by this Directive, including measures adopted pursuant to Article 7(2).

They shall inform the Commission of their reasons for maintaining any existing provisions on the matters referred to in Article 7(1) and of the possibilities for reviewing them at a later date.

Article 9

Within seven years of notification of this Directive, Member States shall forward all information necessary to the Commission to enable it to draw up a report on the application of this Directive for submission to the Council and to propose such further measures as may be required for the implementation of the principle of equal treatment.

Article 10

This Directive is addressed to the Member States.

15. BURDEN OF PROOF DIRECTIVE

COUNCIL DIRECTIVE 97/80/EC

of 15 December 1997

on the burden of proof in cases of discrimination based on sex

O.J. L 14/6 (Jan. 20, 1998), amended, O.J. L 205/66 (July 22, 1998)

THE COUNCIL OF THE EUROPEAN UNION,

Having regard to the Agreement on social policy annexed to the Protocol (No 14) on social policy annexed to the Treaty establishing the European Community, and in particular Article 2(2) thereof,

Having regard to the proposal from the Commission,[1]

Having regard to the opinion of the Economic and Social Committee,[2]

Acting, in accordance with the procedure laid down in Article 189c of the Treaty, in cooperation with the European Parliament,[3]

Whereas, on the basis of the Protocol on social policy annexed to the Treaty, the Member States, with the exception of the United Kingdom of Great Britain and Northern Ireland (hereinafter called 'the Member States'), wishing to implement the 1989 Social Charter, have concluded an Agreement on social policy;

Whereas the Community Charter of the Fundamental Social Rights of Workers recognizes the importance of combating every form of discrimination, including discrimination on grounds of sex, colour, race, opinions and beliefs;

Whereas paragraph 16 of the Community Charter of the Fundamental Social Rights of Workers on equal treatment for men and women, provides, *inter alia*, that 'action should be intensified to ensure the implementation of the principle of equality for men and women as regards, in particular, access to employment, remuneration, working conditions, social protection, education, vocational training and career development';

Whereas, in accordance with Article 3(2) of the Agreement on social policy, the Commission has consulted management and labour at Community level on the possible direction of Community action on the burden of proof in cases of discrimination based on sex;

Whereas the Commission, considering Community action advisable after such consultation, once again consulted management and labour on the content of the proposal contemplated in accordance with Article 3(3) of the same Agreement; whereas the latter have sent their opinions to the Commission;

---

[1]. OJ C 332, 7.11.1996, p. 11 and OJ C 185, 18.6.1997, p. 21.

[2]. OJ C 133, 28.4.1997, p. 34.

[3]. Opinion of the European Parliament of 10 April 1997 (O.J. C 132, 28.4.1997, p. 215), Common Position of the Council of 24 July 1997 (O.J. C307, 8.10.1997, p. 6) and Decision of the European Parliament of 6 November 1997 (O.J. C 358, 24.11.1997).

Whereas, after the second round of consultation, neither management nor labour have informed the Commission of their wish to initiate the process—possibly leading to an agreement—provided for in Article 4 of the same Agreement;

Whereas, in accordance with Article 1 of the Agreement, the Community and the Member States have set themselves the objective, *inter alia*, of improving living and working conditions; whereas effective implementation of the principle of equal treatment for men and women would contribute to the achievement of that aim;

Whereas the principle of equal treatment was stated in Article 119 of the Treaty, in Council Directive 75/117/EEC of 10 February 1975 on the approximation of the laws of the Member States relating to the application of the principle of equal pay for men and women[4] and in Council Directive 76/207/EEC of 9 February 1976 on the implementation of the principle of equal treatment for men and women as regards access to employment, vocational training and promotion and working conditions;[5]

Whereas Council Directive 92/85/EEC of 19 October 1992 on the introduction of measures to encourage improvements in the safety and health at work of pregnant workers and workers who have recently given birth or are breastfeeding[6] also contributes to the effective implementation of the principle of equal treatment for men and women; whereas that Directive should not work to the detriment of the aforementioned Directives on equal treatment; whereas, therefore, female workers covered by that Directive should likewise benefit from the adaptation of the rules on the burden of proof;

Whereas Council Directive 96/34/EC of 3 June 1996 on the framework agreement on parental leave concluded by UNICE, CEEP and the ETUC,[7] is also based on the principle of equal treatment for men and women;

Whereas the references to 'judicial process' and 'court' cover mechanisms by means of which disputes may be submitted for examination and decision to independent bodies which may hand down decisions that are binding on the parties to those disputes;

Whereas the expression 'out-of-court procedures' means in particular procedures such as conciliation and mediation;

Whereas the appreciation of the facts from which it may be presumed that there has been direct or indirect discrimination is a matter for national judicial or other competent bodies, in accordance with national law or practice;

Whereas it is for the Member States to introduce, at any appropriate stage of the proceedings, rules of evidence which are more favourable to plaintiffs;

4. OJ L 45, 19.2.1975, p. 19.
5. OJ L 39, 14.2.1976, p. 40.
6. OJ L 348, 28.11.1992, p. 1.
7. OJ L 145, 19.6.1996, p. 4.

Whereas it is necessary to take account of the specific features of certain Member States' legal systems, *inter alia* where an inference of discrimination is drawn if the respondent fails to produce evidence that satisfies the court or other competent authority that there has been no breach of the principle of equal treatment;

Whereas Member States need not apply the rules on the burden of proof to proceedings in which it is for the court or other competent body to investigate the facts of the case; whereas the procedures thus referred to are those in which the plaintiff is not required to prove the facts, which it is for the court or competent body to investigate;

Whereas plaintiffs could be deprived of any effective means of enforcing the principle of equal treatment before the national courts if the effect of introducing evidence of an apparent discrimination were not to impose upon the respondent the burden of proving that his practice is not in fact discriminatory;

Whereas the Court of Justice of the European Communities has therefore held that the rules on the burden of proof must be adapted when there is a prima facie case of discrimination and that, for the principle of equal treatment to be applied effectively, the burden of proof must shift back to the respondent when evidence of such discrimination is brought;

Whereas it is all the more difficult to prove discrimination when it is indirect; whereas it is therefore important to define indirect discrimination;

Whereas the aim of adequately adapting the rules on the burden of proof has not been achieved satisfactorily in all Member States and, in accordance with the principle of subsidiarity stated in Article 3b of the Treaty and with that of proportionality, that aim must be attained at Community level; whereas this Directive confines itself to the minimum action required and does not go beyond what is necessary for that purpose,

HAS ADOPTED THIS DIRECTIVE:

Article 1

Aim

The aim of this Directive shall be to ensure that the measures taken by the Member States to implement the principle of equal treatment are made more effective, in order to enable all persons who consider themselves wronged because the principle of equal treatment has not been applied to them to have their rights asserted by judicial process after possible recourse to other competent bodies.

Article 2

Definitions

1. For the purposes of this Directive, the principle of equal treatment shall mean that there shall be no discrimination whatsoever based on sex, either directly or indirectly.

2. For purposes of the principle of equal treatment referred to in paragraph 1, indirect discrimination shall exist where an apparently neutral provision, criterion or practice disadvantages a substantially higher proportion of the members of one sex unless that provision, criterion or practice is appropriate and necessary and can be justified by objective factors unrelated to sex.

Article 3

Scope

1. This Directive shall apply to:

(a) the situations covered by Article 119 of the Treaty and by Directives 75/117/EEC, 76/207/EEC and, insofar as discrimination based on sex is concerned, 92/85/EEC and 96/34/EC;

(b) any civil or administrative procedure concerning the public or private sector which provides for means of redress under national law pursuant to the measures referred to in (a) with the exception of out-of-court procedures of a voluntary nature or provided for in national law.

2. This Directive shall not apply to criminal procedures, unless otherwise provided by the Member States.

Article 4

Burden of proof

1. Member States shall take such measures as are necessary, in accordance with their national judicial systems, to ensure that, when persons who consider themselves wronged because the principle of equal treatment has not been applied to them establish, before a court or other competent authority, facts from which it may be presumed that there has been direct or indirect discrimination, it shall be for the respondent to prove that there has been no breach of the principle of equal treatment.

2. This Directive shall not prevent Member States from introducing rules of evidence which are more favourable to plaintiffs.

3. Member States need not apply paragraph 1 to proceedings in which it is for the court or competent body to investigate the facts of the case.

Article 5

Information

Member States shall ensure that measures taken pursuant to this Directive, together with the provisions already in force, are brought to the attention of all the persons concerned by all appropriate means.

Article 6

Non-regression

Implementation of this Directive shall under no circumstances be sufficient grounds for a reduction in the general level of protection of workers in the areas to which it applies, without prejudice to the Member States' right to respond to changes in the situation by introducing laws, regulations and administrative provisions which differ from those in force on the notification of this Directive, provided that the minimum requirements of this Directive are complied with.

Article 7

Implementation

The Member States shall bring into force the laws, regulations and administrative provisions necessary for them to comply with this Directive by 1 January 2001. They shall immediately inform the Commission thereof.

As regards the United Kingdom of Great Britain and Northern Ireland, the date of 1 January 2001 in paragraph 1 shall be replaced by 22 July 2001.

When the Member States adopt those measures they shall contain a reference to this Directive or shall be accompanied by such a reference on the occasion of their official publication. The methods of making such references shall be laid down by the Member States.

The Member States shall communicate to the Commission, within two years of the entry into force of this Directive, all the information necessary for the Commission to draw up a report to the European Parliament and the Council on the application of this Directive.

Article 8

This Directive is addressed to the Member States.

16. RACE DIRECTIVE

Council Directive 2000/43/EC of 29 June 2000

implementing the principle of equal treatment between persons irrespective of racial or ethnic origin

O.J. L 180/22 (July 19, 2000)

THE COUNCIL OF THE EUROPEAN UNION,

Having regard to the Treaty establishing the European Community and in particular Article 13 thereof,

Having regard to the proposal from the Commission,[1]

Having regard to the opinion of the European Parliament,[2]

Having regard to the opinion of the Economic and Social Committee,[3]

Having regard to the opinion of the Committee of the Regions,[4]

Whereas:

(1) The Treaty on European Union marks a new stage in the process of creating an ever closer union among the peoples of Europe.

(2) In accordance with Article 6 of the Treaty on European Union, the European Union is founded on the principles of liberty, democracy, respect for human rights and fundamental freedoms, and the rule of law, principles which are common to the Member States, and should respect fundamental rights as guaranteed by the European Convention for the protection of Human Rights and Fundamental Freedoms and as they result from the constitutional traditions common to the Member States, as general principles of Community Law.

(3) The right to equality before the law and protection against discrimination for all persons constitutes a universal right recognised by the Universal Declaration of Human Rights, the United Nations Convention on the Elimination of all forms of Discrimination Against Women, the International Convention on the Elimination of all forms of Racial Discrimination and the United Nations Covenants on Civil and Political Rights and on Economic, Social and Cultural Rights and by the European Convention for the Protection of Human Rights and Fundamental Freedoms, to which all Member States are signatories.

(4) It is important to respect such fundamental rights and freedoms, including the right to freedom of association. It is also important, in the context of the access to and provision of goods and services, to respect the protection of private and family life and transactions carried out in this context.

---

[1] Not yet published in the Official Journal.

[2] Opinion delivered on 18.5.2000 (not yet published in the Official Journal).

[3] Opinion delivered on 12.4.2000 (not yet published in the Official Journal).

[4] Opinion delivered on 31.5.2000 (not yet published in the Official Journal).

(5) The European Parliament has adopted a number of Resolutions on the fight against racism in the European Union.

(6) The European Union rejects theories which attempt to determine the existence of separate human races. The use of the term "racial origin" in this Directive does not imply an acceptance of such theories.

(7) The European Council in Tampere, on 15 and 16 October 1999, invited the Commission to come forward as soon as possible with proposals implementing Article 13 of the EC Treaty as regards the fight against racism and xenophobia.

(8) The Employment Guidelines 2000 agreed by the European Council in Helsinki, on 10 and 11 December 1999, stress the need to foster conditions for a socially inclusive labour market by formulating a coherent set of policies aimed at combating discrimination against groups such as ethnic minorities.

(9) Discrimination based on racial or ethnic origin may undermine the achievement of the objectives of the EC Treaty, in particular the attainment of a high level of employment and of social protection, the raising of the standard of living and quality of life, economic and social cohesion and solidarity. It may also undermine the objective of developing the European Union as an area of freedom, security and justice.

(10) The Commission presented a communication on racism, xenophobia and anti-Semitism in December 1995.

(11) The Council adopted on 15 July 1996 Joint Action (96/443/JHA) concerning action to combat racism and xenophobia[5] under which the Member States undertake to ensure effective judicial cooperation in respect of offences based on racist or xenophobic behaviour.

(12) To ensure the development of democratic and tolerant societies which allow the participation of all persons irrespective of racial or ethnic origin, specific action in the field of discrimination based on racial or ethnic origin should go beyond access to employed and self-employed activities and cover areas such as education, social protection including social security and healthcare, social advantages and access to and supply of goods and services.

(13) To this end, any direct or indirect discrimination based on racial or ethnic origin as regards the areas covered by this Directive should be prohibited throughout the Community. This prohibition of discrimination should also apply to nationals of third countries, but does not cover differences of treatment based on nationality and is without prejudice to provisions governing the entry and residence of third-country nationals and their access to employment and to occupation.

(14) In implementing the principle of equal treatment irrespective of racial or ethnic origin, the Community should, in accordance with Article 3(2) of the EC Treaty, aim to eliminate inequalities, and to promote

---

5. OJ L 185, 24.7.1996, p. 5.

equality between men and women, especially since women are often the victims of multiple discrimination.

(15) The appreciation of the facts from which it may be inferred that there has been direct or indirect discrimination is a matter for national judicial or other competent bodies, in accordance with rules of national law or practice. Such rules may provide in particular for indirect discrimination to be established by any means including on the basis of statistical evidence.

(16) It is important to protect all natural persons against discrimination on grounds of racial or ethnic origin. Member States should also provide, where appropriate and in accordance with their national traditions and practice, protection for legal persons where they suffer discrimination on grounds of the racial or ethnic origin of their members.

(17) The prohibition of discrimination should be without prejudice to the maintenance or adoption of measures intended to prevent or compensate for disadvantages suffered by a group of persons of a particular racial or ethnic origin, and such measures may permit organisations of persons of a particular racial or ethnic origin where their main object is the promotion of the special needs of those persons.

(18) In very limited circumstances, a difference of treatment may be justified where a characteristic related to racial or ethnic origin constitutes a genuine and determining occupational requirement, when the objective is legitimate and the requirement is proportionate. Such circumstances should be included in the information provided by the Member States to the Commission.

(19) Persons who have been subject to discrimination based on racial and ethnic origin should have adequate means of legal protection. To provide a more effective level of protection, associations or legal entities should also be empowered to engage, as the Member States so determine, either on behalf or in support of any victim, in proceedings, without prejudice to national rules of procedure concerning representation and defence before the courts.

(20) The effective implementation of the principle of equality requires adequate judicial protection against victimisation.

(21) The rules on the burden of proof must be adapted when there is a prima facie case of discrimination and, for the principle of equal treatment to be applied effectively, the burden of proof must shift back to the respondent when evidence of such discrimination is brought.

(22) Member States need not apply the rules on the burden of proof to proceedings in which it is for the court or other competent body to investigate the facts of the case. The procedures thus referred to are those in which the plaintiff is not required to prove the facts, which it is for the court or competent body to investigate.

(23) Member States should promote dialogue between the social partners and with non-governmental organisations to address different forms of discrimination and to combat them.

(24) Protection against discrimination based on racial or ethnic origin would itself be strengthened by the existence of a body or bodies in each Member State, with competence to analyse the problems involved, to study possible solutions and to provide concrete assistance for the victims.

(25) This Directive lays down minimum requirements, thus giving the Member States the option of introducing or maintaining more favourable provisions. The implementation of this Directive should not serve to justify any regression in relation to the situation which already prevails in each Member State.

(26) Member States should provide for effective, proportionate and dissuasive sanctions in case of breaches of the obligations under this Directive.

(27) The Member States may entrust management and labour, at their joint request, with the implementation of this Directive as regards provisions falling within the scope of collective agreements, provided that the Member States take all the necessary steps to ensure that they can at all times guarantee the results imposed by this Directive.

(28) In accordance with the principles of subsidiarity and proportionality as set out in Article 5 of the EC Treaty, the objective of this Directive, namely ensuring a common high level of protection against discrimination in all the Member States, cannot be sufficiently achieved by the Member States and can therefore, by reason of the scale and impact of the proposed action, be better achieved by the Community. This Directive does not go beyond what is necessary in order to achieve those objectives,

HAS ADOPTED THIS DIRECTIVE:

CHAPTER I

GENERAL PROVISIONS

Article 1

Purpose

The purpose of this Directive is to lay down a framework for combating discrimination on the grounds of racial or ethnic origin, with a view to putting into effect in the Member States the principle of equal treatment.

Article 2

Concept of discrimination

1. For the purposes of this Directive, the principle of equal treatment shall mean that there shall be no direct or indirect discrimination based on racial or ethnic origin.

2. For the purposes of paragraph 1:

(a) direct discrimination shall be taken to occur where one person is treated less favourably than another is, has been or would be treated in a comparable situation on grounds of racial or ethnic origin;

(b) indirect discrimination shall be taken to occur where an apparently neutral provision, criterion or practice would put persons of a racial or ethnic origin at a particular disadvantage compared with other persons, unless that provision, criterion or practice is objectively justified by a legitimate aim and the means of achieving that aim are appropriate and necessary.

3. Harassment shall be deemed to be discrimination within the meaning of paragraph 1, when an unwanted conduct related to racial or ethnic origin takes place with the purpose or effect of violating the dignity of a person and of creating an intimidating, hostile, degrading, humiliating or offensive environment. In this context, the concept of harassment may be defined in accordance with the national laws and practice of the Member States.

4. An instruction to discriminate against persons on grounds of racial or ethnic origin shall be deemed to be discrimination within the meaning of paragraph 1.

Article 3

Scope

1. Within the limits of the powers conferred upon the Community, this Directive shall apply to all persons, as regards both the public and private sectors, including public bodies, in relation to:

(a) conditions for access to employment, to self-employment and to occupation, including selection criteria and recruitment conditions, whatever the branch of activity and at all levels of the professional hierarchy, including promotion;

(b) access to all types and to all levels of vocational guidance, vocational training, advanced vocational training and retraining, including practical work experience;

(c) employment and working conditions, including dismissals and pay;

(d) membership of and involvement in an organisation of workers or employers, or any organisation whose members carry on a particular profession, including the benefits provided for by such organisations;

(e) social protection, including social security and healthcare;

(f) social advantages;

(g) education;

(h) access to and supply of goods and services which are available to the public, including housing.

2. This Directive does not cover difference of treatment based on nationality and is without prejudice to provisions and conditions relating to the entry into and residence of third-country nationals and stateless persons on the territory of Member States, and to any treatment which

arises from the legal status of the third-country nationals and stateless persons concerned.

Article 4

Genuine and determining occupational requirements

Notwithstanding Article 2(1) and (2), Member States may provide that a difference of treatment which is based on a characteristic related to racial or ethnic origin shall not constitute discrimination where, by reason of the nature of the particular occupational activities concerned or of the context in which they are carried out, such a characteristic constitutes a genuine and determining occupational requirement, provided that the objective is legitimate and the requirement is proportionate.

Article 5

Positive action

With a view to ensuring full equality in practice, the principle of equal treatment shall not prevent any Member State from maintaining or adopting specific measures to prevent or compensate for disadvantages linked to racial or ethnic origin.

Article 6

Minimum requirements

1. Member States may introduce or maintain provisions which are more favourable to the protection of the principle of equal treatment than those laid down in this Directive.

2. The implementation of this Directive shall under no circumstances constitute grounds for a reduction in the level of protection against discrimination already afforded by Member States in the fields covered by this Directive.

CHAPTER II

REMEDIES AND ENFORCEMENT

Article 7

Defence of rights

1. Member States shall ensure that judicial and/or administrative procedures, including where they deem it appropriate conciliation procedures, for the enforcement of obligations under this Directive are available to all persons who consider themselves wronged by failure to apply the principle of equal treatment to them, even after the relationship in which the discrimination is alleged to have occurred has ended.

2. Member States shall ensure that associations, organisations or other legal entities, which have, in accordance with the criteria laid down by their national law, a legitimate interest in ensuring that the provisions of this Directive are complied with, may engage, either on behalf or in support of the complainant, with his or her approval, in any judicial and/or

administrative procedure provided for the enforcement of obligations under this Directive.

3. Paragraphs 1 and 2 are without prejudice to national rules relating to time limits for bringing actions as regards the principle of equality of treatment.

Article 8

Burden of proof

1. Member States shall take such measures as are necessary, in accordance with their national judicial systems, to ensure that, when persons who consider themselves wronged because the principle of equal treatment has not been applied to them establish, before a court or other competent authority, facts from which it may be presumed that there has been direct or indirect discrimination, it shall be for the respondent to prove that there has been no breach of the principle of equal treatment.

2. Paragraph 1 shall not prevent Member States from introducing rules of evidence which are more favourable to plaintiffs.

3. Paragraph 1 shall not apply to criminal procedures.

4. Paragraphs 1, 2 and 3 shall also apply to any proceedings brought in accordance with Article 7(2).

5. Member States need not apply paragraph 1 to proceedings in which it is for the court or competent body to investigate the facts of the case.

Article 9

Victimisation

Member States shall introduce into their national legal systems such measures as are necessary to protect individuals from any adverse treatment or adverse consequence as a reaction to a complaint or to proceedings aimed at enforcing compliance with the principle of equal treatment.

Article 10

Dissemination of information

Member States shall take care that the provisions adopted pursuant to this Directive, together with the relevant provisions already in force, are brought to the attention of the persons concerned by all appropriate means throughout their territory.

Article 11

Social dialogue

1. Member States shall, in accordance with national traditions and practice, take adequate measures to promote the social dialogue between the two sides of industry with a view to fostering equal treatment, including through the monitoring of workplace practices, collective agreements, codes of conduct, research or exchange of experiences and good practices.

2. Where consistent with national traditions and practice, Member States shall encourage the two sides of the industry without prejudice to their autonomy to conclude, at the appropriate level, agreements laying down anti-discrimination rules in the fields referred to in Article 3 which fall within the scope of collective bargaining.

These agreements shall respect the minimum requirements laid down by this Directive and the relevant national implementing measures.

Article 12

Dialogue with non-governmental organisations

Member States shall encourage dialogue with appropriate non-governmental organisations which have, in accordance with their national law and practice, a legitimate interest in contributing to the fight against discrimination on grounds of racial and ethnic origin with a view to promoting the principle of equal treatment.

CHAPTER III

BODIES FOR THE PROMOTION OF EQUAL TREATMENT

Article 13

1. Member States shall designate a body or bodies for the promotion of equal treatment of all persons without discrimination on the grounds of racial or ethnic origin. These bodies may form part of agencies charged at national level with the defence of human rights or the safeguard of individuals' rights.

2. Member States shall ensure that the competences of these bodies include:

— without prejudice to the right of victims and of associations, organisations or other legal entities referred to in Article 7(2), providing independent assistance to victims of discrimination in pursuing their complaints about discrimination,

— conducting independent surveys concerning discrimination,

— publishing independent reports and making recommendations on any issue relating to such discrimination.

CHAPTER IV

FINAL PROVISIONS

Article 14

Compliance

Member States shall take the necessary measures to ensure that:

(a) any laws, regulations and administrative provisions contrary to the principle of equal treatment are abolished;

(b) any provisions contrary to the principle of equal treatment which are included in individual or collective contracts or agreements, internal rules of undertakings, rules governing profit-making or non-profit-making associations, and rules governing the independent professions and workers' and employers' organisations, are or may be declared, null and void or are amended.

Article 15

Sanctions

Member States shall lay down the rules on sanctions applicable to infringements of the national provisions adopted pursuant to this Directive and shall take all measures necessary to ensure that they are applied. The sanctions, which may comprise the payment of compensation to the victim, must be effective, proportionate and dissuasive. The Member States shall notify those provisions to the Commission by 19 July 2003 at the latest and shall notify it without delay of any subsequent amendment affecting them.

Article 16

Implementation

Member States shall adopt the laws, regulations and administrative provisions necessary to comply with this Directive by 19 July 2003 or may entrust management and labour, at their joint request, with the implementation of this Directive as regards provisions falling within the scope of collective agreements. In such cases, Member States shall ensure that by 19 July 2003, management and labour introduce the necessary measures by agreement, Member States being required to take any necessary measures to enable them at any time to be in a position to guarantee the results imposed by this Directive. They shall forthwith inform the Commission thereof.

When Member States adopt these measures, they shall contain a reference to this Directive or be accompanied by such a reference on the occasion of their official publication. The methods of making such a reference shall be laid down by the Member States.

Article 17

Report

1. Member States shall communicate to the Commission by 19 July 2005, and every five years thereafter, all the information necessary for the Commission to draw up a report to the European Parliament and the Council on the application of this Directive.

2. The Commission's report shall take into account, as appropriate, the views of the European Monitoring Centre on Racism and Xenophobia, as well as the viewpoints of the social partners and relevant non-governmental organisations. In accordance with the principle of gender mainstreaming, this report shall, inter alia, provide an assessment of the impact of the measures taken on women and men. In the light of the information received, this report shall include, if necessary, proposals to revise and update this Directive.

Article 18

Entry into force

This Directive shall enter into force on the day of its publication in the Official Journal of the European Communities.

Article 19

This Directive is addressed to the Member States.

17. FRAMEWORK EMPLOYMENT DIRECTIVE

Council Directive 2000/78/EC of 27 November 2000 establishing a general framework for equal treatment in employment and occupation

O.J. L 303/16 (Dec. 2, 2000)

THE COUNCIL OF THE EUROPEAN UNION,

Having regard to the Treaty establishing the European Community, and in particular Article 13 thereof,

Having regard to the proposal from the Commission,[1]

Having regard to the Opinion of the European Parliament,[2]

Having regard to the Opinion of the Economic and Social Committee,[3]

Having regard to the Opinion of the Committee of the Regions,[4]

Whereas:

(1) In accordance with Article 6 of the Treaty on European Union, the European Union is founded on the principles of liberty, democracy, respect for human rights and fundamental freedoms, and the rule of law, principles which are common to all Member States and it respects fundamental rights, as guaranteed by the European Convention for the Protection of Human Rights and Fundamental Freedoms and as they result from the constitutional traditions common to the Member States, as general principles of Community law.

(2) The principle of equal treatment between women and men is well established by an important body of Community law, in particular in Council Directive 76/207/EEC of 9 February 1976 on the implementation of the principle of equal treatment for men and women as regards access to employment, vocational training and promotion, and working conditions.[5]

(3) In implementing the principle of equal treatment, the Community should, in accordance with Article 3(2) of the EC Treaty, aim to eliminate inequalities, and to promote equality between men and women, especially since women are often the victims of multiple discrimination.

(4) The right of all persons to equality before the law and protection against discrimination constitutes a universal right recognised by the Universal Declaration of Human Rights, the United Nations Convention on the Elimination of All Forms of Discrimination against Women, United Nations Covenants on Civil and Political Rights and on Economic, Social and Cultural Rights and by the European Convention for the Protection of Human Rights and Fundamental Freedoms, to which all Member States are signatories. Convention No 111 of the International Labour Organisa-

---

1. OJ C 177 E, 27.6.2000, p. 42.
2. Opinion delivered on 12 October 2000 (not yet published in the Official Journal).
3. OJ C 204, 18.7.2000, p. 82.
4. OJ C 226, 8.8.2000, p. 1.
5. OJ L 39, 14.2.1976, p. 40.

tion (ILO) prohibits discrimination in the field of employment and occupation.

(5) It is important to respect such fundamental rights and freedoms. This Directive does not prejudice freedom of association, including the right to establish unions with others and to join unions to defend one's interests.

(6) The Community Charter of the Fundamental Social Rights of Workers recognises the importance of combating every form of discrimination, including the need to take appropriate action for the social and economic integration of elderly and disabled people.

(7) The EC Treaty includes among its objectives the promotion of coordination between employment policies of the Member States. To this end, a new employment chapter was incorporated in the EC Treaty as a means of developing a coordinated European strategy for employment to promote a skilled, trained and adaptable workforce.

(8) The Employment Guidelines for 2000 agreed by the European Council at Helsinki on 10 and 11 December 1999 stress the need to foster a labour market favourable to social integration by formulating a coherent set of policies aimed at combating discrimination against groups such as persons with disability. They also emphasise the need to pay particular attention to supporting older workers, in order to increase their participation in the labour force.

(9) Employment and occupation are key elements in guaranteeing equal opportunities for all and contribute strongly to the full participation of citizens in economic, cultural and social life and to realising their potential.

(10) On 29 June 2000 the Council adopted Directive 2000/43/EC[6] implementing the principle of equal treatment between persons irrespective of racial or ethnic origin. That Directive already provides protection against such discrimination in the field of employment and occupation.

(11) Discrimination based on religion or belief, disability, age or sexual orientation may undermine the achievement of the objectives of the EC Treaty, in particular the attainment of a high level of employment and social protection, raising the standard of living and the quality of life, economic and social cohesion and solidarity, and the free movement of persons.

(12) To this end, any direct or indirect discrimination based on religion or belief, disability, age or sexual orientation as regards the areas covered by this Directive should be prohibited throughout the Community. This prohibition of discrimination should also apply to nationals of third countries but does not cover differences of treatment based on nationality and is without prejudice to provisions governing the entry and residence of third-country nationals and their access to employment and occupation.

(13) This Directive does not apply to social security and social protection schemes whose benefits are not treated as income within the meaning

---

6. OJ L 180, 19.7.2000, p. 22.

given to that term for the purpose of applying Article 141 of the EC Treaty, nor to any kind of payment by the State aimed at providing access to employment or maintaining employment.

(14) This Directive shall be without prejudice to national provisions laying down retirement ages.

(15) The appreciation of the facts from which it may be inferred that there has been direct or indirect discrimination is a matter for national judicial or other competent bodies, in accordance with rules of national law or practice. Such rules may provide, in particular, for indirect discrimination to be established by any means including on the basis of statistical evidence.

(16) The provision of measures to accommodate the needs of disabled people at the workplace plays an important role in combating discrimination on grounds of disability.

(17) This Directive does not require the recruitment, promotion, maintenance in employment or training of an individual who is not competent, capable and available to perform the essential functions of the post concerned or to undergo the relevant training, without prejudice to the obligation to provide reasonable accommodation for people with disabilities.

(18) This Directive does not require, in particular, the armed forces and the police, prison or emergency services to recruit or maintain in employment persons who do not have the required capacity to carry out the range of functions that they may be called upon to perform with regard to the legitimate objective of preserving the operational capacity of those services.

(19) Moreover, in order that the Member States may continue to safeguard the combat effectiveness of their armed forces, they may choose not to apply the provisions of this Directive concerning disability and age to all or part of their armed forces. The Member States which make that choice must define the scope of that derogation.

(20) Appropriate measures should be provided, i.e. effective and practical measures to adapt the workplace to the disability, for example adapting premises and equipment, patterns of working time, the distribution of tasks or the provision of training or integration resources.

(21) To determine whether the measures in question give rise to a disproportionate burden, account should be taken in particular of the financial and other costs entailed, the scale and financial resources of the organisation or undertaking and the possibility of obtaining public funding or any other assistance.

(22) This Directive is without prejudice to national laws on marital status and the benefits dependent thereon.

(23) In very limited circumstances, a difference of treatment may be justified where a characteristic related to religion or belief, disability, age or sexual orientation constitutes a genuine and determining occupational requirement, when the objective is legitimate and the requirement is

proportionate. Such circumstances should be included in the information provided by the Member States to the Commission.

(24) The European Union in its Declaration No 11 on the status of churches and non-confessional organisations, annexed to the Final Act of the Amsterdam Treaty, has explicitly recognised that it respects and does not prejudice the status under national law of churches and religious associations or communities in the Member States and that it equally respects the status of philosophical and non-confessional organisations. With this in view, Member States may maintain or lay down specific provisions on genuine, legitimate and justified occupational requirements which might be required for carrying out an occupational activity.

(25) The prohibition of age discrimination is an essential part of meeting the aims set out in the Employment Guidelines and encouraging diversity in the workforce. However, differences in treatment in connection with age may be justified under certain circumstances and therefore require specific provisions which may vary in accordance with the situation in Member States. It is therefore essential to distinguish between differences in treatment which are justified, in particular by legitimate employment policy, labour market and vocational training objectives, and discrimination which must be prohibited.

(26) The prohibition of discrimination should be without prejudice to the maintenance or adoption of measures intended to prevent or compensate for disadvantages suffered by a group of persons of a particular religion or belief, disability, age or sexual orientation, and such measures may permit organisations of persons of a particular religion or belief, disability, age or sexual orientation where their main object is the promotion of the special needs of those persons.

(27) In its Recommendation 86/379/EEC of 24 July 1986 on the employment of disabled people in the Community,[7] the Council established a guideline framework setting out examples of positive action to promote the employment and training of disabled people, and in its Resolution of 17 June 1999 on equal employment opportunities for people with disabilities,[8] affirmed the importance of giving specific attention inter alia to recruitment, retention, training and lifelong learning with regard to disabled persons.

(28) This Directive lays down minimum requirements, thus giving the Member States the option of introducing or maintaining more favourable provisions. The implementation of this Directive should not serve to justify any regression in relation to the situation which already prevails in each Member State.

(29) Persons who have been subject to discrimination based on religion or belief, disability, age or sexual orientation should have adequate means of legal protection. To provide a more effective level of protection, associations or legal entities should also be empowered to engage in proceedings,

7. OJ L 225, 12.8.1986, p. 43.   8. OJ C 186, 2.7.1999, p. 3.

as the Member States so determine, either on behalf or in support of any victim, without prejudice to national rules of procedure concerning representation and defence before the courts.

(30) The effective implementation of the principle of equality requires adequate judicial protection against victimisation.

(31) The rules on the burden of proof must be adapted when there is a prima facie case of discrimination and, for the principle of equal treatment to be applied effectively, the burden of proof must shift back to the respondent when evidence of such discrimination is brought. However, it is not for the respondent to prove that the plaintiff adheres to a particular religion or belief, has a particular disability, is of a particular age or has a particular sexual orientation.

(32) Member States need not apply the rules on the burden of proof to proceedings in which it is for the court or other competent body to investigate the facts of the case. The procedures thus referred to are those in which the plaintiff is not required to prove the facts, which it is for the court or competent body to investigate.

(33) Member States should promote dialogue between the social partners and, within the framework of national practice, with non-governmental organisations to address different forms of discrimination at the workplace and to combat them.

(34) The need to promote peace and reconciliation between the major communities in Northern Ireland necessitates the incorporation of particular provisions into this Directive.

(35) Member States should provide for effective, proportionate and dissuasive sanctions in case of breaches of the obligations under this Directive.

(36) Member States may entrust the social partners, at their joint request, with the implementation of this Directive, as regards the provisions concerning collective agreements, provided they take any necessary steps to ensure that they are at all times able to guarantee the results required by this Directive.

(37) In accordance with the principle of subsidiarity set out in Article 5 of the EC Treaty, the objective of this Directive, namely the creation within the Community of a level playing-field as regards equality in employment and occupation, cannot be sufficiently achieved by the Member States and can therefore, by reason of the scale and impact of the action, be better achieved at Community level. In accordance with the principle of proportionality, as set out in that Article, this Directive does not go beyond what is necessary in order to achieve that objective,

HAS ADOPTED THIS DIRECTIVE:

CHAPTER I
GENERAL PROVISIONS

Article 1

Purpose

The purpose of this Directive is to lay down a general framework for combating discrimination on the grounds of religion or belief, disability, age or sexual orientation as regards employment and occupation, with a view to putting into effect in the Member States the principle of equal treatment.

Article 2

Concept of discrimination

1. For the purposes of this Directive, the "principle of equal treatment" shall mean that there shall be no direct or indirect discrimination whatsoever on any of the grounds referred to in Article 1.

2. For the purposes of paragraph 1:

(a) direct discrimination shall be taken to occur where one person is treated less favourably than another is, has been or would be treated in a comparable situation, on any of the grounds referred to in Article 1;

(b) indirect discrimination shall be taken to occur where an apparently neutral provision, criterion or practice would put persons having a particular religion or belief, a particular disability, a particular age, or a particular sexual orientation at a particular disadvantage compared with other persons unless:

(i) that provision, criterion or practice is objectively justified by a legitimate aim and the means of achieving that aim are appropriate and necessary, or

(ii) as regards persons with a particular disability, the employer or any person or organisation to whom this Directive applies, is obliged, under national legislation, to take appropriate measures in line with the principles contained in Article 5 in order to eliminate disadvantages entailed by such provision, criterion or practice.

3. Harassment shall be deemed to be a form of discrimination within the meaning of paragraph 1, when unwanted conduct related to any of the grounds referred to in Article 1 takes place with the purpose or effect of violating the dignity of a person and of creating an intimidating, hostile, degrading, humiliating or offensive environment.

In this context, the concept of harassment may be defined in accordance with the national laws and practice of the Member States.

4. An instruction to discriminate against persons on any of the grounds referred to in Article 1 shall be deemed to be discrimination within the meaning of paragraph 1.

5. This Directive shall be without prejudice to measures laid down by national law which, in a democratic society, are necessary for public security, for the maintenance of public order and the prevention of criminal offences, for the protection of health and for the protection of the rights and freedoms of others.

Article 3

Scope

1. Within the limits of the areas of competence conferred on the Community, this Directive shall apply to all persons, as regards both the public and private sectors, including public bodies, in relation to:

(a) conditions for access to employment, to self-employment or to occupation, including selection criteria and recruitment conditions, whatever the branch of activity and at all levels of the professional hierarchy, including promotion;

(b) access to all types and to all levels of vocational guidance, vocational training, advanced vocational training and retraining, including practical work experience;

(c) employment and working conditions, including dismissals and pay;

(d) membership of, and involvement in, an organisation of workers or employers, or any organisation whose members carry on a particular profession, including the benefits provided for by such organisations.

2. This Directive does not cover differences of treatment based on nationality and is without prejudice to provisions and conditions relating to the entry into and residence of third-country nationals and stateless persons in the territory of Member States, and to any treatment which arises from the legal status of the third-country nationals and stateless persons concerned.

3. This Directive does not apply to payments of any kind made by state schemes or similar, including state social security or social protection schemes.

4. Member States may provide that this Directive, in so far as it relates to discrimination on the grounds of disability and age, shall not apply to the armed forces.

Article 4

Occupational requirements

1. Notwithstanding Article 2(1) and (2), Member States may provide that a difference of treatment which is based on a characteristic related to any of the grounds referred to in Article 1 shall not constitute discrimination where, by reason of the nature of the particular occupational activities concerned or of the context in which they are carried out, such a characteristic constitutes a genuine and determining occupational requirement, provided that the objective is legitimate and the requirement is proportionate.

2. Member States may maintain national legislation in force at the date of adoption of this Directive or provide for future legislation incorporating national practices existing at the date of adoption of this Directive pursuant to which, in the case of occupational activities within churches

and other public or private organisations the ethos of which is based on religion or belief, a difference of treatment based on a person's religion or belief shall not constitute discrimination where, by reason of the nature of these activities or of the context in which they are carried out, a person's religion or belief constitute a genuine, legitimate and justified occupational requirement, having regard to the organisation's ethos. This difference of treatment shall be implemented taking account of Member States' constitutional provisions and principles, as well as the general principles of Community law, and should not justify discrimination on another ground.

Provided that its provisions are otherwise complied with, this Directive shall thus not prejudice the right of churches and other public or private organisations, the ethos of which is based on religion or belief, acting in conformity with national constitutions and laws, to require individuals working for them to act in good faith and with loyalty to the organisation's ethos.

Article 5

Reasonable accommodation for disabled persons

In order to guarantee compliance with the principle of equal treatment in relation to persons with disabilities, reasonable accommodation shall be provided. This means that employers shall take appropriate measures, where needed in a particular case, to enable a person with a disability to have access to, participate in, or advance in employment, or to undergo training, unless such measures would impose a disproportionate burden on the employer. This burden shall not be disproportionate when it is sufficiently remedied by measures existing within the framework of the disability policy of the Member State concerned.

Article 6

Justification of differences of treatment on grounds of age

1. Notwithstanding Article 2(2), Member States may provide that differences of treatment on grounds of age shall not constitute discrimination, if, within the context of national law, they are objectively and reasonably justified by a legitimate aim, including legitimate employment policy, labour market and vocational training objectives, and if the means of achieving that aim are appropriate and necessary.

Such differences of treatment may include, among others:

(a) the setting of special conditions on access to employment and vocational training, employment and occupation, including dismissal and remuneration conditions, for young people, older workers and persons with caring responsibilities in order to promote their vocational integration or ensure their protection;

(b) the fixing of minimum conditions of age, professional experience or seniority in service for access to employment or to certain advantages linked to employment;

(c) the fixing of a maximum age for recruitment which is based on the training requirements of the post in question or the need for a reasonable period of employment before retirement.

2. Notwithstanding Article 2(2), Member States may provide that the fixing for occupational social security schemes of ages for admission or entitlement to retirement or invalidity benefits, including the fixing under those schemes of different ages for employees or groups or categories of employees, and the use, in the context of such schemes, of age criteria in actuarial calculations, does not constitute discrimination on the grounds of age, provided this does not result in discrimination on the grounds of sex.

Article 7

Positive action

1. With a view to ensuring full equality in practice, the principle of equal treatment shall not prevent any Member State from maintaining or adopting specific measures to prevent or compensate for disadvantages linked to any of the grounds referred to in Article 1.

2. With regard to disabled persons, the principle of equal treatment shall be without prejudice to the right of Member States to maintain or adopt provisions on the protection of health and safety at work or to measures aimed at creating or maintaining provisions or facilities for safeguarding or promoting their integration into the working environment.

Article 8

Minimum requirements

1. Member States may introduce or maintain provisions which are more favourable to the protection of the principle of equal treatment than those laid down in this Directive.

2. The implementation of this Directive shall under no circumstances constitute grounds for a reduction in the level of protection against discrimination already afforded by Member States in the fields covered by this Directive.

CHAPTER II

REMEDIES AND ENFORCEMENT

Article 9

Defence of rights

1. Member States shall ensure that judicial and/or administrative procedures, including where they deem it appropriate conciliation procedures, for the enforcement of obligations under this Directive are available to all persons who consider themselves wronged by failure to apply the principle of equal treatment to them, even after the relationship in which the discrimination is alleged to have occurred has ended.

2. Member States shall ensure that associations, organisations or other legal entities which have, in accordance with the criteria laid down by

their national law, a legitimate interest in ensuring that the provisions of this Directive are complied with, may engage, either on behalf or in support of the complainant, with his or her approval, in any judicial and/or administrative procedure provided for the enforcement of obligations under this Directive.

3. Paragraphs 1 and 2 are without prejudice to national rules relating to time limits for bringing actions as regards the principle of equality of treatment.

Article 10

Burden of proof

1. Member States shall take such measures as are necessary, in accordance with their national judicial systems, to ensure that, when persons who consider themselves wronged because the principle of equal treatment has not been applied to them establish, before a court or other competent authority, facts from which it may be presumed that there has been direct or indirect discrimination, it shall be for the respondent to prove that there has been no breach of the principle of equal treatment.

2. Paragraph 1 shall not prevent Member States from introducing rules of evidence which are more favourable to plaintiffs.

3. Paragraph 1 shall not apply to criminal procedures.

4. Paragraphs 1, 2 and 3 shall also apply to any legal proceedings commenced in accordance with Article 9(2).

5. Member States need not apply paragraph 1 to proceedings in which it is for the court or competent body to investigate the facts of the case.

Article 11

Victimisation

Member States shall introduce into their national legal systems such measures as are necessary to protect employees against dismissal or other adverse treatment by the employer as a reaction to a complaint within the undertaking or to any legal proceedings aimed at enforcing compliance with the principle of equal treatment.

Article 12

Dissemination of information

Member States shall take care that the provisions adopted pursuant to this Directive, together with the relevant provisions already in force in this field, are brought to the attention of the persons concerned by all appropriate means, for example at the workplace, throughout their territory.

Article 13

Social dialogue

1. Member States shall, in accordance with their national traditions and practice, take adequate measures to promote dialogue between the

social partners with a view to fostering equal treatment, including through the monitoring of workplace practices, collective agreements, codes of conduct and through research or exchange of experiences and good practices.

2. Where consistent with their national traditions and practice, Member States shall encourage the social partners, without prejudice to their autonomy, to conclude at the appropriate level agreements laying down anti-discrimination rules in the fields referred to in Article 3 which fall within the scope of collective bargaining. These agreements shall respect the minimum requirements laid down by this Directive and by the relevant national implementing measures.

Article 14

Dialogue with non-governmental organisations

Member States shall encourage dialogue with appropriate non-governmental organisations which have, in accordance with their national law and practice, a legitimate interest in contributing to the fight against discrimination on any of the grounds referred to in Article 1 with a view to promoting the principle of equal treatment.

CHAPTER III

PARTICULAR PROVISIONS

Article 15

Northern Ireland

1. In order to tackle the under-representation of one of the major religious communities in the police service of Northern Ireland, differences in treatment regarding recruitment into that service, including its support staff, shall not constitute discrimination insofar as those differences in treatment are expressly authorised by national legislation.

2. In order to maintain a balance of opportunity in employment for teachers in Northern Ireland while furthering the reconciliation of historical divisions between the major religious communities there, the provisions on religion or belief in this Directive shall not apply to the recruitment of teachers in schools in Northern Ireland in so far as this is expressly authorised by national legislation.

CHAPTER IV

FINAL PROVISIONS

Article 16

Compliance

Member States shall take the necessary measures to ensure that:

(a) any laws, regulations and administrative provisions contrary to the principle of equal treatment are abolished;

(b) any provisions contrary to the principle of equal treatment which are included in contracts or collective agreements, internal rules of undertakings or rules governing the independent occupations and professions and workers' and employers' organisations are, or may be, declared null and void or are amended.

Article 17

Sanctions

Member States shall lay down the rules on sanctions applicable to infringements of the national provisions adopted pursuant to this Directive and shall take all measures necessary to ensure that they are applied. The sanctions, which may comprise the payment of compensation to the victim, must be effective, proportionate and dissuasive. Member States shall notify those provisions to the Commission by 2 December 2003 at the latest and shall notify it without delay of any subsequent amendment affecting them.

Article 18

Implementation

Member States shall adopt the laws, regulations and administrative provisions necessary to comply with this Directive by 2 December 2003 at the latest or may entrust the social partners, at their joint request, with the implementation of this Directive as regards provisions concerning collective agreements. In such cases, Member States shall ensure that, no later than 2 December 2003, the social partners introduce the necessary measures by agreement, the Member States concerned being required to take any necessary measures to enable them at any time to be in a position to guarantee the results imposed by this Directive. They shall forthwith inform the Commission thereof.

In order to take account of particular conditions, Member States may, if necessary, have an additional period of 3 years from 2 December 2003, that is to say a total of 6 years, to implement the provisions of this Directive on age and disability discrimination. In that event they shall inform the Commission forthwith. Any Member State which chooses to use this additional period shall report annually to the Commission on the steps it is taking to tackle age and disability discrimination and on the progress it is making towards implementation. The Commission shall report annually to the Council.

When Member States adopt these measures, they shall contain a reference to this Directive or be accompanied by such reference on the occasion of their official publication. The methods of making such reference shall be laid down by Member States.

Article 19

Report

1. Member States shall communicate to the Commission, by 2 December 2005 at the latest and every five years thereafter, all the information

necessary for the Commission to draw up a report to the European Parliament and the Council on the application of this Directive.

2. The Commission's report shall take into account, as appropriate, the viewpoints of the social partners and relevant non-governmental organisations. In accordance with the principle of gender mainstreaming, this report shall, inter alia, provide an assessment of the impact of the measures taken on women and men. In the light of the information received, this report shall include, if necessary, proposals to revise and update this Directive.

Article 20

Entry into force

This Directive shall enter into force on the day of its publication in the Official Journal of the European Communities.

Article 21

This Directive is addressed to the Member States.

18. CONVENTION ON JURISDICTION AND THE ENFORCEMENT OF JUDGMENTS IN CIVIL AND COMMERCIAL MATTERS ("THE 1968 BRUSSELS CONVENTION")

(Signed at Brussels, Sept. 27, 1968)
Consolidated version, O.J. 1998 C27/1 (Jan. 26, 1998)

PREAMBLE

THE HIGH CONTRACTING PARTIES TO THE TREATY ESTABLISHING THE EUROPEAN ECONOMIC COMMUNITY,

DESIRING to implement the provisions of Article 220 of that Treaty by virtue of which they undertook to secure the simplification of formalities governing the reciprocal recognition and enforcement of judgments of courts or tribunals

ANXIOUS to strengthen in the Community the legal protection of persons therein established

CONSIDERING that it is necessary for this purpose to determine the international jurisdiction of their courts, to facilitate recognition and to introduce an expeditious procedure for securing the enforcement of judgments, authentic instruments and court settlements (2);

HAVE DECIDED to conclude this Convention and to this end have designated as their Plenipotentiaries ... WHO, meeting within the Council, having exchanged their full powers, found in good and due form,

HAVE AGREED AS FOLLOWS:

TITLE I

SCOPE

Article 1

This Convention shall apply in civil and commercial matters whatever the nature of the court or tribunal. It shall not extend, in particular, to revenue, customs or administrative matters (3).

The Convention shall not apply to:

1. the status or legal capacity of natural persons, rights in property arising out of a matrimonial relationship, wills and succession

2. bankruptcy, proceedings relating to the winding-up of insolvent companies or other legal persons, judicial arrangements, compositions and analogous proceedings

3. social security

4. arbitration.

TITLE II

JURISDICTION

Section 1

General provisions

Article 2

Subject to the provisions of this Convention, persons domiciled in a Contracting State shall, whatever their nationality, be sued in the courts of that State.

Persons who are not nationals of the State in which they are domiciled shall be governed by the rules of jurisdiction applicable to nationals of that State.

Article 3

Persons domiciled in a Contracting State may be sued in the courts of another Contracting State only by virtue of the rules set out in Sections 2 to 6 of this Title.

In particular the following provisions shall not be applicable as against them:

— in Belgium: Article 15 of the civil code (Code civil—Burgerlijk Wetboek) and Article 638 of the judicial code (Code judiciaire—Gerechtelijk Wetboek),

— in Denmark: Article 246 (2) and (3) of the law on civil procedure (Lov om rettens pleje),

— in the Federal Republic of Germany: Article 23 of the code of civil procedure (Zivilprozessordnung),

— in Greece, Article 40 of the code of civil procedure (E & thorn;aeeSSo ; ieeoeeoo AeeioiossSSo),

— in France: Articles 14 and 15 of the civil code (Code civil),

— in Ireland: the rules which enable jurisdiction to be founded on the document instituting the proceedings having been served on the defendant during his temporary presence in Ireland,

— in Italy: Articles 2 and 4, Nos. 1 and 2 of the code of civil procedure (Codice di procedura civile),

— in Luxembourg: Articles 14 and 15 of the civil code (Code civil),

— in Austria: Article 99 of the Law on Court Jurisdiction (Jurisdiktionsnorm),

— in the Netherlands: Articles 126(3) and 127 of the code of civil procedure (Wetboek van Burgerlijke Rechtsvordering),

— in Portugal: Article 65(1)(c), Article 65(2) and Article 65A(c) of the code of civil procedure (Codigo de Processo Civil) and Article 11 of the code of labour procedure (Codigo de Processo de Trabalho),

— in Finland: the second, third and fourth sentences of the first paragraph of Section 1 of Chapter 10 of the Code of Judicial Procedure (oikeudenkaymiskaari/rattegangsbalken),

— in Sweden: the first sentence of the first paragraph of Section 3 of Chapter 10 of the Code of Judicial Procedure (rattegangsbalken),

— in the United Kingdom: the rules which enable jurisdiction to be founded on:

>   (a) the document instituting the proceedings having been served on the defendant during his temporary presence in the United Kingdom or
>
>   (b) the presence within the United Kingdom of property belonging to the defendant or
>
>   (c) the seizure by the plaintiff of property situated in the United Kingdom.

Article 4

If the defendant is not domiciled in a Contracting State, the jurisdiction of the courts of each Contracting State shall, subject to the provisions of Article 16, be determined by the law of that State.

As against such a defendant, any person domiciled in a Contracting State may, whatever his nationality, avail himself in that State of the rules of jurisdiction there in force, and in particular those specified in the second paragraph of Article 3, in the same way as the nationals of that State.

Section 2

Special jurisdiction

Article 5

A person domiciled in a Contracting State may, in another Contracting State, be sued:

> 1. in matters relating to a contract, in the courts for the place of performance of the obligation in question in matters relating to individual contracts of employment, this place is that where the employee habitually carries out his work, or if the employee does not habitually carry out his work in any one country, the employer may also be sued in the courts for the place where the business which engaged the employee was or is now situated;
>
> 2. in matters relating to maintenance, in the courts for the place where the maintenance creditor is domiciled or habitually resident or, if the matter is ancillary to proceedings concerning the status of a person, in the court which, according to its own law, has jurisdiction to entertain those proceedings, unless that jurisdiction is based solely on the nationality of one of the parties;
>
> 3. in matters relating to tort, delict or quasi-delict, in the courts for the place where the harmful event occurred;
>
> 4. as regards a civil claim for damages or restitution which is based on an act giving rise to criminal proceedings, in the court seised

of those proceedings, to the extent that that court has jurisdiction under its own law to entertain civil proceedings;

5. as regards a dispute arising out of the operations of a branch, agency or other establishment, in the courts for the place in which the branch, agency or other establishment is situated;

6. as settlor, trustee or beneficiary of a trust created by the operation of a statute, or by a written instrument, or created orally and evidenced in writing, in the courts of the Contracting State in which the trust is domiciled;

7. as regards a dispute concerning the payment of remuneration claimed in respect of the salvage of a cargo or freight, in the court under the authority of which the cargo or freight in question:

(a) has been arrested to secure such payment, or

(b) could have been so arrested, but bail or other security has been given provided that this provision shall apply only if it is claimed that the defendant has an interest in the cargo or freight or had such an interest at the time of salvage (9).

Article 6

A person domiciled in a Contracting State may also be sued:

1. where he is one of a number of defendants, in the courts for the place where any one of them is domiciled

2. as a third party in an action on a warranty or guarantee or in any other third party proceedings, in the court seised of the original proceedings, unless these were instituted solely with the object of removing him from the jurisdiction of the court which would be competent in his case

3. on a counter-claim arising from the same contract or facts on which the original claim was based, in the court in which the original claim is pending

4. in matters relating to a contract, if the action may be combined with an action against the same defendant in matters relating to rights in rem in immovable property, in the court of the Contracting State in which the property is situated.

Article 6a

Where by virtue of this Convention a court of a Contracting State has jurisdiction in actions relating to liability from the use or operation of a ship, that court, or any other court substituted for this purpose by the internal law of that State, shall also have jurisdiction over claims for limitation of such liability.

Section 3

Jurisdiction in matters relating to insurance

Article 7

In matters relating to insurance, jurisdiction shall be determined by this Section, without prejudice to the provisions of Articles 4 and 5 point 5.

Article 8

An insurer domiciled in a Contracting State may be sued:

1. in the courts of the State where he is domiciled, or

2. in another Contracting State, in the courts for the place where the policy-holder is domiciled, or

3. if he is a co-insurer, in the courts of a Contracting State in which proceedings are brought against the leading insurer.

An insurer who is not domiciled in a Contracting State but has a branch, agency or other establishment in one of the Contracting States shall, in disputes arising out of the operations of the branch, agency or establishment, be deemed to be domiciled in that State.

Article 9

In respect of liability insurance or insurance of immovable property, the insurer may in addition be sued in the courts for the place where the harmful event occurred. The same applies if movable and immovable property are covered by the same insurance policy and both are adversely affected by the same contingency.

Article 10

In respect of liability insurance, the insurer may also, if the law of the court permits it, be joined in proceedings which the injured party had brought against the insured.

The provisions of Articles 7, 8 and 9 shall apply to actions brought by the injured party directly against the insurer, where such direct actions are permitted.

If the law governing such direct actions provides that the policy-holder or the insured may be joined as a party to the action, the same court shall have jurisdiction over them.

Article 11

Without prejudice to the provisions of the third paragraph of Article 10, an insurer may bring proceedings only in the courts of the Contracting State in which the defendant is domiciled, irrespective of whether he is the policy-holder, the insured or a beneficiary.

The provisions of this Section shall not affect the right to bring a counterclaim in the court in which, in accordance with this Section, the original claim is pending.

Article 12

The provisions of this Section may be departed from only by an agreement on jurisdiction:

1. which is entered into after the dispute has arisen, or

2. which allows the policy-holder, the insured or a beneficiary to bring proceedings in courts other than those indicated in this Section, or

3. which is concluded between a policy-holder and an insurer, both of whom are domiciled in the same Contracting State, and which has the effect of conferring jurisdiction on the courts of that State even if the harmful event were to occur abroad, provided that such an agreement is not contrary to the law of that State, or

4. which is concluded with a policy-holder who is not domiciled in a Contracting State, except in so far as the insurance is compulsory or relates to immovable property in a Contracting State, or

5. which relates to a contract of insurance in so far as it covers one or more of the risks set out in Article 12a.

Article 12a

The following are the risks referred to in point 5 of Article 12:

1. any loss of or damage to:

    (a) sea-going ships, installations situated offshore or on the high seas, or aircraft, arising from perils which relate to their use for commercial purposes

    (b) goods in transit other than passengers' baggage where the transit consists of or includes carriage by such ships or aircraft

2. any liability, other than for bodily injury to passengers or loss of or damage to their baggage:

    (a) arising out of the use or operation of ships, installations or aircraft as referred to in point 1(a) above in so far as the law of the Contracting State in which such aircraft are registered does not prohibit agreements on jurisdiction regarding insurance of such risks

    (b) for loss or damage caused by goods in transit as described in point 1(b) above

3. any financial loss connected with the use or operation of ships, installations or aircraft as referred to in point 1(a) above, in particular loss of freight or charter-hire

4. any risk or interest connected with any of those referred to in points 1 to 3 above.

Section 4

Jurisdiction over consumer contracts

Article 13

In proceedings concerning a contract concluded by a person for a purpose which can be regarded as being outside his trade or profession, hereinafter called "the consumer," jurisdiction shall be determined by this Section, without prejudice to the provisions of point 5 of Articles 4 and 5, if it is:

    1. a contract for the sale of goods on instalment credit terms or

    2. a contract for a loan repayable by instalments, or for any other form of credit, made to finance the sale of goods or

    3. any other contract for the supply of goods or a contract for the supply of services, and

        (a) in the State of the consumer's domicile the conclusion of the contract was preceded by a specific invitation addressed to him or by advertising and

        (b) the consumer took in that State the steps necessary for the conclusion of the contract.

Where a consumer enters into a contract with a party who is not domiciled in a Contracting State but has a branch, agency or other establishment in one of the Contracting States, that party shall, in disputes arising out of the operations of the branch, agency or establishment, be deemed to be domiciled in that State.

This Section shall not apply to contracts of transport.

Article 14

A consumer may bring proceedings against the other party to a contract either in the courts of the Contracting State in which that party is domiciled or in the courts of the Contracting State in which he is himself domiciled.

Proceedings may be brought against a consumer by the other party to the contract only in the courts of the Contracting State in which the consumer is domiciled.

These provisions shall not affect the right to bring a counter-claim in the court in which, in accordance with this Section, the original claim is pending.

Article 15

The provisions of this Section may be departed from only by an agreement:

    1. which is entered into after the dispute has arisen or

    2. which allows the consumer to bring proceedings in courts other than those indicated in this Section or

    3. which is entered into by the consumer and the other party to the contract, both of whom are at the time of conclusion of the contract domiciled or habitually resident in the same Contracting State, and which confers jurisdiction on the courts of that State, provided that such an agreement is not contrary to the law of that State.

Section 5

Exclusive jurisdiction

Article 16

The following courts shall have exclusive jurisdiction, regardless of domicile:

1. (a) in proceedings which have as their object rights in rem in immovable property or tenancies of immovable property, the courts of the Contracting State in which the property is situated

(b) however, in proceedings which have as their object tenancies of immovable property concluded for temporary private use for a maximum period of six consecutive months, the courts of the Contracting State in which the defendant is domiciled shall also have jurisdiction, provided that the landlord and the tenant are natural persons and are domiciled in the same Contracting State;

2. in proceedings which have as their object the validity of the constitution, the nullity or the dissolution of companies or other legal persons or associations of natural or legal persons, or the decisions of their organs, the courts of the Contracting State in which the company, legal person or association has its seat

3. in proceedings which have as their object the validity of entries in public registers, the courts of the Contracting State in which the register is kept

4. in proceedings concerned with the registration or validity of patents, trade marks, designs, or other similar rights required to be deposited or registered, the courts of the Contracting State in which the deposit or registration has been applied for, has taken place or is under the terms of an international convention deemed to have taken place

5. in proceedings concerned with the enforcement of judgments, the courts of the Contracting State in which the judgment has been or is to be enforced.

Section 6

Prorogation of jurisdiction

Article 17

If the parties, one or more of whom is domiciled in a Contracting State, have agreed that a court or the courts of a Contracting State are to have jurisdiction to settle any disputes which have arisen or which may arise in connection with a particular legal relationship, that court or those courts shall have exclusive jurisdiction. Such an agreement conferring jurisdiction shall be either:

(a) in writing or evidenced in writing or

(b) in a form which accords with practices which the parties have established between themselves or

(c) in international trade or commerce, in a form which accords with a usage of which the parties are or ought to have been aware and which in such trade or commerce is widely known to, and regularly observed by, parties to contracts of the type involved in the particular trade or commerce concerned.

Where such an agreement is concluded by parties, none of whom is domiciled in a Contracting State, the courts of other Contracting States shall have no jurisdiction over their disputes unless the court or courts chosen have declined jurisdiction.

The court or courts of a Contracting State on which a trust instrument has conferred jurisdiction shall have exclusive jurisdiction in any proceedings brought against a settler, trustee or beneficiary, if relations between these persons or their rights or obligations under the trust are involved.

Agreements or provisions of a trust instrument conferring jurisdiction shall have no legal force if they are contrary to the provisions of Articles 12 or 15, or if the courts whose jurisdiction they purport to exclude have exclusive jurisdiction by virtue of Article 16.

If an agreement conferring jurisdiction was concluded for the benefit of only one of the parties, that party shall retain the right to bring proceedings in any other court which has jurisdiction by virtue of this Convention.

In matters relating to individual contracts of employment an agreement conferring jurisdiction shall have legal force only if it is entered into after the dispute has arisen or if the employee invokes it to seise courts other than those for the defendant's domicile or those specified in Article 5(1).

Article 18

Apart from jurisdiction derived from other provisions of this Convention, a court of a Contracting State before whom a defendant enters an appearance shall have jurisdiction. This rule shall not apply where appearance was entered solely to contest the jurisdiction, or where another court has exclusive jurisdiction by virtue of Article 16.

Section 7

Examination as to jurisdiction and admissibility

Article 19

Where a court of a Contracting State is seised of a claim which is principally concerned with a matter over which the courts of another Contracting State have exclusive jurisdiction by virtue of Article 16, it shall declare of its own motion that it has no jurisdiction.

Article 20

Where a defendant domiciled in one Contracting State is sued in a court of another Contracting State and does not enter an appearance, the court shall declare of its own motion that it has no jurisdiction unless its jurisdiction is derived from the provisions of the Convention.

The court shall stay the proceedings so long as it is not shown that the defendant has been able to receive the document instituting the proceedings or an equivalent document in sufficient time to enable him to arrange for his defence, or that all necessary steps have been taken to this end.

The provisions of the foregoing paragraph shall be replaced by those of Article 15 of the Hague Convention of 15 November 1965 on the service abroad of judicial and extrajudicial documents in civil or commercial matters, if the document instituting the proceedings or notice thereof had to be transmitted abroad in accordance with that Convention.

Section 8

Lis pendens—related actions

Article 21

Where proceedings involving the same cause of action and between the same parties are brought in the courts of different Contracting States, any court other than the court first seised shall of its own motion stay its proceedings until such time as the jurisdiction of the court first seised is established.

Where the jurisdiction of the court first seised is established, any court other than the court first seised shall decline jurisdiction in favour of that court.

Article 22

Where related actions are brought in the courts of different Contracting States, any court other than the court first seised may, while the actions are pending at first instance, stay its proceedings.

A court other than the court first seised may also, on the application of one of the parties, decline jurisdiction if the law of that court permits the consolidation of related actions and the court first seised has jurisdiction over both actions.

For the purposes of this Article, actions are deemed to be related where they are so closely connected that it is expedient to hear and determine them together to avoid the risk of irreconcilable judgments resulting from separate proceedings.

Article 23

Where actions come within the exclusive jurisdiction of several courts, any court other than the court first seised shall decline jurisdiction in favour of that court.

Section 9

Provisional, including protective, measures

Article 24

Application may be made to the courts of a Contracting State for such provisional, including protective, measures as may be available under the law of that State, even if, under this Convention, the courts of another Contracting State have jurisdiction as to the substance of the matter.

TITLE III

RECOGNITION AND ENFORCEMENT

Article 25

For the purposes of this Convention, "judgment" means any judgment given by a court or tribunal of a Contracting State, whatever the judgment may be called, including a decree, order, decision or writ of execution, as well as the determination of costs or expenses by an officer of the court.

Section 1

Recognition

Article 26

A judgment given in a Contracting State shall be recognized in the other Contracting States without any special procedure being required.

Any interested party who raises the recognition of a judgment as the principal issue in a dispute may, in accordance with the procedures provided for in Sections 2 and 3 of this Title, apply for a decision that the judgment be recognized.

If the outcome of proceedings in a court of a Contracting State depends on the determination of an incidental question of recognition that court shall have jurisdiction over that question.

Article 27

A judgment shall not be recognized:

1. if such recognition is contrary to public policy in the State in which recognition is sought

2. where it was given in default of appearance, if the defendant was not duly served with the document which instituted the proceedings or with an equivalent document in sufficient time to enable him to arrange for his defence (20);

3. if the judgment is irreconcilable with a judgment given in a dispute between the same parties in the State in which recognition is sought

4. if the court of the State of origin, in order to arrive at its judgment, has decided a preliminary question concerning the status or legal capacity of natural persons, rights in property arising out of a matrimonial relationship, wills or succession in a way that conflicts with a rule of the private international law of the State in which the recognition is sought, unless the same result would have been reached by the application of the rules of private international law of that State;

5. if the judgment is irreconcilable with an earlier judgment given in a non-contracting State involving the same cause of action and between the same parties, provided that this latter judgment fulfils the conditions necessary for its recognition in the State addressed).

Article 28

Moreover, a judgment shall not be recognized if it conflicts with the provisions of Sections 3, 4 or 5 of Title II, or in a case provided for in Article 59.

In its examination of the grounds of jurisdiction referred to in the foregoing paragraph, the court or authority applied to shall be bound by the findings of fact on which the court of the State of origin based its jurisdiction.

Subject to the provisions of the first paragraph, the jurisdiction of the court of the State of origin may not be reviewed the test of public policy referred to in point 1 of Article 27 may not be applied to the rules relating to jurisdiction.

Article 29

Under no circumstances may a foreign judgment be reviewed as to its substance.

Article 30

A court of a Contracting State in which recognition is sought of a judgment given in another Contracting State may stay the proceedings if an ordinary appeal against the judgment has been lodged.

A court of a Contracting State in which recognition is sought of a judgment given in Ireland or the United Kingdom may stay the proceedings if enforcement is suspended in the State of origin, by reason of an appeal (25).

Section 2

Enforcement

Article 31

A judgment given in a Contracting State and enforceable in that State shall be enforced in another Contracting State when, on the application of any interested party, it has been declared enforceable there.

However, in the United Kingdom, such a judgment shall be enforced in England and Wales, in Scotland, or in Northern Ireland when, on the application of any interested party, it has been registered for enforcement in that part of the United Kingdom.

Article 32

[Section 1 of Article 32 lists the courts in each country where applications for the enforcement of Convention judgments may be brought.]

2. The jurisdiction of local courts shall be determined by reference to the place of domicile of the party against whom enforcement is sought. If he is not domiciled in the State in which enforcement is sought, it shall be determined by reference to the place of enforcement.

Article 33

The procedure for making the application shall be governed by the law of the State in which enforcement is sought.

The applicant must give an address for service of process within the area of jurisdiction of the court applied to. However, if the law of the State in which enforcement is sought does not provide for the furnishing of such an address, the applicant shall appoint a representative ad litem.

The documents referred to in Articles 46 and 47 shall be attached to the application.

Article 34

The court applied to shall give its decision without delay the party against whom enforcement is sought shall not at this stage of the proceedings be entitled to make any submissions on the application.

The application may be refused only for one of the reasons specified in Articles 27 and 28.

Under no circumstances may the foreign judgment be reviewed as to its substance.

Article 35

The appropriate officer of the court shall without delay bring the decision given on the application to the notice of the applicant in accordance with the procedure laid down by the law of the State in which enforcement is sought.

Article 36

If enforcement is authorized, the party against whom enforcement is sought may appeal against the decision within one month of service thereof.

If that party is domiciled in a Contracting State other than that in which the decision authorizing enforcement was given, the time for appealing shall be two months and shall run from the date of service, either on him in person or at his residence. No extension of time may be granted on account of distance.

Article 37

[Section 1 of Article 37 indicates, for each country, the courts in which appeals against a decision authorizing enforcement may be brought. Section 2 indicates the forum in each country for challenges to the judgment given on appeal.]

Article 38

The court with which the appeal under Article 37(1) is lodged may, on the application of the appellant, stay the proceedings if an ordinary appeal has been lodged against the judgment in the State of origin or if the time for such an appeal has not yet expired in the latter case, the court may specify the time within which such an appeal is to be lodged.

Where the judgment was given in Ireland or the United Kingdom, any form of appeal available in the State of origin shall be treated as an ordinary appeal for the purposes of the first paragraph (32).

The court may also make enforcement conditional on the provision of such security as it shall determine.

Article 39

During the time specified for an appeal pursuant to Article 36 and until any such appeal has been determined, no measures of enforcement may be taken other than protective measures taken against the property of the party against whom enforcement is sought.

The decision authorizing enforcement shall carry with it the power to proceed to any such protective measures.

Article 40

[Section 1 of Article 40 indicates the courts where appeals against refusals to enforce may be brought.]

2. The party against whom enforcement is sought shall be summoned to appear before the appellate court. If he fails to appear, the provisions of the second and third paragraphs of Article 20 shall apply even where he is not domiciled in any of the Contracting States.

Article 41

[Article 41 indicates the forum in each country where judgments given on appeal provided for in Article 40 may be contested.]

Article 42

Where a foreign judgment has been given in respect of several matters and enforcement cannot be authorized for all of them, the court shall authorize enforcement for one or more of them.

An applicant may request partial enforcement of a judgment.

Article 43

A foreign judgment which orders a periodic payment by way of a penalty shall be enforceable in the State in which enforcement is sought only if the amount of the payment has been finally determined by the courts of the State of origin.

Article 44

An applicant who, in the State of origin has benefited from complete or partial legal aid or exemption from costs or expenses, shall be entitled, in the procedures provided for in Articles 32 to 35, to benefit from the most favourable legal aid or the most extensive exemption from costs or expenses provided for by the law of the State addressed.

However, an applicant who requests the enforcement of a decision given by an administrative authority in Denmark in respect of a maintenance order may, in the State addressed, claim the benefits referred to in the first paragraph if he presents a statement from the Danish Ministry of Justice to the effect that he fulfils the economic requirements to qualify for the grant of complete or partial legal aid or exemption from costs or expenses.

Article 45

No security, bond or deposit, however described, shall be required of a party who in one Contracting State applies for enforcement of a judgment given in another Contracting State on the ground that he is a foreign national or that he is not domiciled or resident in the State in which enforcement is sought.

Section 3

Common provisions

Article 46

A party seeking recognition or applying for enforcement of a judgment shall produce:

    1. a copy of the judgment which satisfies the conditions necessary to establish its authenticity

    2. in the case of a judgment given in default, the original or a certified true copy of the document which establishes that the party in default was served with the document instituting the proceedings or with an equivalent document (37).

Article 47

A party applying for enforcement shall also produce:

    1. documents which establish that, according to the law of the State of origin the judgment is enforceable and has been served

    2. where appropriate, a document showing that the applicant is in receipt of legal aid in the State of origin.

Article 48

If the documents specified in point 2 of Articles 46 and 47 are not produced, the court may specify a time for their production, accept equivalent documents or, if it considers that it has sufficient information before it, dispense with their production.

If the court so requires, a translation of the documents shall be produced the translation shall be certified by a person qualified to do so in one of the Contracting States.

Article 49

No legalization or other similar formality shall be required in respect of the documents referred to in Articles 46 or 47 or the second paragraph of Article 48, or in respect of a document appointing a representative ad litem.

[Title IV deals with recognition and enforcement of documents formally drawn up or registered as authentic instruments (art. 50) and with settlements (art. 51).]

Article 51

A settlement which has been approved by a court in the course of proceedings and is enforceable in the State in which it was concluded shall be enforceable in the State addressed under the same conditions as authentic instruments (40).

TITLE V

GENERAL PROVISIONS

Article 52

In order to determine whether a party is domiciled in the Contracting State whose courts are seised of a matter, the Court shall apply its internal law.

If a party is not domiciled in the State whose courts are seised of the matter, then, in order to determine whether the party is domiciled in another Contracting State, the court shall apply the law of that State.

Article 53

For the purposes of this Convention, the seat of a company or other legal person or association of natural or legal persons shall be treated as its domicile. However, in order to determine that seat, the court shall apply its rules of private international law.

In order to determine whether a trust is domiciled in the Contracting State whose courts are seised of the matter, the court shall apply its rules of private international law.

[Title VI deals with "transitional provisions," including date of effectiveness of the Convention. Title VII treats the Convention's relation with other agreements.]

[The Final Provisions (art. 66) state that the Convention is concluded for an unlimited period.]

19. PROTOCOL ON THE INTERPRETATION BY THE COURT OF JUSTICE OF THE CONVENTION ON JURISDICTION AND THE ENFORCEMENT OF JUDGMENTS IN CIVIL AND COMMERCIAL MATTERS

(signed at Luxembourg, June 3, 1971)
O.J. C 27/28 (Jan. 26, 1998)

Article 1

The Court of Justice of the European Communities shall have jurisdiction to give rulings on the interpretation of the Convention on jurisdiction and the enforcement of judgments in civil and commercial matters and of the Protocol annexed to that Convention, signed at Brussels on 27 September 1968, and also on the interpretation of the present Protocol.

* * *

Article 2

[Article 2 lists the specific courts in each State that may request the Court of Justice to give preliminary rulings on questions of interpretation.]

Article 3

1. Where a question of interpretation of the Convention or of one of the other instruments referred to in Article 1 is raised in a case pending before one of the courts listed in point 1 of Article 2, that court shall, if it considers that a decision on the question is necessary to enable it to give judgment, request the Court of Justice to give a ruling thereon.

2. Where such a question is raised before any court referred to in point 2 or 3 of Article 2, that court may under the conditions laid down in paragraph 1, request the Court of Justice to give a ruling thereon.

Article 4

1. The competent authority of a Contracting State may request the Court of Justice to give a ruling on a question of interpretation of the Convention or of one of the other instruments referred to in Article 1 if judgments given by courts of that State conflict with the interpretation given either by the Court of Justice or in a judgment of one of the courts of another Contracting State referred to in point 1 or 2 of Article 2. The provisions of this paragraph shall apply only to judgments which have become res judicata.

2. The interpretation given by the Court of Justice in response to such a request shall not affect the judgments which gave rise to the request for interpretation.

3. The Procurators–General of the Courts of Cassation of the Contracting States, or any other authority designated by a Contracting State, shall be entitled to request the Court of Justice for a ruling on interpretation in accordance with paragraph 1.

4. The Registrar of the Court of Justice shall give notice of the request to the Contracting States, to the Commission and to the Council of the European Communities they shall then be entitled within two months of the notification to submit statements of case or written observations to the Court.

5. No fees shall be levied or any costs or expenses awarded in respect of the proceedings provided for in this Article.

Article 5

1. Except where this Protocol otherwise provides, the provisions of the Treaty establishing the European Economic Community and those of the Protocol on the Statute of the Court of Justice annexed thereto, which are applicable when the Court is requested to give a preliminary ruling, shall also apply to any proceedings for the interpretation of the Convention and the other instruments referred to in Article 1.

2. The Rules of Procedure of the Court of Justice shall, if necessary, be adjusted and supplemented in accordance with Article 188 of the Treaty establishing the European Economic Community.

* * *

Article 9

The Contracting States recognize that any State which becomes a member of the European Economic Community, and to which Article 63 of the Convention on jurisdiction and the enforcement of judgments in civil and commercial matters applies, must accept the provisions of this Protocol, subject to such adjustments as may be required.

* * *

Article 12

This Protocol is concluded for an unlimited period.

* * *

20. COUNCIL REGULATION 44/2001 OF 22 DECEMBER 2000

on jurisdiction and the recognition and enforcement
of judgments in civil and commercial matters

O.J. L 12/1 (Jan. 16, 2001)

THE COUNCIL OF THE EUROPEAN UNION,

Having regard to the Treaty establishing the European Community, and in particular Article 61(c) and Article 67(1) thereof,

Having regard to the proposal from the Commission (1),

Having regard to the opinion of the European Parliament (2),

Having regard to the opinion of the Economic and Social Committee (3),

Whereas:

(1) The Community has set itself the objective of maintaining and developing an area of freedom, security and justice, in which the free movement of persons is ensured. In order to establish progressively such an area, the Community should adopt, amongst other things, the measures relating to judicial cooperation in civil matters which are necessary for the sound operation of the internal market.

(2) Certain differences between national rules governing jurisdiction and recognition of judgments hamper the sound operation of the internal market. Provisions to unify the rules of conflict of jurisdiction in civil and commercial matters and to simplify the formalities with a view to rapid and simple recognition and enforcement of judgments from Member States bound by this Regulation are essential.

(3) This area is within the field of judicial cooperation in civil matters within the meaning of Article 65 of the Treaty.

(4) In accordance with the principles of subsidiarity and proportionality as set out in Article 5 of the Treaty, the objectives of this Regulation cannot be sufficiently achieved by the Member States and can therefore be better achieved by the Community. This Regulation confines itself to the minimum required in order to achieve those objectives and does not go beyond what is necessary for that purpose.

(5) On 27 September 1968 the Member States, acting under Article 293, fourth indent, of the Treaty, concluded the Brussels Convention on Jurisdiction and the Enforcement of Judgments in Civil and Commercial Matters, as amended by Conventions on the Accession of the New Member States to that Convention (hereinafter referred to as the 'Brussels Convention') (4). On 16 September 1988 Member States and EFTA States concluded the Lugano Convention on Jurisdiction and the Enforcement of Judgments in Civil and Commercial Matters, which is a parallel Convention to the 1968 Brussels Convention. Work has been undertaken for the revision of those Conventions, and the Council has approved the content of the revised texts. Continuity in the results achieved in that revision should be ensured.

(6) In order to attain the objective of free movement of judgments in civil and commercial matters, it is necessary and appropriate that the rules governing jurisdiction and the recognition and enforcement of judgments be governed by a Community legal instrument which is binding and directly applicable.

(7) The scope of this Regulation must cover all the main civil and commercial matters apart from certain well-defined matters

(8) There must be a link between proceedings to which this Regulation applies and the territory of the Member States bound by this Regulation. Accordingly common rules on jurisdiction should, in principle, apply when the defendant is domiciled in one of those Member States.

(9) A defendant not domiciled in a Member State is in general subject to national rules of jurisdiction applicable in the territory of the Member State of the court seised, and a defendant domiciled in a Member State not bound by this Regulation must remain subject to the Brussels Convention.

(10) For the purposes of the free movement of judgments, judgments given in a Member State bound by this Regulation should be recognised and enforced in another Member State bound by this Regulation, even if the judgment debtor is domiciled in a third State.

(11) The rules of jurisdiction must be highly predictable and founded on the principle that jurisdiction is generally based on the defendant's domicile and jurisdiction must always be available on this ground save in a few well-defined situations in which the subject-matter of the litigation or the autonomy of the parties warrants a different linking factor. The domicile of a legal person must be defined autonomously so as to make the common rules more transparent and avoid conflicts of jurisdiction.

(12) In addition to the defendant's domicile, there should be alternative grounds of jurisdiction based on a close link between the court and the action or in order to facilitate the sound administration of justice.

(13) In relation to insurance, consumer contracts and employment, the weaker party should be protected by rules of jurisdiction more favourable to his interests than the general rules provide for.

(14) The autonomy of the parties to a contract, other than an insurance, consumer or employment contract, where only limited autonomy to determine the courts having jurisdiction is allowed, must be respected subject to the exclusive grounds of jurisdiction laid down in this Regulation.

(15) In the interests of the harmonious administration of justice it is necessary to minimise the possibility of concurrent proceedings and to ensure that irreconcilable judgments will not be given in two Member States. There must be a clear and effective mechanism for resolving cases of lis pendens and related actions and for obviating problems flowing from national differences as to the determination of the time when a case is regarded as pending. For the purposes of this Regulation that time should be defined autonomously.

(16) Mutual trust in the administration of justice in the Community justifies judgments given in a Member State being recognised automatically without the need for any procedure except in cases of dispute.

(17) By virtue of the same principle of mutual trust, the procedure for making enforceable in one Member State a judgment given in another must be efficient and rapid. To that end, the declaration that a judgment is enforceable should be issued virtually automatically after purely formal checks of the documents supplied, without there being any possibility for the court to raise of its own motion any of the grounds for non-enforcement provided for by this Regulation.

(18) However, respect for the rights of the defence means that the defendant should be able to appeal in an adversarial procedure, against the declaration of enforceability, if he considers one of the grounds for non-enforcement to be present. Redress procedures should also be available to the claimant where his application for a declaration of enforceability has been rejected.

(19) Continuity between the Brussels Convention and this Regulation should be ensured, and transitional provisions should be laid down to that end. The same need for continuity applies as regards the interpretation of the Brussels Convention by the Court of Justice of the European Communities and the 1971 Protocol (5) should remain applicable also to cases already pending when this Regulation enters into force.

(20) The United Kingdom and Ireland, in accordance with Article 3 of the Protocol on the position of the United Kingdom and Ireland annexed to the Treaty on European Union and to the Treaty establishing the European Community, have given notice of their wish to take part in the adoption and application of this Regulation.

(21) Denmark, in accordance with Articles 1 and 2 of the Protocol on the position of Denmark annexed to the Treaty on European Union and to the Treaty establishing the European Community, is not participating in the adoption of this Regulation, and is therefore not bound by it nor subject to its application.

(22) Since the Brussels Convention remains in force in relations between Denmark and the Member States that are bound by this Regulation, both the Convention and the 1971 Protocol continue to apply between Denmark and the Member States bound by this Regulation.

(23) The Brussels Convention also continues to apply to the territories of the Member States which fall within the territorial scope of that Convention and which are excluded from this Regulation pursuant to Article 299 of the Treaty.

(24) Likewise for the sake of consistency, this Regulation should not affect rules governing jurisdiction and the recognition of judgments contained in specific Community instruments.

(25) Respect for international commitments entered into by the Member States means that this Regulation should not affect conventions relating to specific matters to which the Member States are parties.

(26) The necessary flexibility should be provided for in the basic rules of this Regulation in order to take account of the specific procedural rules

of certain Member States. Certain provisions of the Protocol annexed to the Brussels Convention should accordingly be incorporated in this Regulation.

(27) In order to allow a harmonious transition in certain areas which were the subject of special provisions in the Protocol annexed to the Brussels Convention, this Regulation lays down, for a transitional period, provisions taking into consideration the specific situation in certain Member States.

(28) No later than five years after entry into force of this Regulation the Commission will present a report on its application and, if need be, submit proposals for adaptations.

(29) The Commission will have to adjust Annexes I to IV on the rules of national jurisdiction, the courts or competent authorities and redress procedures available on the basis of the amendments forwarded by the Member State concerned; amendments made to Annexes V and VI should be adopted in accordance with Council Decision 1999/468/EC of 28 June 1999 laying down the procedures for the exercise of implementing powers conferred on the Commission,

HAS ADOPTED THIS REGULATION:

CHAPTER I
SCOPE

Article 1

1. This Regulation shall apply in civil and commercial matters whatever the nature of the court or tribunal. It shall not extend, in particular, to revenue, customs or administrative matters.

2. The Regulation shall not apply to:

(a) the status or legal capacity of natural persons, rights in property arising out of a matrimonial relationship, wills and succession;

(b) bankruptcy, proceedings relating to the winding-up of insolvent companies or other legal persons, judicial arrangements, compositions and analogous proceedings;

(c) social security;

(d) arbitration.

3. In this Regulation, the term 'Member State' shall mean Member States with the exception of Denmark.

CHAPTER II
JURISDICTION
Section 1
General provisions

Article 2

1. Subject to this Regulation, persons domiciled in a Member State shall, whatever their nationality, be sued in the courts of that Member State.

2. Persons who are not nationals of the Member State in which they are domiciled shall be governed by the rules of jurisdiction applicable to nationals of that State.

Article 3

1. Persons domiciled in a Member State may be sued in the courts of another Member State only by virtue of the rules set out in Sections 2 to 7 of this Chapter.

2. In particular the rules of national jurisdiction set out in Annex I shall not be applicable as against them.

Article 4

1. If the defendant is not domiciled in a Member State, the jurisdiction of the courts of each Member State shall, subject to Articles 22 and 23, be determined by the law of that Member State.

2. As against such a defendant, any person domiciled in a Member State may, whatever his nationality, avail himself in that State of the rules of jurisdiction there in force, and in particular those specified in Annex I, in the same way as the nationals of that State.

Section 2

Special jurisdiction

Article 5

A person domiciled in a Member State may, in another Member State, be sued:

1. (a) in matters relating to a contract, in the courts for the place of performance of the obligation in question;

    (b) for the purpose of this provision and unless otherwise agreed, the place of performance of the obligation in question shall be:

— in the case of the sale of goods, the place in a Member State where, under the contract, the goods were delivered or should have been delivered,

— in the case of the provision of services, the place in a Member State where, under the contract, the services were provided or should have been provided,

    (c) if subparagraph (b) does not apply then subparagraph (a) applies;

2. in matters relating to maintenance, in the courts for the place where the maintenance creditor is domiciled or habitually resident or, if the matter is ancillary to proceedings concerning the status of a person, in the court which, according to its own law, has jurisdiction to entertain those proceedings, unless that jurisdiction is based solely on the nationality of one of the parties;

3. in matters relating to tort, delict or quasi-delict, in the courts for the place where the harmful event occurred or may occur;

4. as regards a civil claim for damages or restitution which is based on an act giving rise to criminal proceedings, in the court seised of those proceedings, to the extent that that court has jurisdiction under its own law to entertain civil proceedings;

5. as regards a dispute arising out of the operations of a branch, agency or other establishment, in the courts for the place in which the branch, agency or other establishment is situated;

6. as settlor, trustee or beneficiary of a trust created by the operation of a statute, or by a written instrument, or created orally and evidenced in writing, in the courts of the Member State in which the trust is domiciled;

7. as regards a dispute concerning the payment of remuneration claimed in respect of the salvage of a cargo or freight, in the court under the authority of which the cargo or freight in question:

(a) has been arrested to secure such payment, or

(b) could have been so arrested, but bail or other security has been given;

provided that this provision shall apply only if it is claimed that the defendant has an interest in the cargo or freight or had such an interest at the time of salvage.

Article 6

A person domiciled in a Member State may also be sued:

1. where he is one of a number of defendants, in the courts for the place where any one of them is domiciled, provided the claims are so closely connected that it is expedient to hear and determine them together to avoid the risk of irreconcilable judgments resulting from separate proceedings;

2. as a third party in an action on a warranty or guarantee or in any other third party proceedings, in the court seised of the original proceedings, unless these were instituted solely with the object of removing him from the jurisdiction of the court which would be competent in his case;

3. on a counter-claim arising from the same contract or facts on which the original claim was based, in the court in which the original claim is pending;

4. in matters relating to a contract, if the action may be combined with an action against the same defendant in matters relating to rights in rem in immovable property, in the court of the Member State in which the property is situated.

Article 7

Where by virtue of this Regulation a court of a Member State has jurisdiction in actions relating to liability from the use or operation of a ship, that court, or any other court substituted for this purpose by the internal law of that Member State, shall also have jurisdiction over claims for limitation of such liability.

Section 3

Jurisdiction in matters relating to insurance

Article 8

In matters relating to insurance, jurisdiction shall be determined by this Section, without prejudice to Article 4 and point 5 of Article 5.

Article 9

1. An insurer domiciled in a Member State may be sued:

(a) in the courts of the Member State where he is domiciled, or

(b) in another Member State, in the case of actions brought by the policyholder, the insured or a beneficiary, in the courts for the place where the plaintiff is domiciled,

(c) if he is a co-insurer, in the courts of a Member State in which proceedings are brought against the leading insurer.

2. An insurer who is not domiciled in a Member State but has a branch, agency or other establishment in one of the Member States shall, in disputes arising out of the operations of the branch, agency or establishment, be deemed to be domiciled in that Member State.

Article 10

In respect of liability insurance or insurance of immovable property, the insurer may in addition be sued in the courts for the place where the harmful event occurred. The same applies if movable and immovable property are covered by the same insurance policy and both are adversely affected by the same contingency.

Article 11

1. In respect of liability insurance, the insurer may also, if the law of the court permits it, be joined in proceedings which the injured party has brought against the insured.

2. Articles 8, 9 and 10 shall apply to actions brought by the injured party directly against the insurer, where such direct actions are permitted.

3. If the law governing such direct actions provides that the policyholder or the insured may be joined as a party to the action, the same court shall have jurisdiction over them.

Article 12

1. Without prejudice to Article 11(3), an insurer may bring proceedings only in the courts of the Member State in which the defendant is domiciled, irrespective of whether he is the policyholder, the insured or a beneficiary.

2. The provisions of this Section shall not affect the right to bring a counter-claim in the court in which, in accordance with this Section, the original claim is pending.

Article 13

The provisions of this Section may be departed from only by an agreement:

    1. which is entered into after the dispute has arisen, or

    2. which allows the policyholder, the insured or a beneficiary to bring proceedings in courts other than those indicated in this Section, or

    3. which is concluded between a policyholder and an insurer, both of whom are at the time of conclusion of the contract domiciled or habitually resident in the same Member State, and which has the effect of conferring jurisdiction on the courts of that State even if the harmful event were to occur abroad, provided that such an agreement is not contrary to the law of that State, or

    4. which is concluded with a policyholder who is not domiciled in a Member State, except in so far as the insurance is compulsory or relates to immovable property in a Member State, or

    5. which relates to a contract of insurance in so far as it covers one or more of the risks set out in Article 14.

Article 14

The following are the risks referred to in Article 13(5):

1. any loss of or damage to:

    (a) seagoing ships, installations situated offshore or on the high seas, or aircraft, arising from perils which relate to their use for commercial purposes;

    (b) goods in transit other than passengers' baggage where the transit consists of or includes carriage by such ships or aircraft;

2. any liability, other than for bodily injury to passengers or loss of or damage to their baggage:

    (a) arising out of the use or operation of ships, installations or aircraft as referred to in point 1(a) in so far as, in respect of the latter, the law of the Member State in which such aircraft are registered does not prohibit agreements on jurisdiction regarding insurance of such risks;

    (b) for loss or damage caused by goods in transit as described in point 1(b);

3. any financial loss connected with the use or operation of ships, installations or aircraft as referred to in point 1(a), in particular loss of freight or charter-hire;

4. any risk or interest connected with any of those referred to in points 1 to 3;

5. notwithstanding points 1 to 4, all 'large risks' as defined in Council Directive 73/239/EEC, as amended by Council Directives 88/357/EEC and 90/618/EEC, as they may be amended.

Section 4

Jurisdiction over consumer contracts

Article 15

1. In matters relating to a contract concluded by a person, the consumer, for a purpose which can be regarded as being outside his trade or profession, jurisdiction shall be determined by this Section, without prejudice to Article 4 and point 5 of Article 5, if:

(a) it is a contract for the sale of goods on instalment credit terms; or

(b) it is a contract for a loan repayable by instalments, or for any other form of credit, made to finance the sale of goods; or

(c) in all other cases, the contract has been concluded with a person who pursues commercial or professional activities in the Member State of the consumer's domicile or, by any means, directs such activities to that Member State or to several States including that Member State, and the contract falls within the scope of such activities.

2. Where a consumer enters into a contract with a party who is not domiciled in the Member State but has a branch, agency or other establishment in one of the Member States, that party shall, in disputes arising out of the operations of the branch, agency or establishment, be deemed to be domiciled in that State.

3. This Section shall not apply to a contract of transport other than a contract which, for an inclusive price, provides for a combination of travel and accommodation.

Article 16

1. A consumer may bring proceedings against the other party to a contract either in the courts of the Member State in which that party is domiciled or in the courts for the place where the consumer is domiciled.

2. Proceedings may be brought against a consumer by the other party to the contract only in the courts of the Member State in which the consumer is domiciled.

3. This Article shall not affect the right to bring a counter-claim in the court in which, in accordance with this Section, the original claim is pending.

Article 17

The provisions of this Section may be departed from only by an agreement:

1. which is entered into after the dispute has arisen; or

2. which allows the consumer to bring proceedings in courts other than those indicated in this Section; or

3. which is entered into by the consumer and the other party to the contract, both of whom are at the time of conclusion of the contract domiciled or habitually resident in the same Member State, and which confers jurisdiction on the courts of that Member State, provided that such an agreement is not contrary to the law of that Member State.

Section 5

Jurisdiction over individual contracts of employment

Article 18

1. In matters relating to individual contracts of employment, jurisdiction shall be determined by this Section, without prejudice to Article 4 and point 5 of Article 5.

2. Where an employee enters into an individual contract of employment with an employer who is not domiciled in a Member State but has a branch, agency or other establishment in one of the Member States, the employer shall, in disputes arising out of the operations of the branch, agency or establishment, be deemed to be domiciled in that Member State.

Article 19

An employer domiciled in a Member State may be sued:

1. in the courts of the Member State where he is domiciled; or

2. in another Member State:

(a) in the courts for the place where the employee habitually carries out his work or in the courts for the last place where he did so, or

(b) if the employee does not or did not habitually carry out his work in any one country, in the courts for the place where the business which engaged the employee is or was situated.

Article 20

1. An employer may bring proceedings only in the courts of the Member State in which the employee is domiciled.

2. The provisions of this Section shall not affect the right to bring a counter-claim in the court in which, in accordance with this Section, the original claim is pending.

Article 21

The provisions of this Section may be departed from only by an agreement on jurisdiction:

1. which is entered into after the dispute has arisen; or

2. which allows the employee to bring proceedings in courts other than those indicated in this Section.

Section 6

Exclusive jurisdiction

Article 22

The following courts shall have exclusive jurisdiction, regardless of domicile:

1. in proceedings which have as their object rights in rem in immovable property or tenancies of immovable property, the courts of the Member State in which the property is situated.

However, in proceedings which have as their object tenancies of immovable property concluded for temporary private use for a maximum period of six consecutive months, the courts of the Member State in which the defendant is domiciled shall also have jurisdiction, provided that the tenant is a natural person and that the landlord and the tenant are domiciled in the same Member State;

2. in proceedings which have as their object the validity of the constitution, the nullity or the dissolution of companies or other legal persons or associations of natural or legal persons, or of the validity of the decisions of their organs, the courts of the Member State in which the company, legal person or association has its seat. In order to determine that seat, the court shall apply its rules of private international law;

3. in proceedings which have as their object the validity of entries in public registers, the courts of the Member State in which the register is kept;

4. in proceedings concerned with the registration or validity of patents, trade marks, designs, or other similar rights required to be deposited or registered, the courts of the Member State in which the deposit or registration has been applied for, has taken place or is under the terms of a Community instrument or an international convention deemed to have taken place.

Without prejudice to the jurisdiction of the European Patent Office under the Convention on the Grant of European Patents, signed at Munich on 5 October 1973, the courts of each Member State shall have exclusive jurisdiction, regardless of domicile, in proceedings concerned with the registration or validity of any European patent granted for that State;

5. in proceedings concerned with the enforcement of judgments, the courts of the Member State in which the judgment has been or is to be enforced.

Section 7

Prorogation of jurisdiction

Article 23

1. If the parties, one or more of whom is domiciled in a Member State, have agreed that a court or the courts of a Member State are to have jurisdiction to settle any disputes which have arisen or which may arise in connection with a particular legal relationship, that court or those courts shall have jurisdiction. Such jurisdiction shall be exclusive unless the parties have agreed otherwise. Such an agreement conferring jurisdiction shall be either:

   (a) in writing or evidenced in writing; or

   (b) in a form which accords with practices which the parties have established between themselves; or

   (c) in international trade or commerce, in a form which accords with a usage of which the parties are or ought to have been aware and which in such trade or commerce is widely known to, and regularly observed by, parties to contracts of the type involved in the particular trade or commerce concerned.

2. Any communication by electronic means which provides a durable record of the agreement shall be equivalent to "writing".

3. Where such an agreement is concluded by parties, none of whom is domiciled in a Member State, the courts of other Member States shall have no jurisdiction over their disputes unless the court or courts chosen have declined jurisdiction.

4. The court or courts of a Member State on which a trust instrument has conferred jurisdiction shall have exclusive jurisdiction in any proceedings brought against a settlor, trustee or beneficiary, if relations between these persons or their rights or obligations under the trust are involved.

5. Agreements or provisions of a trust instrument conferring jurisdiction shall have no legal force if they are contrary to Articles 13, 17 or 21, or if the courts whose jurisdiction they purport to exclude have exclusive jurisdiction by virtue of Article 22.

Article 24

Apart from jurisdiction derived from other provisions of this Regulation, a court of a Member State before which a defendant enters an appearance shall have jurisdiction. This rule shall not apply where appearance was entered to contest the jurisdiction, or where another court has exclusive jurisdiction by virtue of Article 22.

Section 8

Examination as to jurisdiction and admissibility

Article 25

Where a court of a Member State is seised of a claim which is principally concerned with a matter over which the courts of another Member State have exclusive jurisdiction by virtue of Article 22, it shall declare of its own motion that it has no jurisdiction.

Article 26

1. Where a defendant domiciled in one Member State is sued in a court of another Member State and does not enter an appearance, the court shall declare of its own motion that it has no jurisdiction unless its jurisdiction is derived from the provisions of this Regulation.

2. The court shall stay the proceedings so long as it is not shown that the defendant has been able to receive the document instituting the proceedings or an equivalent document in sufficient time to enable him to arrange for his defence, or that all necessary steps have been taken to this end.

3. Article 19 of Council Regulation (EC) No. 1348/2000 of 29 May 2000 on the service in the Member States of judicial and extrajudicial documents in civil or commercial matters (10) shall apply instead of the provisions of paragraph 2 if the document instituting the proceedings or an equivalent document had to be transmitted from one Member State to another pursuant to this Regulation.

4. Where the provisions of Regulation (EC) No. 1348/2000 are not applicable, Article 15 of the Hague Convention of 15 November 1965 on the Service Abroad of Judicial and Extrajudicial Documents in Civil or Commercial Matters shall apply if the document instituting the proceedings or an equivalent document had to be transmitted pursuant to that Convention.

Section 9

Lis pendens—related actions

Article 27

1. Where proceedings involving the same cause of action and between the same parties are brought in the courts of different Member States, any court other than the court first seised shall of its own motion stay its proceedings until such time as the jurisdiction of the court first seised is established.

2. Where the jurisdiction of the court first seised is established, any court other than the court first seised shall decline jurisdiction in favour of that court.

Article 28

1. Where related actions are pending in the courts of different Member States, any court other than the court first seised may stay its proceedings.

2. Where these actions are pending at first instance, any court other than the court first seised may also, on the application of one of the parties, decline jurisdiction if the court first seised has jurisdiction over the actions in question and its law permits the consolidation thereof.

3. For the purposes of this Article, actions are deemed to be related where they are so closely connected that it is expedient to hear and determine them together to avoid the risk of irreconcilable judgments resulting from separate proceedings.

Article 29

Where actions come within the exclusive jurisdiction of several courts, any court other than the court first seised shall decline jurisdiction in favour of that court.

Article 30

For the purposes of this Section, a court shall be deemed to be seised:

1. at the time when the document instituting the proceedings or an equivalent document is lodged with the court, provided that the plaintiff has not subsequently failed to take the steps he was required to take to have service effected on the defendant, or

2. if the document has to be served before being lodged with the court, at the time when it is received by the authority responsible for service, provided that the plaintiff has not subsequently failed to take the steps he was required to take to have the document lodged with the court.

Section 10

Provisional, including protective, measures

Article 31

Application may be made to the courts of a Member State for such provisional, including protective, measures as may be available under the law of that State, even if, under this Regulation, the courts of another Member State have jurisdiction as to the substance of the matter.

CHAPTER III

RECOGNITION AND ENFORCEMENT

Article 32

For the purposes of this Regulation, 'judgment' means any judgment given by a court or tribunal of a Member State, whatever the judgment may be called, including a decree, order, decision or writ of execution, as well as the determination of costs or expenses by an officer of the court.

Section 1

Recognition

Article 33

1. A judgment given in a Member State shall be recognised in the other Member States without any special procedure being required.

2. Any interested party who raises the recognition of a judgment as the principal issue in a dispute may, in accordance with the procedures provided for in Sections 2 and 3 of this Chapter, apply for a decision that the judgment be recognised.

3. If the outcome of proceedings in a court of a Member State depends on the determination of an incidental question of recognition that court shall have jurisdiction over that question.

Article 34

A judgment shall not be recognised:

   1. if such recognition is manifestly contrary to public policy in the Member State in which recognition is sought;

   2. where it was given in default of appearance, if the defendant was not served with the document which instituted the proceedings or with an equivalent document in sufficient time and in such a way as to enable him to arrange for his defence, unless the defendant failed to commence proceedings to challenge the judgment when it was possible for him to do so;

   3. if it is irreconcilable with a judgment given in a dispute between the same parties in the Member State in which recognition is sought;

   4. if it is irreconcilable with an earlier judgment given in another Member State or in a third State involving the same cause of action and between the same parties, provided that the earlier judgment fulfils the conditions necessary for its recognition in the Member State addressed.

Article 35

1. Moreover, a judgment shall not be recognised if it conflicts with Sections 3, 4 or 6 of Chapter II, or in a case provided for in Article 72.

2. In its examination of the grounds of jurisdiction referred to in the foregoing paragraph, the court or authority applied to shall be bound by the findings of fact on which the court of the Member State of origin based its jurisdiction.

3. Subject to the paragraph 1, the jurisdiction of the court of the Member State of origin may not be reviewed. The test of public policy referred to in point 1 of Article 34 may not be applied to the rules relating to jurisdiction.

Article 36

Under no circumstances may a foreign judgment be reviewed as to its substance.

Article 37

1. A court of a Member State in which recognition is sought of a judgment given in another Member State may stay the proceedings if an ordinary appeal against the judgment has been lodged.

2. A court of a Member State in which recognition is sought of a judgment given in Ireland or the United Kingdom may stay the proceedings if enforcement is suspended in the State of origin, by reason of an appeal.

Section 2

Enforcement

Article 38

1. A judgment given in a Member State and enforceable in that State shall be enforced in another Member State when, on the application of any interested party, it has been declared enforceable there.

2. However, in the United Kingdom, such a judgment shall be enforced in England and Wales, in Scotland, or in Northern Ireland when, on the application of any interested party, it has been registered for enforcement in that part of the United Kingdom.

Article 39

1. The application shall be submitted to the court or competent authority indicated in the list in Annex II.

2. The local jurisdiction shall be determined by reference to the place of domicile of the party against whom enforcement is sought, or to the place of enforcement.

Article 40

1. The procedure for making the application shall be governed by the law of the Member State in which enforcement is sought.

2. The applicant must give an address for service of process within the area of jurisdiction of the court applied to. However, if the law of the Member State in which enforcement is sought does not provide for the furnishing of such an address, the applicant shall appoint a representative ad litem.

3. The documents referred to in Article 53 shall be attached to the application.

Article 41

The judgment shall be declared enforceable immediately on completion of the formalities in Article 53 without any review under Articles 34 and

35. The party against whom enforcement is sought shall not at this stage of the proceedings be entitled to make any submissions on the application.

Article 42

1. The decision on the application for a declaration of enforceability shall forthwith be brought to the notice of the applicant in accordance with the procedure laid down by the law of the Member State in which enforcement is sought.

2. The declaration of enforceability shall be served on the party against whom enforcement is sought, accompanied by the judgment, if not already served on that party.

Article 43

1. The decision on the application for a declaration of enforceability may be appealed against by either party.

2. The appeal is to be lodged with the court indicated in the list in Annex III.

3. The appeal shall be dealt with in accordance with the rules governing procedure in contradictory matters.

4. If the party against whom enforcement is sought fails to appear before the appellate court in proceedings concerning an appeal brought by the applicant, Article 26(2) to (4) shall apply even where the party against whom enforcement is sought is not domiciled in any of the Member States.

5. An appeal against the declaration of enforceability is to be lodged within one month of service thereof. If the party against whom enforcement is sought is domiciled in a Member State other than that in which the declaration of enforceability was given, the time for appealing shall be two months and shall run from the date of service, either on him in person or at his residence. No extension of time may be granted on account of distance.

Article 44

The judgment given on the appeal may be contested only by the appeal referred to in Annex IV.

Article 45

1. The court with which an appeal is lodged under Article 43 or Article 44 shall refuse or revoke a declaration of enforceability only on one of the grounds specified in Articles 34 and 35. It shall give its decision without delay.

2. Under no circumstances may the foreign judgment be reviewed as to its substance.

Article 46

1. The court with which an appeal is lodged under Article 43 or Article 44 may, on the application of the party against whom enforcement

is sought, stay the proceedings if an ordinary appeal has been lodged against the judgment in the Member State of origin or if the time for such an appeal has not yet expired; in the latter case, the court may specify the time within which such an appeal is to be lodged.

2. Where the judgment was given in Ireland or the United Kingdom, any form of appeal available in the Member State of origin shall be treated as an ordinary appeal for the purposes of paragraph 1.

3. The court may also make enforcement conditional on the provision of such security as it shall determine.

Article 47

1. When a judgment must be recognised in accordance with this Regulation, nothing shall prevent the applicant from availing himself of provisional, including protective, measures in accordance with the law of the Member State requested without a declaration of enforceability under Article 41 being required.

2. The declaration of enforceability shall carry with it the power to proceed to any protective measures.

3. During the time specified for an appeal pursuant to Article 43(5) against the declaration of enforceability and until any such appeal has been determined, no measures of enforcement may be taken other than protective measures against the property of the party against whom enforcement is sought.

Article 48

1. Where a foreign judgment has been given in respect of several matters and the declaration of enforceability cannot be given for all of them, the court or competent authority shall give it for one or more of them.

2. An applicant may request a declaration of enforceability limited to parts of a judgment.

Article 49

A foreign judgment which orders a periodic payment by way of a penalty shall be enforceable in the Member State in which enforcement is sought only if the amount of the payment has been finally determined by the courts of the Member State of origin.

Article 50

An applicant who, in the Member State of origin has benefited from complete or partial legal aid or exemption from costs or expenses, shall be entitled, in the procedure provided for in this Section, to benefit from the most favourable legal aid or the most extensive exemption from costs or expenses provided for by the law of the Member State addressed.

Article 51

No security, bond or deposit, however described, shall be required of a party who in one Member State applies for enforcement of a judgment given in another Member State on the ground that he is a foreign national or that he is not domiciled or resident in the State in which enforcement is sought.

Article 52

In proceedings for the issue of a declaration of enforceability, no charge, duty or fee calculated by reference to the value of the matter at issue may be levied in the Member State in which enforcement is sought.

Section 3

Common provisions

Article 53

1. A party seeking recognition or applying for a declaration of enforceability shall produce a copy of the judgment which satisfies the conditions necessary to establish its authenticity.

2. A party applying for a declaration of enforceability shall also produce the certificate referred to in Article 54, without prejudice to Article 55.

Article 54

The court or competent authority of a Member State where a judgment was given shall issue, at the request of any interested party, a certificate using the standard form in Annex V to this Regulation.

Article 55

1. If the certificate referred to in Article 54 is not produced, the court or competent authority may specify a time for its production or accept an equivalent document or, if it considers that it has sufficient information before it, dispense with its production.

2. If the court or competent authority so requires, a translation of the documents shall be produced. The translation shall be certified by a person qualified to do so in one of the Member States.

Article 56

No legalisation or other similar formality shall be required in respect of the documents referred to in Article 53 or Article 55(2), or in respect of a document appointing a representative ad litem.

CHAPTER IV

AUTHENTIC INSTRUMENTS AND COURT SETTLEMENTS

Article 57

1. A document which has been formally drawn up or registered as an authentic instrument and is enforceable in one Member State shall, in

another Member State, be declared enforceable there, on application made in accordance with the procedures provided for in Articles 38, et seq. The court with which an appeal is lodged under Article 43 or Article 44 shall refuse or revoke a declaration of enforceability only if enforcement of the instrument is manifestly contrary to public policy in the Member State addressed.

2. Arrangements relating to maintenance obligations concluded with administrative authorities or authenticated by them shall also be regarded as authentic instruments within the meaning of paragraph 1.

3. The instrument produced must satisfy the conditions necessary to establish its authenticity in the Member State of origin.

4. Section 3 of Chapter III shall apply as appropriate. The competent authority of a Member State where an authentic instrument was drawn up or registered shall issue, at the request of any interested party, a certificate using the standard form in Annex VI to this Regulation.

Article 58

A settlement which has been approved by a court in the course of proceedings and is enforceable in the Member State in which it was concluded shall be enforceable in the State addressed under the same conditions as authentic instruments. The court or competent authority of a Member State where a court settlement was approved shall issue, at the request of any interested party, a certificate using the standard form in Annex V to this Regulation.

CHAPTER V

GENERAL PROVISIONS

Article 59

1. In order to determine whether a party is domiciled in the Member State whose courts are seised of a matter, the court shall apply its internal law.

2. If a party is not domiciled in the Member State whose courts are seised of the matter, then, in order to determine whether the party is domiciled in another Member State, the court shall apply the law of that Member State.

Article 60

1. For the purposes of this Regulation, a company or other legal person or association of natural or legal persons is domiciled at the place where it has its:

(a) statutory seat, or

(b) central administration, or

(c) principal place of business.

2. For the purposes of the United Kingdom and Ireland 'statutory seat' means the registered office or, where there is no such office anywhere,

the place of incorporation or, where there is no such place anywhere, the place under the law of which the formation took place.

3. In order to determine whether a trust is domiciled in the Member State whose courts are seised of the matter, the court shall apply its rules of private international law.

Article 61

Without prejudice to any more favourable provisions of national laws, persons domiciled in a Member State who are being prosecuted in the criminal courts of another Member State of which they are not nationals for an offence which was not intentionally committed may be defended by persons qualified to do so, even if they do not appear in person. However, the court seised of the matter may order appearance in person; in the case of failure to appear, a judgment given in the civil action without the person concerned having had the opportunity to arrange for his defence need not be recognised or enforced in the other Member States.

[There follow certain specific derogations for particular States.]

CHAPTER VI

TRANSITIONAL PROVISIONS

Article 66

1. This Regulation shall apply only to legal proceedings instituted and to documents formally drawn up or registered as authentic instruments after the entry into force thereof.

2. However, if the proceedings in the Member State of origin were instituted before the entry into force of this Regulation, judgments given after that date shall be recognised and enforced in accordance with Chapter III,

(a) if the proceedings in the Member State of origin were instituted after the entry into force of the Brussels or the Lugano Convention both in the Member State or origin and in the Member State addressed;

(b) in all other cases, if jurisdiction was founded upon rules which accorded with those provided for either in Chapter II or in a convention concluded between the Member State of origin and the Member State addressed which was in force when the proceedings were instituted.

CHAPTER VII

RELATIONS WITH OTHER INSTRUMENTS

[Articles 67–69 deals with the relationship between the Regulation and other instruments (both legislation and international agreements) on jurisdiction and judgments. Article 68, in particular, provides:

... In so far as this Regulation replaces the provisions of the Brussels Convention between Member States, any reference to the Convention shall be understood as a reference to this Regulation.]

Article 72

This Regulation shall not affect agreements by which Member States undertook, prior to the entry into force of this Regulation pursuant to Article 59 of the Brussels Convention, not to recognise judgments given, in particular in other Contracting States to that Convention, against defendants domiciled or habitually resident in a third country where, in cases provided for in Article 4 of that Convention, the judgment could only be founded on a ground of jurisdiction specified in the second paragraph of Article 3 of that Convention.

* * *

CHAPTER VIII
FINAL PROVISIONS

Article 76

This Regulation shall enter into force on 1 March 2002.

This Regulation is binding in its entirety and directly applicable in the Member States in accordance with the Treaty establishing the European Community.

[There are several Annexes.

Annex I enumerates the Member States' "exorbitant" bases of jurisdiction, whose use they basically forswear vis-à-vis other Member States' domiciliaries. They include (1) in Belgium, Article 15 of the Civil Code and Article 638 of the Judicial Code, (2) in Germany, Section 23 of the Civil Procedure Code, (3) in Greece, Article 40 of the Code of Civil Procedure, (4) in France, Articles 14 and 15 of the Civil Code, (5) in Ireland, the rules basing jurisdiction on the fact of personal service within the territory, (6) in Italy, Articles 3 and 4 of Act 218 of May 31, 1995, (7) in Luxembourg, Articles 14 and 15 of the Civil Code , (8) in the Netherlands, Articles 126(3) and 127 of the Code of Civil Procedure, (9) in Austria, Article 99 of the Court Jurisdiction Act, (10) in Portugal: Articles 65 and 65A of the Code of Civil Procedure and Article 11 of the Code of Labour Procedure, (11) in Finland, Section 1 of Chapter 10 of the Code of Judicial Procedure (sentences 2, 3 and 4 of the first paragraph), (12) in Sweden, Section 3 of Chapter 10 of the Code of Judicial Procedure (sentence one of paragraph one), and (13) in the United Kingdom, rules basing jurisdiction on personal service within the territory, transient jurisdiction, and the presence or seizure of property belonging to the defendant.

Annexes II, III, and IV list, respectively, the courts for each Member State that are competent to hear appeals under Article 43(2), 39(1) and 44.

Annexes V and VI presents the certificates referred to in Articles 54, 57(4) and 58.]

†